THE
MONTH-BY-MONTH
BABY BOOK

THE
MONTH-BY-MONTH
BABY BOOK

In-depth, monthly advice on your baby's growth,
care, and development in their first year

Contents

Introduction **8**

Your new baby

Being a parent 12

Adjusting to parenthood 13

Becoming a family 14

Babycare basics 24

Feeding your baby 25

How breastfeeding works 26

Bottle-feeding 29

Sleeping arrangements 30

All about nappies 32

Essential equipment 34

Your baby month by month

Your baby from birth to 3 months 38

The first seven days 40

One month 78

Two months 102

Three months 128

Your baby from 4 to 6 months 148

Four months 150

Five months 172

Six months 198

Your baby from 7 to 9 months 220

Seven months **222**

Eight months **244**

Nine months **268**

Your baby from 10 to 12 months 292

Ten months **294**

Eleven months **314**

Twelve months **338**

Your baby's health

Your unwell baby 362

When your baby is ill **363**

Getting medical help **364**

Looking after your sick baby **366**

Illnesses & injuries 368

Common conditions **369**

Developmental concerns **380**

Everyday first aid **382**

Resources **384**

Index **386**

Acknowledgments **399**

Introduction

In these days of advanced technology when so much can be achieved at the touch of a screen, there is still nothing to compare with the miracle of a baby. For new parents, the reality of having created this little being is life-changing; their baby's future is in their hands. The sense of achievement and responsibility is immense and will change parents' perspectives forever.

By adulthood most of us have learned what is required to get a job, run a home, and have a social life. The one area most first-time parents have not learned about is how to bring up a baby. At one time, families would hand down child-rearing skills, for better or worse. These days, families may be scattered across countries or continents; grandparents may be working. Parents cannot always take family support for granted. At the same time, research and medical care have improved child health dramatically and advanced our knowledge of how best to raise babies. Parents want to have a real input into how their child develops, because they have a vision of the kind of person they hope their child will grow up to be.

The first year of a baby's life is the time of most rapid growth and development. Parents see their baby changing almost day by day. They will be filled with wonder and pride but may be overwhelmed by how much they need to learn. At this time, more than at any other age, they need reliable, balanced, and reassuring information about what to expect and what to do for their baby.

In *The Month-by-Month Baby Book*, parents will find a comprehensive guide to each step of their baby's first year of life. There is specialist advice on each stage of their baby's growth and development, with current evidence-based guidelines on breast- and bottle-feeding, weaning, sleeping, health screening, and immunizations. Common problems and worries are discussed, with friendly, reassuring help. A detailed medical section provides an accessible reference to common illnesses and first aid. Supportive information is given for parents, from breastfeeding and postnatal care, to work options, childcare, family networks, and maintaining parents' identities and relationships.

The book is written for all parents and carers involved in raising children. The aim is to make this first year a happy, rewarding, and confident start to the rest of the whole family's life together.

Dr Ilona Bendefy

YOUR
NEW BABY

Once your baby is born, you'll find that life takes on a new momentum as you grapple with all the first-time experiences that caring for a growing baby involves. The first days – and weeks – can pass in a bit of a blur, so this chapter gives you the kind of background information that's useful to know from the outset. From bonding and parenting approaches to your rights and benefits, to feeding your baby, choosing nappies, and buying equipment, it's essential preparation for parenthood.

Being a parent

IT'S A LIFELONG AND, AT TIMES, DEMANDING JOB – BUT THE REWARDS ARE AMAZING.
You have anticipated this moment for the past nine months, if not longer. Now that your
baby has arrived, you have someone else to love and care for, someone for whom you
must create a safe, nurturing environment, and whose needs come before your own.

Adjusting to parenthood

Your baby is roughly as long as your elbow to your fingertips, yet they are able to turn your whole world on its head. Welcome to parenthood!

Although you may have already made practical adjustments to your life – put up a cot in your bedroom, dedicated a drawer to nappies and another to sleepsuits and so on – the reality of living with and having complete responsibility for your baby can come as a bit of a shock.

Time difference

The most dramatic change you will notice at first is how, by and large, your time is no longer your own – both day and night. Particularly in the early weeks, your baby will need almost constant care. They will wake for feeds when you would rather sleep, and the chances are they will need a nappy change just as you sit down with a cup of tea. This is physically exhausting and a time of both emotional highs and lows as you adjust to your new role. However, even at your most tired, be reassured that this is just a phase.

As you get to know your baby and start to feel more confident as a parent, you should find that life settles down into a more predictable pattern. After about three months, your baby will probably be sleeping longer at night and less during the day. By 12 months, most babies sleep for around 10–12 hours at night and have a couple of naps during the day.

Trusting your instincts

Becoming a parent is the most exciting and fulfilling experience imaginable – but along with the highs comes an entirely new realm of fears and worries. Is my baby feeding too much or too little? Am I playing with them enough? Is my baby ill? Are they developing normally? Trust your instincts and never be afraid to share your concerns and ask for help. You are the best authority on your baby. Nature has an amazing knack of tuning you in to your baby's needs – and if you don't know the answer straight away, you'll soon work it out. If you can't, then seek advice.

Talk to your partner, too. Talking about your hopes, fears, and concerns divides the burden. Even if you don't find the answers, reaffirming that you are in this together is an essential part of coping with the demands of being a parent.

Duty of care You might be surprised at how fiercely protective of your baby you feel – that's your parental instinct kicking in.

Two's company Every parent could do with two pairs of hands, but with twins, sharing the care is even more of a necessity.

The responsibility of a new life in duplicate (or multiple) can be overwhelming. Both you and your partner will need lots of support from family and friends. Try to concentrate solely on your babies, and forget about housework or doing much else for at least the first three months. Delegate making meals and running the home to your partner and family, and spend this precious time getting to know your twins and focusing on the best ways to juggle their needs.

Becoming a family

As soon as you have a baby, you become a family. This changes the dynamics of your relationship with your partner and your relatives.

You and your partner

Before your baby came along, your spare time could be dedicated to one another. If you have individual hobbies, each of you could pursue them without feeling tied to home. However, as soon as you have a baby, your time for each other, and for individual pursuits, is much less of a priority. None of this matters, of course, because your baby is the centre of your world, but inevitably there will come a moment when the full realization dawns of how life has changed for you, particularly as a couple.

Sibling rivalry Giving your toddler time and attention will help her accept the new arrival more readily and lessen feelings of jealousy.

Remind each other every so often that you are in this together. You will be tired and fretful, you may even be snappy or tearful, making it more important than ever that you actively lean on one another for support. Keep talking and try to make time for each other – even if it is just 20 minutes to sit down and eat a meal together – every day. Reassure yourselves that the tiredness of the early days passes soon enough, and that this is the beginning of a journey in which every step you take together in the common goal of doing the best for your baby (even when their old enough to make decisions for themselves) is a step that brings you closer together and reaffirms the strength of your relationship.

One common point of tension in the early months is when a new work-life balance begins as parental leave ends for one or both of you. A stay-at-home parent may feel that they have lost some of their independence, while little has changed in the life of the parent who is back in the workplace. They may feel that the burden of responsibility for the family's day-to-day welfare falls too heavily on their shoulders. On the other hand, the parent who is working may feel left out or alienated, and that their contribution as the breadwinner separates them from the fun part of being a parent.

In fact, you both have crucial roles for the family's wellbeing and it is important that you love, support, and respect one another for the choices you have made. When the weekend comes, try to give the primary care giver even just a few hours' time out, while the working parent immerses themself in family life.

Both of you juggling work and childcare puts its own strain on your relationship. In this case, you both need to share as many of the household tasks as you can, and be ready to ask each other for help when you need it. Try not to make assumptions about what the other is going to take on and which tasks fall to you, as this often leads to misunderstandings. Make lists or notes every morning if it helps, keep talking, and be prepared to be flexible.

Brothers and sisters

If you already have other children, the arrival of a new baby will cause a shift in their lives, too. It is extremely rare that any family completely escapes some form of sibling rivalry along the way (be prepared that it may not happen straight away). If you can show each other and all your children love and respect, siblings are much more likely to show love and respect towards one another, even if they have a wobble at some point about having to share you. Involving all your children with the babycare is important, and so is making time for each child individually – and that goes for step-children or children from a previous relationship, too.

In time, siblings become a support network for you and your baby, providing help for you, and unconditional love for your baby, well into adulthood.

Step-children

A new baby provides step-children with an unmistakable reminder that one of their parents has moved on beyond their original family. Some step-children see the new sibling as the glue that bonds the whole family – old and new – together, and welcome the new life gladly, but others feel resentful. Give step-siblings as much opportunity as possible to play and help with the new baby. Try to avoid terms such as "half brother" or "half sister", which create a distance. Instead, talk about how much the baby is going to love having a big brother or sister.

If your step-child doesn't live with you, keep to the same visiting schedule, and plan activities that you all can enjoy together on those days. Reassure your step-child that your love for them won't ever change.

Extended family

You have become parents, but your parents, your in-laws, and your siblings have become grandparents and aunts and uncles, too. Welcoming your wider family into your baby's life, and ensuring they have regular contact, gives them the opportunity to have a distinct sense of family identity and to know their place in the world. Today, we are often scattered from our own parents or siblings, and it may not always be easy to spend time together. If this is true for you, consider having your parents or in-laws to stay every so often, or going to stay with them. It may be a little daunting taking your baby to stay with relatives, but there are positive gains to be made. Grandparents who see a lot of their grandchildren and are actively involved in their care share a much closer bond than those who become acquainted on the occasional fleeting visit. And the love you all have for

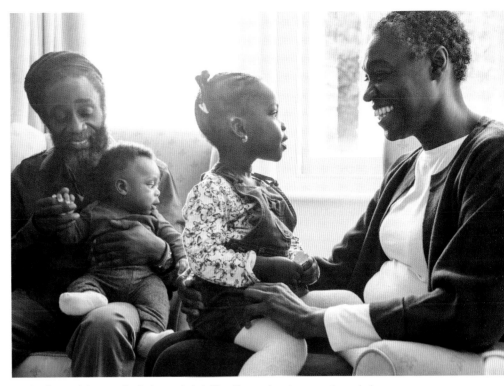

Family ties Involving your family in your baby's life will not only gain you much-needed practical help, but will also allow your child to build close and lasting relationships.

your child gives you a common link that can bring you closer.

For week-to-week contact, join a social networking site through which you can contact relatives and share photos; or download a social chat programme, and invest in a webcam – even if you are at opposite ends of the country, or the world, your baby can still grow up with a sense of their family connections. Finally, babies love to look at faces so, as your baby matures, do show them photographs of relatives, pointing at each and naming them one by one. This is a great way to provide your baby with a sense of their wider family.

SINGLE PARENTING

It takes only two – you and your baby – to make a family and you can provide your baby with everything they need, from food to clothing and especially love. You are also the person who best knows your baby, so your instincts will ensure that you make no more mistakes than any other parent. Being a single parent does not mean that you are alone. If you feel isolated, pick up the phone and talk to someone – a friend, a midwife, or a family member – to share how you feel. Or consider joining a local or online parents' support group to seek advice and encouragement from other parents that may share your feelings. During the first few weeks, be prepared to ask for help from willing friends and family; you may even want to consider staying with someone while you adjust to being a parent.

Parenting approaches

There are no hard-and-fast rules when it comes to good parenting practice. Your own approach to parenting will emerge in time.

Before you had your baby, you may have had some fixed ideas about the right and wrong ways to raise a child. The reality is that as you settle into your new role, some of the ideas about parenting you thought were non-negotiable suddenly become less important, while others move up the agenda. Beyond the fundamental requirements to love, nurture, respond to, feed, and clothe your baby, there is so much to learn as you go along. It is essential to talk to your partner about how you will raise your baby and how, in the years to come, you will set expectations for behaviour.

One thing is for certain – as your baby becomes a toddler, they will soon learn if one of you is a soft touch and one the disciplinarian, and whether or not they can play one of you off against the other. Presenting a united front and giving a clear, consistent message is the key to success, whatever approach to parenting you both decide to take.

Reflecting you

Your approach to parenting will inevitably, in part, reflect the ways in which your parents brought you up. In addition, it will demonstrate your own culture and values, and your faith if you have one. It will also reflect your personality: if you tend to be laid-back, it's more likely that your parenting style will be laid-back; if you are a list-maker and organizer, the chances are that your approach will be more routine-based. No approach is definitive, but you need to be comfortable with the one you choose, so that you can stick by it and provide a secure environment in which your baby can develop.

Setting boundaries

A newborn baby does not yet have the mental acuity to understand right from wrong, yes from no, good from bad. But in only a matter of months, they will begin to explore the world by such actions as reaching and grabbing, at which point, gently setting boundaries gives your baby the opportunity to discover what's around them, while remaining safe.

Furthermore, as your baby becomes more aware, boundaries will make them feel secure in what is otherwise a baffling melee of sight, sound, taste, touch, and scent. Your baby needs you to guide them on appropriate behaviour and actions. Setting boundaries isn't about becoming a disciplinarian with a strict rule book. Rather, boundaries provide an important structure for your baby's life, and when it comes to right and wrong, a moral code for their behaviour. Ultimately, boundaries make them feel secure.

Introducing discipline

During your baby's first year, there are very few reasons for saying "No". You cannot teach a baby to control their behaviour at this age because they are unable to do so – the part of their brain that controls social understanding and behaviour won't be fully developed for another year or two. So "discipline" at this stage should be about gentle correction or distraction, and saying "No" only when your baby is doing something that is unsafe for them, or for others.

Whatever boundaries you set, it is important to follow the same pattern of correction each time. One useful approach is "repeat, remove, distract". So, you repeat the boundary (for example, "Don't touch the vase, it may break"), then remove the temptation (put the vase away) or remove your baby from the danger, if relevant, and then distract them quickly. The next time the baby does the same thing, respond with the same sequence: repeat, remove, distract. Through the consistency of your words and actions, from the age of about nine months, your baby should begin to associate

Perfect parent Of course, there's no such thing, but with plenty of love, kindness, and consistency you'll be the best parent there is.

Out of harm's way Once your baby is mobile, you'll need to remove them repeatedly from danger. Explain why some things are out of bounds, and distract them by moving them to a safer place or activity.

certain commands with certain consequences. This is a vital lesson for the toddler years when all children learn to push boundaries, as your baby will trust that you mean what you say.

Giving reasons

When you ask your baby not to do something, let them know why in very simple terms: "Don't touch the oven – it's hot, ouch", and mime touching something hot. They won't fully understand, but they'll begin to get the idea during their first year. Getting cross with your baby won't achieve anything. As your baby matures, they will listen and respond more readily when you are calm. Get their attention, speak clearly, and show them by acting it out yourself.

ASK A CHILD PSYCHOLOGIST

When does parenting become "pushy" as opposed to "encouraging"? We live in a competitive world and there is a growing trend for parents to fill their children's – even their babies' – time with activities to race them through developmental milestones. However, children will rarely be hurried. Encouraging your child to learn means giving them time to explore the world themselves, and giving them a degree of autonomy to discover what is around them and to discover the principles of cause and effect (whether that's in actions, language, or sounds). It also means giving them lots of praise when they make a new discovery, behave well, or learn to do something for themselves. Above all, children learn best through play, when they are happy, relaxed, and able to work at their own pace. If you allow lots of playtime, and read stories and sing songs together, your baby will have all the encouragement necessary to develop mental acuity at a perfect pace, without being pushed to go too fast.

POSITIVE PARENTING

Whatever your values and the specifics of the way in which you want to raise your baby, there are certain fundamentals of parenting that will make your approach more effective and loving, and some methods that it is best to avoid. Positive parenting is about championing the good in your child. Children thrive on praise, and they also love attention. If they get lots of praise and attention for good behaviour, but find that bad behaviour is reprimanded or ignored, they soon learn to focus on the good.

Key positive parenting traits
• Give lots of extra praise and attention when your baby does as they are asked.
• Show how proud you are of your baby. Celebrate even minor achievements with clapping and cheering. Your baby will love this and soon want to elicit those reactions again.
• Show respect to your baby.
• Be consistent in your rules or expectations and follow through with rewards for positive behaviour.
• Show your baby your love by giving them your undivided attention and lots of physical affection.

Parenting traits to avoid
• Even if you feel frustrated, try not to react angrily towards your baby. If you stay calm, your baby will stay calm and be far more likely to respond positively to you.
• It is never appropriate to criticize your baby. As your baby gets older, focus on behaviour ("You did not share your toy"), not them ("You are selfish").
• Stick to your rules and your routines: babies feel more secure when they know what's expected.

Parental rights and benefits

Once your child is born, you will receive forms that you will need to fill in to register the birth and claim child-related government funds.

In the blur of a new baby's arrival, filling in forms can feel like the last thing you want to do. However, the Government does impose deadlines on registration and claims, so go through the pack you are given as soon as you can. Note that if your child has been born with a disability, you may be entitled to further financial and practical help – talk to your midwife or health visitor who will be able to advise you.

Registering the birth

When you register your baby's birth you will be given a birth certificate, which you'll need to claim child benefit. You have up to 42 days (six weeks) to register, after which you will receive a formal notification to appear before your local registrar and, if you fail to do so, you may face prosecution.

You can go to any registrar in any district to register the birth, not just the district where the baby was born. You usually need to make an appointment. If you register in a different district, your details will be sent on to the district office of birth, and only then will the registrar issue a birth certificate.

There are only certain people who can register a birth. If you and your baby's father are married, either one of you can go on your own to register. If you are not married, you must go together, or one of you has to sign a declaration that you are happy for the other to register the birth alone. This is to ensure that when couples are not married, both parents appear on the birth certificate if they want to. Once you have registered the baby, you will be given a "short" birth certificate, which is free of charge, but you can have a full copy of the register entry for a fee. In most districts it is cheaper to buy the full copy when you register than to order it at a later date. Note that you will need a full birth certificate to apply for your baby's passport (see p.125).

You will also be given your baby's National Health Service number. Keep a note of this and also give it to your doctor. The unique number will belong to your child for life and is used by medical staff to access and update their health records.

Claiming child benefit

If you are responsible for a child under the age of 16 or 17, or for an older one in certain forms of full-time education, you may be entitled to receive tax-free child benefit. The amount you receive is higher for your first child than it is for subsequent children. Usually, child benefit is paid directly into your bank account every month, but if you are on income support or jobseekers' allowance, or you are a single parent, you may be able to arrange to have the money paid weekly. If you or your partner earns over a certain

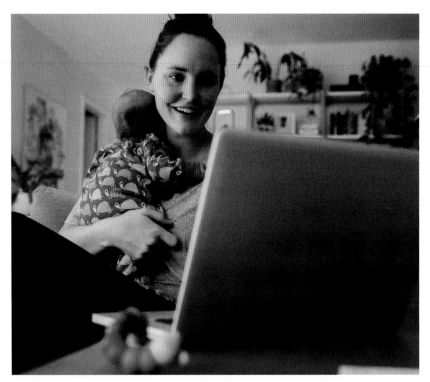

Seeing what help is available You have certain rights and benefits depending on your circumstances so make sure you find out what you're entitled to so that you don't miss out.

Slowly but surely the law is changing to account for the fact that many fathers are more actively involved in their children's upbringing than was the case a generation ago. Presently, once you have been with your employer for a certain amount of time, you are entitled to two weeks' Ordinary Paternity Leave, which you must take consecutively, but not necessarily immediately after the baby is born. You may also be entitled to Ordinary Statutory Paternity Pay (or your company may have a better scheme for new fathers). Together with your partner try to work out the best time to take paternity leave. If you have help from grandparents or other family members or friends for the first week after your baby is born, it might make sense to take the following two weeks off; or if you have other school-age children, you might prefer to wait until their next school holiday.

Increasingly, fathers may be able to take on primary care of the baby while the mother returns to work, with the same rights as the mother would have had, had she stayed at home instead. This is called Additional Paternity Leave, and it must be taken 20 weeks after the birth and before your baby's first birthday. You may even be entitled to receive Additional Statutory Paternity Pay (ASPP) at the government standard rate. If you don't qualify for ASPP, you may be able to take the time unpaid. None of this affects your holiday entitlement.

Is there any additional help available for single parents? If you are bringing up your baby on your own, the Government has several schemes in place that can help you to achieve a good work–life balance. For example, you may be entitled to child tax credit if you are on a low income, and/or working tax credit to help pay for childcare while you are at work. In addition, you may be entitled to receive a maternity grant, which is a lump sum intended to help you buy essentials for your baby. Until your child is five years old, you may also be entitled to free vitamins and milk for them. Single and low-income parents are also often entitled to Council Tax relief. The Government website (see pp.385) has all the information you need on making a claim, or you can call your local benefits office, or the Citizens' Advice Bureau.

threshold, you can still claim child benefit, but it will be taxed. Alternatively, you can opt out of receiving child benefit. You don't need to apply for child benefit immediately after your baby is born, but it will be backdated for only three months from the receipt of your application. You will need to send the original certificate to your local child benefit office, which will process your application. Note that as the law changes frequently with regard to child benefit, check the Government website for up-to-date information.

Your rights and benefits

Assuming that your baby wasn't born earlier than expected, and you were working, you will already be claiming maternity benefit, either in the form of Statutory Maternity Pay (SMP) or according to your company's own policy. SMP is paid for a maximum of 39 weeks (calculated from the start of your maternity leave). You will usually be paid a proportion of your salary for the first six weeks, then a weekly amount from the Government for the remaining 33 weeks. After this, you are entitled to a further 13 weeks off work to care for your baby (making a full year), but during this time you will not receive government-funded maternity pay. Your company may have its own terms to cover this time. If you are self-employed, you may be entitled to Maternity Allowance (MA), a fixed government amount, paid for 39 weeks from the beginning of the week of your first claim. During the time you claim SMP or MA, you may be entitled to do a few days work without losing your benefits – check with your local benefits office.

When you return to work during or at the end of ordinary maternity leave (the first 26 weeks), you are entitled to return to your own job with the same rate of pay. If, however, you return during the second 26 weeks or at the end, you are entitled to return to the same job, with the same pay, as long as that job still exists. If it does not, your employer must offer you a similar position with the same salary and benefits. You need to give your employer eight weeks' notice of when you intend to return to work, if that is before 52 weeks. If you decide to leave work altogether, you must resign according to the terms of your employment contract.

Same-sex parents are entitled to the same maternity leave rights or paternity leave rights as heterosexual couples. Adoptive parents are entitled to statutory adoption pay and leave. Currently, there is no parental leave for foster carers. Childcare rights and benefits may differ from one company to the next, so check with the human resource team at your workplace to better understand your entitlement.

Understanding your child

YOU'LL DISCOVER MORE AND MORE ABOUT WHAT MAKES YOUR BABY TICK AS EACH MONTH GOES BY. Your baby has their own unique genetic make-up, but at least some of their characteristics are inherited. In the first year, as your baby negotiates developmental milestones and develops their own personality, you will gather clues as to what kind of child they will eventually become.

Your child's genes

Friends and family always look to see which parent a baby resembles.
As they grow, you may recognize which traits your baby has inherited.

Passed from parent to child, genes are segments of DNA containing genetic information that determine features or characteristics unique to an individual. A baby's genetic traits are inherited from both their parents. Furthermore, a parent's DNA consists of their parents' DNA, which is why some children show likenesses to one or other of their grandparents.

Eye colour

Certain physical traits are determined by the presence or absence of a dominant or recessive gene, making some characteristics predictable. For example, if both biological parents have blue eyes, their baby will have blue eyes, because they will have inherited recessive blue genes from both parents. However, if one parent has brown eyes and the other has blue, their own parents' genes will play a role in determining eye colour. If one parent's brown eyes are the result of both a brown and a blue gene from their own parents, there is a chance for a blue-eyed baby. However, if one biological parent has two brown genes, even if the other parent has blue genes, the baby will have brown eyes, because they will always inherit one dominant brown-eye gene. Other characteristics that work this way are hair colour – dark hair is dominant, while fair or red hair is recessive, and hair type (curly is dominant; straight is recessive).

Polygenic traits

A polygenic trait, such as height, is a characteristic determined by a combination of genes. Experts say that taking the average of the height of both biological parents and then subtracting 5cm (2in) for a female baby and adding 5cm (2in) for a male baby gives a good idea of adult height. But, genes themselves contain dominant and recessive triggers, called alleles. Even if both biological parents are short, they may still have "tall" (dominant) alleles, it's just these are outnumbered by "small" ones. If a baby inherits genes made up of most or all of a parent's "tall" alleles, and only a few or none of the "short" alleles, they could end up being taller. Polygenic traits are also influenced by environmental factors, such as nutrition. Other polygenic traits include intelligence and skin colour.

Family likeness Spotting family resemblances is an early preoccupation for everyone who will be invested in a baby's life.

ASK A PAEDIATRICIAN

Is my baby likely to be musical like me?
In 2001, geneticists at St Thomas's Hospital in London, working with the Institute for Deafness in Maryland, USA, published a study of hundreds of twins that supported the notion that musical ability is inherited. Certainly, Johann Sebastian Bach came from a long line of well-respected musicians. So, generally, yes, it is likely that your baby will be musical like you, especially if you encourage their innate talent by playing a variety of music to them and offering them instruments to play with. Equally, if you are sporty, you are likely to produce children with the physical build and, say, hand–eye coordination to follow in your footsteps. Inevitably, though, nurture also comes into play. If you are musical, you will naturally encourage your child to love music; if you love sports, you'll encourage them to play sports, which in turn hones their in-built talent.

Your developing child

Your baby's growth in the first year is remarkable. At no other time in human life is development so evident and so rapid.

Soft focus At first, your baby must be up close to see your face; by eight months, they'll identify people and objects from across the room.

ASK A CHILD PSYCHOLOGIST

Can I spoil my baby with love? Babies need to feel secure and you and your partner are the people best placed to ensure that happens. Showing your baby love by giving them lots of attention, in the form of playing with them, attending to their needs, being close at all times and giving them plenty of cuddles and kisses does not spoil them. With a deep sense of security in you, they will develop confidence to explore their world independently. As your baby matures, you can also show love by setting boundaries and limits: giving in to them every time isn't in their best interests; it's more important to show them what is safe and teach them right from wrong.

Physical milestones

The most striking physical change during your baby's first year is their size. By the age of one, your baby will be about 30cm (12in) longer than they were at birth, and about three times as heavy. During that time, muscle tone and physical coordination will develop so that by two months, your baby will be able to hold up their head for a few seconds, and at three months, they may be able to flip over. By 6–7 months, your baby will have developed enough muscle strength to sit unaided, and from sitting will come crawling (usually by 6–9 months), and then, by a year, standing up, possibly unaided. By then, your baby may even be able to walk.

Your baby's fine motor skills will progress from swiping at objects at about three months to holding a small object using a pincer grip at 8–10 months. At around 10 months, your baby can use a trainer or sippy cup and drink with help, and by 12 months can make a mark on paper with a big crayon or piece of chalk.

These major physical milestones are among the most visible, but your baby is developing in many unseen ways, too. Over the first year, their sight will improve from being able to focus only on objects 20–25cm (8–10in) away from their face to being able to distinguish depth and distance at a year. Your baby rapidly learns to recognize sounds, so that by only a few months old, babies can identify where a particular sound is coming from and can turn their head towards it.

Early learning milestones

Your baby's brain has "plasticity", which means that it is able to create, adapt, and change its neural pathways according to all the new experiences life brings. This plasticity ensures your baby's rapid intellectual development. Within a few days of birth, your baby will prefer your face to anyone else's and your baby will recognize your scent. These experiences make a baby feel secure.

By six months, language skills will have developed enough that your baby may recognize their own name when you call it, and by nine months, they'll understand when you say "No" (although they may not always comply), and your baby may even be able to look at the correct image of an object in a book if you name it.

Your baby will begin to make recognizable sounds. At first, at a few months old, your baby may coo, gurgle, or make strange vowel sounds, but by around 10 months, these may become a discernible "mama" or "dada", although it's unlikely your baby will use them discriminately. However, by a year, babies may have managed their first meaningful word – often "dada" when referring to daddy (because babies find the consonant "d" easier to sound out than the "m" sound required for mama), although "cat" and "spoon" are often cited as first words, too.

Behavioural and personality milestones

By the end of your baby's first year, your bundle of mystery will have become a young toddler, who is already showing clear signs of the person they are going to be.

You might be relieved to hear that your baby's behaviour with regard to sleeping will gradually improve month by month, as their stomach grows to hold enough food to prevent them waking for feeds. By the time they are one year old, your baby should be sleeping through the night, going to bed at around seven o'clock and waking about 12 hours later.

At first, your baby will show preferences for certain people – parents, primary caregivers, and siblings – and by six months old, may become wary of strangers. When your baby is six months old, they will begin to display distinct personality traits, such as the sort of things they find amusing and the things that make them frustrated. Your baby may throw away toys when they become cross with them, or cry in anger.

By eight months old, your baby will believe that everything belongs to them and will object to you taking away a toy. They'll still be anxious if they have to leave you, but will be interested in other babies, and will "chat" with other close

We are all born with an in-built genetic blueprint that gives us our relative strengths and weaknesses, and determines certain character traits. However, most psychologists now accept that although a baby might be genetically predisposed to being better at some activities than others, the way in which a baby is brought up, and environmental factors (such as the value of a baby's nutrition) also influence developing skills. Bring out the best in your baby by playing with and reading to them and letting them explore the world (safely). After weaning, give your baby the full spectrum of nutrients, and above all provide a loving, secure environment to give them confidence to reach their full potential. That way, you can nurture whatever gifts nature has bestowed.

adults. Your baby wants to please you and will thrive on your love and affection.

Girls and boys

All children develop at different rates, regardless of their gender. However, there are certain aspects of early learning that seem to favour girls over boys, or vice versa. For example, studies show that girls learn to understand language and talk more quickly and they have more honed fine motor skills (girls will write sooner, for example). On the other hand, boys tend to be more physical and their gross motor skills are often ahead of girls, certainly by the time they reach toddler age.

One study at Cambridge University indicated that boys understand the laws of motion more quickly than girls – for example, they understand the speed and direction of a rolling ball sooner than girls tend to. Girls tend to be more wary; boys more fearless. Needless to say, things inevitably even themselves out, and whether nature or nurture results in stereotypical behaviour for girls and boys is still the subject of much debate.

Head control After a couple of months, babies' neck muscles are strong enough to allow them to lift their heads.

Sitting upright comfortably At around six months old most babies can sit up unaided, and interact with their toys.

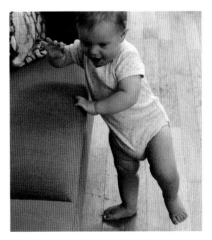

Standing up By the end of their first year, most babies can stand up with a little support.

Baby basics

GETTING TO GRIPS WITH THE BASICS OF BABYCARE WILL HELP TO PREPARE YOU FOR THE FIRST WEEKS. There's an enormous amount to take on board immediately after your baby is born, so the more you can learn beforehand about feeding your baby, putting them down to sleep, changing them, and keeping them clean, the more confident and in control you're likely to feel.

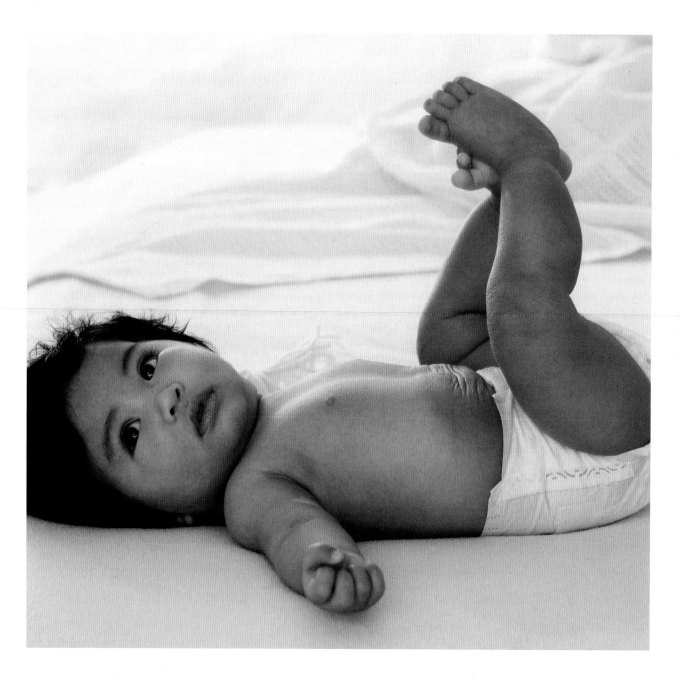

Feeding your baby

Breastmilk or formula provides all the nutrients your baby needs in the first few months and is a mainstay of their diet for the entire year.

Whether you choose to breastfeed or bottle-feed, it's completely normal and understandable to be a little nervous about feeding. Knowing what to expect can make the process easier, more successful, and relaxing.

Why breastfeed?

Breastfeeding is the best way to ensure that your baby gets all the nutrients they need. The composition of your breastmilk will change to meet the needs of your growing baby. It includes healthy fats (including essential fatty acids – EFAs) that are necessary for healthy growth and optimum development (particularly in the brain), and the calcium it contains is better utilized by babies than that found in formula.

Breastmilk contains certain hormones and growth factors that encourage healthy weight gain and development. It also reduces your baby's risk of acquiring diabetes and both childhood and adult obesity, as well as protecting against allergies, asthma, and eczema. Breastfeeding is also thought to reduce your baby's risk of cot death or Sudden Infant Death Syndrome (see p.31), as well as improve bonding. Some research claims that breastfeeding promotes the development of your baby's facial structure, aiding speech and vision.

In some literature, breastfeeding is considered to be the "fourth trimester" in terms of your baby's brain growth and development. You'll also be passing on your antibodies to your baby through your breastmilk, which can help to keep them well until their immune system matures.

Research has found that breastfed babies have fewer incidences of vomiting and diarrhoea, and are protected against gastroenteritis, as well as ear infections, respiratory illnesses, pneumonia, bronchitis, kidney infections, and septicaemia (blood poisoning). There is also a reduced risk of chronic constipation, colic, and other tummy disorders.

Breastmilk contains compounds that are known to destroy bacteria such as E. coli and salmonella that would make your baby unwell. There are other health benefits for your baby, including a reduced risk of heart disease, obesity, and iron-deficiency anaemia. Breastfeeding is by far the best way to feed your baby. For more guidance see pp.26–27.

Benefits for you

Breasfeeding reduces your risk of breast and ovarian cancer and of osteoporosis. There's also growing evidence to suggest that women who breastfeed may lower their risk of heart attack, heart disease, and stroke. Breastfeeding uses up around 500 calories per day, so it can promote postnatal weight loss, as well as delay the return of menstruation. Last, but not least, breastfeeding is very convenient – there are no bottles to wash or sterilize, nothing to prepare, and no equipment to transport.

YOUR BABY'S FIRST YEAR

In most cases, your baby will have a milk-only diet until they are around six months old. Whether you choose bottle- or breastfeeding, they will need an increasing amount of milk over the coming months, and milk should remain the mainstay of their diet throughout their first year (see p.184).

Weaning normally begins by around six months (see pp.236–37), when your baby will start on very liquid purées – usually baby rice mixed with a little of their usual milk – and puréed fruits and vegetables. Once these foods are accepted, a range of others can be introduced – particularly those that are rich in iron and protein, such as meat, fish, and eggs. The texture of foods should change as quickly as your baby finds it acceptable, from purées to mashed to lumpy and then chopped foods. By the end of the year, your baby should be enjoying three meals a day.

Throughout this book, we'll guide you through the stages of weaning, helping you to make the right choices for your baby at the appropriate times. You may decide to choose "baby-led" weaning, in which your baby is weaned on to wholefoods, rather than purées, at their own pace (see p.217 and pp.236–37).

How breastfeeding works

Breastfeeding is a natural process based on supply and demand – letting your baby suckle will trigger your breasts to make more milk to satisfy them.

During pregnancy, your body begins to prepare for breastfeeding. Your areola becomes darker (which some people believe helps your baby to see it and encourages feeding). Tiny bumps around your areola grow bigger and more noticeable (known as Montgomery's tubercles, these secrete oil that lubricates your nipples to prevent drying, cracking, and infections while feeding). Also, your placenta stimulates the release of hormones that make milk production possible.

All women are born with milk ducts (a series of channels that transport milk through your breasts) and during pregnancy, these begin to prepare for feeding. Your milk glands expand dramatically so that by the end of pregnancy, each breast may be up to 600g (1lb 5oz) heavier!

Your lactation system, inside your breasts, is rather like a small tree, with milk glands forming clusters like grapes high up in your breast. These make milk. This milk travels down from the glands through the milk ducts, which widen beneath the areola to form milk "sinuses". These empty into about 20 little openings in your nipple, which release milk when they are stimulated by your baby's sucking.

This sucking sends a message to the pituitary gland to release oxytocin, a hormone that makes you feel calm and loving, and prompts your milk-producing cells to empty their milk into the ducts. This is known as the "let-down" reflex, and it can also be triggered when you hear

your baby cry (and sometimes when you hear other babies!), or even simply think about your baby.

Once your milk is let down, your baby's gums compress the sinuses where the milk begins to pool. If the baby sucks on your nipple rather than the whole areola, they can draw out only a little milk and you may experience discomfort. This is why it is essential to get your baby's "latch" correct from the outset (see opposite).

Your baby's sucking also stimulates nerves in your nipple that send messages to the pituitary gland in your brain to secrete the hormone prolactin. This hormone is responsible for ensuring that your milk is continually produced according to your baby's needs. The more milk that is removed from your breasts, the more milk your body makes to replace it, so even expressing milk can help to keep up your supply if you are unable to breastfeed immediately.

Colostrum

From about 15–16 weeks of pregnancy, your breasts begin to produce colostrum, which is your baby's first milk. This is a very nutritious, dark yellow liquid containing high levels of protein, carbohydrates, healthy fat, and antibodies. It is very easy to digest: just a few teaspoons will provide hugely concentrated nutrition for your baby and keep them hydrated before your milk "comes in". Colostrum has a laxative effect on your baby, helping them to pass their

BREASTFEEDING

• Breastfeeding will be much more successful when you are relaxed, so find a comfortable place to sit down and put your feet up.

• Breastfeeding mums will need (often instant) access to their breasts, so loose-fitting, comfortable clothing that unzips or unbuttons easily is essential. You'll also need a nursing bra that you can open and close with one hand.

• Your baby will feed until they have had enough. If your baby dozes off after a few moments, gently waken them by winding them or stroking their cheek.

• Check that your entire areola is in your baby's mouth; your baby will stimulate the release – and resupply – of your milk by pressing on the milk sinuses (see right). If your baby is only hitting a few sinuses, you could end up with blocked ducts (see p.59), sore nipples, and a hungry baby!

• Don't worry about whether your baby is getting enough. Their weight gain will be monitored over the first few weeks of their life, and as long as the baby puts on weight, has plenty of wet nappies (see pp.44–45), and seems alert when they are awake, all will be fine.

• Try not to give up! Breastfeeding can take a little while to settle down into a comfortable experience, but it does become easier over the first few weeks. Try to remember that you are doing what's best for your baby.

early stools (meconium), which is important for the excretion of excess bilirubin, which may otherwise cause jaundice (see p.372).

Consistency of breastmilk

When your milk comes in two to three days after your baby's birth (although sometimes a little later, if you've had a Caesarean), your breasts will feel engorged and perhaps even a little painful. Each time your baby suckles, your baby will receive two types of milk. The first milk out of the breast is known as "foremilk", which is thinner in consistency and slightly bluish-white in colour. This hydrates your baby and satisfies thirst. Next, your baby will receive "hindmilk", which is the thicker, more nutrient-dense, and calorific milk that provides everything they need for growth, development, and energy.

It's important to empty your breast completely at each sitting to ensure that your baby gets both types of milk. If the baby gets only a little of your foremilk, they may soon be hungry and need to feed again.

Responsive feeding

Feeding your baby whenever they are hungry will encourage your breasts to produce the required amount of milk.

ASK A BREASTFEEDING EXPERT

Is it worth breastfeeding for just a few days? Yes! Breastmilk is the perfect first food and will give your baby a great start to life. Colostrum the first milk you produce is rich in protein and vitamins to support your baby's growth and development, and contains a vital antibody called sIgA. This antibody plays a crucial role in building your baby's immune system, lining their gut and respiratory systems protecting your baby from illness. Breastfeeding has significant health benefits to you too, lowering the risk of breast cancer, ovarian cancer, and cardiovascular disease.

HOW BREASTFEEDING WORKS

LATCH YOUR BABY ON TO YOUR BREAST

Gently stroking your baby's cheek or the corner of their mouth will stimulate the rooting reflex, and your baby will naturally open their mouth to seek out food. The next step is to ensure the baby is correctly latched on to your breast. Getting this right can make breastfeeding more comfortable and efficient.

When your baby opens their mouth wide, bring them to your breast – not the other way round! Their tongue should be down and forwards, and your nipple should be aimed at the roof of their mouth as you draw them on to your breast. When the baby is properly latched on, all of the nipple and some of the breast tissue should be in their mouth. Your baby is correctly positioned if their tummy is to yours – tummy-to-tummy. Their lower lip will be rolled out and their chin will be against your breast. Their lower arm may be tucked under you, and their upper may reach round to hold your breast. Their nose should be away from your breast so they can breathe.

If your baby is correctly latched on, you should hear only a low-pitched swallowing noise – not a clicking or smacking noise – and you should see their jaw moving, a sign that they are feeding successfully. Your breasts may be tender at first; a few different positions can improve comfort (see p.58).

Rooting reflex Help your baby root for your nipple by stroking the cheek nearest to it. They will purse their lips, ready to suck.

Get it right Make sure your baby's tongue is down and forward, and your nipple aimed at the roof of their mouth before they latch on.

Latch on Make sure your baby takes the nipple and a good proportion of the areola into their mouth for a good latch.

Best position Your baby's head and body must be in a straight line so they can swallow easily, and their chin should touch your breast.

While it can be tempting to put your baby on a schedule, they may be left bewildered and hungry, and your breasts will fail to meet demand (see p.58). A good feed normally lasts about 20 to 30 minutes, but a young baby will probably want to nurse every couple of hours, so you might feel as if you're feeding around the clock. If your baby is falling asleep on the breast, or losing concentration and looking about instead, it may be that they aren't very hungry, and you'll be better off trying again later.

Getting support

Breastfeeding is not always easy at the outset, and you may require the support of your midwife, health visitor, or a specialist lactation counsellor to help to get it established, or you may want to attend a baby café. You'll need support from your partner, too. You'll be spending very long hours feeding your baby, and until you are able to express a little milk that can be fed via a bottle (see box, below), your partner won't be very involved and will need to understand that you are breastfeeding to give your baby the best possible start in life. Studies have shown that family and friends play an important role in the decisions that new mums make about feeding. Women who feel supported feel more confident and tend to breastfeed for longer.

EXPRESSING BREASTMILK

Once your milk supply is established – at around a month or six weeks after the birth – you can begin to express a little milk. This will not only buy you some freedom, allowing your partner or someone else to feed your baby from time to time, but it will also provide you with a store of frozen milk that can be used if and when you go back to work.

Not everyone finds expressing easy, and you may need to experiment with different pumps (for example, manual, battery-operated, or electric) or do it by hand (see p.83) to produce enough milk. If you're feeding eight times a day, 90ml (3floz) is usually adequate for a single feed, so don't worry if you do not manage to express much at first. Relaxing somewhere near your baby can make the process more successful, and you may find that if your baby regularly feeds from only one breast in a sitting, you can simultaneously express from the other.

If your baby is born prematurely, they may not be able to feed at the breast initially, in which case you will be helped to express and get your milk supply established, ready for when your baby is physically able to feed themselves.

Manual pump Hand or manual pumps are affordable, lightweight, quiet, and easy to use – you simply operate the plunger to express milk (left). **Electric pump** This pump is automatic, so generally quicker and more suitable if you need to express milk quite frequently (right).

ASK A BREASTFEEDING EXPERT

Is there any reason why I won't be able to breastfeed? Almost all women can breastfeed, and provide sufficient milk to meet their babies' needs. Even women with small breasts or inverted nipples can successfully nurse, so try not to worry. Some women have concerns in advance that it will be too difficult, but with the support of your midwife and partner, you may find breastfeeding a truly rewarding experience.

There are some cases when breastfeeding may not be possible. These include taking some types of medication, which would be unsafe for your baby, or suffering from a breast infection or disease, such as cancer. Very rarely, some women don't generate enough milk for their babies, although current support makes this less likely. Women who have had a breast reduction may find feeding difficult (although not always impossible); or, your baby may be unable to breastfeed because they are premature, too small, have a problem sucking, have tongue-tie, have birth defects in their mouth, such as cleft palate, or have digestive problems. In these cases you may wish to express milk (see box, left).

Bottle-feeding

If you can't or do not wish to breastfeed, or plan to do so for a short period of time, you'll need to get to grips with the art of bottle-feeding.

Mums who cannot, or choose not to breastfeed should not feel guilty. There is a very good range of formulas on the market that will encourage healthy growth and development, and it's perfectly possible to make bottle-feeding sessions warm, nurturing, and positive (see p.59).

Bottle-feeding equipment

You'll need six to eight bottles, teats, and caps, a bottle-brush for cleaning them, a sterilizer, a measuring jug, formula, and a kettle to boil water, which is then cooled to make up the feed. There are many bottles and teats available, and you can purchase anything from anti-colic bottles and those that self-sterilize, to "natural" and slow- or fast-flow teats. You may need to experiment when your baby is born, to see what works best for them.

Teats should be slow-flowing for new babies, and gradually become "faster" as they get a little older. Silicone teats are more durable; however, latex tends to be closer to the sensation of a nipple. Choose from a traditional bell shape, an "orthodontic" teat that manufacturers claim most resembles a nipple, or a flatter teat that is particularly easy for young babies to manage.

Choosing formula

Choose a formula that is appropriate for your baby's age. Most formulas contain roughly the same beneficial ingredients, but you may wish to look for one that contains probiotics to encourage digestive health, and omega oils, which aid brain development. You can make up formula from a powder or a liquid, or buy it ready-made. Breastmilk contains two types of protein: whey and casein. The balance in breastmilk is in favour of whey, with a 60:40 ratio (60 per cent whey, and 40 per cent casein). It is a good idea, therefore, to look for a formula with this same ratio intact. Formulas that have a greater percentage of casein tend to be harder for your baby to digest. Formula is designed to provide your baby with the right amounts of essential nutrients. It is balanced to ensure that it is easily digestible, and meets your baby's needs for both fluid and food. It is, therefore, extremely important to follow the manufacturer's instructions to the letter.

Your first bottle-feed

Bring your own choice of ready-made infant formula to the hospital. No one formula is better than another. The NHS recommends choosing first instant formula (whey-based).

Your midwife will be able to show you the best positions for bottle-feeding (see p.59). Feed your baby responsively rather than adhering to strict timings. Feed little and often, around 15–30mls (1/2–1floz) each feed, and do not force your baby to finish a bottle.

Comforting feed Making eye contact with your baby while you bottle-feed helps to promote bonding and makes them feel secure.

ASK A MIDWIFE

Why do I need to sterilize all my baby's feeding equipment? Washing bottles carefully is important because every trace of milk needs to be removed. However, this is not enough to kill the germs that may cause health problems in your baby. Bottles, and the equipment used to make up your baby's milk, need to be sterilized properly, using high heat, such as steam, or with chemical cold-water treatments that are designed to kill any germs. There is a wide variety of sterilizers available, including those that work in the microwave. It's also fine to use your dishwasher, as long as your machine reaches a hot temperature of at least 80°C (176°F) or more, which is necessary to kill any harmful bacteria or viruses. This will help your baby avoid germs that cause illness.

Sleeping arrangements

Your baby will spend a lot of time asleep in the coming months, so their sleeping place needs to be both comfortable and safe.

There is a wealth of options when it comes to a baby's first bed, and you can spend a lot of money on features that may not be necessary. For example, although a cradle or cot that rocks might look like a good way to settle a baby at night, your baby may get used to being rocked to sleep, and find the transition to a cot or bed more difficult. No matter what your budget, the most important considerations for a baby's sleeping arrangements are safety and comfort.

Portable Moses basket A lightweight Moses basket is ideal as you can move it around and keep your baby close while they sleep.

Little beds

After having been tightly confined in your womb for months, your baby is likely to settle better and feel more secure in a snug environment. For this reason, a "first" bed should be small enough to make your baby feel cosy and comfortable. Experts now recommend that babies sleep in the same room as their caregivers for the first six months of their life, so a "portable" bed, such as a Moses basket, is a practical choice. (Just be aware that you should avoid putting your baby's Moses basket directly on an underheated floor as this puts your baby at risk of overheating.)

Cradles and cots are less mobile, which can be a disadvantage in the early days, but many parents like something sturdier. Your baby's first bed will probably last only a few months, so it isn't usually worth spending a fortune! If you go secondhand, it is recommended that you purchase a new mattress, to help lower the risk of Sudden Infant Death Syndrome (SIDS; see box, right).

If you go for a full-sized cot, there are features that will help to ensure your baby's safety and help you get the most for your money (see p.108). Mattresses can be made of foam, natural, or hollow fibres, and they must fit the cot snugly so that there are no gaps in which a baby could get trapped. The mattress cover needs to be easy to clean. You can put a carrycot or Moses basket inside a cot when your baby is small, which helps to ease the transition to a big cot later.

SUDDEN INFANT DEATH SYNDROME (SIDS)

Sudden Infant Death Syndrome (SIDS or "cot death") is the unexplained death of a baby. It occurs most frequently in babies under the age of four months, but can occur up to the age of one. The cause of SIDS is still largely unknown, but a great deal of research has gone into identifying the risk factors and the measures that can be undertaken to prevent it.

Remember that cot death is rare, so don't let worry stop you from enjoying your baby's first few months of life. However, follow the advice below to reduce the risk.
• Place your baby down to sleep on their back with their feet at the foot of the cot. Use layers of cotton sheets and cellular blankets securely tucked in. Avoid duvets, quilts, wedges, bedding rolls, and pillows.
• Keep your baby in a room with you for the first six months.
• Keep your baby's head uncovered to prevent it from getting too hot.

• Don't smoke in pregnancy and don't let anyone smoke in the same room – or house – as your baby.
• Never fall asleep with your baby on a sofa or armchair.
• Avoid overheating by keeping the room temperature at approximately 18°C (64.4°F).
• Never allow your baby to sleep with a hot water bottle, with an electric blanket, or next to a radiator, heater, or fire, or in direct sunshine.
• Avoid sleeping with your baby if your baby was premature (born before 37 weeks) or if they weighed less than 2.5kg (5½lbs) at birth (see opposite).
• Do not share a bed with your baby if you or your partner are smokers (even if you never smoke in the house), feel very tired, or have recently drunk alcohol or taken medication or drugs that make you sleep heavily.
• Breastfeeding your baby reduces the risk of cot death.
• A dummy can halve the risk of SIDS.

However don't use one for a breastfed baby under four weeks, and use it only when your baby is going to sleep.

Safe sleeping To reduce the risk of SIDS, your baby should sleep on their back with their feet at the foot of the bed.

Your baby's bedding

You will need two or three mattress protectors, three fitted sheets, three flat top sheets, and two to three blankets. Thin cotton sheets and cellular blankets are most practical, as they can be layered (and removed) as necessary to ensure that your baby does not become cold or overheated. Duvets and pillows are not suitable for babies under one year. Although baby sleeping bags shouldn't be used for very young babies, they may be useful once your baby is bigger and begins to wriggle out of the covers.

What temperature?

It is important to keep the temperature of your baby's bedroom on the cool side. Not only will your

baby sleep better, but also they will be at far less risk of overheating – which has been linked to SIDS. A room temperature of 16–20°C (60.8–68°F) is ideal. As a general rule, if the room temperature is 18°C (64.4°F), your baby will need a sheet and two layers of blanket, or a 2.5 tog sleeping bag. The warmer the room is, the fewer layers they'll need.

Early routines

Many babies feel more secure when they have the same sleeping place for naps and in the evening. A space that your baby associates with sleep will help them to settle more easily. Create a sleep corner in your bedroom, or move your baby's bed so that you can keep an eye on them.

Some parents prefer to stick to a regular "bed" at night, and use a carrycot, pram, or pushchair for naps. This approach has the advantage of helping your baby differentiate between daytime sleeps (shorter) and longer night-time sleeps. It allows for a bit more flexibility – your baby can nap in the pram wherever you are.

All about nappies

Your baby will be in nappies for at least a couple of years, so choosing the type of nappy that best suits your lifestyle is important.

Disposable nappies Disposables are very convenient and absorbent, but can be costly.

CHANGING PLACES

Although you may have created a lovely set-up on the changing table in your baby's bedroom, this may not always be practical. Babies often need fairly "instant" changes, particularly in the middle of a feed, or in the event of a sudden explosion at the bottom end! You may find it useful to keep a changing bag handy or to set up mini changing stations in rooms where you plan to feed your baby, near their bed, and where you'll spend time playing. Fill a basket with nappies, wipes, barrier cream, nappy sacks, and/or a plastic bag or tub to contain reusables, and a fold-up changing mat. Check the stations every evening, so that you can keep them fresh, tidy, and fully stocked!

There are two main types of nappies: disposables and reusables, each with advantages – and disadvantages. Many parents choose to use a combination of the two – disposables when they are out and on holiday, and sometimes even at night, because they tend to be more absorbent, and reusables the rest of the time. Work out a system that's best for you. There's not much point in feeling virtuous about doing your bit for the environment if your stress load means you use an environmentally unfriendly tumble-dryer to try to get through a pile of washing. If you do choose disposable, biodegradable disposables are an environmentally kind choice to consider.

If your baby is prone to nappy rashes, their skin may respond better to disposables. If your budget is tight and your organizational skills are immaculate, reusables may be right for you. There is no right way. It's a question of balance and practicality.

Disposable nappies

These are undoubtedly more convenient and there appear to be fewer cases of nappy rash, fewer leaks, and fewer changes necessary with disposables. They are, however, much more expensive, produce a high level of waste, and must be disposed of properly. The majority contain man-made chemicals, too.

Your baby might go through approximately 5,000 disposable nappies from birth to potty-training, and this can have a pretty dramatic effect on the environment. Go for disposables that do not contain any bleaching agents, which are a major source of pollution during manufacture and decomposition.

Nappies that are kinder to your baby's bottom and the environment are those that do not contain gels, perfumes, dyes, and/or latex. Those that are at least 50 per cent biodegradable can help reduce the growing problem with landfills, and nappies that use sustainable materials, that are chlorine-free, and that use less plastic packaging will also make an impact.

If you go with disposables, bear in mind that you'll need an average of 8–12 nappies per day, so make sure you stock up! Ask your midwife to assess the probable size and weight of your baby, so that you don't end up buying a lot of nappies that will instantly be too small. It's best to buy one or two packets of newborn disposables, and then see if your baby is ready to move up. "Bikini nappies", which fold down, will help to keep the umbilical cord free from irritation. Most parents purchase nappy sacks (biodegradable), to efficiently dispose of nappies at home and out of the house. (See also "How to change a disposable nappy", p.44.)

Reusable nappies

Reusables produce less waste and use fewer raw materials in their manufacture. Your baby will also be wearing soft, natural fibres next to their skin. However, washing reusables can waste a lot of water, and requires cleansing agents. It can also be very time-consuming, unless you can afford a laundry service. Your baby will need to be changed more often, as reusables tend to be less absorbent than disposables.

There are two main types of reusables. Two-part nappies consist of a nappy and a wrap. Nappies can be traditional terry towelling, which will require pins or clips, a folded nappy (known as a pre-fold, and which also requires a fastener), or a shaped nappy. On top, you will place a wrap designed to keep the moisture in and prevent leaking. Wraps can take the form of a pull-up pant, or wrap-around with fastenings (often Velcro). All-in-one nappies combine the inner nappy

and the "wrap" in a single waterproof garment. These nappies look a little more like disposables, and are normally self-fastening. Some mums find them harder to wash and thoroughly dry; they also tend to leak. You'll also need disposable nappy liners, which provide a barrier between the fabric and your baby's skin, and make it easier to lift out and dispose of poo. Booster pads can be useful at night to provide greater absorbency. If you choose pre-folds or terry towelling, you'll need nappy pins or clips. Plastic nappy grips are a great alternative to pins, not only because they are easier to fasten, but because they'll prevent accidental pricking.

Finally, you'll need a large bucket with a lid to store soiled nappies, and a plastic carrier to transport dirty nappies when you are out and about.

Reusables also come in "sizes" according to the weight of your baby, and you'll need to purchase about 20 nappies and three or four wraps to begin with. Don't buy too many; your baby will grow and move on to the next size more quickly than you expect. Equally, however, you don't want to be left with only one clean nappy and a pile of unwashed, dirty nappies! Although they can require a hefty investment every few months, reusables should prove cheaper in the long run.

CHANGE A REUSABLE NAPPY

Gone are the days when we had to rely on terry or cotton nappy squares that had to be folded and pinned – no easy task with a small, fractious baby to change. Today's reusables come in a variety of styles and colours, and often use easy-to-manage clips or Velcro tabs to make fastening them quick and efficient. Set up a clean, dry area in a warm room to change your

baby – on a changing table is ideal – and gather all the supplies you need: a clean nappy; cotton wool and water or baby wipes; a nappy bucket or bag to store the dirty nappy; and some barrier cream if your baby is prone to nappy rash.

If you are using flushable liners, you can flush the dirty one away after you remove the nappy; if you have reusable liners, you

will need to shake or rinse off any excess poo before putting the liner in the nappy bucket to be washed.

When you put the clean nappy on, make sure that it fits snugly, but it should not be too tight or it might pinch the skin.

Get ready Lay the nappy out on the changing mat, place the lining on top, then move it to one side while removing the dirty nappy.

Wash your baby Clean the nappy area thoroughly with cotton wool and water or a baby wipe.

Comfortable fit Slide the nappy under the baby's bottom, fold the outer pants over, and fasten the tabs or poppers.

Essential equipment

Although a visit to the shops may suggest otherwise, you don't need a huge pile of new gadgets and equipment – just some key items.

Feeding equipment

Breastfeeding doesn't require any special equipment to start off with. However, there are a few items that make nursing easier and more comfortable and are necessary for expressing milk (see p.28). Bottle-feeding does require a few essentials to keep your baby safe and healthy.

Breastfeeding
• 3–4 good-quality nursing bras that you can open with one hand.
• Breast pads for leaks.
• Breast shells to catch those leaks.
• Nipple cream for sore or chapped nipples; choose a lanolin-based one that can stay on your breast whilst your baby is feeding.
• A pump, if you wish to express, and 2–3 feeding bottles (with caps and teats) to store your expressed milk. You may want more, if you are stocking up the freezer in advance of returning to work. You will also need sterilizing equipment.
• A V-shaped feeding pillow to stay comfortable during long feeds.

Bottle-feeding
• 6–8 bottles; smaller bottles are more suitable for newborns and babies who do not consume much milk at a sitting. You'll need caps and teats, too.
• Sterilizing equipment and a bottle-brush.
• A kettle – you'll need a quick
• and regular source of fresh, boiled water for making up bottles.
• A designated measuring jug, spoon, and knife.

In the bedroom
• A Moses basket, crib, or cradle, which will keep your baby secure in the early days. They are soon outgrown, so if your budget is tight, go for a full-sized cot, which should comfortably fit your child during the first 18 to 24 months of their lives.
• A full-sized cot, although if you are using a "starter" bed, this purchase can wait a few months.
• Bedding (see p.31).
• A changing table. Any hard surface at hip height will work, including the top of a sturdy chest of drawers. If you are purchasing a new chest of drawers, look for one with a lip to prevent your baby from rolling off.
• A changing mat – go for one that is easily washed and comfortable; you may want a few fold-up spares for your mini changing stations.
• A baby monitor; a two-way monitor is ideal, so you can hear your baby and they can hear you!
• Nappies and the other elements of a changing station (see p.32).
• A bouncy chair, which can be moved from room to room.

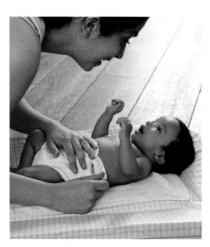

Changing mat Keep a couple of mats in strategic locations around the home, and at least one foldable mat in your changing bag.

Cot Your baby's cot is an important purchase, so do your research beforehand to help you make the right choice.

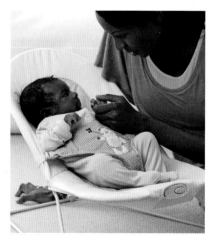

Bouncy chair This compact portable seat is a comfortable and safe place for your baby to enjoy calm time or practise moving their legs.

- A night light, to aid those late-night feeds, or a lamp that will keep the room dim enough to see your baby, but will discourage them from fully waking.
- Large chest of drawers or baskets for storage.
- A nappy bucket for reusables, or a bin for disposables – preferably with a lid!
- If you are planning to co-sleep, you may want to invest in a baby nest, or bed divider (see p.30).

Out and about

- A rear-facing car seat appropriate for your baby's age, with an easy-to-manage five-point harness. Second-hand car seats are not recommended for safety reasons. Your car seat may come as part of a travel system, which can include various fittings, including a pushchair and carrycot that fit on to one base.
- A sling for transporting your baby or keeping them calm when you need your hands free. Choose one with wide shoulder straps to protect your back, and if you and your partner plan to use it, ensure it fits you both.
- A pram or pushchair. Newborn babies need to lie flat, and a traditional pram with a flat base provides a perfect secure environment. Most pushchairs can be adjusted to lie flat, so are suitable from birth, and the seat can be raised so your baby can sit up when they are older. There are many different types, but make sure the one you choose has a five-point harness and a double-locking folding mechanism; is easy to fold and erect; is comfortable for your height; and suits your lifestyle. If you are more likely to shop than jog, storage space may be more useful than reinforced suspension. A first pushchair should be rear-facing – that is, facing you.
- A changing bag. Ideal for transporting all your baby's

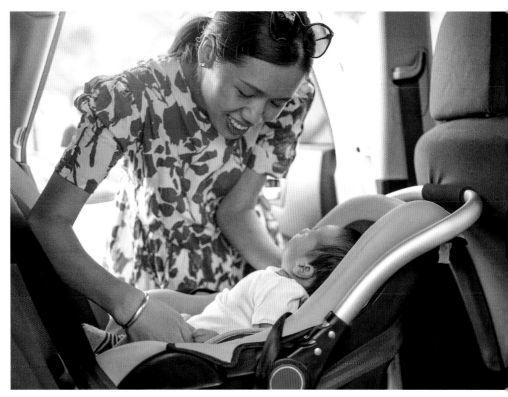

On the move To keep your baby safe whilst they're travelling in the car, it's important that you find the right car seat for them, one based on their height and weight.

paraphernalia while you are out; some come with detachable changing mats. Plenty of pockets mean you can keep things like bottles, nappies, and clean clothes separate.

Staying clean

- Wipes – choose water-based wipes with no fragrance or other chemicals; biodegradable are best.
- Small, thin flannels for reaching tiny folds and crevices, or cotton wool pads (cotton wool balls sometimes leave skin-irritating fluff behind).
- An all-in-one bath and shampoo designed for babies. You'll only need a little, so investing in a good, natural product is probably worthwhile.
- Muslin squares, which can be used to mop up little possets, leaks, and dribbles, and to protect your clothes when you wind and feed your baby.

- Washable bibs that will slip over or fasten behind your baby's neck easily, to protect clothing during feeds.
- A baby bath – although it's perfectly acceptable to wash your baby in a full-sized bath or even the kitchen sink. Invest in a non-slip mat if you use the tub, and line the sink with an old sheet or tea towel for your baby's comfort. If you buy a baby bath, make sure it is sturdy and you can easily fill and drain it.
- A thermometer, if you aren't confident about assessing the temperature of the bath water.
- 2–4 towels – preferably hooded, to keep your baby's head warm and dry while you use the body of the towel to dry the baby off. You'll probably use two at each bathtime (see p.57).
- A bowl for topping and tailing (see p.45).

YOUR BABY
0–3 MONTHS

YOUR BABY
4–6 MONTHS

YOUR BABY
7–9 MONTHS

YOUR BABY
10–12 MONTHS

YOUR BABY
MONTH BY MONTH

Your baby's first year whizzes by so fast, yet every single day is a new adventure for you all, punctuated by triumphs and tears, amazing developments and the odd setback. There's also so much to learn, so this chapter acts as your companion, day by precious day, pointing out the highlights and pitfalls you are likely to encounter along the way. From feeding and sleeping to crawling and communicating (and staying sane as a parent, too), it's a unique and illuminating insight into an unforgettable 12 months.

Your baby from
birth to 3 months

BIRTH

0

MONTH

1

Your baby is
fully dependent,
but their **senses
function well**
– they'll know
the smell and
voices of their
parents.

MONTH 1: ESTABLISH
A SLEEPING ROUTINE

Initially, your baby will sleep up to 18 hours
a day, decreasing to about 15 hours by
three months. However, it's unlikely that
they'll sleep through the night.

NEWBORN: WITHIN DAYS YOUR
BABY WILL RECOGNIZE YOU

Your baby's early vision is fuzzy, but they
can focus on your face if it's within a
30cm (12in) range. From one week old,
your baby will recognize your face.
By six weeks, they can see up to
60cm (24in) away.

Physical contact Being held
and touched makes your
baby feel secure.

> " From a helpless newborn to a smiling baby with a mind of their own, your baby's development is astonishing. "

MONTH

2

MONTH

3

Self-expression

Your baby can now make use of a range of facial expressions to tell you how they feel, or what they need.

MONTH 2: PLACE YOUR BABY UNDER A BABY GYM

By now, your baby may have discovered their haands, but they won't yet recognize them as their own. Your baby will start to swipe at objects within their reach, and try to bat them away.

MONTH 3: KEEP TRACK OF YOUR BABY'S WEIGHT

Your baby's weight gain is probably fairly steady now, but it's still reassuring to get them weighed at the baby clinic every so often. Although every baby is different, most gain an average of approximately 120–200g (4–7fl oz) each week until they are about six months old.

Your baby will **reach out** to swipe at objects within their reach.

The first seven days

SOME BABIES ARE BORN WITH A FULL HEAD OF HAIR WHILE OTHERS ARE NEARLY BALD.
Skin-to-skin contact with your baby immediately after birth as well as in the weeks and months to come helps you to form a close bond with them. Such contact also stabilizes your baby's heart and breathing rates and helps them to maintain a normal body temperature.

After your baby's birth

While you gaze in wonder at your new baby, your doctor or midwife will check that all is well. Then you'll be able to say hello properly.

After nine long months of pregnancy, today you can finally hold your baby in your arms for the first time. You may experience an overwhelming rush of emotions, ranging from tearfulness, pride, and intense love, to exhaustion and elation. You may also feel somewhat daunted by the prospect of caring for such a tiny, fragile human being, and nervous about their health and wellbeing. Labour takes an enormous physical and emotional toll, and you will need time to rest and recover after the birth.

Your baby's appearance

Don't be surprised if your newborn looks nothing like you had imagined. Your baby may be covered in a white, waxy substance known as vernix, which has protected their skin in the amniotic fluid, and they may be streaked with blood from the birth canal. If they had a bowel movement during labour, their skin, hair, and nails may be stained with a blackish, tar-like substance called meconium that forms the first bowel movements. If your baby is premature, they may also have a covering of fine hair, known as "lanugo".

Your baby's genitals may be enlarged and their head may look squashed or elongated, as babies' skulls change shape in order to negotiate the birth canal. Their nose may be flattened and their eyes might be puffy or even sealed shut. If you do glimpse their eyes, they'll probably be blue or grey. All babies have blue eyes in the womb, which are lighter or darker depending on their ethnic origin. The irises develop their final colour between six months and three years after birth.

Many newborns have birthmarks, such as stork marks on the eyelids or nape of the neck that fade over time.

First impressions Newborn babies often look rather squashed and wrinkly, but within a day or two their appearance smooths out.

BREASTFEED

Even if you don't plan to breastfeed in the long term, offering your baby their first feed within an hour of birth ensures that they receive colostrum, your early milk, which contains high levels of nutrients, antibodies, and other health benefits (see pp.26–27). It also reduces your risk of heavy bleeding after birth and stimulates mild contractions that help your uterus shrink back to normal size.

Your midwife will help you into the right position to breastfeed, and your baby may even root around to find your breast and begin suckling on their own. Encourage the baby by lying them next to you under your arm so that they can feed easily. Your baby should open their mouth wide and take in the whole of the areola. This is known as latching on (see p.27).

THE APGAR TEST

Within the first 5–10 minutes after your baby is born, a medical professional will assess your baby's appearance (skin colour), pulse (heart rate), grimace response (reflexes), activity (muscle tone), and respiration (breathing and effort), then will provide a score between zero and two for each criterion. These scores are all added together to calculate your baby's APGAR score. Most babies are born with an APGAR score of around seven, with very few babies receiving a 10. The main purpose of the AGPAR score is to act as a useful tool for medical professionals to check to see if your baby requires any additional medical care or special attention.

You and your new arrival

As your baby begins to acclimatize to their new environment, your doctor or midwife will check that you are recovering well.

After the exertion of giving birth, you'll probably feel sticky, sweaty, and in need of a shower. You may also want to visit the loo. The first time you pass urine it can sting, especially if you've had stitches, so it can help to take a cup to the loo with you, fill it with warm water, and pour it over the area as you pee.

Your body after the birth

It's a good idea to replenish your depleted energy stores – a cup of tea and some toast or a snack should taste delicious right now. The midwife will check your pulse and blood

AFTER A CAESAREAN

A Caesarean section is a major operation, so you need to give your body time to recover. It is normal to feel shaky, tired, tearful, drowsy, and nauseous after the surgery, and you will be given medication to help you deal with the pain. If your Caesarean was unplanned, you may feel the need to talk through why it was necessary with your doctor. Your body will be somewhat compromised by the incision, so your midwife and/or doctor will advise you on how to breastfeed comfortably, use the loo, roll out of bed, and lift your baby without causing damage to the scar. Medical staff will encourage you to become mobile, which will prevent clots forming in your legs. But do try to rest as much as you can.

pressure to ensure they are returning to normal. Your uterus will be gently palpated to observe if it is well-contracted, vaginal blood loss will be checked to ensure it is not excessive, and your perineum will be examined to assess whether or not any cuts or tears need stitching. Your temperature will also be taken. It is normal to experience a slightly raised temperature after the birth, but if it remains high, or begins to rise, this can be a sign of infection. Your urine may be tested to ensure your kidneys are working normally and you'll be asked to confirm that you've passed urine. It's normal to experience continued vaginal blood loss, known as lochia, after birth. The bleeding is usually heavier than during a normal period and small blood clots are common for the first few days. You'll need maternity pads to deal with the flow – you should not use tampons because they could cause infection.

Your baby after the birth

During the first 72 hours, in addition to the APGAR score (see p.41), a paediatrician, midwife, or neonatal nurse will check your baby is well and will check your baby for signs of jaundice, infection of the umbilical cord or eyes, and thrush in the baby's mouth. Your baby may become increasingly alert during the hours following the birth, opening their eyes frequently and gazing at your

The first hours Now you can spend time getting to know your brand-new baby, bonding as a family and admiring every precious little feature as you hold your baby in your arms.

face. You may notice your baby has some mild spots or a rash. After months curled up in the confines of your womb, your baby's arms and legs will be bent but will straighten out over the coming weeks. Your baby will probably respond to the sound of your voice and exhibit some reflexes (see p.47). They may cry, sleep, or look around at their new environment, although they won't see much beyond about 30cm (12in).

The golden hour

The hour immediately after your baby's birth is known as the golden hour because it is an important time for the attachment process between mother and baby. New mums experience changes in brain chemistry straight after birth that increase their desire for nurturing. Holding your baby naked, skin-to-skin, at this stage has been shown to promote bonding, calm your baby, increase resistance to infection, and get breastfeeding off to a good start.

Try not to worry if you miss out on this first hour of bonding, perhaps because your baby requires medical attention straight after birth. It's much more important that your baby receives the care they need first. You can make up for any lost time later by giving "kangaroo care" (see p.54).

On the maternity ward

How long you stay in the hospital after giving birth depends on a few things. If you had an uncomplicated vaginal delivery, and your newborn is healthy and breastfeeding or bottle-feeding, you may well be discharged and be able to go home within a few hours. Before you are discharged, your midwife will do a postpartum check to monitor your vital signs such as pulse, temperature, and blood pressure, as well as check that your uterus is starting to contract to normal size and position and that you can urinate with no problem.

However, if you have had a long or difficult birth, undergone a

Caesarean, or have concerns about your baby's health, you may have a slightly longer stay in the hospital. If you have had a Caesarean providing you are well enough, are able to walk to the bathroom, urinate without the need for a catheter, and can eat and drink without vomiting, you may be able to leave the hospital between 24 and 48 hours after the birth.

If you do need to stay in the hospital, use the opportunity to rest and ask for help with feeding, or any aspect of caring for your baby, from the experienced staff on hand. Having answers to your questions may help to build your confidence in caring for your baby once you are back home.

NEWBORN CHECKS

An examination will be undertaken by a paediatrician or midwife before you return home, or within 72 hours by your GP or community midwife if you have had a home birth. Your baby will be weighed and measured from the top of their head to their heel and around the head. The measurements are plotted on a chart to show you their size in relation to that of other babies. Your baby's stomach will be palpated to check the organs. The opening of their anus will be examined and, if your baby is a boy, the doctor will look at his penis and check that his testicles have descended into the scrotum. Your baby's eyes will be checked for cataracts and they will be given a hearing screening test. If this doesn't take place in hospital, it will be arranged by your health visitor.

Once your baby has passed all the checks (and most babies do without any problems), they will be allowed to go home. Assuming all is well, their next check-up will take place at between six and eight weeks (see pp.92–93).

Heart and lungs The doctor uses a stethoscope to listen to your baby's heartbeat and to check that the lungs sound healthy and fluid-free.

Head shape The head is carefully examined and the fontanelles (soft areas between the skull bones) are checked for irregularities.

Feet and hands The palms and soles of the feet are checked, all the toes and fingers are counted, and reflexes are tested.

Mouth and palate The mouth is examined to check that the roof (palate) is normal, and that the tongue can move freely.

Hips The legs are opened wide and bent upwards to check the stability of joints and look for "clicky" hips or other signs of dislocation.

Spine Your baby will be held up so that the spine can be examined to check that it is straight and there is no sign of abnormality.

Early care

Your initial efforts to feed, change, and settle your baby may well feel a bit clumsy, but never fear – you'll soon be up to speed.

Getting to grips with feeding

If you are breastfeeding, try not to worry if your first sessions haven't got off to a textbook start. Over the next day or two, your baby's attempts to feed may be a little erratic, especially in the first 24 hours after birth, when they're resting. Just let your baby feed when they want to, and don't expect any kind of pattern to emerge. For the next two to three days, your breasts will be producing mainly colostrum. This is a highly

concentrated deep yellow liquidthat is rich in antibodies, immunity boosters, and proteins which help nurture and protect your baby from illness. Your breasts probably won't feel very different at this stage because the amount of colostrum your baby needs is very small – a baby can't fit much more than a few teaspoonfuls at a time into their tiny tummy.

Although your baby doesn't need a lot of milk now, do let them suckle whenever they need to, as this will stimulate the production of mature

milk over the next day or two, and help to prevent your breasts from feeling overly full and engorged when this milk does come in.

Keep going with skin-to-skin contact and encouraging your baby to get a good latch, as this will make breastfeeding more comfortable for both of you.

If you are bottle-feeding, your baby will also want to feed little and often, so offer them a bottle every two to three hours. Let them feed for as long as they want to – if they've

HOW TO CHANGE A DISPOSABLE NAPPY

It's important to change your baby's nappy regularly because urine, combined with the bacteria in faeces, can make a bottom very sore. Nappy changing takes a bit of practice if you've never done it before, but you'll soon be up to speed on the best ways to keep nappies straight and secure (especially after a few leaks). Gather all the equipment you need beforehand to make the change as quick and easy as possible. If your baby doesn't particularly like being changed,

and objects to a cold plastic changing mat, try placing a towel over it to make them feel a bit more comfortable.

When cleaning your baby's bottom, remember to wipe from front to back if your baby is a girl, away from the vagina. This minimizes the risk of infection. If you're changing a boy, keep his penis covered with a clean cloth or nappy so that you don't get caught by an unexpected sprinkle!

Clean his bottom Holding your baby's ankles, lift their bottom, and gently clean with damp cotton wool.

Position the nappy Slide the opened-out nappy under the bottom so that the back of the nappy (with the tabs) lines up with the waist.

Secure tabs Fasten the tabs over the front flap. Fold the flap down ensuring the cord stump is not restricted, then check the fit.

had enough of their bottle, don't press them to drink more.

Your baby's nappies

Your newborn can have eight to 10 bowel movements in every 24 hours, so you'll need to change their nappy about eight to 10 times to keep them comfortable and prevent nappy rash. A bowel movement often happens straight after a feed, but if it doesn't, don't worry: as long as they have at least one movement per day, they're probably fine. For the first couple of days after birth, your baby will pass meconium, a black, tarry substance that filled their bowels before birth. You can tell by the weight of your baby's nappy if it's wet. If the nappy is heavier than a clean one when you change it, your baby is well hydrated.

Staying clean

You don't even need to think about bathing your baby yet. Some experts recommend not giving a full bath until the white, waxy vernix that covered the body at birth has dried and flaked off, in a week or so. For now, it's much easier to top and tail (see box, right). Topping refers to cleaning the top half of the body and tailing applies to the bottom half, or nappy area, which you should clean at every change.

Skin-to-skin contact

If you haven't had the opportunity for much skin-to-skin contact so far, you can indulge yourself and your baby now that you've had a little more chance to recover after the birth. This can help to improve latching on during breastfeeding, which inturn boosts your milk supply.

The optimum time for this type of contact is during feeding. If you are breastfeeding, open your baby's sleepsuit or lift up their vest, and let them tummy press against yours. If it's not too cool, your baby can wear just a

HOW TO TOP AND TAIL

Topping and tailing is a good alternative to bathing for a young baby and to keep an older baby clean between baths. It simply involves gently wiping the baby from head to toe, paying attention to all those little dimply folds and creases in-between. It's important to do this every day because if dirt, fluff, or milk is allowed to accumulate, it can make your baby's sensitive skin feel irritated and sore. It also prevents skin infections.

Gather all you need before you start: a bowl of lukewarm water; a washcloth or cotton wool pads; a towel; clean nappy; nappy cream, if used; and fresh clothes, if necessary. Keeping your baby's vest on to start with, gently clean their face, under the chin, neck, hands and feet, and nappy area. Finally, remove your baby's vest and clean their tummy, paying attention to the cord stump (see p.51) and under their arms, where dirt is often trapped.

Face and neck Clean your baby's face and neck; use a fresh pad for each eye, and then wipe over and behind (but not inside) each ear (left). **Hands and feet** Wipe your baby's hands and feet, taking care to clean in-between all the fingers and toes (top right). **Nappy area** Clean your baby's bottom and thigh creases, changing cotton pads frequently (bottom right).

nappy. Drape a light blanket or sheet over them as protection against draughts. Many women who experience difficulties with breastfeeding in the early days notice that they have more success when there is skin-to-skin contact with their baby.

If you are bottle-feeding, lift up or open your own top to allow skin-to-skin contact. Partners can also

emove their tops and go skin-to-skin to establish their own relationship.

When your baby is a little older, bathing with them to achieve skin-to-skin contact is particularly helpful if they are frightened by the bath. When your baby is difficult to settle, skin-to-skin may be all they need to calm down.

Finding your way

Caring for your new baby may be bewildering at first and you may be unsure what your baby needs from you – try to relax and go with the flow.

If you've had a normal birth, or a home birth, you may settle straightaway at home. You'll probably be most comfortable keeping your baby next to you most of the time and, in fact, experts recommend that your baby sleeps in your room for the first six months. Although it's tempting to hold a newborn constantly, it's important to settle them down so that you can get some rest, too. Your baby will let you know when they need you. In the early days, your newborn will sleep a great deal, and wake when hungry – or simply in need of being held.

Going home

If you are in hospital, you will be discharged when the doctors and midwives are confident that both you and your baby are well, and that you are comfortable with the care you need to give. Most women are discharged within 24 to 48 hours of an uncomplicated vaginal birth, but if you've had a Caesarean you will usually need to stay three or four days. When you are discharged, you'll need to settle your baby in their car seat for the journey home. If you're being driven, you may find it easier to sit in the back seat with them. In the UK, midwives and maternity support workers will visit you at home for seven to 10 days after the birth to check how you and your baby are doing (see pp.50–51). A health visitor will visit 10 to 14 days after the birth.

Feeding

You will continue to produce colostrum, which is your baby's ideal first food. Exactly how much milk your baby needs depends on them, but, on average, a two-day-old baby will take just under 3 teaspoons (14ml) at each feed. Expect a feed to take 40 minutes or longer at the moment. If your nipples feel sore, or breastfeeding is painful, your baby may not be latching on correctly. Try to ensure that you get all your areola into their mouth, and their tummy is against yours (see p.27). Ask your health visitor or midwife, or a lactation (breastfeeding) counsellor for help if needed. Nipple cream can ease discomfort: find a brand that you can leave on while feeding. Pat your nipples dry, then rub a pea-sized amount on to each nipple.

HOW TO HOLD YOUR NEWBORN

You may feel a little daunted at the prospect of handling your tiny baby, but it will soon become instinctive. Your baby is not as fragile as you think, but it is important to handle them gently in order to keep them feeling snug, secure, and safe. Hold them firmly in case they jettison their body backwards. Babies are born with a "startle" reflex (see box, opposite), and will thrust their arms outwards if you fail to support their neck and head.

A newborn's neck muscles are fairly weak and dangling limbs will make them uncomfortable, so hold their entire body by cradling them close to you.

Picking up Slide one hand under your baby's neck to support their head, place the other hand beneath their bottom, and lift them gently (left). **Supporting the head** Rest your baby's head in the palm of your hand, keeping it raised slightly higher than their body (middle). **Face-down hold** Support your baby on one arm with their head near the crook of your elbow and slide your other arm between their legs so that both hands are supporting their stomach (right).

YOUR BABY'S REFLEXES

Your baby is born with over 70 reflexes, which are nature's way of protecting them from harm and promoting their survival. Most of these disappear in six months.

The main reflexes are:

• **Moro or startle reflex** If their neck or head are unsupported, your baby will thrust out their arms.

• **Grasp reflex** This reflex is also known as the Palmar grasp. If you place your finger in the palm of your baby's hand, their fingers will instinctively curl around it and grip on to it tightly.

• **Sucking reflex** Your baby sucks when something is placed in their mouth; this ensures they will get nourishment.

• **Rooting reflex** If you stroke your baby's cheek, it will make them turn towards you, looking for food.

• **Stepping reflex** If you hold your baby upright on a flat, hard surface, they will "walk" by placing one foot in front of the other as you support their weight.

Moro reflex Your baby may throw out their arms in response to a sudden, startling noise (top left).
Stepping reflex Newborns are able to make stepping movements (far right). **Grasp reflex** This reflex may be an evolutionary legacy from primates, who need to cling to their mothers from birth (right).

If you are bottle-feeding, your baby may take more milk – perhaps a few teaspoons (30ml) at each feed. Bottle-feeding tends to be quicker, but not always. A formula-fed baby will likely feed for 20 to 40 minutes.

Weight loss

It is normal for newborns to lose weight during the first week after birth. Breastfed babies tend to lose 7–10 per cent of their birth weight; bottle-fed babies lose about five per cent. Most regain this weight by the time they are 10 to 14 days old.

Provided your baby is feeding well, is passing urine and bowel movements, and appears healthy, there shouldn't be anything to worry about.

Nappy contents

Your baby will continue to pass meconium, which can be very sticky! Warm water and a drop of baby bath can help to clear up the worst of it, but try to use only plain water on your baby's genitals. Your baby's urine should be pale or straw-coloured; if it becomes dark or smelly, talk to your midwife.

My baby sounds very snuffly when sleeping, and is constantly snorting and hiccoughing. Is this normal? Babies can be very noisy sleepers, and you can expect to hear grunts, groans, little mewling sounds, short cries, and even snorts and hiccoughs. Your baby may also appear to stop breathing for up to 15 seconds, which is known as "periodic breathing" and can occur until your baby is six months old. Your baby may have a build-up of mucus in their respiratory system, including their nose, after the birth, which may cause snuffles, coughs, and snorts to clear it. This normally passes by the time a baby is four to six weeks. If your baby's nose seems blocked and they are struggling to feed, talk to your GP; they may have a cold or other infection, and they may need saline nose drops to help clear their nose (see p.376).

How should I care for my baby's genitals? Your baby's genitals may appear swollen for a couple of weeks after the birth, which is caused by pregnancy hormones in their system. A newborn's genitals are very delicate and will need to be carefully cleaned with warm water for a few weeks after the birth; after this, you can use a little of your baby's pH-neutral baby bath to keep the area scrupulously clean. Always clean from front to back in baby girls; lift a baby boy's penis and scrotum to clean around them, and be careful not to pull back the foreskin. If your baby has been circumcised, your doctor will advise you of the best way to keep the area clean. It's normal for there to be a little discharge in the early days, but if it is smelly or yellow.you should report it to your doctor.

Adjusting to your new role

You will soon have been a mum for 72 – mostly waking – hours. It's hard to cope when you're tired, so try to rest whenever you can.

Although your baby may seem impossibly tiny and fragile, newborns grow stronger every day and will be alert for longer periods of time. Your baby's needs are quite straightforward at this stage, and regular feeding, changing, and time in your reassuring presence will help them to feel secure and content.

However, new babies often cry a great deal in the early days, partly in response to the shock of a whole new environment, and also because it is the only way they know how to communicate. This can be very upsetting for new parents, especially when you can't pinpoint what might be wrong. The best thing to do is to work your way through the list of reasons they might be crying and try to address them (see pp.68–69). Bear in mind that this is probably a phase and as you get to know your baby better you will be able to understand their cries and anticipate their needs much more easily.

It isn't possible to "spoil" a newborn baby, and every time you respond to your baby's cries, you will develop a strong bond, encourage trust between you, and teach the baby that their new world is a safe place to be. Some babies undoubtedly cry more than others as they let you know that something isn't quite right. If your baby doesn't respond to being held, winded, fed, or changed, you can try to reduce stimulation around them, which can help to soothe them.

Find a comfortable place in a dim, quiet room and lay your baby on their side. Rhythmically pat their back until they settle down to sleep. Then remember to place them on their back. It's easy to feel inadequate when you can't get your baby to stop crying, but try to relax and remind yourself that this is what babies do, and it is no reflection of your abilities as a parent.

Getting support

If you feel like you'll never have a shower or a hot cup of tea again, you are not alone. Babies have a knack of waking and needing attention just when you think you'll get a break. For the first couple of weeks, have another pair of hands available to hold your baby or even settle them when they're crying, to allow you a little time to relax, wash, and eat.

If you're exhausted and finding it difficult to cope, ask your partner or a family member to take over for a couple of hours so that you can sleep. You'll likely feel much more able to take charge again once you are rested.

If your baby becomes distressed when you put them down, carry them on your chest in a sling, which will free your hands and soothe them. Time showers, meals, and naps when you have someone around to help; don't feel guilty about not playing "hostess". Leave a list of "jobs" on the fridge, so visitors know exactly how they can help around the house.

HOW TO MAKE UP FORMULA

It is essential to follow manufacturer's instructions to the letter. Too much formula powder or liquid can cause your baby to become constipated or thirsty; too little may mean your baby isn't getting what they need nutritionally. First, you need to boil water (to kill any germs) and allow it to cool. Once you have made up the feed, gently warm your baby's bottle in a jug of hot water: the microwave can cause "hot spots", which could burn their mouth. It's best to make up fresh bottles when you need them. If you need to prepare them in advance, store them at the back of the fridge, below 4ºC (39°F), and don't keep them for longer than 24 hours.

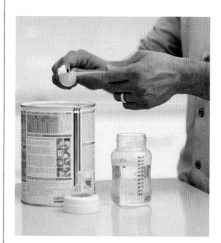

Preparing a bottle of formula Level off each scoopful as you measure out the formula. Add the formula to the cooled, boiled water in a sterilized feeding bottle. Then vigorously shake the bottle so that there are no lumps left and the mixture is completely smooth.

I should be over the moon now my baby is here, so why am I feeling so tearful and emotional? Tearfulness, temporary feelings of inadequacy, exhaustion, and anxiety are experienced by about 60 to 80 per cent of all new mums in the days following the birth. Commonly known as the "baby blues", these emotions are thought to be caused by a drop in pregnancy hormones, combined with a surge in the hormones that are produced for breastfeeding.

You may find yourself in floods of tears, irritable, frustrated, and weary, and you may wonder how you will cope. Baby blues can last for a few hours or up to five days, and you may feel inexplicably under the weather. Don't be embarrassed about crying or feeling anxious. Explain to your partner how you are feeling, and take up all offers of support during this period. If you don't feel any better after a week, talk to your doctor or midwife, who will assess whether you are developing postnatal depression, for which you may need extra help.

HOW TO WIND YOUR BABY

Most babies take in small amounts of air along with their feed. This can become trapped in their intestines, causing pain. Wind can also make your baby feel full, which may prevent them from feeding properly. Winding encourages your baby to burp, helping to release the air trapped in their digestive system and so easing discomfort. You might like to try a little winding session half-way through a feed as well as at the end. If your baby isn't bringing up any wind after 5–10 minutes, don't keep trying. It may be that the baby doesn't have any to burp up, or it may be released later.

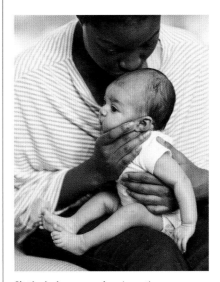

Sit the baby on your lap. Lean them slightly forwards, support their head, then gently rub or pat their back until they burp.

Hold the baby over your shoulder. Gently rub or pat the baby's back until they burb. They may bring up some milk so place a muslin over your shoulder.

Your baby's milk

The chances are that your milk may "come in" today, which means that your breasts will start producing "transitional" milk, a mixture of colostrum and mature milk that looks yellowish and creamy. Your breasts may become harder and possibly slightly engorged, making it difficult for your baby to latch on. Try to get the whole of your areola into their mouth (see p.27), and massage your breast downwards to release some milk and make it easier for them to get your nipple into their mouth.

Over the next 10 days or so, you will produce less and less colostrum, so

that by the time your baby is two weeks old, your breastmilk is said to be "mature". Your body will produce just enough for your baby's needs, so feed as often as your baby wishes to ensure that your supply responds to demand. The more you feed, the more milk you will make. You may find that you are feeding for between 30 and 60 minutes at each session (sometimes longer), and your baby may drop off to sleep when feeding. Gently nudge them awake by stroking their cheek. When your baby comes off your breast, wind them before settling them down to sleep. Most breastfed babies will feed eight to 12 times in a 24-hour period. If

you've had a Caesarean, it may take slightly longer for your milk to come in, but keep the baby suckling at your breast and talk to your midwife about any problems.

Bottle-feeding parents can see exactly how much milk the baby is getting. You'll be feeding every 2–3 hours, and your baby will likely need a couple of teaspoons (30–60ml) at each feed for the first week or so, or until they weigh 4.5kg (10lbs).

Getting checked

In the week after birth, your midwife or health visitor will keep an eye on you and your baby to make sure you are both recovering well.

Your midwife will visit frequently during the first week or so after the birth, which offers you opportunities to ask any questions you may have. If you're breastfeeding you'll be offered support, and the midwife will also check your baby to ensure they are healthy and well and are beginning to put on weight. Report anything that concerns you, no matter how minor it may seem. Being responsible for a new life can be daunting at the best of times, and there may be simple solutions to address any problem.

Checks for mum

If you had stitches after the birth – from tearing, an episiotomy, or a Caesarean – your midwife may take a peek at them to ensure that the area is healing nicely. The midwife will also ask about your blood flow (lochia) to make sure that you are not bleeding too heavily, and will palpate your abdomen to check that your uterus is well-contracted and steadily returning to its pre-pregnancy size. The midwife or health visitor will also take your temperature and perhaps check your blood pressure, too, simply to be certain that they are within a normal range.

Don't hesitate to report any pain you may be experiencing, or any problems you may be facing when breastfeeding; it can be very reassuring to get advice and guidance from a professional.

One important job that your midwife has is to ensure that you are healthy emotionally, too, so don't be surprised if they ask some personal questions about how you are feeling and coping. Try not to be embarrassed by these questions and answer them honestly. Most new mums struggle in the early days, and it's good to get help and support, if necessary, before things spiral out of control.

Baby checks

You'll be asked questions about your baby's feeding and sleeping patterns, bowel movements, wet nappies, and overall happiness, which will provide information about their overall health and wellbeing. Your baby will be weighed during some visits to monitor their weight and see if they are beginning to gain weight.

Weight gain is often slower in breastfed babies, so don't be alarmed if your baby doesn't seem to be filling out as quickly as you'd hoped. Your midwife or health visitor will let you know if they are concerned about your baby's weight, and evaluate your breastfeeding technique. In many cases, improving your baby's latch and allowing them to suckle for long periods in order to build up your milk supply will ensure that they get what they need to put on weight and grow at a good rate.

Your baby will probably be undressed for weighing, and your midwife or health visitor will take a look at any rashes or spots, and offer advice. It's normal for babies to look a little mottled in the early days, but if you have concerns, point them out now. Your baby isn't due for a full health check until they are six to eight weeks old, but your midwife and/or health visitor will keep a close eye on them during the first few weeks, and reassure you if you are worried.

Your midwife or health visitor will record your baby's weight and anything else relating to their health

THE NEWBORN BLOODSPOT TEST

On day five, and sometimes up to eight days after your baby's birth, you will be offered a blood spot (heel prick) screening. This involves taking a small blood sample (normally around 4 drops) to test against one of nine rare but serious health conditions. These are sickle cell disease, cystic fibrosis, congenital hypothyroidism and six inherited metabolic diseases: phenylketonuria (PKU), medium-chain acyl-CoA dehydrogenase deficiency (MCADD), maple syrup urine disease (MSUD), isovaleric acidaemia (IVA), glutaric aciduria type 1 (GA1) and homocystinuria (pyridoxine unresponsive) (HCU).

in their personal health record book, so keep this to hand. If you feel that you are in need of extra support, a midwife can visit for up to a month, which can be reassuring for parents who are finding things more difficult. Some areas offer extra support from a maternity support worker and through a postnatal drop-in centre. Be as honest as you can with your midwife; there is no shame in admitting that you are struggling to cope with exhaustion or a baby who seems to cry inconsolably. Similarly,

don't be afraid to cry or express any anxieties or worries. Your health practitioners are experienced in all sorts of different scenarios and can offer you invaluable help and advice. Don't feel that you have to wake your baby when they visit; in many cases, a chat and a peek at them will suffice. Similarly, don't worry about tidying up the house or playing hostess. The visit is to see you and your baby. They know that housework does not need to be your top priority.

TAKING CARE OF YOUR BABY'S UMBILICAL CORD

It is important to keep your baby's umbilical cord stump clean and dry. It's no longer suggested that alcohol or antiseptic ointments, talc, or liquids be used on it. Instead, plain warm water, with a little baby wash if the area becomes dirty, will do the trick.

Look out for "bikini" nappies, which are fastened below the umbilical area to prevent irritation, or you can turn down an ordinary nappy. You can expect the

umbilical cord area to look a little mucky at the outset. However, if it is very red or sore-looking, or if there is a smelly discharge, see your doctor, who will rule out infection.

Between five and 15 days after your baby's birth, the umbilical cord stump will dry, blacken, and drop off. Underneath there will be a small wound or sore that will heal over the next few days.

Cleaning the cord To keep infection at bay, gently wipe the skin around your baby's umbilical cord stump with a wet soft flannel, then dry the area.

ASK A MIDWIFE

Is my baby suffering from jaundice?
About two-thirds of all full-term babies develop jaundice (see p.372) a few days after birth. Jaundice is caused by a build-up in your baby's blood of the pigment bilirubin: a natural by-product of red blood cells. Most babies with jaundice will not require treatment as the level of bilirubin in their blood will be low. Typically jaundice settles down about 10 days after the birth. Until then, your baby's eyes may look a little yellow. Make sure the baby gets plenty of sunlight and feed them often to help encourage their body to excrete the bilirubin. If your baby's condition gets worse or does not disappear after two weeks, contact your midwife, GP, or health visitor.

I have twins. Will my body be able to produce enough milk to feed them both?
Many new mothers of twins worry that they won't have enough milk to feed two babies. However, breastfeeding works on the principle of supply and demand, so your body will produce milk to the precise requirements of your babies, even during their hungrier periods when they are having a growth spurt.

Should I wake my baby for a feed?
Most parents are reluctant to wake a sleeping baby, as this may offer the only opportunity to get some sleep or catch up on household chores; however, your baby does need to feed frequently (at least every two to three hours) to get enough milk for growth and development, so if they are going longer than this, you might need to wake them up for a feed. It's also important to put them to your breast frequently (ideally, about eight to 12 times in every 24-hour period) in order to build up your milk supply.

Bonding with your baby

Bonding begins in pregnancy and continues throughout your lives as you develop a close, powerful connection with one another.

Gentle touch Touching encourages weight gain and reduces fear and anxiety in both of you.

REGISTERING THE BIRTH

Don't forget to register your baby's birth. You have up to 42 days (six weeks) to register, after which you will receive a notification to appear before your local registrar. Contact the register office in your local authority or any register office in the country to make an appointment (see p.18 for more information) to register the birth.

Bonding is the development of an intense attachment between parents and their baby. It encourages us to love our babies, feel affection for them, and protect and nourish them. It is what gets us up in the middle of the night to feed them! Bonding also fosters a sense of security and positive self-esteem in your baby. Skin-to-skin contact (see p.45) encourages this process. Your partner can also practise this type of contact to establish their own healthy bond.

Babies are tactile, sensory beings. Caressing your baby will trigger the release of the hormone oxytocin in them. Increased levels of this hormone in the bloodstream are associated with feelings of happiness, relaxation, and security. Not all parents find the process of bonding easy, particularly if the birth was difficult. Be patient, look into your baby's eyes, hold them close, and sing and speak to them. Your baby will respond to your smell and touch, and to your voice, which will be familiar to them from the womb.

Family bonding

Your partner may have begun bonding with the baby since the very first ultrasound scan, or when they first felt those magical kicks. It's worth noting that often partners spend less time with their baby directly after the birth, and do need to be given the chance to develop confidence in handling and changing their precious newborn. Give your

partner plenty of opportunities to be alone with their baby and try to stand back so your partner can find their own style. Help if they ask, and make sure they have all they need to change the baby, top and tail them, and settle them down to sleep every so often – this way, they'll get to know them as well as you do and develop that all-important bond.

Bonding with twins

Parents of twins or multiples can find the bonding process more of a challenge because the huge amount of physical energy needed to care for twins can sap you of the emotional energy you need to bond. As with bonding with a single baby, it doesn't always happen instantaneously, and so you need to give yourself time to feel strong attachments to your twins.

Be aware if you are developing more of a bond with one baby than the other. This sometimes happens if one baby needs more time and attention. Try to allocate more relaxed and playful time with the baby you feel less bonded to, as this can help to balance your feelings of closeness more evenly between the two of them.

You may also find that you bond more with one baby, while your partner bonds more easily with the other. This can be a practical measure to ensure both babies develop the security they need for their emotional wellbeing.

Sleeping babies

What a week! Your baby has probably spent most of it sleeping – in-between feeds – although it certainly may not seem like it!

Most newborns will wake up every two to four hours for feeds. They have tiny tummies and are dependent upon a milk-only diet, which digests very quickly. Your baby will wake when they are hungry and sleep when they are tired, and you cannot force them to do otherwise! It's best to have realistic expectations.

If you are breastfeeding, you can encourage them to sleep well now by making sure they fill their tummy. If possible, they should drink from both breasts at each feed. Now that your milk has come in, they will probably feed on demand for between five and 30 minutes at each breast. They should empty one breast before moving to the other to ensure they get the fat-rich hindmilk that comes at the end of a feed.

Bottle-fed babies do tend to sleep a little longer because formula is slower to digest than breastmilk.

Day and night

Many babies wake up for longer periods in the wee hours, and sleep all day. At the outset, it's probably easiest to follow the baby's lead, sleeping when they sleep. You can start to establish a difference between night and day by keeping things quiet and low-key in the run-up to bedtime. Try to settle the baby down while they are still awake. If they fall asleep at the breast, they may experience discomfort from wind. Allow them to suck until they are sleepy, but wind them and put them to bed before they are totally asleep.

Avoid the temptation to overdress your baby. If the weather is warm, just a nappy with a blanket may suffice, and add more layers if they seem cool. When they wake in the night, feed and change them efficiently, without chat.

Most importantly...

Lack of sleep can make you overly anxious and upset. Not only is this transmitted to your baby, making them irritable, it also makes it difficult for you to get a good, restful sleep. Try to be calm when you settle your baby down to sleep. Remember – this is a temporary phase and you will get your nights back eventually.

HOW TO SWADDLE YOUR BABY

Being wrapped up can help to settle a young baby when they are over-stimulated, and prevent them from being disturbed by their own startle reflex (see p.47), which can cause their body to jerk. Choose a soft cotton sheet to swaddle your baby as heavy blankets can cause overheating. The idea is to make the baby feel secure, rather than to keep them warm. Keep their arms free unless they are unsettled, in which case swaddle them loosely with their arms tucked in.

Position your baby Spread out a sheet and fold down a corner to create a long straight edge. Position your baby at top-centre (left). **First tuck** Bring across one side of the sheet and tuck it snugly beneath the opposite side. Ensure it's not too tight (middle). **Second tuck** Wrap the other side of the sheet around the baby. Tuck in the edges beneath them (right).

Your special-care baby

If your baby was born prematurely or was unwell at birth, they may have been placed in a special-care baby unit (SCBU) or a neonatal unit in order to get the best possible medical help and attention from specialist doctors and nurses.

If your baby needs urgent medical care, you may not be able to enjoy skin-to-skin contact or encourage the first feed immediately after birth. You'll probably feel bereft without your baby and extremely anxious about their wellbeing, especially if the baby is in an incubator. However, try not to be alarmed by all the leads and monitors – the incubator protects your baby from infection, provides oxygen if they need it, and monitors their temperature, oxygen levels, heart rate, and lung capacity.

Feeding your baby

If your baby is unable to feed from your breast or a bottle, tubes may be placed in their mouth or nose, or directly into their stomach. It may be possible for you to express your breastmilk, so this can be given to your baby through a tube. You will need to begin expressing (see p.28) as soon as possible after the birth, even if your baby isn't yet ready to take the milk. For a baby who is small or unwell, breastmilk is undoubtedly the best choice. It is rich in proteins, fats, vitamins, minerals, and antibodies, supporting your baby's immune system, growth and development.

Hospital staff will show you how to express your milk: most units have a special room with chairs and an electric breast pump for this purpose. Keep expressing every couple of hours or so to build up your milk supply. Even if you are able to express only a little in the early days, it should make a big difference to your baby's health. Your milk will be fed to your baby through a tube, or possibly via a syringe, bottle, or cup until they are well enough to nurse at your breast.

KANGAROO CARE

Hold your baby close Research has found that babies benefit greatly from being held closely, skin-to-skin.

One of the best ways of promoting the healthy development of a new baby, whether premature or full-term, is to practise kangaroo care. This simply involves holding the baby – dressed only in a nappy and probably a hat – against the skin of your chest, between your breasts. Turn your baby's head so that their ear is pressed near to your heart, and gather them up against you so that they feel your warmth and love. Kangaroo care allows newborns to experience something closer to the containment of the womb while acclimatizing to the world.

There is a wealth of benefits associated with kangaroo care. In fact, research has found that, compared with special-care babies who are not held in this way, those that experience kangaroo care (even for short periods of time every day) benefit from:

• a more stable heart rate
• more regular breathing (including a 75 per cent decreased risk of sleep apnoea, which causes babies to stop breathing temporarily during sleep)
• improved oxygen levels in the blood
• a regulated body temperature
• more rapid weight gain and brain development
• decreased crying
• longer periods of alertness
• more successful breastfeeding
• earlier bonding.

A baby's growth rate increases when held in kangaroo care mainly because the baby is able to fall into a deep, restful sleep when snuggled against either parent. Sleep allows them to conserve their energy for growth and development.

When you do put your baby to your breast, they may not actually suck, but will enjoy your closeness. If you put a little expressed milk on to your nipple, your baby can smell and taste it. A tiny baby will also enjoy catching dribbles of milk in their mouth. Don't expect too much at your first feed, since premature or sick babies tire easily and need to learn how to suck properly. If your baby is showing definite interest, get some help to ensure they are latching on correctly (see p.27).

Your baby needs you

Although your baby may seem fragile, and you may be worried about holding them with all the equipment around them, it is essential that you offer your baby as much close physical contact as you can. They will recognize your voice and smell and will be comforted by the beating of your heart and your warmth. Holding them as frequently as you can – or, if that is not possible, gently stroking their body in the incubator can vastly improve their wellbeing. Your regular touch can promote weight gain, encourage healing, and even help them to develop restful sleep patterns. Sing to your baby, talk to them in a calm voice, and reassure them. Research shows that talking to your baby can help to stimulate the developing connections in their brain, yet also makes them feel more relaxed.

Getting involved

While your baby is in the SCBU or neonatal care, you may feel overwhelmed, especially if they are in an incubator and attached to tubes and wires. Ask the specialist nurses to explain how the equipment works, and ways you can be involved in your

Healing touch It is recommended that you touch and caress your baby, if it is not possible for you to hold them. Spend as much time as possible talking and singing to them.

baby's care. You may be able to help with bathing, changing, or feeding, which will help you become involved in their regular routine.

Look after yourself

Rest often and eat regular, nutritious meals. Get support from family and friends and ask if there is somewhere to stay on hospital grounds, to make it easier to have more time with your baby. Equally, try not to feel guilty if you can't always be with your baby. It's normal to experience guilt, distress, anxiety, and more. Talk to your partner and the health professionals. They are there to support you as well as your baby.

Keep a diary to record your feelings and celebrate milestones, no matter how small. Looking back, you'll see your baby's amazing achievements and find comfort in their progress. Keep a note of questions to ask doctors and nurses and write down the answers so that you can later reflect on them quietly.

HOME FROM HOME

Try to interact with your baby as you would if you were caring for them at home. For when you can't be there, decorate the incubator with photos of family; your baby will become familiar with your faces and reassured to see you there. Play soothing music, or create a recording of your voice to be played during your absences, which will help them to develop their connection to you.

Personal touch Try to forget your clinical surroundings and imagine you're at home.

1 week

DURING THE FIRST FEW WEEKS, BABIES ARE AWAKE ONLY 10 PER CENT OF THE TIME. At this point, your baby's vision will still be blurry, although they will have been able to recognize you since shortly after birth. When they's awake, your baby will show great interest in their new world – and you. They'll be fascinated by your eyes and your voice.

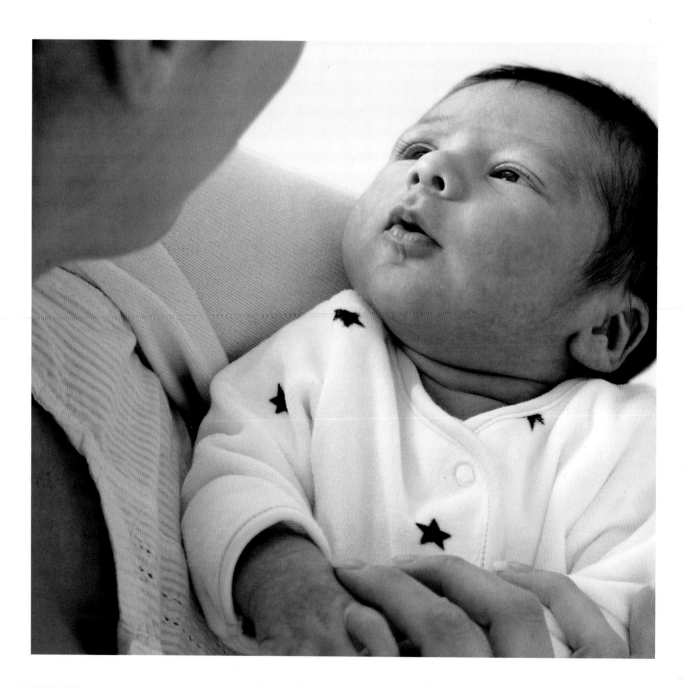

Baby knows you

Your voice and smell have been familiar to your baby since birth, but they now recognize your face and feel secure when they see you.

Although your baby is still too young to focus clearly on your face, they can recognize you and like nothing better than to stare into your eyes. Research has found that babies stare for much longer and with greater determination at familiar faces, so you may find your baby watching you intently. In fact, when your baby is stimulated and interested, they will stop moving and watch you very carefully. Indulge this passion and look into your baby's eyes. Eye contact is not just essential for the process of bonding, but also acts as an early form of communication between you and your baby. Let them get to know you – position your face around 30cm (12in) from theirs – this is the optimum focusing distance for them. Even though your baby won't recognize you yet, they will be drawn to you and want to stare. Your eyes and hairline will offer the most contrast, on which your baby can most easily focus. It won't be very long before they reach up to touch your face.

Forming an attachment

In the early days and weeks after birth, mothers and babies are uniquely primed to want to be close to each other. Continuing with skin-to-skin contact will be reassuring for your baby. They will recognize your heartbeat, and your smell will comfort them and encourage them to feed. What's more, they are growing familiar with your touch and senses a new confidence in the way you handle them, which helps them to feel secure.

GIVING YOUR BABY A BATH

If you haven't yet done so, you might want to give your baby their first bath this week. Lots of infants love the sensation of water, and bath time becomes an enjoyable part of your routine. Ensure the room is warm, and gather a clean towel, fresh nappy, and clothes, so you have everything ready. Half-fill a baby bath with tepid water, testing it with your elbow (37°C/98.6°F on a thermometer). Afterwards, dry your baby quickly so they don't get cold.

ASK A MIDWIFE

Why does my baby cry every time I put them down to sleep? Most babies prefer to be held, particularly in the first week or two when they are adjusting to life outside the womb. Swaddling (see p.53) can help a baby feel more secure, or you may want to put your baby down awake and stroke them until they settle. Bear in mind that most young babies cry between one and three hours a day – it might be that your baby is tired and needs to unwind with a strong cry.

Into the tub Lower your baby into the bathtub, carefully support their head, shoulders, and bottom.

Hair wash Support their head and shoulders, then wet their hair with your hand, a soft flannel, or sponge.

All clean After their bath, wrap your baby up in a soft towel, then gently rub them dry.

Successful feeding

Feeding your baby will be time-consuming but hugely rewarding as you watch them grow and develop on a milk-only diet.

Breastfeeding

There is no doubt that breastfeeding is an art that takes a little practice – for both you and your baby. Getting the latch right can make all the difference when it comes to ensuring your baby gets the milk they need. Once you've both mastered the latch, your baby will feed more efficiently, competently stimulating your breasts to supply them with just the right amount of milk, and you'll be less likely to experience discomfort.

An incorrect latch can make your nipples sore and cause them to crack. It's common to feel "attachment pain" for the first 10 seconds or so, but pain throughout a feed needs checking. If you find you are experiencing problems, don't hesitate to talk to your midwife, health visitor, or breastfeeding counsellor. It can take at least a few days for your milk supply to meet your baby's demands, and maybe a bit longer for you to feel wholly comfortable and confident with the process. Some mums who don't enjoy breastfeeding at first are happy they persevered once it's all going smoothly two to three weeks later.

How long should a feed take? Don't be tempted to time your feeds. Your baby will feed for as long as it takes for them to get the quantity of milk that is right for them. Sometimes your baby may empty your breast within 10 minutes. On other occasions they may be sleepy and take 20 minutes on each side, or even longer. Don't rush. Sometimes your baby will simply suckle for comfort, which is nature's way of increasing your milk supply.

Most newborns feed between eight and 12 times a day. For the first few weeks, your baby may be on your breast every 90 minutes, although they may manage a break as long as three hours after a good feed.

Emptying each breast It's best to empty each breast fully before moving on to the next one, as this ensures your baby gets both the hydrating, thirst-quenching foremilk and the nutritious hindmilk. It can also help to prevent problems, such as blocked ducts (see box, opposite). If your baby doesn't manage both

A GOOD POSITION FOR BREASTFEEDING

For your baby to be able to latch on properly, it's important that you are both positioned well. You should be comfortable, with your back well supported: cushions or pillows may be helpful. There are a number of different positions to try and you'll probably find one or two that suit you best. Cradling your baby at chest level, with their tummy against yours, can be comfortable. A rugby hold with your baby under your arm is good if your breasts are sore, as it stops your baby pulling on the breast. For night feeds, or after a Caesarean, you might find it helpful to feed your baby lying down on your side. Check that the baby's head is able to tip back slightly during feeding. Their chin should touch your breast and they should be able to breathe easily.

Cradle hold Turn their tummy towards yours, cradling their head in the crook of your arm. Use your forearm as support, then tuck your baby's knees in.

Rugby hold Tuck your baby's body under your arm, as if holding a rugby ball to your chest, and support their neck with your forearm.

Lying down Lie on your side with your baby facing you and draw them in close to your breast, cradling them with your arm.

You may wish to begin feeding your babies one at a time until you feel comfortable with breastfeeding. If you take this route, the milk stimulation in one breast may cause a let-down in your other breast (known as the "double let-down"). Place a sterile container nearby to catch any milk that does leak – you can store this in the freezer for later use.

For simultaneous feeding, bear in mind that, in most cases, one twin is a stronger sucker. Put this baby to your breast first, which allows you to spend more time adjusting the position of your second baby. Your second twin will benefit from the simultaneous let-down without having to work too hard for it. If they are small you may be able to snuggle both of them

in your lap, with their tummies against yours. If this is too awkward, try the rugby hold (see box, opposite), in which their heads are at your breasts and their bodies are nestled against your sides.

Positioning your twins This mother uses a combination of cradle and rugby holds. In time, you will find what works best for you.

In most cases an incorrect latch is the cause of discomfort during breastfeeding. Adjusting the feeding position can eradicate niggling problems. Other difficulties include:

Sore or cracked nipples Try rubbing breastmilk on your nipples after a feed, and put a cool flannel or gel pad in your bra to ease discomfort. Emollient nipple cream may help. "Air" your breasts after feeds, and change breast pads frequently.

Leaking It's normal for breasts to leak in the early days. You may leak from one breast while your baby feeds from the other, and your baby's cries can also stimulate "let-down". Wear breast pads and feed your baby often to prevent overflow. Things usually improve within 6–8 weeks.

Blocked ducts Once breastfeeding is established, an oversupply of milk can build up in the breasts, possibly resulting from a poor latch and/or not emptying the breasts completely during feeding. If you have redness or pain in your breast tissue, feed your baby more often to get the milk flowing. If it doesn't improve, inform your midwife or doctor.

Mastitis Inflammation or infection of the breast causes red, inflamed areas and symptoms similar to flu, such as a high temperature. The affected breast may also feel full and tender. Continue nursing your baby frequently, but if you don't feel better within a few hours, call your doctor.

Thrush This can infect the nipples, causing sharp stabbing pains during breastfeeding. Your GP may need to prescribe a gel to treat it and your baby may need to be checked, too.

breasts in one sitting, start them on the full breast the next time they feed to ensure that both breasts are eventually emptied. Make a note of the breast on which the baby last fed.

Bottle-feeding

Make sure you are in a comfy chair with your back well supported and position yourself so that you can look

into your baby's eyes. Just as with breastfeeding, this is a time for bonding, and this will happen more naturally if you imitate a breastfeeding position. Hold your baby close against your chest as you feed them, so they feel comforted. Switch arms regularly to ensure you both are comfortable.

Holding your baby When it's time to feed, stroke their cheek to stimulate the rooting reflex that encourages them to open their mouth. Don't feed your baby when they are lying down – formula can flow into the sinuses or middle ear, causing an infection. Instead, hold them up at a slight angle, and tilt the bottle so that the formula fills the teat and neck of the bottle. A newborn will likely take 60–120ml (2–4fl oz) per feed in the first few weeks and may be hungry every 3–4 hours. Follow their lead: babies will not overfeed, so if your baby wants more milk, they may be feeling extra hungry.

Bottle-feeding position Cradle your baby semi-upright and support their head.

Your baby's weight

At this age, a few grams or ounces matter a great deal, especially when you want your tiny baby to start gaining weight steadily.

If you are breastfeeding, your baby's weight is probably a major preoccupation now. When you can't see how much milk your baby is consuming, you're more likely to worry that they are not getting enough to thrive. This is especially the case if your baby lost weight (as is normal) last week and has been slow to regain it. Being told by your midwife that your baby has gained a minimal amount of weight or – worse – none at all, can be enough to send you into a blind panic.

There is rarely a cause for concern: some babies simply take a little longer than others to start gaining weight. As a rule, once your milk comes in at around three days, your baby should start to gain about 25g (1oz) a day. Most babies regain their birth weight by two weeks, but some do take a little longer. At this age, weight is less of an issue and your baby's general appearance and wellbeing are more important indicators of how your baby is doing: if the baby is generally alert, waking for feeds, has a good skin colour and tone, and is having at least 6–8 wet nappies a day, they should be fine.

If your baby seems lethargic, listless, and pale, poos less than once a day, or does small, dark poos after they're five days old, their skin becomes more yellow, rather than less, after the first week, or their skin remains wrinkled after the first week, it's important to get some help to make sure they are feeding efficiently. Just keep breastfeeding on demand and they should soon start to achieve steady weight gain.

If you are bottle-feeding, you can also expect your baby to gain about 25g (1fl oz) in weight per day from now until the age of three months.

You will need to give your baby about 60–80ml (2–4fl oz) of formula six to eight times a day: babies have tiny tummies and can't manage too much more in one sitting. There should always be a little milk left in the bottle at the end of each feed so that you can be sure they've had enough.

TRIMMING YOUR BABY'S NAILS

Babies' fingernails grow fast, so it's a good idea to clip them to prevent them from snagging their skin. Toenails grow more slowly but they can scratch or occasionally become ingrown. It can be daunting to approach a baby's nails with scissors or clippers, but if you use tools made for babies, you're unlikely to catch the skin. Cut your baby's nails when they are sleeping or feeding, as they're likely to be calmer. Or you can ask your partner to hold their hands or feet still while you get to work. Don't cut them too short – always leave a little of the white showing. Cut toenails straight across, but fingernails can be slightly rounded.

Scissors Use baby nail scissors that have rounded ends to cut your baby's nails.

Clippers The small blades of baby nail clippers are ideal for trimming tiny toenails safely.

Going out

If you haven't yet ventured out, you might be going a little stir-crazy. Try getting out of the house with your baby now – it will do you good.

Tempting as it is to batten down the hatches and stay indoors with your baby, fresh air and a change of scene can give you a break from domestic life and lift your mood. Sunshine encourages the production of vitamin D, which you and your baby need for healthy teeth, bones, and restful sleep; vitamin D also helps to prevent depression and ease baby blues.

You may not feel up to walking far (or getting dressed for that matter), but even a short stroll to the nearest shop or a walk in the local park will help you feel a bit more connected to the outside world and less isolated if you've been ensconced at home with your baby.

If this is your first trip out, time it after a feed so your baby is relaxed. Dress the baby for the weather. In general, put them in the same amount of clothing as you, plus an extra layer to keep out the breeze. If it's cold, a babygro, a warm outer suit, a hat, and a blanket should keep the baby snug. The head should feel warm, not hot, to the touch; the baby's hands and feet should be a little cooler. Don't forget your keys, mobile phone, and purse (tiredness makes you absent-minded), and, above all, enjoy your first outing.

Extra equipment

If you're planning to be out for longer than half an hour or so, you will need to take a few essential items with you. Don't leave home without:

• **Muslin squares** These are perfect for mopping up – and you can drape one over your shoulder whenever you want to breastfeed discreetly.
• **A changing bag** Fill it with clean nappies, wipes, plastic bags for wet or dirty clothes or nappies, a change of clothes for your baby, barrier cream if you use it, and a travel changing mat.
• **Formula and bottles** If you're bottle-feeding, take some ready-made cartons of formula and sterilized bottles.
• **Water and snacks** Take a bottle of water and something to eat in case you feel in need of an energy boost.

Baby carrier A front baby carrier keeps your baby close and snug.

STRAWBERRY MARKS

Also called haemangiomas, strawberry marks are quite common and nothing to worry about. They often form on the head or neck, but can appear anywhere on a

baby's body and may be present at birth or develop in the first few weeks. They may start as a small, bright-red flat area, but usually become raised and look like a strawberry. Strawberry marks grow in size for the first six to 12 months, then often shrink and disappear by the age of seven with no need for medical intervention. Treatment may be necessary if the marks affect your baby's vision or are in an awkward place that impairs feeding or breathing. If concerned, speak to your GP.

Raised swelling A strawberry mark results from an overgrowth of tiny blood vessels.

Taking care of your health

Your focus is on caring for your baby, but don't neglect your own health. Being fit and well gives you energy to cope as a new parent.

While it can be difficult to find time to put together nutritious meals, it's important to make your diet a priority. Grabbing a sugary snack may keep you going between feeds, but your energy levels and your overall health will eventually begin to suffer.

Fill the fridge with healthy foods that you can eat on the run: seeds, nuts, fresh fruit and vegetables, hummus, yoghurt, smoothies, cheese, eggs, wholegrain toast, and lots of water will keep your blood sugar levels stable, and help you feel calm and relaxed.

It is very important to stay well hydrated. Breastfeeding mothers need about 2.7 litres (4.75 pints) of fluids per day. This can be 70–80 per cent from drinks and another 20–30 per cent from food. Smoothies and reduced-fat milk both count. Because caffeine passes into breastmilk, it's best to avoid caffeinated drinks, such as coffee and cola, while you are nursing.

It's possible to eat well, even when time is tight. A nourishing bowl of soup with a wholemeal roll can be produced in minutes, as can scrambled eggs on toast.

Aim to eat at least five or six servings of fruit and vegetables per day to ensure you get plenty of vitamin C, which your body needs to absorb iron. Iron-rich foods include red meat, dried fruit, fortified breakfast cereals, and pulses. If friends or family want to cook for you, take advantage of their generosity. There's no shame in accepting help in the kitchen to allow you to concentrate on your new baby and your recovery.

Exercise

It's still early days yet, but you should try to get outdoors when you can for some fresh air and a little gentle exercise. Fatigue caused by a lack of sleep is compounded by a lack of activity. It's good for both you and your baby and the exertion will encourage a more restful night's sleep. Try to build a brisk walk in the park into your routine, or walk to the shops instead of getting into the car.

If you've had a Caesarean, you might not feel up to going outside for a walk yet, although a gentle daily stroll (even up and down the garden) will aid your recovery. Go out for a walk only if you're sure you feel able to do so. If in any doubt, always check with your midwife or doctor first.

ASK A BREASTFEEDING EXPERT

Can I use nipple shields? These are not generally recommended as they may interfere with proper attachment, as well as reduce your milk supply. Nipple shields are also known to increase the risk of skin irritation, blocked ducts, and mastitis.

Is there anything I shouldn't drink?
Alcohol can pass through your breastmilk, and regular drinking can reduce your milk supply and harm your baby. Restrict your caffeine intake to one cup of coffee a day as caffeine can make babies irritable and restless. Don't overdo herbal teas. Mint teas, for example, are thought to help soothe babies' wind and colic when drunk by breastfeeding mums. However, they can also decrease your milk supply if consumed in large quantities.

Can I smoke while breastfeeding?
You could be putting your baby at risk if you do. Nicotine and traces of smoke in your baby's environment can increase the risk of SIDS (see p.31), respiratory problems, ear infections, and behavioural problems.

If you cannot stop smoking or are finding it hard to quit, it's important to not stop breastfeeding, as breastfeeding will still help safeguard your baby from infections and provide vital nourishment that they cannot get from formula. To protect your baby's health, avoid smoking before feeds as this will limit the amount of nicotine passed into your breastmilk and speak to your GP or healthcare practitioner about safe products and support to stop smoking.

You know your baby

Parenthood can be quite daunting, and you may worry about getting it right. Trust that you know your baby best.

If babies came with instruction manuals, the past week and a half might have been easier. But most parents find this steep learning curve difficult, and worry constantly if they are doing the "right thing" for their babies. Your ability to tune in to your baby's needs will guide you in responding to them. Read your baby's signals, and you will be cuddling, cooing, and feeding, changing, and rocking when they need it.

There is no "right" way to look after your baby – and your baby is an individual, so what is right for another baby may not be right for yours. Try not to compare your parenting skills with those of other parents either; as you get to know your baby, you will naturally do what is best for them, whether your baby manual or friends think differently.

If you are not particularly enjoying caring for your baby's needs at the moment, try not to worry or think that you are failing as a parent. It's not uncommon for new parents to feel that they are just going through the motions rather than actively treasuring every moment with their new baby. For a small number of parents, resentment can start to build about how much time and energy your baby takes up. If this is happening, seek extra support from family and friends and speak to a health professional about how you feel. You may also be exhausted, so do arrange for your partner or a friend to take over to give you time to rest.

Don't push yourself too hard, and try not to panic when things don't go as planned. No two days are ever the same in a household with a young baby, and you'll need to be flexible and sometimes lower your expectations of yourself.

ASK A MIDWIFE

Can I breastfeed when I'm ill? You may not feel up to it, but do continue breastfeeding to keep up your milk supply. Far from passing infection to your baby, you'll provide her with the antibodies you develop against your illness, making it less likely that she'll catch it. Most over-the-counter painkillers are safe while breastfeeding, but check the label or ask your pharmacist before taking anything. Some antibiotics and decongestants, for example, should be avoided. Talk to your doctor about the safety of any medication you take regularly.

FOCUS ON TWINS: CO-BEDDING

Putting your twins in the same cot is called co-bedding. Don't worry that your twins will overheat or smother each other. Studies show that the risks to your babies are exactly the same if they are in the same cot as they would be if they were sleeping separately.

It is important that you follow the same rules as you would for one baby. For example, ensure that each baby is feet-to-foot in the cot. This means positioning the babies so that they are on their backs either head-to-head, with their feet at opposite ends of the cot; or side-by-side, with their feet at the same end of the cot.

The side-by-side position poses no greater risks, even if one baby flings an arm over the other. In fact, the babies may comfort each other like this. Keeping your twins in the same cot is also more practical, because having them in the same room as you for as long as possible – ideally for six months – reduces the risk of SIDS (see p.31).

Sharing a cot It is perfectly safe to have your twins sleep in the same cot, either head-to-head or side-by-side.

Reflecting on the birth

Many new parents want to share and analyse the birth experience.
Talking about it is healthy, particularly if it didn't go as planned.

Whether you had an unexpectedly quick and easy birth experience, or found yourself using every medical intervention going having planned to deliver your baby naturally, you'll probably want to talk about the birth – in detail. Having a baby is a life-changing event and a deeply emotive experience. It's normal to be both proud and unsettled after the birth, and it is equally normal to feel as if you need to make sense of the events.

Some women and their partners feel unhappy with their experience of childbirth and a small number feel traumatized. For women, the birth may have been longer or more painful than anticipated, or complications arose. For men, being out of control and distressed about their partner's discomfort may have coloured their view. You may wish that things had gone as you had hoped they would, or that you had done things differently, or you might wonder why certain procedures or interventions had been necessary. Equally, you may have had a wonderful, positive birth that has left you bubbling with joy and needing to share your encouraging story. However your experience of childbirth unfolded, part of the process of remembering and understanding does involve talking about it – with your partner, your family, the friends you have met in your antenatal classes, and the midwives or doctors who are responsible for overseeing your care.

Don't hesitate to talk to medical staff and ask questions if you feel uneasy or uncertain about any element of the birth. Healthcare professionals are there to support you and will understand that asking questions is part of coming to terms with your experience. The birth of a baby is amazing, and you will find that most people will be fascinated to hear how your baby came into the world.

Focus on the positive

Whatever your experience, try to focus on the positive elements, and the fact that you have succeeded in creating a new life. While it is perfectly normal to feel some disappointment or even guilt when things didn't go as planned – particularly if it seems that everyone else had a much better experience, or achieved that "natural" birth – you have a healthy baby in your arms, and there could be no better result. Take pride in the wonderful new life you have created.

ASK A DOCTOR

My baby's eyes are sticky. Is this normal?
It is very common for newborn babies to suffer from a mild eye infection, which is caused by blood or fluid entering their eyes during the birth. Their eyelashes may appear to be crusty or sticky – or even glued together – after sleeping, and there may be a discharge in the inner corner of their eyes. You can keep their eyes clean by gently wiping off any discharge around them. This condition usually clears up on its own, but if symptoms don't improve after three days, see your doctor.

Cleaning a sticky eye Moisten a cotton wool pad in cooled boiled water. Wipe inside outwards. Use a fresh pad for each eye.

Helping your body to heal

Post-delivery, you may feel uncomfortable and sore if you've had stitches or a Caesarean. Fortunately, there are ways to encourage healing and to feel better.

Your pelvic floor

The weight of your baby, placenta, and amniotic fluid puts a great deal of pressure on your pelvic floor, which supports all the organs in your pelvis. During labour and birth, this area is also stretched to allow your baby out.

If your baby was big or you had serious tears or an assisted birth, your pelvic floor may have become overstretched and weak, causing you to leak urine when you sneeze, cough, or exercise. This is called stress incontinence and it affects almost half of all new mums – but it usually improves. A weak pelvic floor can also cause discomfort and a feeling of heaviness in the vaginal area.

Practise your pelvic floor exercises (known as Kegels) as soon as you feel comfortable (the sooner the better). Do the exercises while you're lying on your back or side, or in the bath.

• Breathe in and as you breathe out gently squeeze your pelvic floor muscles up and in, as though trying to stop yourself passing urine. Hold the squeeze for four or five seconds while you breathe in and out, then relax.

• Repeat five times (stop if you feel at all uncomfortable) five or six times each day. Build up to holding a pelvic floor contraction for 10 seconds.

Although it may feel like nothing is happening initially, you will encourage blood supply to the area, promoting healing, and restoring muscle tone. Pelvic floor exercises will also help to deal with haemorrhoids. If you've had a Caesarean, it's important still to practise Kegels, which should be slightly easier, as your perineum will be less sore.

Your lower tummy

The lower tummy muscle works with your pelvic floor to help support your back and pelvis. Having strong abdominals can also help to relieve back pain. Gentle pelvic tilts (see box, below) are an ideal way to start.

Quick relief

If your perineum or Caesarean scar is tender, apply a cold compress of ice cubes wrapped in a damp tea towel to reduce inflammation and ease pain. Have warm baths or showers to boost circulation and aid healing.

PELVIC TILT EXERCISES

Once you've had the all-clear from your GP or midwife after a vaginal birth, you can use pelvic tilt exercises to strengthen the lower abdominal area. Lie on your back, knees up and your feet flat on the floor. Place your hands on your stomach so you can feel your muscles tightening. Tighten your stomach muscles and push the arch of your back towards the floor. Squeeze your bottom tight. Hold for a count of six, then relax. If you've had a Caesarean, wait 6–8 weeks before working your abdomen. To boost blood flow to the area, suck in your tummy and hold it for a minute or two.

Pelvic tilt Tighten your abdominals and push your lower back into the floor – imagine pulling your belly button in towards your backbone. Aim for three sets of 10, but stop if you feel tired.

Enjoying family life

Adjusting to a new baby can take time for everyone in the family, but maintaining a strong family unit will benefit you all.

Becoming a family is a wonderful event and your life will never be the same again. You may develop a closer bond with your own parents as they settle into the role of grandparents, and spend more time with your extended family. You may have older children, or children from previous relationships, who will need time to adjust to the idea of a new sibling and a different family unit. Your roles may have changed from being simply "partner" to "partner and parent", and

that can alter the way you see and interact with one another. Having a baby offers you an opportunity to build something truly special.

If you have other children, it can be tempting to take turns with your partner to look after the baby while the other cares for the older children, however, creating opportunities for family time will reap rewards. Whether you sit down together to watch a film, head out to the park, play board games, or even just spend

some time in the garden, you will be nourishing the bond that forms the basis of a happy family life.

Spending time together makes every family member feel valued and secure. Even something as simple as cooking or washing up the dishes together helps to spread the load and makes everyone feel they have a role. Affection, play, communication, and relaxation as a family also improve self-esteem and the family dynamic, and create happy memories, too.

JAUNDICE

Jaundice, which causes yellowing of the skin and whites of the eyes, (see p.372) is common in newborn babies, especially if they are breastfed. It usually resolves itself within two weeks, however, about 10 per cent of babies are still jaundiced after two weeks. It is likely to be "breastmilk jaundice", but can also be a sign of an underlying condition such as liver disease, particularly if your baby's stools are chalky white. Speak to your doctor or health visitor: your baby may need to have a blood test.

THE IMPORTANCE OF EXTENDED FAMILY

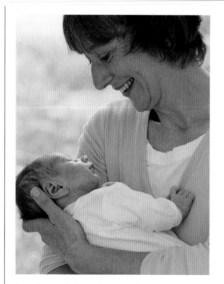

In safe hands Grandparents like to shower lots of love and affection on their newborn grandchildren. This helps build strong bonds between them from the beginning.

Welcoming grandparents or other extended family into your baby's life is part of celebrating your growing family. You may or may not appreciate their help, depending on your relationship with them. Let them know what you need, and how best they can help you. For example, if they live nearby, your in-laws could cover the cooking while your siblings handle the housework. You may also find that too much "help" can be taxing!

Grandparents, aunts, uncles, and siblings are often hugely willing to give advice. Accept it graciously, but believe in your own parenting skills and instincts. There may be gems of wisdom other members of your family can pass on, so listen, but remember – it's okay to make your own decisions.

Time to engage

Now that your baby is alert and awake for longer, playing will help to stimulate the baby's senses and improve their coordination.

Tête-à-tête Making eye contact with your baby, and laughing and talking to them at close quarters stimulates their listening and language skills.

DEVELOPMENT ACTIVITY: BLACK-AND-WHITE PATTERNS

As they begin to interact with the world around them, your very young baby finds boldly contrasting images and distinctive geometric shapes and patterns visually stimulating. To encourage this stimulation, create a black-and-white design for your baby on some card, using felt-tip pens to make patterns and shapes (stripes and angles are particularly appealing to babies), or purchase a baby book with similar designs. These patterns develop your baby's focusing abilities and encourage their spatial awareness and visual perception. Play this game for a minute or two every day, but don't overdo it. Excessive visual stimulation will distract your baby from the "familiarization process" of getting to know and becoming integrated into their new world.

Visual stimulation Bold, moving patterns will hold your baby's attention and also help develop their ability to focus.

At this age "play" simply means engaging with and spending quality time with your baby. It affords them the opportunity to learn much more than you might think, and it will encourage a healthy bond between you, as well as promote their emotional health and wellbeing.

While it is important not to overstimulate your baby, a few 5–10-minute sessions each day, whenever they are calm and alert, will be great fun for both of you, and will help them to develop on all levels. Try to gear your play to the baby's mood – if they are active and alert, try some gentle clapping, tickling games, or carry them outside and show them around the garden; if they're in a quieter mood, chatting and singing may be more appropriate. The point of play is to have fun, so keep it light and cheerful, and forget about what they might be learning. That will become clear before you know it!

Vary the games you play together to develop different parts of your baby's body and brain. Babies instinctively "practise" skills. They may try out their new tricks after the games are finished; for example, if you've been encouraging them to poke out their tongue, they may attempt this when they see your face.

Crying

All babies cry to communicate and it can be difficult to work out what they are trying to say at first. You'll soon learn to differentiate between cries, and find it easier to figure out the very best ways of providing comfort.

On average, even the most contented babies cry for between one and three hours a day, and some seem to cry constantly. Try to relax about crying and think rationally. Most babies cry for the same reasons and working out what's wrong is the first step to finding a solution. If you are anxious, your baby may pick up on it, which will only compound the situation.

Why is my baby crying?

A crying baby is not necessarily unhappy, just good at conveying their needs. So when you've walked around for the fiftieth time trying to settle them, think positively: you are raising a good communicator! It's time to work out what's causing the cry.

Use a trial-and-error approach to soothing your baby. What works one day may not work the next, or you may find a trick that works every time. If there is one thing at which all parents excel, it's adapting. Over time, you will begin to recognize your baby's cries – you'll know that they are hungry or lonely, or that it's time for a nap. You'll recognize when the baby needs a cuddle or even a little time on their own. They may not enjoy nappy changes or getting dressed, but you'll create techniques to make these more fun, or become adept at getting them done quickly.

Hunger Babies cry when they are hungry or thirsty and will not stop until sated. During growth spurts,

Crying for attention Young babies do not cry without reason; they usually have a genuine need that requires your attention.

when your breasts are struggling to keep up with demand, your baby may be hungrier than usual and cry more. Let them suckle at your breast – for comfort and to build up milk supply.

Feeling too hot or cold Young babies cannot regulate their body temperature. Check that your baby is not wearing too many or too few clothes. Dressing your baby in and putting them to sleep under thin layers can make it easier to cool or warm them quickly. If your baby is

How can I tell if the crying is caused by colic, or reflux? About a quarter of young babies suffer from colic. The cause is unclear, but it is linked to excess wind and is characterized by uncontrollable crying (often around the same time of day or night), and drawing up of their knees in clear discomfort. Most babies outgrow it by three months. (For help with easing colic, see p.75).

Reflux occurs when the acid content of the stomach rises into the oesophagus, causing burning and discomfort. This can make a baby very irritable. With reflux, crying often occurs during or just after a feed, unlike colic where crying tends to be worse in the evening. Reflux can also cause babies to regurgitate frequently, sometimes in large amounts. If you suspect that your baby has reflux, talk to your doctor.

small or slim, they may need more clothing to maintain their body temperature. Chubby babies are often happier with fewer layers.

Wet or uncomfortable A wet or soiled nappy can cause discomfort. Some babies are particularly sensitive and need a barrier cream applied to their skin to protect it. If your baby's skin is red, bumpy, or raw in the nappy area, the baby may have nappy rash (see p.73 and p.373). Leave the nappy off for short periods of time to encourage healing.

Loneliness Babies are sociable and love to be held close. Your baby is stimulated and entertained by your presence and will feel more secure knowing you are there. Don't hesitate to pick your baby up when they cry – there is a genuine need to satisfy.

Understimulation Babies get bored! If the baby has been lying in the cot or car seat for hours, they may need interaction. Gentle play, chatting to them, moving them to a different location, or simply a mobile over their cot can help to keep them happy.

Overstimulation A little stimulation encourages development, but babies also need quiet periods, during which to consolidate skills and information. They also need to relax in order to sleep well. If your baby is fractious after periods of activity, it may be time to help them wind down and sleep. Baby massage (see p.119) or a long feed can encourage this.

Tiredness Tired babies become irritable. Being overstimulated, or not being given the opportunity to unwind in order to fall asleep, can distress your baby. If your baby seems to be crying for no reason, rubbing their eyes and yawning, rock them until they settle, wrap them up, and lay them down to sleep. Don't try to put them down when they're upset, or you may compound the problem.

Wanting comfort Sometimes babies simply want to be held in a parent's arms, have a cuddle, a gentle massage, or the comfort of suckling – on a breast or a dummy. While you do not want to encourage "snacking", sometimes nothing else will work.

Feeling unwell An unwell baby may cry as a result of discomfort. Check your baby's temperature (see p.363), which can indicate an infection. It's almost impossible for parents to diagnose illness in a young baby, so if you notice any signs, see a doctor.

SOOTHING YOUR FRACTIOUS BABY

• Babies respond to being held and rocked. If your baby is eased off to sleep by rocking, bring the pram inside and settle yourself in a position where you can comfortably rock it with a free hand or foot.
• If your baby needs constant comfort, carry them against your chest in a sling so they can hear your heartbeat.
• Rhythmical sounds, such as low music, or even the sound of the vacuum cleaner, soothe many babies.

• Many babies like to feel swaddled (see p.53). Try wrapping them snugly in a cot sheet before settling them down.
• Some babies need to suck to get to sleep, or to settle, which is why they feed almost constantly when they are upset. If they're not hungry, they may find comfort from a dummy.
• Calm them down by giving them a light massage (see p.119).
• If crying begins after feeding, after switching from breastmilk to formula, or after switching formula, talk to your health visitor or midwife. The formula they are taking may not be suitable.
• Take a deep breath, and relax yourself. If necessary, put them down safely for a few moments and leave the room to give yourself some space to calm down. Crying babies can be exhausting, and you may be at your wits' end. It will do your baby no harm to be left in a safe place for a few minutes while you take a quick break.

Face-to-face chat Look into your baby's eyes and talk to them to distract them from crying.

Rocking Simply rocking your baby gently to and fro can soothe and comfort them.

Dummy Babies like to suck for comfort and a dummy can help soothe a restless or upset baby.

Baby sling Your baby may love being held in a sling, but make sure their neck is well supported.

Copycat

Your baby mimics your facial expressions, opening their eyes and mouth as you do, and copying the tone of your voice when they coo.

When a newborn's parent sticks out their tongue and moves it from side-to-side, their baby responds in kind. Researchers conclude that imitation is the key learning tool in your baby's "kit" of instincts. Babies watch and imitate other people, then practise the new skills to hone them.

What's more, if you regularly make the same faces when you play, your baby will consider them "familiar" and respond more quickly. Imitation is a sign that your baby is processing information in a sophisticated way:

not only do they need to work out what you are doing, they also have to control different parts of their body to copy you. This process can start hours after birth, and continues throughout the first months of life. Your baby will also cry with an inflection that matches your accent, which they have picked up in the womb. Researchers have found that babies also cry in a way that mimics mum's "native" language (for example, French newborns cry with a rising "accent"), aiming to form an early bond.

Making faces Using exaggerated faces frequently when you chat with your baby makes it easier for them to copy expressions.

Baby sounds

Your baby is already learning to talk. "Oohs" and "aahs" will soon develop into babble that is the basis of early speech. Listen carefully!

Crying is your baby's primary method of communicating, but they'll begin to utter little sounds when they are alert, and may respond with sounds when you speak to them or stimulate them, in response to being startled, or when they recognize something like you or your partner's voice.

The first sounds will be vowel sounds, usually "oooooh" and "aaaaah", and little cooing noises. Apart from attempts to chat with you, you can expect to hear plenty of hiccoughs and sneezes as well!

Encourage your baby to "chat" – move close so they can see your face, and talk to them. When your baby responds with sounds of their own, "reply" by mimicking those sounds. Your baby is starting to understand basic communication and will respond to this interaction. Chat constantly; tell them what you are doing, for instance, when you are changing a nappy. They'll become familiar with the words you use, so when it's time for speech, they'll have a good vocabulary to draw from.

REGISTERING WITH A GP

When you register your baby's birth (see p.18) you will be given a registration form (GRO 4), which you should take to your doctor's surgery so that your baby can be registered as a patient. Alternatively, you can use their NHS number. It's best to do this sooner rather than later, in case your baby needs to see a doctor.

Babywearing

All babies love being held. Carrying your baby against your chest will not only settle and reassure them, it will also encourage bonding.

Your baby was tightly confined in your womb for many long months, and so became dependent upon touch to feel secure. After the birth, touch is equally important – and reassuring – for babies. Research has found that touch is calming and helps babies adapt to their new surroundings. It encourages bonding and promotes healthy growth, development, and even immunity. In fact, newborns need constant soothing touch to become healthy, happy children. Studies in orphanages have found that babies who are not soothed or nurtured by touch fail to thrive, are slow growers, and develop social problems later in life.

While there can be nothing more rewarding and relaxing than holding your new baby for hours on end, there are things that you will need to get done to keep the household running. Using a sling to carry your baby is a good way of keeping them in close proximity to you while you get on with chores. Your baby is likely to sleep for longer periods when they are held close to you, or is rocked gently to sleep listening to your familiar heartbeat. Your breathing patterns will stimulate theirs, and they will be reassured by being able to feel you right there, next to them.

ASK A BREASTFEEDING EXPERT

Can I express yet? Unless you need to express your breastmilk straightaway, it is recommended that you wait until both you and your baby feel happy and confident with breastfeeding before you start expressing. This is because sometimes, babies can experience "nipple confusion" (see p.85) as the muscles and movement that your baby uses to latch on and suck a teat are different to when latching onto your breast. However, there may be a variety of reasons you may wish to express milk, including, if your baby is premature or in a special-care baby unit, you are returning to work or study, if your breasts feel uncomfortably full, or when your baby is unable to latch on or to suck well.

SOOTHING YOUR BABY THROUGH TOUCH

Your baby will respond very positively to your touch, and will be soothed and reassured by it, so use touch often, especially when they need to be comforted and settled. Hold them close while bottle-feeding or breastfeeding, ideally with their bare skin against yours (see p.45). Be tactile – stroke their little face, gently rub their back, pat their hands, and feel and explore their body with your hands. Rock or hold them close when they're crying – leaving a newborn baby to cry sends the message that you are not always there for them, and makes them feel insecure. Infancy is no time for "sleep training". Cuddle your baby after their bath – they'll be relaxed and ready to settle down when you put them to bed, resulting in a deep, restful sleep.

Gentle strokes Softly caressing your baby's body and talking to them as you change them can help them feel less vulnerable.

Feeling lonely?

If your partner has gone back to work and any other family help has headed home, you may find yourself alone with your baby for the first time.

Not only can it be difficult to get to grips with caring for your baby on your own, but also you may find that long hours without adult conversation can be, well, a little boring. Use local social media groups to find out about parent and baby activities in your area, where you can meet other new parents, and engage in a new activity. If you took antenatal classes, try arranging get-togethers, and taking turns to host. If your baby's grandparents are nearby, you could organize regular visits, to give you something to look forward to. Talk to your partner about your feelings, too; they may be able to check in by phone more regularly or come home earlier sometimes. Ultimately, though, take this time to adjust and put your feet up while you bond with your baby. Why not watch a favourite film or binge-watch an online series if you get the chance!

ASK A HEALTH VISITOR

Can I give my baby water to drink?
Breastfed babies receive a perfect balance of fluid from breastmilk and don't require anything else, even if a little dehydrated during illness. Bottle-fed babies should get the fluid they need from formula, but if it's very hot outside, or they have a bug, offer a little water. Use only previously boiled, cooled water in a sterilized bottle.

Breastfeeding in public

Many new mums may feel apprehensive about breastfeeding in public, but breastfeeding in public isn't just accepted it's protected.

At first, you may feel self-conscious about breastfeeding in public. But it doesn't have to be a difficult experience, and your confidence will grow the more you go out with your baby. You have the right to breastfeed in public and should never be made to feel uncomfortable about nursing.

Preparation is key – practise different breastfeeding positions at home so you can find one that feels most comfortable and helps your baby to latch effectively. Look online for local breastfeeding-friendly places to go. You may also wish to go on your first few outings with your partner, a family member, or a friend for moral support and company.

Breastfeeding is a convenient way to feed your baby, and there are many ways of doing it discreetly. Try wearing a loose top that can be easily lifted or use a shawl or large muslin cloth to cover your breast and baby. Look online to find feeding-friendly clothes (see p.107) or try layering tops so that you can tuck your baby underneath one and still be fully covered. Choose a bra that you can easily open, ideally with one hand. Try out a few options to find what feels best for you.

Discreet feeding A loose top will allow your baby easy access to feed and will not reveal too much of your flesh.

Your baby's thermostat

Babies cannot regulate their own body temperature until they are much older, so it's important to check that they are not too hot or cold.

Babies' bodies are unable to regulate temperature effectively. They lose heat from their heads when very hot but, otherwise, rely upon parents and carers to keep them at the right temperature.

It isn't necessary to take your baby's temperature (see p.363) unless they feel very hot and may be suffering from an infection. Instead, examine them regularly by putting your hand against their cheek, which should feel warm to the touch, and checking that their feet and hands are cool, but not hot or cold. Dress your baby in layers, which you can add or remove as necessary. You'll need to use your instincts to assess the right balance.

Aim for a bedroom temperature of around 16–20°C (60.8–68°F), which is just right for babies. Overheating has been linked with SIDS (see p.31). At night, dress your baby in a vest and babygro, then add layers of light cotton sheets and cellular blankets until they seem cosy.

During the day, your baby should wear roughly the same amount of clothing as you, plus one extra layer. Avoid putting their recliner next to a radiator or fire or in direct sunlight. Keep them away from draughty open windows. Hats are a good idea when it's cool outside, but babies should not wear hats in bed unless very small or premature, so they can cool down when necessary by losing heat from the head. Babies often become very warm in the car, so they don't need a blanket over them unless it is very cold or you have the air conditioning on. Always remember to remove your baby's outdoor clothing when inside.

Most importantly, relax. In most cases, your baby will look and/or feel obviously cold or hot, and you'll soon know at a glance whether they need a cardigan or their socks removed!

CONTRACEPTION

You should decide on the form of contraception you want to use now, and discuss it with your doctor. While the time it takes for fertility to return is very variable, it's important not to take risks. It's possible to find that you are pregnant again within weeks of your baby's birth. Your periods usually return between four and 10 weeks after birth if you are bottle-feeding or combining breast and bottle. Exclusive breastfeeding day and night gives 98 per cent protection against pregnancy until your baby is six months, provided your periods have not returned.

DEALING WITH NAPPY RASH

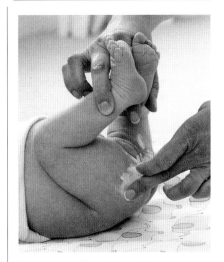

Barrier cream Zinc oxide topical cream can soothe any inflammation as well as protect your baby's skin when their nappy is soiled.

Contact with urine or faeces irritates your baby's delicate skin and can result in nappy rash. To prevent this, change your baby's nappy frequently. If their bottom does become sore, let them play and kick about without their nappy on at least twice a day, to allow the air to get to the area. If you use reusable nappies, give them an extra rinse. Apply calendula or metanium ointment to encourage healing, but if their rash does not clear in a couple of days, see your GP who will check for thrush and may prescribe an antifungal cream.

Getting your baby to sleep

If you can recognize when your baby needs to sleep, you can catch their wave of tiredness and send them off into a peaceful slumber.

An overtired baby can fail to settle, so settle them to sleep as soon as you notice they are tired, when they will be more likely to fall asleep quickly and sleep deeply. The length of time your baby goes between naps will be individual to them, so it's important that you recognize when they ready to sleep. In general tiredness comes after a period of wakefulness.

Throughout the day and night, your baby will have drowsy periods when they are more ready to fall asleep. If you miss one window, you may have to wait an hour or so for the next. Look out for yawns and eye-rubbing, obvious signs of drowsiness. They may cry a little for no obvious reason, or make little grunts or growls that eventually reach a full-blown cry. Some babies acquire a frown when they are tired, while others become a little jerky – probably in frustration! Don't try to keep your baby awake when they're tired – overstimulation takes that much longer to unwind.

ASK A DOCTOR

My baby brings up a little milk after each feed. Are they ill? It's normal for babies to "posset" a little milk after feeds, resulting from trapped air surfacing, bringing up a little milk with it. It doesn't cause any pain or discomfort. To prevent possetting, handle your baby gently after a feed and when winding them. If they are bringing up large amounts of milk, they may have reflux (see pp.369–70), so take them to see the doctor.

Taking a break

Although it can be tempting to assume full charge of your baby, especially if you are breastfeeding, regular breaks will refresh you.

Family time Family members need to get to know your baby and understand their care, too.

You may be one of the many parents for whom it's difficult to relinquish control. However, it's important to take time off to recover fully from the birth. Whether you have a long soak in the tub, meet a friend, exercise, or get some sleep, a break from routine will make all the difference to your physical and emotional health.

Your partner, or other trusted family members, will welcome the chance to hone their skills and spend time bonding with the baby. They will develop confidence in their care, reducing the pressure on you. Set up a regular time for them to take over – perhaps bath time, or on weekend mornings. Even short periods help to establish their relationship – and give you a rest.

After around four weeks, if you are breastfeeding you can start to express milk (see p.28) and your partner or other family can take over feeding from time to time. You can then go further afield during your breaks.

Responsive feeding

Your baby is learning what hunger feels like, and by satisfying their appetite you reassure them and help them feel more secure.

Food and security Let your baby feed whenever they want to. Their tummy is still tiny and can only take small amounts, so they need to suckle on a regular basis.

It is important to continue to feed your baby on demand – whether breast- or bottle-fed – because they are learning how to respond to their own hunger cues. They will let you know when they are hungry, and when you satisfy that hunger you are not only encouraging trust and security by meeting their basic needs, but you are also teaching them to eat when they are hungry. This can help to prevent problems such as obesity in later life.

By now, your baby may be going three or even four hours between feeds, but don't be surprised if this pattern suddenly shifts. Growth spurts and increased physical activity during the day can make babies hungrier, and they may seem to suckle endlessly as they work to build up milk supply!

DEALING WITH COLIC

To ease symptoms of colic (see p.68) wind your baby carefully after feeds (see p.49). Try a warm bath to calm them down, and then rub their abdomen and lower back with a little warm olive oil or grapeseed oil, using circular motions.

A breastfed baby may react to Mum's diet. Reducing the amount of dairy products you eat may make a difference, as may avoiding processed foods that contain milk protein – look at food labels to help guide your choice. Avoiding garlic, onions, cabbage, beans, and broccoli may also help. If you are bottle-feeding, try an anti-colic bottle, which can reduce the amount of air your baby takes in while feeding. You may also try a different formula but ask your health visitor first. Colicky babies are soothed by motion, so try a ride in the car, or pram, or gentle rocking in a sling. For babies over one month, gripe water (a herbal remedy with bicarbonate of soda), may help. Colic normally subsides at around three or four months of age – but if you are concerned, finding it hard to cope and nothing seems to be alleviating your baby's symptoms call the NHS helpline or contact your GP.

Colicky babies Hold your baby face down along your forearm with your hand firmly between their legs. Try walking around a little, too.

Conflicting advice

There is no harm in listening to well-meaning advice given by friends and family, but don't feel under any obligation to carry it out.

Everyone, from your mother-in-law to the butcher, has very clear ideas about how babies should be treated and cared for, and how children should be raised. It can be very disconcerting to find that, in the eyes of some people, you are doing everything, well, wrong.

One of the most important skills you can learn as a new parent is to sift advice – develop a thick skin, listen politely, and then ignore what doesn't fit in with your parenting philosophy. This skill will be useful not just now but throughout your parenting years. When people are offering advice, no matter how experienced, remember that times change, and that everyone has their own ways of doing things. So what may have been standard 20 or 30 years ago, may not be appropriate now. Also, every baby requires tailor-made care. Trust your own knowledge, and politely deflect advice and criticism. Try anything that sounds useful, and take on board practical tips if you want to, but stick to your guns and do things your way.

ASK A DOCTOR

My baby's scalp has large patches of loose, dry skin. Is this eczema? Your baby has cradle cap, a common condition characterized by yellowish, greasy, scaly patches on the scalp. To help control the itching and discomfort, lightly massage a baby-friendly emollient (moisturizer) onto their scalp to loosen the scales. Using a soft brush, gently brush over their scalp to loosen the scales, then carefully wash your baby's scalp with baby shampoo.

Little explorer

Your baby is starting to show an interest in all the new things in their world, and nothing is more fascinating to your baby than their own little body.

Oral discovery Babies examine and test things out using their tongues and lips.

Around this age, your baby discovers their hands and, possibly, their feet. They'll look at their hands in wonder, and bring them to their mouth. This provides entertainment and develops early hand–eye coordination. Within a baby's line of vision, hands are easy focus – wonderful "toys" that appear in and out of the horizon and capture attention for long periods. Your baby won't know the hands belong to them for some months yet, though.

As your baby's neck muscles get stronger, they will turn their head towards noises and try to manoeuvre into a position to see you. Their eyes may open with interest when a face or a toy is held within a line of vision, and if you move it away, they may make an effort to follow it. This is the beginning of tracking (see p.79). Hang a mobile so that the objects are about 30cm (12in) from their head. Your baby's eyes will move to examine it.

Switching nappies

Now you're feeling a little more settled, you might consider different ways of doing things, such as changing to reusable nappies.

Many parents go for disposables in the early days because they are more convenient, and save the presence of an ever-growing pile of dirty nappies. But as life begins to take on some semblance of a routine, you may find that you can now rearrange your time to launder nappies – or even investigate a nappy service. Babies grow very quickly, so if you have already been using reusables, you may need a new set now.

If you haven't yet used reusables but are thinking about doing so, now could be a good time to make the switch. Once your baby is about 4.4kg (10lbs), you can purchase nappies that can be adjusted to see them through to potty-training days. So at least you won't have wasted any money on buying the tiny ones. According to a 2023 review by Which?, reusables were more cost-effective and environmentally friendly than disposables. There's also research to suggest that the shape and design of reusables offer better support for your baby's posture, and can help to keep their legs apart, in a "frog" position, that benefits the development of their hips.

Of course, disposable nappies have their advantages, too, including being super absorbent and easy to put on and take off. So there's no reason to change if you don't want to. Even if you prefer reusables, disposables are handy from time to time – on holiday, out and about, or even when you're busy and washing and drying nappies is a task too many.

YOUR POSTNATAL CHECK

There are just a couple of weeks to go until your postnatal check by your doctor to make sure you have fully recovered following the birth of your baby (see pp.92–93 for more information). In some cases, an appointment will be made for you by your doctor's surgery, but you should ring and check what the procedure is in your area – you may need to arrange the appointment yourself. It's a good idea to start jotting down any questions you have now so that they don't slip your mind later on.

SMILING YOUNG BABIES

It is possible that you've seen your baby smiling in their sleep, and giving a fleeting grin from time to time. This type of smiling is known as "reflex" smiling, and it can occur from birth until a baby is about eight weeks old. It is believed to make infants more attractive so that they are cared for. Social smiling, which occurs in response to stimuli (such as your smiling face, or a familiar song) is known as "learned" smiling, and can occur as early as four weeks, although usually at 6–8 weeks. But even contented babies might be 12 weeks before they smile. You'll know it's the real thing when your baby smiles with their entire face, including their eyes.

Is your baby smiling? In the early days, a baby's smile is the result of an in-built reflex rather than a responsive gesture.

1 month

BABIES HAVE OVER 300 BONES; MANY FUSE TOGETHER OVER TIME TO MAKE 206 ADULT BONES.
Although your baby still needs plenty of support, they are already trying to hold up their head on their own. They may even lift it briefly when they are resting against your shoulder or on their tummy. Their hands are held in fists for the first few months, but they'll soon start to open and close them.

Tracking objects

One of the most exciting developments in your baby's vision is the fact that they can now begin to "track" an object as it moves.

Focusing with both eyes Your baby can focus but they can't see very far, so keep objects of interest within 30cm (12in) of their face.

At the outset, your baby moves their head in order to move their eyes, so a massive movement is required to keep their eyes pinned on a moving object. Initially, they move their head only horizontally to track objects, largely because it is easier to move a head from side to side than to lift it up and drop it down. If you pass a rattle in front of their eyes, they'll try to move they head to the side to follow it.

In time your baby will start to move their eyes independently of their head and develop "eye-teaming" skills, in which they use their eyes together. So don't worry if they look cross-eyed from time to time – in the coming weeks, their eyes will be better coordinated as they will have more control of the nerves and muscles to keep them from crossing.

Your baby will find it easier to track objects that are highly contrasting – your face, for example, or black-and-white geometric shapes and lines, will catch their attention and encourage them to focus. Hold the object of focus in their line of vision and move it slowly from side to side. Their eyes will lock on to it. Gentle movements are easier for them to follow than fast, jerky movements.

Over the coming weeks, you'll notice that they will track things for longer, and show much more interest in the things they track. By three months, you can begin to encourage their vertical tracking skills. For now, though, celebrate their wonderful new achievement.

FOCUS ON TWINS: TELLING IDENTICAL TWINS APART

Although every parent of identical twins will tell you that there are subtle differences between their babies, the truth is that most parents of identical twins do struggle to tell them apart from time to time, especially in the early weeks, when the different personalities of each baby are not yet established. It can be much easier to know which is which if there is an obvious difference, such as a birthmark, a fuller head of hair, or a different timbre of cry.

Many parents choose to colour-code their children – with red for one and blue for the other, for example. You can choose to keep on your baby's hospital band for a little longer than usual, just to differentiate between them, and then colour-code their clothes so that you'll know who is who. Rest assured that, within a few weeks, their minute differences will become clear, and these will become very big differences with every month that passes.

ASK A DOCTOR

I seem to be leaking urine when I cough or laugh. Shouldn't things have tightened up down there by now? It can take a while for ligaments and muscles to tighten up after pregnancy and childbirth. Like all muscles, your pelvic floor, which supports your bladder, needs to be exercised regularly to become "fit". If you didn't practise these exercises (known as Kegel exercises, see p.65) during pregnancy, it can take longer to tone them after the birth, but it's never too late to start.

Taking time out

It's easy to forget that you and your partner had a relationship before parenthood. Take up any offers of babysitting and find time to be together.

No matter how much you enjoy being a new parent, there are times when you probably long for a little adult conversation and to get out of the house. Yet, parenting is tricky, and requires plenty of planning, negotiating, and agreement.

Equally, your relationship requires the same input and effort that it always did to keep it strong, so it is important that you and your partner spend time alone together. While there is no reason why you can't schedule "dates" at home, it's very refreshing to go out and focus on each other, without the interruptions and distractions of life with a new baby.

A grandparent or close, trusted friend can care for your newborn for an hour or two. Choose a time when your baby is usually happy and fed, or likely to be asleep. Use this time to enjoy your partner's company; try not to talk only about the baby. Talk about other things, and relate as adults in a relationship, not just tired parents. Your relationship will enjoy a new lease of life, as will you!

ASK A DOCTOR

When will my baby sleep through the night? Most babies don't sleep through until around six months (and sometimes later). Your baby's tummy is tiny and digests feeds quickly, so needs regular refuelling, even at night. Also, they need the reassurance of being close to you. Comparatively, breastfed babies sleep lightly and wake more often. Don't panic. Rest when they do, keep night-time feeds quiet, and remember – this stage won't last forever.

Enjoying sounds

Your baby is now starting to make sense of the world's sounds and will respond to loud and soft noises and, best of all, music!

Your baby will listen carefully when a sound catches their attention. They'll turn their head to find out what's causing sounds. Loud noises may startle, and a lullaby may soothe. Watch you baby's response when you whistle or drum your fingers on the table. Play lively music and watch as they kick their legs or listens with interest. Play a softer melody and your baby will likely quieten and relax. Some studies show that music can affect a baby's nervous system, easing anxiety.

Use music in playtime to stimulate and add to the sense of fun. Play different types of music according to your mood and point out the sounds that make up your baby's environment. Your baby will begin to associate sounds with the activities they denote, so they'll hear the bath running and eventually realise this means bathtime.

Great shakes Your baby will be interested in hearing a variety of different sounds.

Night and day

Many babies don't automatically have their body clocks set to your schedule, spending long hours awake at night, and sleeping through the day.

Daytime sleep To help your baby differentiate between daytime sleep and night-time sleep, keep the room light during the day, and don't block out household sounds.

Although it makes sense to sleep when your baby does in the early weeks, they do now need to be edged more towards a practical sleeping plan so that you both get the rest you need. Babies need plenty of sleep during the day, but there should now be periods of activity between naps. At night, aim for the opposite.

In the daytime, put your baby to sleep in a pram or Moses basket in a light room other than the bedroom. The light entering the room will work on the baby's pineal gland in the brain, which governs sleep and wakefulness, and they'll be much less likely to sleep for very long periods than if the room were dark. Also, they'll be more likely to wake at an appropriate time if there is a little background noise going on.

Make the day stimulating enough to promote sleepiness at night. If your baby is napping and feeding all day, they are unlikely to be physically tired enough for prolonged night-time sleep. Wake them up from long naps with plenty of cheery chat, play, and songs, and fill the waking day with stimulating activity.

At night, handle the baby very quietly and efficiently, and resist the temptation to chat. Put the baby back into the cot after changing and feeding, making it clear that playtime is not at night. Your baby may grizzle, but will soon get the message.

DEVELOPMENT ACTIVITY: MOBILE ENTERTAINMENT

A mobile over your baby's bed, floor mat, or even changing table, if you have one, will be visually stimulating and encourage the baby to "track" objects (see p.79), which also strengthens spatial perception. Choose bright colours to catch attention, and, if possible, a model that can be wound up to move in a gentle, baby-friendly circular motion. Music is a bonus, as it can soothe or stimulate, depending on what's best.

Your baby's Moses basket or floor mat is a safe place for them to relax and play, and you can get on with other household activities while your baby watches and listens to their toy.

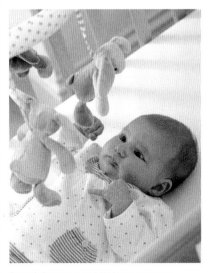

Round they go A mobile hung over your baby's cot gives them something to focus their attention on.

Feeling up and down

Having a new baby changes life dramatically, and it can be difficult to manage to begin with, which can leave you feeling a little low.

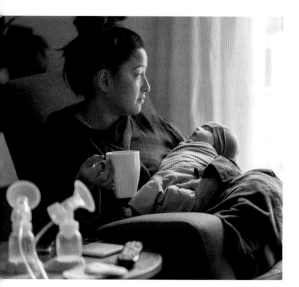

No matter how happily you anticipated your life with a new baby, the reality can be exhausting and, for some parents, a little stifling. You may miss regular contact with friends and colleagues and feel lonely. You may be shocked by the fact that you can't manage to get anything done during the day other than care for your baby, and long for the days when you could be spontaneous.

Don't feel guilty about such emotions – they don't mean you don't love your baby or enjoy being with them. This is a period of adjustment to a new way of life, guided completely by another person.

It can help to arrange get-togethers – with friends from your childbirth classes or other groups in the area. Pop your baby in a sling and take them into work to visit. Get out into the fresh air and change your routine occasionally. Rest assured, soon, life will take on a more regular pattern and you can plan more. Ask your partner to take over for an hour and give you a welcome respite from babycare while you read a book, or even just feel the sun on your face.

Downtime Caring for a new baby can be very tiring and it's perfectly normal to have mixed feelings in the early days.

Your post-birth body

Pregnancy and birth can change a woman's body. Although that can feel surprising or strange, the new you is something to celebrate.

After childbirth, many new mums glow, even if they feel tired; others feel a bit flat and body conscious. Your tummy is likely to be less swollen now, and for most mums, it's good to feel that their bodies are their own again, free from the rigours of growing a new life! If you're not quite at that stage yet, don't worry. You have adjusted to the physical rigours of pregnancy, and it will take time to restore a sense of normality in your body. If your breasts are bigger now you're breastfeeding, enjoy your voluptuousness. If you have stretch marks, remind yourself that they'll fade over time. Eat healthily and enjoy some physical activity when you can, and do this to remain healthy and give you energy, rather than feeling you need to fit back into your skinny jeans.

ASK A DOCTOR

I'm breastfeeding and my periods have returned! Is this normal? Although most women do not see the return of their periods until around six months, they could start as early as four weeks or as late as a year after the birth. For this reason, do not presume that breastfeeding offers you a reliable form of contraception.

Expressing milk

Expressing your milk allows you to buy yourself a little freedom and your partner to get involved with feeding your baby.

Some women start expressing around now with a view to continuing to breastfeed when they return to work, or because they want more flexibility and someone else to be able to give their baby a feed every so often. You can express milk using a pump (see p.28) or by hand (see box, right). The best time to express is when you are relaxed. You'll soon work out when in the day you have most milk – many women find that they have very full breasts first thing in the morning. Give your baby a feed from one breast, and either simultaneously express from the other or take a warm bath, pop your sleeping baby in their basket next to you, and express what's left.

When you express, your breasts will produce more milk. However, it can take a few days for your milk supply to catch up, so express small amounts and let your baby suckle at your breast often. You might notice that your breastmilk looks watery in comparison to formula or cow's milk – but it's the perfect consistency for your baby.

If breastmilk is immediately frozen, it will last for up to four months. Store it in plastic feeding bottles with secure tops, or you can buy sterile bags made for this purpose. Write the date on the bottle or bag so that you know when you need to use it by. Freezing breastmilk destroys some of the disease-fighting antibodies it

EXPRESSING MILK BY HAND

Some women find it easier to express by hand than they do being attached to a pump. Make yourself comfortable, preferably with your baby nearby. A warm bath first may relax you. Cup your breast with one hand and use the other to press the breast so the milk in the milk channels travels downwards towards the areola. Now use your thumb and forefingers to squeeze the breast tissue to press out the milk, but try not to touch the areola. Keep pressing and releasing – you'll find a comfortable rhythm. It can take a few minutes for your milk to flow. If you are struggling, imagine your baby suckling or even reach over to touch them to encourage let-down. Rotate your hands to reposition them from time to time, which encourages flow by stimulating the sinuses (see p.26).

Have a clean bowl or sterilized bottle ready to collect the milk. Express each breast until the flow slows down – for perhaps five minutes or so. You can go back and forth between them until your breasts feel empty. If you are putting your freshly-expressed milk into the freezer, remember to add a label with the date.

Manual release Press the breast to start milk flow. Then, avoiding the areola, gently squeeze and release the breast between thumb and forefingers, using both hands.

contains, but its nutritional value is not affected. Defrost frozen milk in the fridge overnight, or place the bottle or bag in a bowl of warm water. Don't use the microwave or a hob to heat milk, as this kills some of its nutrients.

Freshly expressed breastmilk can be stored in the fridge for up to five days at 4ºC (39ºF) or lower, in the ice compartment of the fridge for up to two weeks, or in the freezer for three to six months at no higher than -18ºC (0.4ºF).

Baby talk

Constantly talking to your baby can help them develop their language and communication skills.

You may be surprised to find that you are, quite unexpectedly, speaking "baby talk" in a high-pitched sing-song voice – and that your baby is responding. This is a natural, instinctive method of communication that parents use, known as "parentese" (or "motherese"), and it occurs in every language in the world. Studies have found that babies pay more attention to and prefer this type of speech. It encourages communication between parent and child and helps babies to learn the rudiments of language. Using baby talk doesn't just interest your baby and hold their attention, but it helps them to pick up words more quickly than without it, and contributes to their mental development.

You may feel uncomfortable speaking in a slow, high-pitched voice with a simplistic vocabulary (or even babble) and lots of repetition, but your baby will find it soothing and will actually begin to understand you – and the nuances of language. Talking to your baby has an incredible impact on their development, so don't hesitate to chatter away as you look after them.

Explain what you are doing as you go along. They won't understand the meaning of words at first, but over the coming months they'll learn that these sounds are labels for your actions or objects around them.

Studies suggest that talking to babies helps them to identify where words begin and end, and provides them with the clues needed for them to develop language skills. You'll find that most adults – and even children – adopt parentese when speaking to babies, and this is an instinctive way of speaking that will reap long-term rewards.

Sharing the load

Co-parenting has never been more usual for families than it is today, so if you plan to share childcare, it's important to start as you mean to go on.

It's good to share babycare with your partner – your baby gets to bond with both of you and ensures neither of you feels less confident than the other. Your baby will enjoy cuddles from you both, and will become familiar with the ways each of you has worked out how to care for and soothe them.

Taking turns When you and your partner take an equal share in babycare, you divide the load and both learn new skills.

Talk to each other about how best to divide the workload of caring for your baby and running the home. When either one of you is in charge of babycare, try not to undermine each other – if your baby is happy, it's fine. If you're bottle-feeding, it's preferable that only the two of you feed your baby in the early days as this is prime bonding time. If you're breastfeeding, once you've settled into it, you can express so your partner can feed the baby, too.

Bottle-feeding know-how

Whether you're using formula or you plan to start, or you've been expressing milk, here's how to ensure bottle-feeding goes smoothly.

If you are breastfeeding, most experts advise against offering babies a bottle before about 4–6 weeks to avoid "nipple confusion". Sucking from a bottle requires less effort and babies can get used to drinking milk more quickly. However, if you can establish breastfeeding successfully over the first six weeks, your baby will develop the skills they need and find it less daunting to switch between breast and bottle.

Remember that your milk supply is based on your baby's demands. If your baby is getting milk from a bottle, they won't be "demanding" it from you, and your supply will run down. If you are planning to return to work, you should introduce the occasional bottle around now. Some babies will reject a bottle if you leave it too late. Once you have expressed milk (see p.28 for more on pumps, and p.83 for information on manual expressing and storing breastmilk), offer a bottle once a week or so to make the transition to bottle-feeding easier. Heat the milk so that a drop on your wrist feels just warm, and discard unfinished milk. Throwing away expressed milk may seem a waste, but there's a risk of bacteria building up, which can lead to tummy bugs.

Sometimes even babies who have been bottle-fed from birth can experience problems. If your baby struggles when feeding, check the teat flow. If it takes longer than 20 minutes to finish a bottle, your baby may need a faster teat. If they choke or splutters, the flow may be too fast.

INTRODUCING A BREASTFED BABY TO A BOTTLE

Choose a time when your baby is calm and not very hungry. Some babies take to bottles easily, while others are more resistant. If your baby is reluctant, try expressed milk rather than formula, and smear a little of your usual nipple cream around the teat. Choose a slow-flow teat that is shaped like a nipple to mimic the breastfeeding experience, and open your shirt so that the baby feels your skin – and warmth. It may take a few attempts for your baby to accept it.

If you are having no luck, try asking your partner or another trusted family member or friend to take over. Sometimes babies smell their mum's milk and know that they are being offered something different. They may be more likely to accept "different" from someone else. If your baby becomes distressed, leave it for another day and breastfeed as usual. The last thing you want is for the bottle to have unhappy associations.

Giving the bottle Gently stroke your baby's cheek to elicit the rooting reflex and insert the teat carefully into the mouth.

During the feed Chat with your baby and let them pause mid-feed if they like. Change sides to give your arm a rest.

Removing the bottle Gently slide your little finger into the corner of their mouth to stop them sucking the teat.

Thinking about safety

Now that your baby has a little more control of their movements, use these tips to keep them safe.

Ensure your baby is supported, positioned, and held at all times, so that they don't suddenly jerk themself out of your grasp or roll off the bed. Remove electrical leads and dangling cords for curtains or blinds away from your baby's bed, play, changing, or feeding areas. Never leave medicines, small objects, household plants, or plastic bags within your baby's reach. Always remember to fasten the harness on your baby's bouncy chair and car seat, even when they are sleeping and immobile. Avoid leaving your baby alone, even for short periods, unless they are on a flat, safe surface (ideally the floor) or strapped into their seat or pushchair. Keep your baby's bedding tucked safely under their arms, so that they don't draw it up and over their face. Similarly, put them to sleep at the bottom of their cot so that they don't wriggle down under their covers.

COMFORT ITEMS

Your baby has the mental capacity to remember familiar objects, so now is a great time to introduce a comfort item. A soft toy or blanket are ideal – buy two, in case one gets lost. If you bring out their comfort item whenever you soothe them, they will associate it with comfort. This encourages them to learn to self-soothe by giving them a tool to encourage happy, positive, relaxing feelings.

Making new sounds

Your clever baby may have increased their vocabulary already, moving on to double-syllable sounds with the odd consonant.

Make baby talk Encourage your baby's communication skills by "chatting" to them.

Cooing and gurgling, and even giggling, may be becoming second nature to your baby, and they'll be excited about communicating with you, and other members of the family. Their babbling is their first attempt at speech, and you'll notice huge leaps in their baby vocabulary over the coming months as they practise the sounds they've been learning to make.

Your baby is learning the basics of conversation and the art of listening and responding. According to linguists, babies can tell the difference between similar syllables, such as "ma" and "na", from about four weeks. Repeat the sounds they make back at them. They'll love to know that you understand what they're trying to say, or the emotion they're attempting to communicate. They are most responsive when they are with familiar people, and when they are spoken to in parentese (see p.84).

Vowel sounds, such as "ah", "uh", "ooh", and "oh", are the first sounds babies make. These graduate to double vowel sounds, such as "ah-uh" and "ooh-ah", before a consonant such as "g" or "m" appears. "Ahh-gooo" may become your baby's favourite means of expressing pleasure.

Listening and learning

Your baby's hearing faculty is quite sensitive. This makes them a great listener and means that sound is a good source of information for them.

Even before your baby was born they could hear your voice and the voice of your partner. Now that the baby hears it every day outside the womb, and understands the link between those voices and continued wellbeing, they find them highly comforting. Given that your baby likes to hear your voice so much, make the most of it – talk to them (see p.84) and sing songs. Hearing you around helps your baby to feel safe.

Repetitive sounds

Particularly when they are accompanied by repetitive actions, such as the "pop" in "Pop Goes the Weasel", repetitive sounds help babies learn expectation and predictability, and cause and effect. Some experts believe that repetitive sounds can help to improve babies' memories.

New sounds

Unexpected sounds can make your baby startle – they might fling their arms in the air, raise their knees, or even cry. Reacting negatively to sounds affirms that your baby's hearing is working as it should. Comment on the noises your baby hears to teach that noises are normal and have meaning. Babies who live with noisy siblings may even learn to zone noise out!

Spotting a problem

Your baby should be noticeably calmed or become distracted by your voice – although that pause may be only brief. And, if you clap your hands behind the baby's head, they should startle. If you think your baby consistently doesn't seem to respond to your voice or loud noises, consult your health visitor or GP, who can arrange a hearing test.

Often, though, babies simply learn to ignore the noises around them, and young babies can sleep through a great deal of noise. Full-term babies rarely experience hearing problems, unless there are other members of the family who have them.

Listening to mum Your baby is your devoted audience; they love to hear your voice.

DEVELOPMENT ACTIVITY: PLAYING MUSIC

Exploring sounds Introducing your baby to new sounds, such as the sound of crinkling paper, is good for sensory development.

Some studies suggest that babies who are exposed to many musical styles develop a good ear for sound and musical appreciation when older. Music, particularly classical music, may encourage neurological pathways to develop in the newborn's brain, improving thought processes and stimulating "alpha" brainwaves, which are associated with feelings of calm.

Bring different styles of music into your baby's life. Perhaps play lively, upbeat music in the morning, sing nursery rhymes at playtime, and play soothing classical music when you want to create a sense of calm for a sleep.

Downtime for baby

Raising a relaxed child partly depends on how relaxed you are, so it's important to include a little bit of wakeful downtime every day.

It is healthy for babies to spend some time each day looking around, taking in their world without you directing them. Otherwise you will have a fractious overstimulated infant. It takes time to find the balance between playtime and downtime, but as you learn to read your baby's signals this will become easier.

Downtime is important, but make sure your baby has short bursts of tummy time every day, too. Be mindful of the amount of time your

Quiet time Give your baby quiet time on their back to explore the world independently.

baby spends lying on their back, particularly if they are awake and active. When your baby is born, their skull is soft. Too much time lying flat can result in some babies developing flat head syndrome causing the head to look asymmetrical (plagiocephaly) or to widen causing the forehead to bulge out (brachycephaly). Usually, neither problem is a cause for concern and both are quite common, affecting about one in every 5 babies at some point. Over time, the head shape usually improves by itself requiring no medical intervention.

Your social network

Meeting friends lifts your spirits, gives you a change of routine, and introduces your baby to the idea of sociable company.

Whether you meet up with friends from your antenatal group, visit a parent-and-baby group, or join an online parents' support group sharing experiences, swapping tips, and enjoying adult conversation can be invaluable. Having other parents to talk to can reassure you that your concerns are likely to be common.

Spend time with positive people who respect your philosophies. If you come away feeling as if you are not

living up to collective expectations, it may be the wrong group for you. This should be an uplifting experience that increases your confidence.

Be mindful of what you post online; "sharenting" is the action of parents using social media to share news, images, or videos of their children. This practice raises issues around consent and leaving a long-lasting digital footprint, which may have implications long term.

ASK A PAEDIATRICIAN

My baby hates tummy time. Is there any way to encourage them? Babies need about 30 minutes of tummy time each day in order to develop important muscles, but it doesn't have to be all at once. Plan three 10-minute sessions. If your baby grizzles, distract with a song or a toy to eke it out! Choose a stimulating play mat, and get down on your tummy too, stroke their back, and chat to them.

It's bedtime

Now that your baby is almost six weeks old, they'll probably respond well to their bedtime routine and feel happier about being left alone.

It will probably be some time before your baby sleeps through the night, and they will continue to wake up frequently for feeds or comfort as the weeks go by. No matter how tired or frustrated you may feel by these night wakings, try to stay calm and respond to their needs as quickly and quietly as you can. A baby who knows that their parents will come when they need them is more secure, and will more likely develop self-soothing skills early on.

Good sleep patterns are dependent upon a gentle bedtime routine, which helps your baby unwind and anticipate the series of events that will ultimately lead to longer periods of restful sleep. High jinks with a parent who returns from work won't relax them, so keep things calm and quiet, giving them a wash, a lovely feed, and a lullaby before settling them down. Babies love repetition, so sing the same song each night to help them to understand what's coming next and anticipate it with pleasure.

Stay with your baby if they need you and reassure them of your presence. Don't tiptoe around the house when they drift off – let them hear the familiar sounds of your voice and normal household activities. They'll know you're there, and will get used to sleeping in noisier environments, so won't be startled awake by tiny sounds.

All babies need daytime naps, and babies who have regular naps find it easier to sleep well at night as they are well rested and accustomed to being settled. If you get your baby down at the first sign of sleepiness (see p.81), you'll miss their second wind of energy.

Finally, don't sleep train your baby yet or leave them to cry. At this stage, they need a warm, loving routine that makes them confident enough to fall asleep and settle back to sleep when they waken, knowing you're there if they need you.

YOUR BABY'S HAIR

When your baby is born, their hair may be thick or thin, dark or light, standing on end, or neatly coiffed as if they've just stepped out of a salon. What a baby's hair will be like at birth is as unpredictable as anything else. Even if both the baby's parents have blond hair, they may be born with dark hair and vice versa. Very often, if your baby is born with hair at all, it will fall out over the course of their first few months of life, to be replaced by something more in keeping with the rest of the family!

Your baby may develop a bald patch on the back of their head, where their head rests when they're lying down; this is perfectly normal, and once their "proper" hair comes through, the patch will disappear.

Thick hair Any hair your baby had at birth may fall out in the first six months and then grow back in a different colour or texture (left). **Fine hair** Babies born with no hair, or very fine hair, may stay like that well into the first year (right).

Extra feeds

By this time most babies start to sleep for longer at night than they do during the day.

Around now, many babies have a growth spurt, making them hungry and demanding, so be prepared for extra feeds during this time. If you're lucky, your baby might just smile properly for the very first time about now. However, many babies don't manage to smile until around two months of age.

Between now and 3 months, your baby will start to respond to certain sounds – first by turning their head and changing their facial expressions, and then by actually cooing and gurgling. They're really beginning to communicate.

First smiles Up until now, a baby's smiles are likely to be a reflex action or as a result of wind. However, they will move on to giving gorgeous, purposeful smiles.

Time for a growth spurt

You can expect a rapid and intense period of growth any time now – sometimes it can seem as if your baby has grown bigger overnight!

Restlessness during sleeping, extended periods of sleeping, and, most obviously, an increased demand for food are all signs that your baby might be having a growth spurt, especially when they appear in combination. Many breastfeeding mothers mistake increased restlessness and feeding demands for signs that they are not producing enough milk – however, if these signs occur around the six-week mark, a growth spurt is more likely the cause.

During a growth spurt, it can be really difficult to establish a fixed routine of feeding your baby, and any routine you thought you'd established can seem to disappear as your baby constantly seems hungry. Your milk supply will respond to your baby's demands, so it's important that you feed them whenever they ask for food so that your body steps up the quantity of milk it produces to satisfy them. It's also important to encourage your baby to empty each breast fully, so that they get plenty of fatty, filling hindmilk. Usually, the feeding pattern will settle down again pretty quickly as the growth spurt passes, often within only a few days.

If you are bottle-feeding your baby, it may be time to increase the amount you give, but only by 25ml (1fl oz) at a time. Consult your health visitor if you are unsure.

Hungry baby Feed your baby as often as they want; the amount of milk you produce depends on how much they nurse.

TOO BIG FOR NEWBORN SIZE?

If your baby was over 3.6kg (8lbs) at birth, they may not even have worn newborn sizes; however, the average baby normally outgrows the smallest-sized baby clothing between five and eight weeks – sometimes sooner. If things are starting to look a little tight (particularly at the feet), keep them comfortable by moving them up a size. Clothes designed for 0–3-month-old babies should get them through the month, but be prepared to be flexible. Take the baby along when you go shopping and hold the clothes up against them; allow for shrinkages in the wash and the upcoming growth spurt. When in doubt, go a size larger. Your baby will be into 3–6-month outfits in no time at all!

ASK A BREASTFEEDING EXPERT

My baby seems hungry all the time. Can I give a bottle of formula as well as a breastfeed? Although your milk supply should now be established, it will increase over the coming months to meet your baby's needs. Around this time, your baby will be undergoing a growth spurt, and want to feed more often to fuel that growth. Suckling will increase your supply to match the baby's new demands, so it is important to put the baby to your breast as often as they wish. It's not a good idea to give extra bottles of formula at this stage because your breasts will not be stimulated to make enough milk for your baby. So if you want to continue breastfeeding successfully, try to avoid doing so. It usually only takes a few days for your breasts to catch up, so bear with it and feed frequently.

Postnatal checks

When your baby is around six weeks old, you will be asked to visit your GP. This routine examination is to check that you and your baby are doing well, and that you're coping with your new life as a parent. This is a chance to discuss any concerns you have.

The postnatal check, also known as the six-week check, is usually performed by your GP at your local surgery, although some health trusts invite you back to see a doctor at the maternity unit in which you had your baby. There is no reason why you might go to the hospital instead of a surgery – it will entirely depend upon the protocol in your area.

Checking your physical health

It is likely that, as with your antenatal appointments, the first checks your doctor will perform will be to take your blood pressure and, possibly to test a urine sample. Six weeks after birth, your blood pressure should have returned to normal levels (below 140/90), even if you suffered from either high or low blood pressure during your pregnancy. Your urine may be checked, especially if you had high blood pressure during pregnancy, have high blood pressure now, have any urinary symptoms, or if you had gestational diabetes.

If you are breastfeeding, your doctor will ask you about your breast health – whether you have any soreness or cracked nipples, and so on – and will perform a physical examination if you want one. They will also be ready to answer any concerns that you may have about breastfeeding.

Increasingly, doctors are concerned that mothers adopt good dietary and exercise habits after giving birth to speed their recovery and to help them achieve appropriate weight loss. For this reason, your doctor may weigh you and advise you, if necessary, about appropriate diet and activity that will help you regain your pre-baby weight. It is advisable to wait until you have this check before embarking upon any significant exercise programme, as your body will take at least six weeks to recover properly from childbirth.

Your doctor may ask if you would like them to check any stitches and healing in your perineum if you had a tear or episiotomy. They will ask if your vaginal bleeding or discharge has settled down and if you've had a period yet. You will also be asked whether or not you have had intercourse, and if so whether you experienced any pain. This is also a good time to talk about contraception, and whether you have any concerns. If you haven't had a smear test in the previous three years, the doctor will encourage you to book yourself in for one once the baby is over three months old.

Checking your emotional health

Your doctor will want to know how you are feeling emotionally following the birth. They will ask if you have experienced any low patches, how well you are sleeping, and how you are coping with the demands of being

My baby's belly button sticks out. Could there be a problem? Belly buttons come in all shapes and sizes, so how your baby's umbilical stump will detach and what their belly button will look like is entirely unpredictable. However, if it protrudes significantly, especially when your baby strains or cries, they may have an umbilical hernia. This harmless condition occurs when there is weakness in the muscles around the umbilicus, where the cord was attached. Most umbilical hernias sort themselves out in the baby's first year without medical intervention. Occasionally, however, babies need a simple operation. It is worth mentioning a protruding belly button to your doctor, so that, if there is a hernia, the condition can be diagnosed and monitored.

When will my piles go away? Piles (haemorrhoids) are common in pregnancy, and can also occur as a result of pushing during labour. In many cases, they disappear within a couple of months of the birth, and you can encourage this by eating a diet rich in wholegrains, fruit and vegetables, drinking plenty of water, and exercising regularly (including pelvic floor exercises, see p.65). Raising your feet on toilet rolls can help when opening your bowels. If it's painful, not improving, or you have bleeding, see your GP.

a new parent, including asking about your support network. None of these questions is intended to catch you out, and it's important that you answer honestly, voicing any worries or concerns you have (about any aspect, physical or emotional) about your own or the baby's wellbeing. Your doctor will be mindful to look for signs of postnatal depression so that, if you do seem susceptible, you can receive the support you need as quickly as possible.

Questions about the baby

As well as checking the baby's physical health, the doctor will ask you about the baby's feeding habits and whether or not you have any concerns about the baby's wellbeing. They will also ask you if your baby wees and poos regularly, and if they have started to smile yet. If you're lucky, your baby will oblige and answer that question for you!

Because most babies are carefully monitored from birth, the six-week check is a formality that rarely throws up new concerns. However, if your doctor has any worries about any aspect of the checks, they will suggest appropriate follow-up appointments to ensure that any potential problems are caught and tackled, or dismissed, at the earliest opportunity.

AFTER A CAESAREAN

Your doctor will check that your incision scar is healing, and that you do not have any discomfort. By six weeks, most women can do most of their essential everyday activities, such as bathing, housework, babycare, and some gentle lifting. However, some women continue to find it difficult to lift heavy things and to have sex until much later. Don't do anything that feels uncomfortable. You can drive again as soon as your doctor confirms that it's safe. Check your insurance cover: some companies require your GP to certify that you are fit to drive.

CHECKS FOR YOUR BABY

Your baby also receives a six-week check, either at this appointment or on another occasion. The examination is similar to the one they had at birth. You'll need to undress them, so dress them in clothes that are easy to put on and take off, and take a spare nappy.

- **Bones, joints, and muscles** The doctor will lay your baby on their back and gently manipulate each leg to check that their hip joints offer the full range of movement. The doctor will straighten the baby's legs to ensure they are the same length, and also check that the spine is straight and their other joints are functioning properly. The doctor will check the baby's fontanelles have a healthy appearance (that they aren't bulging or sunken; see p.97), and may check how the neck muscles and head control are developing, either by observing your baby as you hold them on your shoulder or by placing them on their tummy.
- **Heart** Your doctor will check your baby's heart sounds and pulses to help rule out congenital heart problems.

- **Reflexes** Your GP may use some simple tests to check how your baby's reflexes are developing.
- **Eyes** Looking into your baby's eyes with an ophthalmoscope will reveal any congenital problems, such as cataract. The doctor will also check that your baby can track objects (see p.79).
- **Other** Your doctor will feel your baby's abdomen to check for hernias. If you have a boy, the doctor will check that the testes have descended properly into the scrotum sacks.

Weight check Weighing your baby and plotting the reading on their growth chart will help ensure that the baby is gaining weight at an appropriate rate for their age.

Checking the head Your baby's head circumference provides an indicator that their growth is normal and that there are no problems beneath their skull.

Heart check Listening to your baby's heart with a stethoscope enables a doctor to check whether there are any abnormal heart sounds or murmurs.

Little smiler

Your baby's first smile is a precious moment, as it shows things are going to plan and that your baby is happy.

Babies don't smile until they are ready to – even the most contented babies may not break out their first smile until about seven weeks old, sometimes later. However, evidence does suggest that talking to your baby, smiling at them, and making lots of eye contact with them helps the process along. Baby boys may be slower to smile than girls, but are just as open to encouragement. Once your baby does break that first smile, they'll be so happy with your reaction that they'll do it again and again.

First smile The more you smile at your baby, the more they'll try to copy you and smile back.

Your baby's first smiles will take place in response to familiar auditory stimulation, such as the sound of your voice. By two months, as their vision improves, they will begin to smile in response to things they see – usually their favourite, most familiar people.

Once your baby has learned to smile, they have reached the first milestone in their ability to communicate in a manner other than crying. This first smile seems a wonderful reward for all your work! Soon they'll be smiling at other familiar faces, such as siblings and grandparents. The bigger the fuss you make of those smiles, the more you'll see them repeated.

Grasp reflex

Your baby has little control over their movements yet, but they'll try to grasp if you give their something to reach for.

Your baby will automatically grasp anything that is placed in their palm, because the newborn grasp reflex is still in place. However, they're also becoming more aware of what's around them, so if they see something that attracts them, they may try to stretch out or wave their arms to grasp it.

Instead of just watching that toy, they may lift an arm towards it in an uncoordinated motion. It will be a long time before they can actually open their hand and then close it around the object in a conscious movement, but they may well grasp something by accident rather than by design, even if many of their movements are undertaken with a clenched fist. Now's a good time to make sure that there's nothing within their reach that they could pull down on top of them. They may also reach for dangling hair, jewellery, or scarves, so watch out!

Your baby's kicks and arm motions are probably still a little jerky, but they will slowly become more graceful and intentional as the their muscles and nervous system continue to develop. They may also start to kick and wave their arms in excitement or enjoyment.

Improving vision

By now, your baby's eyesight will have improved dramatically compared to how it was at birth.

Your baby is now able to focus at distances of up to around 60cm (24in), because their brain has become more effective at interpreting data and processing it into clear pictures than it was at birth. You may also find that they start to discover and focus on parts of their body, particularly their hands (see p.106).

Your baby has developed some special cells called binocular cells that help to improve their ability to distinguish depth. However, they still can't move their eyes in perfect unison, and their ability to perceive depth properly is still a month or so away.

Colour and shape

It takes a while for the brain to distinguish between different colours, and especially between various shades of a single colour. By the time your baby is six weeks old, their brain will begin to decipher the colours red, green, and yellow, with blue coming a little later. They prefer distinctive shapes to straight lines, and some research suggests that a special part of a baby's brain is acutely attuned to recognizing faces, which is why they will fix on a face, and learn to smile in response to it.

Movement

Your baby should be able to follow movement with their eyes, if only briefly (see p.79).

| ASK A DOCTOR

My baby boy has an undescended testicle – will they have to have an operation? Normally, the testes (testicles) develop inside your baby's abdomen, then drop into the scrotum during the second half of pregnancy. By the time your baby is born, their testicles should have descended into his scrotum. Sometimes they remain in the groin, and this is known as "undescended testes". If they are not released into the scrotum, they will not be able to produce sperm in later life – and are at an increased risk of developing cancer. Try not to worry. In some cases, testes move down on their own, usually by 12 months. If your baby's testes don't do so, he may need an operation, known as an "orchidopexy", which would be carried out just before his first birthday. Your doctor will monitor the situation, and talk you through the procedure.

Sometimes when I'm washing or changing my baby, I notice they have an erection. Is this normal? Yes, this is normal. The penis is very sensitive and all baby boys have erections from time to time, some more than others. They have even been observed to have erections in the womb.

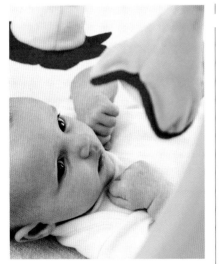

Seeing in colour At six weeks, your baby's brain starts to decipher the colours red, green, and yellow, and, a little later on, also blue.

EYE EXAMINATION

A follow-up physical examination is available for babies up to the age of eight weeks old to identify any problems not picked up at birth. As part of this examination, your baby's eyes will be checked. While the examination is not painful, your baby may find parts of it uncomfortable. Using a special torch, the healthcare practitioner will look into your baby's eyes to check how their eyes look and move, and for any signs of eye problems.

Resuming intimacy

Sex might not be high on your list of priorities right now, but making time to be intimate together keeps you connected as a couple.

Between six and eight weeks after the birth, the woman's body should have almost completely recovered. Any stitches or tearing should have healed, bleeding (lochia) should have stopped, and the vagina should have returned to its pre-pregnancy size.If it was a Caesarean birth, the incision site should be well on the mend.

However, after birth, most women experience a significant drop in oestrogen levels, which can lead to vaginal dryness. For most new parents, however, lack of desire has more to do with tiredness and adjusting to new parental roles than with hormones.

If you're the woman and you're worried that penetration might be painful, talk to your partner and let them know what you are comfortable with. If you don't feel ready for full intercourse, consider foreplay instead. Be sensitive to each other's needs and patient with one another. If you want to have intercourse, take it gently at first and try using a vaginal lubricant to ease penetration.

If you are breastfeeding, be aware that sex can trigger the let-down reflex, which may cause milk to leak from your breasts during lovemaking. Also, you'll need to use some form of contraception, unless you are relying on exclusive breastfeeding as a birth-control method.

Peak period for crying

If your baby seems to be wailing non-stop today, take heart: studies show that crying is at its most fervent around this time.

Frequent crying At around six weeks, crying is often as bad as it will ever be and should become less of a problem by three months.

Usually babies cry because they want attention, a feed, or a nappy change, but there are also other likely causes.

Some doctors believe colic (see p.68) peaks at six weeks, causing persistent bouts of crying, often during the evening, which can be distressing for all. If this is the case for your baby, there's little you can do except to wait and reassure yourself that it is usually significantly reduced by about three months of age.

A growth spurt (see p.91) makes your baby more hungry and more liable to fuss. Some theories suggest that this is because crying triggers the mother's body to manufacture more milk to meet the baby's demands.

Learning new skills, such as smiling, and becoming increasingly alert, can be tiring for young babies and crying provides a release for this.

Carry your baby in a sling or rock them gently in your arms to reassure them. Take comfort that this phase will pass. Enlist the help of friends and family if you're struggling to get things done or need to take a break for an hour or so. If you are finding it difficult to cope, your health visitor and GP can support you.

Starting to get active

If you were given the all clear at your six-week health check, now might be a good time to start easing your body back into physical activity.

Fitting in movement Some postnatal yoga classes incorporate baby yoga, too. Yoga can help you regain strength in your back, stomach, and pelvic floor muscles.

Every female body responds to pregnancy in its own way – so be realistic. If you were very toned before becoming pregnant, and if you had an active pregnancy, you are likely to regain your fitness more quickly – but it isn't a foregone conclusion. Whatever your underlying fitness level, make your goals achievable and don't expect too much too soon – the truth is that you may never get back the same body you had before, but you can certainly be as healthy, if not healthier.

Take it easy

Pregnancy and childbirth put your body through a major trauma. Ease yourself gently into exercising, taking things at a slow pace to start with. Your joints and ligaments will still be loose for around three to five months, so stick to low-impact exercise and avoid anything too vigorous or jerky, which could potentially cause injury.

Spend some time both before and after exercising doing a few gentle stretches to warm up and cool down. If, at any point during exercise, something hurts, stop immediately.

How much, how often?

Initially, aim for about 5–10 minutes of toning exercises every day, and 20 minutes of gentle aerobic activity three times a week, if you can. You can increase both as you become fitter and your body feels stronger. Never push yourself beyond what feels comfortable or achievable.

You'll have to work out ways of fitting in exercise with a baby:

THE FONTANELLES

There are two soft spots on a baby's head, one at the back and the other on top of the head. The fontanelles allow a baby's head to pass through the birth canal. The posterior, triangular fontanelle, located at the back of the head, will close when a baby is about four months old, while the one on the top of the head (the diamond-shaped, anterior fontanelle) takes between nine and 18 months to close.

It is normal to see your baby's head pulsating in time with their circulation. When your baby cries, the fontanelles may bulge a little, and then return to normal. If they bulge more than usual or become sunken, contact your GP. Sunken fontanelles may be a sign of dehydration while bulging fontanelles might indicate a serious illness, head trauma, fluid build-up, or internal bleeding. Seek medical advice if your baby shows signs of distress.

perhaps sharing babycare with a friend so that you can take turns to exercise. You could even take your baby with you to a pram-pushing exercise class, held in a local park.

Include your pelvic tilts and your Kegel (pelvic floor) exercises (see p.65) to help prevent postnatal incontinence. And try yoga. Postnatal yoga classes adapt the yoga postures to account for the fact that you have recently had a baby.

Active baby

Your baby is beginning to practise their new muscle control – wriggling a lot more, kicking, and twisting their body from side to side.

This is the perfect time to introduce a baby gym. Your baby's control over their body has improved so they will enjoy batting at hanging toys, and reaching out towards things. They may even manage to grab them, although they won't be able to intentionally close their fist around them yet. If you put something in their hand, they'll hold on – and chances are, they won't let go!

Their arms and legs will wave furiously when they are excited – or even angry – and nappy changing will become much more trying. You may find that they respond to music by slowing down their movements or speeding them up, accordingly.

Their new interest in using their body may keep them awake at night as they work on honing their skills and inadvertently kick off their covers. Some parents introduce a baby sleeping bag at this time, so that the baby stays warm throughout the night. If they have a low-hanging mobile, move it up a notch, as they may decide to bat it down.

ASK A DOCTOR

Is it okay to let my baby have a dummy? A dummy won't harm your baby's health or development provided you use it responsibly. If it helps to soothe them, there's no reason why not. But be careful if you're breastfeeding that you don't give your crying baby a dummy when what they really need is a feed, as this could affect your milk supply. Try not to use a dummy all the time, just keep it for when you're trying to settle or comfort them.

Studying shapes and colours

Your baby is showing much more interest in complex designs and shapes, and is now able to distinguish more colours.

Your baby can now focus both their eyes on an object, and will show a preference for more complicated designs, colours, and shapes. They'll still love faces the most, but they'll be very intrigued by high-contrast, colourful objects, which will be able to keep them mesmerized for many minutes at a time.

Colourful toys Your baby will enjoy looking at brightly coloured objects, especially those with faces. A mobile in their line of vision is bound to attract their gaze.

Encouraging them to look at objects that interest them will help to strengthen pathways in their brain and develop their vision further. Try hanging a new mobile over their cot, or attach one to their play mat, close enough for them to focus on.

While your baby could once focus only on black-and-white and bright colours, they can now recognize interesting patterns and a wide range of colours, which is one reason why baby toys are manufactured in a rainbow of colours.

Your baby's vaccinations

An important part of preventative health care is immunizing your baby against illnesses that may seriously harm them later on in life. Your baby will be given an immunization timetable, which it is important to follow.

While a baby's immune system develops life-long immunity against illnesses by acquiring them, many are dangerous, with a high risk of complications or death, so over the coming months, your baby will be immunized against serious illnesses to protect them. By immunizing them, you also help largely to eradicate diseases from the population.

Immunization begins at two months and prepares your baby's body to fight diseases it may catch in the future. For example, the polio vaccine stimulates the immune system to produce antibodies against the polio virus, which later recognize the disease if and when it enters their body, and are ready to fight it.

In most cases, vaccines provide life-long immunity, although some need topping up every 10 years or so. It is possible to show symptoms of mild forms of some diseases by immunization, but the risk of complications is much lower than if your baby acquired the full-blown disease. It's natural to be concerned that combining several vaccines could overload your baby's system, but there is no need to worry. Your baby's immune system becomes more mature by the day, and is already capable of protecting them from a wide range of organisms causing infections that they come into contact with all the time. Their system can very easily cope with the existing combined jabs.

There is a small risk of side-effects, such as a mild fever and some weak symptoms of disease. It is unusual for a baby to experience an allergic response, but natural to experience some tenderness, swelling, and redness at the site of the injection. They may be irritable, and sleep more than usual. A dose of paracetamol and a quiet feed should soothe them. Rest assured: vaccines have a well-researched high safety record.

Keeping track

Your baby's immunizations will be noted down in their health record book, but you may wish to keep your own record of the date of each immunization and any symptoms or side-effects. Some parents like to note down the brand name of the vaccine for future reference, in case they move to another part of the world at some point, or the schedule of immunizations changes for any reason.

Making your baby comfortable

Give your baby a feed before their vaccination to settle them. Stay calm and talk to them and reassure them in a soft voice, or distract them with a dummy. It will be over in a few seconds, and they may not even notice it's happened. If they cry, hold them and talk to them gently. They'll be back to their usual, happy self in no time.

IMMUNIZATION SCHEDULE

2 months:
• Diphtheria, hepatitis B, Hib (haemophilus influenzae type b), polio, tetanus, and whooping cough (pertussis), given as a 6-in-1 single jab
• Rotavirus vaccine
• MenB (Meningococcal group B) vaccine (first dose)

3 months:
• 6-in-1 vaccine (second dose)
• Rotavirus vaccine (second dose)
• PCV (pneumococcal) vaccine (first dose)

4 months:
• 6-in-1 vaccine (third dose)
• MenB (Meningococcal group B) vaccine (second dose)

Between 12 and 13 months:
• Hib/MenC (haemophilus influenzae type b, meningitis C) vaccine (first dose), given as a single jab
• MMR (measles, mumps, and rubella) vaccine, given as a single jab (first dose)
• PCV (pneumococcal) vaccine (second dose)
• MenB (Meningococcal group B) vaccine (third dose)

Note: If your baby was premature or suffers from health problems, your GP may recommend a seasonal flu jab. Talk to your GP to find out if your baby needs one.

More regular feeds

Your growing baby should have settled into a pattern and be able to take in more milk at each sitting, and go for longer between feeds.

ASK A DOCTOR

My baby seems to be uncomfortable after a feed, and is suffering from diarrhoea. What should I do? If you are breastfeeding your baby's poo will often be soft, runny, and yellow in colour. Whereas if you are using formula milk, your baby's poo will tend to be firmer and a pale brown, green, or yellow colour. It is quite normal for your baby to have occasional runny poos while their digestive system adapts. You will be able to tell if your baby has diarrhoea if their poo has a stronger odour than usual, is more watery, causing leaking nappies, or if your baby is pooing more frequently than normal. If your baby's diarrhoea persists and they have other symptoms such as vomiting, arrange to see your GP.

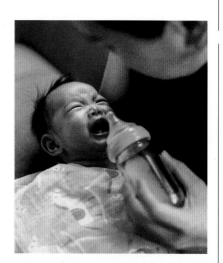

Upset tummy Speak with your GP if your baby appears distressed after a feed.

Milk is still your baby's only source of nutrition and liquid, so it's important not to "schedule" them into a routine that leaves them hungry or thirsty. Breastmilk is digested more quickly than formula so, a breastfed baby may feed more often than a bottle-fed one, but the gap between feeds will increase over time. Bottle-fed babies often sleep longer through the night than breastfed babies, but that's no reason to make the switch to a bottle.

You'll ideally want to empty both breasts at every feed, so that your baby gets the right balance of liquid and nutrition (see p.27); however, you may find that your baby is satisfied after just one breast. Make a note of the times you feed your baby and the breast from which they last fed to remind you which breast to offer first at the next feed, and also see if there is a pattern to the feeds. If the baby is not gaining weight as expected, they may be snacking a little too often, rather than taking in a full, long feed.

If you are bottle-feeding, keep a note of feeding times and the amount. At this age, most babies are having six to eight bottles of 120–180ml (4–6fl oz) in 24 hours.

If you wish, tweak your baby's schedule in small ways: you may feed on demand during the day, then wake your baby before you go to bed to fill them up so that they sleep longer at night, for example.

LACTOSE INTOLERANCE

Some babies find it hard to digest the natural sugar (lactose) found in both breastmilk and formula milk. Babies who are lactose-intolerant suffer digestive discomfort, such as diarrhoea, vomiting, and colic, which can cause distress and result in constant crying.

Lactose intolerance is very rare and occurs when there is a lack of the enzyme lactase, which helps the body digest the sugar in both breastmilk and formula milk. Lactose intolerance is more common in premature babies as the level of lactase builds up towards the end of the last trimester of pregnancy. Sometimes, babies can develop lactose intolerance for a short period of time after suffering from a stomach bug, or prolonged use of antibiotics.

A baby suffering from a cow's milk allergy may present with similar symptoms. While it is one of the most common baby allergies, it is still relatively rare with less than 2% of babies diagnosed in the UK. If you are worried your baby has a cow's milk allergy or is lactose intolerant, you should seek medical advice.

Fun bathtimes

If your baby has so far been reluctant to have a bath, a few toys and gentle splashing games may persuade them to start enjoying one now.

Bathtime can be much more fun now you can add a few bath toys to the tub for your baby to play with. They may be excited by the fact that they can cause waves by kicking their legs.

Gently splash the water and use a small cup or bath toy to pour warm water over them – they'll love the experience, and be interested in the movement of the water. Sing, laugh, and speak in a gentle, upbeat voice to encourage them to see bathtime as positive. They're more likely to enjoy themself if they see you smiling. Singing a song that relaxes them, or finding one they can begin to associate with bathtime, can help to keep them calm and happy.

Now they're a little more mobile, make sure that you have a good grip on them, as they will be very slippery, particularly if they're determined to manoeuvre themself into a different position. Don't make bathtime too long, just a few minutes is ample at this stage. Take them out of the bath and wrap them quickly in a warm towel so that they don't feel cold.

If your baby still resists a bath, try bathing with them. Get everything ready by the tub so you can step into a robe and get them dried off first. You may need your partner to hold them while you get into and out of the water. Remember that babies can't tolerate hot water

in the same way we can, so make the bath cooler – around 32–37°C (90–98.6°F).

Fun time Bath time is a great opportunity to have fun and to bond with your baby.

Sleeping well at night

Catching a nap when your baby sleeps may be your only option in the early weeks, but you will, over time, want a good night's rest.

Being woken in the night can be frustrating, no matter how much you enjoy feeding your baby. If your baby is right next to your bed (or sleeping with you), you can feed them quickly while still half-asleep yourself. If their nappy isn't too wet, you can probably leave a change until later, too. It may sound difficult to believe, but you'll soon go on to "auto pilot" at night and

feed them without really waking up!

If you do wake up and can't get back to sleep, do some of the relaxation exercises you practised during pregnancy, and try not to focus on how many hours of sleep you are not getting. Avoid alcohol or caffeine in the evenings. Try a glass of warm milk, a banana, or a bowl of oatmeal before bed; these foods

contain the amino acid "tryptophan", which will encourage restful sleep. If you are breastfeeding, it may enter your milk supply to help your baby sleep well, too!

Finally, about an hour before bed, have a warm bath (not hot, which can be overstimulating), and take some time to unwind. Doing chores is not an ideal pre-sleep routine!

2 months

AN INVOLUNTARY RESPONSE, THE "GRASP" REFLEX THAT BABIES ARE BORN WITH PERSISTS FOR THE FIRST FEW MONTHS. As your baby's muscles become stronger, they may be able to push themself up a little when they're on their tummy. They "discover" their hands around now and find them endlessly fascinating. They'll want to reach out and grab things, but may not succeed for several weeks.

Your baby's immune system

Now that your baby has reached the two-month mark, they may need a little more help from you to protect them from illness.

At two months old, your baby's "reserve" of antibodies (primarily from their time in the womb) begins to run dry, and they are more susceptible to illnesses. This is the point at which babies begin their immunization programme (see p.99).

If you are breastfeeding now, you will continue to protect your baby with the five most important types of antibodies. Breastmilk also contains a type of white blood cells, called lymphocytes, that help your baby fight off illness. This is "passive immunity", because it is passed to your baby rather than developed by them. Your baby will be protected against many, if not all, of the diseases to which you are immune. Breastfed babies have been shown to get sick less often, and experience less severe symptoms when they do become ill. Your baby's own immune system starts to kick into action in the first few weeks of life, but does not mature until later in childhood, which is why children can get so many colds!

Hygiene

Keeping your environment clean will help to protect your baby against illness. This doesn't mean dousing the household in antibacterial solutions, but simply keeping anything that they could put into their mouth (such as bottles, teething rings, equipment for making up feeds, and dummies) scrupulously sterile. This will prevent a build-up of bacteria that could cause stomach upsets, and also prevent the transmission of viruses from other members of the family.

Vet your guests

Although it can seem absurd to turn away visitors who are suffering from a cold or another illness, it is a good idea in the early weeks of your baby's life while your baby is less able to fight off the infection. Bacterial infections can also be very dangerous in little ones. Ask guests (and family members) to wash their hands regularly, dispose of any used tissues, and avoid holding your baby until they are fighting fit.

Sick babies tend not to feed well, and even a little weight loss can impact on a baby's overall strength and development. Any baby with a fever should be seen by a doctor as a precaution (see p.369).

A close eye If your baby seems unwell, keep monitoring them and call your GP if they worsen.

ASK A DOCTOR

How do I tell if my baby has an ear infection? It's difficult to tell without seeing a doctor. Ear infections are particularly common after a cold, but there aren't many specific symptoms. The ear won't look red, and although some babies rub or bat their ear when it hurts, many also do this when tired. Crying, irritability, high temperature, vomiting, and even diarrhoea can all be due to ear infection (see p.378). There may be a discharge from the ear, which suggests that the infection has perforated the eardrum. By this stage your baby may appear better, but it's still important to see the doctor. Antibiotics aren't routinely offered as many ear infections are viral, but the sicker the child, the more likely they are to have antibiotics, and this is often the case with babies. Paracetamol syrup and cuddles can help with pain.

Dressing up

Spending a fortune on baby clothes isn't practical, but shopping for a special occasion will be fun and provide some priceless photos!

A special occasion may give you just the excuse you need to buy something beautiful for your little one.

Before you head straight for the frills and ribbons, consider the nature of the occasion. If your baby will be passed around lots of people, or expected to get through a whole day outside their usual environment, try to be practical. Go for something that won't make their skin itch or make them feel uncomfortable, and ensure that it can be fastened and unfastened for quick changes. Fiddly buttons, tight collars or waistbands, or anything that constricts your baby's movement or causes them to overheat probably aren't ideal.

Avoid anything too expensive – one leaky nappy or heavy possett and off it comes! (Washable is essential.) It may also be a good idea to go for separates so that a quick part-change can save the day. Bring along a couple of spare tops and/or bottoms, just to be on the safe side.

BUYING SECONDHAND

If you have to dress twins for a smart occasion, two outfits will obviously hit your bank balance harder than one, so look online or at twins' sales. Most special outfits only get worn once or twice before babies outgrow them, and smart clothes are often given as gifts and never worn, so you may be able to find something new or next-to-new, for very little outlay.

Developing memory

Your baby is developing their "recognition memory", which means that they can remember and identify familiar people and objects.

Tuned in Your baby identifies objects and people and remembers more than you think.

From birth, or shortly afterwards, your baby was able to recognize your voice and smell, and soon showed a preference for familiar faces. Now, they will be able to make some general associations. For example, if their older sibling always makes the same silly face, your baby may try to imitate it when they see them. They may gaze at a rattle, waiting for it to make its familiar sound. They will associate you with milk and comfort.

Your baby is now building associations based on the repeated link between an action and a feeling; for example, you hold out your arms towards them and they anticipate a feeling of being safe. Over the next few months, these and other associations build rapidly.

This type of memory is a natural, protective instinct that encourages babies to form strong attachments with their primary caregivers. Remembering and preferring familiar faces and objects is a method of keeping themselves safe from danger.

Healthy eating

Being a new parent is demanding work. One of the most important things you can do for yourself, is to eat healthily and be well-nourished.

All new parents need plenty of healthy, nutritious food. If you are short on nutrients, you will be prone to illness, fatigue, and mood swings.

Try to base your diet around fruits and vegetables, wholegrains (such as wholemeal bread and brown rice or pasta), proteins (such as lean meats, dairy produce, eggs, fish, nuts, seeds, and pulses), and healthy fats (olive and sunflower oil, avocados, and oily fish). Eating this type of healthy diet will provide the essential nutrients you need for optimum health. If you are breastfeeding, these nutrients, in turn, enter your breastmilk, so you'll enhance your baby's diet, too.

Eating right It's important to eat lots of fresh fruits and vegetables that are nutrient rich.

BOOSTING YOUR ENERGY LEVELS

A good way to maintain energy as you cope with the demands of early parenthood is to eat little and often. Reduced-fat cheese with apple slices, an oatcake with low-fat spread, or some dried apricots can keep you going between meals and keep your metabolism active. Try the following to help you feel healthy and energized.

• Get a little gentle exercise every day. Walking, swimming, aerobics, and/or yoga (with your baby, of course) can help to build muscle, which encourages your metabolism to work efficiently.

• Stay hydrated. Thirst is often mistaken for hunger, and breastfeeding (if that's relevant for you) is thirsty work. You'll need about 2.7 litres (4.75 pints) of fluid each day to replace what's been lost.

• Take up all offers of meals made by friends, and get into the habit of batch cooking when you do get a moment in the kitchen. With a small baby, having some standby meals is always a good idea. If you've got a freezer full of nutritious soups, casseroles, or even delicious fruit-and-oat muffins, you are more likely to eat well, and you'll be less likely to rely on highly fatty or salty takeaways. It's just as easy to make a quick salad as it is to prepare a ready meal, and you will reap the rewards.

• Keep plenty of healthy snacks. Pre-cut some carrots, celery, or cucumber and pop them in some water with a squirt of lemon juice to keep them fresh. Buy salsa, low-fat dips, or hummus. If you long for something sweet, whiz up a fresh fruit smoothie, eat a couple of small squares of dark chocolate, or try a bowl of wholegrain cereal with fruit compote and yoghurt.

ASK A NUTRITIONIST

How many more calories should I eat each day while breastfeeding?
Breastfeeding mums use up about 500 extra calories each day, but you don't necessarily have to replace them. If your diet is much the same as it was pre-pregnancy, you will naturally lose about 450g (1lb) per week without making any changes, as your fat stores will be called upon. If you are exercising a little, you are likely to lose even more. It's best not to think about calories: if you focus on eating a healthy diet, your body will find balance and that means you will feel and look healthy, too – and your baby will be getting the nutrients they need.

Sleeping like a baby

Your baby may now be going longer between feeds, and sleeping more soundly at night. You'll probably be able to get more sleep as well.

It is more likely that your baby will sleep well if they are comfortable, so it is important to alternate their sleepwear and bedding as outside temperatures change. A hot or cold baby wakes frequently, even if tired. Keep your baby's bedroom cool, even in winter, using layers of thin sheets or blankets that can be easily taken off or put on. If it's hot outside, it's fine to put your baby to bed wearing just a nappy and a vest, with a thin cotton sheet on top. To keep air circulating around the room try using a fan, facing it away from your baby's bed. A gentle breeze will keep them comfortably cool.

If your baby is starting to kick off their covers at night, tuck the ends firmly under the base of the mattress, or around their legs. If your baby is waking themselves up in the night with little jerks and startled movements, consider swaddling.

A baby sleeping bag might come in useful to keep your baby warm no matter how active they are. Choose a quilted cotton sleeping bag that fastens at the shoulders for quick night-time changes. Bags are available in "togs", much like duvets, so choose a weight that suits the temperature in your baby's room.

Fascinating hands

Your baby's favourite "toys" at the moment are their own hands, which entertain them as they move in and out of their line of vision.

Increased dexterity Your baby now has better control of their hand movements.

Now that your baby is starting to open and close their own hands, they may begin to stare at them in fascination, bringing their hands or fingers towards their mouth, or even aiming them in your direction touching your face or body. They may attempt to bat at objects dangling above their bed or baby gym, or at a toy if you hold one out to attract their attention.

Your baby is a tactile little person and will enjoy feeling new textures. They may unconsciously stroke their own face, clothes, comfort blanket, or anything they come into contact with. Your baby may look up in amazement when you offer something new with an exciting texture, such as a soft toy with fur or a textured teething ring. Everything is new and interesting, and your baby will enjoy exploring using their mouth and hands.

Try offering a rattle to hold for a moment (they are likely to drop it) or attach a wrist rattle to your baby's arm to attract their attention. Give your baby the space to explore and find out what they can do by themselves.

Stylish nursing wear

If you have breastfed since birth, you're probably ready to ditch the baggy T-shirts and functional nursing bras and update your look.

While there's no reason to change or buy new bras unnecessarily, be aware that your breasts do change size during these early months. For this reason, it's worth going for a professional re-measure every so often to be sure you are wearing the correct size. If you do need new bras, nowadays there's a wider range of colourful, feminine maternity lingerie to choose from, so this might be a good opportunity to treat yourself.

It's a similar situation with clothes for breastfeeding. At first, the most important consideration is comfort, but once you start to feel more like your normal self again, you may want to shop for "normal" clothes in your favourite stores. You can still follow fashion when you breastfeed – just go for wrap tops, or low scoop-neck and loose-bottomed T-shirts that can be lifted up and tucked over your feeding baby. Choose cotton and other natural fabrics that won't cause you to overheat while your baby is pressed against you feeding. Look for clothes that will be easy to wash and dry. There are also stores and online boutiques selling practical and stylish clothes designed specifically for breastfeeding mums, so you may wish to check these out, too. Take the time to try on any purchases – your shape may have changed. Some stores offer a personal styling service, so take advantage of expert advice.

Nursing top There are tops available that are both practical and stylish.

DEVELOPMENT ACTIVITY: FUN WITH SOUNDS

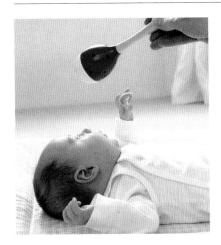

Rattles are wonderful toys for young babies, and as your baby becomes more interested in the world around them, they'll be mesmerized by the sight and sound of their favourite toy in action.

Whether you choose a rattle that attaches to their wrist or a hand-held model that can be placed in their hand, you will be providing your baby with a perfect first toy. They'll learn hand–eye coordination and develop their muscle control as they work out how to operate it. Choose a brightly coloured rattle that makes a sound easily. The idea is that they will be able to make the toy work themselves – even if it is not through conscious effort. Most toys will end up in your baby's mouth, so choose something soft and easy to clean. The handle should also be easy for their little hand to hold. Take care, too: their movements are still very jerky and they can easily bop themselves on the head in excitement.

Rattle stimulation Offer your baby a rattle that is light enough for them to grasp. They will no doubt want to mouth and taste the rattle, too!

Getting used to a cot

Help your baby to familiarize themselves with this new space, by putting them in their Moses basket first before moving them into the cot.

Your baby might be touching the sides of the basket by now – and even waking themselves up when they do so. If this is the case, you'll want to move them into a cot. A big cot can be daunting for a baby who is used to a smaller and cosier environment, so it's a good idea to get them used to it gradually before you put them down to sleep in it for the first time.

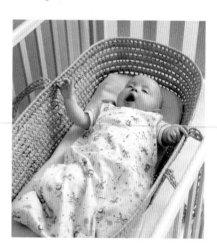

Moving to a cot Placing your baby's Moses basket in the cot for a few nights makes the transition easier for your baby to cope with.

If you've already bought a cot, it can be a safe place for your baby to play while you busy yourself with other things in their room. A mobile and a few toys scattered about, or a baby mirror fastened to the side, will capture their interest. They'll become accustomed to the space, so when it is time for them to sleep there, they will find it familiar.

Before you make the transition, put their Moses basket or crib inside the cot (or nearby) for a few nights. If, when you do come to move your baby, they seem distressed at the outset, try putting them in their cot for daytime naps only. This way, they'll be able to see what's around them and grow more confident. When they're settling nicely in the day, you can consider moving them at night-time, too.

ASK A HEALTH VISITOR

What do I need to consider when positioning my baby's cot? You should keep your baby's cot in your bedroom for the first six months to reduce the risk of sudden infant death syndrome (SIDS, see p.31). Also, position the cot so that it's out of direct sunlight and well away from windows, blind cords or strings, radiators, lamps, bookshelves, and hanging wall decorations or pictures.

Can I use a second-hand mattress? Always buy a new mattress, even if your baby's cot is secondhand. It should fit the cot snugly, so your baby can't slip between the cot and mattress. Check that it conforms to current safety standards and does not contain fire-retardant poly-brominated diphenyl ethers (PBDEs).

YOUR BABY'S COT

If you haven't yet bought a cot, now's a good time to do so. Your baby will probably be sleeping in a cot until they are two or three years old, so both the frame and slats need to be strong and sturdy, with no jagged edges or sharp points. Also, bear in mind the following:

• If you are buying a new cot, check that it conforms to current British safety standards. Bars should be no less than 2.5cm (1in) and no more than 5cm (2in) apart. Avoid decorative cut-outs in the head or foot boards which could trap your baby's limbs.

• Most cots have drop sides and an adjustable base height to make it easier to lift your baby in and out.

• A teething rail is a protective covering – usually made of clear, non-toxic plastic – that lines the side rails of the cot. This helps to protect your baby's gums (and the cot) once they're teething and they start to chew.

• When assembling the cot, check that all screws and bolts are secure, so there is no danger of the cot collapsing. Also, badly fitted screws could scratch your baby or even work themselves loose and pose a risk of choking.

• Bear in mind that cots made or painted more than 30 years ago may have been finished with poisonous lead-containing paint. In this case, the paint must be stripped and the cot repainted to make it safe.

Your baby's sleep cycle

Just when you think you've got your baby to sleep, they stir and wake up. What's happening as your little one settles down to rest?

Babies, like adults, experience two different types of sleep: deep sleep or "NREM" (non-rapid eye movement) and light sleep or "REM" (rapid eye movement) sleep. In deep NREM sleep, the body and mind are quiet, breathing is shallow, and limbs are relaxed. In light REM sleep, the eyes move under the eyelids and the brain is active, which is when dreams occur.

Sleep and brain activity

Over an eight-hour night, adults typically spend 75 per cent of the time in deep NREM sleep and 25 per cent in light REM sleep, which occurs in cycles throughout the night. In the first few months of life, babies sleep for about 18 hours a day, half of which appears to be spent in light REM sleep. One theory is that babies need lots of REM sleep during the steep learning and growth curve of early life, to allow the brain to develop

new connections. Blood flow to the brain nearly doubles during REM sleep, so your baby may appear restless, with fluttering eyelids and twitching arms or legs. Your baby is unlikely to adopt any kind of regular sleep pattern with identifiable NREM/REM cycles until about 4 months old. At this point, they'll probably spend about 35 per cent of their sleeping time in light REM sleep and 65 per cent in deep NREM sleep.

What to do when

If possible, put your baby down just before they drift into light sleep, so that they get used to settling themself. Once they drift off, avoid moving them from one place to another, as they're likely to wake.

If they seem about to wake up, resist patting them on the back or talking. Leave them, and they'll be

Sweet dreams Your presence will reassure your baby, helping them to feel safe and secure.

more likely to drift back to sleep. As your baby grows older and enjoys longer REM sleep cycles, they should sleep more soundly and be less likely to wake.

ASK A PAEDIATRICIAN

Does my baby dream? There is evidence to suggest that babies not only dream from the moment they are born, but have been doing so for several months in the womb. Dreams take place during REM sleep (see above), when your baby isn't sleeping quite so deeply and their brain is active, and because they have so many more hours of this type of sleep than we do, they'll be dreaming frequently. Their dreams will usually be based around their

experiences of the day, which consolidates learning, emotions, and development. They may have upsetting dreams from time to time, but will be calmed by your soothing voice.

When can I sleep-train my baby? Your baby will sleep as much as they need to, whenever they need to, and won't be ready to sleep through the night without a feed for some weeks. Sleep-training

techniques aren't generally started until babies are several months old, and involve encouraging them to sleep longer at night with minimal attention from their parents. This doesn't mean leaving them to cry, but helping them feel safe enough to fall asleep alone. But it's not too early to adopt a calming bedtime routine, such as a bath, feed, and a lullaby, so that your baby begins to associate this soothing sequence of events with sleep.

Post-baby health issues

If you can't seem to shake off the baby blues and still feel low or upset, it's possible that you're experiencing postnatal depression.

The baby blues affect most mums about three days after the birth of their babies as a result of hormonal changes wreaking havoc on their emotions (see "Ask a… midwife", p.49). The baby blues should normally ease within a couple of weeks, so if you continue to feel low or exhausted, you may be experiencing postnatal depression (PND).

What is PND?

Feeling distressed as the weeks go by, having a sense that other mums are coping when you are not, or becoming low during your baby's first year means it's likely you're suffering from postnatal depression. PND can last for a few weeks or for months – but the

sooner you get professional help, the more quickly you are likely to recover.

Typical signs of PND include:
• Feeling exhausted even when you've only just woken up.
• Crying often; feeling empty and sad.
• Guilt and shame that you're not happy or don't love your baby enough.
• Being overanxious in yourself or fearful for your baby.
• Feeling scared to be alone or go out.

One or two mums in every ten will suffer from postnatal depression. The important thing is to recognize that you are unwell and to get help as soon as possible. Your health visitor or GP will recognize your situation and know how to get you help, often linking you into local services to support you. Your doctor may recommend medication, such as anti-depressants, and may refer you for counselling.

Postnatal psychosis

A very few women (about 1–3 in 1,000) develop a condition called postnatal psychosis, symptoms of which include severe depression, delusions (believing everyone is conspiring against them or they or others are possessed), hallucinations, and an inability to think clearly. It is essential if you feel this way to visit your GP. Medication, such as anti-depressants or anti-psychotics, and therapy mean postnatal psychosis can usually be treated in a few weeks.

Long-lasting blues If you are still feeling upset, tearful, or depressed, don't hesitate to ask your health professionals for advice.

POST-BABY HORMONAL CHANGES

The pregnancy hormone relaxin softens collagen and elastin in the tissues. It remains in your body for up to five months after birth. If you are breastfeeding, prolactin, the hormone that produces milk, has a similar effect. As a result, your gums may soften and be prone to bleeding, which can lead to tooth decay. See your dentist to have your teeth cleaned and the state of your oral health assessed.

After pregnancy, hair follicles enter a "resting phase", causing excess hair loss (moulting). This occurs any time between two and nine months after the birth. Once your hormones return to pre-pregnancy levels, moulting stops and your hair will regrow.

Breastfeeding affects your bones. Mums lose 3–5 per cent of their bone mass while breastfeeding, although this is recovered within six months of your periods restarting or weaning your baby from the breast. This won't have any ill-effects; in fact, breastfeeding prevents osteoporosis (thinning of the bones) in later life, but breastfeeding mums do need plenty of calcium in their diet – roughly 1,250mg per day.

Your wider family

Cherish your relationships with your extended family. They'll provide a support system for you and your baby for many years to come.

Over the past couple of months, you may have seen more of your relatives than ever before, as they flock to admire the new addition to the family. No matter how independent you have been until now, relying little on extended family, and perhaps only meeting on special occasions, all that is set to change. You may already have found that your bond with your own parents is strengthened. Now you may realize how important other family members will be in your baby's life. However, not every parent has close family ties, but there are many ways to find a support network (see p.170).

Try to encourage relationships with family and create frequent opportunities for visits. Relations can become strained when you have conflicting views on caring for your baby, and you may be the recipient of plenty of unsolicited advice. Gently encourage family members to respect your ideas and approach, even if they don't agree. Allowing them to establish a loving relationship with your baby is the most important thing.

If you are a single parent, your family will be more valuable than ever for support and guidance, as well as love. It's hard raising a child on your own. You may feel you lack opportunities to talk about your baby's development or even your worries. It can be a pleasure to share your baby's milestones with family.

Staying close A strong bond with your extended family will enrich your baby's life.

Distracted baby

Your baby is fascinated by everything that's going on around them, and attracting their attention while feeding and changing may be difficult.

It's easy for your baby's attention to be drawn elsewhere now, which can be challenging when you're trying to nurse. Try feeding your baby in a quiet room that offers fewer distractions. Turn off the TV when you are feeding and talk to your baby quietly so that their focus remains on you. Gently turn your baby's head back to you if they become distracted. Try to establish feeding times when they are genuinely hungry and want a long feed. If your baby is snacking or feeding for comfort, you may find yourself putting them back to your breast or bottle again and again.

When changing their nappies or clothes they may resist you or wriggle and roll about in order to see what's going on around them. Try to engage your baby by making nappy-changing a more interesting experience: hang a colourful mobile over the changing mat, tickle or talk to them, and work fast so that you don't have to deal with their wriggling for long!

Working out distances

Your baby can now discern a variety of colours and is also starting to develop depth perception, marking the progression to seeing in 3D.

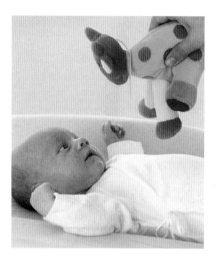

Depth perception will not be fully developed for another four months (usually at least six months), but as your baby's brain and coordination develop, they will be able to discern an object's position, size, shape, and relative distance more effectively. This will eventually allow successful reaching out and grasping to take hold of things. Before this can happen, though, their eyes have to be able to work together. You'll notice

Toy time Fun toys that are different shapes and colours will hold your baby's attention.

your baby's depth perception slowly improving – their eyes will move together but won't always be coordinated in the early weeks, but gradually that will get better and better. It takes a while for babies to see their world as a complete picture.

Depth perception will eventually help to keep your baby safe by preventing them from crawling off the edge of the porch, for example, but bear in mind that being able to discern the distance is not all that's needed to stay safe – curiosity will often get the better of them.

Hygiene and allergies

Good hygiene prevents illness but don't go overboard with the antibacterial wipes: some contact with germs is important for your baby.

Overuse of antibacterial cleaning products has now been linked with a higher incidence of allergies – probably because a baby's immune system will not be given the opportunity to develop properly without having things to fight. Allergies are a sign of a dysfunctional immune system, and anything that hampers its development in baby- and childhood could make your baby more susceptible. The general rule should be to keep things clean, rather

than sterile. This will ensure that your baby's environment is safe from harmful germs, yet suitable to allow their immune system to develop.

Hot water and soap are perfectly adequate for cleaning your baby's toys (although these should still be sterilized once in a while). If plastic, the toys may be able to go in the dishwasher. Stick with natural cleaners wherever possible around the house. Filling your baby's environment with a host of chemical

cleaners can also trigger an allergic response, as well as overload their sensitive system. Normal cleaning products, soap, and water will be enough to keep your house clean and fresh the natural way.

Don't worry about a little dust settling; studies have found that early exposure to dust mites can prevent allergies to them, and it will take the pressure to clean off you. The same goes for pet dander (see also p.122).

Relationship roles

Your lives have changed dramatically and you may feel surprised or unsettled by the altered dynamics of your relationship.

No matter how much you adore your baby, if you worked before the baby's birth you may feel bewildered by how much your life has changed, and resentful that your partner is able to go out to work while you take on the day-to-day care. Your career may be on hold and you may worry about taking time out from your career and the effect on your future progress.

What's more, because you're at home, it probably makes sense for you to take on more of the domestic chores. This can cause an imbalance in the way you perceive your relationship – and the equality within it. Also, you may not enjoy the same financial independence, which can be difficult to adjust to.

Work out a fair division of labour, bearing in mind that many workplaces now permit new parents to share childcare in the first year. Take advantage of keep-in-touch days with your own work, and proactively approach home-life niggles, by talking respectfully and openly, before they become problems.

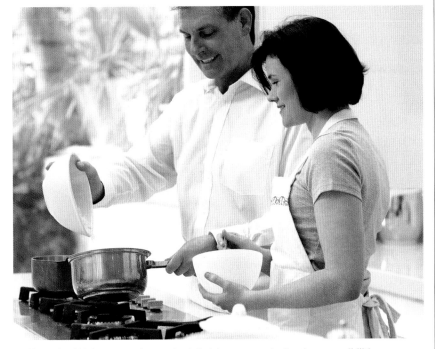

Feeling valued It's important that you both feel that you are sharing the responsibilities of family life as fairly as you can, even though your home life will have changed to adapt to parenthood.

ASK A DOCTOR

I had a Caesarean and although the scar has healed, I'm still feeling low and tired. How long will it be before I'm back to normal? Every woman recovers from a Caesarean birth differently, and although the visible scars may heal within six weeks, some women will take up to six months to regain their full energy. It's also quite common for numb areas on your skin to persist many months after the operation. Try to take each day as it comes, as with any new mum, and rest if you feel tired. If you experience any pain in the pelvic area, or you feel low and tired, talk to your GP: there maybe a reason (such as anaemia or postnatal depression) which can be treated.

I've noticed some very slight spotting of blood following intercourse. Should I be worried? Sometimes, just the manipulation of the cervix, which is still healing, or orgasm (which makes the uterus contract) can cause light spotting. It could also be related to hormonal fluctuations, or if you are using contraception, notably birth control pills. Occasionally, small skin tags form at the site of tears or incisions, which can bleed when rubbed against. Certain infections, such as chlamydia, can also cause spotting after sex. If you have any bleeding after sex, make an appointment to see your GP.

Planning childcare

Going back to work may feel a lifetime away, but it's important that, sooner rather than later, you think about who will care for your baby when you resume your career. Deciding on the right childcare strategy is not something you want to feel rushed into.

The best way to begin your search is to draw up a shortlist by word of mouth – ask friends to recommend nurseries, nanny agencies, and childminders. You can then look at their inspection reports on the Ofsted website (see p.384). Ofsted is the government department that inspects and regulates childcare providers. Your baby's wellbeing is paramount, and childcare may well be your single biggest outgoing once you go back to work, so it's vital to get it right.

Childminders

A childminder looks after your baby in their own home, probably along with several other children. All childminders need to be government-registered and inspected. Always take time to visit prospective childminders in their own environment, and bring along your baby to see how they fit in. Take time to compile a list of questions to ask, and leave time to discuss issues important to you. Ensure that your childminder has plenty of experience with babies and very young children. Is the house clean and welcoming, with lots of suitable toys and books, and space to play outside? Is there a smoker in the house? Or a lot of TVs? Is your childminder flexible? You don't want to end up with a series of fines when you are running a little late. Consider the number of children the childminder has in her care, and ask how they can balance the needs of

differently aged children. A young baby needs a great deal of individual care, and you need to be certain that your baby will get it. If you feel comfortable in a childminder's home and your baby seems calm, chances are they will be happy there.

Nurseries

Most nurseries provide childcare from three months old (some take babies from as young as six weeks). Visit every nursery on your list to get

a feel for whether or not it has a caring atmosphere and an ethos compatible with your own. Ask about staff turnover, as long-serving staff suggest a happy, supportive environment. The best nurseries have long waiting lists, so it's never too early to start looking.

Nannies

Hiring a nanny means you'll have someone to look after your baby in your own home. Use a reputable

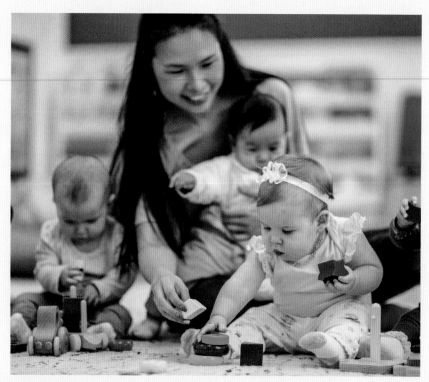

Choosing a childminder Your prospective childminder should have plenty of experience of looking after young babies and juggling their needs with those of older children in their charge.

agency and interview each nanny on your shortlist. Have a list of questions ready, covering such topics as how they handle discipline and what kinds of games they would play with your baby. If you need them to be able to drive, ask about that too. Start by drawing up a full job description, describing every aspect of your baby's day-to-day care – and what you'd like to see happening in the future. Talk these through with each interviewee to make sure that the nanny's working practices, beliefs, ideas, and ethics match your own.

Make sure that you interview nannies with your baby, and watch how they interact. You'll want someone who is interested, playful, and affectionate with your baby. Check references, ensure that the nanny has emergency first-aid training and a DBS (police) check (which shows they can safely work with children), and talk through issues such as nutrition, exercise, stimulation, and TV watching. Ask for an example of a daily routine, and assess how flexible the nanny might be. If they have to leave on time every evening, you might find that the arrangement won't work. It's also worth asking where the nanny sees herself in five years' time. If you are hoping for continuity over the coming years, it would be good to know now if they are planning to emigrate!

You will need to draw up a formal contract of employment and meet your legal obligations as an employer, such as paying tax and national insurance contributions. For more information, visit HM Revenue and Customs' website.

Other options

There are government initiatives that allow parents to work flexible hours – and even from home – when their children are young. You may be able to plan your schedule so that both you and your partner can take on some of the childcare, and get in extra help on the days you can't. You may decide to work at home, and try to juggle work and your baby – perhaps with the support of an au pair or a home help. An au pair is not permitted to have continuous sole charge of children under the age of two, but can help around the house or supervise older children. Ideally, use a recognized, approved au pair agency.

Sometimes grandparents are happy to step in and take care of children, but this is an arrangement that should be treated with respect, and carefully discussed in advance. Payment may not be necessary, but you should be flexible and also feel confident that your approach to childcare is honoured. It can work beautifully when you establish good communication. Equally, however, it can lead to resentment on both sides, so tread cautiously.

Finally, you may wish to consider working part-time, or changing your hours so that childcare is less frequently required; for example, if you can work from seven till three every day, and your partner takes over the early morning care, you may be able to get away with just five hours of care a few days a week. Talk through the different scenarios with your partner, and make sure you are both in agreement. If you are a single parent, make sure that you have some back-up support so that your baby will be cared for when you are running late, or your baby or carer is ill. Being solely responsible for a baby can be overwhelming at times, so do take up any offers to help you out when you just can't be there.

CHOOSING A NURSERY

When selecting a nursery, above all else, trust your instinct. If you see contented, happy babies, and warm, caring staff, you are probably on to a good thing. If it feels good, it may be right! Focus on nurseries with:

• A high staff-to-child ratio. There are laws about the number of little ones that can be cared for by each responsible adult; you are looking for better-than-average ratios.

• An arrangement in which younger and older children are separated, so babies get the right care without the distractions of older children.

• A strong, fair discipline policy that matches your own beliefs.

• Permanent staff members with good first-aid experience, and experience dealing with childhood illnesses and providing medical attention. If your baby has any health concerns, check that carers can deal with them effectively.

• Well-trained, experienced staff who constantly update their knowledge, and understand child nutrition and development, and the common issues of childhood.

• Warm, loving staff with affection for and interest in the children.

• A designated staff member for every child, to ensure that individual needs are met.

• A sound policy and clear evidence of safety and security.

• A good selection of clean, tidy toys, and age-appropriate books.

• Plenty of opportunities for your baby to be stimulated.

• A quiet place for babies to sleep and

• a clean place for them to be fed.

• A policy of updating parents on their babies' progress daily.

• A good open-door policy, so you can visit at any time.

Target practice

Your baby's hand–eye coordination is developing fast. They are working hard to get their arms and legs to go where they want.

Coordination Your baby will enjoy practising skills, such as reaching and grasping.

By now, your baby will have come to realize that when they hit an object it moves, thereby making a link between cause and effect. Each time your baby reaches out for a toy important information is being fed back to their brain about muscle and body movement. They will now hit and grab with greater meaning.

Lay your baby on their tummy and put a toy a little away from them to encourage them to move towards it. Help your baby to grasp the toy by placing it in the palm of their hand: grasp reflex will cause their fingers to tighten around the toy.

Place your baby under a baby gym and position them so they can easily reach one or more of the hanging toys. If your baby is successful, some of the time, at reaching and grasping the hanging toys, they will enjoy the experience much more. In the coming months, your baby will be able to target objects more accurately and pull them towards them.

Tummy time

It is safest to put your baby to sleep on their back, but they also need dedicated time to lie on their front to develop upper body strength.

Your baby should now be able to lie on their front and attempt to lift their head to look up or to the side. They may try to lift their head by using their forearms to push upwards. It will be another month or two before your baby pushes up with confidence. This important milestone in their development is the start of the motor skills that will lead to rolling over and, eventually, crawling. Your baby should have dedicated time to lie on their front when they are alert, as studies show that because babies sleep on their back, extra tummy time gives much-needed practice in looking and pushing up. However, stay close as your baby's neck muscles are still relatively weak and unable to hold up their head for long. If left on their front for too long they may get distressed and need your help.

Put toys around your baby to encourage them to reach out and even move (see "Target practice", above). Lay your baby on your chest while you're on the floor. It will make them happier to see your smiling face when they lift up their heads.

Developing muscles Your baby can probably lift up their head to see what's around them.

Out and about

Your baby can see quite well now and their sight is improving all the time, so give them lots of opportunity to explore the world around them.

If you haven't used a pushchair yet, you can now consider one that allows your baby to sit upright with support. Some pushchairs are designed to face outwards, while other models face inwards so that your baby can see you.

Some experts say that inward-facing pushchairs are best, as they allow your baby to continue bonding with you, learn from your chatter and facial expressions, and be comforted by your visible presence. A pushchair that faces outwards, on the other hand, encourages your baby to look at what's passing them by. If they're daunted by your absence, chat to them as you walk, and reach over and stroke their face to remind them you are there. Occasionally, crouch down in front of the pushchair and have a reassuring little chat. They are learning information about speech, content, tone, and rhythm as you talk, even though they can't understand the meaning of the words.

Stay safe

Always fasten your baby's harness carefully, and check that they are comfortably upright, not slouched forwards. Adjusting their bottom so that it is a little further forwards should help them to sink back in comfort. You may also wish to invest in a headrest or neck support, to make them feel more secure. A good pushchair will fully recline so that you can gently ease them down, ideally without waking them if they're asleep. Don't forget to put the brake on whenever you stop, even if there is no obvious incline. Accidents can and do happen. Avoid hanging heavy bags on the handle of the pushchair; it can easily topple over. It's best to invest in a pushchair that allows you to store items under the seat, which gives it a good, firm base. Bear in mind that upright collapsible buggies with only one seat position are not suitable until six months.

For mums of more than one child, there are many double (and triple) buggies, some more practical than others. While some parents like the "one-in-front-of-the-other" (tandem) set-up (as it allows them to negotiate tighter spaces), although these can be hard to manoeuvre and require brute force to turn them.

Out and about Being in, or out, of their buggies gives babies opportunity to experience the new world around them.

"Twin" buggies tend to be popular because your babies can see, hear, and communicate with one another. This form of "entertainment" may be invaluable if an outing takes longer than expected. The drawback to this type of pushchair is its width and use in narrow entrances and aisles.

DEVELOPMENT ACTIVITY: BOARD AND FABRIC BOOKS

Brightly coloured books with faces of babies and/or animals are perfect for your baby's stage of development, and they will love to gaze at the pictures.

Sturdy board or fabric books are good, as they can often be easily cleaned and can double up as toys for your baby when they want to entertain themself. Books that have a variety of different textures on their pages will appeal to your baby. Encourage them to reach out and touch the pages. Make up your own stories as you go, or repeat the name for the object on the page to help them learn.

Reading your baby's cues

Sucking fingers? Yawning? Reading baby cues is an important first step in communication. It lets your baby know that you understand and will respond.

As you repeatedly offer your baby what they want as soon as you see the signal, they learn that you will meet their needs without having to resort to crying. The baby will build up a larger repertoire of cues and gestures to get messages across, and in the coming months will begin to anticipate your response. In this way, your baby's communication and trust are starting to develop.

Looking for clues

You can probably already recognize the different pitch and tone of a cry that means "I'm tired" compared to the one that tells you "I'm hungry". Now it is time to look out for more specific vocal and non-vocal signs. You should watch out for cues such as leg-kicking, a reddened face, and fist-waving because these signs or actions may mean your baby is overstimulated, frustrated, or in need of a nappy change. Look for mannerisms that suggest tiredness – perhaps rubbing eyes, yawning, or sucking on fingers. As you gain more understanding of your baby's signals, you'll predict evermore quickly what it is they need.

To play or not to play?

Your baby can also give you signals about whether or not it's the right time to play, or whether they need time to unwind quietly on their own. These are known as "withdrawal" and "approach" cues. If your baby becomes still, looks at your face, reaches out to you, moves their arms and legs smoothly, turns their eyes (wide and bright) or head towards you, coos, smiles, babbles, and raises their head, you're being given classic "approach" signals. Your baby is in the mood for interaction!

If your baby turns away their head, arches their back, squirms or kicks, pulls away, turns their eyes away from you, wrinkles their forehead, hiccups, or frowns, these are "withdrawal" cues. They are a sign that your baby needs a break or a rest from what is going on. They may want to stop playing, feeding, or even being held. It may well be time for a change in activity or even a nap.

ASK A DOCTOR

My baby seems to be constipated – is this likely? Babies' stools can vary greatly, but a change from what is normal for your baby may suggest a problem. Babies can open their bowels anything from three times a day to once every other day.

Breast-fed babies tend not to get constipated as breastmilk contains the right ingredients to keep the stool soft and easy to pass. Lots of babies strain when passing a motion, which is quite normal. However, signs of constipation can include hard, pellet-like stools, straining without producing stool, or pain on passing stool, sometimes with a tiny amount of fresh blood on the nappy due to a small tear in the anus. If bleeding occurs, you should consult your GP.

What do I mean? Sucking his fingers could signal tiredness, hunger, or watchfulness.

Winding down Your baby's yawn means that playtime is over and it's time for a nap.

Baby massage

Massage can relax and soothe your baby, help to ease the discomfort of wind and colic, and even promote restful sleep.

There are plenty of baby massage classes should you wish to learn the proper techniques (your health visitor may be able to recommend one locally), but you can also use gentle strokes you practise every day as you rub their back to soothe them, or play with their hands or feet. The main aim of baby massage is for you to have fun together, and for your baby to enjoy your loving touch.

Try to choose a time when your baby is relaxed – so not just after a feed or when they are hungry – and make sure that the room is warm and your baby is lying comfortably on a soft surface. Try stroking their arms and legs firmly to begin, then massage their abdomen lightly in a clockwise direction. Talk to your baby as you massage and watch their cues: if they seems unhappy at any point, stop the massage. Try a mixture of gliding, fluttering, and rotating strokes to see which your baby likes best.

Legs and feet Start by gently squeezing the thigh, and then rub the ankle and foot.

Your social baby

Your baby is smiling more and may be gurgling and cooing to "talk" to you. Your social baby is emerging.

You and your partner have the greatest influence on your baby's developing sociability. As you talk with them, wait for them to respond and then react back to them. In doing so, you are teaching your baby how to engage in two-way communication.

Your baby's smiles are now becoming more frequent and you will find that smiles come not just in response to your smile, but even perhaps in response to your voice. Your baby will also begin to smile at other willing adults who might grin at them. These are all signs that your baby is now widening their social network. Spend plenty of time throughout the day having face-to-face time. Look into their eyes, mirror back their expressions, speak, and then wait for your baby's reaction.

Around this age, babies become aware of who is familiar and who is a stranger, and may even begin to express preferences for certain people. You can help your baby to feel relaxed around trusted others by ensuring grandparents and friends get lots of cuddles and opportunities to smile at and coo over them. Babies are also fascinated by other babies and often become mesmerized by another baby's face, perhaps even smiling at it. It will be a while yet (up to two years away) before your baby makes firm friendships, but early interaction is good for long-term positive sociability.

Smile!

A baby's mouth has more nerve endings per square millimetre than any other area of the body.

Because a baby's mouth is supersensitive, they explore the world by mouthing anything they can get hold of. Your baby also learns by watching. Babies have "mirror neurons" in their brain, specialized nerve cells that enable them to imitate the facial expressions and movements of others.

Even though your baby may smile and excitedly wave their arms when they see you, they may not be so friendly with strangers. That's because they're beginning to develop the ability to remember people and objects. When they are unfamiliar, they may get a little anxious and need reassurance.

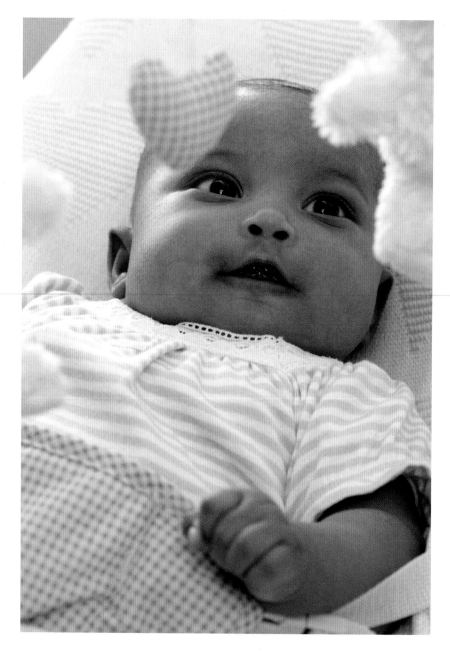

Do as I do Your baby will copy your facial expressions, from smiles to frowns to tongue-poking! Have some fun making faces at each other.

Listen + watch = learn

Everything your baby sees and hears helps them learn how to adapt to their new environment, so what's fun for them is also good brain fodder.

Your baby was born with plenty of brain cells already connected so they could perform essential tasks such as sucking and swallowing straight away. Also, all the baby's senses have been soaking up information from the moment they were born. Every experience forges connections between brain cells, which means learning. Your baby will also copy your facial expressions and make a sound after you've spoken.

Imitating your baby's facial expressions teaches your baby to express their feelings without words, learning that others can do what they can do – psychologists believe this plays a crucial role in developing a sense of self, others, and belonging. At 11 weeks, your baby is gleaning more and more information, creating a detailed picture of their environment. From watching siblings dance to music to looking at a light, then turning away from it, the baby has myriad nerve impulses firing through the brain to make connections between, say, music and movement and light and dark.

Bright colours stand out best at this stage, and your choices for stimulation needn't be expensive. Position the baby (safely) next to a mirror, or on a warm day, seat them in the shade beside a bright paper windmill that spins in the breeze.

Mirror play Your baby will be fascinated by their own reflection in a mirror.

Time out as a family

A family outing can be a welcome change of scene and gives your baby the experience of different environments.

Now that your baby is increasingly interested in all sights and sounds, an outing can be refreshing and stimulating. Seek out some family-friendly experiences to share. Try to keep car journeys relatively short and look for places that will give new smells, sights, and sounds. A simple picnic in the park, lying with you on a rug under some trees watching the pattern of leaves and branches moving is enough. Even a walk through the park or along the busy streets in the buggy provides scope for entertainment.

What's more, whenever you do things together as a family, at home or away, you are building up a store of shared memories and stories to tell relatives, especially details of your baby's cute or amusing reactions to new experiences. You are also beginning a tradition of family activities that will become a positive habit as the years pass.

Do take plenty of photographs of these early experiences. As your child grows older, they will love to look through them and see what they did with you when they were a baby.

Pets and your baby

It's not only your own pets that you need to be careful about, but also friends' and family's animals, too.

It will still be a while before your child is old enough to build a safe relationship with pets. For now, remain mindful that even the best-trained animals can become unpredictable, and it is important never to take anything for granted between your baby and your pet.

Animals, and dogs in particular, can become jealous of the new kid on the block. If you have a dog, try to give it special attention when you can, so that it doesn't feel neglected. Make sure your dog still gets routine walks and meals at normal times so that the baby's presence doesn't disrupt life too much. Don't let the dog go upstairs if this is where your baby sleeps; install a stair gate if necessary to keep the dog away.

As your baby nears three months old, they will have grown used to being able to grab and pull the objects they can reach. When this is a pet's tail or ear, there is a risk of a warning shot from the animal – a nip or a scratch, say. Never leave your baby unattended around your pets, and keep the pets out of the room while your baby is free to play. Under no circumstances should any pet be allowed to sleep in your baby's bed.

Cats, in particular, may go looking for warmth in a cot (or a pram), which makes them especially dangerous. Always use a cat net to prevent this.

Health-wise, make sure your pets are regularly immunized and kept worm- and flea-free. Pets, especially puppies and kittens, may carry parasites that cause toxocariasis, so always maintain proper hygiene to minimize the risk of infection. Never allow either cats or dogs to lick your baby, especially on the face. If you're visiting friends who have pets, the same precautions apply – keep your baby safe within sight.

DEVELOPMENT ACTIVITY: DANCING

Do you have a favourite song that you love to dance to? If so, why not make this song the anthem of a regular activity that you or your partner can share with your baby? Put on the favourite song, hold your baby securely, and sway with them to the music. You can make the movements rhythmic and gentle or a little bolder as the music dictates, as long as your baby is safe. They will love the feeling of being moved around in your strong arms, and may even chuckle as you move around.

In time, your baby will learn to associate the music with a positive experience with their favourite people, and hearing it will make them feel good, even if one of you is out at work, or if you both are and you have left your baby in a trusted other person's care.

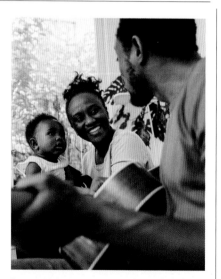

Song and dance Babies usually love being rocked to music – and at this age, they won't be embarrassed by your dancing!

PET SAFETY

• If you own a cat, buy a cat net to cover the baby's cot and always use it.
• No matter how trustworthy you think your dog or cat is, don't leave them unattended with your baby: the slightest movement or baby swipe could cause the animal to lash out.
• Wash your hands after handling pet food or pet bowls to reduce the risk of spreading pet-food-related diseases, such as salmonella infection. Also, wash your pet's food and water bowls in a separate sink or bucket.
• Reptiles are associated with a high incidence of salmonella infection which can be caught by handling them. Some experts recommend that they should not be kept as pets if children are under five years old.

Exploring by mouth

Your baby's mouth and lips are full of nerve endings and taste buds to provide information on flavour, texture, and consistency.

Your baby will by now be putting their fingers into their mouth and trying to grasp objects and bring them up to their mouth. They will enjoy exploring each item, discovering its taste, its feel, and the resistance to pressure as they bite down.

Mouthing helps your baby to practise moving their tongue, lips, and jaw so that, over the coming months, they gain finer motor control of each. This will aid speech development, chewing, and swallowing.

Exploring their world Your baby will mouth objects to get a sense of their feel and taste.

Your baby will be indiscriminate about what goes into their mouth, so just make sure that there's nothing within reach you wouldn't want them to chew on. There are plenty of toys available that are specially designed for babies to chew, including cloth books with rubbery edges. Teething rings are good too, especially when they double as noisy rattles. They're often narrow, too, so easy for tiny hands to hold.

You might find that your baby enjoys sucking on the corner of a soft toy or muslin square – babies often do this for comfort, as a sort of alternative dummy.

Caring for your baby's skin

Babies often suffer from dry skin, spots, and rashes, so it's important to treat their skin gently and ensure that they're comfortable.

Babies' skin is thinner, more sensitive, and less oily than adults', making it particularly prone to drying out, especially during winter when the air indoors is dry and overheated.

If your baby's skin is dry, try not to bathe them too often (once every 3–4 days is fine, with top and tailing at other times) and avoid using soap or bubble bath. Plain warm water, a drop of hypo-allergenic or organic

baby bath is enough. Keep bathtimes brief and afterwards, pat them dry and apply a little hypo-allergenic moisturizer or emollient cream.

Washing powder residues can cause irritation, so use a baby-friendly detergent and fabric softeners, and put baby clothes through an extra rinse cycle. Avoid clothes made from woollen or scratchy fibres, and synthetics.

Spots, or tiny pimples, on your baby's face are known as neonatal acne. Leave them alone – they are common and will disappear on their own. If your baby has a bright red rash around the neck, armpits, or nappy area, they may have heat rash. Remove clothing to allow air to circulate and cool their skin. A red rash may be a sign of thrush (see pp.373–74).

Keeping track

Your baby's weight gain is probably fairly steady now, but it's still reassuring to get them weighed at the baby clinic every so often.

Although every baby is different, most gain an average of between 120–200g (4–7fl oz) each week until they are about six months old. By this age, they have usually doubled their birthweight, and weight gain then gradually slows.

Breastfed babies tend to grow more rapidly than formula-fed babies for the first three months, but then they grow more slowly and, by the time they are 12 months old, breastfed babies are on average just over 0.5kg

(1lb) lighter than formula-fed babies. Most parents like to visit their local baby clinic to get their babies weighed in the early months. These clinics are run by health visitors, and provide a chance for new parents to get together and to ask questions or raise any concerns. Your baby's weight will be recorded in their red book and plotted on their growth chart. If they are following roughly the same centile line, their rate of growth is perfectly healthy. Growth spurts or

bouts of illness may lead them to jump up or down to the next centile occasionally, but you are looking for a fairly regular pattern of growth overall. Provided your baby is doing well, aim to get them weighed at the baby clinic about once a month.

If your baby's weight gain does dip, or increase significantly over an extended period, talk to your health visitor, who can assess whether or not there might be a problem, and refer you if there is cause for concern.

Towards sitting

Your baby's neck muscles are probably strong enough to support the weight of their head for a few seconds now.

Stronger neck muscles Carrying your baby so that they can look over your shoulder encourages them to lift their head.

In order to sit upright, your baby needs to be able to support their neck and back, and work out how to use their legs to steady themself and their arms to stop toppling forward – that will probably take until they are about seven months old, but they can certainly start to practise.

Even if your baby can perform confident push-ups, they will need to

develop greater neck stability. Tummy time (see p. 116) is great for this, as is carrying them on your shoulder.

You can help your baby develop core stability by propping them up in a reclined sitting position. Make sure they are well cushioned to the back and sides and stay with them at all times. Be ready to pop them back on their back or tummy when they tire.

Once your baby is strong enough to hold their head securely for prolonged periods, getting the balance right is a matter of practice – and lots of cushions to fall into.

Travelling with a young baby

Your baby's stronger now and they's also very adaptable, so if you've been thinking about going away, this could be a good time. With a little advance planning, there's no reason why you shouldn't all enjoy a relaxing, hassle-free break.

Now that your baby is two months old, they should be quite a good traveller. They're less fragile than they were and probably won't mind too much where they sleep. Also, they're still too young to have a set routine yet, so a little disruption shouldn't disturb them too much.

Planning ahead

If you intend to stay in a hotel and your baby sleeps in a cot, you'll either need to take your own travel cot, or reserve a cot for your room. If you are hiring a car at your destination, it's important to reserve an infant seat during the booking process. If you're travelling abroad, you'll also need a passport for your baby. If you plan to travel to a country where vaccinations are needed, check with your GP to learn whether your baby is old enough to have them. Some, such as yellow fever, are not safe for babies under six months old.

MALARIA

The WHO advises against taking infants to areas with malaria. If you decide to go, seek expert medical advice on how best to protect your baby and yourself, especially if you are breastfeeding. Seek immediate medical help if your baby develops a fever during or after a trip to a malaria region, even if you have taken all the precautions.

Travelling by car

In some respects, car journeys are the most straightforward – provided you have plenty of boot capacity – as you load up everything you need. Fit window sun shades to protect your baby's eyes and skin, but remove their outdoor clothing. Make sure that the car seat is securely fixed to the back seat and that the seat belts are properly threaded. Avoid rush hour, and consider driving at night, when your baby can go a bit longer between their feeds.

Travelling by plane

Check your airline's baggage policies. Nappies, creams, clothing, formula, feeding equipment, and other necessities add a lot of weight, so book extra allowances in advance. Weigh your cases before you leave.

You are allowed to take enough baby milk and sterilized water (in a baby bottle) in your hand baggage to last you the journey. In some cases, this may be over 100ml (3fl oz). You may be asked to verify the liquid (or baby food) by tasting it.

You can often take your baby in their pushchair all the way to the plane door, at which point you'll need to collapse it so it can be taken to the hold. Or you can use a baby carrier.

Packing Being prepared for every eventuality is the key to successful travelling with a baby.

ASK A DOCTOR

When is it safe for my baby to fly? It's safe from two days old but practically, you're unlikely to fly with them until they are at least two weeks old because they'll need a passport. Mothers who've had a Caesarean will be unable to fly until 10 days after the birth. It's advisable to check with your airline to find out their policy.

Give your baby a feed during take-off and landing: swallowing will help prevent ear discomfort owing to changes in cabin pressure. Most planes have special carrycots, and changing tables in the toilets.

3 months

CHARACTER TRAITS PRESENT FROM BIRTH ARE PART OF WHAT MAKES UP YOUR BABY'S PERSONALITY.
Your baby's eyes now work better together and vision is becoming more three-dimensional. The
baby's muscles are stronger, and your baby may be surprised to find that they can flip from tummy to
back. Your baby likes to kick, which strengthens leg muscles in preparation for crawling and walking.

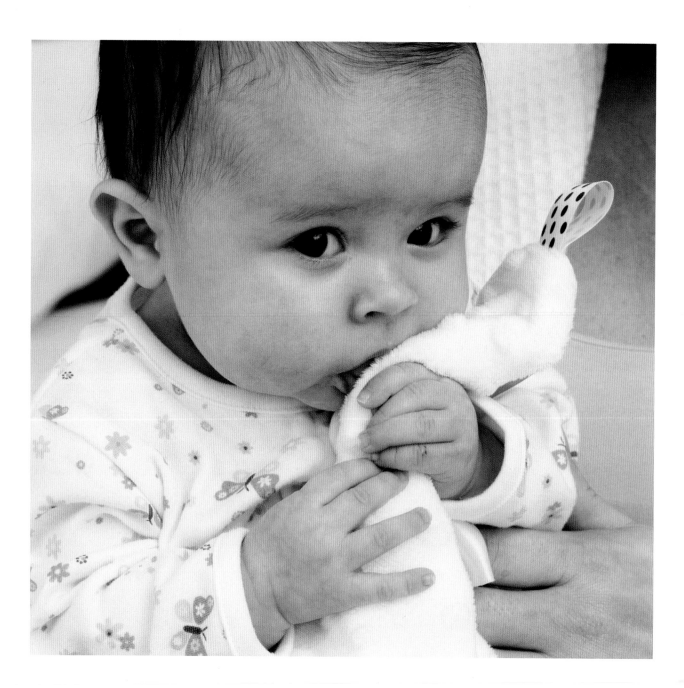

Another growth spurt

Your baby's due for a second growth spurt at around three months, so prepare for another feeding frenzy – and a restless night or two.

Supply and demand Your baby's frequent demands for milk are nature's way of making your body step up its milk production.

Now you're more settled, the three-month growth spurt shouldn't come as too much of a surprise. Your baby may demand food as frequently as every two hours for a few days, which can be exhausting for you, but there's no fighting it, so as much as you can, try to go with the flow. If you're breastfeeding, stock up on healthy snacks, drink plenty of water, get a good book to read while feeding, and prepare to be in demand for a while. Your body will increase milk production to meet the baby's increased needs.

Formula-feeding

You may need to make up an extra bottle for your baby during the day, or increase the quantity of each bottle by 30ml (1fl oz). Be guided by your baby's appetite and take care not to overfeed. Your baby shouldn't have more than 150ml (5fl oz) of milk per kilogram (2.2lbs) of weight per day. So, if your baby weighs 6kg (13lb 3oz), they shouldn't have more than 900ml (30fl oz) over 24 hours. Keep some emergency cartons of formula in your cupboard, which can provide a good back-up, too.

Sleeping

You may find your baby sleeps more during the day and is restless at night, perhaps waking more than usual. Or they may wake earlier from naps because they're hungry. This sleep disruption may last a couple of days to a week but it will pass.

FOCUS ON TWINS: COPING WITH GROWTH SPURTS

To have two babies going through a growth spurt at the same time or one after another can be exhausting. Routines tend to be disrupted, so one baby may wake frequently for feeds (that is, has entered their growth spurt), while the other doesn't. To relieve the burden, express some breastmilk so that someone else can give the baby who is going through a growth spurt an extra feed.

Alternatively, when the twin demanding extra wakes for a feed, you wake the other one, too, even if it's for a smaller feed. Many mothers of twins find

this simply means the less hungry baby eats little and often, but remains happy. However, once the growth spurt is over, you may find that you have established a routine of frequent feeding in both babies that you then have to break.

Most importantly, sleep when your babies sleep, and enlist the help of friends and family to keep the rest of the household running smoothly.

Twice the work To feed two babies as they each experience a growth spurt will require plenty of patience on your part.

Looking further afield

Everything your baby sees is new and exciting, and they'll begin to focus intently on objects that are further away.

Your baby will be fascinated by everything they see, near and far. By three months, their eyes are more coordinated, working well together. They will not look quite so cross-eyed and can track a slow-moving object with much smoother eye motions. Their depth perception is improving, and their world is becoming more three-dimensional. Their distance vision is beginning to develop, and they can now make out the shape of your face when you enter a room. You'll notice your baby watching things that are several metres away.

Provide your baby with plenty of things. Hold the baby turned outwards so they have a chance to see what's going on around them, and point things out to them. Call from the other side of the room, and watch their delight when they make out your familiar face. Shake noisy toys from a little further away, encouraging your baby to turn and look.

Up to about 12 weeks, many babies may squint as their vision develops. This is a normal phase of growing, but if your child continues to squint after three months, tell your GP so that they can catch any anomalies early and take steps to correct your baby's vision, if necessary.

Doing the flip

Your baby may be about to flip over from tummy to back. But watch out – just in case any acrobatics are going to begin...

Tummy time (see p.116) helps your baby to strengthen the muscles they use to roll over. It's easiest for babies to flip from front to back, so this usually occurs first. In most cases, it won't be due to any conscious effort on your baby's part – it will just happen. It's unusual for babies to flip over at 12 weeks, but as soon as they achieve it once, they'll manage it again and again, so be mindful about where they might end up and what's within reach. Don't leave them on the bed or changing table, even for a second. Bear in mind that some babies never roll. Skipping this milestone is nothing to worry about.

Rolling over By three months, your baby's movements will become smoother. They may lift their head and shoulders high, perhaps to roll over and get closer to you or investigate a toy.

Your baby's personality

Babies, like the rest of us, have their own individual personality. Getting to know your baby's unique traits and characteristics will help them to flourish.

In their first few weeks and months, your baby's personality will start to show. They may be easy to please, excitable, or even a little grumpy and difficult to settle. If you have a child already, you may be surprised to find your new baby may have a very different temperament.

Your baby's personality is shaped by a combination of inherited traits, present needs, and environment – including the way you respond and communicate. You may find it interesting to ask your parents whether you were similar to your own baby at this age. Your reaction to your baby and state of mind can affect how the baby responds on a day-to-day basis too.

If your baby is calm, responsive, and smiling, you may find them easier to parent and to respond to; however, if they are less settled, perhaps distressed because of difficulties such as colic, you may find you have to be particularly alert to their needs and spend more time soothing them and introducing activities such as baby massage (see p.119), which can relax and quieten them.

Some babies are less sociable and easily overwhelmed and over-stimulated by groups of people and noisy, bright environments. If your baby has opportunities to meet new people in a warm and welcoming way, they'll soon overcome their natural fears.

Sensitive soul Babies who are less eager to go to new people need extra reassurance.

At ease Some babies enjoy more interaction and cope better when visitors come along.

Your baby may be energetic and enjoy physical exercise, or calm and laid-back, and take everything in their stride. They may be easily unsettled and need a routine to feel secure. All babies are unique. Getting to know and understand your baby's personality can help you to adapt and learn which activities to offer. Try not to label your baby; embrace them for who they are and they'll flourish in your care.

SUN AND SAFETY

Babies need vitamin D from sunlight for strong bones and teeth, but their delicate skin can easily burn, and they can easily overheat. Avoid direct sunlight and keep your baby indoors during the hottest part of the day (from 10am to 3pm). Use a high SPF sunscreen (factor 30–50 is fine) that's hypo-allergenic and blocks the sun rather than filtering it. Your baby's sunscreen should contain protection against UVA and UVB rays, and be applied 10 minutes before you take them out into the sun, and reapplied in a few hours or after swimming. Put a sun hat on your baby and keep them in the shade. Choose a bathing suit that extends down their legs and arms and offers UV protection. Offer plenty of feeds if you're breastfeeding; bottle-fed babies may need a little extra water to stay hydrated.

Working parent

If you need to return to work, you will undoubtedly have some juggling ahead of you. Remember that you don't need to be superhuman.

Depending upon the demands of your career, you may decide to return to work while your baby is still very young. The key to a smooth transition is to find excellent childcare that will give you the confidence in your baby's wellbeing while they are away from you. Don't rush this process – take your time to find the carers who perfectly suit you and your family.

Remember that daily reunions with your baby, when you walk through the door, will nourish the bond between you both. Hold off on chores and instead spend as much quality time as your schedule allows soothing, chatting, and playing quietly together at the end of the day. If you can make it back for bathtime, this is a great opportunity to bond. If you are worried about keeping the house tidy, do a quick surface clean after your baby is in bed, or if appropriate, consider paying for a weekly clean to give you more time with the baby when you're home.

Time to connect

Don't worry about taking shortcuts. If you can't manage to put together a meal from scratch every night, investigate some of the quality, ready-prepared meals now available that can be put into the oven when you get home. Or, batch cook at the weekend while your baby is napping or being entertained by your partner, friend, or family member, and use your freezer to make workday meals

I'm home! Your daily reunions are time to reconnect.

simple – just a case of defrosting and serving. Sauces and stews are great time-savers, too – while heating them up boil pasta or rice, or hydrate some couscous. Even a hunk of bread dunked in a reheated stew is a quicky and tasty option.

Over time, things will settle into a routine, and you'll find the best ways to manage both work and home life. Making time for your baby and your partner whilst you're at home will reap rewards in years to come – a little dust or clutter now is a short-term problem. With a supportive and healthy home life, you'll be surprised at how capable you feel, ready to tackle anything and everything!

ASK A DOCTOR

I'm still feeling very tired and low – could I be anaemic? Many new parents feel tired and generally low not as a result of anaemia due to iron deficiency, but because they are trying to cope with the challenges of parenthood on little sleep. If you are a mother, it could also be a sign of postnatal depression (see p.110) or an underactive thyroid gland. Anaemia can also cause the following symptoms:

- shortness of breath;
- heart palpitations;
- cravings for particular foods or substances, such as crunchy vegetables or ice;
- food tasting different to normal;
- sore tongue;
- headache.

If you have any of these symptoms or feel excessively tired, see your GP.

VACCINATIONS

Around the 12-week mark, your baby is due for second vaccinations, which act as a booster to the set they had at eight weeks, plus a first dose of the Meningitis C vaccine. If you haven't heard from your doctor, ring the surgery for an appointment. Try not to be anxious when you take the baby for their jabs or they'll pick up on this and experience more distress while they're there.

Naps and night-time sleep

Your baby may now be awake longer during the day, but they'll still need three naps and a good night's sleep to get the rest they need.

By around three months, your baby will be sleeping about 15 hours in every 24-hour period. About 10 of those hours will take place at night (probably punctuated by one or two feeds) and the other five will be broken into three naps across the day.

Some parents complain that their babies don't nap, but if you put in place a good sleep routine, you'll find that your baby will eventually settle down into a good pattern of daytime naps and a long night-time sleep.

Babies who don't get enough rest during the day can become over-stimulated and take much longer to settle at night. Putting your baby down regularly during the day – even if they just kick and play in their cot – will get them into the nap habit, and they'll soon learn to accept that this quiet time is for sleep.

If your baby sleeps for more than 10 hours in the night, try waking them in the morning to help "programme" their body clock.

| ASK A HEALTH VISITOR |

My baby never seems tired – particularly around bedtime. How can I settle them down? It's normal for babies to acquire a second wind when it's time to put them down. This is a sign that they are overtired and getting energy from adrenaline. Try moving the baby's bedtime to half an hour earlier, while they are genuinely tired, and look out for sleep cues.

Little kicker

As your baby's legs get stronger and they become more coordinated, the baby will enjoy kicking so much, they'll even wake up at night to practise.

Kicking and stretching the legs prepares your baby's leg muscles for crawling, walking, and even rolling over. To promote her leg development, offer colourful toys just out of reach, and provide a safe environment for them to explore. Their curiosity will encourage them to become mobile in a few months' time, but they'll build up the skills and strength to do this by moving towards things of interest.

Tummy time mainly encourages the development of your baby's upper body, neck, and arms, and also provides an opportunity to bend the legs back from the knees, and to push forwards with them later on. When they spend time on their back, they'll perfect their bicycle kick and a wide range of leg movements. You can encourage weight-bearing a little by carefully holding the baby upright. When you do this, the baby will naturally bounce – don't let go!

Now is the time to be extra cautious; your baby will wriggle and use their legs to move. They might even begin "creeping" – slowly and steadily from one place to another.

Kicking up a storm Your baby may try to kick away their clothes during nappy change.

131

Observing the world

Babies often gaze intently at objects of interest, as if observing and memorizing every little detail.

Your baby will follow you with their eyes, and will enjoy taking in the sights, sounds, and smells around them. They are beginning to understand and react to their world. Their social skills are starting to flourish, and they will try to communicate in new ways to attract your attention, They may smile, coo, or gurgle.

Although your baby was born with a full set of primary teeth, they were hidden underneath the gums. Their first few teeth may now be making their way upwards, making their tiny gums feel uncomfortable, and causing your baby to become unsettled.

Look and learn By watching you and others around them, your baby will be learning how to react to changes they may observe.

Cooing baby

Your baby's early attempts at speech represent their new way of communicating with you, so make sure you respond to them!

Babies start to understand speech long before they can speak themselves. During this time, your baby will love to engage you in conversation, listening intently when you talk and practising new sounds in response. This exchange is important for helping them develop language and communication skills. Your baby may start responding to their name, smiling at you, then waiting for a response. Say the names of favourite toys or objects your baby shows interest in. At this stage, babies are able to tell the difference between happy and angry tones of voice.

As your baby's language develops, they will start crying less and start to make cooing sounds and noises to communicate. Your baby will attempt to imitate sounds and intonation, and will begin to experiment with making "bubbling" sounds caused when their tongue contacts their lips and also "raspberry" sounds when they squeeze their lips together. This stage is very important for your baby, as it allows them to practise and develop control of the muscles that they will later use for talking. Encourage your baby to develop their own memory bank of sounds. Engage in conversation with your baby as often as you can, giving them lots of praise. They might not look as if they are listening, but they are absorbing it all.

Little chatterbox Encourage your baby to use their voice by giving them opportunities to speak. Show clear pleasure at these attempts.

Teething and sleep

Most babies will experience some teething discomfort, waking frequently at night, often wanting the comfort of a feed, even when they're not hungry.

Although the jury is out on whether or not teething can cause a baby to suffer bouts of diarrhoea, most parents find that their babies' stools are looser for short periods of time during teething, so more frequent nappy changes may be required.

If you know your baby is teething, ensure that they're comfortable before bed. Give a warm bath and gently massage the baby's face around the jawline and under their chin. This helps to relax the area and ease inflammation. You can offer infant paracetamol and rub a drop of teething gel into the affected area of the gums. (Don't use more than the manufacturer's recommended amount, this could be dangerous for your baby's health.) Give a feed before your baby goes to bed and ensure they get as much as possible, so that hunger doesn't wake them too early. If the baby does wake in the night, offer one more dose each of paracetamol and teething gel – as long as it is at least four hours since the last dose – and try massaging the jaw again. Give lots of cuddles and be patient – this will soon pass.

Peek-a-boo!

Gradually, it will dawn on your baby that an object they can't see may still be there – and peek-a-boo games help them to understand this.

The understanding that objects continue to exist even when they cannot be seen, heard, or touched is known as "object permanence", and is a major milestone in a baby's first year. The term was first used by child psychologist Jean Piaget, who believed that most babies grasp this concept between eight and 12 months old. However, all children are different, and some babies have been known to begin to develop this concept as young as four months. Games of peek-a-boo now are great fun, because your baby will be pleasantly surprised each time you cover your face with your hands and then "magically" reappear again. They also test your baby's memory: the baby is learning to anticipate, so they will wait excitedly for your face to appear, and to hear you cry "Peek-a-boo". If you leave your hands over your face for longer than usual, they may reach out to prompt you to move them! Learning that things – including you – can still be there when they can't see them is also good for their emotional security. When you vanish for a few moments, leaving them in the care of someone else, your baby won't feel as concerned as they may have previously.

Learning to sit

Your baby is not ready to sit unsupported but they'll love to be propped or held in a sitting position to get a different view of the world.

Your baby is ready to start gaining the muscle strength and coordination that form the basis for sitting upright. If they can lift their head during tummy time and roll confidently, you can introduce some play ideas to build their readiness to sit. For example, prop your baby up securely so they have a stable position, then give them noisy, bright rattles to reach for, or encourage them to stretch to grab a cloth draped over their legs. Each time they lean out they're refining their balance. They will topple over so be ready to hold them, and make sure there are plenty of cushions around to break their fall.

When you prop them do not leave them alone even for a few moments. Until their muscles, coordination and balance are improved they will tire easily and even become frustrated so watch for signs that they'd rather do some less strenuous play. At this age they may not be ready for this sort of activity at all and that's fine, too. The average age for sitting is six months with some babies not reaching this milestone until around 10 months.

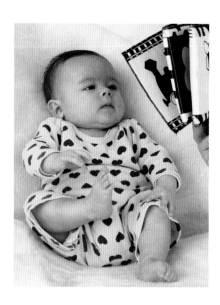

Good vantage point While your baby's sitting propped up, it's a good opportunity to hold up a book so that they can see it easily.

Making associations

Even the most acquiescent baby will go through a stage of expressing not just their likes, but also their dislikes – and you'll know about it!

As your baby's memory develops, they will begin to make positive and negative associations. Soon, they will light up when you walk into the room, smile at an older sibling, and gurgle when they see their baby gym. However, their car seat may produce an instant cry of protest; they may actively resist being laid down for tummy time, and your attempts to leave them alone in their bed at night may well end up in tears of frustration – and even anger! They're starting to know their own mind and express their opinion. In fact, browse any baby forum on the Internet and you'll see that 12-week-old babies have a wealth of dislikes, including their cots, the family dog, bedtime, slings, the bath, getting dressed, and even being winded. So get ready for a few disagreements!

Positive associations

In the early days, the best way to deal with dislikes is to create positive associations. Maybe your baby has been stuck in their car seat for too long in the past, so a few short journeys with the nursery rhymes on and their favourite cuddly toy next to them may make a difference.

Change your routine slightly if they're showing a dislike for the bath or bedtime. Perhaps share a bath together. If they dislike being put into their cot, try staying close by, putting a containing arm around them while they lie there. Softly tell them stories,

Distraction often helps – hum, or sing to them; hang a mobile over their change table; festoon their car seat with new toys; put them in a sling facing outwards; dress them in a different place and play "This little piggy" while you do it.

Gentle guidance

Ultimately, this is a developmental stage that you'll have to work through. Most activities to which babies object are necessary, and you'll have to guide them through – gently, kindly, and patiently. Talk to them, make them laugh, maintain eye contact, and try to control your own frustrations. Until your baby can use words to express themself, try to negotiate, and understand why they must do things they dislike, you'll have to persevere as best you can.

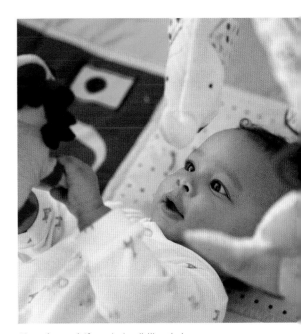

Changing tack If your baby dislikes their bouncy chair, they might be better off somewhere else for a change, such as under a baby gym that offers colourful distractions.

ASK A HEALTH VISITOR

My twins don't enjoy the same activities; how can I keep them both occupied and happy? Try to encourage solo play. Set each baby up with an activity they enjoy, putting one baby on each side of you. There will be some to-ing and fro-ing involved to keep them both occupied, but you'd probably be doing that anyway. It is good that your babies are expressing their individual characters, however hard it is to facilitate two very different sets of needs. If one hates the bath, top and tail them and put them in their baby chair while you bathe the bath-friendly sibling. If one resists bedtime, settle down the happy twin first and introduce a new element to your bedtime routine for the other. As they get older, they'll begin to look with interest at what the other is doing, and probably want to join in. Be as flexible and creative with your arrangements as you can, and bear in mind that this is just a stage.

Routines to suit you

Your baby's sleeping and feeding patterns are now more predictable, so try adjusting their schedule to work better for you.

By now, your baby may be able to be a little more flexible than they were previously because they can go longer between feeds and, probably, sleep for extended periods of time. Many parents find this a positive development. It means that you are not quite so tied to your baby, and they will be much more amenable to fitting in with a routine that suits you a little more.

You can now anticipate when they are likely to be hungry, and squeeze in a good feed before heading out to meet friends or catch up with some jobs. When they're usually alert and happy, you can set them up in their recliner with a couple of board books, or in their baby gym surrounded by toys, in order to get on with some phone calls, or sift through your emails. Adjusting their routine slightly from time to time will help them to become more flexible and buy you a little freedom. Routines are great for providing young babies with security, as they learn to anticipate what comes next; however, they can become overly binding – the last thing you need is to find yourself in a position where all lunchtime social engagements are put on hold while your baby has their nap. Don't hesitate to create a little time for yourself by involving others, too. If both parents can take turns with the bedtime routine, you'll both develop the knack of settling your baby – and they'll be equally happy in either scenario. Life will soon be getting much easier!

DEVELOPMENT ACTIVITY: PLAYTIME

Your baby will enjoy exploring their toys while held securely on your lap. Encourage them to reach for, grasp, and examine toys with different textures, sounds, and shapes. Noisy toys will get their attention, leading them to look, reach, and turn. Scrunch a crinkly toy, or shake a rattle a bit above and to the side of them and encourage them to reach and grab. These activities help hand–eye coordination, muscle control, and their ability to grasp by opening their hand and curling their fingers around a toy.

Busy fingers Your baby will love to grasp things, and any new toys will be grabbed and examined carefully.

COLIC

If your baby is still crying frequently and you are convinced they have colic, take heart that most babies outgrow colic around this time, and the distress, discomfort, and bouts of crying should soon stop completely.

In some cases, colic can go on for up to four months, or more. If your baby's colic continues much beyond three months, and nothing helps to make them more comfortable, see your doctor to ensure that nothing else is at the root of the problem, such as a reflux disorder.

New challenges

Your baby is ready to play with toys they can grip, shake, and squeeze – they're ready for a new challenge!

The mobile, floor gym, activity quilt, and textured toys are still important to your baby's development, but you can add toys with new textures, sounds, and even buttons. Give them a rattle or squeaky toy and they'll learn that they can make things happen. They will enjoy waving it, and squeezing and shaking it to make a noise, and will in time grasp the concept of cause and effect.

Toys with a variety of bright colours, lights, and sounds, will be popular. Babies of this age also find toys with friendly faces comforting as well as fascinating. Your baby will respond well to a toy face, especially if you help them identify it by pointing

out the toy's facial features, then your own, and then gently touch your baby's face as you name each part. Don't box away old favourites. Babies benefit from being able to master a toy easily, along with learning about more challenging ones. A mixture means there is always a successful activity at hand.

Great shakes A rattle is an ideal toy now as it helps your baby learn that by shaking it, they can cause it to make a noise.

FUN TOYS FOR NOW

Your baby's favourite plaything will always be you, and the time you spend with them is invaluable for their emotional development. But there are some toys that they will enjoy playing with, and that are great for this stage of their development.

- **Rattles** are a perennial favourite and they help your baby learn to control their movements.
- **Textured fabric books** are great fun, as are chunky board books with firm lift-up flaps.
- **Blocks** with "surprises" in them will entertain your baby endlessly. Ensure they are chunky enough for them to grasp – eventually.
- **Stacking pots** make a satisfying noise when banged together; and they'll enjoy learning to stack them.
- **Bath toys** that squeak, leak, and float will make bathtime enjoyable.
- **Toys that can be clipped** to your baby's pushchair will keep them occupied when you're on the move.
- **A music box** that responds to your baby's touch with nursery rhymes or lively music will delight them.
- **Toys that pop up** when buttons are pressed, such as a jack-in-the-box, will provide endless entertainment and encourage your baby to develop their hand–eye coordination.

TOYS AND SAFETY

Always give your baby age-appropriate toys. Toys intended for children aged over three years may have small parts that could cause choking if they come away. Ensure stitching is firm in soft toys, and that labels are well sewn in.

Do not attach toys to your baby's cot or playpen using string or elastic: a length of 30cm (12 inches) or more can wrap around a baby's neck and create a strangulation hazard. And remember that your baby can't yet tell a toy from a household implement, so make sure that you place

anything that should not go into their mouth well beyond their reach.

If you have older children, store their toys separately, and try to train your older children to keep their toys away from the baby in case they injure themselves.

Most importantly, never leave your baby unattended when there is anything within their reach, or with anyone who is not responsible enough to ensure that they do not put into their mouth something that might cause them to choke.

What a giggle!

Your baby has probably blessed you with smiles over past weeks, but any time now their first giggle will melt your heart all over again.

Finding something that makes your baby laugh becomes addictive. Babies respond best to eye contact, so looking them straight in the eye and smiling is the best way to start. To turn their return smiles into a giggle, you can try tickling their toes or under their armpits, or gently squeezing the fleshy, ticklish parts

Tickles Many babies giggle when tickled. Make a fun game of tickling your baby to get them to laugh with you.

of their thighs. They will likely respond with a giggle that lets you know they find it funny. Try pulling a funny face (such as an exaggerated look of surprise) while you tickle their thighs or their toes, to add another humorous dimension to the game to help to bring on the laughter.

Babies are more likely to be engaged and remember things if an experience stimulates more than one sense. So if you make a funny sound as you tickle your baby, they are even more likely to find it funny.

Forming attachments

Your baby can now identify your face, voice, and smell. When they hear you speak or sing, they will know you are just round the corner.

At around 14 weeks, your baby's sight improves dramatically. As you walk around the room, their eyes will follow you more, because they now have greater muscle control. As they become more aware of your coming and going, they may object or begin to cry if they can't see you any more.

Talk to them in reassuring tones as you move around. If you leave the room momentarily, tell them that you will be back in a second – they will soon begin to make connections between what you say and your

actions. When you come back, smile to let them know all is well.

As babies begin to understand that they are a separate person from you, having something comforting to hold on to can help them feel secure. It's wise to have two identical comfort objects, so that if one gets grubby you can replace it while it's washed (and you have a spare should it ever go missing!). Your baby may also get attached to its odour, so regular washing is useful to ensure the baby doesn't reject it when it smells fresh!

ASK A PAEDIATRICIAN

Why does my baby drool? All babies will drool either a little bit, or a lot, from time to time – this is normal and nothing to worry about. Drooling is something they will grow out of over time. Most babies drool more when they are teething, or if they have a cold or a blocked nose. Saliva contains protective proteins that provide a germ-fighting barrier against bacteria, so drooling can be helpful when your baby reaches the stage of automatically putting everything they pick up in their mouth.

Accidental rolls

At three months old, it can happen that your baby will begin to roll, but this is more often by accident rather than by intent.

Once your baby has achieved the flip from their tummy to back (see p.128), they'll be working on mastering the art of rolling over, every which way! Most babies can roll over by the time they reach six or seven months old, so it's unusual for them to be doing it now, but not unheard of.

Once they've done it once, that doesn't mean that they has mastered rolling: it takes muscle strength, coordination, and planning to make this happen each time they try.

Encouraging rolls

Short periods of tummy time and encouraging your baby to lift their head and push up with their hands are great practice for this milestone. As it is much easier for a baby to roll from front to back, put your baby on their tummy. If they can support themself well on one arm, hold a favourite, easy-to-grab toy to one side of them, but slightly above them, just out of reach. Try to coax them to tip their head back to look up and reach for the toy. As they reach, move the toy further behind them and see if you can coax them to lean towards the toy, encouraging them to flip over on to their back. If they do so, reward them with clapping, and reassuring smiles, especially if they seems a bit bemused by what just happened, and be sure to give them the toy. Encourage them to turn to both sides.

Rolling safety

Once your baby can roll over, never leave them on any raised surface. Change them on a changing mat on the floor. Keep one hand on them as you reach for things. Also, never leave your baby unattended in a room that hasn't been babyproofed.

DEVELOPMENT ACTIVITY
BACK-TO-FRONT ROLLS

Reaching out Once your baby twists their body and leans over in one direction, they'll soon learn to take the movement all the way over into a back-to-front roll.

The back-to-front roll happens only once the reflex that forces out your baby's arm as they turn their head is overruled by their improving coordination. They also need enough muscle tone to support their head, body, and legs, and the coordination to be able to pull in their arms so they do not prevent the roll. To encourage a back-to-front roll, lay them on their back and place a toy to one side of them, just out of reach. Get them to reach for the toy. If they reach far enough, their centre of gravity will shift to bring them over on to their front. Once they've mastered the move, they'll combine it with the front-to-back roll, for complete rolling-across-the-floor freedom.

Tummy time to rolling All it takes is one stronger-than-usual push up with one arm and a slight rocking from side to side, and your baby will have tipped themselves over on to their back.

Your baby's financial future

It may seem early to be thinking about saving for your baby's future, but some forward planning now really can pay off later on.

It may seem precipitous but saving now for your baby's future can reduce the financial burden of being a parent (driving lessons, a first car, perhaps further education fees) when your baby becomes a teen or young adult. A small regular investment now will grow into a decent sum by the time your little one reaches 18 years old.

Grandparents or relatives may want to give you a lump sum to invest on your child's behalf. It can make sense to open up something in your child's name to benefit from special tax savings that may apply. If you do this only your child will be able to access the money, and they will usually have to wait until they are an adult to do so. Some children's accounts can be operated by the child from the age of around seven, but these are more like junior bank accounts for managing pocket money. A guardian's signature is often needed for withdrawals.

Do your research Whichever type of investment you choose to make for your baby, ensure you put some time into researching where to find the best deals.

Savings accounts

A simple way to invest is the Junior Individual Savings Account (Junior ISA) is a tax-free account into which you can pay up to a certain amount, set by the government, every year. Interest is not taxed, regardless of how much income is generated in your child's name elsewhere. This is a relatively risk-free way to save, but the rate of return on savings is likely to be low. If, over the course of 18 years, the rate of inflation outstrips the rate of interest on the Junior ISA, the savings become worth less than they were to begin with, in real terms.

Trusts and bonds

An investment trust is intended to bring a healthy return through the stock market, but there is a greater risk of the value of your investment falling. Money paid into bonds is also invested in stocks and shares. You can choose the length of the bond, so you might wait until your child is 18 before they can cash it in, but you have to invest a regular amount each month for a set period of time. Cashing in a bond early may give a negative return. If you're considering investing, talk to a financial adviser, or look for advice online.

SMALL CHANGE SAVINGS

One lovely way to save even a little for your baby – with the added dimension of handwritten notes to discover later – is to make or buy a "sealed" piggy bank (sometimes called a terramundi) that you can pop loose change into over the weeks, months, or even years – slowly, slowly building up a little pot of cash to spend on something fun in the future. From time to time, write a little note about something funny that your baby did or a milestone they reached, and post it through the opening. Invite visiting family members to do the same. In years to come – perhaps a 13th, 16th or 18th birthday – your "baby" can crack open the pot, pocket the spoils, and read all the memories of their younger years.

Structuring sleep and feeds

Your baby's tummy can now hold enough milk to allow them to sleep for longer periods, and so your baby will be settling into a more regular routine.

In the morning, wake your baby when you do, so that they're more likely to sleep when you want to relax for the evening. At this stage most babies need six to eight feeds in a 24-hour period, including breakfast, mid-morning, lunch, mid-afternoon, and teatime. If your baby wakes in the night to feed, try instead waking them for a feed just before you go to bed. Keep them calm, with stimulation kept to a minimum. In the daytime, introducing playtime after a feed will help your baby to distinguish between the night and day.

On average, babies sleep for about 10 hours at night and five in the day, but each baby is different. If it suits your baby, try a mid-morning nap, an afternoon nap, and, if necessary, a short power nap around teatime. If your baby's bedtime is around 7pm, try two longer daytime naps instead.

Good morning Waking your baby for their first feed helps them adapt to your routine.

Physical play

Now that your baby's stronger, physical games such as knee rides and tickles encourage confidence and physical awareness.

Fun faces Hold your baby close to your face as you pull faces, make funny noises, and rub noses – you may even elicit a giggle or two!

Whether it's tummy time, tickles, or bouncy play, your baby will benefit from having the opportunity to move and take part in activities that make them aware of their body.

With your baby on their front, roll a ball in front of them. They may move their legs and body to reach it. Sit on the floor with them and prop them securely in a baby nest, or hold them safely between your legs, then build towers of soft blocks. they will try to reach out to bat them, and will enjoy watching the bricks scatter across the floor. Your baby will love to be rocked from side to side if they are supported well. If they protest, stop, or try rocking more gently. If they can hold their head up, raise them into the air, and "bump" noses as you bring them down. Try water play: in a bath or paddling pool, sit with your baby firmly in your arms. Let them splash, and use a toy watering can to sprinkle water over their arms. Never leave them unsupervised near water.

Being active

So your baby may not be up and toddling yet – but when it happens, you'll need to be fit and healthy, with lots of stamina!

It can be difficult to motivate yourself to be active, especially if you're feeling tired. However, regular physical activity will help to decrease feelings of stress, and promote relaxation and better sleep, which in turn will leave you feeling more energized. Among the benefits of being active as new parents are stronger bones, muscles, and joints; lower body fat and better weight control; good balance, coordination, and agility; improved self-esteem, and a more positive mental outlook.

If you're a new mum, physical activity will help reduce your likelihood of suffering from postnatal depression, anxiety, and low mood. For breastfeeding mums, invest in a quality sports bra that offers good support to ensure you have a comfortable workout.

Resuming a sporting activity A few quick laps of your local swimming pool, a buggy-jog in the park, or a game of tennis with a friend are all great ways of getting some exercise.

What kind of activity?

About 14 weeks after giving birth, a woman's body will have regained enough strength for moderate aerobic exercise. Cycling, swimming, dance, pilates, and yoga are all good options. Aim for becoming slightly out of breath but still able to hold a conversation. If it hurts, stop.

Fitting around the baby

Most gyms and local sports centres offer crèche facilities, and most will take a baby from three months old. The prospect of leaving your baby in someone else's care can be daunting, but classes often last for only up to an hour. The feel-good factor of doing something for yourself can be a just reward for an hour's separation.

If you are not comfortable leaving your baby in a crèche, try to find a window for physical activity once your partner is home, giving them some bonding time with the baby, too.

If you can't get to a gym, you could enrol on a programme of online dance or aerobic classes, or join a park "pram" walk, organized by local groups, where you are likely to meet other like-minded parents, too. Also, there are community centres that run outdoor activities that allow you to take your baby along.

FEEL-GOOD FACTOR FOR YOU

It is very easy in the first weeks of having a new baby to become completely tied up with the business of parenthood and forget that you need looking after, too. This week, agree a time with your partner for them to look after the baby so that you can take some time out to pamper yourself with something you enjoy for you – a lunch or a trip to the cinema with friends; a visit to a sports fixture; or just an hour out in a local café with a good book. It's even better if it's something you need to book, so that you don't get tempted to cancel. Whatever you choose, it should feel like a treat, enabling you to come away feeling fabulous.

Feeding and teething

Babies often experience the symptoms of teething before their first tooth is perceptible under the gum, which can cause them discomfort.

Upset baby Many teething babies feel irritable and restless and, sometimes, pain as the tooth cuts through the gums.

Many babies lose their appetite when teething as their gums are so uncomfortable. If your baby has flushed cheeks, red gums, is drooling excessively, or is chewing on toys or fingers more than usual, or if their sleep is disturbed, they may have a tooth coming. Some associate a low-grade fever with teething, but doctors are reluctant to make this link. If your baby does have a fever, or seems unwell, do not assume this is down to teething. Instead, ask a doctor to check for an infection.

Each tooth pushes up through the gum to become visible in your baby's mouth. You may be able to feel a hard, protruding bump in the mouth if you rub their gums with a clean finger, and the area may look inflamed.

Some breastfed babies respond to teething by wanting "comfort" feeds and this may be the best way to settle your baby. Other babies find being nursed uncomfortable, cry, and come on and off the breast, only to want it again soon afterwards as they are still hungry. While this is frustrating for you both, keep offering your breast as usual until your baby settles.

Bottle-fed babies may also fuss while teething. A little teething gel before a feed can ease the pain for long enough to get some milk into them. If you have any worries, see your health visitor.

ASK AN EXPERT

My baby has a tooth and bites me when I breastfeed! How can I discourage this?
Often, babies bite when they are experimenting with their new teeth. Release them from the breast while saying "ouch", then reattach them. They will begin to understand if your reaction is to shout in pain. It may shock them and be enough to stop them doing it again! They're more likely to bite if they're not hungry, so take them off your breast when they have had enough. Do they have a cold or congested nasal passages? If so, they may be clamping down with their gums and teeth to hold your nipple in place as they breathe through their mouth. For a remedy to this, call your GP.

TEETHING RINGS

Invest in some non-PVC teething rings that can be cooled in the fridge or freezer. These are invaluable if your baby's gums are sore or inflamed. Although it may be a few weeks, or even months, until the first tooth emerges, getting them used to gnawing on a teething ring now can help to prevent symptoms before they start and your baby will know what to do when those first teeth start appearing.

Cool relief Keep a few teething rings in the fridge so there is always a cold one on hand to help ease your baby's discomfort.

Help from family

If your parents or other trusted family members are willing, you may want to consider enlisting their help so you can take a whole night off.

RECORDING YOUR BABY'S VOICE

It may seem impossible to believe that you could ever forget the sound of your baby's earliest sounds, but each stage of a baby's development is so absorbing, it can be easy to lose track of those momentous, heart-warming attempts at communication. This week, make time to record your baby chatting away. Perhaps you can continue to do so regularly, each time making a note of the date. Record the gurgles, coos, and other sounds using your smartphone and email the recordings to family and friends, or just dowload them to an external hard drive to keep your recordings safe for that trip down memory lane in the future.

LONG-DISTANCE GRANDPARENTING

Relationships with grandparents can be rewarding for your baby and on into their adulthood. Getting things right in the early days can ensure that relationships flourish. If your baby's grandparents live far away, they may feel they need an invitation to visit – always articulate the offer, even if the practicalities make accepting it tricky; don't assume that they simply know the offer is open. Keep them involved by chatting to them using video calls, with your baby on your lap, or send them weekly emails with lots of photos. Don't forget to report all those amazing "firsts" to keep them in the loop.

Now that your baby's routine is more established, you've got expressing down pat (if breastfeeding), and caring for their needs has become easier, you might want to think about indulging in some time with your own friends or your partner, or time out to enjoy your own passions or need for unfettered me-time. If grandparents, say, or other trusted family members or close friends are able to babysit for the night, you can plan a trip to the theatre, dinner out, or even a night away – a proper break that gives you time to focus solely on each other or on yourself.

While some parents don't feel comfortable with leaving their baby early on, others find that the benefits to their relationship or self-care outweigh their anxieties. Letting your nearest and dearest help out allows your baby to begin to develop a loving and significant relationship with them – and those significant others will almost certainly relish the opportunity to spend bonding time with your baby. However, leaving your baby for the first time is a personal choice, and in the end it comes down to what feels right for you.

If you agree that the time is right to get away, decide whether your baby will be staying at your home or the home of the person or people entrusted to look after them. At this age, your baby will probably sleep wherever they are. Then, talk through

An extended family Grandparents and other family will enrich your baby's life, especially if their bond is developed early on.

every aspect of the baby's care: when to give a feed; change a nappy; put the baby down to sleep; and what to do if they wake up. Make sure that your family or friend is aware how best to offer comfort if your baby becomes upset. It's important that you feel you have covered every eventuality. Once you have left clear instructions and contact numbers, there's no reason to worry. Ask your parents, partner's parents, or other family member or friend to call you straight away if they have any concerns.

Encouraging social skills

Your baby will gurgle, chatter, and coo in your company, and be pleased to meet new people if introduced to them with care.

Babies naturally favour their primary carer, so you can make things easier for your partner and other family members by encouraging your baby's social skills. At 15 weeks, your baby is ready for this – social skills are developing apace.

Ensure you set a good example by interacting positively with the people around you. After a busy day with just you for company, your baby will be keen to see and play with someone new. Do give your partner a moment to get through the door, but don't keep your baby to yourself. A shared cuddle makes a nice handover as your baby transfers interest to the other parent. Spend time together as a family as much as possible, so your baby witnesses how you relate positively to each other. Your baby will learn and take cues from you. Share childcare duties between you and your partner. As long as you stick roughly to the same routine, it won't matter if your techniques differ. Your baby won't mind if one of you sings the bedtime song differently!

A parent-and-baby group gives your baby contact with other adults. All babies are unique in their willingness to go to others. If your baby is reluctant, introduce new people gently, shortening visits or interactions, if necessary, until your baby builds up confidence.

Reading as a habit

Developments in your baby's vision and comprehension mean that they are now able to enjoy books and stories much more than before.

Reading aloud to your baby teaches them about communication, encourages their listening skills, memory, and vocabulary, and introduces concepts such as "story sense" (which is essential for reading skills later on). Books provide an exciting view on the world, in an entertaining and comforting way.

Sit down with your baby at least once a day to explore books. Encourage them to look and listen as you point at and talk about the pictures, and lift flaps. Fill your voice with emotion and expression to capture your baby's attention, and help them to experience positive social interaction with you during reading, which promotes healthy emotional development.

Babies love repetition, so your baby may want the same book over and over. You'll be encouraging memory skills by repeating the same stories.

Most things go straight in the mouth at this stage, so choose books that can withstand a good chew. Sturdy, colourful books with rhymes, pictures of babies and animals, and interactive elements (such as lift-up flaps and textures) will engage your baby and involve them in the story.

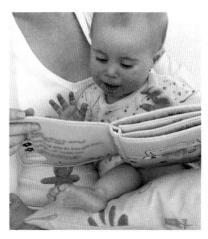

Reading time Establish a reading habit that your baby can enjoy alone when they're older.

Reaching and grasping

Now that your baby knows that there are hands that belong to them, they will start to practise their reaching and grasping skills in earnest.

Your baby has been batting at and trying to grasp objects for a few weeks now. They have worked out that their hand is their own, and their goal now is to direct it towards an object without looking at their hand first.

Once your baby can confidently direct their hand towards an object, they will be able to reach out and grasp small, easy-to-grip, brightly coloured toys or rattles. These will probably go straight to their mouth, although they may spend time looking at them, dropping them (usually by accident), and reaching for them again.

At this point in your baby's development, reaching and grasping occur at the same time. Your baby can't yet correct any mistakes while reaching. If they can't get hold of an object that they see first time, they'll try again, reaching and grasping together. They'll close their hand when they see that they've reached that interesting toy. With every attempt, they improve their hand–eye coordination.

To encourage your baby to reach out, surround them with light, sturdy toys that fit easily in one hand. Choose a variety of shapes, but ensure each one is easy to grip and has a shape, edge, or texture that would fit into your baby's palm. Offer your baby both still and moving objects – there are plenty of toys that vibrate, or can be rolled to draw their attention. Praise their efforts to reach

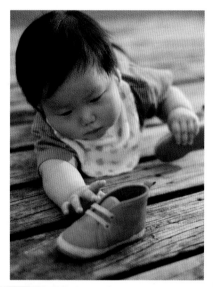

Practice makes perfect With practice, your baby's attempts to reach out and touch or even grab things will become more accurate.

and grab. Move toys a little closer if they're just that bit too far for eventual success to avoid your baby becoming disheartened. Try not to intervene and do things for them, though. Your baby needs to practise and learn from own their mistakes.

Once your baby can grab things, keep hazards well out of reach. For example, remove your handbag (which may contain small items a baby could choke on); hot drinks or food; pets; strings or cords; hard or unhygienic items (which will end up in your baby's mouth); electrical leads; houseplants; and medication.

DEVELOPMENT ACTIVITY: CLAPPING GAMES

Although your baby will not be able to clap their hands until about seven to nine months, or later, clapping games, in which you move their hands gently to make a clap, give them the experience of bringing their hands together in front of their body. Sing songs while you clap their hands together. Let their hands fall, then clap your own hands, singing as you do so. Encourage your baby to grasp your hands, one in each of theirs, then bring your hands together again – they're clapping your hands now! The song "If you're happy and you know it, clap your hands" is perfect for this activity. Your baby will associate it with the actions, and will be ready to join in as their own ability to clap develops in the coming months.

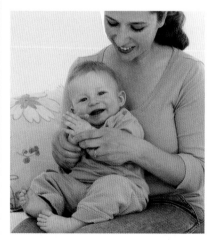

Clap and sing Babies love the drama of clapping their hands and will enjoy singing songs and playing games, too.

What baby sees now

Your baby's vision is improving all the time. They're still drawn to bright colours, but can distinguish more subtle colour contrasts now, too.

Your baby's eyesight has notably sharpened and now they will be able to notice objects across the room, although they will still prefer to look at objects close-up.

Your baby's eyes should move together smoothly and follow objects and people around the room. If you notice a squint or any other vision problems, mention them to your doctor or health visitor.

Your baby may now be able to distinguish between more subtle colour contrasts, such as red and reddish orange, although subtle differences between pastel shades may still prove elusive. You may also notice that your baby's eyes are starting to change colour. Lighter-coloured eyes may go through several changes before settling on their final shade at about six months.

Maturing vision At around this time, your baby will be able to see colour and perceive depth more accurately than previously.

Changing friendships

Having a baby shifts your life and focus dramatically, and you may find that some friendships alter as your needs change.

It may be that many of your friends and family share your enthusiasm for your baby. Others, however, may find your new focus bewildering.

It is natural for friendships to wane and surge throughout our lives. You may well make a new set of friends among your baby crowd, and probably have more in common with them at this point. Equally, however, old friendships are not dispensable, and you may need to make an effort to keep some of them going. Make time to go out with friends without your baby and show an interest in their lives. Keep talk of your baby to a minimum and focus on what you have in common. Your friends are no less worthy if they fail to share your passion – try to remember a time when you were not interested in nappies and teething yourself!

Your friendships will continue to evolve in the future, and you may one day find that you can play a supportive role when friends go on to have their own babies. Keep things simmering away for now, and remember that this is a phase that will eventually be resolved.

ASK A DOCTOR

My baby has started to suck their thumb. Is this a problem? About 80 per cent of babies suck their thumbs or fingers, which causes their brains to produce endorphins ("feel-good" chemicals) that soothe and calm. Thumb-sucking is a sign your baby is learning to comfort themselves, which is a useful skill. Don't worry about their teeth. As long as you discourage the habit by the time your baby's milk teeth fall out (at about five years of age), there won't be lasting damage. Most suck their thumbs much less by the age of three.

Your baby from
4 to 6 months

MONTH

4

MONTH

5

Full-out belly **laughs** may appear around five months of age.

MONTH 4: ENCOURAGE YOUR BABY TO ROLL

Your baby may learn to roll over with surprising speed. Most babies roll from tummy to back before mastering the more difficult back to front roll. Not all babies roll over – some skip this stage and go directly to sitting and crawling.

MONTH 5: SUPPORT YOUR BABY TO SIT UP

Towards the end of their fifth month, your baby can hold their head up well and is able to sit upright with plenty of support. While sat up, your baby will enjoy taking in the world around them.

Your baby will **grasp** and inspect an object that interests them, before instinctively **putting it into their mouth** for further exploration.

> " Your baby is exploring, laughing, and interacting more with you as well as gaining mobility and coordination. "

MONTH

6

MONTH 6: TIME TO WEAN YOUR BABY

By six months your baby is ready to move to solid foods that will complement their milk diet. Gradually, your baby will have fewer milk feeds as they get used to eating more solid food and enjoying new flavours and textures.

By experimenting with new sounds, your baby is developing their **language skills**.

Your baby should be able to **reach out** and **grab things** with greater accuracy.

4 months

BABIES' BABBLING AT THIS AGE SOUND THE SAME, NO MATTER WHAT LANGUAGE THEY HEAR.
Your baby should enjoy tummy time more now that they are stronger. If they haven't done so already, they're about to push up on their arms and support the weight of their upper body – if only briefly. They'll be using a wider variety of sounds, and perhaps even joining syllables together.

Look who's "talking"

Your baby may start joining sounds and syllables together so that they sound like "words", but they don't have any meaning yet.

Facial expressions Have a "conversation" with your baby, by encouraging them to "talk" by imitating your sounds and "words".

Around now, you may well notice, as your baby practises their vocal skills, that many different vowel sounds have crept into their "language", and that they are making more sounds when playing on their own. They may growl and gurgle, and even squeal and shriek unexpectedly. The odd consonant may now sneak into their vocabulary, and they may create some peculiar words, such as "ibcooo" and "gipgooo". Your baby may also begin to recognize that the way your mouth moves affects the sounds you make, which is more or less lip-reading!

You can encourage the development of your baby's verbal skills by answering them when they make their little noises. They'll be learning the rudiments of language and conversation, which includes both speaking and listening. They have been exposed to language since they were in the womb, and they were born with a very basic understanding of speech patterns and different sounds. Now, they will attempt to replicate those patterns and sounds, and you may find that they mimic the high- and low-pitched voices you use when you speak to them, and also that their babbling and coos sound much more like language.

Bilingual baby

If more than one language is spoken in your household, don't hesitate to use both languages regularly. Research suggests that being exposed to two languages early on affects brain development, making such babies receptive to new languages for a longer period. This is especially true if a baby hears both languages in the first year of life. Also, speaking more than one language helps your child's learning. Speak to your baby in whichever language feels comfortable to you. One of you may speak the first language while the other uses the second, community language. Your baby will adapt and learn to use them individually as they move between home and community.

Sometimes it's thought that children who learn two languages will have delayed speech. This isn't usually the case and such an assumption can mean that a speech problem is ignored. If you have any concerns about your baby's speech, consult your GP.

DEVELOPMENT ACTIVITY: ROCK, SWAY, AND SWING

The part of your baby's brain that senses motion and balance is known as the vestibular system. As this system matures, it helps them to keep their head upright and, eventually, to keep their balance when sitting and standing up. Rocking, swaying, and swinging your baby up and down, both gently and more playfully, will encourage the development of this system, and they will love the activity. There is good research to suggest that these types of movements help to improve a baby's sense of balance, their gross motor skills, and their perception of movement in advance of crawling and walking. Try to make movement part of your regular playtime.

Your parenting style

Around this time, you'll have developed your own ideas about raising your baby, but it's good to keep refining your thinking.

Whether to take on board others' advice is a tricky area for parents. One set of grandparents frowns on the use of a dummy; your sibling thinks your baby should be potty-trained pretty much from birth; your best friend thinks that even young babies should be "sleep-trained" to last through the night. Not your philosophy? Don't worry. Establish a culture of respect – you do it your way, I'll do it mine. It's always worth listening to the ideas of others, but if you and your partner are in agreement about how to raise your baby, you are perfectly within your rights to carry on.

The basis of your parenting should always be the provision of a warm, responsive, and loving family. It is too early for rules, but it is the right time to discuss with your partner your joint approach. Talk about how each of you was parented, which will shape your own attitudes. Discuss dos and don'ts: one of you may be keen on rewards, while the other thinks smiles and praise are enough. Find a compromise that suits you both.

FOUR-MONTH VACCINATIONS

It's time for your baby's third set of immunizations (see p.99). At four months, your baby is due a third dose of the 6-in-1 vaccine to protect against diphtheria, hepatitis B, tetanus, whooping cough, polio, and Haemophilus influenzae type b (Hib). They'll also be given a second dose of the MenB injection to protect against meningococcal infections, such as meningitis. Call your GP to ensure your baby's immunizations are up to date.

Growing appetite

Your baby may be hungrier than usual around now, and they may demand constant bottle-feeds or spend long hours at the breast.

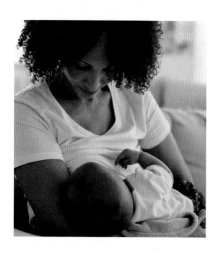

More milk Your baby may feed more around now to fuel their increasingly energetic play and their rapid physical growth.

Your increasingly active baby needs more fuel to keep going, which may be why they're hungrier. If you are breastfeeding, feed on demand. If you are bottle-feeding, an empty bottle is your cue to give them an additional 30ml (1fl oz) of formula. If they drain the bottle and seem dissatisfied, give them another 30ml (1oz). Do not exceed 150ml (5fl oz) of milk per kilogram (2.2lbs) of weight per day. If you're unsure, speak to your health visitor or GP. You may want to offer some cooled boiled water between feeds to ensure your baby isn't thirsty.

Your baby's nutritional needs are still being met by milk, so don't be tempted to introduce solids quite yet; their digestive system won't be ready. If you are considering weaning them before six months, discuss with your health visitor who can help you decide if your baby is ready (see also pp.154–55).

The importance of play

Playing with your baby supports their development in so many ways, and promotes healthy communication with you in the years to come.

Playing with your child supports emotional health – for example, by encouraging self-esteem and trust. Play is essential for healthy development in babies and children, providing opportunities to develop motor, cognitive, perceptual, and social skills. It encourages creativity, imagination, and self-sufficiency, and it helps babies to discover new things, solve problems, and, above all, relax and enjoy themselves.

Play allows your baby to learn about the world. Whenever they hear, see, touch, taste, or smell something, messages are sent to their brain, prompting the creation of important mental connections. So when you play with your baby, you're helping to shape their brain. Giving your child a variety of activities to experience will result in more brain connections, and repeating these activities will make these associations stronger. Physical play encourages gross motor skills, spatial awareness, and much more; while books, shape-sorters, rattles, cause-and-effect toys, and "conversation" promote cognitive development, hand–eye coordination, and fine motor skills. Mixing different types of play will allow your baby to grow into a healthy, stimulated child.

However, don't fall into the trap of thinking you need to stimulate your baby constantly, or make every play session a learning opportunity. Play should be relaxed, spontaneous,

DEVELOPMENT ACTIVITY: PLAYING WITH HOUSEHOLD ITEMS

Your baby doesn't need expensive toys; in fact, babies tend to enjoy playing with the things you use and copying what you do. Plastic cups are great for stacking up, then knocking over. A clean wooden spoon (keep it light to avoid it being too sore if the baby inadvertently bonks themself on the head) and an empty plastic mixing bowl are great for banging and "stirring". Scrunch up a large piece of paper to investigate the texture and crunchy sound it makes. Even a cardboard box or plastic measuring spoons can be fun for your little one to play with. Avoid hazardous items, such as plastic bottles with screw lids that can be chokeable.

Fascinating new world Things we would consider ordinary are positively exotic to your baby. Almost anything can make a good plaything, as long as it is safe for the task.

and fun. Your baby will learn just as much from a tickling game as they will from expensive, developmentally appropriate, high-contrast flash cards. Play never needs to be structured – just do what comes naturally, simply encouraging your baby to attempt new feats, enjoy your company, explore their environment, relax, and have fun. Most important, give your baby lots of your time; you will promote their emotional wellbeing by simply being there for them.

Weaning

It's little wonder that new mums are often baffled by weaning – differing opinions and contradictory advice about the process abound. So here's a straightforward guide to what it is, how to decide when it's best to start, and what you'll need to get going.

Finger sucking A baby who is ready to move on to solids may demonstrate the classic tell-tale sign of sucking fingers or fists.

What is weaning?

This is the gradual process of introducing foods other than milk into your baby's diet. It is sometimes called complementary feeding as the foods, or "solids", are given alongside milk. It doesn't mean encouraging your baby to stop breastfeeding or drinking formula; milk will continue to be a mainstay of your baby's diet. However, as your baby becomes bigger and more active, they'll need the extra nutrients from solid foods to ensure healthy growth and development.

When should we start?

Over the next couple of weeks, your baby might start showing signs that make you think they're ready for some solid food. Perhaps they seem consistently hungry and normal feeds seem unsatisfying, for example, or they've started waking in the night for a feed when previously they slept through. Perhaps parents of other babies you know are giving solids already, and you're wondering if you should, too. Or an older family member may have told you that weaning happened much earlier in their day. All of these factors can prompt parents to start weaning – but is this really the right time?

The Department of Health (DoH) and the World Health Organization (WHO) advocate waiting. They recommend exclusive milk feeds for the first six months of life, after which your baby should able to sit in a high chair, take food easily from a spoon, and/or pick up and hold food to feed themselves.

However, some experts disagree that waiting until six months is a good idea. There is a growing body of evidence that this increases the risk of iron deficiency in babies, as well as the risk of allergies. Babies' iron stores begin to run down at six months, so if they are only just starting on fruit and vegetable purées at this time, they're unlikely to be getting all the iron they need. The most recent recommendation from the British Dietetic Association (BDA) is that feeding just breastmilk or formula for six months is a desirable goal, and that weaning should begin by six months at the latest, but not before four months. Also, breast- or bottlefeeding should continue

WEANING EQUIPMENT

• A high chair or a seat that clips on to your dining table. Look for a sturdy high chair, ideally with moulded corners and crevices to make cleaning easy, a harness or five-point belt, and an insert to hold younger babies snugly. A detachable tray is a plus (see p.206).
• A splash mat for under the chair.
• Two or three small plastic bowls, preferably with a suction cup at the base for stability.
• Two or three plastic or soft rubber weaning spoons with a small, easy-to-use "scoop".

• A plastic cup or beaker with a spout; choose a "slow flow" one.
• Easy-to-clean bibs.
• A food processor or hand-blender. An electric grinder is useful for foods that become glutinous in a food processor and foods with tough skins, such as peas or soya beans.
• A flexible ice-cube tray with a secure lid, and mini pots with lids to freeze larger quantities of your baby's favourite purées.
• Stick-on labels or freezer bags so that you can note the type of purée and the date that you make it.

throughout weaning, particularly in the early stages.

The BDA also supports research that indicates that introducing foods containing gluten between four and seven months while breastfeeding may reduce the risk of coeliac disease, type 1 diabetes, and wheat allergy. Furthermore, high-allergen foods, such as eggs and fish, do not need to be delayed until after six months. Other research suggests that babies who are weaned before six months are more likely to enjoy a wider variety of flavours and textures than those weaned at or after six months.

The right time

Before you begin, be certain that your baby is absolutely ready to take this step. Every baby is different, physically and emotionally. If your baby is healthy, happy, and growing well on their milk-only diet, there is no need to wean for the sake of it.

The earliest you should introduce solids is at four months, or 17 weeks. Before this time, your baby won't have the digestive enzymes required to digest and extract nutrients from solids; the baby's jaw and tongue won't be sufficiently developed to "chew" and swallow food; and the kidneys will not be mature enough to deal with solids. The baby needs to have lost the "extrusion reflex" (which causes a baby to push out anything that goes into their mouth), and to have the motor capacity to move food from the tip of the tongue. Once your baby is at least four months old, they may be ready for solids if they are doing some or all of the following:
• sitting up unaided (encourages digestion and helps to avoid choking)
• showing interest in your food, and perhaps reaching out to grab it
• hungrier than usual, and often

dissatisfied after a usual feed
• waking up in the night for an extra feed after previously sleeping through
• double their birth weight
• able to control their head
• attempting to put things into their mouth, and "gumming" them rather than pushing them out
• making "chewing" motions.
Talk to your GP or health visitor, who'll be able to reassure you whether it's the right time or not and give you advice.

The right pace

If you start weaning before six months, you can take the whole process at a relatively leisurely pace. If you wait until the recommended six months, you will need to progress swiftly from fruit and vegetable purées and baby rice (see p.210 and pp.216–217) on to dairy, meat, fish, eggs, and cereals and grains (see pp.236–37). This is because by then, your baby will need the additional iron contained in protein-rich foods. By the time your baby is 10 months old, you'll have introduced texture (lumps and bumps) as they move towards a balanced diet (pp.286–87).

WEANING A PREMATURE BABY

If your baby was born prematurely (before 37 weeks), it may be advisable to wean early. The reason for this is that babies born prematurely or with a low birth weight miss out on some of the normal nourishment that occurs in the womb in the latter stages of pregnancy. Each baby should be treated individually, and advice on when to wean them will depend on their history, growth pattern, and weight gain. Usually, weaning for premature babies is recommended between five and eight months after their actual birth date. It's important that babies have adequate head control before they are weaned. If your baby suffers from gastric reflux, solids may also be introduced a little earlier to help control symptoms. Seek advice from your health visitor as to the best time to wean your premature baby.

Gumming Frequent "chewing" on objects can be a sign that your baby is approaching the time when they are ready for solid foods to be introduced into their diet.

Sleeping longer at night

Now that their tummies can hold more food, many babies are capable of sleeping for a decent stretch at night, but that's not to say they will!

If your baby is still waking in the small hours, it's likely for comfort than needing food. Ensure they have a good feed and are winded at bedtime, so you'll know they're likely not hungry or uncomfortable.

Then, rather than offering a middle-of-the-night comfort feed, offer an alternative comfort. Stroke their back, sing to them, and reassure them that you are there. This may be enough for them to settle back to sleep. Because they have become accustomed to "snacks" during the night, and to being picked up and held at regular intervals, they may be a little resistant to this approach at first. Do pick them up but don't feed them unless they appear to be ravenously hungry.

You can start to encourage them to self-soothe. Do go to them when they call so they know they can trust you. (Leaving them to cry may exacerbate things – they'll learn not to cry eventually, but that doesn't mean they'll be secure and happy.) If they are secure that you are there and will offer them comfort if they need it, they will begin to learn to settle themselves back to sleep. See to their needs and, over the next few weeks, you can expect them to go longer between waking up until – eventually – they sleep for the most part of the night.

Feeling rundown?

A busy life and sleepless nights may have left you feeling lacklustre. You may need to make small lifestyle changes to get back on top form.

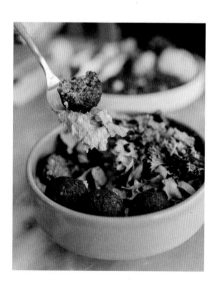

Lack of energy is often related to a lack of sleep, exercise, or decent nutrition, so if you're feeling under par, you may need to do something about one, or more, of these areas. Getting out in the fresh air will help you feel more energetic and could help you sleep better.

It's just as important to eat well. Parenting a new baby is so busy and exhausting that it can be easy to forget to eat properly. Eat healthy food that provides you with a sustained source of energy, such as a baked jacket potato stuffed with tuna, or a homemade vegetable soup with a wholegrain roll. Eating well when breastfeeding is especially important as milk quality is influenced by diet.

Take time to unwind before bed. If your baby wakes up at the crack of dawn, consider adjusting your own schedule to sleep and wake earlier. If you feel debilitated with exhaustion, see your GP. You may be suffering from low iron (causing anaemia), an underactive thyroid, a low-grade infection, or postnatal depression.

Wholefood diet Try to eat three meals a day, including fruits, vegetables, and wholegrains, with some dairy, fish, and unprocessed meat.

Getting ready to crawl

Although the average age to begin crawling is around eight to nine months, your baby is already practising the moves!

Over the coming weeks, your baby will start to lift their head during tummy time, dig their toes in to see if they can propel themselves forwards, and push up with their arms. They'll also be getting ready to roll, and in a few cases may flip from front to back. Each time your baby moves, they are learning where parts of their body are and working out how they can move together.

During tummy time, your baby may move their arms and legs in a "crawling" motion, and, although they can't boost themselves forwards yet, they might rock forwards on their tummy. This helps them develop the coordination needed to be able to crawl. They might wriggle their torso to achieve some movement, and will look around with their head raised and chest pushed up using forearms or hands. They are interested in the world around them, but though keen to be mobile, they won't crawl until they can sit well without support, some time after their sixth month.

The agile "one-arm-in-synch-with-one-leg" crawl is quite a sophisticated development in terms of coordination and gross motor skills, so most babies won't have this down pat until they approach their first birthday. Don't worry if your baby doesn't ever crawl – some babies skip this step and decide to go straight for walking, and end up pulling themselves up on the furniture instead of shuffling around on all fours.

DEVELOPMENT ACTIVITY: GET THAT TOY

Move a toy just out of your baby's reach when they are sitting upright or during tummy time to encourage them to practise their hand–eye coordination and the skills necessary for crawling. Ensure you set the toy at an achievable distance; if your baby can't reach it, despite their best efforts, move it a little closer and encourage them to try again, so your baby doesn't feel frustrated and give up.

The power of determination Your baby's impetus to crawl may spring from a burning desire to get hold of something just beyond their reach. You'll be amazed at their perseverance!

It's interesting to note that, since SIDS guidance that babies should sleep on their backs came into play around 1994, crawling has begun much later in many babies. It's likely that, because they spend more time on their backs, they aren't getting as much practice time on their tummy, and so crawl later. You can encourage your baby to spend time on their tummy and enjoy moving their legs by lying down with them and entertaining them during tummy time. Also, when they're on their back, dangle toys above them to encourage kicking, or gently "cycle" their legs. These activities will assist crawling when they have developed the balance, strength, and coordination to do so in a few months' time.

Baby gymnastics

Your baby now has greater strength and coordination, so they can bend their body to explore parts they couldn't previously reach!

Tasty toes Your baby's flexibility is in-built at this stage, so you may see them perform yogic feats of bendiness that would be difficult for an adult to achieve.

Babies are born flexible, but up until now, they haven't had the strength or sufficient control of their gross motor skills to do anything much with this innate flexibility. However, around this time, their ability to perform circus-like contortions develops apace. You can encourage their flexibility by holding their legs together, then gently moving them apart to say "peek-a-boo". Stretch up their arms in a cheer, too.

Strength and coordination
Your baby's muscles are significantly stronger now: their neck muscles are fully supporting their head, and their chest and back muscles are enabling them to sit with support for up to 15 minutes at a time. Babies learn to control the muscles closest to the torso first. For instance, your baby learns to move their arm at the shoulder before they work out how to bend it at the elbow, then at the wrist. Skilful manipulation of the fingers, or fine motor skills, comes last. Now, your baby will probably be reaching out and grabbing an object with both hands. They'll wrap their hands around it, study it, and most likely put it straight into their mouth.

With stronger back and neck muscles, they will love "pony ride" games, such as "Horsey, horsey, don't you stop".

VITAMIN D

Formula milk contains vitamin D, and breastmilk has vitamin D passed on by mums who obtain it through food such as oily fish and fortified cereals, as well as by manufacturing it when their skin is exposed to the sun.

However, babies born to black or Asian parents (dark skin hinders absorption of vitamin D through sunlight) can suffer from lack of vitamin D, and there have been recent concerns that breastfed babies may not be getting enough vitamin D. A lack of vitamin D can cause rickets, which weakens bones.

Current advice is that full-term breastfed babies need vitamin A and D supplements from the age of six months; if the mother's vitamin status was low in pregnancy, supplements should be given from one month.

Full-term formula-fed babies need vitamin A and D supplements when they are over six months and are drinking less than 500ml (16fl oz)of formula a day.

Premature breastfed babies are given supplements from birth; premature formula-fed babies receive vitamins in special formula, but should start supplements once they move to a normal formula. In some areas with a high incidence of vitamin D deficiency, supplements may be advised from birth.

Running commentary

Tell your baby what you're doing and describe what goes on around them to help them connect your words with objects and concepts.

As you go up the stairs, count the steps; count the toys as you put them back in the basket, and count your baby's toes in the bath. Show them the cat's tail and the leaves on the plant. Point out their tummy, eyes, fingers – and yours. Give them the names of all the things around them to be filed away in their brain. Before long they will have the developmental ability to access and use it.

Repetition is by far the best way to cement your baby's learning. If they have heard you count 1, 2, 3, 4 as you climb the stairs dozens of times, they will find counting that much easier when they are older. Every time you dress your baby, give them the names for all of their body parts. You may

find that they start to imitate the basic sounds of the words you use. They won't understand them yet, but they are beginning to associate sounds with objects.

Talking to your baby about what you are doing also helps them to understand how things work, the order of events, and how activities such as cooking, cleaning, and shopping unfold. Tell them what you are preparing for dinner, show them the taps that fill the bathtub, and the light switch on the wall, and demonstrate how it works. Explain what you are doing as you tidy up and put things away. Chat to them about what you are going to do each day, and who you'll see.

Describing emotions

Help develop emotional intelligence, too. You can also describe the emotions you think your baby is feeling: if they are crying, say "sad". If they are laughing, say "happy". Many of their emotions are felt as physical sensations. Make sure that you soothe them when strong feelings are evident to help them learn that you and they can cope with these feelings together.

ASK A CHILD PSYCHOLOGIST

My baby wants to be picked up all the time. Is this normal? Your baby is used to plenty of physical comfort in your arms and still needs that reassurance from you. However, you can begin to teach them that they can cope for a few moments without you holding them. Encourage them to play with their toys – for example, get down on their mat with them, and spend time showing them how things work. Move a short distance away, but come back if they want you, stroke their back, then move away again. Over time, move further away, talking to them as you go, so that they are reassured by your voice. They'll soon realize that, even if you aren't in their immediate vicinity, you are still there and will come when they need you. If they get distressed and you can't pick them up right away, reassure them with your voice. In a soothing tone, tell them you are there: they'll start to cope for longer and need fewer pick-ups.

Learning words Point to your nose and your baby's and say the word "nose". Bring their little hand to your nose, repeating the word. Soon, they will point to it themself when you give them a cue.

Building self-esteem

Even at four months, your baby is building up a self-image that will affect their self-perception and perception of the world for the rest of their life.

The most important way in which you can let your baby know that you value and love them is to respond to their needs as soon as you can. If they are hungry, offer food; if they are cold, wrap them up; if they have a soiled nappy, change it straight away. Come to them when they need a cuddle, and play when they need to play. Overwhelming evidence suggests that babies whose needs are met quickly grow up to become secure and self-assured individuals.

Your baby needs to know that all the minuscule things they learn to do every day are worth celebrating (and, therefore, doing again). When your baby bats the baby gym and makes a sound, cheer in appreciation to reinforce that this is a success. Kisses, cuddles, clapping, and cheering for even seemingly minor achievements let babies know that they are a successful little person who can do things worth celebrating, in turn developing a sense of self-worth.

ASK A HEALTH VISITOR

I need to go back to work. Can I breastfeed part-time? Yes, you can. You may even be able to continue exclusive breastfeeding if you have access to a pump at work and can get your milk home in a cooler. Or substitute formula for the feeds you can't give, and breastfeed your baby outside of your work schedule. Your milk production will adapt as needed. See p.185 for more information on breastfeeding while working.

Playing alone

It's important for your baby's development to learn to occupy themselves for short periods of time and discover ways to entertain themselves.

Babies need moments on their own to gradually understand that they are independent from their caregivers.

Look for occasions when you can place your baby under a baby gym or on a blanket or rug on the floor with some soft toys within easy reach. Leave the baby there for a short time to explore the environment and learn to be alone and amuse themself momentarily. Over a few weeks, try to stretch the amount of time your baby has to themself. Keep watch and read the signals: pick your baby up before they start fussing. For safety, keep your baby within sight – they can just as easily learn to amuse themself while you sit nearby. Being able to sense your presence is likely to make your baby feel happier, and willing to play by themself for a little longer.

Learning to occupy themself paves the way for a much easier toddler, who will be more able to find a toy and play with it without always needing your help or participation.

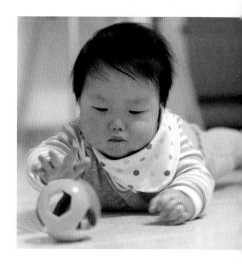

Developing self-sufficiency Give your baby lots of opportunities to play on their own.

Nature versus nurture

Being aware of how your baby's character is shaped by environment as well as by their genes can help you give them the best possible start.

Natural ability Whether your baby seems naturally curious or particularly active, positive interaction with you on a daily basis can help them to thrive and develop new skills.

Nature versus nurture is an age-old debate. Whereas in the past, views tended to be fairly polarized, today it's more widely accepted that it's the interaction of genes and upbringing that determines how we develop. Your baby's environment and everyday care therefore are crucial components in how they interact with you and others, and learn new skills. This is especially true in the early years, as it's thought that the care and stimulation a baby receives can affect brain development. Every primary carers' vital role in a baby's positive development is undisputed.

While your baby's genes may favour certain traits, for example being particularly dextrous, or, say, musical, your baby needs to be in a stimulating and secure environment for these traits to flourish. At this stage, new skills come at a rapid rate, and senses are constantly bombarded with new information. Your job is to help make sense of each new experience and ensure sufficient stimulation without overwhelming. It's thought that positive interaction with your baby on a daily basis actually enhances brain development, and responding to needs will help your baby to thrive. On the other hand, failing to respond to your baby and/or limiting the time you spend interacting can make them feel less secure, and more likely to act out negative character traits.

ASK A CHILD PSYCHOLOGIST

Do girls and boys develop differently in the first year? Boys and girls do have differences in their development but these tend to show as they reach the toddler years onwards. In this first year, if you compare a boy and a girl, you will notice plenty of variation in personality and development, but this is the natural outcome of being two separate individuals, rather than related to their sex at birth.

There is one significant difference between boys and girls in the first year that is useful to know about. Studies have found that boys are more vulnerable to stresses in the family, such as adult conflict and parental depression. Boys are more likely to react to this by being sad or showing withdrawn or aggressive behaviour, compared to girls, who tend to be more resilient and less distressed by it. The reason behind this difference is not clear. If you are depressed or have family tensions, getting help will benefit your children, especially your son, as well as yourself.

While talking to, playing, and interacting with your baby are crucial nurturing skills, it's important, too, to be in tune with your baby's needs, recognizing when they have had enough, and letting your baby develop at their own pace. That way, they will have time to process each new piece of information, and consolidate each new skill with you providing support on cue.

Tooth care

Some time between four and seven months, your baby will cut their first tooth. As soon as they have it, you need to start taking care of it.

Your baby's first tooth might come through any time now, and it will usually be one of the two lower front teeth, which tend to appear first (followed by the upper front teeth). Although baby teeth eventually fall out (a process that usually begins at around six years of age), they are important because they enable your baby to speak and eat (chew) properly. For these reasons, you need to look after them as soon as they appear to avoid infection and promote good dental hygiene habits that will hopefully last throughout your baby's childhood and into adult life.

There is no need to use toothpaste while your baby is so little. Instead, use a little water on a very soft infant toothbrush or piece of clean gauze, and sweep it lightly over the tooth in the morning and evening.

Change your baby's toothbrush or gauze regularly. In addition, avoid allowing your baby to fall asleep with a bottle in their mouth because formula and breastmilk contain sugars that will remain on their teeth all night and can lead to tooth decay. Offer cooled, boiled water as a supplementary drink rather than cordial or diluted fruit juice, which contain high amounts of sugar.

Picking things up

Not too long ago, your baby could only just curl their fingers around objects, but now, at 4 months old, they hold on to them confidently.

While your baby still uses the broad "palmar" grasp, a reflex present from birth that causes them to grasp anything placed in their palm and which remains until around six months of age, they are able to hold on to objects for longer now and shake a toy as they hold it. Offering rattles, cups, and other objects will help your baby develop their handling skills. Blocks are great for learning to pick up and hold.

Developing skill As your baby's grasp develops, they can hold on to objects for longer.

Your baby might love to hold a ball and then release it on the floor and watch it roll away (ensure the ball is too large to fit in their mouth). Many baby balls have specially designed grip holes that the baby can fit their fingers into.

Interestingly, babies at this age are not as competent at letting go of objects as they are at picking them up, and will release something they are holding only when they feel the object is up against a hard surface, such as the floor.

Whatever your baby picks up will end up in their mouth: keep choking hazards well out of reach.

Fun baby classes

From the age of about five months, fun baby classes abound! They are good for your baby and also provide a way to meet other babies and parents.

Have a look online or in local magazines to see what's happening in your area. While some can be expensive, others, such as those at the local library, are often free of charge. Among frequent offerings are:

Baby gymnastics

From four – and certainly six – months classes are designed to build up babies' core body strength, using exercises such as forward rolls.

Sensory development

This aims to give babies a wide range of visual, auditory, and tactile experiences to encourage learning. Fibre-optic light shows, bubbles, bells, musical fun, baby signing, and puppet shows are among the attractions on offer. With so much variety, these classes might be good for babies who are easily bored!

Music

There are lots of courses aimed at introducing young babies to music, most of which involve singing songs and nursery rhymes, dancing, and playing percussion instruments. Babies do enjoy listening to new sounds but at this age, they have a short attention span, so parents might enjoy them more than baby.

Baby yoga

Yoga classes are said to be great for helping babies to sleep. A typical session involves stretching and movements such as swinging, rolling, and lifting that will all help strengthen a baby's muscle tone and encourage coordinatio and flexibility. Some classes enable parents and babies to exercise together.

DEVELOPMENT ACTIVITY: UP AND DOWN

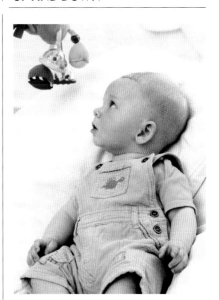

Vertical tracking Being able to watch an object as it moves up and down is a skill that develops after horizontal tracking.

Your baby is now able to follow objects with their eyes as they move vertically. To hone this ability, move a brightly coloured toy up and down in front of them. Hold the toy still to begin with, until you see them focus on it, then slowly move it down, watching their eyes as they track the movement. Once you have reached the bottom of your baby's field of vision, slowly move the object back up again. Describe what you are doing as you go. Move slowly at first, so that their eyes have a chance to keep up with the object.

POSTNATAL DEPRESSION IN MEN

While postnatal depression (PND) in women is well documented, it's less well known that around one in 10 men suffers depression after the birth of a baby. Although the hormonal triggers are not present for men, many of the other triggers that contribute to PND in women are relevant, such as sleep deprivation, isolation, and changes in their relationship. In men, these factors can be compounded by additional financial responsibilities, and worries about combining the demands of work and fatherhood. Dads may also feel resentful if partners, maybe unwittingly, undermine their babycare skills. Symptoms can include exhaustion, anxiety, irritability, poor concentration and appetite, and worries about the future. As with women, it's important for men to seek professional help from their GP if feelings persist, and to talk to amily and friends about their feelings.

Milk matters

If your bottle-fed baby seems ravenous all the time now, you might consider using a formula specially designed for hungry babies.

First-stage formula is specially designed to reflect the composition of breastmilk closely and be easily digestible. It's fine for your baby to stay on this formula for the entire first year. However, if your baby is no longer satisfied after a feed, even when you've offered some more, you may want to consider using a special "hungry baby" formula, which contains more casein than normal formula, making it less easy to digest and supposedly keeps your baby feeling fuller for longer, even though the calorific content is the same. Ask your health visitor for advice before changing, but if you do change, follow the manufacturer's instructions exactly. Be aware, too, that the transition may cause constipation. In that case, offer some boiled, cooled water in addition to the usual feeds.

FLU JABS

In most cases, babies do not need to be vaccinated against seasonal flu, but it may be recommended that your baby has a flu jab when outbreaks of virulent strains occur, if your baby is over six months old. Babies with heart or lung disease should be vaccinated as a matter of course once they are over six months.

Action rhymes

Action rhymes provide a fun way in which to enhance your baby's coordination, memory, language – and even social – skills.

Singing to your baby helps them to identify different sounds, timbres, pitches, and patterns of language, and engages them in a way that speech may not. "Incy wincy spider", "Round and round the garden", "If you're happy and you know it", and "This little piggy" all encourage singing along and practising the actions. Show your baby how to move their hands in time, and repeat the rhymes to help with memory.

Rhyme time Get a friend or relative to recite a favourite rhyme – it's familiar to your baby, but also novel because someone else is doing it.

Making sense of sounds

Your baby is now able to make connections in their brain between what they see and what they hear. They're recognizing more sounds every day.

Your baby is now making and becoming familiar with more sounds. They are accustomed to the noise of the rattle, the sound of your voice, and the creak of the door opening and shutting. They are also beginning to associate objects and sounds, and the ability to anticipate is just emerging: they may respond with squeals when they hear your voice as they know your arrival will follow.

Your baby's hearing has been good since birth, but they may have now made the leap to processing what they hear and linking it to what they know about their world in a more complex way. They may expect you to sing "Pat-a-cake" when you set them up for their clapping game, because they have learned to associate this song with the movements that always accompany it, and may be surprised if you clap but don't sing to them when they're expecting to hear the familiar words. They will also watch your tongue and lips intently now as you speak: they are starting to link the sounds you make with the movement they see in your lips. Let them see your face when you talk to them and sing to them to encourage this skill.

While loud or sudden noises may distress your baby, they will be soothed by familiar sounds, so you can calm them in bustling, noisy environments they find disturbing by quietly singing a familiar song; they will be able to focus on your voice and relax more easily. It is likely that your

DEVELOPMENT ACTIVITY: ANIMAL NOISES

Nothing fascinates a baby more than unusual sounds, and animal noises are ideal for stimulating your baby and helping them to understand that different animals make different sounds. Show them pictures in a book and explain that the cow goes "mooo", the sheep says "baaa", the chicken says "cluck", and so on. Exaggerate your voice and let them see your lips so that they can see how you shape your mouth to form sounds. Point to the picture of the animal – or show them a plastic or soft-toy version – so that they make the association. While your baby won't repeat animal noises until they're into their first year, they will have fun listening and learning in these early months.

Seeing and listening As you mimic the sound of an animal, show your baby a toy or picture of that animal, so they can make the association between the animal and the sound it makes.

baby associates their favourite lullaby with rocking, so if you wish to calm them by singing them the familiar lullaby, you'll need to rock them, too.

Interestingly, recent subtle changes in their hearing mean that your baby also understands more about the tone of your voice. When you are happy, your baby will respond in kind; if you are stressed, they will pick up on this and may become anxious. Using positive body language – turning to face them and making plenty of eye contact when you talk to them – will enhance your communication.

Bundle of laughs

First your baby got the giggles – now they're really game for a laugh. The simplest of things can make a baby chuckle over and over again!

Pop-up toys, silly faces, gentle tickles under the chin or arms, and hiding your face behind your hands before revealing yourself with a "boo" may well invoke a fit of laughter. Your baby is just gaining the cognitive ability to anticipate what happens after a certain event. As this ability emerges, your baby may, for example, laugh the moment you put your hands over your eyes, or when you press down on their pop-up toy.

Fun and laughter Incorporate fun into your daily routine so that your baby has plenty of opportunity to enjoy laughter with you.

This marks a key developmental milestone that shows your baby's socialization and language skills are developing. They have learned to communicate by crying, cooing, and grunting, and are now learning to interact by giggling and laughing. Sometimes the best distraction for a grizzly baby is to bring out a silly hat or pop a favourite toy out from a blanket and play peek-a-boo.

Laughing produces chemicals in your baby's brain that will make them feel happy and secure.

Falling asleep on their own

If your baby is used to being rocked to sleep, or to being picked up during a night waking, you'll need to teach them how to go to sleep on their own.

Encouraging your baby to get back to sleep without you there will help them quickly drift back off by themself whenever they wake and, therefore, have a better sleep.

This does not mean you should leave your baby to cry, rather that you should try to put them down while still awake, allowing them to begin to associate the cot with falling asleep.

Lay your baby down snugly after their feed or story. Dim the lights and

offer a soothing hand on their back. Say goodnight in a calm voice, or choose a phrase you will always use to settle your baby so they learn to associate "sleep tight", say, with sleep. Leave the room and see how your baby gets on. If they resist, return and stroke them again, speaking gently to reassure that you are there. Come to your baby every time they call, but, if possible, try to comfort them without picking them up and rocking them to

sleep. Eventually, they'll get the message that it is safe to sleep, secure in the knowledge that you will come when they need you. However, if your baby really isn't settling and simply continues crying, then do pick them up for a reassuring cuddle before settling them back down.

If your baby cries each night having previously been easy to settle, they may be in pain or unwell. Consult the GP or health visitor.

Nappy leaks

A leak every so often is to be expected, but if you're mopping up on a regular basis, you might need a different nappy.

Leaking nappies are a rite of passage for all parents. But, if leaks happen all the time, you need to investigate.

First, check that your baby is wearing the right size of nappy. Nappies are sized by weights, but these do overlap and vary between brands, so you may need to experiment. The right nappy should fit well around your baby's legs, without digging into the flesh, and fit snugly around the waist with no ruching or gaps. If the nappy is leaking urine, try going down a size; if poo is the problem, the nappy is probably too small.

Second, check that you're changing your baby's nappy frequently enough – about every two-and-half hours during the day now. However, if your baby looks uncomfortable or the nappy feels full, change it more regularly. Change a poo-y nappy immediately so that the acid in poo doesn't harm the baby's delicate skin.

Your baby's bladder is larger now, so it can hold a lot of urine and, as a result, your baby will urinate regularly in the night. If your baby is waking with a soaked sleepsuit and bedclothes, you could try adding a booster pad to the nappy (disposable or reusable) to absorb the excess urine. Alternatively, you could try using ultra-absorbent "night-time" nappies. Also, if you use disposables, it may be worth trying another brand, if only just for use during the night-time, to see if it prevents leaks more successfully.

ASK A DOCTOR

My baby has diarrhoea. What can I do? Diarrhoea in babies can have a number of causes, the most common being gastroenteritis and, less often, milk intolerance. It can also be a temporary problem after antibiotics. Diarrhoea can be dangerous in babies, quickly causing dehydration. See your GP or health visitor if your baby has a few loose stools in a day, especially if they vomit or refuse feeds, have a fever, are floppy, sleepy, or pass blood in their stools. Your GP will decide on the best treatment and whether they need a stay in hospital if dehydrated. Meanwhile, breastfeed on demand, and offer cooled, boiled water if they are bottle-feeding: it's important that they get as much fluid as possible.

My baby coughs a lot in the night – what should I do? The most common cause of a cough is a cold. Secretions from the mouth trickle down the back of the throat, causing irritation and a cough. Raising the head of their mattress a little may bring relief. Another cause of a recurrent cough that is often worse at night is narrowing of the airways caused by an infection such as bronchiolitis. Some babies need a short stay in hospital to help their breathing. See your GP if your baby struggles for breath, is off feeds, has a fever, is sleepy, unwell, or coughs for over a week. Follow your instincts, too: if you are worried, take your baby to the GP.

The right size As your baby grows and requires progressively larger nappy sizes, ensure their nappy fits them snugly around the leg and waist, without either ruching or digging into their flesh.

Your baby and infections

Babies do fall ill, but symptoms are a sign that your baby's immune system has kicked into action, and is fighting the infection.

It's normal for babies to become more prone to infections in the first year as the immunity they gained in the womb wears off. Breastfed babies have immunity for longer from the antibodies in breastmilk. Babies' own immune systems are immature at birth and develop over the first year. Try not to worry if your baby seems to catch one infection after another. As long as your baby continues to gain weight, is happy, content, well between illnesses, and developing as expected, they should be fine. With every infection, your baby's immune system becomes more mature and efficient and, in future, will be far better at quickly fending off low-level illness. If you're concerned, though, talk to your GP or health visitor.

The very best way to prevent illnesses is to avoid large groups of people, and to ensure that all family members and friends wash their hands before play. Also, don't smoke, and don't allow anyone else to smoke near your baby.

If you are breastfeeding, continue to do so as normal while your baby is ill. Breastmilk boosts your baby's immunity while providing them with your own antibodies.

Restful sleep is also important for a strong immune system, so don't be tempted to skip the naps or keep the baby up too late; your baby still needs at least 15 hours of sleep in every 24-hour period. Finally, when your baby begins solids, make sure that

Signs of illness Disruption in your baby's usual patterns of feeding, sleeping, and responses will alert you to any changes in their state of health.

everything you give is fresh, healthy, and nutritious. You'll be giving only little tastes at the outset, but every vitamin and mineral will contribute to overall health and wellbeing.

Seeking advice

If you think your baby is ill or you are unsure about how to care for them, consult your GP or health visitor first. If the baby stops feeding, develops a rash, or has a fever, do not delay in seeking help as babies can deteriorate quickly.

IS MY BABY ILL?

Babies who are inexplicably tearful, more tired and clingy than usual, fractious, not smiling or playing, and experiencing a change in feeding patterns (for example, appearing uninterested in their feeds, or feeding poorly) may be ill. Being aware of the signs of illness will ensure you respond promptly and seek help if needed.

Obvious signs include:
• A fever (over 39°C / 102.2°F)
• Diarrhoea or vomiting
• A rash or spots, or bruises
• Pale, clammy, or mottled skin
• A weak or high-pitched cry
• Being unusually quiet
• Blood in the stools

Less obvious signs include:
• Unusually long sleeps
• Not sleeping
• Failure of your baby to smile when they normally do
• Irritability or clinginess
• Excessive drooling

Always seek medical help immediately if your baby:
• Develops breathing problems
• Has a convulsion
• Seems blue around the mouth
• Feels floppy or limp
• Has a bulging or depressed fontanelle

Pelvic floor exercises

In the busy schedule of caring for a baby, many new mothers let their pelvic floor health slip – but it's worth keeping these important muscles in shape.

Strengthening your pelvic floor (see p.65) and increasing your abdominal exercises will stand you in good stead. Carrying even the smallest baby for long periods can strain your back and cause discomfort, but you are less likely to suffer if your core is strong.

If you haven't exercised yet, it's not too late to start – they will not only help to improve your posture and reduce niggling back pain, but will also improve your circulation and help your pelvis "knit" back together where it joins at the front. Your ligaments, including those in your pelvis, became more elastic during pregnancy to allow for birth, and regular exercise is necessary to bring your core muscles back in line.

Pelvic floor exercises practised every day will strengthen the muscles supporting your womb and bladder. This will get you back in shape for subsequent pregnancies, and help to prevent urine leaking when you laugh or cough. There's no time limit on how long you should continue these exercises; in fact, it's worth carrying on with them indefinitely.

Continue to practise your pelvic tilts, to help strengthen your abdominals. Sucking in your tummy and holding for a few seconds will help to flatten it and encourage correct posture – which helps to avoid back pain. Aim to perform pelvic tilts 8–10 times once or twice a day – perhaps while your baby is occupied under their baby gym.

Touch and feel

Your baby's senses are continuing to develop. The sense of touch, in particular, teaches babies a great deal about their environment.

Show your baby how to stroke their soft toys, feel the crunch and crackle of scrunched-up paper, and experience warm water running through their fingers. Books, play mats, and toys with different textures come into their own at this age. Let your baby roll in the grass, and feel the texture of the carpet or their soft blanket. Use words to describe what they're feeling: soft, rough, hard, smooth, and so on. This helps your baby to learn more about their world.

Stimulating your baby's sense of touch can improve curiosity, memory, nervous system development, and attention span. They'll also develop confidence in unfamiliar situations, as their curiosity rather than their fear is piqued by the things they can feel around them. Soon, they'll be introduced to solid food – a whole new world of textures. If they've had experience of textures in the lead-up to this, they'll feel less daunted by a squishy avocado or a dry rusk.

Water play Wash your baby's hand under a running tap. They'll enjoy the feel of water flowing through their fingers.

Taking a tumble

No matter how careful you are, accidents can and do happen. Try not to worry where minor tumbles occur, though – babies are remarkably resilient.

No matter how minor, most parents feel mortified when their babies take a tumble, and suffer paroxysms of guilt and anxiety over what harm the baby may have come to.

However, fortunately, most babies emerge from minor incidents almost entirely unscathed. So, while not down-playing the importance of keeping your rolling baby safe at all times, and being mindful when you hold or carry them, try not to feel too

Kiss it better A comforting cuddle and plenty of kisses will help your baby get over the upset of a minor accident more quickly.

anxious if your baby has a small fall or knock. If they cry right away, or almost right away, all is likely to be well, especially if they smile soon afterwards and calm down quickly.

However, do get medical advice if your baby has a sizeable bump after a fall, especially if the bump is on the head, or if they have trouble moving a limb or they have significant bruising.

If your baby vomits or becomes unusually sleepy, or you have any other concerns about the severity of the fall, consult a doctor urgently (in the UK, you can call 111 for instant medical help and advice).

A parenting team

Adopt a team mentality to tackle the sink full of dirty dishes, towering laundry pile, and caring for your baby's every need.

The simple truth is that you and your partner are probably never going to see eye to eye on every parenting issue or household responsibility. Try to develop a strategy that gives you both an opportunity to shine at the things you like and are good at, and allows relaxation time for all.

Different parenting styles are not grounds for a clash. Everything that you and your partner bring to the team will provide important gifts and

opportunities for your baby. Avoid criticizing each other – there is no single "right" way to raise and care for a baby. Respect and celebrate your differences and be prepared to compromise from time to time.

Attack that to-do list together. Make a list of everything that has to be done around the house and to care for your baby. What do you enjoy? What jobs does your partner enjoy? What does each of you loathe? Where

you're both vying for the good stuff and trying to shake off the unenjoyable, agree to take turns or split the good, bad, and indifferent equally between you. There are always compromises, as long as you are willing to communicate and plan. Resolve these issues now to avoid any build-up of frustration, which could affect your relationship. As a team, you can give your baby the best possible home life.

Body language

Until your baby is able to communicate verbally, you can rely upon their body movements to work out what they're trying to tell you.

With every day that goes by, you and your baby are getting to know each other a little better, and not only is their body language becoming clearer to you, you are getting better at interpreting it, too. Learning to read your baby's cues (see p.118) can be an invaluable method of anticipating their mood changes and diverting their attention before they enter a meltdown stage.

Yes, I am bothered

Babies can get annoyed and frustrated just as much as adults can. They may narrow their eyes, lower their eyebrows, and grimace or purse their lips into a square shape. If your baby's facial expression seems to darken, think about what may be bothering them. You may be offering the wrong set of toys or playing the wrong game; equally, they may think that it is not the right time for a nappy change or to undress for a bath. A little distraction and the usual tricks that make them laugh should be enough to ease them gently out of their strop.

Babies also sometimes wrinkle their noses to show an aversion. They may not want that silly rattle game again; they may not want to be held by someone unfamiliar; they may not want what you just had for lunch via their breastmilk. Watch their nose!

If they arch their back and flex their fingers and toes, with their eyes open wide, they may be in pain. Wind them to see if trapped air is the culprit. Or, if they're bottle-fed, think about their last bowel movement – it's possible that they could be constipated (see pp.371–72).

Party on or party over?

If your baby is purposefully averting your gaze, fidgeting, and turning their head away when you are playing, they may simply need time away from stimulation and interaction and are ready for a break. This is a good moment to try a quieter activity to help them unwind: pop them into their cot under a mobile, or on the floor under their baby gym, and let them have a little "alone time". You may also notice that they cover their eyes with their hands, which is their way of avoiding excess stimulation and loud noises.

If they're kicking up a storm, however, and breathing rapidly, they're probably excited and happy, and boisterous games and tickle time will definitely be appreciated! Similarly, if their hands are clasped at the front of their chest, they are ready for playtime.

DEVELOPMENT ACTIVITY: DO WHAT I DO

Your baby is a natural mimic and will learn emotional expression and control of the face, mouth, and tongue muscles by copying what you do. Stick out your tongue at them, then put it back in slowly. Repeat, and watch them try to do the same. Make sure you applaud their efforts – they may not even know they've succeeded. Open your eyes wide and make a funny face. Continue to repeat it until you see that they're trying it, too. Your baby will soon start this game on their own when they settle down to play with you.

Copy-cat Make faces and expressions and watch as your baby tries to copy them.

5 months

BABIES WILL COPY FACIAL EXPRESSIONS, WHICH HELPS THEM TO LEARN HOW TO EXPRESS EMOTIONS.
Learn to read your baby's signals for when they are up for noisy toys and physical play and when they are more in the mood for a quiet "chat" with plenty of smiles and eye contact. Getting to know their body language will help you to understand what they're in the mood for.

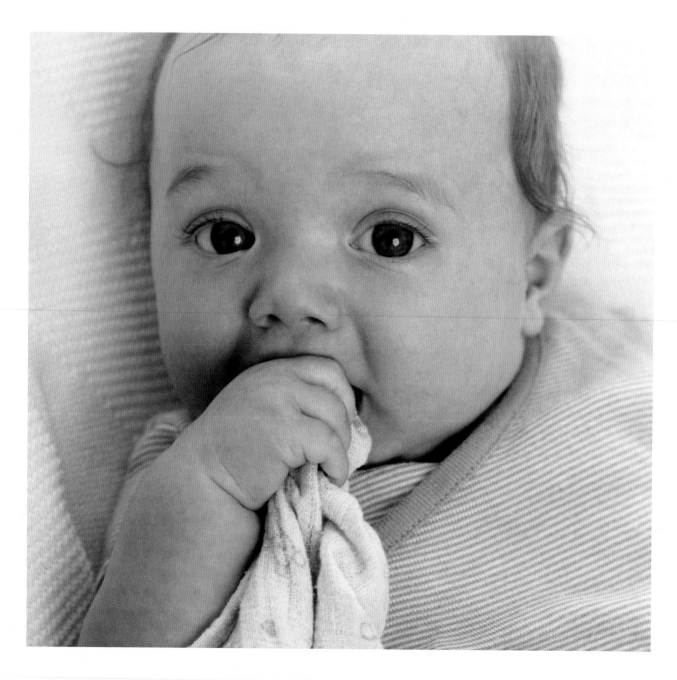

Competitive parenting

Child-rearing isn't a competitive sport even if some parents treat it that way. All babies grow and advance at the right pace for them.

Enjoying groups Being with other parents and babies can be valuable for you and your baby, so long as you don't take it to heart if another baby sleeps for longer or reaches a milestone earlier.

PREMATURE BABIES AND TWINS

Consider your premature baby's corrected age when reviewing whether or not they are meeting milestones at appropriate times. Little ones who had an early start can take much longer to catch up, but that doesn't mean they don't! In the vast majority of cases, premature babies catch up by school age, and go on to succeed at the same level as their peers.

Similarly, try not to compare your twins to one another; it's common for one twin to leap ahead a little on the developmental front, which is the legacy of sharing resources and space in the womb. Again, celebrate their unique characteristics, personalities, and achievements, and give each of them the support they need to be the best they can be at the time that is right for them.

Individuals It's easy to forget that twins pick up skills at different rates. Enjoy their individual achievements.

Being with other parents whose babies are a similar age provides an opportunity to socialize and access to support. However, occasionally, a hint of competitive parenting emerges. It is natural to talk about and compare milestones, and positive for a parent to be proud of their own child, but watch out if there are suggestions of superiority if one baby is a little ahead of the others. Avoid being drawn in – remember that your baby will develop in their own time. Choose friends well, disassociating from those who undermine your confidence. If, though, you are worried about your own baby's milestones and if there is a clear, consistent difference between your baby and others the same age, seek professional advice. For the small number of babies whose development is delayed, early help is most effective.

Your baby is unique; they will develop, learn, and grow at a rate that is right for them, and shine in some areas more than others. Moreover, early crawlers or talkers don't necessarily go on to be "early" achievers. Celebrate your baby's individuality and personal milestones at their unique pace.

Are you listening carefully?

By five months, your baby may be using sounds to try to tell you something. You simply need to figure out what it is!

It's common for babies to create their own sound vocabulary in advance of proper words. Sometimes your baby might be experimenting with sounds by copying. For example, if you always say "Gooood baby" when changing their nappy, they may start to make an "oooo" sound when they're being changed. At other times, they may use a sound to say that they're tired: grunting is common, as is a slightly whiney, grizzling sound. They may try to let you know they are hungry by smacking their lips and plaintively "babbling" while trying to manoeuvre themselves into a feeding position. If they're in the mood for fun, they may coo, gurgle, or squeal. Throughout, it is important to respond by listening, replying, and seeing to their needs.

Getting the message

As well as the different sounds your baby makes, their tone and body language will also give clues. When you respond to them quickly and "read" their sounds, expressions, and movement, they know that you understand. Respond with words of your own and wait for them to react: they are learning the turn-taking and listening skills vital to conversation. Listen to their babbles and you will hear sounds repeated over and over: respond and encourage, and they will want to communicate all the more.

If sometimes it's hard to work out what your baby is communicating, look at their body language, follow their gaze, and point at things they might want, then watch. If you've got it right, you are bound to get a smile of appreciation. Name objects, activities, and feelings. You are filling your baby's memory with words to retrieve when their verbal skills develop. These first conversations are an important step in their cognitive and speech development, and, as they reach the 12-month mark, you'll be rewarded with their first words.

10 GOOD THINGS ABOUT BEING A PARENT

When you're feeling exhausted, remind yourself of some of the reasons why being a parent is so fantastic!

• The immense pride you feel at having created a life from a single moment.

• That lurching feeling when your baby first returns your smile.

• Reliving your own childhood. Even while they're so young, it's exciting to anticipate all the things you can share.

• The realization that this is forever – scary, but amazing too! Putting another's needs first is liberating.

• That intoxicating baby smell, and those incredible cuddles!

• Looking at things as though for the first time through your baby's eyes.

• Rediscovering the art of giggling – you never realized how infectious your baby's giggles could be!

• Enjoying a new sense of closeness with your partner.

• Watching your parents fall in love with your baby, too.

• The first time your baby says "mama" or "dada" – that's you!

Baby love Raspberries, gurgles, and giggles – a baby's endearing attempts to communicate are enough to melt any grown-up heart, but particularly that of a parent.

Daytime play

The more your baby enjoys playtimes during the day, the more they'll learn and the stronger your bond will become.

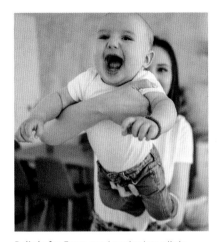

Built-in fun Every good routine has a little time set aside for playing together.

Daytime play sessions. expend some of your baby's exuberant energy, and encourage them to use their muscles, practise coordination, and increase awareness of how their limbs move. They also provide opportunity for learning in a relaxed, fun way. Plus, they nourish and support your bond.

Your baby will anticipate your play times with pleasure. Think of different ways to keep them entertained and stimulate or challenge them a little; for example, you could sway and dance with them in your arms, hold toys out for them to bat or kick, or blow bubbles for

them to swipe at (make sure they don't pop in their face). Try giving them some different smells to sniff – rubbing a little cinnamon spice or lavender on your hand, for example.

Keeping playtime fun and upbeat is important, as they will learn best in a calm, happy environment. Some parents worry that their baby is not reaching developmental milestones as quickly as others, and usc playtime to push them to achieve skills before they are ready. Avoid falling into that trap. Play should be about stimulation and fun in a supportive environment.

Your baby's role models

Adults are not just your baby's first caregivers, but also role models who set an example and teach positive lessons for life.

As a parent, you (and your partner, if you have one) are already sensitive to your baby's needs, providing both the day-to-day care and the love that is the cornerstone to healthy emotional development. In addition, the other adults in your baby's life – their grandparents, aunts, uncles, cousins, godparents, and close family friends – provide extra role models.

While it may seem too early to be setting a good example for your baby,

they are learning all the time, so it's important to start demonstrating now all the qualities you want to see in them as they grow up. All of the adults in your baby's life can teach them fundamental qualities such as empathy, good manners, fostering a positive outlook, responsibility, and healthy social interaction. Your baby will observe positive characteristics and, eventually, copy these and use them in their own life.

Your baby is learning all the time, and absorbs most about their world – and how to interact within it – from the people around them. Supplying them with strong, responsible, and loving role models will give them a series of influences that will guide them through childhood and into adulthood in the most empathetic ways possible, as well as providing a support network they can trust.

Daytime naps

Some babies may be ready to drop a nap now – probably the late-afternoon one – while others continue happily with three naps a day.

Your baby still needs around 15 hours of sleep in every 24, broken into naps during the day and including a longer night-time sleep. At this stage, they may well be ready to have two longer naps during the day, rather than three or four short ones. They're probably going longer between feeds, too, which means that naps can last a little longer. Often, the late-afternoon nap is first to go, and babies of this age often manage well on a mid-morning nap followed by a longer sleep after lunch. However, babies are naturally more playful at this age, so don't assume that your baby is ready to drop the nap just because they're harder to settle. They may need a pre-nap routine to encourage sleep. If your baby is not really sleeping, but playing, they probably don't need to be asleep. There's no reason why they can't spend some quiet time in their cot – a little solo play will relax them and give them (and you) a break.

When you first drop a nap, it may be a struggle to reach bedtime without your baby dozing off. Push bedtime forwards by half an hour or so, until your baby adjusts.

Receiving affection

At this age, your baby loves attention from you – but is also learning how to return your love and affection. Enjoy!

The simple exchange of physical affection between you and your baby is a potent way to express your relationship. At first, affection is largely one way as you offer cuddles, hugs, massage, and stroking. Now, though, as your baby gains control over their body, they will respond. Give and take will begin as they put their arms around your neck when you hold them, or squeal in delight when you tickle them. Very soon, they will reach out their arms to invite you to pick them up or give them a hug.

Reaching out Your baby loves to be held close and will begin to reach out for you – if you're wearing jewellery, they might want that, too!

This early gesture is important in their developing ability to communicate. Responding to their gesture shows them that they have successfully communicated their need, and will encourage them to continue communicating with you.

Your baby also displays affection when they snuggle into your body, and, in turn, feels safe when you hold them against you. Support their head and let them nestle into your shoulder, which allows them to take a good look at their world from the security of your arms. Keep interacting with your baby positively, giving them plenty of attention and responsive communication.

Using their initiative

Your baby needs brief periods each day for experimentation on their own to play without your direction and explore at their own pace.

It is certainly time to give your baby brief periods when they can play unaided. Your role is to make their toys available, whether attached to their buggy, or beside them on their rug, then supervise, but don't interfere for a few minutes. Solo play allows your baby to direct their attention without prompts, so that they can spend as little or as much time as they want feeling, mouthing, and watching their toys or mobiles. This should not be their main form of play, however, as they gain most when you talk to them about their world, and play and interact together.

When they do play on their own, set them up so that they are either well supported by cushions, lying on their back on the rug, or securely strapped into their buggy or bouncy chair. Place a selection of toys within reach, but not so many as to overwhelm them. They may enjoy a basket of small, easy-to-grasp, noisy toys so they can grip them and explore texture and sound as well as bring them to their mouth. Provide toys that they can work themself, such as pop-up toys and fixed items, such as those on a baby gym, that won't roll out of reach and frustrate them.

When they play without your intervention, they'll keep trying to reach their goal, whether kicking upwards to hit a toy dangling from their play gym, or pressing buttons on a buggy toy. They may try a bit longer when you aren't there, but they can also get frustrated, so do intervene if they need you. If they become distressed or get into an awkward position, be ready to help out. Solo playtimes should be brief, and you need to be nearby and attentive, even though you are not involved.

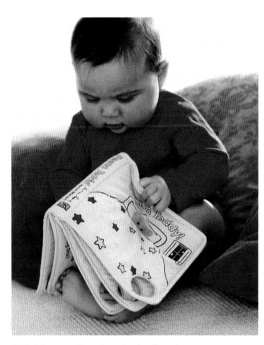

Satisfying toys To make solo play fun, give your baby toys that are easy to use, such as textured fabric books that squeak easily.

SETTLE AN OVERSTIMULATED BABY

It's important to help your overstimulated baby gain some peace when they need to have the volume on life turned down. You'll have to follow their lead to work out what they need in order to settle them. Sometimes "alone time" can be just the thing. Try lying them in their cot on their back. Turn on their mobile and let them watch it go round, or put a few easy-to-manage (or chew) books in their cot and let them lie quietly.

Alternatively, your baby may need some comfort. Hold them on your lap and sing their favourite night-time song or recite a familiar rhyme that has calming associations. Speak quietly and stroke their back. Physical touch has a calming impact on their nervous system, so a gentle touch is always soothing.

Babies who are overstimulated often respond positively to a cool, dark environment. Pull down the blinds and turn down the heating, open a window, or undress them a little to help them cool down (but keep checking them as they can quickly become too cold).

Your baby's first foods

So you've decided that the time is right to start your baby on solids. Going about it the right way from day one will help make the experience more enjoyable for you and your baby and encourage them to try new flavours.

Choose a time when your baby is alert and not too hungry. About an hour or so after a feed is usually a good time to start. Put the baby in the high chair or bouncy chair, and have everything prepared well so that the baby doesn't need to wait. The purée should be lukewarm – test a little on the inside of your wrist, as with milk.

New flavours Choose healthy and tasty foods for your baby, using a hand-blender or food processor to purée them.

Offer the spoon

Use a spoon to scoop up a little purée and, coming from the side, put the spoon against your baby's lips. If they open their mouth, gently insert the spoon. In the beginning, your baby will "suck" the food from the spoon, rather than use their lips to remove it. Hold it there until it's gone; if the baby doesn't do this, gently scrape the spoon against the upper gums so that the purée is left in the baby's mouth. Your baby may look a bit shocked, or spit the food out again. (If spitting happens repeatedly, your baby may not have lost the "extrusion" reflex, in which case you may have to wait a couple of weeks and try again.) If your baby doesn't open their mouth, rub a little purée on their lips. Their tongue will eventually appear to lick it up.

Clear up any purée on your baby's chin with the spoon and scoop it back into their mouth. Then start with a fresh spoonful. Most babies will only have one or two spoonfuls on the first few occasions, so be patient. If your baby seems reluctant, stop.

Sociable mealtimes

Talk to your baby as you offer the spoon, and open your own mouth to show what to do. You may even take a taste from a different spoon to make it clear that it's delicious. Let your baby play with the food – this is part of the process of learning to eat. Your baby may dip in their fingers and suck them, or try to scoop up some of the food and eat it themselves.

At the outset, offer your baby just a spoonful or two per day, usually in one sitting. Offer a new food every day or so. If your baby doesn't like something, introduce it again a little later. For more information on how to progress, see pp.216–17.

Baby-led weaning

Over the past 15 years, this approach has become increasingly popular. From the age of six months, babies are

GOOD BEGINNINGS

All babies start with fruit and vegetable purées, as well as a little cereal, such as baby rice, which can be mixed with their usual milk. Start with vegetables – babies who begin on fruits tend to develop a sweet tooth and then later resist anything more savoury. Try a variety of vegetables of different colours – orange, red, white.

• **Vegetable purées:** Potato, carrot, butternut squash, parsnips, swede, pumpkin, sweet potato, spinach, broccoli.
• **Fruit purées:** Apple, pear, banana, peach, nectarine, mango, papaya.
• **Baby rice or millet:** (Can contain gluten, introduce after four months).

• **Consistency:** First purées should be liquid, then gradually thicken them as they get used to puréed food.
• **How often to feed:** Once a day for the first week or two if weaning earlier than six months, or for the first few days if after six months.
• **Best time to do it:** After a milk feed so your baby is calm and not ravenous.
• **How much to feed:** 1–2 tsp at first; you can give more once your baby becomes accustomed to purées and if they want more (see pp.216–17).

encouraged to feed themselves. To date, there is little empirical evidence to support this method and more research is needed to assess its impact on babies' nutrient and energy uptake, and on their eating behaviour and weight.

Keeping a food diary

Keep a note of every new food you introduce, when you introduce it, and any reactions your baby has. Introduce new foods in the morning or at lunchtime, as this makes it easier to monitor your baby's reaction to it.during the rest of the day.

HOW TO MAKE PURÉES

To make first purées, steam your chosen vegetable or fruit until it is soft. (Vegetables such as carrots can be boiled, or cooked in the microwave.) Use either a tiered steamer pan, or a steamer basket that fits in a regular pan. (Some purées, such as ones made with very ripe peach, papaya, mango, and banana, don't need to be cooked.)

You can purée a large batch of baby food in a food processor, or use a small bowl attachment for little amounts. Alternatively, use a hand-blender or food grinder (mouli) to achieve the correct consistency. First foods should be semi-liquid and almost milk-like in consistency to make them easy to swallow. You can add your baby's usual milk or a little cooled, boiled tap water to thin purées if they are too thick.

Prepare batches of purées, then chill them straight away, and freeze them in portion-sized, freezer-safe containers. Ice-cube trays produce ideal baby-sized portions. Batch cooking helps you give your baby a variety of tastes every day, and provides you with a series of great stand-by purées when you're busy. To preserve nutrient content, cover ice-cube trays or freezer pots. Fill them almost to the top and put them in a freezer at -18 °C (-0.4 °F) or below within 24 hours. You can keep purées in the freezer for up to a month.

Light steaming Peel and dice your chosen vegetable and put it in a steamer basket inside a pan containing a little boiling water, or in a tiered steamer pan, and steam until the dice are soft (above). **Puréeing** Put the steamed dice in a bowl to cool, then blend with a hand-blender, food processor, or mouli to achieve the correct consistency (top, right). **Freezing** Divide the purée into portion-sized containers, cover, label with the date and contents, then freeze (right).

Can I give my baby fruit juice to start off the weaning process? No. Bottle- and breastfed babies do not need juice before they begin eating solids. Until one year of age, their main drink should be their normal milk or plain water. Drinking juice won't help them to learn to chew while swallowing, nor will it help in the development of the jaw and tongue muscles. Furthermore, juice offered in a bottle can damage a baby's emerging teeth as it "swirls" round their mouth before being swallowed. If you do offer juice after your baby has begun to eat solids, ensure you dilute it to a ratio of 1:10 parts water to reduce the natural sugar levels, and offer it in a cup.

Is there anything my baby shouldn't eat under the age of six months? While official advice has been to avoid gluten and other potentially allergenic foods before six months, the British Dietetic Association recently updated its advice based on evidence that introducing gluten between four and seven months while breastfeeding can reduce the risk of coeliac disease, type 1 diabetes, and wheat allergy. Also, they state that if you are breastfeeding, high-allergen foods such as egg, fish, and dairy products do not need to be delayed until after six months as there is no evidence that this reduces allergies. (See p.217 for foods to avoid under a year.)

Can I reheat purées in the microwave? Yes – but do stir it carefully before serving as it may have hot spots. You can also use the microwave to defrost foods. Defrost thoroughly, then heat them well in a little boiled water and allow to cool to the right temperature.

Safe rolling

Some five-month-old babies can roll – often at speed – right across the room. Now is the time to babyproof your home!

If your baby can roll themselves along the floor, you might be surprised at how much ground they can cover within just a few seconds. Make sure there is nothing that could harm them along the way.

Most importantly, check your floors and remove anything that you don't want them to put in their mouth. Also, remove anything that, if grabbed, could cause something to topple over and hurt them, such as loose wires attached to lamps. Your baby's perspective is much lower than yours – get down on your tummy to see what dangers lurk beneath sofas. Keep an eye out for small toys older children may leave lying around.

When you change your baby's nappy, dry them after a bath, or get them dressed, do so on the floor so they can't roll off an edge. If you have no choice but to put them on a raised surface (say, when using a changing table in a public bathroom), keep one hand on them at all times.

ASK A HEALTH VISITOR

Do I need to sterilize my baby's toys?
Bottles, teats, and dummies should be sterilized, and some do advise sterilizing mouthed toys, too. However, as your baby needs exposure to some germs to build their immunity, common sense is the key. If the dog has licked a toy, or an ill sibling or adult has touched it, clean it in a hot dishwasher or washing machine, or in a sterilizer before letting the baby play with it again. Otherwise, use common sense.

Frustrated baby

Some babies are determined to get ahead in life – and want to do more than they are physically capable of. No wonder they're frustrated!

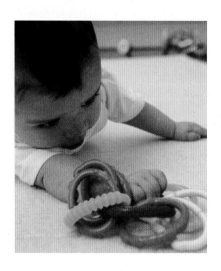

While some babies are content to sit back and watch the world go by, others really do want to run before they can walk! If yours is the latter, you are going to have to expect tears of frustration when your baby sits up and reaches forwards to support themselves on their arms, but then collapses; and anticipate a meltdown if they become "stranded" on their tummy. Although it might be difficult to witness on a daily basis, just accept that this is an essential part of the learning process – without it, your baby would be content to sit still. You have a baby who will likely be much happier once they are able to crawl.

Of course, if your baby begins to get very upset and frustrated, sometimes it's best to step in. If they are reaching for a toy, gently stretch them towards it so that they can grab it themself; if it is being stranded on their tummy that is upsetting them, move in and reposition them gently, praising their efforts as you do so.

Striving and success Your baby will feel less frustrated when they achieve their goal.

Feeling connected

Parenting is both wonderful and stressful. At times, the road ahead seems tough, but there are lots of resources you can tap into.

Connecting with other parents can be invaluable, not just for new parents, but also for parents with older children. By sharing experiences and advice, you can find and offer reassurance on parenting issues and concerns.

If you are a new parent, and not many of your existing friends have yet started families, local parent-and-baby groups are a great way to meet other families. Groups are often run in community centres or church or village halls, so have a look at notice boards in your area, or in local newspapers or support forums on social media for details. You can also research online (see also the resources section of this book, pp.384–85) Some baby clinics run "stay-and-play" sessions to enable parents to socialize with other new parents and babies.

Government-run family services

Sure Start children's centres offer help and guidance to parents. The centres offer advice on all aspects of family health and wellbeing, and some offer dental treatment, physiotherapy, and nutritional advice, as well as parenting classes and advice on coping with children with special needs. They also provide childcare services or guidance on where to find appropriate childcare.

Your local council may also run a branch of the National Association of Family Information Services. These provide guidance for parents of children of all ages – from infancy to adulthood. They can give details of local parent-and-baby groups and activities, as well as advice on finding childcare support if you have a baby with special needs or disabilities. Some offer an "outreach" programme, in which team members can talk impartially about any help you need, from childcare to special services.

Internet resources

Social networking has boomed in recent years, and among the many chat rooms and blogs lie parenting websites that offer invaluable advice. Many facilitate live chat and give advice on topics from feeding to sleeping, and information about local groups and activities.

BabyCentre, Babyworld, Netmums, and Mumsnet all provide local listings and advice, as well as the opportunity to log on and share experiences. Above all, they can provide a sense of community, and, if your baby does something that worries you, or doesn't achieve a key milestone, you will find other parents who have gone through the same thing and can offer practical advice, or at least a reassuring voice. However, if you remain concerned about any aspect of your baby's health, seek professional medical advice from your GP or local healthcare practitioner.

SINGLE PARENTS

Good times Both you and your baby may benefit from socializing with other families.

From advice on finding appropriate childcare to arranging contact with your baby's other parent (if there is one), single-parenting websites help you to negotiate the particular twists and turns of looking after a baby on your own. Many provide extensive advice on rights and benefits, as well as case studies and guidance on how to deal with the challenges of juggling work and looking after a baby on your own. Downloadable fact sheets, help lines, and email advice are just some of the services they provide, and, if you become a member, all tend to offer a chat forum so that you can share your concerns and successes with other single parents. OneSpace, Gingerbread, Lone-Parents, and OneParentFamily are among the most popular sites.

Brain development

Your baby's experiences build up to create trillions of neural networks in their brain, forming the basis of their understanding of the world.

Babies are born with all the brain cells they will ever have but, at first, there are only a few connections between them. With every passing week, whatever your baby sees, hears, touches, smells, or tastes creates unique connections or neural pathways. These complex connections lay the foundation for thinking, feelings, and behaviour, and are responsible for your baby's many mental milestones. Your care and your baby's environment play into how these connections are formed. The more experiences you provide, the more your baby's brain will absorb: talking helps form language pathways; attending to your baby's needs helps to develop the emotional intelligence, and so much more.

BABY'S BRAIN CELLS

Your baby's brain has 100 billion brain cells, or neurons; their brain is shaped by experiences taken in by the five senses, which help to form connections between these cells. By the age of three, your baby's brain has formed approximately 1,000 trillion connections.

Diversion not discipline

You can't explain anything to a baby, so if yours is doing something they shouldn't, the best tactic at this age is to divert them.

Diversion tactics Occupy your baby with a favourite toy to keep them calm and cooperative when carrying out less than welcome tasks.

Your baby does not yet have the capacity for naughtiness – the mistakes they make are merely the result of their inquisitive mind and their investigations into cause and effect. There are certain lessons in safety you'll want to reinforce, but at the moment, one of the most effective ways to do that is through diversion. If they pick up something they shouldn't and chew it, offer them a safer object and remove the original object from their grasp.

Similarly, if your baby reaches for something you don't want them to have – a mug of hot drink, say – simply move the object away from them and divert their attention with one of their toys. Babies are fickle – you'll probably find that they switch with barely a blink.

With every diversion, offer them a firm, but calm, "No" so that over the months, the meaning of "No" sinks in. Be consistent about activities that elicit a "no" from you, so they don't become confused.

Finally, never become angry with your baby and, above all, avoid physical discipline. They are more likely to learn in a safe, loving, nurturing environment, and listen to you if they trust you. If you shout, they will cry, but if you are calm, consistent, and firm, they will begin to understand the boundaries.

Instant energy fixes

It's important to keep your energy levels up, so if you're feeling sapped, take time out to review your diet and routine and make a few quick fixes.

Try to make time for breakfast each day – a bowl of porridge, yoghurt, or a smoothie will keep hunger at bay. If you don't have time to eat at home, pack a banana or oat cakes to eat on the go. Aim to drink eight glasses of water a day (more if breastfeeding). As well as water, try herbal teas, decaffinated drinks, and fresh soups. Fruit and vegetables provide fluid, too. Avoid high-sugar or high-fat snacks; instead, have a bowl of unsweetened muesli, or plain yoghurt with fresh fruit to get a more sustained release of energy. Opt to home cook family meals as much as possible. Choose simple, freezer-friendly batch cooking recipes that you can prepareahead of time.

Take some exercise

A brisk 30-minute walk (at a pace that gets you breathing quite hard) will push up your heart rate and boost your circulation and energy.

Take some deep breaths

Deep breathing allows a more efficient intake of oxygen, making you feel energized. Sit back on your heels and rest your hands on your knees. Sitting upright with your head facing forwards, breathe in slowly and deeply through the nose, then slowly exhale, forcing the air out of your lungs. Repeat these deep, slow breaths in and out three to five times, then return to normal breathing again.

Take a cold shower

If you can bear it, try alternating the shower temperature between hot and cold. This technique is said to speed up your metabolism and boost circulation, increasing the oxygen flow to the body, so making you more alert.

Super foods Healthy food choices will give you the nutrients and energy to stay strong and motivated.

ENERGY NAPS

Being a mum is a great excuse to revive the siesta! Research shows that the body is designed to have a short rest in the afternoon, and that doing so improves energy levels and cognitive function significantly. When you put down your baby for their afternoon nap, take the opportunity to have a nap yourself. A longer nap of about an hour or an hour and a half should put you through a full sleep cycle, which has excellent restorative effects on your energy levels for the afternoon. However, if you also have jobs to do while the baby is sleeping, aim for a nap of 20 minutes, which will be enough to refresh you, but not send you into such a deep sleep that you wake up feeling groggy. Set an alarm so that you don't have to worry about judging the time.

Milk still rules

Even after your baby starts on solid food, milk should remain the mainstay of their diet throughout their first year.

Your baby's diet is about to change during the next month or so as you begin to introduce them to new tastes, textures, and foods. This coincides with their ability to master the skills necessary to chew, swallow, and digest. However, that doesn't mean that milk feeds become any less important. In fact, milk is still the most important part of their diet.

When your baby first starts on solids, they'll have only a few spoonfuls of very liquid purées (see pp.178–79). Although these should be nutritious and healthy, your baby will rely on their usual milk to supply them with key nutrients, fats, proteins, and carbohydrates.

As your baby progresses from their first tastes towards regular meals (see pp.286–87), you can reduce the number of milk feeds you give, or the amount of time you spend feeding (and, therefore, the amount of milk they receive). But you'll also need to play it by ear – if they're hungry, they'll need to be fed.

Until they are a year old, babies need at least 500–600ml (17fl oz–1 pint) of formula or breastmilk per day, and that means regular feeds. Formula or breastmilk added to purées will count towards your baby's overall milk intake, too.

Comfort feeds

Quite apart from needing the nutritional value of their usual milk, your baby also enjoys the familiar comfort that sucking offers. At 22 weeks and beyond, babies still require lots of physical touch to nurture their emotional development. Also, by continuing to breastfeed or bottle-feed your baby, you are helping them to establish positive associations between food and feelings of love and security.

There's no doubt that some babies are a little reluctant when weaning commences. However, they soon begin to accept the difference and enjoy the new tastes and textures. They will feel reassured that milk – their old favourite – is still available.

It's better to wean your baby gradually from the breast or bottle as this helps both you and your baby adjust both physically (the sense of physical closeness) and emotionally to the change.

Staple diet Milk, whether in the form of breastmilk or formula, continues to constitute the greater part of your baby's diet.

ASK A PAEDIATRICIAN

When will I be able to tell whether my baby will be right- or left-handed? You'll have to wait until your baby is at least 18 months before you notice any marked preference, and, particularly if your child uses both hands equally, it might not be until they are 5–6 years old that they make a final choice. Right- or left-handedness is determined as one or other side of the brain becomes dominant; if the right side prevails, your baby will be left-handed, and vice versa. However, babies rarely show a preference for using a particular hand in the first year. They tend to grab with the hand nearest to what they want.

About 10 per cent of people are left-handed, a trait that is thought to be influenced by genetics. If both parents are left-handed, their child has a 45–50 per cent chance of being left-handed too. Try not to influence their preference as this may affect their psychological wellbeing and interfere with writing later on.

Breastfeeding while working

Returning to work doesn't have to spell an end to breastfeeding. With careful planning, your baby can still receive your nourishing milk.

If you are returning to work soon and hoping to express your breastmilk, you will need to plan for this at least several weeks before you return. You should inform your employers in writing before you return to let them know your intention so that they can provide a suitable, safe environment for you to express your milk. Employers are advised to provide a private, clean, comfortable area for you to express (toilets are not suitable), and to help you plan dedicated time out during your day to do so. How often you will need to express will depend on the age of your baby and the frequency of their feeds, so discuss this with your employer when planning your working day. They should also ensure there is fridge storage space for your milk.

Try to start expressing your milk at least several weeks before your return so that you can practise and perfect your technique. You will also need to ensure that your baby is comfortable taking your milk from a bottle. Again, introduce a bottle gradually several weeks before your return date.

If you are planning to partially breastfeed, and for your baby to receive formula milk from their carer during the day, you will need to reduce your breast feeds gradually to avoid your breasts becoming engorged. Drop one feed every four to five days until the remaining feeds fit around your working day. You may need to stick to this routine as far as possible during weekends and holidays so that your milk supply remains consistent.

Getting organized As well as your pump, you will need sterilized bottles or bags to store your milk, and ice blocks to transport it home.

CREATING A MEMORY BOX

Your baby's hospital wristband, a lock of their hair, pictures from your pregnancy scan, a recording of their coos and giggles, a book noting down their "firsts", and even a print of their hands or feet – such items can form the basis of your baby's memory box, which you can build up over the years to produce a perfect record of all those memorable moments. Pop anything in that will evoke memories, such as their first vest or rattle, when they've outgrown them. Keeping special mementoes in one place will allow for a wonderful trip down memory lane in years to come.

Collecting memories Start a collection of items that will help you remember your baby's infancy. Include a scrapbook in which you can jot down accounts of memorable milestones.

Little wriggler

With so many things to do and new skills to practise, it can be difficult for your baby to stay still. It's time for a little distraction!

Distraction skills A bit of fun is often all it takes for your baby to forget for a while that they dislike having their clothes changed!

Changing your baby's nappy or clothing and feeding them can become more challenging as they wriggle a bit more, and become distracted by their surroundings. This normal development can last for a few months, so parenting tactics are key.

Try catching them unawares. Change them or get them ready for the bath in a new spot. A little break in routine may intrigue them, and they may forget to try their escape techniques. Put a mobile over their changing table and a few toys nearby to attract their attention. Sing and chat to them, keeping eye contact. Count their toes, tickle their tummy,

blow a raspberry on their neck, buy a new bath toy, talk about the colours of their clothing, and, meanwhile, do your job as efficiently as you can!

If they wriggle when you feed them, move to a place with no distractions. Set up a "feeding association" that imparts pleasure, comfort, and relaxation, such as a new lullaby. Sing it to them when you settle them down for a feed; they'll soon realize that it signals the time to be calm and enjoy close, quiet time with you. When they are eventually reintroduced into noisier, busier environments, their feeding lullaby will help them to concentrate on the job at hand.

Weight-gain checks

It is normal to be concerned that your baby is putting on the right amount of weight, and growing at the right rate for their age.

With the current focus on childhood obesity, you may worry that your baby is too chubby and may go on to have a weight problem; or if they are small, you may be concerned that they are underweight and will always be small. Generally, if your baby remains on, or close to, the "centile" line (a line showing the expected pattern of growth) on which they were born, they're doing well.

Exclusively breastfed babies tend not to be overweight, and regular weight checks will pick up potential problems if your baby's underweight. As long as they are alert, active for periods during the day, sleeping well, and feeding and filling their nappies normally, all is well.

A bottle-fed baby may be more prone to weight gain, simply because they can be overfed more easily.

During weaning, reduce their milk appropriately. Babies can be reliant on milk for comfort as well as nutrition and hydration. So, cut out feeds slowly over the next few months so that your baby has plenty of time to adjust physically and emotionally.

If you're concerned about your baby's weight, your health visitor can check their weight and height and reassure you.

Early rising

Just when your baby begins to sleep through the night, and you think you may get some rest, they begin to wake early – to play!

Babies this age vary in the amount of sleep they need, with a few managing 11 hours a night, some eight hours, and many still waking for a night feed. If your baby is going to bed at 6.30pm, and rising again, fully alert, by 5am each day, try putting them to bed a little later. Don't be tempted to cut down on their daytime naps, though, as this will not encourage them to sleep longer at night, and your baby still needs two to three naps. Instead, try timing their naps to ensure that they don't sleep past 4pm.

Think about whether they are waking early because they are being disturbed by something in their environment. Morning light, perhaps. If so, consider installing a black-out blind. Are other family members getting up early and rousing them? Try to keep noise to a minimum.

Make sure your baby is physically active in the day, with plenty of playtime and stimulation. If they're regularly sitting in their chair or in the back of the car for too long (which is anyway inadvisable), they simply may not be physically tired enough to sleep for long periods. A good balance of stimulation and rest will ensure they are tired enough to fall and stay asleep, and will give them more information to "consolidate" at night.

If they're happy to play on their own a little when they wake up, leave something safe (no choking hazards) for them to look at such, as a fabric book or soft toy.

However, if they wake and need your attention, go to them and give them the feed, change, or playtime that they need. If you think they're stirring rather than waking, try your usual techniques, such as rocking, stroking, singing, humming, or simply patting them as they settle themself.

If all else fails, take turns getting up with them and enjoy their high spirits, even if you would rather be under the duvet!

Early riser If your baby is waking up earlier than usual, you may need to make some slight adjustments to their routine to encourage them to wake up at a more sociable time!

FOCUS ON TWINS: SLEEPING PATTERNS

Even if both twins are sleeping through now, at some point in the next few weeks or months you can expect one of them to wake up earlier than the other, and disturb the other. Perhaps one twin needs more sleep, or has adapted more readily to a regular sleep pattern. Although it is important for them, and for you, to synchronize their sleep patterns as much as possible, if one of your babies is waking up a lot earlier, it's easiest to separate them. If your twins are still sharing a cot, it might be the time to explore separate cots across the room.

Small is beautiful

As your baby's eyesight improves, they'll take an interest in the tiniest things – dials, knobs, little flowers, and even your smallest earrings.

Around this time, you may find your baby looking with interest at the polka dots on their dungarees, the eyes on their teddy, and the clip that fastens your changing bag. The smallest items will now capture their attention, and they will reach out to touch them and try to pick them up using a whole-hand grasp, even if that's a little clumsy. This practice develops their fine motor skills. By now, your baby can also stretch out with one hand to grasp toys and other objects, and can hold them, examine them, and even lift them up to suck.

Encourage your baby's curiosity by giving them lots of different objects to look at and pick up. Transparent plastic balls with "surprises" inside, toys with fine design details, and activity boards with buttons, dials, and knobs will all fascinate them.

Equally, however, beware and keep everything that is smaller than their fist out of their reach. Watch them carefully. Ensure that buttons are firmly sewn on to clothing (their and yours), and avoid leaving your handbag or anything else that may contain choking hazards near them.

Fast learner

Your baby's development continues to surge ahead. You'll be amazed at your baby's ability to learn and remember new things.

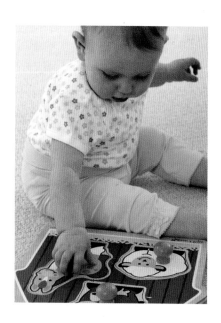

Repetition is the best way for your baby to learn about their physical and social environment. Developing the ability to reason (working out patterns for things and learning about how the world operates) requires repetition for your baby's neural pathways to process information well. Although, at this stage, social interaction is best for stimulating their senses and building emotional security, your baby will also enjoy some independence to explore things at their own pace,

Ring ring Your baby won't make a connection between pushing buttons and hearing noise yet but they might if they do it it many times over.

fathom how things work, and experiment. If you pick up their toy each time they drop it, you won't be giving them a chance to retrieve it independently, and so learn a number of valuable skills, including hand–eye coordination, fine motor skills, and some self-sufficiency.

Give your baby toys they can play with on their own without too much help – it won't speed up their development to give them toys intended for older children. In fact, mastering skills with familiar toys helps to reinforce new pathways in their brain and will give them the confidence to move on to more complicated toys when they're ready.

Into the big bath

If your baby is getting too big for their baby bath, it might be time to introduce them to the full-sized tub.

Bathtime support A bath support leaves your hands free to wash your baby. It prevents your baby from slipping and keeps their head out of the water.

HAIR TIME!

If your baby, like the vast majority of babies, does not like having their hair washed, squeeze warm water over their head during regular bathtime so they become used to the sensation, and distract them with a toy as you wash their hair unobtrusively. While supporting them with one arm, place a drop of shampoo on their hair, then press a damp flannel to their forehead to prevent water or soap entering their eyes. Massage the shampoo into their hair and scalp, then wet a second flannel or sponge and squeeze this over their head. Continue until the suds disperse. If they still resist, consider buying a special shampoo rinse cup, which has a lip to prevent water reaching their face or eyes. While you wash their hair, make soothing noises to calm them.

Some babies take to a big bath right away and enjoy the freedom of being able to splash about; others are daunted by the expanse of space so may need to get accustomed to it gradually. You know how your baby is likely to react, so if you think they'll be fearful, pop their baby bath into the big bath a few times before taking the plunge fully. Or you may want to get into the bath with your baby.

When you do put your baby in the big bath on their own for the first time, make sure that they're safe. Use a non-slip mat for the base of the tub. Get the water temperature right, around 37°C (98.6°F) – run the cold tap first, then add hot water until the bath water is just warm. Keep a flannel over the hot tap while your baby is in the bath to catch drips. Always supervise your baby in the bath – don't leave even for a second.

Make bathtimes fun and relaxing: place their favourite bath toys within easy reach, and add some exciting new ones. Bob the toys up and down and gently swish the water around them. Speak gently, as your voice will probably echo in the bathroom, and if your baby shows any sign of distress, sing a familiar song.

Bath supports

You may want to use a bath support suitable for young babies, which holds your baby securely, leaving your hands free to wash them. Sit-up bath seats aren't suitable for babies under six months old, as babies need to be able to sit without support in them so that they don't slip down in the seat. Look for ergonomic bath supports that recline and are moulded to support a baby's head, shoulders, and back, which are suitable for babies who can't yet sit upright very well.

Introducing a cup

If your baby can sit steadily with support, you might like to let them experiment with a trainer cup now so that they don't resist it later on.

The longer a baby drinks from a bottle, the more difficult it tends to be to get them to drink from anything else. Trainer cups can be useful especially for breastfed babies who refuse to drink from a bottle. While the advice is to start babies on trainer cups at six months, some babies accept them readily at five months. The main prerequisite is that your baby is able to sit up with support. If they're not sitting properly upright, there is a risk that they may choke. Giving your baby a cup doesn't mean giving up the breast or bottle altogether; it is simply an additional means of giving them fluids.

The right cup

Choose a sturdy plastic cup with a lid that won't break when dropped to the floor. Try experimenting with a few different cup styles until you find a combination of handles and spout that your baby finds comfortable. Some babies prefer to hold a cup with no handles between their palms; others like a handle to grasp. Babies who have been bottle-fed sometimes prefer soft spouts, which are more like teats, while breastfed babies often prefer the harder, flip-up type, which release liquid more easily. Many babies become quickly frustrated with spouts that require a strong suck. Bear in mind that a slow-flowing spout offers a good way to start on a cup, as the first few times they use a cup, your baby may gag.

What to put in the cup

You don't need to start expressing milk into a cup; nor do you need to switch to giving your baby their formula in a cup if you are bottle-feeding. Instead, put in a little cooled, boiled water and allow your baby to sip on it just a few sips at a time. Once they start on solids, you can offer a cup at mealtimes and stick to the bottle or breast for their milk feeds. Avoid juices, cordials, or squashes, as the sugars can damage their teeth.

HANDLING A CUP

Taking hold You will need to hold the cup for your baby at first, but as they become more dexterous, they will be able to hold it themself.

• Put only tiny amounts of fluid in the cup to begin with, because your baby won't be able to take too much at a time. It will also make it easier for them to learn how to handle the cup.
• Teach your baby how to bring the cup up to their lips and tip it back to enable them to take a sip.
• Put them in a bib. Your baby is likely to swallow only small amounts of the liquid they take into their mouth, and the rest will run down their chin and onto their bib, if you're lucky, or their clothes, if not!
• If they can't hold the cup for themselves effectively, give them a helping hand, supporting the bottom as they take sips.

• Once your baby turns their head to indicate that they don't want any more, don't force the issue. Put the cup away and try again tomorrow or next week.
• Cups, lids, and spouts should be sterilized until your baby is six months old, after which they just need careful cleaning by hand or in the dishwasher. However, if you're giving your baby milk in a training cup, it's advisable to sterilize the lids and spouts until your baby is one.
• Never leave your baby unattended while they are learning to drink from a cup, in case of choking.

Learning through imitation

Your activities fascinate your baby. Your baby will enjoy having their own versions of objects and tools you use regularly – to be just like you!

Babies learn by imitating their parents and carers, and enjoy age-appropriate toys that mimic common household objects they see being used in front of them day to day. Toy keys, mixing bowls and spoons, pots and pans, mobile telephones, and even a baby guitar can provide endless hours of entertainment and, better still, your baby will be learning as they play.

Show your baby how to stir their bowl. Have a pretend phone call, each on your own phones. Teach them how to bang a drum like their big brother, or jingle toy keys. Your baby is making sense of the world, and these activities provide the opportunity to experiment in a safe environment.

Choose toy versions, or real household objects, such as bowls and spatulas, that are very clean and easy to handle, so that your baby doesn't hurt themself. The more you repeat activities and sounds, the greater the baby's understanding of the world will be, and the larger their memory bank – and their ability to retrieve information from it.

Vocal imitation

From around five months of age, babies imitate not just movements and facial expressions, but also sounds. You may find that your baby hums while they "stir" their bowl with a spoon, as you do when you are cooking; they may make noises that are louder and more excited than

It's for you! Activities such as having a pretend phone conversation will encourage your baby to act out what they see in real life, which stimulates their imagination and enhances their creativity.

usual when they are "talking" on their phone; they may even "sing" when they bang on their drum.

Your baby's vocalizations take on a similar tone and energy to yours when you perform certain activities. For example, they may coo in a quiet, melodious way at bedtime, just as you are likely to talk softly; shout and squeal during playtime, or murmur in the bath if they are used to you soothing them while they splash.

Interestingly, your baby's vocalizations with female caregivers may be higher pitched than those with male caregivers, in a close imitation of the tones they hear.

ASK A CHILD PSYCHOLOGIST

Should I say "no" to my baby? Yes, you can say, "No", but use the word judiciously – and only when you pair it with an action. Babies reach an understanding of the concepts of "yes" and "no" when they are around 9–12 months old. Start using these words now and you are preparing them well to reach this milestone. As you pair the word "no" with an action, such as holding your baby back from touching the hot oven, you teach them that the word "no" means they should stop. They want your approval, and "yes" and "no" will soon become clear signals as to what you do and don't want them to do.

Creating memories

Your baby's memory is developing quickly. They remember sequences of repeated events, and anticipate what comes next.

You'll notice that your baby's face lights up when they see a familiar book or favourite toy. They may quieten when you snuggle up with a book at bedtime as they recognize this as part of their evening routine.

The things your baby will retain first are those that are most frequently repeated and those that most engage their interest. They will remember and imitate actions that they've seen you do many times. Through repetition, they'll know where their toys are, or how to activate sounds on a favourite book with buttons. Repetition is the most effective way of encouraging your baby to learn; don't expect them to recall things after just one try. Your baby's memory skills are still rudimentary. They may show recognition with a very familiar story, but not with one they have heard only a few times; and will master more quickly a regularly presented toy. This need for repetition means they may delight at seeing a grandparent who regularly cares for them, but be less willing to accept a cuddle from a relative who visits less often.

Emotional baby

Your baby won't hesitate to express their emotions, and you may find that they're capable of picking up on and expressing your moods, too!

High emotions Your baby can't understand or control their emotions yet, and may be happy one minute, and crying the next.

Your baby may throw a toy in frustration, or become angry, tearful, and anxious when you leave the room. They may be excited and happy one moment, giggling and squealing as they play with an older sibling, then annoyed and angry the next, when the games stop. They aren't able to control or understand their emotions: which are simply there and can feel overwhelming. Knowing this and understanding that they are not misbehaving can help you feel less frustrated by emotional outbursts.

From a very early age, your baby has been sensitive to your emotions, too, and often responds to things in a way that's similar to your responses. If you are stressed and anxious, you may find that they become tearful or fractious; if you are happy, they may exhibit a sunny, smiley demeanour.

It is important therefore to try to keep calm. Research suggests that children not only pick up on stress, but also become stressed as a result. If your baby is regularly stressed by your emotions, their ability to learn can be affected and they may become oversensitive to adverse experiences, which makes it hard to respond well to stress in later life.

Good nutrition for babies

Your baby's nutritional requirements are different to yours – so it's good to know the basics before you begin to introduce food.

Now is a great time to think about what the essentials are for your baby's diet, in preparation for the time when you begin to wean your baby. Naturally, their diet will be different from your own, as they have particular needs; their diet must include adequate nutrients and energy to support healthy growth and development. There are four main constituents that should feature, in varying proportions, in a balanced diet – fats, proteins, carbohydrates, and vitamins and minerals.

Fats

Your baby has high energy needs in relation to their size, so breastmilk or formula provides a high proportion of fat, which is a concentrated source of energy (calories). When you start to introduce solid foods to your baby (see pp.178–79), it is a good idea to combine them with a little breastmilk or formula as the flavour will be familiar to your baby and may encourage them to try new foods. Small amounts of cow's milk can also be mixed with food, but not given as a drink until your baby is 12 months old. You can introduce full-fat dairy products, such as plain yoghurt, fromage frais or low-sodium pasteurised cheeses. Avoid fatty foods, such as chips, crisps, cakes, and biscuits, opting instead for wholefoods in which fat is naturally present, such as avocados.

Carbohydrates

Lactose, or milk sugar, is the main carbohydrate in breastmilk, which is why it is sweet. Formula also provides lactose. As your baby's diet widens, they will encounter starches and other natural sugars in fruits, vegetables, grains, and potatoes. Although not as concentrated a source of energy as fat, carbohydrate-rich foods contain different vitamins, minerals, and protective plant chemicals (phytonutrients). Your baby's diet should gradually become lower in sugars and higher in starches as more foods are introduced and milk plays a less dominant role.

Proteins

Every cell in the body contains protein, and milk is a great supply. However, it's important to introduce other protein-rich foods into the diet as they also provide important minerals and vitamins. Red meat, for example, provides essential iron and zinc. Vegetarian sources of protein, such as tofu, are easy to mash or purée and are a good source of iron and calcium, too.

Vitamins and minerals

These are essential for health. Fruit and vegetables are excellent sources – the more colourful the range, the better. Include green vegetables, such as broccoli and spinach early so your baby gets used to the flavour of these nutritious vegetables.

BABY'S BALANCED DIET

Below are foods from each of the four main groups to include in your baby's diet after beginning weaning.

- **Fats:** Cheese; yoghurt; fromage frais; butter and spreads; cow's milk (in cooking); eggs; vegetable oils (such as olive and rapeseed); oily fish (such as salmon, mackerel, and sardines); smooth nut butters (salt-free).
- **Carbohydrates:** Baby rice; potatoes, yam and sweet potato; cereals and foods containing gluten; such as wheat, rye, barley, and oats (usually after six months); followed by pasta, bread, and unsweetened breakfast cereals.
- **Vitamins and minerals:** Fresh or frozen vegetables, including cooked (soft) carrot sticks, green beans, and baby corn or raw cucumber. Fruit may be fresh, frozen, or canned in natural unsweetened juice. Good choices are sliced banana, pear, avocado, grapes and blueberries (both halved to avoid choking), plus dried unsweetened fruit, such as chopped dried apricots, figs or prunes.
- **Proteins:** Lean red meats (cooked through); chicken or turkey (opting for the darker cuts, which contain more iron); white fish fillets and oily fish such as salmon, or canned fish in oil; lentils, beans, and peas cooked as dhals; low-salt hummus; eggs (hard-boiled).

Playing alongside others

Although it will be a long time before your baby can play properly with other babies, at six months will play happily side by side.

Play date Playing with other children helps your baby discover new activities and toys, and they may get their first experience of sharing.

Your baby is fascinated by faces, and will probably watch other babies and children with amazement. Your baby will be interested in the sounds they make and the things they do, and will learn new skills by watching and mimicking others. In fact, one study found that babies of this age copy other babies, for instance by picking up a rattle if that's what another baby is doing. Your baby may cry when another baby cries, and smile and "talk" to other babies. Regular play dates with other babies will provide your baby with opportunities for social interaction. Although it is far too early for them to absorb social skills, they will see all sorts of relationships in action.

Your baby is likely to absorb themselves in their own play, even in the company of other babies. Your baby is not necessarily shy. Their behaviour simply reflects their developmental stage. Furthermore, new faces and experiences involve a period of adjustment. Once social experiences become familiar and they remember them as fun, they will be keen to repeat them.

Who's that baby?

Your baby does not understand the concept of "you" and "me". For now, their identity is inextricably linked to you.

Your baby is experimenting all the time with how their body moves: they will begin to copy you and others in simple ways, deeply interested in their interactions with you. Your baby does not yet recognize, or see, themselves as an individual. Put your baby in front of the mirror and you'll find that they are excited by the "new baby" they can see, completely unaware that it is a reflection of themselves, even if they recognize you and know that they are in your arms.

You may find your baby looking back and forth between you and their reflection and wanting to reach out and touch both.

It will not be until your baby is around 16 months of age that they will begin to recognize themselves as a separate individual, a stage of development called differentiation. At this point, they will finally realize that they are a separate individual able to make their own choices, which may begin with saying the word, "No!"

ASK A DOCTOR

My baby sucks their thumb constantly. Will they ever break the habit?
Thumb-sucking is very comforting for babies and gives them a convenient way of soothing themselves. It is more irritating to parents than it is harmful to children, so try not to worry about it. Your baby will stop when they're ready and developed other ways of soothing themself. Provided it ceases by the age of five, there's no evidence that it harms the teeth.

You're not only a parent

No matter how much you love and enjoy caring for your baby, it's normal to need a little time without them to just be yourself.

Every parent needs a little time to themselves to pursue their interests, enjoy some adult interaction, and re-establish a sense of self outside of parenthood. In fact, creating a satisfying life alongside your life with your baby will not only make you more relaxed and happy, but will probably make you a better parent, too. It won't be helpful for you or your baby if you feel isolated and never take the time to recharge your batteries.

While it is important not to overload yourself with new projects and activities that can leave you tired and frustrated, it is beneficial to achieve a balance in life that allows you some space to follow your own interests and maintain your identity as an individual.

Your baby is approaching six months old, so can be left with a family member, trusted babysitter, or friend for short periods of time. In fact, if your baby is weaning, they'll probably be able to go a little longer between feeds and be happy to take a spoonful of purée to keep them satisfied while you are away.

You may enjoy using social media and staying in touch with friends via your smartphone, but it's important to enjoy time away from technology, too. Take time out to curl up with a book or magazine and relax, or maybe plan regular trips to the gym. If you have career aspirations, or are thinking about changing careers

when you return to work, you may want to consider investigating the opportunities available to acquire new qualifications. Even time out with friends whose focus is not on babies and children can be rewarding and remind you that, while your role as a parent is paramount, there are other aspects of your life that are valuable and need to be nurtured.

Talk to your partner about making time to pursue individual interests. You could also discuss things you can do together without your baby to help to cement your relationship. Ultimately, you are a role model for your baby. If you show them how to live a balanced, satisfying personal life, in which individual interests and family both play an important role, they are much more likely to follow your lead as they grow, and develop friendships and interests.

Alone time Having time to yourself to relax and see to no one's needs but your own will refresh you so that, when you return to your baby, you'll be that much more ready for action!

ASK A CHILD PSYCHOLOGIST

My baby makes a big fuss when I pay attention to my other children. Is this normal? You are the centre of your baby's world and, at this stage, they will naturally think you belong to them. They won't understand that you have other responsibilities or grasp the concept of sharing time yet. Involve them when you are with your other children; chat to your baby and encourage your other children to do so as well. As long as your baby is getting attention, they'll probably be content. If you are playing with another child, set your baby up with some toys nearby so they can have fun while you're occupied. Show affection to all of your children regularly so your baby becomes used to sharing your time. Sharing will then become natural to them in time.

6 months

IF YOUR BABY LOST THEIR HAIR IN THE FIRST MONTHS AFTER BIRTH – WHICH IS VERY COMMON – IT MAY LOOK PATCHY FOR A WHILE BEFORE IT STARTS TO GROW BACK. Bald patches on your baby's scalp may be the result of sleeping in the same position, which gently rubs away the soft, downy hair that they are first born with. This is completely normal – the hair will grow back once the baby is sitting up.

Six whole months

Can you believe how grown-up your baby seems? They're on a roll now – or rather on to much more purposeful, strategic moving around.

Your baby is already half-way through their first year. You have probably settled into your roles and grown more comfortable and confident with the responsibilities of parenthood. Can you even imagine now what you did with your time before your baby was born?

Your six-month-old baby is more sociable than ever, and loves to be with people. They'll be smiling and laughing with gusto in company – but may be a little more selective about whom they want to engage one-to-one with. Take advantage of their sociability to introduce them to a variety of people and encourage them to say hello and wave goodbye.

There is a sudden burst in awareness. Your baby is curious and wants to explore everything. They also appear to make decisions when choosing which toys to play with. They will love playing face to face with you, and their sense of trust and confidence is growing. They'll enjoy studying faces, touching, poking, and pulling them to understand their separateness from other people.

Big and beautiful

Most babies have doubled their birth weight by six months so, having filled out nicely, they're probably looking particularly bonny now. If you haven't done so already, it's definitely time for weaning (see pp.178–79 and pp.236–37 for more guidance). You may be thinking about introducing

Giggle all the way Your baby will enjoy games that involve an element of surprise or silliness. Hide them under a blanket and then "discover" them. They'll be amused and burst into laughter.

supplementary bottles of formula, or expressing extra milk, if you are breastfeeding, stopping breastfeeding (see pp.254–55), or changing to follow-on formula (see p.207).

Your baby may be able to sit without support, and be capable of bearing some weight on their legs and bouncing when held upright. They'll use their entire hand to rake over a small object and then pick it up, and will purposefully grasp, shake, and bang items. If they drop things, it probably won't be deliberate yet (that will appear around nine months).

BABY WALKERS AND BOUNCERS

It's best to avoid these toys. Baby walkers can be dangerous as they give your baby extra height, allowing them to reach out-of-the-way hazards, and can tip over, causing distress, and injury if they collide with something. There are more accidents with these than with any other toy. Moreover, your baby needs to learn to sit, roll, crawl, and play on their tummy to gain the skills for walking, and baby walkers prohibit these activities. Baby bouncers are no longer recommended as they put too much pressure on bones, joints, ligaments, and muscles at too young an age. Also, accidents can result if they're not attached properly.

Your baby's teeth

Your baby's teeth started developing in their gums in early pregnancy –
now the first of their 20 primary (milk) teeth may begin to come through.
Some babies experience discomfort, while others sail through teething
with barely a dribble.

Most babies begin teething between
four and eight months old, although
some can start as late as 12 months.
   The bottom incisors (bottom front
teeth) are the first to come through,
followed by the top incisors a month
or so later. At nine to 12 months, come
the top lateral incisors (either side of
the top front teeth). The bottom
lateral incisors emerge about a month
later, then the canines (the pointy
teeth on either side of the bottom and
top incisors) at about 16 months.
Molars (back teeth) might appear
before the canines; and second
molars, at the back, may not appear
until after 20 months. By the age of
about three years old, all the milk
teeth will be through.

Cleaning their teeth Make brushing fun for your baby, and start to get them into
the habit of brushing each morning and evening now, so that it becomes a
familiar part of their routine.

Caring for milk teeth

As soon as your baby cuts their first
tooth, clean it regularly (see p.162).
Once they have three or four teeth,
move on to a toothbrush designed for
babies, with super-soft bristles and a
small head that can reach gently into
the corners of your baby's mouth. Use
a tiny speck of children's lower-
fluoride toothpaste (1,000ppm) on the
brush. A small amount of fluoride
strengthens tooth enamel and helps
to prevent tooth decay. Don't allow
your baby to eat the toothpaste.
   Wait at least half an hour after
feeding before brushing to allow the
antibacterial properties of saliva to
get to work first. Brush gently in a
circular motion, cleaning the area
around the gums in particular, as this
is where plaque can build up.
   If your baby resists having their
teeth brushed, make a game of it.
Count their teeth when you brush
them, and give them the toothbrush
after brushing so they can experiment
on their own. You'll need to brush
their teeth for them until they are
about seven years old.

Seeing the dentist

Take your baby with you to your
dental appointments, to familiarize
them, then expect your baby's first
full appointment to be at around six
to 12 months old.

ASK A DOCTOR

**Is it normal for my baby to have
diarrhoea when they are teething?**
Although there is no reason why your
baby should experience a runny tummy,
some parents do report that their babies
tend to have looser bowel movements
during teething. If the diarrhoea is
short-lived, there shouldn't be anything to
worry about. However, it should never be
assumed that teething is the direct cause
of diarrhoea. If your baby's diarrhoea
becomes persistent, they seem at all
unwell, or have a temperature, take them
to see your doctor just in case.

Tearful parenting

It's often said that once you're a parent, tears tend to flow at the slightest provocation. Read on and don't weep.

A distressing story on the news, a poignant picture, even a troubling episode of your favourite show can have you feeling extra-sensitive, particularly in all matters concerning children. It seems to come with the territory of being a parent. Perhaps this change has to do with becoming more empathetic – feeling intense love for your own child makes you more aware of other people's – especially children's – suffering. If you talk to other parents, you'll probably discover that they are just as sentimental as you are.

However, if you're a breastfeeding mother and your propensity for tears is accompanied by severe pre-menstrual syndrome (PMS), and you are in the process of weaning, your feelings may be a result of hormonal changes.

When you stop breastfeeding, prolactin, which helps you feel calm and relaxed, declines and progesterone and oestrogen levels increase, triggering symptoms. The feelings of aggression, or anger, or low mood associated with PMS should lift once your hormones settle. If your low mood persists, see your GP or health visitor – you may be experiencing postnatal depression.

Hands free

Once your baby can sit propped up, they'll be able to practise using their hands more, and will soon use them more effectively and efficiently.

Having two hands free allows your baby to practise their hand–eye coordination more readily and to develop the ability to pass a toy from hand to hand. They may also choose a toy for each hand and bang them together, or examine them both with interest before dropping one to concentrate on the other.

The ability to use both hands together to manipulate an object is known as bilateral coordination, which usually develops throughout your baby's first year. Any two-handed activities provide good practice. Toys with dials to turn, strings to pull, and buttons to push, as well as busy boxes, activity boards, shape-sorters, stacking blocks, and toy rings are all ideal.

Not every baby develops this skill quite so early, so if at six months, your baby can grasp an object and put it into their mouth, bring their feet to their mouth, hold smaller objects, and even release objects purposefully from time to time, they're on track with the developmental milestones necessary for bilateral coordination.

Two-handed exploration Give your baby toys that require them to use both hands to develop their "bilateral" coordination.

199

That looks yummy, mummy

Your baby is looking longingly at your food and reaching out
to grab a taste, but can they have it yet?

Tempting It's best to avoid introducing certain adult foods, such as biscuits.

ASK A NUTRITIONIST

Will weaning my baby early make them more prone to allergies? Your baby's digestive system can cope with solid foods from about four months, but weaning is generally recommended from six months. Talk to your GP if you do plan to introduce solid foods earlier. It is now recommended that you aim to introduce common allergenic foods, such as wheat, dairy, egg, peanuts and other nuts, shellfish, and fish, before 12 months of age to induce tolerance and lessen the risk of allergies. Studies on this topic are ongoing. However, if your baby shows signs of intolerance, such as swollen lips, face, tongue, eyes, or itchy skin rashes or abdominal pain or vomiting seek urgent medical attention. See pages 225 and 376 for more information on food allergies.

Watching you eat and looking at foods is one of the developmental signs that your baby is ready to start weaning, or "complementary feeding". However, not all the foods that you eat are going to be suitable for your baby in the early months, and some are best avoided. One aim of weaning is to introduce your baby to family foods, but you will need to adjust your meals to ensure they are suitable and safe for your baby to eat. This is because adult food often contains ingredients that are not suitable for babies.

Too much salt Many foods – especially highly processed foods – contain salt. Babies' kidneys are not fully developed, so can't cope with more than 1g of salt (sodium chloride) per day before the age of one. That amount includes the salt naturally found in vegetables and grains, and through your breastmilk. An average bag of savoury snacks contains at least 0.5g salt, and a few baby-sized pieces of pizza could easily exceed your baby's recommended daily amount.

Too little fat Your low-fat yoghurts are great to help you with weight control, but they do not contain sufficient fat, and therefore calories, to support your baby's growth and development. Full-fat dairy products, including cow's milk used in cooking, are useful additions to your baby's diet up to the age of two, with a gradual reduction recommended up to the age of five.

Too much sugar Your baby is born with an innate preference for sweet food, so it is important to begin introducing vegetables and savoury foods early on. Foods with added sugar may encourage your baby to choose sweet foods over savoury, which may cause a dietary imbalance, and increase the risk of tooth decay, once teeth have erupted.

Too much bulk Avoid giving your baby too many high-fibre foods. It's fine to encourage your baby to eat fruit and vegetables, but not to the exclusion of higher-calorie foods. Vegetables, fruit, and grains are filling, so it can be easy for a baby to feel full without having eaten many calories. It is a good idea to mix your baby's first solids with their usual milk, and move on to other higher-calorie foods. You'll probably know if you are giving your baby too much fibre to eat as the number of nappies you change will increase!

Sweeteners Sugar substitutes were developed to help adults and older children reduce their intake of added sugar. They are not suitable for babies or toddlers, so drinks and foods that contain sweeteners should be off limits.

Alcohol Some adult desserts may contain alcohol, which your baby is unable to process, so be very careful. not to allow your baby to eat these.

Repetitive sounds

You can encourage your baby's recognition of sounds and words by talking to them constantly, and naming everyday objects.

At this age, your repetition of words and sounds is a vital component in your baby's language development. They will constantly be babbling and running strings of sounds together. Your baby is busy improving their control of their mouth, lips, and tongue to form sounds. Your job is to keep talking to them, to show natural gestures, and to be responsive by listening to their babbles, repeating them back, then waiting and listening while your baby responds.

You can gradually develop their understanding of language by demonstrating in your everyday speech that words can be labels for an object. So repeatedly saying "teddy" when a teddy bear is held out is an excellent way to build the connection between something and the name for them.

Familiarizing your baby with sounds will assist them with word recognition later on, helping them to take the next developmental leap.

ASK A DOCTOR

Is it safe for my baby to play in the playground sand pit? As long as they are supervised, they will probably enjoy this experience and learn a lot from watching other children, feeling the texture of the sand, and seeing how it moves in their hands. Choose a pit that is protected from dogs and cats and cleaned regularly. Ensure they don't put sand in their mouth, and wash their hands afterwards.

Nature trail

Whether your baby is lying on a rug in the garden or enjoying a wildlife tour in your arms, they will love the sights and sounds outdoors.

The big outdoors can be a source of fascination for babies. Feed your baby's interest by giving them an increasing number of things to see, smell, and touch. Pop your baby on a blanket in the shade in your garden, or in a safe area of your local park, and let them experience the fresh air and the wealth of stimuli that surrounds them. Point out a squirrel leaping between trees, a fragrant flower, a colourful bird, and a quacking duck in a pond.

Encourage your baby to touch the soft blades of grass, some gritty sand, and the coarse bark of a tree. Take your baby's socks off and place their feet into a children's sand pit. Each new experience will stimulate their senses and expand their knowledge.

Continue to add to your baby's memory bank of words. Tell them the names for everything around them, sharing words such as "rough" or "soft" to describe the different textures they may encounter.

Environmentally friendly Help your baby to explore all the exciting sights, smells, and textures of the great outdoors.

Story time

At this age, your baby begins to anticipate story time with pleasure
and will want to become actively involved in the process, too.

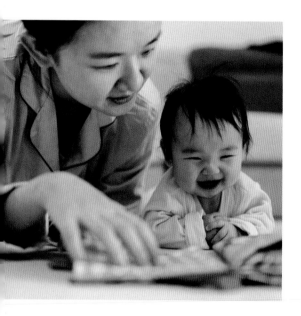

Your baby will love familiar stories
and shows anticipation about what
comes next. They may pat or try to
grab the book, and show their
unhappiness with a frown if you stop
reading or put the book away. As well
as the enjoyment they get, reading to
your baby introduces them to a wider
vocabulary, different tones and
pitches of speech, their first
experience of looking at letters and
words, and following a sequence of
events. All of these assist speech
development, and are good

Involved reader Encourage your baby to
explore books by getting them to help turn
the pages, lift flaps, and stroke textures.

preparation for the future when
they starts to read themself.

If you've got twins, you can
probably manage to read to both of
them from time to time while they're
settled on your lap. However, it's
good, too, to read to each baby on
their own, to give both an opportunity
to have one-on-one time with you
and develop their own reading
preferences. Prop up one baby on the
floor with their own books and toys
while you read to the other. While it
can be tough for parents of multiples
to apportion reading time to each
child, this really will benefit their
language and learning, particularly
if they were born prematurely.

Building independence

When your baby finds a task difficult, resist the temptation to leap
right in! Give them a chance to learn by trial and error.

Babies learn best through repetition,
trial and error, and your guidance,
but it can be difficult to get the
balance right when it comes to
necessary help and stepping in too
early. Your baby may repeatedly drop
a toy, or be unable to get their little
fingers into just the right position to
make their pop-up animals pop, and
they may fumble as they try to turn

the pages of their book. However,
try to resist doing everything for
them. On their first attempt, guide
them through the actions: hold their
hand or support their body in the
right position as they try. Next time,
give them less, or no, help as they try
independently. Make positive sounds
of pleasure when they attempt
something new, and a cheerful "not

quite" or "uh-oh" when they don't
quite manage it. If they become
frustrated, step in and help.

If they get attention for trying,
and are frequently encouraged from
the sidelines to carry on, they are
much more likely to continue their
efforts. Their problem-solving skills
will be enhanced, and so will their
confidence, effectiveness, and pride.

Learning by experience

Now that your baby is more interested in their surroundings, and feeds are easier to plan, you might enjoy venturing further afield.

Your baby is now more aware of what's going on around them and are very receptive to new experiences. For your part, it's probably much easier to anticipate what they need and when they need it. This means that you can be a bit more adventurous and enjoy longer outings occasionally, because you'll know when to take a pit-stop to feed or change them while you are out and about. So perhaps now is the time to visit that friend or relative who lives a bit further afield, organize a day out with other parents and babies, or spend a day at the seaside *en famille*.

Visits to grandparents or aunts and uncles help your baby get to know their extended family better: the more familiar they and their homes become, the easier it will be to plan short stays for them in future.

Babies at this age love the great outdoors and so will be fascinated by parks, playgrounds, and beaches (as long as they have some shelter from the sand, heat, and sunlight). Your baby will also enjoy activities where there are other children to watch, such as soft play areas where there are separate designated areas for babies, or stays with your own siblings who might also have children – the bond between cousins can often become quite special.

If you are planning to use a public transport route with your baby for the first time, it's probably worthwhile checking in advance what the facilities are for buggies. For example, check if you will be able to push your buggy on to a bus rather than have to fold it up; and whether there are lifts at the station.

MONTHS 4–6

BEING PREPARED

Outings with your baby can be lots of fun for both of you, especially if you are prepared for every eventuality. Nothing can spoil an outing more effectively than running out of clean clothes for your baby if their nappy leaks, or not having enough toys to distract them if they become grizzly. Ensure you are armed with everything you'll need, and a little more, in the event of an unexpected change of plan. Make sure your changing bag is fully packed, and that you have enough nappies, baby food (if you are weaning), formula (if you are bottle-feeding), toys, and a comfort item to help to soothe them, and changes of clothes for you both.

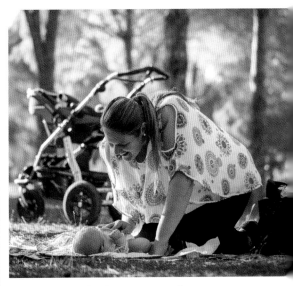

Quick change Clothes that are easy to take off and put on make for hassle-free nappy changes on the run.

ASK A DOCTOR

A friend has come down with chickenpox. We saw her recently – could my baby have caught it? It's possible, but unusual, for young babies to contract chickenpox. This is because most babies get antibodies against the virus from their mothers while in the womb, giving them immunity for the first few months. After being exposed to chickenpox, symptoms usually appear within three weeks and last for between five and 10 days. If your baby has caught it, they may be tired, off their food, and a bit feverish. You may notice small red spots, typically on the trunk, and sometimes on the face. Chickenpox in babies tends to be mild, so is not usually a cause for concern. If you think your baby has chickenpox, consult your health visitor or GP.

Legs bearing weight

Your baby may love to bounce when held upright, which strengthens their leg muscles in preparation for crawling and walking.

Now, when held in a standing position, your baby's legs may be able to bear most of their weight. This position helps strengthen their bones and muscles. It's important not to force a baby to stand who is not ready. It's worth noting that some babies prefer to shuffle on their bottoms. These babies tend to be later walkers.

Many parents share a few common concerns when they start to hold their babies upright, such as whether encouraging them to stand will make them bow-legged. Here, you'll find answers to issues that might arise now.

Bow-leggedness

Holding your baby as they stand and bouncing them won't give them bow legs. Most babies have legs that curve outwards from the hip, then in again around the ankle, giving them a "bow-legged" appearance. In the womb, the legs take on this shape to make the most of the space available.

When your baby begins to stand, and then, eventually, to walk, new bone grows and is remoulded in order to support their weight. The result of this is stronger, straighter legs. By the age of three, your baby's legs should be as straight as they will be in adulthood. If you have any concerns, call your GP.

Slender legs

Parents of slim-framed babies with slender calves and thighs often worry that their babies' legs are not physically strong enough to bear

Learning to stand Bounce your baby on your lap to help them develop balance and build her lower-body strength.

their weight. If, when held upright, your baby is strong enough to bear their own weight, they're fine. Leg muscles develop through movement and play. Try placing your baby on their back and cycle their legs, then hold their hands to encourage them to pull themselves up. Tummy time will help strengthen your baby's arms and hands, helping them to propel themselves forwards.

Flat feet

All babies appear to have flat feet, partly because of "baby fat", which masks their foot arch, and partly because the arches don't develop until about the age of two, once they have been walking for about a year.

ASK A PAEDIATRICIAN

One of my baby's legs looks shorter than the other, and I can't get them to put any weight on that leg when I hold them upright. What could be the reason for this? Your baby could have a condition known as developmental dysplasia of the hip (DDH). This occurs when there is an abnormality in the shape of the head of the femur (thigh bone), or in the hip socket or its supporting structures. The abnormality may be mild, where there is incomplete contact between the femur and the hip socket, known as subluxation; or it can be more severe, where there is no contact, known as dislocation. DDH affects 1–3 per cent of newborns, is more common in girls, and runs in families. It also occurs more in breech and multiple births, and in babies with club foot (talipes).

All babies are checked at birth for DDH, and at 6–8 weeks of age, and those at high risk are also given a hip ultrasound. However, as it can develop after eight weeks, consult your GP with any concerns, including if your baby won't take weight on one or both legs by about seven months; if their legs seem to be different lengths; or if they always turns one foot outwards when taking weight on their legs. After four months of age, a pelvic X-ray can be used to confirm a diagnosis of DDH. If treatment is given early enough, the prognosis is excellent, and most babies with DDH do not walk late.

Sensing something's wrong

Your baby is affected by your feelings, so it's important to try to shield them from negative emotions and accentuate the positive.

You may find that your baby watches you carefully if they hear a note of sadness or frustration in your voice; if you make an angry phone call, they may stop what they are doing and turn to check that everything is okay. If they see that you are sad, distressed, stressed, or angry, they may cry and hold out their arms to be held. They don't understand your change of moods, but want you to be happy because it makes them happy. They still feel very much an extension of you, and your emotions will guide theirs. When you are sad and anxious, they will become clingier and in need of reassurance and comfort. Of course, this is a paradoxical situation because the very last thing you need when you are feeling dispirited or distressed is a fractious baby; however, what they're doing is reminding you that they are there. Some experts believe this "antennae" is a primitive instinct that helps a baby ensure their mother doesn't become too preoccupied and ignore them!

Your baby is becoming more sensitive to your moods and in tune with them as they learn about their world. They are watching you and picking up clues about how to react in each new situation. If you become angry or frustrated in different situations, they will learn that this is the correct and appropriate response. If you are happy and cheerful, and sociable with others, they'll be more inclined to adopt this frame of mind, too. Although no-one can be even-tempered all of the time, try to make an effort to keep your voice and your facial expressions bright and positive. Your baby will feel much more secure as a result, and will learn to react positively in difficult situations.

Safety first

It's exciting to see your baby's interest in exploring their world, but ensure you keep potentially dangerous objects out of reach.

Fascinating objects Your baby may be drawn to dangerous objects such as scissors and keys that have sharp or pointed edges.

A major hazard for young babies is button batteries, which are used in a variety of portable devices around the home such as in children's toys, remote controls, watches, musical greetings cards, and indoor lights. These tiny batteries are bright and shiny, which make them attractive to young children, and as these batteries are small, they can become a choking hazard if placed in the mouth or if poked up a nose or into an ear can become lodged. When these batteries get wet, the acid in the battery can break down and become corrosive, causing burns or serious internal injury if swallowed.

Babyproof your home and try to take sensible precautions. Avoid storing cleaning products in low cupboards where they're within easy reach of a curious baby. Household objects such as scissors, string, and glue present the risk of choking, strangulation, or injury. Sharp objects in handbags also present a risk.

Speech development

At around six months, your baby repeats sounds and uses more consonants. They'll begin to try out sounds such as "ma ma ma" and "da da da".

Much as you may want it to be, your baby's first "mama" or "dada" will not be said with meaning: they just happened to get certain sounds in the right order. But your excited response will encourage them to repeat it, and when you answer their call, they'll eventually (in three or four months' time) learn that Mama is you!

Don't be surprised if "Dada" is your baby's first recognizable word. Hard consonants, such as D and B, are learned before soft ones, such as N and M, so Dad may get the honour of being named first.

Your baby will love it when you repeat their babbles back to them, and benefits when you name objects and people, as this strengthens the concept that they can be represented by words, something they'll start to grasp over the coming months. At this point, speaking is a game, and your baby is experimenting with using their vocal cords, tongue, and teeth to make many sounds. Babies have similar patterns of speech development and babbling vocalization regardless of their native language, so around the world there are babies making sounds like yours! They'll make sounds that they find interesting and fun, and repeat them when they provoke a response, or just because it feels good!

High chairs

Your baby's high chair will help them master their eating skills, and make them feel part of the family as they join in the fun of eating together.

A high chair can be a considerable investment, so be armed with a list of requirements before you buy one.

Practicality

Your baby's chair should be easy to clean (a detachable tray is easier to wash and dry than a fixed one) and be suitable for the size of your kitchen. If space is tight, you may prefer a model that folds, or one that can be pushed up against a dining table and, therefore, doesn't require a tray. Some models can be raised and lowered, which can be useful if, say, you don't have a dining table, in which case you can lower the chair and push it up to a coffee table. Or you may prefer a model that adapts to become a table and chair for toddlers.

Comfort

The seat should preferably be padded or able to hold a padded insert that supports your baby in an upright position. Removable, washable padded inserts are best – buy two, so there's always one available while the other is being laundered. A chair with an adjustable foot rest and seat heights may prove useful as your baby grows.

Safety

Make sure the base of the chair is wide, so that the chair can't topple over without considerable force. The high chair should also have a five-point safety harness, which should be used each time your baby is in the chair – babies have an astonishing ability to slither out of high chairs. Finally, ensure that a foldable seat has a safety catch and won't trap your baby's fingers or fall down while they're in it. Secondhand chairs are perfectly acceptable, but ensure they adhere to British safety standards with Kitemark BS EN 14988.

Changing your baby's feeds

You might be thinking about stopping breastfeeding, or you may wish to mix breast- and bottle-feeding, or try a new formula now.

If you have been breastfeeding and are going back to work, you can arrange to express and store your milk during your working day (see p.185) if you don't want to switch your baby onto formula. Or you may decide to mix bottle- and breastfeeding in a way that works for your schedule and your baby's needs.

If you have difficulty getting your baby onto a bottle, try smearing the teat with a little of your usual nipple cream, or mix formula and expressed breastmilk to make the feed more palatable. Also, try changing teats, or offering formula in a lidded cup.

A new formula

It's not necessary for your baby to move on to follow-on milk as they can remain on their first formula until the age of 12 months. However, whether you have been breastfeeding and are moving onto formula, or have been bottle-feeding, and your baby seems to be hungry even after a good feed, another type of formula may be more appropriate. The idea of follow-on milks is that there is more nutrition in a smaller amount of formula – in particular there is a greater quantity of iron, which babies will increasingly need.

However, your baby will be slowly and gently weaned off their regular milk as they eat more solid foods, and, if you are careful to provide your baby with a variety of healthy foods, they'll undoubtedly receive an increasing amount of vitamins and minerals from solids and become less dependent upon milk for their nutrition

That said, if your baby is fussy and slow to take solids, consider milk designed for older babies – not only because it often contains more calories and is, therefore, more satisfying, but also because it's designed to provide more iron, omega oils (EFAs), and vitamin D.

Whatever milk you choose, it should satisfy your baby and they should continue to put on weight as normal. Talk to your health visitor for advice on formula milks and feeding.

PLANNING TO STOP BREASTFEEDING

If you have a date in mind in the next few weeks for stopping breastfeeding, you may wish to start replacing a breastfeed with a bottle-feed now. This is because it's not a good idea to stop abruptly, as your baby is likely to be distressed by the withdrawal of their main source of comfort and sustenance. Also, stopping suddenly can cause your breasts to become engorged and may result in mastitis. Instead, you need to cut down the number of breastfeeds your baby has and slowly replace them with bottle-feeds over a period of a few weeks. The advice is to drop one feed every 4–5 days.

You may want to start by dropping the early evening feed. If your partner or another carer can give the feed in another room so that your baby won't smell your milk, so much the better. Usually the last feeds to go are the late evening and morning feeds, which your baby will associate with security, cuddles, and contentment.

If you do have to stop breastfeeding suddenly and your breasts become uncomfortably engorged, you'll need to express some milk. Express just enough to relieve the discomfort; if you express too much you will produce more. It may take a few days to feel comfortable and up to a couple of weeks before your milk completely disappears. (For more information about planning to stop breastfeeding, see pp254–55.)

New experience Switch from breast to bottle slowly so your baby has time to adjust.

Rest and recharge

Your baby's eyes are working together to form a three-dimensional view of the world and all the learning and consolidating as a result is exhausting!

Your baby needs their daytime naps more than ever now – learning so much about the world and their early attempts at moving about will use up lots of energy and tire them out.

As they become increasingly mobile your baby will make good use of their developing hand skills to reach out and grasp objects. They are also experimenting with cause and effect, and learning fast that when they push a ball or rolling toy they can make it move away.

Your baby may be able to bear some weight on their legs if you hold them in a standing position, but don't force them to if they're not keen.

Daytime naps Short naps will help your baby to re-energize so they are ready for their next adventure!

On your marks, get set...

Your baby is about to get going! Whether rolling, commando crawling, or crawling on their hands and knees, they're entering a new mobile phase.

On the move Once your baby begins to experiment with creeping or crawling, carpets or rugs on the floor provide soft cushioning during practice sessions.

It's still early for babies to roll or crawl, but some babies do start to become mobile this early – so it's just as well to be prepared.

Babies learn to manoeuvre themselves in different ways. Some babies rock on their hands and knees to move forwards or backwards; others develop an efficient bottom shuffle and never make it on to hands and knees at all. Some babies roll across the floor, wriggle on their tummies, or pull themselves along with tummy to the ground. Some babies crawl backwards rather than forwards; others skip the crawling stage altogether and pull themselves up on furniture and try to walk. If you have twins, you may find they move in different ways and, of course, in different directions!

Road to independence

The way in which your baby moves is not as important as the fact that they do move. Mobility is a step towards emotional and physical independence, and a developmental milestone that must, obviously, be reached before your baby is able to walk. It allows them to explore their environment at their own pace, satisfy their curiosity, entertain themself, and develop coordination, balance, and muscle strength. What's more, it exercises their heart, and lungs, lifts their spirits, and promotes deep, restful sleep.

Encouraging your baby to be mobile helps them to enjoy physical exercise, understand how their body works, and, ultimately, have fun as they pursue what interests them.

ASK A HEALTH VISITOR

Is it OK to use an activity centre?
Activity centres foster fine motor and problem-solving skills, imagination, and independence. A sturdy activity centre, in which your baby is seated and surrounded by dials to turn, flaps to lift, shapes to sort, and buttons that produce sounds, can stimulate and amuse them. Stationary activity centres are appropriate once your baby can sit unassisted, and many adjust to different heights to ensure that they can reach the activities while sitting upright. Once they start to stand or walk, these centres are no longer safe.

When my baby starts crawling, can I put them in a playpen when I want to keep them safe? Once your baby is mobile, a playpen prevents a baby from doing what they really want to do: get around and explore; so they're likely to protest loudly at being confined. It's important to give them as much freedom as possible to investigate and move physically at this stage of development, so try to make sure that they have a babyproofed area where they can scuttle about freely (under your supervision, of course). On the other hand, there are times when you can't watch your baby every second, and if you want to make sure that they're safe when your attention is focused elsewhere – while you make a phone call, for example – and you have plenty of space, a playpen can be useful.

Learning to eat solid foods

When you start to give your baby foods other than milk, bear in mind that it takes time to learn to adapt to food coming on a spoon.

At the outset, your baby will enjoy purées of baby rice with fruits or vegetables. The purées should be thinned with milk, so your baby can suck the liquid from the spoon. As they become accustomed to taking purées from a spoon, you can make them a little thicker by adding less milk, or by adding more baby rice. Baby rice on its own is also a good starter food because it is bland, easy on your baby's digestion, and most brands are fortified.

Depending on when you start the process and how well your baby receives foods, you'll probably find that for the first few days your baby will only try one or two spoonfuls at one meal a day. However, if your baby seems to want more, allow them to eat more. They will turn their head, get upset, or close their mouth when they've had enough. If reluctant to try altogether, simply stop and wait until the next day to try again.

It is important to make mealtimes pleasant and upbeat so that your baby establishes a healthy association with food right from the outset. Ensure, too, that you offer a variety of foods, even ones you don't enjoy. Don't be tempted to add salt or sugar to foods to make them taste better, neither are healthy or necessary.

First foods should be nutritious. One of the most important parts of weaning involves introducing your baby to the flavours and textures of wholefoods. The earlier your baby

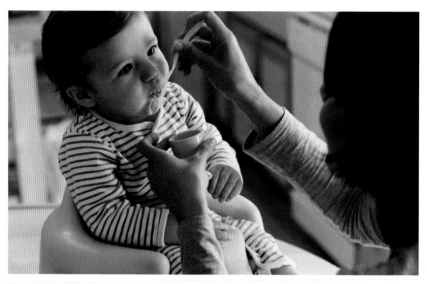

New tastes and textures Eating solid food from a spoon is an entirely new experience for your baby, and they will need time to adjust to it.

learns to eat vegetables, for example, the more likely they will continue to eat them throughout their childhood and into adulthood. So, giving in and offering your baby their favourite apple purée because they refuse the broccoli purée will not encourage them to enjoy broccoli. Remember your baby may respond to your cues about food, so your dislikes may become theirs. Offer your baby one new food every day or so. If they refuse, try again another day. It can take up to several encounters for a baby to consider a food to be familiar, and it may well take that long for them to take to something that was previously refused.

TIPS FOR SUCCESS

To help the process of weaning get off to a smooth start for you and your baby, try the following:
• Find a time when your baby isn't too tired or too hungry – a good time is often after a small milk feed.
• Be relaxed and happy yourself.
• Expect a mess, be prepared for a range of reactions, and don't allow yourself to become flustered.
• Give praise and encouragement for each mouthful.

Sleeping alone

If you're planning to move your baby into their own room, start getting them used to the space now, before you make the transition.

From the age of six months, it's safe for your baby to sleep alone. Help them to make the transition from your room to their own room. Settle them down in their own room for naps at first, so they can become familiar with the feeling of falling asleep in this new environment. Slowly increase the number of naps they take in their own room before you take the plunge and put them there for the night.

You may find that your baby sleeps better in their own room because they won't be disturbed by your night-time coughs and movements. Alternatively, your baby might wake more often because they miss the rhythmic sound of your breathing, and may feel a little lonely and frightened at first. If they cry in the night, go and soothe them so that they learn that you're still there if you are needed.

Give them a comfort object to help them settle. Being able to see, touch, and smell something familiar can help soothe them to sleep. Don't forget to remove objects from their cot overnight

You may wish to invest in a baby monitor for your own peace of mind. Many parents experience sleepless nights when their babies first sleep in their own rooms. You may find yourself waking repeatedly to check on your baby. If you can hear cries and breathing, you will feel reassured that it's safe for you to fall asleep. If you can find a monitor that allows your baby to hear your voice, too, they may also sleep better with a few whispered words from you, or listening to a gentle lullaby.

Tip and tilt

Gently tipping your baby or changing their position gives them a whole new perspective on familiar surroundings.

When held in different positions, your baby benefits from sensory feedback. While supporting their neck, tip them back so they can look at the ceiling; lay them on their back over your knee and tickle, or blow raspberries, on their tummy or neck. Your baby may wriggle with pleasure or remain still as they take in this new perspective. Hold your baby's body firmly, rather than by their limbs.. Try tipping back their pushchair seat when you are out so that your baby can look up towards the sky.

This type of play stimulates a baby's vestibular system (which controls balance). Your baby will rely on different muscles, and the coordinated effort to maintain balance and support. Being held in different positions will give your baby new and exciting perspectives, which benefit both your baby's muscles and neural development.

A new perspective Tilt your baby's body to give them different sensory feedback about how their body moves.

Eagle eyes

Their eyesight has greatly improved. Your baby will watch you like a hawk, and notice the subtlest of changes around them.

Babies first develop depth perception between the ages of three and five months, and by now your baby's brain can efficiently interpret the images from each eye to create a sophisticated three-dimensional view of the world.

Depth perception requires visual experience, good eye–muscle coordination, and sufficient maturity of the nerve cells in the eyes and brain. At this stage, your baby's level of vision is approaching that of an adult's, and by the time they are about eight months old it will be almost perfect. Although objects at close range will interest your baby most, they can now see and recognize things from across the room. They'll notice the curtains stirring in the breeze, a toy lodged under the sofa, and your handbag tucked away in the corner. Once they can make out these objects, they'll be determined to get to them because now they're attracted by novelty, whereas previously they were probably more interested in looking at familiar objects.

AS A MATTER OF FACT

Studies of depth perception in babies involved a "visual cliff" – a glass surface with patterns creating the illusion of a drop. Babies crossed the "shallow" side, but most reacted with fear to the "deep" side, suggesting that, by the time they crawl, most babies understand depth perception. This won't keep them safe though, so precautions (such as stair gates) are vital.

Sunshine and vitamin D

Vitamin D is important for you and your baby. It is needed for the development of bones and teeth, and for immunity and cell growth.

Ideally, we should all get at least 10 minutes of sunlight a day (without sunscreen) to maintain vitamin D levels, which the body manufactures when the skin is exposed to sunlight.

Natural sunlight in the shade is as effective as direct sun, so in the warmer months, pop outside for a brief spell of shady play without sunscreen, each day if you can, avoiding the hours between 10am

Outdoor play Ten minutes per day in the shade allows your baby's body to produce vitamin D.

and 3pm when the sun is strongest. For the rest of the day, protect your baby's skin with a high factor (30–50) sunscreen outside, even in winter. Some babies are vitamin D deficient, so it's appropriate to give a vitamin D supplement; for example, for breastfed babies and for babies with darker skin (such as those of African, African-Caribbean, and South-Asian origin), because their bodies are not able to make as much Vitamin D naturally (see p.158). Ask your healthcare practitioner for advice.

Separating gently

If you plan to go back to work, try to ease your baby into the idea of separation, and give them confidence in the fact that you'll be back.

Happy goodbyes Make the separation as easy as possible for both of you by ensuring your baby is familiar with their surroundings and the people who are caring for them in your absence.

Use the following strategies to make the parting easier on you both. Introduce your baby to their carer, and have a few sessions together so your baby can get to know their new carer secure in your presence. The first time you leave your baby and their carer alone, do so only briefly (say, for 15 minutes).

Avoid leaving your baby if they are tired, hungry, or unwell. The happier they feel, the more likely hey are to settle quickly. To helpthem feel secure, give them a comfort object (see p.282) to hold on to while you are gone – something you have enjoyed playing with together, for example.

Adopt an exit ritual – your baby will find security in the routine. Give them a kiss, and a firm goodbye. Keep your tone positive and expression happy. If they cry, reassure them that you'll miss them, but will soon be back. (Later, you can provide a marker for your return, such as "after lunch".) Say goodbye again and leave. Avoid the temptation to return to soothe any crying – put yourself out of earshot. If you are worried, call the carer after about 15 minutes to see if your baby has settled down – in most cases, babies are easily distracted.

DEHYDRATION

This occurs when a baby isn't getting adequate fluid, for example through poor feeding because of illness, making them sleepy, breathless, or uninterested in feeding. It also occurs when a baby loses too much fluid, for example through vomiting and/or diarrhoea, as in gastroenteritis, or through sweating, caused by a fever or overheating.

Dehydration is a potentially dangerous condition, and your baby should be seen immediately by your doctor if you suspect they are dehydrated. Continue to feed them as often as possible, offering bottle-fed babies some cooled, previously boiled water alongside regular feeds. Rehydration solution, which replaces lost fluids and body salts, may be necessary to maintain their body chemistry.

If left untreated, dehydration can develop into a medical emergency causing brain damage, so if your baby shows signs of lethargy or drops in and out of consciousness, call an ambulance, or, if quicker, take them to an emergency department, at once.

Signs of dehydration include:
• A sunken fontanelle
• Listlessness
• Sunken eyes
• Dry mouth, eyes, and lips
• Strong-smelling urine
• Clammy hands and feet
• Far fewer wet nappies (fewer than six per day).

Showing a preference

Your baby is becoming more aware of themself, you, and other people.
They may even indicate who they prefer to have looking after them.

Even if you both spend time with your baby, the primary caregiver is likely to be the one whom your baby prefers during moments of insecurity. Equally, the parent who comes home and focuses on play carves a special place in affections. Try to keep the babycare as balanced as you can when you are at home together. Take turns to do bathtime or bedtime.

Wary of strangers Your baby may feel shy with less familiar people, and may "nestle in" to a parent for some comfort and reassurance.

Some parents worry that their baby will come to love a childminder more than them. There is nothing to worry about on this score. Babies know instinctively who their parents are, and, as long as the time you spend with your baby is spent happily (with lots of interaction), your baby will never switch allegiance from you. Try to remain thankful that your baby loves their childminder, because it would be much harder to leave them if they didn't, and were crying for you.

Sleep at six months

In theory, your baby should enjoy eight to 10 hours of blissful sleep each night. In practice, a good night's rest may still be a distant dream.

Babies vary widely in the amount of sleep they need, although on average most will sleep 12–14 hours out of 24, and for twice as long at night (8–10 hours) as during the day. If your baby is still waking for feeds, now might be a good time to try to break the pattern of night-time waking. If your baby is still sleeping with you in your room, you might be disturbing them. Consider moving them to their own room (see p.211); this may prove disruptive while they get used to it, but better for you all in the long term.

If you're breastfeeding and you think your baby is waking in the night through hunger, you could try giving extra feeds, known as "cluster feeds", in the early evening before their bedtime. You could also try rousing them very gently, but without waking them properly, if possible, for a night-time feed just before you go to bed, between 10pm and midnight. You could also try this late feed to help a bottle-fed baby sleep longer at night (but cut out a daytime bottle-feed to keep the calorie intake appropriate). These tactics may not work, but they're worth a try.

At six months, your baby might be showing the first signs of separation anxiety (although this generally happens at around eight months), so they may wake up and worry that you're not there. Go in to reassure them and help them settle down, so that they feel secure enough to go back to sleep.

If your baby is still waking after trying these steps and you want to try more strategies, see pp.324–25.

Parenting in shifts

Whether one of you stays at home full-time, or you share your baby's care, switching traditional roles can present challenges for parents.

Parents who take a more active role in childcare are known to find it enormously rewarding, regardless of stereotypes. But there are stresses that can develop as a result of one parent being the main carer and the other the main "breadwinner". The breadwinner may feel resentful or guilty at being separated from the baby. The parent at home can feel isolated. Even if both parents work flexibly and split babycare more or less equally, it's common for one parent to feel that they shoulder most of the domestic burden.

Do whatever it takes to make sure you are comfortable with your roles and responsibilities. Remember that the baby is forming a relationship with each of you, so parenting collaboratively is essential. Talk about every aspect of your baby's care and make decisions together. Apportion the household chores fairly; plan your baby's menu for the week; make sure you're both consistent about naps and bedtimes; discuss what to do if your baby is upset or won't eat; and check that you're in agreement when it comes to setting boundaries. It's important to make sure that you both are equally involved in your baby's life.

Hands-on Many dads are spending more time at home, building strong bonds with their baby, and enjoying the rewards of playing with and watching each milestone.

AS A MATTER OF FACT

Studies show that babies who have spent quality time playing with and interacting with their fathers in the first 5–7 months of their lives achieve more in school and find it easier to form strong relationships.

Interestingly, it doesn't seem to be the amount of time a father spends with his children that has the most influence in this way, but his immersion in the activity with them during the time he has.

Even if you are out at work, and have only evenings and weekends to play with your baby, studies suggest that if you give the baby your full attention, they'll grow up to be more self-assured. In addition, your enthusiasm for fun and physical play develops trust in you and their own confidence. In the coming months, rough-and-tumble play promotes mental and physical strength in both sexes.

Stage one weaning – starting solids

If you have waited six months before introducing your baby to solid foods, now's the time to start weaning in earnest. If your baby has already enjoyed some first tastes, now you can start expanding the repertoire.

From six months on, breastmilk or formula alone isn't sufficient to meet all your baby's nutritional demands. Additionally, your baby is more likely to accept new flavours, tastes, and textures between five and seven months of age, so if you've waited until six months, as soon as the baby accepts food from a spoon, move on quickly using lots of variety.

How to start

Offer your baby single flavours of vegetables, fruits, or baby rice each mixed with their usual milk. Try each food on its own so that you can tell what your baby likes or dislikes and make a note of it. You don't need to wait to see if your baby has an adverse reaction unless you are introducing potentially allergenic foods (eggs, cow's milk products, wheat, fish, and nuts and seeds). These are best introduced one at a time, and then you should wait a day or so to see if your baby reacts (see p.241). Your baby is more at risk of a reaction if they have a family history of atopic conditions – for example, if either you or the baby's other parent or any siblings have a food allergy, eczema, or asthma. If this applies to your baby, keep breastfeeding while weaning as this seems to provide some protection against developing these conditions. If there's a family history of atopic conditions and you're bottle-feeding, don't give allergenic foods before six months.

What next?

When your baby is happy with a few single flavours, start to offer blends (more than one fruit or vegetable blended together). The more flavours and combinations you offer, the more likely your baby is to go on to enjoy many different foods.

(see p.241)

SIMPLE STARTERS

As soon as your baby accepts simple single purées, you can blend them to create new flavour combinations.

• **Fruit and vegetable blends** Such as carrot and parsnip; pea and cauliflower; spinach and sweet potato; peach and banana; apple and pear; avocado and banana.

• **Vegetables and meat/fish/poultry** Try carrot and chicken; broccoli and beef; potato and cod; sweet potato and lamb; salmon and sweet potato.

• **Starchy foods and/or vegetables with milk and cheese** Such as cauliflower cheese; baby breakfasts or wheat biscuits with cow's milk; mashed potato with grated cheese.

• **Starchy foods with fruits and/or dairy** Such as stewed puréed apricots with baby breakfast cereal; mashed banana with wheat biscuits.

• **Consistency** Semi-liquid purées quickly progressing to thicker purées and mashed foods.

• **How often?** 1–2 meals a day, progressing to 3.

• **How much** 4–6 tsp (more if your baby is hungrier) of 2–3 different foods at each sitting.

• **Milk** At this stage, your baby won't need to drop any milk feeds.

First tastes Gently place the spoon with some puréed food in your baby's mouth. They may take a while to get used to taking food from a spoon, and may push out more than they take in to begin with. Simply scrape it up with the spoon and try again.

BABY-LED WEANING

Baby-led weaning is a different approach to introducing solids that involves skipping purées and spoon-feeding and allowing babies to feed themselves from the outset. Foods are chopped, grated, or cut up so that little fingers can manage them.

Some babies who are weaned this way may find the transition to lumpy foods easier and manage family meals much earlier. And because they are given an element of choice, some people think that babies who are weaned in this manner enjoy the process of eating more than traditionally weaned babies, and are less likely to be fussy eaters.

Good "starter" foods include steamed potato wedges, lightly steamed carrots, apple chunks, slices of banana, and broccoli florets. Some babies simply play with, gnaw, or suck on the food, however, as they become accustomed to the tastes and textures, they eat more. There is a risk of choking with this approach – so babies must be supervised when eating.

Some health professionals are concerned at the lack of clinical trials that properly assess the adequacy of nutrition using this method of weaning or confirm claims that babies eat better as a result. The DoH and WHO recommend giving well-mashed or puréed foods at the start of weaning, and introducing finger food once babies can grasp it.

However, what is important is that the foods babies eat should be highly nutritious (see p.210). Finger foods tend to be bulkier than purées and babies may fill up without having adequate calories, so the right foods are key.

Helping themself At first, a baby may simply play with food, grabbing chunks of whatever is in front of them, and sucking it.

New routines

Some babies find it hard to adjust to food coming on a spoon. Be patient, and try again each day. You may want to let your baby suck some food from your clean finger. Keep offering different foods, but don't force it. Perhaps your baby prefers to be more in control and feed themselves (see box, above), or need a slower pace.

Expanding the menu

As soon as your baby is happy eating vegetables and fruit, you can introduce other foods such as puréed or blended meat, poultry, or fish. White fish, such as cod, haddock, sole, or plaice (responsibly sourced), are good first bets because they are mild in flavour and easy to digest. Chicken is an ideal first meat. The dark meat contains twice as much iron and zinc as the breast, so try to give dark meat, too. You can also introduce well-mashed lentils, split peas, chickpeas, or other pulses; and full-fat dairy products, such as yoghurt, fromage frais, and hard cheese.

FOODS TO AVOID

Some foods are not suitable for babies until they are over 12 months old, so those listed below are off the menu until then.

• **Some types of fish** Shark, marlin, and swordfish can contain high levels of mercury that could damage a baby's developing nervous system.

• **Salt** Don't add salt to your baby's food – if you are cooking for the family, season your meal after taking out your baby's portion. Avoid salty and processed foods, such as bacon, ham, olives, sausages, ready meals, and pizzas.

• **Honey** Because of a tiny risk of a potentially serious food poisoning bacteria (Botulinum), it's safest not to give honey to babies under one year.

• **Unpasteurized dairy products** All dairy produce should be pasteurized because of the risk of bacterial infection.

• **Eggs** A Lion Mark stamp shows the flock has been vaccinated against a certain type of salmonella. Cook egg yolks until they are firm.

• **Artificial sweeteners and food colourants** These ingredients are not designed for use in foods for babies, so keep them off limits.

• **"Adult" foods** Avoid deep-fried foods, chips, crisps, oily dressings; sugar and sweetened foods, such as adult desserts; and tea and coffee, which contain caffeine and can interfere with your baby's ability to absorb iron; and low-fat or diet foods (see also p.200).

• **Whole nuts** These are not suitable for children under five years because of the risk of choking.

As new evidence emerges, guidance is updated. For latest dietary advice check online at food.gov.uk and nhs.uk.

Nappy news

On a milk-only diet, your baby's poos were yellow, and mousse-like in consistency. That changes with the introduction of solids.

Your baby's gut can't yet absorb their food fully. And this means multi-coloured poo! If you give your baby broccoli, you are likely to find that their poo is slightly green; give them carrot, and what arrives in the nappy will be bright orange.

Consistency

When you start your baby on solids, expect to find some soft lumps in your baby's nappy. If, however, you find that the lumps are dry and hard, your baby isn't getting enough fluids and may be constipated. If your baby is eating finger foods, chunks may make their way through the digestive tract almost undigested.

Smell

The poo of a baby on solids begins to smell more like adult poo. Where possible, shake the loose poo into the toilet so that you can flush it away. If you don't already have a dedicated nappy bin with a lid, now might be the time to invest in one – or, put the soiled nappies into the main bin outside as soon as possible. You will definitely want to invest in some scented nappy bags, too!

Unhealthy poo

Look out for stools that are too hard or too loose, which might indicate either constipation or diarrhoea, and speak with your doctor if you spot mucus or blood in your baby's poo. Some believe that babies who are teething have slightly looser stools, but if your baby is also unwell or has a fever, consult your doctor.

Having fun with mirrors

Your baby is developing socially all the time. Babies are natural mimics, and you will often see your expressions reflected in their faces.

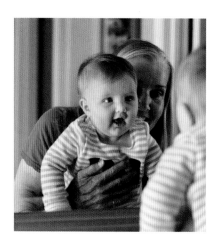

Most experts agree that self-recognition doesn't happen until around 14 months. However, babies love looking at faces – their own and yours – and will respond to the different expressions they see you make, often copying them. This behaviour shows they are developing as social beings, learning that they can increase their interaction with you by responding to your expressions with ones of their own, and back and forth on and on.

Build on this interaction by holding the baby up to a mirror and interacting with their reflection. Pull a range of faces and expressions – silly faces; a sad face; a happy, smiley face; and a surprised face. Exaggerate your expressions to help your baby read emotions. As well as watching you, your baby will see the delighted response of the baby in the mirror!

Here's looking at you Hold your baby in front of the mirror so that they can see you both. Say their name and point to parts of their face.

Vitamins for babies

Vitamins are vital for your baby's healthy development – which is why supplementation of vitamins A, C, and D is now recommended.

Because of concerns that some babies and children are not getting enough of the key vitamins in their diet, the Department of Health recommends that babies are given vitamin drops containing vitamins A, C, and D from the age of six months.

Ask your health visitor for advice on supplements and where to get them – some families are entitled to free vitamin drops. Supplements can also be bought over the counter in pharmacies, but these usually contain other vitamins or ingredients, so talk to your pharmacist about which supplement would be most suitable. Remember that having too much of some vitamins is as harmful as not having enough. Do not give your child two supplements at the same time.

Vitamin A

This is essential for the normal growth of cells, and plays an key role in the maturation of your baby's lungs. A lack of vitamin A can lead to a susceptibility to infection as well as the poor functioning of the lungs and other tissues. Food sources include: egg yolk; butter or spreads; oily fish, such as salmon; yellow and orange fruits; green leafy vegetables.

Vitamin C

This is an important vitamin for general health and the immune system. It also helps your baby's body to absorb iron. Good fruit sources of

PLAYING WITH WATER

Your baby will enjoy playing with water, splashing about and getting a soaking in the process. Ensure that your baby is supervised at all times: play alongside them, and keep their body stable and well supported so they can safely lean forwards. Half-fill a washing-up bowl with warm water, put in some bath toys, and encourage your baby to fill and empty cups, bob the ducks, swirl the water with a spoon, or simply to splash with their hands. Your baby is used to water at bathtime, but this activity teaches them how water works in a confined space, and how their actions can cause it to ripple, pour, bubble, splash, and seep. They will also learn how things float and sink. Encouraging water play helps to increase their confidence in water.

Water play Babies are fascinated by water and they relish the opportunity to pour, splash, or sprinkle.

vitamin C include oranges, kiwi fruit, tomatoes, and strawberries; vegetables include peas, broccoli, sweet potatoes, green beans, and butternut squash.

Vitamin D

This is important for bones and teeth. Low vitamin D can lead to rickets (weakening of bones). Vitamin D is mostly made in the body by the action of sunlight on skin. Few foods contain vitamin D, but spreads and breakfast cereals are often fortified with it.

Iron

The manufacture of red blood cells and the development of the nervous and immune systems rely on iron. Red meat is the best source, but dark poultry and oily fish are also good. Tofu, pulses, and dark green leafy vegetables are plant sources.

Your baby from
7 to 9 months

MONTH

7

By now, your baby will enjoy **feeding themselves** with simple finger foods.

MONTH 7: ENCOURAGE THEIR PASSING SKILLS

There's quite an art to passing an object from hand to hand, as your baby needs plenty of hand–eye coordination and to be able to open and close their grip efficiently. Once they've mastered this skill, they will enjoy practising.

MONTH

8

MONTH 8: SEPARATION ANXIETY MAY HAPPEN

Around eight months is when your baby is most likely to become anxious about strangers or separating from you, so, therefore, may need extra reassurance.

Your baby's **problem-solving** and fine motor skills are developing fast.

" From sitting to standing to doing simple puzzles to trying new foods, your baby is a busy little person. "

9

MONTH 9: PRONE TO EMOTIONAL OUTBURSTS

At this age, babies may cry from frustration at not being able to master something, or become sad when you leave the room. Emotions often feel overwhelming, so calm, patient handling is key. In time, your baby will learn how to better regulate their emotions.

Using a piece of furniture for support, your baby may be able to pull themselves up to a **standing position**.

As their comprehension improves, your baby will **want to copy** your sounds and movements.

7 months

EARLY BABBLING USUALLY CONSISTS OF ONE SYLLABLE REPEATED, SUCH AS "MAMAMA". AROUND THIS TIME, BABBLING AND PLAYING START TO COME TOGETHER. Sitting without support means that your baby's hands are free so that they can take full advantage of their increasing dexterity. They want to play constantly, and enthusiastically explore – and "talk" about – anything within their reach and beyond!

One hand to another

You'll notice that your baby has more control over their hands, and seems quite enthralled by passing things between them.

RAISING AN AVID READER

Make books a part of your baby's daily life to support the development of their verbal skills, their understanding of language and pleasure in listening, and to promote a habit that may one day become a passion. Select age-appropriate books and get them to turn pages and lift flaps. Use an expressive, exaggerated voice that will appeal to them, and don't hesitate to read the same book frequently. Repetition will spark their memory and help them to learn. Look for chunky books with simple stories. Books with peep holes will stimulate curiosity. Keep a selection of books around the house, and in your handbag or the pushchair to pass the time when you are out and about.

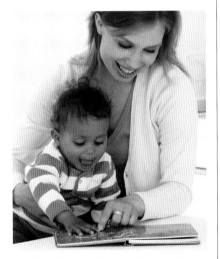

Book fun Make reading part of your routine so your baby anticipates it and develops a positive association with books.

Your baby is developing the ability to transfer objects from one hand to the other, and to accurately place them in a container. They will visually explore whatever they are holding. For example, they might hold it at a distance, then pass it from hand to hand to find out about its properties. This enables them to learn that objects don't change size when moved closer or further away, even though they look bigger or smaller.

Manipulative movement

Suitable toys and opportunities for play will support the development of your baby's manipulative movement. This involves the controlled use of their hands and feet – grasping, opening and closing their hands, and waving are all examples of manipulative movement. This type of movement develops throughout childhood, and involves fine motor skills and hand–eye coordination.

Give different-sized objects to handle, as well as items with varying textures. Small bricks and blocks are ideal at this age – while your baby won't be stacking or building for a good while yet, they will be able to grasp with their fist and pass objects between their hands, and will enjoy exploring the shape and feel. You may find, some time between seven and nine months, that they start to clap on their own, as you do, when they hear their favourite action rhyme.

Improved grasp Your baby can now scoop things up with one hand and transfer them to the other. Give them plenty of objects, such as soft blocks and toys, to help them practise this skill.

While your baby is keen to discover the world and practise their growing bank of skills, they will also continue to imitate you. You are their role model; so while you move around the room engage them and demonstrate different actions, such as picking an object up or placing it into a basket.

Let me investigate

Your baby will attempt to do everything they see you doing to find out all about it, and want to investigate anything that looks exciting.

Your baby's growing ability to perceive depth and see at a distance allows them to spot new things constantly, and they'll make an effort to get to them. The baby may become fixated on objects, such as the pot plant you moved out of reach, or your car keys, and become quite vocal in attempts to get to them. They may stretch, reach, and wriggle towards

Learning touch Your baby's explorations and experiments teach your baby about the properties of different objects.

what they want, so make sure dangerous items are put away. Watch out for your cup of coffee on the table, fragile ornaments, and small parts from toys left lying around by older siblings. You may need to do frequent sweeps of your home to be safe.

Curiosity leads to learning and babies respond to sensory experiences with a desire to find out more about the world. Playing with and exploring different textures, tastes, and consistencies all give valuable feedback about the world.

When's a good bedtime?

Your baby doesn't have to be in bed at 7pm; provided they get enough quality sleep, you can adjust bedtimes to suit your lifestyle.

Consistent bedtimes are important because they help to set your baby's body clock and form part of a good sleep routine. However, settling your baby down to sleep at 8pm instead of 7pm is certainly possible, and gives working parents more opportunities to spend some quality time together. If you do go for the later bedtime, ensure the room is dark enough to allow the baby to sleep a little later in the morning – they will still need at least 8–10 hours a night, regardless of when it starts and stops.

If you're waiting for a parent to get back from work, make sure they don't overstimulate the baby with exciting fun and games in advance of bedtime. While it is a happy occasion for all of you to be together, keep activities low key and relaxed.

Avoid the second wind

If your baby becomes overtired, they may get a second wind and find it difficult to settle. Giving a late-afternoon nap can help to prevent this. You may need to experiment a

little to work out how much sleep is right for the late afternoon to last until the absent parent comes home.

Early bedtime

If you prefer to have some time on your own in the evenings, and your baby naturally tires at around 6–7pm, then put them down at that time and get the rest you need. The habits you establish now should not be hard to alter later. Babies are generally quite adaptable up until the age of about 12 months.

Food allergies

It's natural to worry about allergies when weaning. Knowing what the symptoms are, and where to turn, means you're equipped to cope.

Food allergies are on the increase, but they are still relatively uncommon in babies, and are very often outgrown in childhood. Your baby is more likely to develop allergies if there's a family history of eczema, asthma, hayfever, or food allergies. If this is the case, when you start weaning (see pp.236–37), you should introduce milk, eggs, wheat, fish, and shellfish (the most common allergenic foods) so that you can watch for any reaction. You don't need to delay introducing these foods if you are breastfeeding, but if you are bottle-feeding don't give them before six months (see p.217).

Some food allergies are easy to spot, particularly if a reaction occurs soon after the food is eaten. See your GP, if your baby displays any of the following symptoms: flushed face, or a red and itchy rash around the mouth, tongue, or eyes, which can spread across the body; mild swelling, particularly of the lips, eyes, and face; runny or blocked nose; sneezing; nausea, vomiting, stomach cramps, and diarrhoea. Very rarely, foods can cause a severe allergic reaction called anaphylactic shock (see p.372).

In some cases, reactions to certain foods are not so easily identified because the symptoms are less obvious and may not appear for hours to days after the food has been eaten. These are known as "delayed food allergies" as they involve the immune system. However, they do not cause anaphylaxis. Common culprits are milk, soya, egg, wheat, and gluten, and symptoms can include eczema, colic, reflux, diarrhoea, and constipation.

If an allergy is suspected, your GP may refer your baby for a skin prick test and/or a blood test for a definite diagnosis. Sometimes you may be advised to eliminate the suspected food or foods to see whether the symptoms subside. It may be possible to reintroduce these foods back, or you will need to use alternative foods.

Don't be tempted to cut out food groups from your baby's diet without professional guidance. (See p.241 for further information.)

Food labels It is important to develop the habit of reading food labels to check the suitability of the ingredients for your baby.

ASK A NUTRITIONIST

I'm worried that my baby might be allergic to peanuts. Should I avoid them? There's no reason to avoid offering foods containing peanuts, or any other nuts or seeds from 6 months of age but introduce them in small portions. Advice suggests that your baby may be at a higher risk of developing a food allergy if they have early-onset or moderate-severe eczema or already have a food allergy. In these cases, your baby has a higher risk of developing a nut allergy, and you should talk to your health visitor or GP before giving your child food containing nuts (such as peanut butter) for the first time.

Can I arrange for my baby to be tested privately to diagnose a food allergy? It's very important to see your GP in the first instance to rule out any other possible cause for any symptoms your baby is experiencing. The NHS does offer allergy testing, usually in hospital outpatient clinics. If you choose to go private, it's important to see an accredited, trained specialist (see the Allergy UK website for details, p.385). Some commercial allergy-testing kits, such as hair analysis tests and VEGA tests (where electrodes on the skin detect allergies), aren't recommended by doctors. There is little scientific evidence to support them, and some may even be dangerous for babies.

Less vital statistics

If you are still struggling to return to your pre-pregnancy weight and fitness levels, cut yourself a bit of slack.

Most women put on weight steadily over the nine months of pregnancy, so it makes sense that it may take time to lose any extra pounds after the birth. While exclusive breastfeeding can encourage continual weight loss, some women say that any extra pounds refused to shift until they stopped breastfeeding. Losing weight can depend on your individual build and metabolism. Most women's bodies change completely during pregnancy and never return to their pre-pregnancy shape. You may find,

for example, that while you've lost the weight, your waist is thicker, your breasts may be smaller or heavier, and your hips may be broader or rounder. Change doesn't have to be viewed as a bad thing. Focus on what amazing things your body has done and continues to do for both you and your baby.

If you are a healthy weight try to reframe your thoughts from negative to positive, or just neutral. If your healthcare practitioner does advise weight loss, take a look at your diet to

see if there are areas where you can make healthier choices. Reducing the size of your portions can help, as can cutting back on foods high in fat or sugar. Avoid highly-processed foods, opting instead for wholefoods, filling up on vegetables and wholegrains. Switch to low-fat versions of milk and cheese. Don't forget to stay well-hydrated: try adding a squeeze of orange or cucumber slices to water.

Exercise helps weight control, as well as firming muscle and skin tone, all of which can help you feel better.

Sound combinations

Speaking is a complex process that requires lots of nerve and muscle control, which is one reason why speech comes slowly.

When we speak, we coordinate many muscles, including the larynx, which contains the vocal cords; the teeth, lips, tongue, and mouth; and the respiratory system.

By now, your baby has laid some of the groundwork for speech acquisition. They are using a combination of vowels and consonants: lip consonants with

vowels that are generated in the centre of the mouth, with the tongue flat ("mama", for example); tongue-front consonants in front of vowels that come at the front of the mouth ("dada"); and tongue-back consonants in front of vowels that are created in the back of the mouth ("gaga").

Your baby is starting, therefore, to create some sounds that sound more like adult speech. At this stage, though, it's still baby babble. Always respond to their babbling and be very interactive and positive.

Words of praise Encourage your baby with praise when they try to communicate with you and uses their "words".

Not so silent nights...

Your baby's sleep may not be quiet. You may hear the baby snort, breathe irregularly, bang their head, and rock themself to and fro as they sleep.

Not all babies sleep in utter tranquillity – many snore and snuffle, have irregular breathing patterns, or even rock or bang their heads to soothe themselves. Most of the time, this is nothing to worry about and babies grow out of whatever peculiar sleep habit they happen to adopt, but occasionally you may need to take action.

Snoring and snuffling

Babies often snore, snort, or snuffle when they have a cold or a blocked nose. Try using a vaporizer in the bedroom to add moisture to the air, which can ease breathing. Or place a damp towel over a warm radiator in the room. You can also raise the head of the cot a little to help mucus clear from the nose. Talk to your GP if you see a noticeable change in your baby's habits (snuffling much more than usual, say). Also consult your GP if the baby has difficulty breathing, has a fever or seems unwell, or has difficulty feeding due to congestion.

Irregular breathing

Lots of babies experience changes in their breathing patterns while they sleep. For example, your baby might breathe rapidly, then slow down, and even pause for several seconds before breathing again. Breathing may also change as they become excited or frightened by dreams. These pauses in breathing should start to happen less frequently now, but if they continue and you are concerned, talk to your GP. If the baby seems clammy or blue, get urgent medical help.

Very occasionally, a pause in breathing may be caused by sleep apnoea, although sleep apnoea is more common in babies who are one year or older. Your doctor will need to diagnose it and suggest treatment.

Head-banging and rocking

After the age of six months, some babies adopt rhythmic activities, such as head-banging and rocking, to soothe themselves. From their time in the womb, they are used to rocking as well as being in a head-down position, so may feel comforted by rhythmic pressure on the top of the head. If your baby isn't harming themself, leave them to it. Most children outgrow this by the age of three, and many stop long before that.

There is no indication that rocking or head-banging is a sign of an emotional disorder. Sometimes babies bang their heads to distract themselves from the pain of a sore throat, teething, or an ear infection.

Comfort habit Your baby can find it soothing to suck their thumb or fingers, which can help them to settle and fall asleep.

ASK A DOCTOR

I've heard of something called ALTE. What is this? Rarely, babies stop breathing for a longer period than a few seconds, which causes oxygen levels in the blood to drop. This can give the skin a white or blue appearance, and the baby can also choke or gag, and/or become floppy or stiff. Such an episode is called an Apparent Life-Threatening Event (ALTE), which used to be called a "near miss cot death". This should be treated as an emergency, and the baby may need resuscitation. Even if a baby recovers fairly rapidly on their own, an ambulance should be called and they should be assessed in hospital, and their condition prior to the episode assessed. Monitoring over the weeks following ALTE is important to ensure that the baby has recovered fully.

Separation anxiety

Your baby is approaching the age at which separation anxiety sets in, which can be difficult not just for the baby, but also for you.

Suddenly, it seems, your happy, independent baby may cry each time you leave the room or put them down. They may hate to be alone, and look for you rather than engaging in the activities they usually enjoy. This is completely normal, even if it is a little frustrating. Your baby doesn't want to be without you, and will do what they can to prevent your departure.

At this age, your baby is learning to develop trust, so to support this it is important that you recognize their fears and emotions, and do whatever you can to help them feel secure.

Go to them whenever they call you, and give a little cuddle to help them feel more confident. Talk to them when you are out of sight, so that they know you are there, and return frequently so they understand that you will always return.

While frequently stopping whatever you are doing to reassure your baby can be time-consuming at the outset, the baby needs to learn to feel safe and to understand that you will always be there, even when they can't see you. When you leave, the baby must learn that you will always come back. These feelings are the foundation of trust and emotional wellbeing, so constant reassurance at this stage will go a long way towards encouraging confidence and independence later on.

Hands together

Your baby is now aware that both hands are theirs, and they're beginning to work out that they can operate those hands simultaneously.

Your baby may reach for a toy with one hand and peruse it. Suddenly, their attention is captured by another toy. They know that one hand is busy, so they'll put the other to work to grasp what they see. They may look at both toys with interest, or perhaps drop one to focus on the other. They may see something else and the process will begin again. Your baby can use both hands, but they haven't quite worked out how best to use them together for even better results! They may pass a toy from hand to hand, and bang toys together, but those actions are likely to be slightly clumsy as they are probably not intentional. They may manage to place two hands on the same object, pick it up, and turn it over, but when something else catches their attention, they'll forget that they're holding something at all, and drop it.

With help, your baby may be able to hold a beaker with both hands, but they're likely to let go unexpectedly and may find it difficult to pick it up and guide it to their lips.

Better grasp Babies develop hand skills by touching, reaching, exploring, and grasping, so give lots of opportunity to do just that.

Your baby's drinks

Are follow-on formulas beneficial for your baby, and what else should they be drinking – or not – in the second half of the first year?

If you're breastfeeding, breastmilk is the ideal drink for your baby for the first six months and, together with an increasingly varied diet, can form the basis of nutrition up until one year.

If your baby is formula-fed, you are mixing breast and formula, or thinking of weaning them off breastmilk, you may wonder which type of formula is suitable after six months, and whether you should switch to one for older babies.

Formulas contain two types of protein: whey and casein. First formulas, suitable from birth, are whey-based, which is easy for your baby to digest. Follow-on and "hungry baby" formulas marketed at babies over six months, are casein-based, which takes longer to digest and is thought therefore to keep babies satisfied for longer. However, there is no significant nutritional difference between the two, and first formula is suitable for your baby for the whole of their first year.

Soya formula is not suitable before six months. After this, some choose soya if they wish to exclude animal proteins from their baby's diet. Soya is also promoted as an option for babies allergic to cow's milk formula. However, these babies can also be allergic to soya milk, and there are more suitable formulas, known as fully hydrolysed formulas, that GPs prescribe for babies with an allergy. Soya also contains glucose, which can damage your baby's teeth. Talk to

your health visitor or GP before giving soya formula milk.

Goat's and sheep's milk and oat drinks are also promoted as an alternative for babies with cow's milk allergy. However, these are not suitable under one year as they contain insufficient iron and other nutrients. Goat's milk also contains lactose so isn't a good low-allergenic alternative. Don't give full-fat cow's milk until one year.

Quenching thirst

Once your baby is on solids, you can supplement feeds with another drink at mealtimes. Tap water is best, and after six months there's no need to boil it. Avoid bottled water, but if you have no choice, buy water with under 200mg sodium per litre. Fruit juice contains vitamin C and can be especially beneficial if your baby is vegetarian. It's fine after six months, but to protect your baby's teeth, give it only at mealtimes, in a lidded cup,

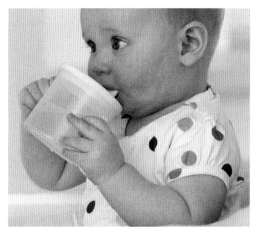

Mastering a cup Encourage your baby to start drinking from a cup after six months.

and diluted to a ratio of one part juice to 10 parts water. Fruit drinks, squashes, and flavoured milks should be avoided under one year, and limited or avoided after this; and fizzy drinks, and other caffeine-containing drinks, shouldn't form any part of a young child's diet.

ASK A PARENT

My baby cries and spits out all the solid food I offer. What can I do? Offer some breastmilk on a spoon to get the baby used to the idea of the spoon itself. Mix the vegetable purée with breastmilk to make it seem more familiar, then slowly reduce the amount of milk you add. Give your baby their own spoon with a chunky handle and a little purée in a bowl. Let

them use their hands and spoon to play with their food; most will probably end up in their hair, but their instinct will be to put some into their mouth. This may be an easier way to make the transition to new tastes and textures. If your baby still resists, leave it for a little while, then try again when you know that they're hungry and in a more receptive mood.

Using the right words

Your baby is too young to understand instructions, but it's valuable to begin using the words "yes" and "no" to introduce these concepts.

While your baby will not yet understand the concepts of "yes" and "No" (and no is often overused when it comes to children, making it ineffective), do use them to start conveying their meaning. It is helpful to use "no" paired with a firm tone and a shake of the head or finger if your baby is in danger. When you say "no" like this, you will also need to act quickly as your baby won't stop on your say so at this age. As your baby grows, it is most helpful to tell them what you want them to do, rather than not to do: for example, "Hold the teddy", rather than "Don't drop it". Children respond quicker when they know what you do want.

Use distraction – entertaining with a new toy or pulling funny faces – to deter unwanted behaviour. It's not appropriate to introduce discipline now, as telling off a baby is likely to distress them at this age.

Equally, don't hesitate to say "yes" when your baby does things correctly. Praise, a big smile, and a positive, cheerful "yes", while you nod your head, will encourage them to continue in the same vein.

Enjoying music

The best way to teach your baby musical appreciation is to fill their life with all kinds of music and enjoy it with them.

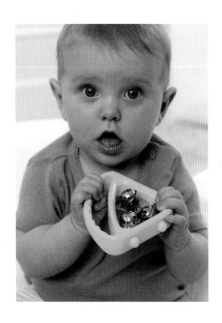

Making music Pass over the baby musical instruments and create music together. Dance along as they shake and rattle.

Your baby may display a preference for certain types of music. There may be a calm song that always soothes them if they are frustrated or helps them fall asleep, and some favourite playtime music that makes them giggle and has the power to entertain even when they are unsettled.

Music encourages the development of speech, and research suggests that babies exposed to lots of music are better able to understand the patterns of speech and grammar, and language development is enhanced. Also, studies show that soothing music can reduce the stress hormone cortisol, while lively music will engage your baby, but may overstimulate them if they're tired. One study on the effect of music on young children found that soft music (in this case, lullabies) relaxed restless children.

Whatever the long-term effects, there is no doubt that your baby will enjoy listening to and making music. Sing along and hold them in your arms or on your lap as you move to music. Bear in mind that they can learn from all types of musical genres. It isn't only classical music that works on their brain's neural pathways – any music will do the same.

Practical babywear

Now that your baby is bigger and more mobile, you may need a few more items of clothing that allow them to move about comfortably.

Loose clothing Choose garments that do not restrict your baby's movements. Stretchy baby leggings are ideal and are very versatile.

Choose garments that are a little on the large size to give your baby space to manoeuvre. They'll be on their hands and knees a lot, so patches, reinforcements, or padding on the knees will help to keep them comfortable (and the trousers intact). Long-sleeved shirts can protect little forearms and elbows. Find fabrics that will wash well, not require ironing, and that will be kind to your baby's skin (there will be a lot of chafing as they learn to crawl and walk).

T-shirts and vests with easy-to-fasten poppers at the crotch will keep them cosy and clothes with poppers and elasticated waists are excellent for quick changes as your baby inevitably tries to wriggle away.

All change!
Weaning is a messy business and you can expect several changes of clothes a day. Go for tops and bottoms that can be mixed and matched. Don't spend a lot of money – clothing will be stained (and then outgrown)!

Feet first
Your baby may be trying to move, so they'll need to get a grip on the floor. Socks with little grip pads on the soles are ideal. If the weather doesn't call for socks, let them go barefoot – the best grip of all. Babies need socks and bootees only for warmth; they don't need shoes to learn to walk and should not, in fact, be fitted for their first pair until they are cruising or walking confidently.

ASK A HEALTH VISITOR

I have always put my baby to sleep on their back to lower the risk of SIDS. But now, they've started to flip over and sleep on their stomach. Should I turn them back? There isn't much point in turning them on to their back again once they've learned to roll over. If they prefer sleeping on their stomach, that's where they'll end up. While you keep putting your baby to bed on their back until they are one year old, the high-risk period for SIDS is generally passed by the time a baby can turn over. Just make sure that your baby's cot is safe and continue to follow the guidelines for preventing SIDS, such as avoiding pillows and duvets (see p.31). But try not to worry if their position changes during the night.

My baby's hands and feet are very cool at night, but they are sleeping well. Do they need more layers? Their hands and feet will always be cooler than the rest of their body. A better gauge is to put your hand under their neck and feel their face. If these are warm, they're probably dressed appropriately; if they feel cool, try another light blanket or pop on a pair of bed socks. Sweating around their face, head, or neck is a sign that they are overheating – it is very important to avoid this. Provided your baby's room is kept at a temperature of around 16–20°C (60.8–68°F), ideally 18°C (64.4°F), they shouldn't become too cold or too hot.

Talking with gestures

Your baby is beginning to understand how words and gestures go together. Activity rhymes can encourage this development.

Your baby may begin to make gestures, such as raising their whole hand towards something they want, which will rapidly develop into pointing over the next couple of months. Encourage your baby to pat or touch things in their books by saying, "Where's the cow?", "Where is the dog?", then point to them to help your baby make the connection. When they look at and gesture to their favourite toy, bring it to them so that they know their signal is understood. They may direct you to what they want with their gaze, and babble, or wave their hand.

Until they learn to point, your baby may gesture with their fist: they may ball up their hand and stretch out their arm. At about nine months, they will learn instrumental pointing, involving an outstretched arm and an extended index finger.

Imitating gestures

Around this time, your baby may be able to imitate some hand movements in activity rhymes, and copy you when you stroke a soft toy. Say, "Pat-pat" when you stroke the toy, so that your baby may learn that actions and gestures are associated with words, too. Two studies found that babies who are encouraged to gesture in advance of, and then in conjunction with speech, learn to speak more quickly and have faster cognitive development.

Giving clues Help your baby learn simple concepts such as "hungry" or "tired" by pairing hand gestures with your words.

USING A CUP

Once your baby can hold onto things and starts to eat finger foods, you can introduce a cup for drinking water. Choose one with a spout, preferably soft, and a large handle they can easily get hold of. It will be dropped, so look out for one that will bounce without the lid falling off! Learning to drink from a lidded cup is important, as by now your baby should be giving up bottles with slow-flowing teats. If you choose to give diluted fruit juice, it should only be given in a lidded cup at mealtimes so that emerging teeth are not bathed in sugars for longer than it takes to finish a drink (see also p.229).

ASK A DOCTOR

My baby is constantly teary-eyed. Will this clear up? Newborn babies have tiny tear ducts in the corner of each eye. When tears start being produced, at around one month, they drain away through these ducts. Occasionally, the ducts in newborns are blocked. However, this is not a cause for concern, and most blocked tear ducts resolve themselves by the end of the first year. Your GP may show you how to unblock them. If the eye becomes crusty, clean them with cotton wool pads dampened with cooled boiled water. If you notice any redness in the eye or a yellow discharge, consult your GP as your baby may need antibiotic drops.

Should my baby be vaccinated against swine flu? If your baby is healthy, they don't need this vaccination. It is only recommended for babies over six months with a long-term health condition who risk complications if they catch the flu.

Is it normal for my baby to pull up their legs and grimace when they do a bowel movement? They're just helping their bowels move. Drawing up the legs creates a squatting position, which makes it easier to poo. It doesn't mean that they have a problem or are in pain. As long as their movements are regular and there's no blood in their stools, they're fine.

Building awareness

Your baby's grasp of the concept of object permanence is maturing. They will delight in games of hide and seek and may hide from you!

Your baby's cognitive development is continuing apace, and they will now show that they're beginning to gain the concept of object permanence – that an object exists even when they can't see it. This means that they may continue to look for a toy if it is covered with a cloth or has fallen out of sight, and will delight in games that involve the disappearance and reappearance of an object, face, or toy.

They will apply this understanding to other parts of their life, too, for example, pulling the covers away from your head when you are sleeping to check that you are still there, and moving toys to find something underneath.

Emotional implications

Your baby is approaching the age when separation anxiety starts to set in (see p.263). This development, coupled with their increased understanding of object permanence, may make your baby much clingier than usual. While once they may have played happily on their own, oblivious to your presence even when you popped in and out of the room doing chores, they will now start to wonder where you are when they can't see or hear you. After all, you are not in sight, so you must be there somewhere. It's no longer "out of sight, out of mind", and they may shout and cry to bring you back. Reassure your baby by responding to them when they cry out so that they begin to feel confident that you are nearby even when they can't see you, and that you are still there to answer their needs when they call out.

DEVELOPMENT ACTIVITY: PEEK-A-BOO

Your baby will be a big fan of peek-a-boo games now and will love to play them with you. They may think they're invisible when they can't see you, and find it great fun to "reappear", even though they've been there all along.

Playing peek-a-boo at this age can reinforce their understanding of the concept of object permanence. With lots of chances to rediscover that "missing" things are not gone forever, your baby will eventually learn to cope more effectively with feelings of anxiety when you are not able to be with them.

Surprise! As your baby gets used to this game, you can make it even more enjoyable by using a range of silly expressions.

ASK A PAEDIATRICIAN

How can I reduce the risk of my baby getting asthma? If one of you, or another one of your children, has asthma, breastfeeding your baby for as long as possible will reduce the risk of developing asthma. You can also reduce the risk by both you and your partner avoiding smoking during and after pregnancy. Replacing old thick-pile carpets and rugs with laminate, wood, or lino flooring, and replacing old bedding and cushions reduces your baby's exposure to dust, which in turn reduces the risk of getting asthma. Some children experience increased symptoms with certain pets, so research this before introducing a pet into the home.

Emotional awareness

Your baby's emotional antennae are sensitive. They'll pick up on stress in their immediate environment and will be affected by it.

We know that if babies are hungry and not fed, or not given comfort when distressed, they experience symptoms of stress. As babies are still developing their sense of security, and are not equipped physically or emotionally to deal with high levels of stress, this can have a profound effect on their wellbeing. Your baby needs you to reduce their experience of stress by meeting their needs for food,

warmth, and love, and by soothing them when their emotions run high. When you respond rapidly to calm their emotions, they learn that feelings need not be overpowering. As a result, they'll learn to self-soothe when they do experience stress.

Studies have shown that babies have sensitive social barometers and pick up on parental stress, causing them to feel unsafe, afraid, and even

unwell. If an argument becomes heated, even if raised voices aren't directed at them, they'll be startled and upset. Work hard to ensure discussions are calm; agree that if they get heated, you both take a break. Your baby doesn't understand the context of your disagreements, but calm resolution helps them learn that disagreements are healthy when respectfully handled.

Gentle guidance

Your baby certainly knows their own mind, so if they're veering in an unsuitable direction, you'll need to steer them gently elsewhere.

Guiding your baby towards appropriate objects, activities, and behaviours is a technique all parents will need to adopt. Babies may be single-minded, but they are also easy to distract as their memories are still fairly short and their interest in new things is limitless.

When your baby wriggles while being changed, heads for the potted plant for the twenty-fifth time in a row, or tries to eat their outraged

Look at this! If your baby is doing something unwanted, divert their attention by grabbing a toy that you know will distract them.

siblings' crisps, it's time to employ some diversion tactics. Keep toy stashes dotted around the house for the job. Change the toys frequently so they always seem new. Choose a song or activity rhyme and launch into it when your baby is heading for trouble. Pick them up and move them to a different room, tickle their toes, or point out a bird in the sky.

Your baby is too young to reason with, so avoid battles and instead divert. Over time, your baby may begin to realize that they won't be allowed to wriggle away from you while they're being changed – although they may well trying!

Toys for seven months up

At seven months, your baby will be ready for new toys that stimulate their reasoning, coordination, and gross and fine motor skills.

Toys don't have to be expensive to entertain your baby and promote their development. In fact, many household items can keep them occupied. There are, however, some great toys for this age.

Balls and toys on wheels encourage mobility and promote hand–eye coordination. Rolling a ball back and forth encourages motor skills and coordination. Also, go for a toy on a sturdy string that you can pull just out of their reach, or that they can pull towards them.

Toys that make your baby think will sharpen their reasoning skills. Look for toys with features that hide behind or inside part of the toy. Very basic puzzles with chunky handles or lifting and moving will stimulate your baby. Ensure they are not too difficult or they will become frustrated and give up.

Toys that help your baby explore different shapes and sounds as well as cause and effect, nurture their thinking and motor skills. Shape-sorters, noisy blocks, toys that ring, rattle, and crinkle when you squeeze or touch different parts of them, and stackable toys that fit inside one another will all entertain them. Musical instruments designed for their age, such as a baby rain-maker, can intrigue them with the sounds they make.

An activity board attached to their cot or the back of a chair will help them to practise their coordination, and they'll love learning that they can open doors, twist, squeeze, shake, and pull things to get a good reaction. Blocks that can be piled, knocked down, banged together, and dropped in and out of containers are a good investment, as they'll be put to different uses over the coming years.

Finally, don't forget books! If books form a regular part of playtime, your baby will develop an avid interest in stories and reading, and their vocabulary and speech will continue to improve. A love of books will help promote lifelong learning.

ASK A CHILD PSYCHOLOGIST

Is there such a thing as a toy for a boy or a toy for a girl? Toys are toys and are genderless. Focus on the quality, design, and purpose of the toys you give your baby – aiming for those that are designed to stimulate development (which includes emotional and physical development) as well as to entertain. Until they are three or four years old, children will have no real understanding of gender differentiations in either themselves or anything else in the world, so encourage them to play with anything and everything that captures their attention.

DEVELOPMENT ACTIVITY: TREASURE BOX

Fill a basket or box with a selection of baby-friendly objects, and encourage them to investigate the contents one by one. The box doesn't have to contain toys – household items such as a lemon, and clean kitchen implements, such as a whisk, are ideal. Your baby can rummage through the box and touch, bang, chew, smell, and study the items. This type of game encourages hand–eye coordination, imagination, speech development, and, above all, a sense of fun!

Box of fun Place an assortment of child-safe items in a box for your baby to investigate.

Stage two weaning – lumpier foods

As soon as babies are enjoying a variety of puréed foods, they are ready to move on to the second stage of weaning. Now you should introduce your baby to a greater range of foods as well as new textures and some finger foods.

A TYPICAL DAY'S DIET

To give you an idea of what your baby should be eating at this stage, below is an example of a day's food intake for a 6- to 7-month-old baby. Your baby should still be having around 720ml (24fl oz) of milk each day. At first, some parents prefer to feed their baby at breakfast and lunch to give them time to digest their meal before sleeping at night. A simple, easily digestible meal can then be introduced in the evening.

• **Breakfast** Breastfeed or formula; wholewheat cereal with usual milk or full-fat cow's milk and mashed fruit; or yoghurt or porridge with mashed fruit; or scrambled egg and lightly buttered toast fingers.

• **Lunch** Meat, poultry, fish, or lentils with vegetables and mashed potato, or baby pasta shapes or sweet potato; soft pieces of fruit; water to drink.

• **Mid-afternoon** Breastfeed or formula.

• **Tea** Vegetables with cheese and starchy foods, for example baked potato mashed up with Cheddar cheese, or macaroni cheese with canned tomatoes, or creamy pasta with vegetables; plain full-fat yoghurt with fruit or rice pudding; water to drink.

• **Bedtime** Breastfeed or formula.

As your baby starts this next stage, they will begin to cope with soft lumps in foods, as well as mashed foods rather than runny purées. They don't need to have teeth to deal with lumps, but they do need to learn to chew rather than just suck.

Your baby will start to learn to move foods around in the mouth, and this will be a new sensation. So it's important to vary the textures of your baby's food to get them used to chewing and moving food around, which will also help to develop the muscles used for speaking.

Moving on from purées

Your baby will be familiar now with the taste and consistency of the usual purées, so it's important to alter the texture of food, doing so fairly quickly if you have waited until six months to start weaning. You can adjust the texture of these familiar foods as well as adding new foods to them. For example, you can add finely chopped, mashed, grated, or ground "new" foods to purées. This will provide a different texture and flavour as well as improve their nutritional value.

Add very tiny, soft lumps to familiar foods. Don't be surprised if the lumps reappear – scoop them back up and spoon them back in. Try well-cooked, baby-sized pasta shapes, mashed potato, or soft cooked vegetables that you can mash with a fork.

Introduce some finger foods – a little bowl of bite-and-dissolve foods such as baby bread sticks, soft cooked carrots, courgette and potato cut into fingers, slices of banana, pear, and cubes of melon, papaya, or avocado. Your baby will investigate these foods and over time will learn to chew or "gum" them, and then swallow. Make sure you stay with your baby in case they choke.

Larger lumps

After this, it's time to introduce some slightly bigger lumps and textures, and some different new foods. For example, roughly blend some cooked chicken breast or fish so it is not a smooth purée and stir into mashed potato with puréed peas. Grate hard cheese into cauliflower purée; and mash banana into baby rice.

If you are bringing up your baby as a vegetarian, try ground nuts, such as almonds, mixed into yoghurt with fruit purée, or add to sweet potato or carrot purée to thicken the texture.

The idea is to introduce a much wider variety of foods over the next few weeks, mixing them with their favourite fruits and vegetables, while increasing the number and size of the lumps until the baby is able to move towards eating a similar texture of food to the whole family. The atmosphere around mealtimes is really important, so give your baby plenty of encouragement and praise and don't press them to eat if they obviously don't want to. If your baby is really reluctant, check how much milk they are having and perhaps avoid giving a milk feed in the hour or two up to mealtime to see if this helps.

How much?

Most babies won't eat much more than a tablespoon or two of a purée at the beginning of this stage, but this can dramatically increase as milk feeds start to decrease. Your baby needs a diet that contains protein, carbohydrates, and fat as well as a range of vitamins and minerals. To achieve this, they need to have foods from the four food groups (see p.193). You'll be able to work all these foods into two or three small meals per day.

Checking for reactions

If your baby has not reacted to foods up until now, you may just prefer to jot down what they like and keep on trying the foods they seem to dislike. However, if your baby has reacted to foods, it is likely you'll have discussed this with your health visitor or GP. They will advise you how to introduce other potentially allergenic foods.

IDEAL FINGER FOODS

• Vegetables steamed or cooked in the microwave until soft: carrots, sweet potato, baby corn, green beans, broccoli or cauliflower florets.
• Plain cooked potatoes cut into wedges, steamed new potatoes, slices of courgette or parsnip.

• A few flakes of white fish, with a vegetable purée for "dipping".
• Toast soldiers or fingers of grilled cheese on toast.
• Miniature, unsalted, and unflavoured rice cakes.
• Cream cheese spread on pitta bread fingers, or sliced chapatti bread.
• Hard-boiled eggs cut into wedges.
• Chunks of cheese.
• Soft ripe fruit, such as sliced pear, melon, banana, avocado, nectarine, and berries.
• Cooked pasta shapes served plain, or with a small amount of sauce or a little olive oil drizzled over.
• Dried fruit, such as ready-to-eat apricots or figs, cut into pieces; large raisins or sultanas (you can soak them in a little water first to make them easier to manage).

Happy meals Babies love to grab food and some may be happier if allowed to feed themselves. Learning to feed themselves is a huge step in your baby's physical and intellectual development, so encourage all their efforts and don't worry about the mess.

NEW FLAVOURS AND TEXTURES

It's time to introduce new flavours and meals with lumps by adding mashed, minced, and roughly chopped ingredients.
• **Meat, poultry, fish, eggs, and pulses** Once thicker purées are going down well, add small chunks or minced pieces of cooked poultry, meat, or fish to get your baby used to lumps. A casserole with vegetables can be pulse-blended to keep some texture. Add to mashed potato, couscous, or baby pasta shapes.
• **Fruit and vegetables** Introduce a wider variety of fruits, including berries and dried fruits, and offer green vegetables such as spinach and broccoli.
• **Carbohydrates** Provide a range of cereals: unsweetened breakfast cereals can be softened in milk and used as finger foods. Try pasta, couscous, sweet potato, rice, and potatoes, as well as chapatti, toast, or pitta bread.
• **Dairy produce** Use full-fat milk to make sauces, and add grated hard cheese. Spread cream cheese on toast fingers. Try full-fat yoghurt or fromage frais with fruit purée.
• **Consistency** Mashed foods at first with tiny lumps and progressing to larger soft lumps.
• **How often?** 2–3 meals a day.
• **How much?** 4–6 tsp (more if your baby is hungry) of 2–3 different foods at each meal, with at least 2–3 vegetables and one fruit each day, plus some foods from the other food groups.

Growing up fast

The way your baby looks is changing as they grow, and you may also find that their little rolls of fat are starting to disappear.

Million-dollar smile Your baby may now have four to eight teeth, just two, or even none, but their cheeky smile is still irresistible!

Some babies look a little leaner as they become more mobile – all the activity burns off fat stores so that they begin to lose some of their chubby rolls of dimpled flesh.

Your baby's fontanelles are closing over, and, as your baby begins to bear weight and then walk, their feet will begin to flatten. Although they will continue to bounce up and down when held upright, they will straighten their legs at the knees for longer periods of time. Their head is becoming more rounded as they spend far less time on their back, and,

as their body grows, it looks more in proportion to the rest of them than it did previously. They may have a full head of hair by now or a just few delicate wisps covering their head.

Your baby will continue to grow at a tremendous rate in the lead up to their first birthday, but a little slower than previously. They will probably put on about 450–600g (1–1¼lbs) per month, and grow about 6cm (2½in) before they turn one. Babies usually develop their final eye colour between six and nine months, and variations in hue until age three.

Kitchen hygiene

Preparing your baby's food requires good hygiene; their immune system is still immature so they're susceptible to food-borne illnesses.

Use one chopping board and set of knives for meat and another for veg and fruits. Keep raw and cooked foods separate. Cook meat and poultry until it is well done, and wash fruits and veg or peel them before puréeing.

Use your baby's food immediately or freeze it. If you store leftover food in the fridge, keep it in there for only two or three days, then discard it. Tip out a portion of jarred food into a bowl for serving, and refrigerate the remainder for later.

Wash all your baby's spoons, bowls, and food containers in hot, soapy water or in the dishwasher to kill any germs. You don't need to sterilize them, but it is important to continue to sterilize bottles properly, particularly the teats that your baby sucks, as warm milk is a perfect breeding ground for bacteria. Also, wash your hands (and your baby's) before you handle their food, clean surfaces frequently, and change kitchen cloths fairly regularly.

YOUR BABY'S FEEDING AREA

Clean your baby's high chair after every meal with hot, soapy water and, if you wish, a little disinfectant. Pay attention to crevices around the tray and seat, where they may have dropped bits of food. Mop the floor around the chair and look for food that they may have fired across the room; they'll undoubtedly spend some time on the kitchen floor and put anything that looks interesting straight into their mouth, even if it is a week-old meatball.

Coping with chaos

Babies are messy! You may find that your once-tidy kitchen is a shambles, and your sitting room looks like a cyclone has hit it!

Try not to let the mess get to you. You may have to lower your standards and expect things to look less tidy than usual. Time with your baby is precious, and it's much more important to spend it interacting with them than it is to follow along behind them clearing up.

Having said that, you can put into place a few routines to help keep things a little more organized. Clear away the toys at the end of every play session. Make this easier by keeping them in baskets or boxes placed on open shelves, or screening off an area of your sitting room in which toys are piled out of sight.

Create baby areas in several rooms in your home, each with a large basket or a shelving unit in which to keep all your baby's things together. At the end of the day, do a sweep-around, gathering the single socks, dropped toys, bibs, wet towels, and books, and pop them back into their homes, or give them a wash. Take a few minutes to top up your changing bag, so you are ready to go out on impulse the next day.

When you're loading the dishwasher, give your baby some toy crockery and cutlery to organize too – just like you. If you're washing up by hand, a little bowl of warm water with bubbles from a spot of baby shampoo is the perfect play thing (even better if the bowl has sucky pads to prevent it going on the floor!). Protect the floor around the high chair with a mess mat – which is as useful at mealtimes as it is when playing at washing up.

If you can afford help with cleaning, don't hesitate to organize it – if some of the heavier cleaning is done regularly, it's easier to stay on top of the general tidying. If a cleaner isn't right for you, spend some dedicated time each weekend cleaning with the help of your partner while your baby sleeps; or pick one room a day – it may feel like your home is never completely clean and tidy in one go, but it means you can stay on top of things.

DEVELOPMENT ACTIVITY: TIDY-UP TIME

Encouraging your baby to become involved in clearing up their toys at the end of a play session will help to establish good habits, and they'll soon accept it as part of their routine. Show them how to pile their toys back into the basket and put their books on the lowest shelf of the bookcase. Demonstrate how to neatly line up their soft toys and put everything in its place. Explain what you are doing, and repeat the fact that you are making things "nice and tidy" to establish a positive association with the activity rather than making it sound like a chore! Praise them when they manage to put a toy in the basket. Your baby will enjoy this activity because it's with you, and as they notice your pleasure, they'll be more likely to join in next time, too.

The tidy-up game Make a game out of clearing away the toys so that your baby learns what to do after playing with them. This is a great way of introducing the concept of tidying up.

Bottom shuffling

Not all babies like to crawl, so don't be surprised if your baby seems determined to stay on their bottom and move in their own sweet way…

Learning to move around can be frustrating for babies, which is probably one reason why they all have different approaches. Some crawl before they walk, some don't crawl until after they walk, and others don't crawl at all. Instead, they shuffle on their bottoms, sometimes using a hand behind and a foot in front to propel themselves. As bottom shuffling involves being able to sit and wriggle forwards on their buttocks, it typically develops two to three months after a baby is able to sit unsupported.

Around nine per cent of babies are bottom shufflers and it is thought to run in families, so if you or your partner were shufflers, there's a chance your baby will be one, too. Many bottom shufflers walk a bit later than usual, often because they are so successful at scooting around on their bottoms that there's less incentive to stand up. As long as your baby can get about, it doesn't matter how they do it.

Taking turns

From time to time, your baby may express a strong preference for one parent, and even cry or hide their face from the other. What's going on?

Showing favouritism Many babies go through phases of "preferring" one parent to another, so try not to take it personally.

As your baby develops, they may at times show a preference for one of you over the other. Try not to be disheartened by this favouritism – it will swing around to you again at some point, and is not because you have made a mistake, or because they aren't bonded with you. Most often, your baby will show a degree of preference for the person most tuned into their needs and communication, and who knows all the best ways to soothe them. This is usually the parent who spends the most time with them, and who therefore has more opportunity to "read" signals and gain confidence in responding.

The opposite, though, can also be true. For example, a fresh face may be what your baby wants at the end of the day. So if you are returning from work, you may be the one getting the squeals of delight and a greeting of raised arms ready for a cuddle.

Balance your baby's preferences by taking turns with the childcare. Each establish your own special activities with the baby when you are together, and don't be disheartened when they do show an unashamed preference for the other parent. They don't know it may feel hurtful, and they are definitely not doing it deliberately to upset you.

Coping with a food allergy

Having a baby with an allergy can present a number of challenges. Thankfully, many babies outgrow their allergies with proper care.

There is often confusion between allergies and food intolerances. A food intolerance is when your baby has difficulties digesting a specific food or group of foods. A reaction will often take several days to detect, and presents as mild symptoms such as diarrhoea, skin rash, bloating, and flatulence. If you suspect that your baby has a food intolerance, speak to your GP and always check with them before removing and eliminating any foods from your baby's diet.

On the other hand, a food allergy is when your baby has an abnormal immune reaction to a particular food or substance that will occur within just minutes of eating it. Symptoms of an allergy can include itchy skin and rash, swollen lips and throat, blocked and runny nose, sore and itchy eyes, a cough, vomiting, and diarrhoea. If you suspect your baby has an allergy, speak to your GP who can refer you to an allergy specialist. They will conduct a skin prick or blood test, so you know exactly which food or group of foods you should avoid.

Occasionally, an allergy can lead to a severe and life-threatening reaction, called anaphylaxis. This normally occurs within minutes and symptoms come on and worsen quickly. Symptoms include clammy skin, wheezing and difficulty breathing, rapid heartbeat, signs of confusion, collapsing, and losing consciousness. Call an ambulance immediately.

If your baby has an allergy, you should speak to your doctor about whether you need an antihistamine that's appropriate for babies. If your baby's allergy is severe, you may also need to carry an EpiPen Auto-Injector for emergency anaphylaxis. You should also ensure that anyone else who spends time with your baby knows about their allergies, and how to administer any medication.

Prepare food using implements that have been washed to avoid cross-contamination, and rigorously inspect labels on foods that you buy.

DEVELOPMENT ACTIVITY: WASHING-UP TIME!

Babies like nothing more than joining in with your activities, and a little help with the washing up can provide an opportunity for fun. Give your baby a washing-up bowl of warm, soapy water, set them up on their mess mat on the floor, and allow them to "wash" their own dishes using a big sponge and a clean kitchen cloth. Your baby will love being involved and doing things they see you doing, and they'll also learn a helpful skill, develop their hand–eye coordination, and enjoy the sensation of playing with water.

Soapy fun Set your baby up with a big bowl of soapy water, a sponge, and a few "dishes", toy cars, or even cuddly toys to wash, and let them enjoy doing their version of what the grown-ups do.

Maintaining a food diary

Keep a food diary to help you identify a food or group of foods that cause a reaction in your baby. It's important that you try not to introduce feelings of anxiety around food and eating, as your fears may make your baby nervous about eating, trying new foods, and relaxing during mealtimes. A food diary may prove a useful reference for a dietitian or allergy specialist should your baby be referred to a specialist.

Bed sharing

Your baby may be sharing your bed – perhaps it's time to encourage them to sleep in their own.

Unless you plan to co-sleep with your baby for an indefinite period of time, getting them used to their own bed and sleeping space will, in the long term, benefit both of you.

Try to resist the temptation to bring your baby into your bed when they wake up. Instead, stroke them, sing to them, and snuggle them into their covers, then leave the room.

Return whenever they call to reassure them that you will come whenever they really need you – if you leave them to cry, they'll simply become more insecure. Implement this new policy for the first time on a night when you don't have to wake up early the next morning. Be calm and patient and remind yourself that even if it takes an hour or so for your baby to

fall back asleep, only to wake up again an hour or so later, it's worth the effort in the long run.

Over the coming nights, your baby will complain for shorter and shorter periods of time, until it becomes clear that no amount of grizzling will lead to sleeping in your bed.

For more advice, ask your health visitor and see pp.324–25, too.

Time-saving strategies

Most parents feel that there are never enough hours in the day, but there are ways to save time and buy a little more freedom for you.

Now that life has settled into some sort of routine, you may hanker after a little spare time in which to pursue an interest or hobby, or to rest. To gain yourself a bit more freedom, start by taking an objective look at how you prioritize your day and how much time each activity takes up. This can be a really good way of taking control of your time and assessing where too much is devoted to unimportant things, and too little to what really matters, such as your

relationship, friendships, and health. Then try to find ways of reducing time spent on what you least enjoy, such as household tasks. If you iron regularly, for example, think about hanging out your washing as soon as it's done to prevent creasing, and then smooth out and fold the items before putting them away. Or tumble-dry clothes on a low heat for 5–10 minutes and then fold them. If you're cooking a meal, make double the amount and freeze the rest. Shop online for food and other staples, if you find it quicker, and then pop to your local grocer (with your baby) for fresh foods to top up, rather than making long trips to the supermarket in the car.

Speedy shopping Save staples in your online grocery basket to save time having to find and add them week to week.

Pulling up to standing

Your baby may start to pull up to standing with support, but they probably won't find it so easy to sit back down again.

Over the next few weeks or months, your baby will start to pull themself into a standing position. At first, they may need your help, but eventually, they'll realize that by putting one hand above the other, they can haul themself upwards. From this new vantage point, they'll be able to see lots of exciting new places – yet more motivation to get moving!

Unfortunately, at first, what goes up doesn't always come down easily: your baby might well get stuck. They won't immediately work out how to use their hands and feet to make their way along the edge of a piece of furniture. They don't know how to walk. Neither do they know how to lower themself back down to the floor. You may need to help them sit back down gently and reassure them many times before they feel confident enough to plop down safely on their own. They may even begin to have as much fun dropping down with a thump on the floor as they did pulling themself up in the first place.

While they're standing supported, they'll be practising maintaining their balance, supporting their weight on their legs, and shifting their weight to enable them to lift one foot or the other. Once they've mastered the art of standing and balancing, they will at some point take a step while holding on to whatever they have used to pull themself up. This is called cruising, a precursor to walking (see p.249).

Pulling up A favourite toy positioned on an armchair provides your baby with an incentive to pull themself up. From there, they can cruise around, using the chair as support.

Update your babyproofing

Once your baby starts to pull up to standing, consider what they can now reach. Also, is there any furniture that might topple over if used as a support, or might they climb on something and topple off. Is your bookcase securely fastened to the wall? What is reachable from on top of the sofa? Your baby is intrepid and curious, and will be out of sight in no time, so make sure that you are prepared and you have done everything you can to keep them safe.

ASK A PAEDIATRICIAN

My baby's feet are curving inwards. Is this normal? When your baby is born, their feet turn inwards and their legs bow slightly, which is a result of living in the small confines of your womb for many months. As they grow and develop, their legs become straighter and their feet flatter, to aid their ability to walk. Later on, as they approach the age of three, their flat feet will usually develop arches.

At about 7 months, your baby's feet should sit quite flat on the floor when they are held upright. They may balance on the outsides of their feet from time to time to establish their balance, and then adjust their position. Sometimes a baby's feet, or even lower legs, may be slightly misaligned, and turn or even twist inwards (known as intoeing). Your doctor will be able to check if there is a problem. Be reassured that in virtually all cases, intoeing will correct itself naturally, and will not hinder your baby's ability to walk.

8 months

TOYS THAT ENCOURAGE EXPLORATION OF DIFFERENT SHAPES STIMULATE A BABY'S MIND.
Shape-sorting and stacking toys test motor and cognitive skills and encourage problem solving.
Help your baby to learn about sequences and sizes by demonstrating how these toys work. Your
baby's speech is more complex now, and they're getting better at imitating the pitch of speech.

Babies and antibiotics

Antibiotics are not a cure-all for every illness or infection – you may like to know why they might or might not be prescribed.

Should your baby become sick, their illness is likely to have been caused by one of two main types of germs: bacteria or viruses. Bacteria are organisms that can be found inside and on the body (such as on the skin) and can cause infections including tonsillitis or strep throat and ear infections. However, not all bacteria are bad – some help to keep your baby's body in balance, such as the beneficial bacteria in their intestines that help them use the nutrients in milk and food.

Viruses are organisms that cause disease by invading healthy host cells in the body. Viruses can cause chickenpox, measles, flu, and many other diseases.

Antibiotics are used to treat bacterial infections. They have no effect on viruses, so will not work for coughs, colds or flu, or sore throats (except strep throat), or runny noses.

Frequent and inappropriate use of antibiotics encourages strains of bacteria that can resist treatment. These resistant bacteria require higher doses of medicine or stronger antibiotics to treat. Doctors have even found bacteria that are resistant to some of the most powerful antibiotics available today.

More complex chatter

Your baby's chatter is changing all the time, and they now have a greater variety of sounds than they did in their first six months.

Moving on to solid foods encourages your baby to develop lip control as they learn to keep their lips sealed when they chew and swallow. Their chewing takes on a circular motion, which in turn helps with tongue control. These changes allow them to create more complex vocalizations.

Your baby's babble now contains more syllables and different consonants and vowels. They're starting to combine syllables, for example, saying "digabu", "apaba", or "babamado". They're also becoming more accomplished at imitating the pitch and intonation of the speech they hear around them, and maybe even imitating individual sounds. So at a lively gathering, they may babble more loudly and in a higher-pitched voice, and when you read to them at bedtime, they may murmur and use a softer tone of voice, just as you do. This is known as echo "talk": instead of simply imitating the tone and vowel sounds of your speech, as they have been doing over the past few months, they start to pay more attention to pitch.

Early speech Your baby is beginning to communicate in a more consistent way now, which makes it easier to understand them.

245

Positive relationships

Grandparents are a wonderful part of your child's life, as they will often lavish them with their love, attention, and gifts.

It is very normal for grandparents to want to "spoil" their grandchildren, and it can give them great joy to provide your baby with things that you may not be able to afford yourself. While it can be a godsend to have some of the more expensive items provided by your baby's grandparents, you may feel it conflicts with your desire to be independent, or there may be a tricky inequality between what different sets of grandparents are able to offer.

Material posessions aside, you may find that grandparents are more relaxed about behaviour and rules than you are, which can be confusing for a baby or young child.

Talk to your baby's grandparents about your concerns. Explain that, while you appreciate their generosity, you would prefer that expensive gifts were agreed with you first, and that, as your baby grows up, you want them to realize that sometimes we have to wait for what we want, and to value love and care above gifts.

Share with them the values you want to teach your child. Whether these are about positive relationships, working for what they want, or a cultural ethos. Open dialogue will help you understand each other.

Taking turns

This is a good stage to begin teaching your baby about cooperation by taking turns when you do things together.

My turn When you take turns playing with toys, your baby learns the give and take of communication and social interaction.

Roll a ball to your baby and encourage them to push it back to you. Push the button on a toy (my turn), then ask them to do it (your turn). They can lift the flaps or turn the pages of the book, then you can; they can "wash their face" with the flannel in the tub, then you can; or they can hold their teddy and hug them, then you can, too.

Your baby will begin to experience satisfaction when they have an opportunity to experiment and become involved in activities, which over time will build their self-confidence and it will help to introduce the notion of sharing and even (way down the line) that it's okay for other people to do things for us, too. However, they won't begin to fully understand what it is to share for a while yet, even when taking turns at play. In fact, it won't be until they are around 3–5 years old that they'll begin to understand how to put sharing into practice.

With twins, while it's a good idea to set up both babies with their own toys and important to remember that they are individuals as well, and will behave as such, you can also start to encourage them to play "together", taking turns with toys –although you'll need to supervise.

Healthy food on the go

As well as your baby's regular meals, it's a good idea to have a supply of healthy snacks and drinks at hand.

It is a good idea to get into a pattern of giving your baby a healthy morning and afternoon snack, including a drink, in addition to their three main meals. This helps to prevent them from grazing, which can lead to them being too full to eat a proper meal, increase the exposure of their teeth to food, and override their innate capacity for appetite control.

Watch how much your baby drinks, too. If you are using formula milk, make sure that you don't let them drink more than the recommended

Healthy snacks Bananas are a perfect convenience food, whether you're at home or out. They don't need preparation, are easy to digest, and contain important nutrients, including vitamin C.

ASK A NUTRITIONIST

Won't regular snacking make my baby overweight? Nutritious snacks are part of your baby's healthy diet, helping to ensure they get the nutrients they need throughout the day. It's important to look at snacks as part of their overall diet, rather than as treats, to help you choose nutritious foods. Try to avoid feeding them snacks to distract them when they are bored or unhappy. While it may seem like a good quick-fix solution, they may learn to use food to alleviate boredom, and to associate food with comfort. This may increase long-term risk of becoming overweight. Offer regular snacks when they seem hungry, and at regular intervals, leaving a good gap between snack and mealtimes, to ensure they develop an appetite. Water is the best drink at snack time as an alternative to milk (see "Your baby's drinks", p.229).

amount, and use a fast-flowing teat or cup so that they can finish the drink quickly. If they constantly have a bottle of milk at hand, their appetite may be poor for other foods.

A healthy snack can be a useful way of adding important nutrients to your baby's diet. So opt for a piece of cheese, a baby bread stick, and a few grapes, which supply essential calcium, vitamin C, as well as calories, sugar, and fat. Dried foods such as mini rice cakes, raisins, and dried apricots will not go off quickly and are good for keeping in your change bag. A fresh banana, hard-boiled egg,

chunks of cheese, tomatoes, and peppers make a good baby picnic.

Meals on the run

If you're going to be out at a mealtime, pack a purée and find out if you can heat it up to piping hot and let it cool. Alternatively, keep it hot in a wide-necked thermos flask. Carry some foods that can be puréed, mashed, or cut into chunks on the spot, such as bananas, melon, papaya, avocado, carrots, and ripe pears or peaches. Chunks of soft chicken, and fingers of pitta, chapatti, or bread are good cold.

Fidgety baby

Your mobile baby is less content to sit and watch the world go by – so you may need to adapt your routine to give them a bit more action.

Now that your baby is older and more mobile, you may find that they're less keen to be confined to their pushchair or car seat for even short periods of time. Generally, they are now more restless and likely to become fractious if expected to remain still for too long.

This is all part of growing up, so your best bet is to adapt your routine a little to suit you both. For instance, you might want to arrange to meet friends at a soft play area where you can grab a coffee and chat while you watch your babies crawl, climb, and explore. You could take turns with other parents to host get-togethers in each other's homes (your babies will love to discover an entirely new range of toys) or, in the summer, arrange picnics in the park. If you dread shopping with a wailing baby, go alone when your partner is at home and can take over the childcare.

ASK A NUTRITIONIST

I'm trying to move my baby on to solid foods but they gag. What can I do?
Rather than backtrack to familiar purées, offer soft finger foods or a spoon so they feel in control. On their high chair table place small pieces of food so they can explore with their fingers. If all else fails, have a couple of days on familiar purées then try small spoonfuls of lumpier foods, such as mashed potato.

Night-time acrobatics

Your baby isn't only active during the day; they may turn while they sleep and roll over onto their tummy.

If your baby is strong enough to roll onto their tummy on their own, don't worry if they flip over onto their back during the night. At this age, the risk of SIDS (see p.31) is greatly reduced, as some 90 per cent of cases occur before a baby is six months old. It's important that you don't restrict your baby's movements or try to force them to sleep on their back.

Roly poly Although they may roll over in their sleep, still place your baby on their back when you first put them in their cot.

Avoid swaddling, too. Confining them will disrupt their sleep and possibly encourage them to develop negative sleep associations.

A wriggly sleeper may kick off their blankets. Firmly tuck in the covers at the base of the cot to stop them riding up to cover your baby's face as they move about in their sleep. Or, invest in a baby sleeping bag appropriate for their age. Start them off on their back at night (the position they will probably find most familiar) and continue to avoid pillows and duvets, and placing soft toys in the cot.

Learning to walk

From standing and balancing to cruising around the living room holding on to the furniture, your baby's progression towards walking may occur any time from now on, so make sure you are prepared!

First steps may happen any time from as early as nine months, right up to 18 months, so if your baby is in no hurry to walk, there's no rush. Help them to develop strength in their legs by holding their hands and bouncing them up and down. Give them some tummy time to strengthen their back and neck muscles and improve their coordination and balance, and provide them with a good, sturdy toddle-truck that will tempt them to get up onto their feet and push it along when they are ready.

Before your baby can walk, they'll need to master getting themself up into a standing position while holding a support, then bending their knees and sitting down. It can take many months for them to develop these techniques. When they can stand for short periods without support, they may be ready to take their first steps.

First steps

Your baby's first steps represent an enormously important milestone in their physical development as they put together balance, gross motor skills, control, coordination, and especially courage! In advance of walking unaided, they will spread out their feet to increase their balance, giving them a waddling gait. They may launch in the direction of something stable, such as a table or even you, and probably throw out their arms to cushion a fall.

Over the coming weeks, your baby will learn to take a single step at a time, stopping to regain balance before continuing. One thing they won't be able to control for a while is speed – at first they tend to hurl themselves forwards, then lean too far back to redress the balance, resulting in a series of stumbles and falls. Brush them off and help them back up. They'll learn through their mistakes and soon realize that they must learn to walk before they can run!

Twinkle toes Your baby should practise walking barefoot, as this encourages good balance, coordination, and grip.

MONTHS 7–9

WALKING SAFETY

Check that your baby's environment is safe when they are learning to walk. Although they'll take many tumbles, you can help to cushion their falls.

• Tape down loose rugs or carpets, so they don't become a trip hazard.
• Watch out for obstacles around the room that may hamper your baby.
• Keep out of reach small objects that could be swallowed and cause choking.
• Tidy away loose or tangled cords that could cause entanglement.
• Erect baby gates at the top and bottom of the stairs.
• Install guards or locks on windows.
• Secure or remove any furniture that is unsteady and could tip over when your baby grabs it to help them balance.
• Consider padding sharp corners or edges on furniture (such as tables), or remove the piece of furniture.
• If you have a glass-topped coffee table, consider temporarily replacing the top with Perspex.
• Keep drawers shut – your baby may use open drawers to climb up onto uneven or slippery surfaces.
• Cover heated surfaces, such as radiators, and install a fireguard if you have an open fire.
• Ensure the toilet seat is kept down; get a clip to lock it into place.
• Position pan handles facing inwards on the stove.
• Keep dangling electrical appliance cords out of your baby's reach.

Strong emotions

Your baby will be unable to control their emotions, and may end up in tears of frustration or become sad when you need to leave the room.

A young baby has highly changeable emotions, one minute squealing with delight, the next upset or frustrated. While these changes may be difficult to predict at times, each is an important communication from your baby to you, telling you about their needs and wants. Try to remember that what they are doing is communicating with you, and that this is a good sign.

In their first year, your baby will experience strong emotions as physical feelings in their body – their task is to separate out these emotions gradually, and, eventually, with your help and guidance, to label each one.

At first, strong feelings can be frightening for your baby, and they will need your help to tolerate the sensations and to return to a calm, regulated emotional state. According to "attachment" experts (who study the deep relationship between a child and their main carer during the first few years of life, and the profound influence this has on a baby), your role is to show them you accept their feelings, that they don't scare or overwhelm you, and that they don't need to feel out of control or afraid.

One way to do this is through "mirroring", which involves reflecting your child's emotions, but in a milder version. You may naturally tilt your head during mirroring to signal your understanding. Holding them while a feeling grips them can reassure that they are safe. You can mirror your

Reassure, comfort, and calm Your baby can't handle their emotions and will look to you to calm them down when they're feeling angry or frustrated.

child's emotions no matter how young they are. Your steady reaction will give them confidence that feelings need not be overpowering. Help your baby to put a name to their feelings. Say things like "You look angry" or "Is that a sad face?"

Good role model

Be a positive role model for your baby by showing how you are able to manage your own strong feelings and recover from them. If you find yourself struggling to cope with a prolonged period of distress from your baby, seek help from your partner, or a trusted friend or relative, while you take a break. It's important to be realistic about your own limitations, and to recognize when you need time out yourself.

ASK A DOCTOR

Why has my baby suddenly developed regular bouts of diarrhoea, even though they don't seem ill? A change in your baby's diet may cause diarrhoea and/or constipation, as their digestive system makes the transition to solid foods. Sometimes, new foods can appear undigested in the runny stools as they're introduced in the diet, a phenomenon known as "toddler" diarrhoea (although this is more usual after one year). If this is the reason, your baby will be otherwise well, and the diarrhoea should settle down as the bowels get better at digesting new foods. Make sure that your baby drinks plenty of fluids – give cooled boiled water on top of the usual milk feeds – and, if you are giving any fruit juice, ensure that it is well diluted.

Is fresh always best?

Using a mixture of homemade and bought baby food can increase the range of flavours your baby experiences and gives you more time.

Many parents feel they should feed their baby exclusively homemade food, and feel guilty about using commercial baby foods. Nutritious homemade food is preferable, but there are some ready-made baby foods available that are nutrious and are also salt-, sugar-, and additive-free. In fact, combining homemade and quality shop-bought foods may introduce your baby to a wider variety of flavours, colours, and textures. Also, a pouch or jar of ready-made baby food is a convenient option to use when you're out and about.

Further reassurance is provided by the stringent regulations over the nutritional content of baby foods. In the past, parents worried that baby food contained added sugar and salt, or fruit concentrates. However, these additions, along with synthetic preservatives, flavours, and colours, are no longer permitted. There are also regulations over the amount of protein, fat, and calories, as well as the vitamin and mineral content. Manufacturers are keen to provide what parents want – a convenient ready-made version of food you would make at home.

As well as shop-bought meals, ensure that other commercially produced food you give your baby is suitable. For example, your baby needs "baby" cereals as these are fortified with vitamins and minerals and don't have added salt or sugar; and baby yoghurts are made with full-fat milk and contain no artificial sweeteners, colourings, or other additives found in regular yoghurts. They also come in baby-sized pots so there's less danger of overfeeding your baby.

Measuring nutrients

Some baby foods have been treated at high temperatures to ensure they keep safely on the supermarket shelf at room temperature. This can destroy some vitamins, but these are often added back in. On the other hand, some baby foods are frozen at high speed, which ensures that a high proportion of vitamins is kept.

When making your baby's food, look for the freshest ingredients and steam or lightly boil vegetables to ensure that your baby's purées have the optimum nutritional content.

While shop-bought foods are convenient and offer reasonable nutrition, it's important that they do not become the mainstay of your baby's diet.

ASK A NUTRITIONIST

Which is more cost-effective – shop-bought or homemade baby food?
Commercially produced baby food is a comparably expensive way to feed your baby. Making meals at home gives you complete transparency on what ingredients make up a dish, plus you can make a dish in bulk and freeze batches. Also, it's easy to give your baby some of your own meal by putting a portion aside before seasoning, and then pulsing it to the desired consistency.

SHOP-BOUGHT BABY FOODS

If you are out and about, a jar or pouch of baby food that doesn't need to be kept cool can be extremely helpful, and many restaurants and cafés will heat them for you. (See p.247 for more ideas on healthy food on the go.)
• When buying commercially produced baby foods, make sure that your baby doesn't stay on thin purées for too long. Take care that the progression of textures and tastes that you make for them at home is reflected in the shop-bought foods that supplement their diet.
• If your own diet is restricted in any way through choice or intolerance, commercial baby foods are a convenient way to give your baby flavours you don't tend to eat. However, do try to ensure that you also cook foods at home specially for your baby, so that they don't develop an aversion to homemade foods.

Developing a personality

Your baby's personality is beginning to unfold, and you might notice certain traits that seem very familiar – and a few that are unique.

Your baby is their own little person, with their own likes, dislikes, and foibles. If these don't match yours, it's important to accept this and allow them the space to grow in their own way. It can be easy to regard your baby as a "mini-me", but don't be surprised or frustrated if they don't behave as you expect. If they are an extrovert, who loves attention and being around others, but both you and your partner are shy, try to give your baby lots of opportunities to socialize. (This may change in the coming months as they experience separation anxiety – see p.263.) Equally, if they are shy and from a family of extroverts, don't force them into situations that cause them anxiety. Let them play on your lap while you chat; they will probably get bored and, in time, choose to investigate what else is going on at their own pace.

Likewise, if you are fairly laid-back and tend to go with the flow, it doesn't follow that your baby will enjoy this; on the contrary, they may crave routine. As their parent, you need to try to structure their day so that they feel comfortable and secure, even if you are not the sort of person who relishes routine.

Caring for your baby's hair

As your baby gets more active and makes more of a mess at feeding times, you will find regular hair care becomes essential!

If your baby was born with a full head of hair, by now they may need their first hair cut. Be gentle and – if you are doing this at home – very careful, combing the hair through first, and ensuring that cut hair doesn't go into their eyes or ears.

Baby hair doesn't need washing every day: twice a week is usually enough. However, you will inevitably find bits of food in their hair as they get more involved at mealtimes, so you may need to wet sponge it after they've eaten. When you do wash their hair, gently tease out any tangles with your fingers or a fine-toothed comb first. Start at the tips and work your way up to the roots to avoid tugging the roots. Use a baby shampoo that doesn't contain harsh chemicals (such as parabens and sulphates) or perfume that could sting their eyes, and has a balanced pH of between 4.5 and 6. If your baby has very curly hair, you might want to comb conditioner through to help keep it soft and loose. Sponge it off with water.

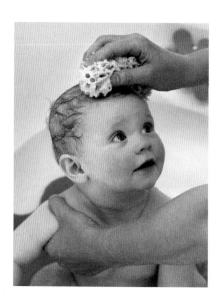

Hair care Using a sponge or wet flannel to rinse the shampoo from your baby's hair will stop soapy water trickling into their eyes.

All sorts of sounds

As your baby hears words repeated regularly, many will start to sound familiar to them and they will be stimulated to babble even more.

Although babbling seems nonsensical, studies show that the way babies babble is modelled on how we talk, in that they use the right-hand side of their mouths slightly more in the same way that adults talk (watch yourself in the mirror!). Research shows that the left brain, which controls the right side of the body and is responsible for understanding and language, is also instigating babbling, confirming that babbling is important in language development. Psychologists believe that babies begin meaningful talk long before we realize (as early as between eight and 10 months) – we just don't recognize the words!

Toot! Toys with sounds can help language development. "What noise does a train make?"

Question time Ask "Where's the ball? Give a running commentary as they play.

Speech development

While most babies won't utter their first comprehensible word until close to a year, or older, babies are like sponges, soaking up sounds, so keep talking. Your baby will watch your mouth intently as you talk, so face-to-face chatting helps speech development, as do games that involve distinctive sounds. Point to animals in books with phrases such as "What does a cow say? A cow says moo!" Even if they don't make the sound, they might copy the shape of your mouth. Talk to them about things that make a noise ("an aeroplane goes wheeeee!"), and talk to them constantly during everyday tasks such as dressing and bathing.

Naming people and objects all the time, including using your baby's name, helps their word recognition. Although a baby's recognition of their own name is usually around nine months, there are clear indications that before this, babies grasp that words have associations.

If your baby isn't babbling by now, or doesn't respond to loud noises or you calling their name out of their range of vision, speak with your healthcare practitioner who may suggest a hearing test for your baby.

DEVELOPMENT ACTIVITY: SONG AND SPEECH

Studies suggest that babies who are sung to a lot learn to speak more quickly than those who are not. Singing separates out syllables in words, breaking them down so that they are easier to pronounce, and listening to songs helps to improve attention spans in young babies. There are lots of musical and singing activity groups for parents and babies, but simply singing to your baby at home is enough. Don't worry if you think you're tone deaf; your baby won't mind and will enjoy being held by you as you sway and move to a song. Sing nursery rhymes and introduce your baby to songs with actions to help them get involved.

Stopping breastfeeding

Many mums continue to breastfeed throughout the first year – and beyond. However, if the time is right for you and your baby to stop, take things slowly and drop one feed at a time to make it a painless experience for you both.

ASK A NUTRITIONIST

Our family has a history of allergies. Should I wean my baby on to soya or goat's milk formula instead of cow's milk formula? If you are concerned that your baby has a higher risk of being allergic to cow's milk formula, it's essential to talk to your doctor or health visitor before deciding how to wean your baby off breastmilk; the medical professional will be able to give you unbiased advice on the pros and cons of different types of formula. They may also advise you not to make any assumptions before you have started weaning.

Goat's milk also contains proteins that your baby may react to, so is not a good alternative. Most importantly, though, goat's milk isn't advised for babies because the level of proteins are too concentrated.

Soya is sometimes promoted as an alternative for babies allergic to cow's milk. However, a significant proportion of babies who are allergic to cow's milk also react to soya milk formula. If, while weaning your baby, you notice that they develop a rash or is experiencing stomach upsets, for instance, talk to your doctor, who can prescribe a special type of formula called fully hydrolyzed formula (see p.229), in which the proteins are broken down so that they are easier to tolerate.

Some babies lose interest in breastfeeding, preferring to drink their milk from a bottle or a cup because it's an easier way to feed. If they enjoy formula, this allows you to wind down breastfeeding fairly easily. Other babies enjoy the comfort of sucking and breastmilk long past the point at which mum has had enough, and it can be hard to wean them.

The length of time you breastfeed is a personal decision. Common reasons for reducing, or stopping, breastfeeding are that you want to allow other carers a chance to feed your baby; or, if going back to work, you need to wind down breastfeeds (you can still express milk, mix breast- and formula milk, or you may want to stop altogether). Whatever the reason, it is kindest to your baby, emotionally, and better for you physically, to drop feeds one at a time.

A successful transition means planning ahead and carefully timing the dropping of feeds. Try to avoid times when your baby may feel unsettled, for example, if they've just moved to their own room, or they are feeling unwell.

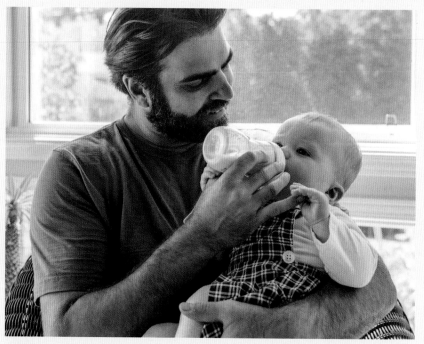

Breast to bottle Giving your baby formula allows your partner and other relatives to get involved in their care, helping them to strengthen their bond with your baby.

Milk, whether breastmilk or formula, remains the most important source of nutrition for the first year of your baby's life. When your baby starts on solids, milk still forms the bulk of the calories, while the baby gets used to new textures and tastes. Weaning your baby off breastmilk in the first year, then, means substituting formula (not cow's milk) for breastfeeds.

You can begin to substitute one breastfeed at a time for formula in a cup or bottle. While there is no set timescale, it's recommended that you drop just one feed a week to start with – or allow a minimum of four to five days in between dropping feeds, to give your baby and your breasts time to adjust. Make the first feed you switch one where your baby isn't ravenously hungry – a mid-afternoon one, say.

Many mums like to continue the evening feed for as long as possible, as it is a natural way to unwind before bed and often a cherished part of the routine. Your baby may also be more resistant to losing this feed. You can continue to give your baby one or two breastfeeds a day for as long as you both want.

When your baby resists

If your baby is finding it hard to give up breastfeeding, ask your partner or a friend to give the formula feed in a bottle or cup. Change your routine slightly so that your baby isn't as aware that the bedtime breastfeed hasn't materialized. Distract the baby with a book away from the place that you usually give the feed, and offer a cup of formula before the story instead of after, or the reverse. Try to keep your baby away from your breasts, and avoid changing in front of them – sight and smell can remind your baby of what they're missing!

You could try enticing them onto a bottle or cup by offering expressed milk at first so that it's a familiar taste.

Dealing with discomfort

A slow approach helps prevent your breasts becoming engorged or leaky. If they feel full, a cold flannel can soothe. Wear a supportive bra. If your breasts are very full and the excess milk does not leak out naturally, try expressing a tiny bit extra, at feeding times only, to relieve the fullness without stimulating them to make more. Taking off small amounts of milk can decrease the milk you make so your body adjusts. If it doesn't and you become feverish or suspect mastitis (see p.59), see your doctor.

Weaning can be difficult for you both; rest assured your baby won't starve themself, and will be happy if they otherwise get the comfort and affection they are used to.

Bedtime hugs Make sure you still have a long cuddle before bed so that you continue to feel physically close to each other.

ASK AN EXPERT

My friends are giving up breastfeeding, but I want to continue. Is it a good idea to carry on? There is absolutely no reason why you can't continue to breastfeed for as long as both you and your baby enjoy it. This could be for their first year, or much longer. Plenty of research suggests that breastmilk continues to offer antibodies well into toddlerhood, which can help your little one to resist infection. It also contains protein, essential fatty acids, vitamins, and minerals, complementing a healthy, varied diet. There are also health benefits for mum: breastfeeding beyond infancy has been shown to lower women's risk of developing certain forms of cancer, for example.

Breastfeeding offers emotional nourishment and comfort, and can play a strong role in a healthy mother–child relationship. If you are worried that returning to work means an end to breastfeeding, it may reassure you to know that many working mums keep it up with a little organization (see p.185). You can express and freeze milk so your baby can be fed in your absence. This can be a comfort for your baby and means you will keep up your supply of milk. Of course, many working mums keep up the evening feed to enjoy that bond at the end of the day.

It's important to focus on what's best for you and your baby, and try not to be swayed by the actions or opinions of others. In retrospect, the time you spend feeding your baby can seem all too fleeting, so follow your instincts and enjoy this special bond with your baby for as long as you want. (For more on extended breastfeeding, see p.331.)

Encouraging good behaviour

Your baby is now establishing patterns of good behaviour that will help them grow into a kind and helpful child.

Your baby is highly inquisitive, which sometimes means that they do things you would rather they didn't. While they don't understand "good" and "bad", you can start to set boundaries to establish the foundations for good behaviour later. Make lots of positive noises when they do something you approve of, and make little fuss if they do something you would rather they didn't! If they pass you a toy or offer some of their food, praise them. Likewise, if they let you dress them without a fuss, tell them, "Well done!" and offer up a big cuddle. Gently patting pets is also worthy of praise.

Babies of this age don't intend to be naughty, so respond appropriately to unwelcome behaviour. For example, snatching is normal at this age. Holding their hands, making eye contact, and saying, "No, you mustn't snatch" is adequate boundary setting. If they repeatedly snatch, gently move them away so that they sense their actions are not welcome.

YOUR FRUSTRATED BABY

As your baby grows, they become more aware of their needs, yet have a limited ability to convey them – and no concept of patience! Pay attention when they're frustrated, and help them to cope by communicating all the time. Respond to their babbles and cries, talking to them and vocalizing what you think might be wrong: "Are you hungry/tired?". Knowing you're paying attention will be the first step to calming them.

Regular "me-time"

Now that you and your baby have a more predictable routine, you might want to book a regular "slot" off to pursue your own interests.

Caring for your baby and making sure they are entertained, stimulated, and content leaves very little time for relaxation. However, by now, you and your baby have probably settled into some sort of routine. Rather than feel overly anxious about how your baby will cope if you're not there, reassure yourself that regular "me-time" will recharge your batteries and help you to maintain a balance between self and family that will allow you to tackle parenthood with a clear head and a sense of calm. Entrust your partner or a grandparent to look after your baby for an hour or so. Ideally, join a weekly class so that you make a commitment to take time out. Alternatively, reading the newspapers in a local café for half an hour, going for a swim, or just settling down with a book, will all give you rewarding and rejuvenating time off. Your baby will be in good hands and you will be a more relaxed, happy parent.

Time for you Give yourself a little space – read a book, go for a run, or just indulge in a long soak in the bath. You deserve it!

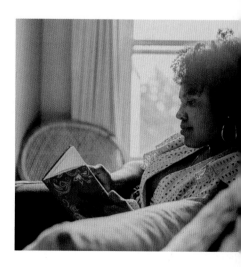

The monthly cycle

If you've recently stopped breastfeeding your baby, you may find that your periods have returned and you are fully fertile again.

All the hormonal changes that your body experiences during pregnancy and breastfeeding can affect your body in a number of ways. You may find that problems such as PMS are no longer as debilitating as they were before you became pregnant, or that you now experience stronger symptoms. Your previously regular cycle may be all over the place now, or the opposite may be true – some women who have never had a reliable cycle find that everything works like clockwork once they've had a baby.

If you do find that having a baby has made your periods heavier or more painful, see your GP. They can check that there is no underlying cause, ascertain that you are not anaemic, and discuss ways to relieve pain and reduce heavy bleeding.

MONTHS 7–9

Still breastfeeding

If your periods have returned and you are still breastfeeding while your baby moves towards solids and therefore starts to drink a little less milk, you may find that your cycle becomes a little unreliable. You may skip periods for a month or two, and sometimes experience only spotting at the time when your period would usually appear.

If it's usual for you to experience some breast tenderness during the lead-up to your period, this can make breastfeeding uncomfortable. Although easier said than done, try to relax during feeding, as any tension

---

THINKING AHEAD

Even if you have not started having periods, once you are not fully breastfeeding, you are likely to be fertile. You may have decided to try for another baby straight away, for example if it took a long time to become pregnant, or your biological clock is ticking, but bear in mind that having two babies under two years of age can be exhausting. Also, caring for a baby while pregnant is no easy task. You won't get to catch up on your sleep this time, and may find it hard to juggle your pregnancy needs with those of a young baby. You may have an exhausting third trimester just as your toddler is into running and climbing! If you are struggling to cope now, it might be right to take a break and wait until your baby is a bit older and more independent.

Having said that, extending a family is a joyous experience and our baby will no doubt benefit from having a loving relationship with their sibling. If they are close in age, they are likely to be doing fairly similar activities as they get older, and you and your partner will experience the wonderful, but tiring, early years all in one go, rather than have to readjust to nappy-changing mode a few years down the line.

---

will increase the discomfort. To help ease the pain, hold a warm cloth on the side of the breast from which your baby is feeding, and massage the milk downwards. If all else fails, try a mild painkiller, such as paracetamol, to relieve discomfort.

Return of fertility

Breastfeeding stops being a reliable form of contraception once your baby is over six months old, or you begin to reduce breastfeeding. In fact, ovulation can occur before your periods return making it possible to get pregnant again. You may want to discuss contraceptive options with your GP. If you are still breastfeeding, the combined oral contraceptive pill is not recommended as it can interfere with your milk supply. Your doctor may suggest the progesterone-only mini-pill, the progesterone implant (Nexplanon), or an intra-uterine device (IUD or coil).

Scaling new heights

When your baby starts to negotiate their way around, it's time to make some changes to your rooms. Everything moves upwards!

As soon as your baby can pull themselves up to standing, they will realize that this newfound technique means they can climb. The first step is often the stairs, which requires a great deal of both brain and brawn, so it marks an important stage in your baby's development. The hands, legs, and feet move in synchronicity to keep their weight stable with each upward movement. The hoist they need to push themself up comes from the coordinated efforts of one arm and the opposite leg, which alternates with the opposite arm and leg at each step. The whole movement requires quite sophisticated control of limbs, and considerable muscle strength.

Babies know danger only because we alert them to it, and although scaling stairs is potentially risky, it is an activity that, with constant, close supervision, helps to develop a baby's confidence. Allow your baby their foray into the danger zone of the stairs, but stand right behind them; they will have a surge of self-confidence, especially with you there praising every effort.

Safety considerations

Never leave your baby unattended on the stairs. Although going upwards is a fairly foolproof adventure, the slip of a hand or knee can make a tumble likely. Furthermore, coming down requires a completely different skill set and, at this age, it's important to teach your baby to descend in the

ASK A HEALTH VISITOR

Our home isn't ideal for safe climbing. What can I do to help my baby climb safely? You can encourage your baby to climb in a completely safe environment by making regular visits to your local soft-play centre. Most centres have areas that are cordoned off for tots which are furnished with small, baby-friendly play equipment designed for their little limbs, and with soft spongy mats to break their fall when they tumble. Your baby will learn from watching other children as they move themselves up and down the play equipment, and will enjoy the sociability of play. However, your child will still want to practise climbing at home, so if your home isn't safe, you will need to be extra vigilant.

least risky way possible. Feet first and on their tummy is best (forward facing, even bumping on a bottom, risks gravity toppling your baby over).

Install stair gates at the top and the bottom of the stairs and shut them when you are not there to help. If you have large gaps in your banisters, consider investing in a mesh to fill them for the time being. Now is also the time to look afresh at the rest of your home and ensure it's safe for your baby.

Mini mountains

It's not just stairs your baby will want to climb. On to and over sofas or chairs, cots, and low tables are other common options for infant explorers. Try to babyproof these as much as you can. Keep sofa backs against walls, and try gently to steer your baby away from unstable items of furniture.

If your baby is trying to climb out of their cot (a leg over the side is a risky feat of agility), adjust the base of the cot so that it's at the lowest height and remove anything inside the cot that might give the baby a leg up.

Getting up It's very tempting for your baby to use any furniture they can pull themself up on as a climbing frame.

Post-pregnancy fitness

Usually it takes at least six months to lose any weight gained during pregnancy, but the more important focus is health and fitness.

Feeling good about yourself helps you to give the most to your baby. Try to focus on feeling healthy and more energized – rather than on the goal of fitting back into an old pair of jeans. Opt for a nutritious wholefood diet rich in vitamins and minerals, especially if you're planning another baby in the future. Also, if you're breastfeeding, you need a slightly higher calorific intake so don't actively diet unless advised to do so. Keeping fit also helps you to stay trim, as well as enabling you to keep up with the physical and emotional demands of motherhood.

Getting active

The key to reaching your health goal lies in getting active. You may feel that your baby never lets you sit down, and this constant activity is definitely beneficial. There are other simple changes you can make to bring fitness into your routine. Whenever possible, walk your baby in their buggy, rather than drive. If you walk at a fast pace (enough to raise your heart rate a little) for 1 mile it will take about 15 minutes – there and back is 30 minutes good exercise.

Resisting temptation

Try to resist picking at your baby's finger foods. Eat your lunch when your baby eats, introducing the notion of sociable eating to your baby and reducing the temptation to your picking at their food.

Motivating yourself Being active quickly becomes a habit, but to get started requires a little bit of self-motivation.

HEALTHY EATING

While you may be eager to shed the extra pounds gained during pregnancy as soon as possible, it's judicious to avoid faddy diets and quick-fix solutions. Instead, concentrate on maintaining a nutritious diet and moderating your portions. This will help you lose weight steadily and instil healthy eating habits that will enable you to maintain a constant healthy weight, rather than yo-yoing on the scales. The following tips can help to keep you on track.

• **Eat regular meals** Eat three meals a day and ensure that each contains at least one vegetable portion, as well as fruit.

• **Choose foods that give a sustained release of energy** This will help you to feel full for longer and resist snacking between meals. Try porridge and wholewheat toast for breakfast along with some fresh fruit. Lunches and dinners should contain wholegrains, lean meat or fish, and, ideally, two portions of vegetables.

• **Opt for low-fat dairy products** Fat contains twice the amount of energy as carbohydrates and proteins, so choose reduced-fat milk, spreads, yoghurts, and cheese, and measure out oils, mayonnaise, and salad dressings with a spoon. It's important, though, not to eliminate dairy altogether as it plays an important role in your diet. There's also evidence that calcium has a part to play in weight loss.

• **Include protein** All meals should include some protein, which helps to keep hunger at bay.

• **Maintain your fluid intake** Drink water regularly; this helps to keep you hydrated and can stop you mistaking thirst for hunger. Try adding in a squeeze of lemon for a zesty, fresh flavour.

• **Eat healthy snacks** Keep cut-up carrots, celery, and cucumber in the fridge for quick, healthy snacks.

A flexible routine

Planning a day out or a short break can play havoc with your baby's routines, but by using familiar cues you can help them adjust.

A certain amount of predictability can make a baby feel secure, and most babies respond well to having a routine. However, it's not a timetable; your baby notices and understands a series of events, not a clock.

So if occasionally it suits you better to shift your baby's nap time on by half an hour, this is fine, as long as they aren't grizzly. They are unlikely to expect to have a nap until you take out their sleepy-time story and settle them into their cot. With these in hand, they will probably offer up no more or less resistance than they would have done had they been put down for their nap at the usual time.

Thinking of their routine as a sequence of events allows you to be flexible, for example when you go on holiday or want a spontaneous day out. Indeed, implementing a familiar routine on trips and visits can help them to settle. As far as possible, do the same things, so if it is a quiet game, bath, book, then lullaby, do it in the same order as usual and keep it up while you're away. They'll recognize the cues and realize what's coming, whatever the time or place.

How strictly to schedule your baby's day is a subject of debate. Most experts suggest a degree of routine, with mealtimes, play, and sleep as the predictable elements help your baby feel secure. It's up to you to tailor-make the day. Of course, no routine should stop you seeing to your baby's needs for food, comfort, or rest.

Question time

Your baby is beginning to understand that objects (and people) have names. Have fun with simple questions that reinforce this learning.

The more you read to your baby, sing songs to them, and chat to them, the quicker they will learn that everything has a name. Brightly coloured board books with clear pictures can help you teach them the names of objects. Ask them, "Where's the ball?" and guide their hand towards it. One of the best ways to teach your baby names is through song – try "Head, shoulders, knees, and toes", putting your hand on the different parts of the body, then follow on with a game. Ask them, "Where is [their name]'s nose?" Then touch it yourself, saying, "Here it is", and move their hand to touch it. Use the third person, as their language skills are not developed enough to understand possessive pronouns and adjectives (such as their, your, my).

They'll want to please you, so if you ask them something simple like "Bring me the book" while pointing to it, they'll enjoy fetching it for you.

Where's my nose? Asking simple questions as you point to your nose is a game they'll enjoy. Soon they may point to it themself!

Using a babysitter

You and your partner may want to go out and leave your baby with a sitter, but how do you find someone you feel happy with?

BABYSITTING CHECKLIST

- Leave a list of emergency contacts – your mobile numbers, the land line number of where you will be, and details of a trusted neighbour and your baby's doctor.
- Very importantly, ensure the babysitter knows if your baby is allergic or intolerant to any particular foods or medicines.
- Tell your babysitter about your baby's health or state of mind that day. For example, whether your baby is teething, was grumpy, or refused food, so the minder is prepared.
- Tell your babysitter how to settle your baby if they wake up, or explain their bedtime routine if the babysitter will be settling them.
- Show your sitter any bottles, or meals, your baby is allowed to have during your absence, and how to heat them appropriately.
- Leave clear instructions on whether or not the babysitter should answer the door or phone, for example if you are expecting a delivery.
- Make sure your baby has all their necessary comfort toys, and let the babysitter know what they are and how they are used.
- Be prepared to return in a hurry if necessary, and ensure the babysitter knows they can call you at any time.

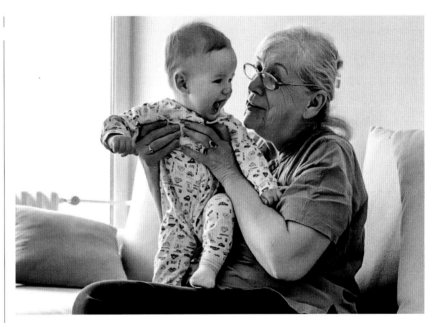

Getting to know you Give your baby and babysitter the chance to get used to one another before you leave them on their own for the first time.

Family and friends who have spent time with your baby are an obvious choice for babysitting, but that is not always an option. If you are back at work, you might consider asking your baby's childminder, or a favourite nursery staff member to sit instead. Or perhaps friends can recommend a local childminder.

A professional babysitting agency that specializes in finding carers, and who will check their credentials and suitability, is a good option. Or is there a parents' babysitting circle in your area – your local library or health visitor will have details. If not, perhaps you could set up your own babysitting circle with your antenatal group or families you know well.

Teenage children of neighbours are a traditional option. There's no legal minimum age, but if the sitter is under 16, you remain legally responsible. You should always feel confident that the babysitter is right. Talk to them and find out how they would settle your baby if they woke up and how they would handle an emergency. Ask a new sitter to arrive at least half an hour before you put your baby to bed, so they aren't a total stranger, should your baby awake.

261

Getting creative

It's time to get arty! Your baby will enjoy trying a new activity and they might even create something to treasure.

Simple painting activities that don't involve holding brushes or creating neat lines are easy to organize with your baby. An ideal place on a warm day is outside on grass; otherwise, clear a space on the floor, or a low table, and put old towels down to soak up spills. Have water and cloths at the ready.

Non-toxic, ready-mixed paints are easy to find. Check that the ones you buy will not stain your baby's skin or clothes (wearing just a nappy is good).

You'll need large sheets of blank paper or a roll of lining wallpaper. Spread the paper flat on the floor, pour some paint into an old dish or saucer. Daub their hand in paint or let them put them hand in it, then help them press on to the paper and make prints. You can do that with their feet, too. Their first attempts will probably be splodges, but you should get at least one lovely hand print to frame or put in a book. Remember to date them! It's a great way to record their growth, too.

Fussing at bedtime

Resistance at bedtime needs careful handling to prevent bad habits forming. What should you do when your baby wants to stay up?

It can be unsettling for everyone if your baby suddenly starts to create a fuss about going to bed. Many babies go through a phase of resisting bedtime about this age. Your baby has realized that events in their life follow a predictable sequence, and they will begin to know what's coming next. They are also increasingly aware that sleep time means separation from you. Separation anxiety (see p.228 and opposite) is a normal developmental stage, and can lead to tears when you try to leave them at bedtime, or when they wake up and

Resisting bedtime Being firm about sticking to the bedtime routine will encourage a reluctant baby to settle down for the night.

you're not near. How you react now can affect their future routine, so do your best to get them back on track. Ensure they have had an active day so that they are physically tired. There's no need to cut back on naps, but stimulate them with trips to the park or a soft play area. Stick to their bedtime routine, making sure it's an enjoyable experience that they want to take part in: say goodnight to the pictures on the wall or their soft toys, read a story, or sing a song. Finally, be firm that this is bedtime; don't be tempted to let them play a bit longer. Be reassuring when you settle them, and return if they call, but try not to pick them up. Eventually, they will settle again.

Separation anxiety

Your baby's growing independence reminds them that they are separate from you, and they may become anxious about you leaving.

From around eight months, your baby is very likely to experience separation anxiety. This milestone signals their deep attachment to you and their recognition that you are their primary source of care and protection. At the same time, they are gaining the concept of object permanence, becoming aware that when not in sight, you have gone away. The source of their safety and care has left them and they're unable to understand that you'll be back. They'll show how they feel through genuine distress, tears, and tantrums.

Reassuring your baby

When you leave the room, keep your voice calm and positive, and tell them you'll be back in a moment. If this phase coincides with a return to work, try to leave them for short periods only to begin with, getting them used to the fact that you always return. When you leave them with their carer, talk about what you're doing, "Mummy is going to put you in the car and do up your strap". Avoid sounding anxious, and don't be impatient – they are more likely to settle if you are calm, even if you have to be firm. Leaving a transition object, such as a comfort toy, blanket, or piece of clothing smelling of you, will help to soothe them while you're apart.

When you drop them off, don't prolong the agony by spending too long cuddling, or telling them you

DEVELOPMENT ACTIVITY: TICKLING GAMES

Now that they has a greater sense of anticipation, your baby will squirm and giggle with excitement and expectation long before the moment at which a tickling rhyme actually becomes a tickle! Among the traditional favourite tickling rhymes are "Round and Round the Garden" (in which you say the rhyme while making circles on your baby's palm with your index finger, then run your fingers up their arm to them armpit for "tickle you under there!") and "This Little Piggy" (you take each toe in turn and, at the end, you cry "This little piggy went weeeeee all the way home!" while tickling them feet).

Tummy tickling You can tickle your baby on their tummy to squeals of delight. Their reaction will probably make you giggle, too!

wish you didn't have to leave – at their age, this sends a mixed message because the outcome will be the same. Talk to them while you hand them to their carer, tell them you love them and will see them soon (or after lunch/their nap/at teatime); give them a big kiss, a wave, a smile, and leave. Wait until you are out of sight and earshot before you burst into tears, if you need to!

Like most things in a baby's life, this is a passing phase (although one that often lasts, albeit in a milder form, up until the age of three).

However, if you think they are genuinely unhappy with a carer, you may want to consider other childcare options. Bear in mind, though, that a change may not make a difference. You may simply have to ride out the storm and build their self-confidence so they learn to separate more willingly. Visit play areas with them so they get used to being around other babies, and grow in confidence while in your company.

Learning to focus

Your baby's brain is not yet mature enough to stream sounds, which means that they cannot select what they hear by focusing on it.

Adults can filter out background noise, but babies are less able to do so, which is one reason why babies startle so easily at loud noises – everything is heard at full-blast at the same time as the other sounds in the environment. Try to keep things quiet from time to time to allow your baby to concentrate on their activities and focus on your voice. They are learning all the time, but this learning can be hampered if they are subjected to constant background noise. This doesn't mean that your household has to be completely silent, but many sounds will distract them from their activities. Turn off the television when you are reading or playing together, and turn off or reduce the volume of any music during playtime.

Try to tone down the overall noise level at your baby's bedtime, but don't try for silence or near silence, as falling asleep with a little background noise means your baby is less likely to wake to the sounds of the evening.

If your baby is struggling to reach some of their developmental milestones, give them some peace and space in which to try again.

Problem solving

While learning through play, your baby develops skills that enable them to look at a problem and find solutions on their own.

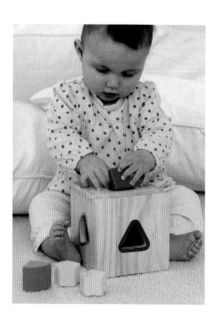

Studies show that, once they reach eight months of age, babies' cognitive awareness has developed enough to enable them to understand cause and effect ("If I want to drink from my cup, I need to tip it"), and that one problem might have several solutions.

To encourage these important skills, simply allow them to play with toys that require your baby to move objects around or press a button and see what happens. Sorting cups (which you can stack, and they can enjoy knocking over), shape-sorters of different kinds, and toys with lids that need replacing or removing (ideally to discover something hidden inside) are all fantastic toys for encouraging your baby's problem-solving skills.

Watch as your baby uses their ingenuity to solve tricky situations such as how to reach a toy that isn't immediately at hand – they might crawl to it, or protest until you get it for them, and by nine months, they may start to point at it! These are all signs of their developing cognitive skills. As always, offer your baby plenty of encouragement and praise their efforts.

Think and play Shape-sorting toys help to improve your baby's problem-solving skills as they try to fit the pieces into their proper slots.

Your baby and screen time

Is it okay for your baby to watch television briefly, or is any screen time bad for their development? There are arguments for and against.

Many of us will have an abundance of technology in our homes – smartphones, tablets, TVs, laptops, and game consoles to name a few. Handing over your smartphone or tablet to your baby, or popping on the TV may seem like a blessing, providing a little distraction for a fretful baby, or keeping them temporarily amused while you get on with other tasks or catch up with friends. However, after decades of research on screen time and child development, there remains mixed evidence revealing both positive and negative developmental outcomes.

Who's right?

The information available can be confusing, and contradictory. Some research suggests that high-quality TV programmes and apps designed for babies can help with their language development, shape, and colour recognition, as well as promote problem solving and visual thinking. While other studies link babies who are overstimulated by screen time to physical health concerns such as obesity, diabetes, and poor sleep patterns, as well as negative impacts on their mental health later on including issues with anxiety and low self-esteem. Also, research has shown increased links between excess screen time and attention deficit disorders (ADHD). Although more conclusive research is needed, there's little doubt that watching a screen eats into your

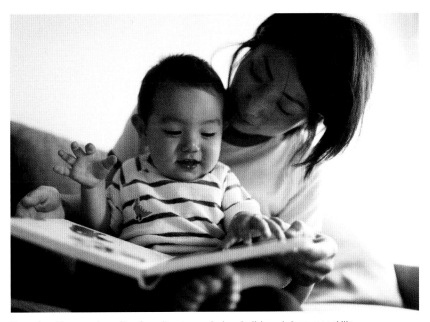

Storytime There are benefits of reading to your baby – builds early language skills, introduces first concepts, and nurtures a bond between you and your baby.

baby's time to play, observe, and explore the real world, and to be stimulated by physical games, reading, and creative play.

Research has shown that screen time cannot match the educational value of time spent with you, family, or friends. For example, studies show that language is acquired most effectively through face-to-face interaction rather than from passive observation of TV shows, however, child-centred. Rather than ban screen time, the best solution is probably to use technology mindfully and for limited periods only.

Keeping it interactive

Make sure that your baby is not in front of a screen for long, encourage your baby to engage with a book or enjoy some playtime. Interact with your baby while they watch a show or programme to bring any learning to life. Point out objects and name them as they appear, and repeat any rhymes featured on the programme to reinforce the rhythm. Try acting out the roles of their favourite characters using different facial expressions and voices. This level of interaction will make the experience together more fun and memorable.

265

Testing your reactions

When your baby does something repeatedly, you may notice that they're watching you carefully to see how you will react.

This will usually work to your advantage as they'll repeat sounds, actions, and behaviours that make you smile, or give them praise, attention, or a hug. But babies will also repeat behaviours and actions that get a reaction from you – including a negative one!

No baby is wilfully naughty, they just want your attention. You can begin to teach that things such as hair pulling or snatching are not okay simply by calmly saying, "Stop, that hurts" and showing in your expression (a frown, say) that it's painful or unwanted. You can go on to demonstrate gentle, for example moving your baby's hand to stroke your arm, saying, "Let's touch gently." Ignoring negative behaviour is not a recommended strategy at this age as you need to stop the baby if they are doing something potentially harmful to themself or others. If your baby receives the best reactions from you for the positive things they do, they will repeat those actions. So if they stroke the cat gently, eat their food without throwing the bowl, and copy you by putting a toy in a box after playtime, praise them, clap your hands, and give them plenty of attention. In this way, you will begin to teach them the boundaries of acceptable behaviour.

Great communication

Your eight-month-old baby is open to learning, so explain things to them and respond to their communications to support their development.

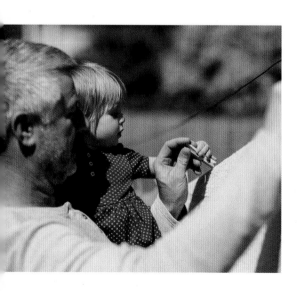

Chat to your baby to describe your activities throughout the day so they develop an understanding of the world. Everything is new and exciting to a baby, so stop and look at the cracks in the pavement and the butterfly perching on a pretty flower. Lie on your backs in the grass and look up at the clouds and show them the leaves on the trees.

Also, listen and respond to your baby's communications as if you are having a conversation. Show an interest when they babble to you, repeat their sounds and intonation, and allow them to respond. Pay attention when they shout, laugh, gurgle, or gesture towards something they want. Responding to their needs and efforts to communicate will help them to become confident about expressing themself. They'll also get an early grasp of the subtleties of sociability and manners. Everything you help them to understand in these formative months forms the basis of their curiosity, self-belief, memory, vocabulary, imagination, and more.

Running commentary Explain to your baby what you are doing around the house, and what comes next in their daily routine.

Going swimming

Swimming with your baby is fun and relaxing. It also promotes a healthy respect for water and encourages their development, too.

Water supports your baby's weight, which means that they're able to move around freely in a swimming pool even if they're not yet mobile on dry land. This gives them a feeling of freedom and independence, and allows them to work their muscles while kicking and splashing around. It also helps them to build their confidence in the water so that they don't feel afraid of it.

Before you go

You'll need to buy a swim nappy for your baby (ordinary disposables are not suitable in a pool as they disintegrate). You can choose between disposable or reusable nappies – just make sure that whichever you choose fits snugly. You may also wish to invest in some inflatable baby arm bands or a swimsuit fitted with buoyancy inserts, to help keep your baby afloat.

If you're using a public pool for the first time, check the water temperature beforehand. If it's below 30°C (86°F), your baby may find it too chilly. Plan your visit for when the pool is not too busy or noisy. Make sure that you feed your baby at least an hour beforehand – don't go swimming just after a meal – and take a drink and snack for afterwards.

Getting started

Take things slowly. Introduce your baby to the water gradually, holding them close to you and giving them

Free movement Once your baby learns that they can kick their legs and splash about in the water, they'll love the freedom of movement that being in the pool gives them.

time to get used to the sensation of the water before you start to play. Once they are comfortable, splash gently, sing, and kick their legs for them so that they realize the range of movement they can achieve in the water. Show them how to blow bubbles, which helps to teach them to avoid inhaling water.

Keep your first session reasonably short – 20 minutes or so – and supervise your baby at all times. If, at any point, your baby seems cold, or if their skin or eyes are irritated by the chlorine, it's time to get out. Give them a warm shower afterwards and dress them before you dress yourself.

ASK A DOCTOR

My baby has eczema. Is swimming okay?
While chlorine can be a potential irritant to children with eczema, taking a couple of precautions can help to ensure it's an enjoyable and stress-free activity. You can apply a barrier cream first to protect their skin from the chlorine. However, as this can make them slippery in the water, you might want to put them in a UV swimsuit or baby wetsuit after applying the cream so that you can hold them securely during the swim. After swimming, make sure that you shower them to wash off the chlorine, then pat them dry, and apply their usual emollient cream.

9 months

ABOUT 12 PER CENT OF BABIES ARE WALKING BY THE AGE OF NINE MONTHS. Now that your baby is increasingly active and alert throughout the day, they may be tired enough at night to sleep through until morning. This shift in their sleep pattern may also affect their daytime naps. What remains the same is that when awake, they'll be keen to play and learn.

Going cruising

Once your baby pulls up to standing, the next step is to start edging their way around the furniture – it's time for cruising.

Over the next few weeks, or months, as your baby experiments with their new ability to stand upright and step, they will be cruising from one piece of furniture to the next. Try to arrange your furniture so that they always have something to hold on to. As they become more confident, you can create small spaces to encourage a few tenative, free steps. Just make sure the furniture is sturdy and never leave them alone to explore. Cruising is a developmental milestone of its own, but one that some babies never go through, preferring instead to bottom-shuffle (see p.240) to get around before going straight to unsupported walking.

There are several defined stages of cruising. A first-time cruiser uses both hands to hold on and will keep close to the item of support. Later, they'll stand a little further back from the support, holding on with one hand only, and then – at some point – they will try letting go. Your baby may also develop an interest in climbing – over cushions, up the stairs, and even up on to the sofa. Keep an eye on your babyproofing and make sure your baby can't get into danger. Once they're feeling confident about their balance and control, they will enjoy walking while holding your hands and may even attempt a step or two on their own. Take off their socks so that their toes can grip the floor and help them balance more effectively.

Baby steps Your baby may spend weeks pulling themself up to a standing position before they are willing to step out and cruise between items of furniture.

MONTHS 7–9

ASK A HEALTH VISITOR

How many milk feeds does my baby need at this age? At nine months, most babies need 2–3 milk feeds a day, along with 2–3 meals of solid foods. It's recommended that they have approximately 600ml (20fl oz) – or one pint – of breastmilk or formula each day alongside a varied diet until they are one year old, at which point they can drink cow's milk. If in doubt, be guided by your GP, or health visitor, who will be able to advise on the correct amount.

My baby is cruising on their tiptoes – is this normal? Don't worry – quite a few babies do this. Before long they should start to use their whole foot to support themself while moving around. If it continues, though, do mention it to your health visitor or GP.

Tiny tears

At this age, your baby is sensitive to other people's distress. Their cries in reaction to your tears are a forerunner to their later empathy.

By now, you will have noticed that your baby is mimicking some of your facial expressions and tone of voice, and engaging in exchanges of babbles and sounds. They have also been noticing others' emotional reactions and reacting with distress if someone else is upset. This is known as "reflexive" crying. You may have noticed this when, for example, your baby starts to cry when another baby cries, or reaches out for you if you cry.

This gesture of comfort is probably copied from you and, although it is not truly empathic, such gestures will gain genuine meaning in time – it won't be until their toddler years onwards that they will really start to identify emotions. Over the coming years, they will gradually gain an understanding of others' perspectives and recognize the effects of their behaviour. To help them develop an understanding of emotions, it's important not to hide your own feelings; but you also need to ensure that if you are showing strong feelings, your baby sees you cope with them rather than seeing you become overwhelmed.

When you soothe your baby, you are teaching them to comfort themself. This is an invaluable life lesson, and they will use methods such as stroking or hugging to show their empathy for others.

Changing sleep patterns

If your baby is sleeping through the night, they may be ready to drop their morning nap and make it through the morning in good spirits.

Siesta time Your baby's afternoon nap may last longer once you drop the morning nap.

Some babies will need two naps a day well into their second year of life, but if your baby is happy in the mornings, and resists attempts to settle down, they may be ready to switch to one nap. Settle them for their morning nap. If they play quietly instead of sleeping, they'll still get a little respite from their busy day and will benefit from the quiet time. There will, however, come a point when they resist being put down.

For a smooth transition from two naps to one, alter your routine a little to give your baby their lunch and midday feed a little earlier and put them down for their afternoon nap an hour or so earlier than usual. Watch for signs that they are becoming overstimulated. Without a morning nap, they may sleep for longer in the afternoon, so if they don't stir, wake them after a couple of hours, or they won't be tired enough to sleep at bedtime. If they seem tired the next day, they may need two naps again, then just one longer one the day after. Let them be your guide.

Keeping love alive

Parenting a baby is tiring, so while being intimate together may seem like too much effort for new parents, it will help to keep relationships strong.

Falling into bed (straight to sleep) well before your partner; feeling a little resentful that you've been at home with your baby all day; being too busy to make time for each other – these are all common reasons why sex can end up on the back burner in early parenthood. The physical closeness you share with your baby, and the affection you lavish on them, can also leave you feeling as if you need space rather than touch. If you're breastfeeding you may feel that your body isn't your own.

A healthy relationship can cope when there is a period without regular sex, but it is a powerful way of expressing feelings, and it can also lift your mood and help you to relax. Eventually, it will help to keep your relationship strong; for now, being more affectionate with one another will help to revive your physical relationship over time.

Romantic moments

Try booking in a few "date nights" to spend time together. Curl up in front of the TV or, better still, switch it off, light some candles, and give each other a massage. Share a bath or just snuggle up in bed and chat. Simply savouring the warmth of each other's bodies and becoming familiar with them again is a good stepping stone towards regaining a sex life.

Respond positively to each other's suggestions. Even if you aren't in the mood for sex, a positive response to

Staying close Make time to be physically close with your partner. Even if it doesn't lead to sex, the intimacy will help you both to feel more connected and in tune with each other.

gestures of tenderness will reassure both of you that you are still lovable and attractive. A little foreplay or even some passionate kissing can help you to feel more in the mood and rekindle a little sexual excitement.

Equally, however, sex may not be a priority at the moment, and if you are both happy with the situation, it's absolutely fine to show your love in other ways. If you and your partner's sexual desires do not match at the moment, and one or both of you is feeling pressured – or lonely, frustrated, and isolated – try to come to a compromise. Expressing your love is an important part of your bond, whether you do this sexually or through words and actions.

ASK A DOCTOR

Sex is still painful after my baby's birth. Is this normal? If you had a difficult birth, your body may still be recovering, and you may feel emotionally bruised, too. The anticipation of pain may be making you tense, which will increase discomfort. Using a lubricant can help, especially if you are not becoming aroused due to fear of discomfort. Take things slowly and experiment with positions. Practise pelvic floor exercises (see p.65) to improve muscle tone and encourage circulation. Occasionally, episiotomies or tears cause long-term discomfort, as can an infection such as thrush. If you continue to feel pain, see your GP who may refer you to a physiotherapist or gynaecologist.

271

New tastes

Although it can be tempting to feed your baby exactly what they like, it is important to expand their menu to include new foods.

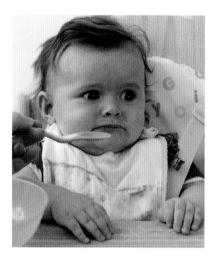

Keep offering them new foods, using different accompaniments to alter the flavour, texture, and appearance of the meal, if your baby resists.

If you've got into the habit of batch cooking, use these as a base for new meals. So if your baby loves mashed sweet potato, you could stir in some minced chicken and a few crushed peas – an instant casserole, packed

Not sure about that! Some babies actively resist trying new foods. Don't give up – keep re-introducing, using some new tactics, if you need.

with nutrients. If they're a fan of potatoes, mix mashed potato with finely chopped white fish, a grating of mild Cheddar, and chopped spinach for a "fish pie". If they like mashed carrot, blend it with sweet potato, parsnip, and butternut squash.

Dippers are a good option, too. Show your baby how to dip healthy finger foods, such as carrots, cucumber, or toast fingers, into their favourite mashed foods. Try chopped spinach in with mashed carrot with buttered pasta pieces and cucumber sticks to dip.

Getting dressed

Your baby may be far too busy for anything as trivial as getting dressed! Distraction tactics will help to get their clothes on them.

When you want to dress them, catch your baby off guard! If they get dressed at the same time or stage of their routine each day, alter things occasionally so that they don't begin to resist as soon as they anticipate what's coming. Alternatively, if you have a baby who thrives on routine and always likes to know what's coming next, ensure you dress them at the same point each day, as this type of personality will probably resist less if they know what's coming.

You may find it easier to dress your baby on your knee, so you can hold them firmly to stop them wriggling away. This change to the norm might surprise them into cooperation. Or, as long as they will be warm enough, dress them in stages, letting them play between layers.

Do your best to make dressing fun for your baby. Give a commentary to distract them – for example, "Here are your pretty red leggings and we'll pull them up over your legs and around

your tummy! Now it's time for your stripy T-shirt. Arms up, over the head. Hooray!" Tickle them when you pull down their T-shirt, encourage them to help you put on their socks, play "This little piggy", or sing one of their favourite songs. If they're engaged and having fun, they'll forget that they don't like getting dressed. Whatever you do, aim for speed and efficiency, and it will be over before they know it!

Successful childcare

Whether you leave your child with a family member or paid carer, it's important to foster a good relationship with them.

Whoever looks after your baby, trust, understanding, and mutual respect are key, along with good two-way communication, which will help childcare run more smoothly.

Paid-for care

If you have a nanny or childminder, keep your relationship both friendly and formal. You don't need to be best friends, but you do need to be a good boss. Listen to their concerns, pay them on time, keep to the agreed hours, and be willing to oblige if they need you to be more flexible from time to time. You'll definitely need the same from them, too.

Remember that they aren't just an employee. You may be paying them, but they are the most important "other" person in your child's life, so make time to get to know them, remember birthdays, and ask about things that are important to them.

Communicate as fully as possible. Pass on salient information – teething, attachment to comfort objects, particular clinginess. Similarly, your baby's carer must report on all developments, no matter how minor, at the end of each day.

Share your philosophy on childcare and take time to explain why you want your baby to eat the food they eat, or why you'd rather they didn't watch television, and how you are maintaining their routine at home. If your carer feels involved, they're more likely to follow your

lead. Show respect for their experience, though, and open your mind to new ideas – you may well learn some important tips from them.

Set up regular reviews to air any concerns (from either of you) and give a sense of being a team. Show sensitivity to their needs and they're likely to do the same in return.

Family help

If a family member is caring for your baby, show them your appreciation

regularly. It is not easy caring for a young child all day, and if no (or little) money is changing hands, the situation can become resentful. Talk through any problems as soon as they arise, and show willingness to shoulder extra responsibilities if they are finding it difficult to cope. Understand that anyone caring for small children needs a break from time to time, as well as some adult company. Show that you do not take them for granted.

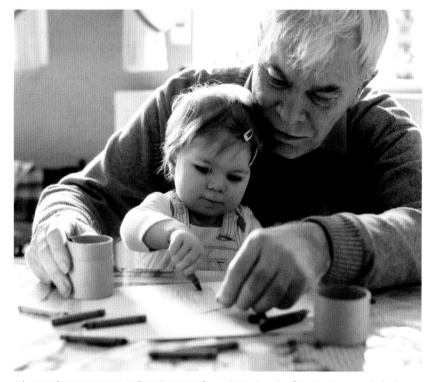

A harmonious arrangement Grandparents often take on the role of carer; ensure your baby's grandparent feels valued and respected, even if they feel it's a privilege to help out.

Self-chatter

Your baby will happily babble away whether you are listening or not, and they'll start to experiment by turning up the volume.

Range and volume As your baby goes about the important business of playing, they may hum, blow raspberries, squeal, make burring noises, and laugh as they entertain themselves.

At this stage, your baby will be practising their speech patterns and inflections by chattering, singing, and even shouting to themself. This is an important step in the development of their language skills. Don't be surprised if they practise a single sound for a long time, before joining it with another. They'll also be keen to experiment with volume, and emit some loud, high-pitched shouts that may make them laugh at their own capabilities. Listen out for raspberries and other funny noises as they practise their vocal range!

As your baby hits the nine-month mark, they continue to respond to you by mimicking the sounds you make, including the pitch and inflection. This copying helps to cement the rhythm and cadence of language. You may notice that they end some of their "sentences" with a higher-pitched sound like a question, or even an exclamation. Repeating what they say helps this process. Your baby will watch your mouth closely, but their understanding comes from association, so keep pointing to things and explaining what you are doing.

DEVELOPMENT ACTIVITY: BYE-BYE!

Waving goodbye as someone leaves is one of our most common gestures, and one that babies love to watch and copy. Most babies give their first meaningful wave between 10 and 12 months. Some do so earlier; especially if either of you has held their arm to wave from an early age. If your baby isn't waving on their own, you can show them how as you say "Bye-bye". After plenty of repetition, they'll start to respond. Soon they will automatically raise their hand and wave unprompted when leaving friends or at buses and in shops!

Waving Around now your baby may be linking the action of waving to hearing the words "bye-bye".

274

Growing up fast

Your baby has now evolved from a helpless newborn to an active, curious infant, trying out sounds ready for their first word.

Your baby may be two or three times the size that they were at birth, and the dramatic developments in their physical and cognitive skills are increasingly evident. Their milk-only diet has made way for a variety of foods. They are increasingly independent and happy to play on their own at times, and learn from their experiments and explorations on a constant basis. They're a willing communicator and like nothing better than a good "chat". While crying was once the only way for your baby to express their needs, signals, gestures, increasingly sophisticated sound combinations, and even the odd "real" word make up their new repertoire of communication skills. What's more, their ability to interact and respond to people shows a huge leap in their social competence, fostered by their sensory awareness.

Your baby's gross motor skills have developed to the extent that they can hold up their head and sit unassisted, and also roll over, crawl (possibly), and perhaps pull up to standing. Their fine motor skills continue to mature, so they can manipulate objects with both hands, and may be able to use their fingers efficiently.

If your baby seems slow to reach their milestones, you may wonder if they're developing at the right rate. If they haven't yet achieved the same social, language, cognitive, and gross and fine motor skills as their peers – or your other children – don't panic. All babies develop at different rates. However, if you are concerned, do speak with a health professional for reassurance or help.

If your baby was born prematurely, you can expect them to lag behind on some developmental tasks. This is entirely normal. Use your premature baby's adjusted age when you assess their development, and as with any developmental issues, seek advice if you're concerned.

DEVELOPMENT ACTIVITY: PUPPET TIME

Your baby will love to watch a puppet show, and probably want to take part! Make a sock puppet using an old sock, a marker pen or embroidery to mark out eyes, or purchase an animal hand puppet. Make the puppet play hide and seek behind a cushion, and laugh, cry, and even tickle your baby! Pop your baby's hand in the puppet and show them how it works. Finger puppets are ideal for playtime, and can easily slip onto your baby's little hands. Make your finger puppet whisper, giggle, shout, dance, and jump up and down, and ask your baby if their puppet can do these things, too. Puppets encourage creativity and imaginative play and aid concentration and visual skills.

Was that a quack? Puppet games are great fun for your baby, and they won't even notice if your skills as a ventriloquist aren't up to scratch.

Slowed weight gain

Although they're more hungry these days, your baby may gain weight more slowly at this age because being mobile burns lots of calories.

It's normal to be worried about your baby's weight, but if it continues to follow the same centile line on the growth chart in their health record book, they'll be doing just fine. Continue to have them weighed regularly, around once every two months, to keep tabs on their progress and to reassure yourself.

Your baby's growth rate rapidly slows down during their first year of life, reaching a near plateau by 12 months of age. Breastmilk and formula are more calorific than the foods your baby will be tasting and eating now, and it can take time for them to be able to eat enough to make up the difference in calories. Don't panic if they don't seem that interested in solid food at first; many babies take a while to show an interest. Be reassured that milk still provides the basis of their nutrition at the moment, and that your baby needs time to get used to and accept new tastes and textures.

ASK A DOCTOR

My baby's fontanelles are still soft – is this normal? It can take up to 18 months for a baby's skull bones to fuse together. By 11 months, the smaller gap (the posterior fontanelle, towards the back of the head) has usually closed, leaving only the larger gap (the anterior fontanelle, at the top of the head) still soft. So there's no need to worry for seven months or so, but if your baby's fontanelles are sunken or bulging, see your GP immediately.

Mouthing toys

Now that your baby is able to hold on to toys without dropping them, they can move them around their mouth to explore all of their surfaces.

Your baby's jaw and tongue movements are quite coordinated, and their "mouthing" skills are sophisticated, allowing them to extract sensory information from whatever enters their mouth. Using their tongue, lips, and jaw, your baby will explore toys and other objects to find out about their size, shape, texture, and weight. They will use this skill to find out about the food they eat, assessing every mouthful.

Tool for discovery Your baby's mouth is often the first port of call when investigating objects.

Your baby will begin to gnaw on toys to ease the discomfort of teething. Chewing helps to soothe gums. You can help by offering cold non-PVC teething rings to chew. Mouthing prepares your baby for chewing and swallowing solid food, and for speech, working the muscles of the jaw and tongue.

Now that your baby is more mobile and is in the throes of mastering their pincer grip (see p.311), be very careful not to leave potential choking hazards within reach.

Cot safety

Once your baby is able to pull themself up to standing in their cot, you'll need to take some steps to ensure they remain safe in there.

ASK A CHILD PSYCHOLOGIST

My baby wants to be picked up all the time. When I put them down, even for a couple of minutes, they cry. It makes life very difficult – what can I do? Some babies feel more insecure than others (perhaps as a result of separation anxiety, see pp.228, 263). Your baby feels safe in your arms and that's where they wants to stay. However, carrying your baby around the clock not only prevents you from getting things done, it also stops your baby from practising new skills such as creeping and crawling, that will eventually enable them to get around without being carried. Neither does it allow them to learn how to entertain themself for short periods.

Babies also cry to be picked up because they want comfort and attention. So ask yourself whether you are spending enough one-on-one time with them. Is their nappy dirty or is it time for lunch? If their needs are being met, then try to lengthen the time between pick-ups. Give them enough toys to keep them entertained and leave them to their own devices for a short while. If they start fussing, play with them for a few minutes, and then move away. If they cry to be picked up, try distracting them by engaging them in an activity. Be realistic – all babies need lots of cuddles and carrying around. Once they start crawling and gains a sense of independence, they're less likely to want to be held all the time (and you'll probably miss it!).

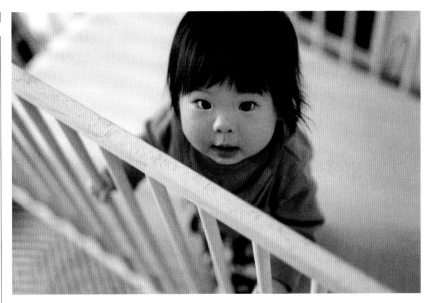

Safe height By now, the base of your baby's cot should be set at its lowest height. Ideally, your baby will be completely behind the bars, even when they are standing up.

Ensure your baby's cot base is set at its lowest possible height now. Once they can stand up in their cot, your teething baby is likely to chew on the top rail. If the cot is painted, check that the paint doesn't contain lead. You may be able to purchase a plastic teething rail that sits over the top rail, to protect your baby from paint and splinters, and also keep your cot looking a little nicer, too!

Remove mobiles and adjacent wall shelves that your baby could reach and hold on to for balance as they manoeuvre themself up and out of the cot. Tie cords for lamps, blinds, or curtains up and out of reach.

Check that the mattress fits snugly. A moving baby can become trapped if their foot gets lodged in a gap between the cot and mattress. Cover cut-out designs or other spaces in which their arms or legs could get caught. Check that the spacing between the bars adheres to British Safety Standards (especially if the cot isn't new). There should be no more than 5cm (2in) between the bars, to prevent a baby's head from becoming lodged between them.

Finally, as a precaution, place a thick, soft rug on the floor by your baby's cot. With an intrepid baby, where there's a will, there's a way!

Brain power

Your baby's brain is developing faster than at any other time in their life. What's going on in there?

Your baby's brain grows more during the first year of their life than at any other time. By 12 months, their brain will have doubled its volume and reached about 60 per cent of its adult size. Your baby was born with their full complement of nerve cells (called neurons), but as they grow those used most frequently grow stronger and branch out to make more connections that enable your baby to think and to learn new skills. By the end of the first year, your baby's brain will have made millions of new connections – and the more it makes, the more advanced their mental development will be. In addition, each of your baby's neurons has a coating called myelin, which insulates and protects it, and helps messages move faster.

Stimulation and repetition While your baby's brain is developing, experiencing repeated stimuli will encourage the development of neural pathways, which is how information is stored.

Repetition

Neural pathways are formed as your baby's brain processes the experience of the world. Repetition in words, actions, and play cements these connections, and is much more beneficial to your baby's neural development than one-off actions.

Building skills

Your baby's development occurs in logical stages, with each milestone providing the building block for them to go on to reach a more complex or demanding milestone. For example, mastering the ability to lift their head and push up provides them with the skills for rolling, and enables them to practise the movements they will need for crawling. Once you add strength and balance, they will be able to combine all of these separate skills and start to crawl in earnest.

Stimulating their senses

All of your baby's experiences – what they smell, taste, see; each voice, song, or noise they hear; and every texture they feel – will help develop their brain building a strong foundation. New neural pathways are made while others are reduced through a process called "pruning", which helps your baby's brain become more efficient. Give your baby plenty of stimulation, and keep repeating experiences so that their brain grows strong.

SOFT PLAY AT HOME

Babies love dens. Set up a soft-play den in your living room – your baby will be fascinated by the transformation of the room, and playing in the den will encourage the development of their gross motor skills. Collect as many quilted or fleecy blankets and duvets as you can and cover the floor with them to give a soft landing. Use cushions and upturned plastic boxes to create obstacles to climb over, and a cardboard box (open at both ends) to make a tunnel to crawl through. Don't leave your baby unattended while they explore this fascinating play zone and, if they need it, help them to negotiate the ups and downs of your homemade adventure course.

Testing times

Your adventurous baby is pushing the limits of their ability, and sometimes they are going to get stuck!

Being endlessly curious, your baby may manage to pull themself up to standing, then feel unsure how to get back down. They may crawl up the stairs, then look back to see that they've gone a bit too far, and not know how to get back down. They may cry when they hear a dog barking or another loud noise, and even express a sudden dislike of their dark room at bedtime. These reactions are a form of self-protection. They may encourage them to be cautious, but this is often overpowered by their curiosity and hunger to learn or practise emerging skills. There may come a time when they've really overreached themself and need your support, reassurance, and comfort.

Show them how to climb and descend the stairs and sit down from standing. Encourage them to repeat the actions until they beam with confidence. No matter what situation they've got themself into, stay calm. If you're frantic, they'll quickly grow alarmed. Help and reassure them, then let them have another go with your help. Don't show them your fear of accidents, and be confident in unfamiliar situations. Set up opportunities for playtime success to boost their confidence and praise them when they do well.

Bumps and falls

It is inevitable that your baby will end up with bruises and bumps as they become more mobile and interested in doing things themself.

If you teach your baby that making mistakes, with bumps and tumbles part of normal life, they'll take these minor setbacks in their stride and carry on trying. Be careful not to overreact when your baby does take a tumble. They'll gauge your reaction before deciding how to respond, so if you panic, they'll do the same. If they become fearful of new experiences because they associate them with being hurt, they'll be much less likely to engage in healthy experimentation and exploration.

If your baby becomes distressed after an accident, comfort them, place a cold compress on any bumps, and check them carefully. Any bump to the head, awkward fall, or a cut that bleeds for longer than a few minutes should be discussed with your GP particularly if your baby seems distressed. Consider contacting an organization such as St John's Ambulance (see pp.384–85) to learn first aid, a useful skill for a parent.

Baby tumbles Take the sting out of falls and minor cuts with some fun plasters and lots of attention and cuddles.

Music and brain development

Listening to music will stimulate your baby's brain, improving their memory and cognitive skills. Making music is even more beneficial.

Listening to and making music supports the development of your baby's sensory coordination and memory. Singing nursery rhymes promotes their language skills and teaches them about about rhythm.

Your independent baby will love to make music by themselves, so encourage this as much as possible. Their memory is improving, and they are making connections between sounds and objects. Toy musical instruments help to develop your baby's fine motor skills.

Music can have a significant impact on your baby. Soothing music can calm them, while lively music can lift their spirits, proving an excellent distraction when they're tired or fractious.

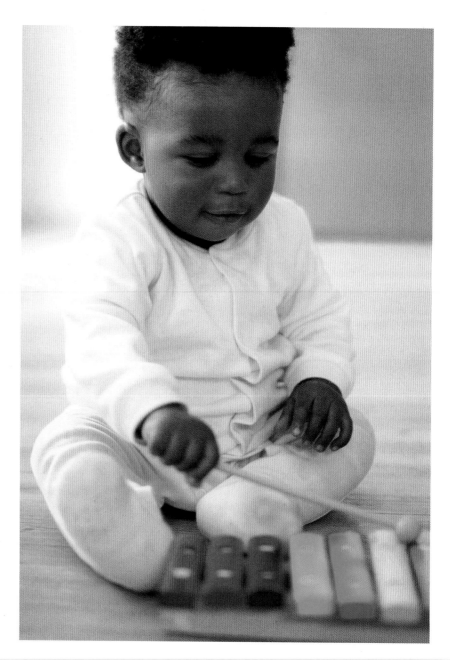

Xylophone Encourage your baby to explore music by making up their own tunes.

YOUR BABY MONTH BY MONTH

Music and movement

Stimulate your baby's natural sense of rhythm and encourage their enjoyment of listening to music and moving their body in rhythm.

Dance practice

Encouraging your baby to move in time to music will help them develop a sense of rhythm, improve their coordination and body awareness, and express themself creatively. Put on a tune you know they like, and they'll instinctively move their arms and legs when they're little, and bounce and sway as they get older.

Sing, clap and make music together. Share your favourite tunes, dance to the rhythms, and sing out loud. Hold your baby's hands to support them and "dance" with them, lifting them up for a twirl. Or put on a waltz or a tango and glide around your living room – ballroom style – with your baby in your arms. They will love to be swayed and twirled!

Research suggests that babies are born with a predisposition to move rhythmically in response to music. In a study of 120 babies between five months and two years old, researchers played recordings of classical music, rhythmic beats, and speech to them, and videotaped the results. They found that the babies moved their arms, hands, legs, feet, torsos, and heads in response to the music much more than to speech. The study suggested that the reason for this was because dance and music-making were important to our ancestors for social cohesion.

Music and movement will help your baby express their feelings and emotions, building their self-confidence and creativity. Besides encouraging their self-expression and imagination, music and movement stimulates the development of physical skills including hand-eye coordination and balance. Learning how to play music and dance with others will teach your baby social skills such as taking turns and sharing a musical toy.

Musical life Make listening to music – and making it – a part of your baby's everyday life. It will stimulate them on every level.

DEVELOPMENT ACTIVITY: HOMEMADE BAND

Improvised instruments Anything can be a musical instrument, as long as your baby is able to make plenty of noise.

Your baby will enjoy making lots of noise with safe household objects. Make a shaker from a plastic bottle full of pasta or rice. Do make sure the top is securely sealed and taped so that nothing can escape to create a choking hazard. Use pots and pans and plastic bowls and containers, together with a spatula or a wooden spoon to create a homemade drum kit. Use their rattles as maracas. If you have a keyboard or piano, let them bang away on that, too. Make music together, but also leave space for them to make their own sounds. Play lively then quiet music and watch how your baby reacts to each; does their banging slow down when the tempo changes?

Comfort objects

If your baby has a comfort object, they've probably become very attached. It may be difficult for them to settle at night without it.

At this stage of their babyhood, when separation anxiety sets in (see p.228 and p.263), a comfort toy can ease your baby into new situations by providing a link with the familiar. With their "comforter", they'll find it easier to sleep without you or sit on a stranger's knee. If you are going back to work, their comfort object can help them feel more at ease with their carer, and they can use it to soothe themself when they are distressed.

If your baby doesn't have a comfort object already, it's not too late to offer one. Choose a toy that they like with a soft, smooth texture they can rub or chew, or a blanket that's light enough for them to carry. Pick one that is machine washable, and safe for them to handle – and, ideally, something that's easy to replace if lost! Tuck it under their arm when feeding, and ensure they have it with them when they go to sleep. Use it to soothe them when they're tired and grumpy, and they will soon associate it with comfort.

Your sociable baby

Your baby is fascinated by other babies. They will chatter away to them, imitate their actions, and enjoy playing alongside them.

Parallel play Your baby will play alongside others but won't share for a couple of years yet.

Around now, your baby will engage in parallel play – alongside another baby, each doing their own thing. They may chatter to one another and look over to see what the other is doing. They may even tussle for the same toy or copy each other's activities, but they are largely playing independently. In fact, they may even forget the other is there.

However, they love to see others who are just their size and these early interactions allow them to become used to the company of other children. They'll learn things by watching other children, and make "friendships", which, at this age, means other babies become familiar and, therefore, favourites. They'll gravitate towards babies they know when you enter a playgroup or meet up with friends.

Don't be surprised if your baby wants to examine their companion and give their hair a good tug or poke at their face as they would with a new toy. They may enjoy getting a good reaction when they bash them on the head or climb on top of them. Be patient; this is experimentation, not aggression. Show them how to pat other people gently, then distract them.

Repetition

You'll have to pick things up a lot over the coming weeks as your baby discovers the fun in dropping things, and does it over and over again.

So far, your baby hasn't had the motor coordination to be able to open their hands purposely to release an object they are holding. At around seven months of age, they begin to make the transition from involuntary release to intentional release. At first, this is almost forced – in passing an object from one hand to the other, the giving hand has to let go as the receiving hand pulls the object free. Also, when your baby feels the object they are holding pressing against another surface, they learn to let it go. Over time, they learn to extend their fingers and thumb to release an object deliberately. Although it seems obvious to us, for your baby this action is fascinating to practise.

At around the same time, your baby has an increasing understanding of object permanence (see p.233). They soon realize that if they drop something over the side of their high chair, it hasn't disappeared, but is now on the floor. In addition, they are learning to point – so they can also tell you that the object is down there, and "request" that you pick it up.

Dropping objects also compounds lessons in cause and effect. When an object hits the floor, it makes a noise. Your baby will want to hear that noise repeatedly, each time reinforcing the connection between the drop and the thud as it hits a surface. The delay between the action and the noise teaches them important lessons about timing and space.

Pick and drop Your baby may decide that dropping objects is lots of fun, and will spend plenty of time playing this fascinating new game – if you'll help them!

Dropping objects is an important game, as irritating as it might be to repeatedly pick things up. Humour your baby for as long as you can bear to, reminding yourself that dropping something, looking for it, and pointing to it are all important developmental milestones. Once they get a little bit older, you can adopt the "rule of three" – once it's been thrown on the floor and you've picked it up three times, the fourth time means it stays on the floor! Your baby will soon understand and adapt.

DEVELOPMENT ACTIVITY: PLAY CATCH

Your baby is definitely interested in dropping their toys, and is about to find out about throwing. They're learning to let go of objects, so play catching games with them. Sit them in their high chair and throw a soft bean-bag toy onto their tray. They will pick it up and, with any luck, go to drop it from the chair. As they do so, catch it and gently toss it back onto the tray. Before long, they will get the hang of the idea that they are to pick it up and drop it again, perhaps even copying your movement and giving the beginnings of a throw themself. You could follow the same principle when rolling a ball along the floor to them – now that they can let go purposefully, they'll eventually learn to bat or roll the ball back. These new experiences will help the development of cognitive and coordination skills.

Nap time

Your baby's naps, probably now down to one a day, continue to be important for their wellbeing, whether they think so or not!

Your baby may not want to miss out on any fun, but that doesn't mean they don't need to sleep. In fact, their rapid development and all the activities they enjoy will make them very tired, even if they don't admit it!

If you are having trouble settling them, try putting them down a little earlier. Set up a short pre-nap routine with a milk feed, a wash, and a comforting lullaby. They may begin to anticipate these activities with pleasure and unwind sufficiently to sleep. Some babies will sleep in broad daylight, while others need silence and a good black-out blind. Work out what works best for your baby.

If your baby is flagging but resisting a nap, have some quiet time. A nice long walk in their pushchair, or snuggling with a book on the sofa can be enough to keep them going.

Schedule play dates, shopping, or social visits for when your baby is alert. There will be times when they fall asleep in the car and you will have to transfer them to the cot, or they may doze off in their pushchair, where you can leave them as long as they are strapped in and safe.

Developing recognition

As their memory improves, your baby may turn their head when you call them, and start to show they recognize familiar objects you name.

Your baby may be starting to point when they see something that they want, and they show excitement and recognition of familiar places.

They will now recognize people they haven't seen for a few weeks, and will therefore be happier to settle with a familiar babysitter. They will recognize the toys they enjoy, and maybe even vociferously request them with an urgent "uh-uh-uh" and a dramatically pointing finger.

Encourage their attempts to communicate by trying to work out what they are saying and what they want. It may involve a lot of holding up objects and saying, "This?", but they will appreciate your efforts to understand them, and when you get it right, you will be rewarded with a very big grin.

If you keep broadly to a daily routine, your baby will come to recognize the stages of the routine. They understand much more of what you say now, and will love to become involved in what is going on. They may even adopt a cheeky grin when you hold up your camera! They recognize what comes next, and they're game to do what is required.

I know that! Your baby may be able to gesture to things that you name in a favourite book.

Preventing tooth decay

The enamel on your baby's teeth is weaker than yours, and even a little sugar or inadequate oral hygiene can put them at risk of tooth decay.

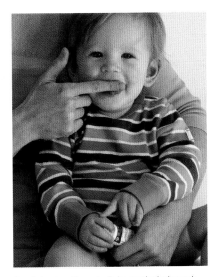

Applying toothpaste Rub your baby's teeth with a little children's toothpaste containing fluoride to prevent build-up of bacteria.

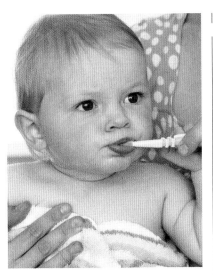

Brushing teeth Let your baby try brushing their teeth.

FLUORIDE AND BABIES

Fluoride is a natural mineral found in many foods and in drinking water. Fluoride promotes good dental health because it strengthens tooth enamel, making it more resistant to decay. It reduces the amount of acid that bacteria on your teeth produce. It can also prevent grooves forming in teeth, reducing areas where plaque can collect. For these reasons, it's added to most toothpastes to help make brushing more effective.

Since 1945, fluoride has been added to water in some areas in an effort to improve dental health. Water fluoridation has been proven to reduce decay by 40–60 per cent. However, it is not added in every area, so you'll need to check with your local water authority if you want to find out whether your supply is fluoridated.

Regardless of whether or not your water contains added fluoride, the British Dental Health Foundation recommends that all babies and children up to three years old should use a toothpaste with a fluoride level of at least 1,000ppm (parts per million). After the age of three, they should use a toothpaste that contains 1,350–1,500ppm.

Too much fluoride isn't good for children either, and can cause discolouring of the teeth. For this reason, you should use only a tiny smear of fluoride toothpaste and keep it well out of reach to make sure your baby can't eat it.

Your baby doesn't yet have a full diet of solid food, and therefore they have less of the saliva that builds up when they eat (saliva helps to protect the teeth and make them stronger). For this reason, it is important to take steps to guard against tooth decay, and to give their teeth every chance to become strong and healthy.

Encourage your baby to eat foods that contain lots of calcium, which will help both their baby teeth and the next set of teeth to develop properly. Leafy green vegetables, dairy products, and soya are the best sources, so try to include these in their daily diet. Of course, they will be getting plenty of calcium from their regular milk feeds, but you're setting up good eating habits for later.

Clean your baby's teeth regularly and effectively (see p.200). Even if they don't have many teeth yet, rub or brush them with a little children's toothpaste that contains fluoride. This will keep their teeth clean enough to prevent bacteria building up, and will encourage strong enamel.

Offer treats at mealtimes, when saliva is at its best. Similarly, offer fruit juice – which contains natural sugars – only with meals. Snacks should be accompanied by water when at all possible, or milk, as the protein and calcium content of milk help to keep teeth healthy.

Stage three weaning – a varied diet

As soon as your baby is enjoying a variety of puréed foods, they are ready to move on to the third stage of weaning. Now they'll be introduced to a greater range of foods as well as new textures and some finger foods.

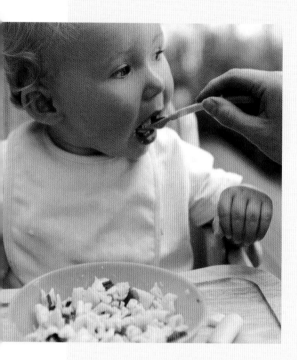

The third and final stage of weaning basically involves carrying on with all the good work you've done so far, but adding more texture to meals – in the form of bigger lumps and foods your baby needs to chew – as well as a wider range of flavours.

Your baby should now be able to eat some finger foods as well as enjoy mashed meals. They may also be able to drink water from a lidded cup.

In this third stage, which is generally from about the age of nine months, you can introduce finely chopped or minced foods as well as hard finger foods as they'll be able to

Expand your baby's diet Once your baby is happy with solids, it's important to introduce a variety of textures and combined flavours.

bite and chew more confidently. Some babies will also be very happy trying to feed themselves at this stage even if the result is quite messy. Although they will be happy holding a spoon, the dexterity required to find their own mouth without tipping off the contents comes later on in their second year, so don't expect success overnight. Some babies like to eat meals composed of finger foods, which they can hold more easily than a wobbly spoon that seems to have a mind of its own. However, it is good to let your baby try a spoon as it's a skill they'll eventually need to master.

Your baby should now be eating three meals a day, plus snacks, and sampling a wide variety of different foods. If you're still mainly spoon-feeding, you shouldn't need to do much more than roughly mash the food with a fork first; by nine months, just chop or pulse the bigger lumps.

Whether you're spoon-feeding or baby-led weaning, you can also now take advantage of your baby's fast-developing pincer grip (the ability to bring their thumb and first finger together to pick things up) to offer smaller finger foods, such as raisins, berries, peas, and halved cherry tomatoes or grapes. Or something altogether squishier.

Good eating habits for life

At this stage, it's important to introduce your baby to more complex recipes that combine different flavours, as well as

THREE MEALS A DAY

It's time to introduce more lumps, new textures, and a wider range of flavours and finger foods.

• **Protein** Your baby should have at least three servings of protein a day. One serving is approximately 40g (1 ¾ oz). Sources include eggs, meat, fish (check for bones), dairy produce, tofu, nut butters, pulses, and seeds.

• **Fats** Around half your baby's calories come from fat, some of which comes from the milk. Include healthy fats such as avocado, olive oil, and full-fat dairy.

• **Fruit and vegetables** Aim for five servings per day.

• **Carbohydrates** Your baby should have approximately three servings a day. Include cereals, bread, pasta, couscous, potatoes, rice, chapatis.

• **Consistency** Mashed, chopped, and minced foods with larger lumps.

• **How often?** Three meals a day, plus a few snacks.

• **How much** Be guided by your baby; they may be hungrier on certain days. Start with a small amount so they aren't overwhelmed, and give them more if they want it. Bear in mind that they're unlikely to be hungry if they are having more than two milk feeds a day.

herbs and spices. Simply adding a sprinkle of mixed herbs to spaghetti, for example, can turn a bland meal into something new and exciting for your baby. Hot spices may be difficult for babies to manage, but other fragrant options, such as coriander, cinnamon, lemongrass, thyme, and basil, are all good options. And broadening your baby's palate now can help to make them less fussy about food in future.

Meals like shepherd's pie, tuna pasta bake, and casseroles provide an appealing mix of flavours, as do mixed fruit desserts, and fruity breakfasts.

Dishes that contain different combinations of ingredients add variety that educates the taste buds.

It's important your baby has a balanced diet that includes proteins, fats, carbohydrates, and vitamins and minerals. Offering your baby a wide variety of foods will ensure they get the nutrients and energy they need to grow and develop properly. It may take time for your baby to adjust to new foods, flavours, and textures. This is normal, don't worry. Be patient. (For more information on nutrition for babies, see p.193).

Following your lead

Try to sit down and eat as a family so you can lead by example. Children who eat with their parents often have a better idea of healthy foods and are more likely to be adventurous eaters – your baby is more likely to try a new food if they see you, your partner, or a sibling eating it. They'll learn about table manners and the sociable aspects of mealtimes. Don't push your baby to eat a new food if they really object; take it away without comment. Offer praise, even for eating only small amounts.

MEAL IDEAS FOR OLDER BABIES

Breakfast
• Porridge or unsweetened cereal with cow's milk and banana
• Toast fingers with hard-boiled egg and slices of fruit, such as peach or pineapple
• Puréed apple, natural yoghurt, and unsweetened cereal
• Bagel and cream cheese, with a handful of blueberries.

Lunch
• Baked potato with tuna or cheese
• Picky bits: for example, chunks of cheese, sliced cherry tomatoes, pitta bread, cucumber sticks, and hummus

• Reduced salt-and-sugar baked beans and toast
• Mini sandwiches: for fillings, try cream cheese or hard-boiled egg or chopped chicken and a little mayonnaise
• Spaghetti with tomato and basil sauce
• Homemade tomato soup with bread and butter fingers
• Margarita pizza slices with chopped cherry tomatoes and cucumber
• Fish (check for bones) or chicken goujons with carrots and tomato sauce
• Bread sticks and vegetable crudités with fresh dips.

Dinner
• Minced or chopped meat, mashed potatoes, and carrots
• Fish fingers, peas, and mashed potatoes
• Chicken casserole and rice
• Lasagne with broccoli
• Vegetable risotto with grated cheese
• Beef or lentil burgers, courgettes, sliced tomato, and boiled potatoes
• Cauliflower cheese and green beans
• Meatballs with broccoli and carrots
• Poached salmon with rice and chopped up vegetables
• Chicken and vegetable kebabs.

Breakfast Baby oat porridge with milk, yoghurt, and mashed banana.

Lunch Fillet of white fish and vegetable sauce, with a sprinkle of cheese.

Dinner Baby pasta shapes with a simple tomato pasta sauce.

Feeling displaced

If you're back at work, you may be a little envious that your baby's carer is able to witness your baby's milestones before you do.

A professional carer will be aware that parents struggle with a sense of missing out, so do express how you are feeling. To help you feel close to your baby, ask your carer to keep you up-to-date with everything that occurs in the day, even if it means ringing you while you're at work. Make it clear that you appreciate the efforts your baby's carer makes and comment positively on the things they have taught your baby. If you feel a little left out, remind yourself that your baby is with you many more hours than they are looked after.

Don't be surprised if your baby fusses or even cries sometimes when you come to collect them. Transition moments can be stressful. You may be interrupting play or a nap; they may be feeling comfortable where they are, and don't want to be moved. Take your time and hold the baby while you ask the carer about the day. Wave goodbye to mark the end of the time with the carer and then spend some one-to-one time together, even if there are other jobs to do. Your baby will appreciate some time with you now. Be reassured that most parents feel some degree of guilt about spending time away from their baby; you are not alone.

First words

You may find that your baby has their own words for familiar objects. For example, point to their comfort item to see what they call it.

What's that up there? Ask your baby to tell you their words for everyday objects.

If your baby repeats a sound each time you show them an item, chances are they've developed their own word for it. It's common for babies to blend some of the sounds from the name for an object to create an identifiable "word". They may call the bottle a "baba"; they may say "mi-mi" for milk or "dob" for the dog. Encourage them to name things, and applaud their efforts. Listen carefully for patterns in speech – do the same "words" crop up regularly? What might they mean?

Your baby may become frustrated when they try to communicate with you, pointing and repeating their words to get across their message. To ease frustration, hold up familiar items to hear what the baby calls them. Repeat those words and give the correct word as well. For example, say, "Yes! Dob! This is the dog!"

Give your baby opportunities to practise new words. Ask them to point to different objects in a picture book. Give them the correct words and see how they respond. If you've been practising your animal sounds together, they may well use the noise that an animal makes rather than attempt to say its name. Celebrate the fact that they are linking words and sounds with objects, and encourage them to continue.

Family holidays

Holidays with your older baby can be fun. As long as you are well prepared, they'll love having an adventure with their family.

Many babies feel unsettled in a new environment, so it is a good idea to take a few of your baby's familiar toys when you go on holiday. Pack some toys and books into your hand luggage, too, to distract them while you are in transit. If you are staying in a hotel that provides a cot, or taking a travel cot with you, take your baby's usual sleeping bag or a familiar blanket – they may find it easier to sleep in a different place if there is something else that's familiar about it. Let them play in their new bed before you settle them down, so that when they wake up in the night they will know where they are.

THINGS TO REMEMBER

On p.125, you'll find lots of tips for travelling with a young baby. Now that they are a little older, you may also want to consider bringing some of the following:
• A sunshade for the car, and a shade or sunpod for the beach.
• A first-aid kit with some infant paracetamol and teething gel.
• A baby monitor or night light.
• A canopy for their pushchair.
• A baby backpack carrier.
• Buggy books and buggy toys.
• A universal bath plug that fits all plug holes so that a shower can be run to become a bath.
• Some laundry detergent so that you can clean clothes after messy meals.

Milk and food

If your baby is bottle-fed and you are going abroad, take a supply of their regular formula in case you can't find the same brand at your destination. You might also worry about which solid foods they're going to be able to eat while on holiday. If they're used to jars or pouches, take a few with you so that they still have some familiar meals as they adjust to a new place and different food. These also serve as a standby in case of emergencies. Individual sachets or pots of fruit purée usually appeal to most babies, and if there is a fridge at your destination, you can take squeezy yoghurt and individual cheeses.

Pack a few favourite snacks, too, such as boxes of raisins, bread sticks, and rice cakes. Small boxes of baby breakfast cereal may also prove useful.

Between local supermarkets, markets, and your own plates, it's usually fairly easy to cobble together enough food for your baby to get by on. Fresh fruit and vegetables purchased in their country of origin are also particularly delicious – and you may be able to tempt a fussy baby to expand their palate by offering them tastes of fresh local produce.

Sensible precautions

Wash fruit and vegetables carefully, and peel fruit when possible. If you buy bottled water for your baby, make sure it's low in sodium. If you order a poultry or meat dish from

Go prepared Pack your baby's essentials in a changing bag that you can carry with you.

a restaurant, always check that it is well cooked.

On arrival at your accommodation, check for potential hazards. If your baby is crawling, starting to pull to stand, or even cruising, look to see if there are any steps, wires or cords, accessible electrical sockets, unstable furniture, or anything else that could lead to an accident. If you are worried about your baby's safety, speak to someone in charge to have it rectified. Finally, don't forget in all that to take your travel documents with you – including your baby's own passport, if you're going abroad!

Shining locks

From a fine downy covering to a mass of unruly tangles, babies' hair grows very differently and so needs caring for accordingly.

During their first year, most babies lose their soft downy hair as new, thicker hair grows. However, as with all things baby-related, there's huge variation. Some babies might still have very little hair at nine, or even 12, months; others may have a mop of unruly curls, or hair down to their shoulders. If your baby is still lacking in the follicle department, don't worry – the hair will grow, and at least for the time being, it's easy to look after.

This is the way... we brush our hair. Make routines more fun by involving your baby and making them an active participant.

A wash with a gentle shampoo a couple of times a week, and a brush with a soft-bristled brush, is perfect.

For parents of babies with lots of hair, particularly if it's curly, use a small amount of conditioner after a shampoo and rinse, and then comb through with a fine-toothed comb to ease out tangles.

Thick, coarse, curly, or wavy hair requires special care because of its texture and curl pattern. Treat it gently as the hair can be prone to breakage. Overwashing can also strip the hair of its oils, so it's best not to wash it more than once a week.

Hot and cold

Your baby's body is now better able to regulate its own temperature, but you still need to ensure they don't overheat or become too cold.

Your baby may pull at their clothes or become fractious if they're too hot, or come to you for a cuddle if it's chilly.

In cold weather, dress your baby with the same number of layers you put on yourself. In the pushchair, they'll be less active and will probably feel cold more easily, so pop a hat on their head and tuck a blanket around them. A double layer of socks will keep feet warm inside the buggy blanket. Mittens may be a challenge as they restrict hand skills, but if it is cold enough for you to need gloves, your baby should have some, too.

When it's hot, allow your baby to play outdoors in just a hat, vest, and nappy, or dispense with the vest, too (make sure they're wearing sunscreen). A red face, damp and clammy skin, or frequent tongue-poking may indicate the baby is too hot. Offer a drink and remove a layer of clothing.

KEY TEMPERATURES

The temperature of your baby's bedroom should be kept somewhere between 16°C (60.8°F) and 20°C (68°F). Your baby's bath water should be at a temperature of about 37°C (98.6°F). A "normal" temperature for a healthy baby is 37°C (98.6°F) when taken in the mouth. This can be up to one degree Fahrenheit lower when measured from the armpit.

Your baby's memory

Since birth, your baby's memory has come a long way. They remember many things and retain information for increasing amounts of time.

Your newborn baby operated primarily by reflex, and while your smell, touch, and voice would be familiar, out of sight was, quite literally, out of mind. From there, their memory has developed on a gradual basis.

One of the first things your baby remembered was your face, which allowed them to form a strong bond with you. Before they were six months old, they began to remember things that were significant to them on a short-term basis. This was evident in their ability to anticipate certain actions and events, indicating that they were drawing from their memory. For example, they would know what was about to happen next when their book was brought out or you sat them down in their high chair for a meal, and they may have shown excitement at seeing their comfort object or a favourite toy.

By the time your baby was six months old, they recognized you and your partner as the most important people in their life, and by now they turn if you call their name, indicating that they remember that this sound refers to them. They will recognize familiar objects, too, and will remember where their toys are stored, or where their snacks are kept, and will recognize familiar faces and everyday routines.

There are, of course, some disadvantages to your baby developing a memory. For example,

they may remember that they hate having their hair washed and begin to fuss and wriggle the moment they hear the bath water running.

Developing long-term memory

The development of your baby's memory is such that they have a steadily increasing ability to store and recall information. The more they see and experience something, the more likely they will be to recall it.

They are also gradually increasing the amount of time they can hold a memory. For example, if they see their grandparents infrequently, they may recognize them immediately if they see them again within a month, but will probably take a moment or two and/or need a reminder if it's been a longer break than this. How much your baby remembers can depend on various factors, such as familiarity and the reminders they receive about certain pieces of information.

DEVELOPMENT ACTIVITY: MESSY PLAY

Your baby is interested in textures, consistency, and generally getting their hands dirty. You'll already notice they want to put their fingers into their food, stirring it around, squeezing it, and patting it on the high-chair tray. They may also enjoy smearing it on their face and clothes. This playfulness with different consistencies is all part of understanding the properties of familiar items in their world so that, eventually, they'll be able to predict or anticipate how things feel. Give them some sloppy porridge or springy jelly; let them pull the leaves off Brussels sprouts or push their hands into pliable pastry – it's all about learning how things look and feel.

Flour power Making lots of mess with foodstuffs is not only fun but teaches your baby about texture and form.

Your baby from
10 to 12 months

MONTH

10

MONTH 10: SAYS THEIR FIRST WORDS

There might be one or two words that your baby says regularly now – whatever the sound is, if they use it often, with meaning ("bah" for bottle, for example), it counts as a word. You might hear "dada" and "mama" said with meaning now, too.

Your baby may be able to **turn the pages of a chunky board** book now and enjoy the pictures.

MONTH

11

Your baby will start to enjoy complex play, such as **stacking and sorting**.

MONTH 11: LEARNS TO SAY THE WORD 'NO'

Understanding "no" Your baby is beginning to realize what "no" means but they won't always cooperate. They're more likely to think it's a game!

> **"** Your baby is now a sociable little person with a host of new skills and much greater control over their body. **"**

MONTH

12

Your baby sees their **peers as objects** and wants to know how they look and feel.

A few babies will take their first independent **steps** during their first year.

MONTH 12: BECOMING A TODDLER

Your baby is becoming more independent, and will have their own ideas of what they want to do and when. With their improved speech, they will combine first words and gestures to try and communicate with you about what they want.

10 months

ALTHOUGH YOUR BABY MAY START TO SUFFER FROM SEPARATION ANXIETY, THEY WILL BE GAINING MORE CONFIDENCE IN OTHER AREAS. Your baby can use both hands simultaneously with confidence. Give your baby plenty of praise for their achievements. They will be more sociable now, and will enjoy and benefit from spending time with others.

Expressing self-will

As your baby grows up, there are occasions when they might be less cooperative than you would like. Time for you to hone your skills in patience!

DEVELOPMENT ACTIVITY: PICK IT UP

As your baby approaches 10 months of age, you'll find they use their fingers to "rake" small items that they want to hold until they have positioned them so that they can pick them up between their thumb and forefinger. Mealtimes provide the perfect opportunity for practice – a raisin placed on their tray, or small pieces of soft fruit or lightly cooked vegetables are tempting treats to pick up. Place two or three pieces at a time on their tray and let them pick them up and release them into their mouth by themself. They'll enjoy dropping everything onto the floor from their high chair. This is known as "casting", and to your baby it's great fun.

Motor skills Your baby will find many practical applications to practise their fine motor skills.

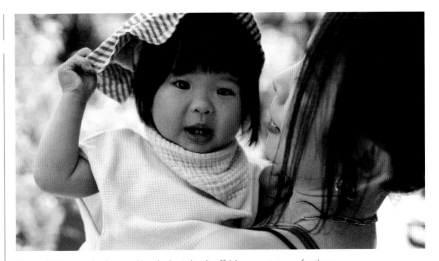

Hats off! You put the hat on. Your baby takes it off. It's a great game for them and a test of patience for you – especially if you're in a hurry to get out of the door to enjoy a sunny day!

Although your baby won't be striving for their own independence quite yet, they're certainly capable of objecting to or taking an instant dislike to something you are trying to do. What happened to your biddable baby?

Perhaps you want them to have their hat or socks on and they keep taking them off, or they're objecting to having their nappy changed or their coat put on, or they empty their food bowl all over the floor. There may be days when you feel that your patience is being sorely tested. Keep a sense of perspective and remember that your baby – even though they seem to have developed all of a sudden – is still very much a baby and doesn't mean to be difficult.

Time and compromise

Try to build some time into your plan so that if your baby doesn't cooperate straight away, you don't become flustered under time pressure.

Try to respect their wishes when you can – if they don't really need their socks on and you can cover their feet with a blanket, let it go. If they prefer a cosy cardigan to a coat, take the easy option. If they become frustrated, offer help; if they push you away, let them experiment and try to achieve whatever they're trying to do.

Above all, don't get angry. Your baby won't understand and they'll be upset by it. Try to see the funny side and don't expect too much – after all, nine months old is still a baby.

Consistent nap times

One of the keys to ensuring that your baby sleeps through the night is to give them a consistent nap time during the day.

Good-quality naps Your nine-month-old baby needs one good nap each day.

Although at this age babies can cope with little shifts in their routine for the odd day out, it's important that, by and large, nap times are consistent and that your baby gets good-quality sleep when they nap. If they are overtired at bedtime, they'll be harder to settle and may be fretful at night.

Most babies at this age are down to one longer nap in the afternoon. If the nap is well scheduled (coinciding with your baby's signs of sleepiness) and of a good length (2–3 hours), your baby should be able to make it through to bedtime without becoming overtired, then sleep well at night.

A consistent nap-time routine that is similar, but not identical, to your baby's bedtime routine is important. Keep to the same pattern each day so your baby learns to anticipate that nap time is coming and prepares for it, so that they're more likely to settle happily and fall asleep quickly.

Going naked

Our ancestors would be amazed at how we wrap up our babies. When cold isn't a factor, it can do a baby good to go naked at times.

Your baby will love some nappy-free time every day. For obvious reasons, summertime is best to do this, although just before bathtime in the safety of a well-heated and tiled bathroom is good at any time of year. Or, invest in a waterproof mat, covering it with a couple of towels to quickly absorb accidents.

Giving your baby two or three short nappy-free periods each day helps to prevent, or clear up, nappy rash. It also enables your baby to become familiar with the sensations

of weeing and pooing, which means that, in time, they will learn what it feels like just before they need to go. In fact, some experts believe that nappy-free time every day hastens potty training. Although that might be a happy end-product of nappy-free time, don't make it the reason. Your baby is still very young, and their nappy-free hour should be nothing more than an opportunity for them to get a sense of freedom in their body, and for their bottom to get a good airing!

HISTORIC CLOTHING

The babies of our ancestors had very little in the way of clothing – in the Middle Ages, for example, cloth was considered a luxury. Babies were usually swaddled in linen strips until they were old enough to sit up on their own. Then they were often simply naked, or wrapped in blankets against the cold. They may have been clad in simple gowns. It wasn't until the 18th century that baby boys were dressed in jump suits and girls in simple shift dresses.

Eating as a family

Your baby will benefit from regular family meals. This will encourage good eating habits and a willingness to try new foods.

It might not be practical to sit down as a family to eat all the time, but try to do it a few times during the week and also when you have more time at the weekend. Babies are sociable and they tend to be less choosy in their eating habits when everyone is round the table together. If your baby sees their family eating foods they haven't tried, they'll be more willing to try them themself. Offer them suitable foods from your plate, and if you can, cook meals that you can all eat.

Your baby will see you using cutlery, drinking from cups or glasses, and perhaps using napkins. They'll notice that you don't throw your bowl across the room, and that family members may ask to leave the table and help with the dishes. Although they won't develop these types of social skills for years, you are providing them with an excellent example of how people eat together and the kind of behaviour and manners that are expected. Keep mealtimes cheerful. It's best if you don't use the time for heated debates.

Involve your baby in social or larger family meal gatherings – perhaps at Sunday lunch or festive occasions. Even though they may be naturally wary of strangers, the more opportunities they have to meet new people, with you at their side, the more confident they will become.

FAMILY MEALS

There are many family meals your baby can eat too, remembering that they shouldn't have salt and sugar added to their portion, or hot spices and some condiments, such as mustard or vinegar, which may upset their tummy. Make sure the texture is right for them by puréeing, mashing, or finely chopping. Ideas for baby-friendly family meals include:
• Chicken casserole with vegetables and herbs, mashed potato, and green vegetables.
• Thick vegetable or lentil-based soup with toast fingers.
• Baked cod with spinach, peas, and potatoes.
• Homemade meatballs in tomato sauce with noodles or rice (if you blend the meat finely and make the meatballs small enough, they can eat them as finger foods).
• Broccoli, leek, or cauliflower and cheese bake.
• Tuna pasta bake with tomato sauce.
• Fishcakes with avocado (form their cakes into small, firm balls and mash avocado, or leave in slices).
• Shepherd's or fish pie – take care with stocks, which are high in salt.
• Dhal (avoid curry spices and pastes that contain salt).

Social mealtimes Family meals offer a good opportunity for interaction. Your baby will observe your table manners, and when they see you eating something they're more likely to want to try it.

Learning to be sociable

It's common for even the most sociable of babies to become fearful and uncomfortable in the presence of strangers around this time.

Your baby's anxiety about strangers and separating from you may become more intense now. They understand that their relationship with you is special, and that other people need to be treated with caution. Instead of beaming with pleasure when they see the lady at the supermarket check-out, they may cry, cover their eyes, and cling to you.

This is a normal part of their development but can be tricky for close family and friends. Try not to be embarrassed if your baby fails to be always sociable. Some form of separation anxiety (see p.228 and p.263) can last until a child is three.

Introduce them to social situations slowly, and reassure them constantly, using a low, gentle voice. Give them time to warm up around strangers before you pass them to be held. If they really don't want to go, don't force the issue. If you feel the need, explain to strangers that they're not too keen on people they don't know right now, and not to take it personally. Show friends and family a few tricks that make your baby laugh, to relax them and make positive associations. Even if they want to be held by only you, let them get used to meeting new faces. As long as you are there, reassuring them, they will gain confidence. Above all, be positive and sociable in the company of others. If they see that you are relaxed and having fun, they'll soon realize that there's nothing to worry about.

Having a laugh

Laughter is a developmental milestone – it shows your baby can respond positively to stimuli and is developing a sense of humour.

Your baby finding something funny is the clearest sign you have that they enjoy the company and actions of those around them. They have probably been able to let out at least a little giggle since they were about three months old but, by now, their giggles may well have turned into full-blown belly laughs.

All sorts of silly behaviour will leave your baby in helpless laughter – blowing raspberries on them, tickling their thighs, or pretending that their feet are very smelly. As they are now better able to read other people's expressions and feelings, they will love it that their feet have made you groan in horror. You'll probably find that they thrust them into your face for you to groan again! And when you find a thing that makes your baby giggle uncontrollably, you'll want to repeat it, too – because, for most parents, your baby's laughter is pure, feel-good parenting joy.

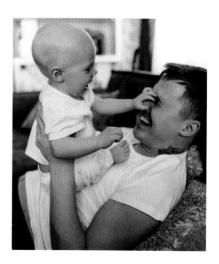

Cheesy! Try pretending that your baby's feet are really smelly – they may find it hysterical!

What's my baby eating?

Your baby can now eat food that is more like your meals. They may eat three meals a day with snacks, and can tolerate lumpier textures.

Now is the perfect time to introduce a wider range of finger foods into your baby's diet. Apart from finger foods, the rest of their food will be mashed, and you can progress to giving them cut-up chunks of food (see Stage three weaning, pp.288–89).

Your baby will probably have a few teeth by now, and their jaw and tongue have developed enough to allow them to "gum", chew, and swallow food efficiently. The more lumps, bumps, and different textures they are given, the less likely they are to become a fussy eater.

Mashing together vegetables, rather than using a food processor, is a good way to provide plenty of texture. You can also mash well-cooked and raw fruits, or several vegetables and/or fruits together. Finely mincing foods such as meat also produces pieces that have a little bite, but are soft enough to be chewed and swallowed by your baby.

Once minced and mashed foods are acceptable, finely cut and chop your baby's food. As they become used to eating food in pieces, make the pieces gradually bigger. Some babies prefer large identifiable chunks to smaller lumps that take them by surprise.

Variety of textures

Work towards giving your baby a dish made up of all sorts of textures. For example, you could mince chicken, mashed potatoes and carrots, and sweetcorn pieces. Or whizz together some spinach with cream cheese and nutmeg, and serve this alongside fresh or canned flaked tuna, pasta shapes, and steamed green beans or broccoli florets for them to pick up.

By the end of your baby's first year, they'll be eating three meals a day, although the amount of food they eat at each meal can vary considerably. If they find breakfast hard to manage, try giving them less milk in the morning so that they have more room for a breakfast meal. If they still have a milk feed during the day, give it after a meal, and not before.

Don't fret if your baby doesn't eat everything at each meal. As long as you offer three balanced meals and two healthy snacks over the course of the day, they will be getting the nutrition that they need.

Changing diet Solid foods now become more important in your baby's diet, and the food they eat is much more like your own food.

ASK A HEALTH VISITOR

My baby won't breastfeed. What should I do? As they get older, they're likely to be more easily distracted from feeding by all the things going on around them, and may feel impatient with how long a feed takes. Usually, the problem is temporary. Try the following tactics to get your baby interested in feeding: feed them away from the action, as they may settle once the distractions are removed; feed them when they are sleepy and less likely to be distracted; offer a little skin-to-skin contact to encourage them to recall positive early bonding experiences; feed them when they are most relaxed and when they are in their favourite, familiar spot. Continue to offer feeds around the usual times, working around their mealtimes, and begin a session by rubbing a little breastmilk on their lips. They may just need to be reminded about how nice it all is. If all else fails, offer them breastmilk in a cup or bottle and express regularly to keep up your supply. Eventually, you'll be able to coax them back.

Shopping with your baby

Any parent knows that supermarket shopping with baby in tow can be a trial, so here are some ways to navigate the aisles without tears.

Write a shopping list before you go. If you know the supermarket layout, you can write your list in the order of the aisles you visit so that you're super efficient when you get there!

Plan your shop around meal- and nap times so that your baby isn't either too hungry or too cranky. Try to avoid going at peak times, so that you don't have to negotiate long queues. Take a snack, such as some rice cakes or a bread stick, that they can munch on as you're walking around. If you're putting them in the baby seat of the trolley, make sure the harness is safely fastened. Bring a couple of their pushchair toys, too, to keep them amused. Park as close as you can to the supermarket entrance and trolley bay, so that you only have to cover a short distance to return the shopping trolley after loading the car.

Last but not least, involve your baby in the shop. For example, pick up a pineapple, explain what it is, and let them touch it before you put it in the trolley. Keep talking to them as you walk around the supermarket, and praise them, touch their hand, and make plenty of eye contact with them to let them know that you're pleased they're sitting nicely.

Standing tall

If your baby had already started to move around gingerly while holding onto furniture, they may begin to cruise more confidently now.

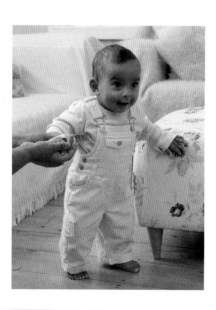

The average age for babies taking their first steps is 13 months. Before then, your baby will be concentrating on spending lots of time pulling up to standing, and becoming an increasingly confident cruiser. By now, they may be very happy working their way around the room holding onto furniture, and may stand more upright, leaving a bigger gap between their body and the furniture as their confidence grows. At some point, they may even let go momentarily and stand with no support at all.

While you will want to wait until your baby is walking properly to buy their first pair of sturdy outdoor shoes, there are plenty of soft shoes available that can be ideal for your baby around now, especially when they are outside (see p.302).

Don't fret if your baby favours other methods of getting about, such as bottom shuffling. As long as they are showing an interest in being mobile, they are fine. Many bottom shufflers are so proficient that they are less interested in taking to their feet than other babies.

I'm almost off Your baby will totter when they first walk because their feet will be set quite far apart to help them stay upright.

Home safety checks

With your increasingly mobile baby often on the prowl, it's a good idea to reassess your babyproofing to ensure they are safe from harm.

The best way to keep your home as safe as you can for your baby is to get down on your hands and knees and look at it from their height. If there are loose wires, tuck or tape them away; buy safety plugs to fill sockets; and look for any head-height edges and corners that might cause bumps or cuts. Babies often use the space between the door and the frame on the hinged side to hang on to, because their little fingers can get in the gap – if the door swings closed, fingers get squashed. Invest in doorstops to hold doors open to prevent little fingers from getting trapped.

Leave floor spaces clear by removing rugs, if you have them, for the time being. It might also be a good idea to put away your coffee table temporarily. Not only will it have sharp corners and edges but, inevitably, drinks will be left on it, presenting spilling hazards and, in the case of hot drinks, the possibility of scalding.

Buy a cover for your oven door if your baby can reach it, and put child locks on cupboards that contain items such as knives and chemicals. Also, unplug hair dryers or straighteners and avoid leaving them lying around.

Keep the washing machine, dishwasher, and tumble dryer doors firmly closed so that they can't open them and climb in. Internal glass doors should contain safety glass; if yours don't, you can arrange to have a special film placed over them to make them safe. If you have pets, keep their food and water shut in a room that your baby can't get to, or put them out when they are out of the room.

DEVELOPMENT ACTIVITY: MAKING FACES

Making faces to each other is important to their social development; they are mirroring your expression and you are reflecting this back to them. They are learning social turn-taking, and these facial movements eventually have meaning for them as in later years they connect the raised eyebrow to questions, or a frown to anger. Pairing an expression with a label such as "cross" or "happy" is the very beginning of teaching your baby the labels for different emotions. They won't make the connection right now, but it's a good idea to start this emotional education early.

Making faces also helps to develop your baby's facial muscles, which, in turn, helps to develop their speech.

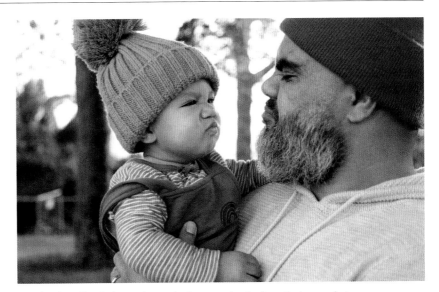

Copying faces Your baby can learn a lot from copying the faces that you make to amuse them, and will have lots of fun with you at the same time.

Sweet tooth

Your baby may prefer sweet foods over savoury, but avoid giving them processed sugary foods that could harm their emerging teeth.

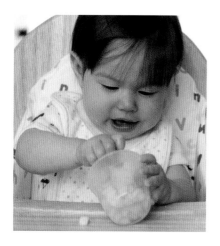

Many studies suggest that a sweet tooth is learned. Older babies can have their need for sweet foods satisfied easily with healthy foods.

Sugar is naturally present in many foods, including fruits, vegetables, and milk. Sugar in wholefoods is less damaging to teeth than extracted sugar, such as that found in fruit juice, which acts on teeth in the same way as table sugar. As your baby's

Natural sugar Fruit is full of sweetness and flavour, so appeals to a baby's sweet tooth.

teeth are emerging, monitor their sugar consumption. Avoid giving refined sugar products such as cakes, biscuits, sweets, and chocolates. A treat in the form of grated apple or a mashed banana is sweet enough. Restrict sticky dried fruit such as raisins to mealtimes as they can lead to tooth decay. For a drink, offer primarily water. If you give juice, dilute it one part juice to nine parts water. While your baby is still fairly suggestible, though, offer savoury foods as much as possible.

Shoes for cruising

Once your baby starts cruising confidently, you may wonder whether their feet need support and protection.

Going without socks and shoes allows your baby to work out how to use their toes to balance. So, as much as possible, let your baby practise walking in bare feet. Their feet are going through an important phase of development, and walking barefoot also helps to build the arches and encourages the ankles to strengthen.

You may be concerned, though, about whether a standing baby's feet need more protection, especially when they are outdoors or moving about on slippery surfaces. Many

outlets sell shoes specially designed for "cruising". While there is some debate as to whether or not these are a good thing for babies, proponents of cruising shoes state that they provide support for toes and heels, which gives a baby confidence on their feet.

Soft "cruising" shoes give complete flexibility, allowing your baby's feet to bend and ensuring that they can still feel the floor. Choose a soft material and make sure you have them fitted at a shop by a trained fitter used to working with babies.

ASK A PARENT

Even "cruising" shoes are expensive. Can I buy a secondhand pair? It's not a good idea to buy cruising shoes secondhand because they mould to the shape of the previous owner's foot, which isn't advisable when your baby's feet are developing. If they'll be wearing them regularly, it's worth buying a new pair. You could make an exception if you want an "occasional" pair for special events that won't see much action.

A real personality

Your baby's personality is increasingly evident now as they learn more ways to express themself and have distinct behaviour patterns.

Many aspects of your baby's eventual personality have already emerged. They may be strong-willed or easy to please; they may be calm and quick to laugh or a little more highly strung and sensitive.

Whatever the case, avoid labelling. Calling them "easy" or "difficult" can influence their personality. If your baby grows up thinking they are "the fussy one", they're more likely to act in this way. This is particularly important if you have twins or other multiples, which makes it more tempting to compare and label.

Celebrate your baby's individual characteristics, even when they are at odds with your own personality or, in the early years, somewhat frustrating. A non-stop, highly energetic baby may be exhausting for new parents, but bear in mind that these qualities will be admired when they are older.

Some characteristics may be a little extreme, and you can work to ease them during these formative months. For example, if your baby is relaxed to the point that they don't respond much to their surroundings, play lively music and encourage them to be physically active. If they're easily frustrated when things don't go right, show them how it's done, or distract them with another activity until they're calm. Their temperament may not change, but they'll develop the ability to tolerate frustration.

It is possible to stifle your baby's natural characteristics by trying to impose your own. If you are quiet, you may find their ebullient personality exhausting. However, actively avoiding situations in which these characteristics shine through could leave your baby slightly bewildered, without an outlet to express themself.

Try to celebrate your baby's unique characteristics, even those that you find a little challenging, and look for ways in which to support your baby. With a gentle guiding hand, even the trickiest babies can become settled, well-behaved children and adults.

A real character Celebrate your baby's personality and find good ways to channel it.

DEVELOPMENT ACTIVITY: MAKING MOVES

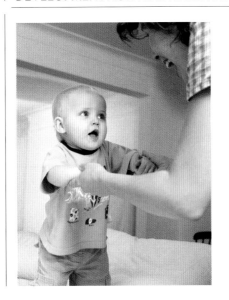

Wiggling, swaying, bouncing, clapping – these are all dance moves that your baby can now achieve with very little effort. If they are comfortable with standing and holding on to something, you can put on some music, hold their hands or lightly grasp their waist to keep them steady on their feet, and dance with them. The bouncing in their knees will encourage them to bend and straighten, which is another step on the road to walking, and will also build strength in their legs.

Dancing together Get your baby moving to some music. Doing it on a bed allows for soft landings when things get rowdy!

Was that "dada"?

Studies suggest that babies are most likely to utter their first word at around 10 or 11 months. But what will it be?

Your baby has now developed enough control over their vocal cords to be able to make sounds purposefully. Any friendly competition that vies for your name to be their first word can only help speech development as the adults in your baby's life concentrate on getting them to talk.

"Dada" is the most common first word, followed by "mama", most probably because the "d" sound is

First words More babies say "dada" before "mama", but that has more to do with how speech develops than relationships.

easier for babies than the "m" sound. So don't be surprised if your baby says "dog" or "duck" before "mama". Other popular first words are "cat" (although it will probably come out as "tat") followed by "milk" ("mah") or "ball" ("bah"), while less popular but frequent contenders include "juice" (usually as "juh"), "popper" (or "pop"), "shoe", "dog", "bye", "ta", and "nana".

Words with easy consonant sounds (p, b, d, m, n, s or sh, g, and so on) tend to be the basis for first words, with words made up of trickier sounds (k, j, th, l, for example) coming later.

How your baby grows

It now seems inconceivable that your newborn baby was ever that small – just look at the size of them now!

Between now and 12 months, your baby should weigh somewhere between two and three times as much as when they were born. However, these are just guidelines and all babies gain weight at slightly different rates. They should also have grown by about 25cm (10in) by the time they reach their first birthday.

If you notice slowed growth or a drop in weight, it could be due to illness – a couple of days of not eating, especially if combined with

vomiting or diarrhoea, can lead to weight loss that your baby will regain when they recover. Or it could happen if your baby is crawling, cruising, or walking, as these all burn calories. If your baby is alert, happy, feeding well overall, and filling their nappies normally, all is likely to be well. If there's any cause for concern, see your health visitor or GP.

If you are worried that your baby is too plump, check their weight with your health visitor, who will tell you

straight away if there's a risk of your baby becoming overweight. Never withhold feeds, but pay attention to cues that the baby is full.

If your baby is a little overweight, make sure that their calories come from nutritious sources – like fruits, vegetables, healthy fats, and cereals – rather than sweets and processed food. Play with your baby to encourage physical activity, making sure that they have a safe space in which to practise being more mobile.

Balancing work and baby

It's not easy to balance work and home life: add a baby in the mix and you'll need to put all your organizational skills into practice.

Nobody is perfect at everything, so don't try to be superhuman. If the housework slides or your baby doesn't get a bath one night, the world won't end. Making things easy at home is the secret to survival. Babies are hugely resilient and their needs are actually very basic. As long as your baby is loved, cared for, and stimulated, they'll be fine. Sometimes they will be glad just to be in your presence, so relax with them, too.

Also, learn to say, "No". Your baby, family, and job are your priorities. Maintaining these will sometimes be all you can manage. Work out the parts of and people in your life that you enjoy and say no to anything or anyone that doesn't add positivity.

Similarly, don't succumb to guilt. If staying at home with your baby is not an option financially, embrace your situation and find ways in which you can make it healthy and happy for all of you. In other words, be positive. How can you get the most from the time you have with your baby? Focus on the things you can do, rather than the things you can't.

Work boundaries

You may once have been able to work full-time and even more but this will be hard now. It helps for your work colleagues to know your needs when you return to work. You may wish for more flexible or part-time working arrangements; don't be afraid to ask for these. Most workplaces value their employees and are willing to try to accommodate the work-life balance you hope for. If you are in charge yourself, consider delegating some of your workload to give you more time.

Take care of yourself

An exhausted, underfed, emotionally drained parent isn't any good to anyone! You'll be able to keep more balls in the air if you eat well and sleep well. Time alone for yourself and your partner is also important for a healthy emotional life. Sometimes both home and work can feel tricky, but even if there isn't much time to spare, you both need to take time out without guilt and with support.

FOCUS ON TWINS: DIFFERENT INDIVIDUALS

Your twins' personalities will be emerging in earnest now, and no matter how alike in some ways, they will probably have different character traits, even if they are identical. You may find that one wants to crawl, and the other isn't interested, or one is relaxed and placid while the other is easily frustrated. The challenge with twins is to avoid comparing or labelling them. A label can stick, and one child being labelled the "shy one" and the other the "loud one" could put each child into a category that is difficult to change later on. As your babies grow, it's important that they feel valued as individuals as well as have a close relationship as twins.

Same but different One twin may be more dominant or gregarious early on, but that doesn't mean it will always be so – the dynamics of the relationship will change as they grow.

305

Troublesome teeth

First-year molars often surface towards the end of a baby's first year. They are blunt, square teeth, used for grinding and chewing.

First molars can cause much pain as they erupt through the gums. A flap of gum may loosen, and your baby may rub the side of their face or their ear, feel the area with their tongue, and dribble more. Both sides of your baby's mouth may be affected. Girls tend to teethe earlier than boys. Your baby may want to chew to ease the discomfort. Offer hard foods such as bread sticks, rice cakes, toast, or apple slices. Cold smoothies can help to soothe inflammation.

Emerging molars Your baby might rub the side of their face or put their fingers in their mouth where it's feeling tender.

ASK A DOCTOR

My baby's milk teeth look mottled and almost striped. Is this normal? It is normal for a baby's teeth to have mild ridging and appear bluer rather than white. If there are distinct marks on their teeth, there may be a few possible causes. Certain antibiotics, in particular tetracycline, shouldn't be prescribed in pregnancy as they can cause baby teeth to become mottled, as they form in your baby's mouth early in pregnancy. There may also be problems with their enamel if it has formed unevenly. Ask your dentist to check their teeth if you are worried, but rest assured that most problems will not affect your baby's permanent teeth.

How clean?

Your baby is exposed to many germs during their daily activities, so is there any need to continue sterilizing their feeding equipment?

The simple answer is, for the most part, no. Your baby's mobility means their hands make contact with the floor wherever they go, and if they go to playgroups or have siblings, they frequently play with toys handled by other children. They put their fingers and toys in their mouth all the time. However, do wash plastic toys in warm, soapy water regularly and put cuddly toys through the washing machine on the hot cycle from time to time to minimize risk.

Wash plastic spoons and bowls in hot, soapy water, or in a normal dishwasher cycle, but don't worry about sterilizing them now. Continue to sterilize bottles and cups that have had formula or breastmilk in them, as the fatty deposits on the insides of the bottles can be hard to remove from washing alone, and residue can cause tummy upsets.

Keep your floors clear of debris and wash wooden and tiled floors regularly. Also, wash your baby's hands before mealtimes and after handling pets. Don't be too anxious – your baby has to be exposed to germs to build their immunity.

Encouraging independence

To support your baby's development and ease separation anxiety give them the opportunity to explore their world without you always guiding them.

Ensure that wherever your baby can go is safe, of course, and free from hazards, but then let them travel from room to room, without you if they'll let you hang back. Chat to them as they move so they know you are near. Slowly, their confidence in the idea that in fact they are okay without you for a little while will grow, along with their independence.

Playtime leader

Give your baby a basket containing a few suitable toys and let them choose what to play with. Once they have selected one, engage with them in their play to show them that you are interested in the choices they make and that you will follow their lead.

There are certain toys that are particularly good for encouraging independent thinking. Shape-sorters, stacking cups, and building blocks will all help your baby try to solve problems on their own.

Self-feeder

At mealtimes, allow your baby to have a spoon of their own so that they can try to feed themself, even if you have another spoon so you can ensure some of the food actually finds its way into their stomach! Finger foods are great for independent feeding.

What to eat

As your baby gets older, you will relish the days when you could choose their food without them making any objection. You can give them a little independence by offering them two healthy choices for a snack, encouraging them to point to the one they prefer. Whatever they choose, they get. If they then want the other snack, too, let them have it, as the exercise should be fun and will help them feel as if they have a degree of control over their own life, which, in turn, helps them to understand the advantages of independence.

DEVELOPMENT ACTIVITY: HIDE AND SEEK

Your baby has understood the concept of object permanence (see p.233) for some time now. Playing peek-a-boo (see p.136) has helped them to realize that you are still there even when they can't see you, and hide and seek is the perfect progression for a mobile baby, as it encourages trust in your presence and absence. Play it in one room only and as a family first to allow your baby to get the idea of how it works. One of you hides while your baby and the other parent count and then "seek" together. Next time, you and your partner swap roles, so that your baby knows that either one of you may disappear but you will always come back. Once your baby understands the concept of the game, they can play it with just one of you hiding while they seek. The first few times, call from your hiding place to give them a clue and, more importantly, to reassure them that you're still there close by. Then, encourage your baby to "hide" (often unconvincingly!) while you pretend to find them.

Ready or not! Your baby will love playing hide and seek with you, and learning not to panic when they can't see you.

Constant colds

Your active, sociable baby contracts lots of germs from many people and environments. It may seem as if they have a constantly runny nose.

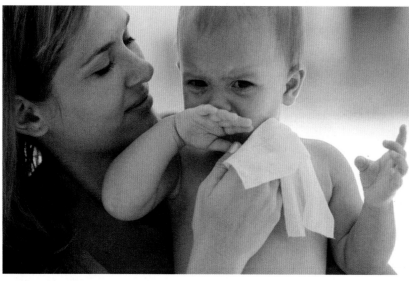

Sniffles and sneezes Babies do tend to suffer a lot from colds during their first year – but each minor illness helps to build their immunity so they can fight off similar viruses in the future.

While a cold may disturb your baby's sleep, contracting relatively harmless bugs is an important part of building immunity. Your baby will inevitably be exposed to germs through toys at the homes of friends or at playgroups, which is fine. However, avoid clearly very poorly children, especially those with infections such as croup or a chest infection. Ideally, you don't want your baby catching anything more serious than a common cold.

Treating colds

It is normal for your baby to have up to eight or more colds a year. The majority pass within a week. Make your baby as comfortable as possible. Take their temperature – if your baby has a fever or a high temperature of about 38°C (around 100.4°F) you may want to give infant paracetamol according to the dosage instructions.

If your baby has a blocked nose, try using a baby vapour rub to help clear their sinuses, or put a few drops of eucalyptus oil on a clean muslin and leave it in their room, but not in their cot, as they could rub their face in it.

Give plenty of fluids and lots of rest. Don't force them to eat if they don't want to – babies often lose their appetite if unwell. Offer small amounts of food often.

DANGER SIGNS

If your baby has a cold and shows any of the following complications, contact your doctor urgently.

Fever A temperature of 39°C (102.2°F) or higher, or one above 37°C (98.6°F) that persists for more than two days, should be checked by your doctor.

Drowsiness We all feel a bit more sleepy when we are trying to beat infection, but if your baby is hard to rouse from naps, or floppy or unresponsive, seek medical help.

Dehydration Babies need fluids to fight infection, so if they have refused their bottle, the breast, or water for more than eight hours, seek advice. See p.215 for signs of dehydration.

Rash While some rashes are relatively harmless symptoms of a virus, any rash is worthy of medical attention.

Ear rubbing If your baby is rubbing their ear and seems very unhappy, they may have an ear infection.

Persistent cough If they have a cough that lasts more than a week, they may have a chest infection, especially if they also have difficulty breathing.

Laboured breathing If your baby is struggling for breath at any time, go straight to the doctor.

Showing caution

Your baby's life is full of new experiences and not all are to their liking, so they'll naturally show caution and even distress at times.

Just a couple of weeks ago, your baby may have been fearless in their curiosity and exploration but now, after a few tumbles and one too many startling discoveries, some babies will be a little more cautious in their exploration. Separation anxiety can also mean they're more easily distressed in new situations, especially if they think you may be leaving them. This is a natural progression as they learn about their world and may vary from day to day or week by week as they gain confidence in each situation.

Gently encourage your baby to keep exploring and engaging in new situations. Stay by their side while they scan the room or begin to investigate a new toy or play equipment, for example, or push them in the ride-in car, but keep talking so they know you are there, even if they aren't able to see you.

You may find they startle easily at loud or unfamiliar noises; these often can't be avoided so handle this with plenty of cuddles and reassurance, and very simply explain, "Oh, that's a car going 'beep beep'."

Gradually, they'll become accustomed to most sounds as they experience them but, of course, being startled is a natural response to keep us safe, so it's bound to occur occasionally when there's an unexpected noise. Don't make fun of your baby's wariness or reluctance to do something, or use the phrase "Don't be silly!" It's important to keep reassuring them until they feel more comfortable in any new situation.

Building confidence If the height of the slide is an issue, help them come down it slowly and reassure them that you've got them and it's safe.

ASK A CHILD PSYCHOLOGIST

My baby doesn't seem to like the dark, how can I help them get used to it? For some babies, being in total or almost total darkness can be frightening (even some adults prefer to sleep with some light at night). A small night light may be enough to reassure your baby that all is well if they wake, and allow them to recognize their surroundings quickly. This reluctance to be in the dark does not need to be changed or "treated" – trying to force them to sleep in total darkness is more likely to cause distress than teach them that darkness is okay. If your baby insists on having the light on at night, then use a dimmer switch to turn the light down over a period of a week or two.

Eating out

It's never too soon to get your baby used to being in a restaurant with you, but certain things can help to make the experience easier.

A good indicator of a baby-friendly restaurant is that it has high chairs, baby-changing facilities, a children's menu, and kiddie activity packs. If you're unsure, call ahead to check. If you want to bring your own baby food, ask about facilities for warming it. Also, it's a good idea to book a table by the window so your baby has quick distractions to look at throughout the meal, if necessary.

Take plenty of tabletop activities with you. A few building blocks, board books with flaps, and a small shape-sorter will keep your baby occupied. Time your booking to coincide with your baby's lunchtime so that they are preoccupied with eating while you are (even if you have to feed both of you simultaneously). This should also give you plenty of time before they need a nap.

Finally, remember that talking, playing with, and involving your baby throughout the meal will make this an experience to repeat.

ASK A DOCTOR

How do I clean my baby's ears? The ear is self-cleaning – ear wax removes dust and debris from the inner ear. It may look unsightly but it's beneficial, so don't remove any lumps of wax while they are still in your baby's ear cavity. You can wipe away wax from their outer ear with a damp cotton wool pad. Never put a cotton bud in their ear. Even if your hand is steady, they are liable to move and you could damage their eardrum.

Learning through touch

Your baby's senses teach them everything they need to know; now that they are more aware, capitalize on their ability to learn through touch.

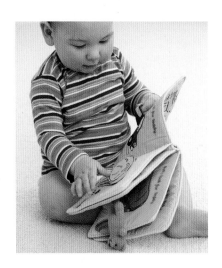

Support this learning through touch by offering different textures to feel and experiment with.

Sit your baby in their high chair and present them with two or three bowls of different textures to get their fingers into. Ensure the contents are safe for mouthing. Some mashed-up banana, a bowl of cereal hoops, some pasta shapes, and a bowl of cooked rice are all interesting to explore.

Exploring textures Books that feature a variety of textures allow your baby to explore and learn through the sense of touch.

Babies also love to stick their fingers in jelly! Keep an eye on what goes into their mouth (to prevent choking) and be ready with a clean muslin to clean any gooey fingers.

Give your baby books that feature a variety of fabrics and textures aimed at teaching babies the meaning of words such as silky, soft, squashy, rough, and so on. Sit with them and read these books together, and encourage your baby to touch the different textures in the book and say the words that describe them.

Using objects correctly

Your baby can associate objects with actions and anticipate sequences of events, which inspires them to use objects as they see you doing.

Your baby understands that their beaker holds water or juice, and is able to bring it to their mouth. They know what their toothbrush and flannel are for, and they may try to use their spoon to eat. They will enjoy practising these skills on a regular basis, as they learn from you.

Let your baby have a go at squeezing toothpaste onto their toothbrush. Let them brush their teeth alongside you, put your socks

Who to call? As your baby gains control over their hands and fingers, they'll be keen to employ them "correctly" when using objects.

on together, and stir the cake batter with the spoon. Having a go enhances understanding of the relationships between objects and activities. Prompt this understanding by giving them the words for the objects they use and the things you do with them. Soon your baby will point to named items, and even retrieve them.

Ask your baby to pass you their flannel in the tub, or their cup at teatime. If they hear an instruction and the correct words, while watching you point to and use objects, they'll soon make the links necessary to understand your requests.

THE PINCER GRIP

The pincer grip is a fine motor skill that begins developing from around eight months of age. To perform it, your baby uses their index finger and thumb together to pick up and hold items. It is this grip (or grasp) that will allow them to button their shirt, use a pencil, play musical instruments, and operate a mouse on a computer in years to come. Being able to perform the pincer grip is a developmental milestone that indicates that your baby's brain, nervous system, and muscles have become much more coordinated and synchronized. It also opens up a world of possibilities for them. With a pincer grip, your baby can stack blocks, feed themselves, manage a shape-sorter, and much, much more.

You'll notice that your baby began to pick up objects by brushing their hand over a toy, then curling their palm and fingers around it. Then they'll grasp things using all four fingers and thumb, which is still quite awkward. As they approach 12 months, the ability to hold something between their forefinger and thumb in a pincer grip enables them to pick up and manoeuvre objects much more easily and precisely. To encourage the refinement of your baby's pincer grip, give them small things to pick up from their high-chair tray at mealtimes, such as raisins, cereal hoops, and cut-up grapes, or give them a simple lift-out puzzle to tackle. Avoid small objects that might pose a choking hazard if they put them into their mouth.

Better grip Give your baby toys that fit in their hand to help improve their whole-hand grip and, eventually, their pincer grip.

311

Encouraging self-feeding

Your baby loves to put their fingers in their food and transfer it to their mouth. Although messy, this is the start of them feeding themself.

Many babies want to be independent and feed themselves but, at this age, most lack the hand–eye coordination to get food onto a spoon and into their mouths. Finger foods come into their own as they allow your baby to enjoy more independence.

Use this to try to introduce a wider variety of tastes and textures: crunchy foods, such as bread sticks, rice cakes, toast, and dry breakfast cereals are all ideal finger foods. Also try cucumber sticks, cubes of mild cheese, and cooked pasta shapes. As your baby gets better at feeding themself, you can introduce a daily meal of "picky bits" – for example, mini sandwiches, pitta breads, or toast soldiers with cheese; veggie sticks with hummus; chunks of cheese; cooked vegetables; some chopped grapes, apple, pear, or banana. Ensure that your baby's finger-food meals are balanced and healthy (see Good nutrition for babies, p.193).

You could encourage them to try new foods by adding just one new item to their finger-food meal among others you know that they like.

All this practice with finger foods is great for their fine motor skills and coordination, which will help when they start to use a spoon (see p.339).

Fun with animals

Young children adore animals and soak up everything to do with them, whether looking at animal pictures, or meeting the real thing.

Family pets Contact with pets increases your baby's confidence around animals. Supervise animals around your baby at all times.

Learning about animals is a natural part of your baby's development. Familiarize them by looking at pictures in books, and watching programmes about animals. Talk about the animals, pointing out each one by name with the noise it makes. Sing nursery rhymes, too, that have animal noises, like "Old MacDonald".

If you have a garden, consider putting up a bird feeder and let them watch the birds feeding. Or point out regular visitors such as squirrels. On outings, point out birds, cats and dogs, and ducks and geese in ponds or rivers. Or take them to a children's animal farmyard. While they may be too young to stroke the animals, their senses will take in everything, and they will build up their confidence around them. Hygiene is of course essential to remember when handling animals. Wash your baby's hands well after being with farm or domestic animals, and make it routine to wash their hands after playing in the sandpit or garden and before mealtimes. Teach your baby, even now, to ask before petting a dog.

The importance of affection

Showing your baby love and attention is probably second nature by now and they will thrive on as much physical affection as you can give.

Some of the most important work on babies' need for affection and attention was carried out by psychologist John Bowlby in the 1960s and it has defined our way of nurturing and creating security for children ever since.

Their attachment theory taught us that the bond between parent and child is the foundation for your baby's security and creates a positive pattern they will repeat in the relationships they go on to make.

A baby who has been brought up in a secure, loving environment where affection is given and received freely through hugs and kisses, pats and snuggles, is more likely to grow up to be an affectionate adult.

There have been plenty of different ideas about the "best" way to raise your baby, from the old adage that children should be "seen and not heard" through to schedule-based and more baby-led methods. Whichever approach you prefer, there's no doubt that fundamentally your baby needs your love, attention, and affection in order to develop their sense of security, stability, and confidence. When you comfort your baby, offer them lots of warm physical affection. They also need your consistency, so that they can predict what reaction they will get and what pleases you. As they get older, it will be important for them to know which behaviour is preferred by you and which is unacceptable.

Undivided attention

Laughing with your baby, having a tickle and a giggle, and giving them undivided attention is another way to show them how much you love them. Studies have shown that if you are watching them playing but doing something else as well, such as reading or talking on the phone, their play will be less complex than if you watch them with your full focus.

Follow their lead at playtime – sometimes they will want to be held, at other times, to get down because they want some freedom. Sometimes all they need is a gentle stroke on the cheek or head to know that you love them. By responding to, and respecting, the peaks and troughs in their need for affection, you show them that you value their feelings, which means that they learn to value them themself.

Secure and happy Consistent love, comfort, and protection from parents and caregivers helps babies develop good mental health.

BEING GENTLE

A 10-month-old baby doesn't have any real sense of their strength, and still lacks the necessary coordination to monitor how hard they pat or hold on to things. However, it is never too early to teach them to be as gentle as they can be. Encourage your baby to stroke their cuddly toys or dolls, gently holding their hand so that they get a sense of the lightness of touch. Choose one special toy and give it a cuddle in front of your baby, then encourage them to do the same, saying, "Ahhhh, teddy". Gently put the teddy down, cover them in a blanket, and give them a kiss, then encourage your baby to do the same. Such role play reinforces a baby's understanding of the need for care and kindness with others.

11 months

MANY BABIES HAVE A FAVOURITE COMFORT OBJECT THAT THEY WANT TO TAKE EVERYWHERE. As your baby becomes more mobile, they will develop greater self-confidence and be very definite about what they do and don't want to do. Be patient but firm about the limits you've set. From their first smile at about six weeks, your baby may have progressed to fits of full-blown laughter.

Letting your baby help

Your baby might enjoy giving you a little "help" with some small tasks, and will think it's fun to be just like you.

Tidy up time Ask your baby to perform simple tasks, such as putting their bowls and plates back in the cupboard.

The simplest and most useful thing that your baby can do for you is to help put their toys back into the toy boxes at the end of the day. If you make it part of their end-of-day routine, you may also find that, by the time your baby reaches toddlerhood, this behaviour has become second nature. Empty a toy box in the middle of a room and turn tidying into a game: "Can you find the rabbit? Brilliant! Now put the rabbit in the box." Give them lots of praise and even take turns – "Now I can find the train. Here it is! Into the box." Use the time as an opportunity to reinforce colours, shapes, animals, and so on in your baby's experience and learning.

Slowly, but surely, the tidying up will be done, if a little slowly!

Cleaning

Give your baby a clean duster and let them wipe the surfaces they can reach as they cruise around the house. Even if wiping down the sofa is not altogether very helpful, give them lots of praise and encouragement for helping you. Similarly, give them a damp cloth after mealtimes and ask them to help you wipe the table – although their wipes will be in one area back and forth in front of where they're sitting, they'll get the idea, and in years to come, perhaps they'll even do it truly helpfully!

DEVELOPMENT ACTIVITY: STACKING FUN

Stacking helps to develop your baby's hand–eye coordination, encourages them to work out logic puzzles, and reinforces what they have learned about cause and effect. Good stacking toys include cups that fit inside one another and also sit on top of one another if turned upside-down (plastic measuring cups will do the job just as well), coloured bricks, and hoops that go over a central cone.

To stack cups and hoops appropriately, your baby has to work out their shapes and relative sizes and pass the objects from one hand to the other. The bricks require skill with balance, fine motor skills, and the gentle touch that's needed to get items of the same size to rest securely one

on top of the other. With either type of toy, these tasks introduce your baby to the beginnings of mathematical problem solving, which gives them a head start with mathematical skills for later in life.

Start your baby off by showing them how the stacking is done, then tell them it's their turn. Watch as they carefully try to work out which item goes next and give them a hand if they need it. If the toy topples over, that doesn't matter – it's all part of the learning process, and they will love building things back up again.

Early maths Stacking toys introduces your baby to maths skills, all in the name of fun.

Meeting other children

Your baby will benefit from growing up with children of all ages – babies their own age will play in parallel; older children will encourage interaction.

Older children can engage in a variety of games such as peek-a-boo and hide and seek, and will enjoy reading to your baby and crawling around pretend "dens". Your baby might find it easier to engage with children, who they can play near to, rather than with new adults who may want to interact, or interfere with their play. Children may also love the chance to "look after" your baby and – given clear "do's and don'ts" – can be surprisingly good carers. Even though you have to be there, it will help your baby feel more independent. Older siblings make home-grown playmates. But if your baby is your first or only, look for opportunities for them to interact with others – at a childminder, nursery, or crèche, for example. If you have nephews and nieces, ask them to visit or supervise a visit to their home. Meeting regularly, if practical, can build close family ties beyond your immediate circle.

If it appeals, you could consider going on holiday with friends with children. However, make sure there's enough space in your accommodation and you know the other family well enough to be able to speak freely about your wishes for your baby and yourselves.

Time to yourselves

You and your partner need some time to focus on each other, and to pursue some of your favourite individual activities again.

You might pay a babysitter for the evening to go out together, or booking a night or two away, leaving your baby with a trusted friend or family member. You could set up a babysitting circle with your friends with babies so you can take turns to look after each other's babies once in a while. However you manage it, your relationship will thrive on having time to enjoy each other's company, taking in activities as a couple.

Just the two of you You and your partner need time away from your baby to relax and enjoy being on your own together.

You can also give yourselves "permission" to resume individual activities you used to enjoy. You may want to restart a sport you have put on hold. Seeing friends socially can be a boost; whether it's shopping, watching sport, grabbing a coffee, or going to organized activities, this gives you time to recharge your batteries. Whatever the activity, the important thing is that you both have some time and space to do the things you enjoy and that make you each feel special, both together and as individuals.

Home comforts

There's no doubt that a comfort object is helpful, especially when your baby is anxious, but what if it starts ruling your life?

Your baby encounters new experiences every day. The bombardment of learning, and understanding comes thick and fast at 10 months, and the whole process can be both exciting and unsettling for a baby just getting to grips with the notion that they are independent from you. It's little wonder, then, that comfort objects (sometimes called transitional or security objects) provide a constant. They represent your love, they smell of home, and they have positive, safe associations. Your baby will need their comfort object when you are not nearby, when they experience something new, or they feel ill or tired. Sometimes, they may rely on their comfort object so heavily that they can't bear to let it go.

This is all very well, but such dependence can start to fray the most patient of parent's nerves after a while. It's difficult enough to remember everything you need when you go out, but simply frustrating if you're half-way down the road with baby safely in the car seat when they start wailing – because you've left their "best friend" behind! Plus, you are saddled with the huge responsibility of looking after – and never, ever losing – your baby's most precious possession.

Go with the flow

There's little you can do about this situation other than accept it and make contingency plans. Once your baby has formed an attachment to a particular thing, taking it away will make them feel insecure and upset. So ideally, they should be able to reach their comfort object whenever they need it, wherever they happen to be. Eventually, they'll either grow out of it, or you'll need to help them let go of the object gradually, but not until they're older. For the time being, do all you can to safeguard it. If possible, buy a couple of spares in case the original goes missing. If your baby is attached to an irreplaceable blanket, consider cutting it in half so that you can wash one half, while the other is being used. Try to wash the comfort object before it becomes too deeply embedded with your baby's scent so that they don't reject it when clean (and are less likely to notice when you swap it for one of the spares while the original is in the laundry).

DEVELOPMENT ACTIVITY: TUNNEL TIME

Babies of this age love playing in toy tunnels. Nylon tunnels are readily available, but a tunnel made from three cardboard boxes taped together with their ends open can work just as well. Customize it with peepholes along its length so your baby can see you. Encourage them to crawl inside the tunnel, perhaps by placing a few toys inside, and play peek-a-boo as they emerge from one end. Or surprise them yourself by appearing "magically" at the opposite end. If they seem confident within it, you could hang a blanket over one end for them to peep out of. Don't force them to play with the tunnel if they seem nervous about going inside – just leave it on the floor until they are ready to explore.

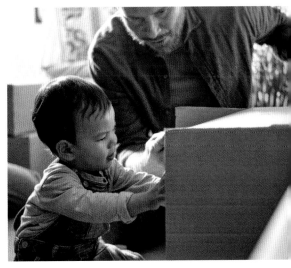

Tunnel play Exploring a toy tunnel helps to develop your baby's gross motor skills and their powers of anticipation.

Story and rhyme sessions

As well as enjoying books at home, it can be fun to join in with story and rhyme activities with other babies and parents.

Most libraries now offer membership to children from birth, and actively encourage babies and toddlers to make the most of their facilities, including dedicated activity sessions for babies, using rhymes, stories, songs, and possibly pictures and puppets, to help keep little ones entertained and interested. Not only is this sociable and interactive for your baby, it also provides an opportunity for you to meet other parents and explore the wealth of books on offer in the library. Visiting the library from an early age and encouraging your baby to explore and enjoy books will set them up for reading activities as they grow older. If you don't have a library close to your home, your local parent and baby group may have a story-time session that you can join in – if not, why not suggest that you start one? A book club for babies!

LAUGHTER

Babies laugh much more frequently than adults: an average baby laughs around 300 times a day, compared to an average adult, who laughs around 20 times a day – although how much we laugh also depends on personality. Between nine and 15 months, babies understand that when Mum puts a nappy on her head or "moos" like a cow, she's doing something unexpected – and that it's funny.

Quality time

If one or both of you are out at work all day, it's important to make sure that you have some one-to-one quality time with your baby.

Babies derive different things from each parent, so it's important that they get individual time with both of you. This can be difficult to manage when one or both of you work, but your different ways of parenting are equally stimulating for your baby, which broadens their understanding of human uniqueness. One of you may be calmer and more peaceful while the other may enjoy more boisterous play. Attention from you both helps promote social, emotional, and intellectual development.

If you're both at home in the evenings, try to organize your routine so that whoever is at home earlier does bathtime, whoever comes in later does the bedtime story, then you both get to kiss your baby and say goodnight. Or try to plan things so that one or other of you gets to sit down and have breakfast with your baby before you leave for work. When you do have time off, make sure that you play individually with your baby, as well as together.

Reading style Each parent may have a unique reading style that stimulates your baby's enjoyment of story time in different ways.

On the way to walking

At this age, your baby will probably crawl, possibly pull themselves up to standing, and may even cruise – but when will they walk?

It's natural to look forward with excitement to witnessing your baby's first steps – after all, as they totter unsteadily towards your waiting arms for the very first time, they're taking huge strides on the road to independence.

If your baby is by now cruising reasonably confidently around the furniture, it's possible that they may take their first independent steps at any time. However, since the average age for babies to take their first steps is at 13 months, it is unusual – though not unheard of – for them to start walking this early.

Walking depends on the development of gross motor skills, coordination, and build (a baby with a long body and short legs, for example, might find it harder to get their balance). If your baby was late to hold their head up or sit unaided, they're likely also to be late to walk – their gross motor function is taking a little longer than average to reach each milestone. There's no apparent correlation between early walkers and sporting prowess or intelligence – some babies simply do it sooner than others.

Slowly, slowly

Your baby's first steps are more likely to be a side-to-side shuffle that gradually inches them forwards rather than a striding march. Only once they have developed much better coordination and balance (often not until the age of two) will they pick up one foot to place it in front of the other. Until then, they will take lots of little steps, barely raising their feet from the floor at all. Babies also keep their feet wide apart and bend their knees, making them look bow-legged, and they tend to walk with a slightly arched back and toes pointing inwards. Early walking may not look elegant, but it'll seem miraculous to you.

Once your baby starts walking, patience will be your biggest virtue. They'll need you to hold their hand and match their snail's pace as you walk to the car, or to fetch something from another room. Progress can be frustratingly slow, especially when you're in a hurry. But try to avoid scooping them up too often – they need all the practice they can get!

Enjoying mobility As long as your baby is moving, it doesn't matter whether they do it on their bottom or their legs for now.

DEVELOPMENT ACTIVITY: CRUISE CONTROL

If your baby is at the stage where they're pulling themselves up but not quite cruising yet, you can encourage them by putting a toy a few feet away from them on the sofa so that they have to side-step to get it. The more stepping they do, the better their stability and coordination become.

All this movement is good exercise for their leg muscles, making them stronger; and good practice for lifting and planting their feet. Once they're more competent at cruising, you can place their toy a little further away, or on the next chair, to encourage them to move between pieces of furniture.

Parenting with confidence

As you race towards the end of your baby's first year, reflect on just how much you've learned – and be proud of yourselves as parents.

YOUR BABY MONTH BY MONTH

Happy family Being confident in your decisions and abilities as a parent will help you, your partner, and your baby enjoy family life that much more.

You are not alone. Your parents, your friends, and your GP and health visitor are all there to offer advice and support if you need it. Together, you and your partner demonstrate that confident parenting isn't solitary.

Have faith

Your baby looks to you for guidance – and will for years yet. No parent always gets it right, just have faith that your decisions are made with the best intentions. Believe in them, but also to be able to abandon them if you realize you made a mistake. It is a sign of confidence to be able to admit when you are wrong, take responsibility, and move on.

Be firm

Your self-confidence as a parent shines through in your ability to be able to set boundaries for your baby. No matter how much they protest at something you have good reason to say no to, hold firm. Your baby is more likely to grow up into a confident individual if they see that you mean what you say.

Be happy

Finally, love the job you're doing. Every day, as you watch your baby grow and learn something new, be proud of them – and yourself. They will feed off your delight, which means they will be happy, too.

CONFIDENT PARENTING TIPS

Do...
• **Take the positives** from your own upbringing and repeat the good practices your parents had, and take on board the best aspects of other parenting styles you see around you.
• **Think about the negative parenting** traits your parents or others might have had – and avoid repeating them.
• **Treat your baby with respect,** which doesn't mean giving in to them all the time – but instead gently setting firm boundaries.
• **Talk to your baby** as you would like to be spoken to, listen to them as you'd like to to be listened to, and be there to comfort them whenever they need you.
• **Always show love** – tell your baby how much you love them, and let your actions speak louder than your words.

Don't...
• **Be hard on yourself** if things don't go to plan – there's no parenting rule book and, if your baby is growing and happy, you're doing fine.
• **Be critical of your partner** – talk to each other about your differing approaches and be open-minded about the specifics of your parenting styles. Remember, you both have your baby's best interests at heart.
• **Be afraid to ask for help:** there are lots of resources out there, so do use them if you need to.

Breastfeeding and your bust

Breastfeeding doesn't change the shape or size of your bust – it's pregnancy that does that. Here is some key know-how for new mothers.

During pregnancy, a surge in hormones causes your breasts to increase in size. They stay like this throughout pregnancy and, if you breastfeed, will stay this size more or less until you wean. (If you don't breastfeed, your breasts will return to their pre-pregnancy size a few weeks after giving birth.)

Your breasts don't contain any muscle, but are attached to the muscles of your chest wall by thin ligaments. As your breasts increase in size, these supportive ligaments may stretch, which happens regardless of whether or not you breastfeed. If you gained a lot of weight during pregnancy, and go on to lose it, this can have an effect on your breasts, too. It's important to wear a properly fitted feeding bra when breastfeeding to support your breasts.

Your breasts are made up of fatty tissue, so if you gain weight your breasts will grow larger, and if you lose it, they shrink. The amount they shrink should be in proportion to your weight loss, so if you become slimmer than you were prior to pregnancy, your breasts are likely to be smaller than they were, too.

Your breasts might be a little less firm when you stop feeding, but in the six months or so after stopping, fatty tissue will gradually replace the milk-producing tissue in your breasts, leaving your breasts feeling fuller. Exercising your pectoral muscles (see box, below) can help your breasts become firmer and more lifted. Well-hydrated skin has more elasticity and looks smoother, so drink plenty of water and use moisturizer to keep your neck line feeling soft and supple.

Get re-measured by a professional bra fitter when you stop feeding in case your breast size has changed.

STRENGTHENING YOUR PECTORALS FOR A FIRMER BUSTLINE

A pair of hand-held weights or a couple of small bottles of water will help you gain the best results with some techniques.

Push-ups If you're new to push-ups, place your hands on the floor, extend your legs out behind you, and rest your knees on the floor. Cross your ankles. Support yourself on your arms, keeping your back straight. Bend your elbows to lower your upper body so that your nose touches the ground, then straighten your arms to raise yourself again. Repeat 10 times, rest, then do another 10 times. If you are concerned about straining your abdominals or uterus, try an inverted push-up. Stand facing a wall with your arms outstretched and palms placed on the wall at shoulder height. Gently bend your elbows to move your body towards the wall, then straighten them to return to the starting position.

Chest press Lie on your back with your arms above you, elbows slightly bent, and a weight in each hand. Slowly and deliberately lower your arms out to the sides, keeping your elbows bent, until your fists hover over the ground. Raise your arms to your starting position. Make 15 repetitions, rest, then make 15 more.

Overhead press Stay on your back with a weight in each hand, arms above you, elbows slightly bent. Gently lower your arms over your head until you feel the weight touch the floor behind your head, then bring your arms back up to the starting position. Make 15 repetitions, rest, then make 15 more.

Chest stretch To wind down, stretch the muscles you have been exercising. Sit with your back straight and hold your hands behind your back, bringing your shoulder blades together to open up your chest. Hold for a count of 10, then release.

Baby talk

Listen very carefully – your baby might well be saying actual words, but you may not have noticed. Encourage them by repeating their first words.

In some cases, it's not always easy to recognize the words your baby says, but at other times, they may be obvious. Perhaps if they are keen on trains, they might say "toot toot", or they might say "yeow" when they see a cat. Their increased vocabulary doesn't have to be full of the actual nouns that we attribute to objects.

Consider, too, that their words might lack an ending. It is perfectly normal for babies to be unable to

Clever! Your baby loves to babble, but if you listen carefully to what they're saying, you might hear some actual words!

make the hard sounds at the ends of words when they first begin to talk. In which case, the train noise might be more a "too" than a "toot", a cat might be a "cah", and a dog, a "doh".

Although your baby might be closer to two years old before they master the knack of finishing their words, you can help the process along by keeping background noise to a minimum when you talk to them, so they can hear you clearly. Also, be careful to finish your words. From time to time, feel free to exaggerate the hard sounds at the ends of words a little to help them focus on them.

Sheer determination

Babies are remarkably resilient and steadfastly tenacious when it comes to achieving something they have set their minds on doing.

The utter determination of babies is what drives them to learn new skills and develop the ones they already have every single day. Of course, if there is a downside to your baby's will to try again and again, it is that they might be unwilling to let you help them, which can mean that some practical tasks – such as putting on a hat so that you can go out – take significantly longer than they might if you stepped in.

Teachers increasingly report a pattern that suggestss that when students struggle, they are unwilling to go back to a task to see it through. Try to encourage stickability in your baby by praising their willingness to keep trying, and giving them lots of chances to repeat until they succeed, have had enough and turn away naturally, or allow you to help them. Above all, give them lots of praise for their continued efforts.

ASK A PARENT

My baby has started biting me and it hurts. How do I stop them? Your baby has no idea they're hurting you, but it's not a habit that you want to encourage! Make sure you don't react too strongly but do say, "Ouch, that hurts" and give a matching expression. Pop them on the floor for a minute and distract them. They'll soon get the message that this is something you don't like.

Time for playgroup

Helping your baby to socialize will teach them important life skills, from communicating with peers to learning to be kind.

Now is a good time to start taking your baby to playgroup, because they'll enjoy playing near other children and playing new games and with different toys. The closer the playgroup is to home, the better, as your baby can make friends with children who live nearby, and who one day might even go to school with them. Some groups are run by the council, others by local churches or a group of dedicated parents (who will pass on the baton as their own children head off to school). Try out a few in your area, finding one (or more) that feels the friendliest and that your baby seems to enjoy most.

What to expect

Much of what happens at playgroups depends upon their size. A small playgroup might have a room or area for toddlers, with a few climbing toys and art or craft activities, and a separate room or area for babies. Larger playgroups will have whole rooms dedicated to aspects of play – perhaps a room for painting (or other messy play), a room for babies, and a room for active play for toddlers. All offer cups of tea and coffee, and biscuits, as well as drinks and snacks suitable for the children. At the end of the session, there is usually a circle time, when everyone joins together to sing some songs, celebrate birthdays, and give notices about activities.

As a rule, playgroups are informal and relaxed, and parents are free to play with their children and talk to other parents as they wish. Some groups will ask for a small contribution each time you visit (or termly) and some will ask if you would be willing to help out one week – perhaps by manning the tea hatch or doing some craft preparation at home. Getting involved is a great way to feel part of a community.

Baby doesn't want to play

The noise levels and frenzied activity at some playgroups can be quite daunting for some babies, and if your baby doesn't want to get off your lap the first few times they go, don't despair. Find an activity that the two of you can do together, or simply find a book and read to them. Once you have been several times, their natural curiosity will get the better of them, and they'll go off to explore. However, bear in mind that, at only 10 months, they will be happy playing alongside other babies, but won't necessarily want to play with them.

DEVELOPMENT ACTIVITY: FLOUR PAINTING

Find a shallow tray that is ideally of a dark colour. Sprinkle some flour over the tray and rock the tray back and forth so that there is an even covering across its surface. Now show your baby how to trace their finger through the flour to "draw" patterns and shapes. This activity is far less messy than using paints! Flour "painting" is a great way of bringing out the budding artist in your baby, and it will help them to develop their fine motor skills, which are so important for drawing and writing later on in life.

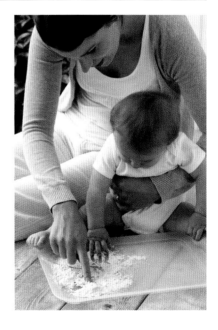

Budding artist Flour painting is a good way of introducing your baby to the concept of mark-making. They'll enjoy drawing shapes as well as the tactile quality of this activity.

323

Sleeping through the night

If your baby isn't sleeping through the night yet, don't worry – you will certainly not be alone. A 10-month-old should, though, be capable of a proper night's rest, so it's worth considering whether some of the ideas below might help you both get the sleep you need.

Your baby needs sleep so they can process the events of their day, and in order to grow. You and your partner need sleep, too. Generally, having too little sleep makes us irritable, impatient, and uncompromising – hardly a recipe for family harmony.

While it may seem hard to tackle your baby's night waking now, erratic sleep patterns will become harder to rectify as your baby gets older.

Assuming that your baby's nap times are working well, at night a 10-month-old baby should be able to sleep for a good stretch, perhaps 10–12 hours. By this age, they should be eating 2–3 meals a day, with snacks in-between, so there should be no need for night-time milk feeds.

Reasons for waking

If your baby isn't used to settling themselves back to sleep during the lightest phase of the sleep cycle (which, as adults, we don't notice), they will rouse fully and call out for comfort or for milk. This can become a habit if you always comply. Babies aged between nine and 12 months often also suffer from separation anxiety, which can become acute when they wake alone in the darkness. Other reasons for waking might be that your baby is having too much sleep or napping too late in the day, or is struggling to re-establish good habits after a bout of illness or teething pain that caused night-time waking.

The key thing is to decide which approach you feel comfortable trying to re-establish your baby's night-time sleep, and stick to your guns. If your baby has been consistently wakeful in the night (that is, you've never had a period during which they have slept through), breaking the habit can take up to three weeks of persistent effort. Don't give up!

Bedtime basics

Your baby will benefit from a strict but loving and happy bedtime routine. Give plenty of positive and soothing signals that it's time for bed. Spend the last hour of the day engaged in quiet interaction together. This way, your baby will get lots of positive attention to make them feel secure. Give them a bath, get them dressed for bed, and read them a bedtime story. Saving one story specifically for bedtime is an clear signal that it's time to settle.

When the time comes for sleep, give your baby a reassuring cuddle and kiss, put the baby in the cot, settle them down (with a comforter or teddy if there is one), say good night, then leave the room. You can leave a night light on if you wish, and perhaps soothing music. Keep the cot a happy place – avoid using it as a convenient means of confinement while you do something else. Make it a place where a favourite cuddly toy sleeps, and where your baby sees a big smile from you last thing at night and first thing in the morning.

Cosy bedtime routine Keep the last hour of your baby's day restful as you prepare them for bed with lots of reassuring cuddles and kisses. Encourage them to self-sooth while slumbering in their cot.

Midnight mayhem

If your baby has a tendency to wake up and want to play, you need to reinforce that night-time is a time to rest. If the baby is crying, soothe them calmly, but don't chat or engage. If your baby's nap times are too long, or they are still having a late afternoon nap, the baby may not be tired enough at bedtime to sleep through the night. Try moving the afternoon nap forwards by 15 minutes, and making it 15 minutes shorter, too. You don't want your baby to be overtired at bedtime, but they do need to be ready for sleep.

Waking for a feed

It can be hard for you or your baby to give up a night-time breast- or bottle-feed, if it's a time you are close and calm together. If you suspect this feed is merely one of habit, it's time to take steps to drop it. Gradually reduce the amount of milk you give, either by reducing the time you spend breastfeeding or by gradually decreasing the amount of formula in the bottle over several nights. Or offer your baby water instead of milk – over time they may not consider it worth waking up for! Plus, if your baby settles with water, you know that it's not true hunger that's causing the waking, but the habit of it.

Waking for a cuddle

If your baby is determined to have your reassuring presence in the night, it can be tempting to bring them into bed with you (see box, opposite). Be aware that this can later make it harder for a baby to learn to settle in their cot – and that a toddler takes up a lot of room in your bed! If you prefer to have your baby sleep in their own space, soothe them by going to them when they call and patting them in the cot, hushing calmly or humming softly, rather than lifting for a cuddle. Some babies need a short wind-down cry before they go to sleep, so try to make sure the baby is really summoning you before you go in.

Sleep "training"

Other frequently mentioned techniques include gradual withdrawal or controlled crying. Gradual withdrawal is the gentler method that involves soothing your baby to sleep at bedtime in the usual way, but then laying them in their cot just before they drift off, and sitting in the room (without engaging) until they fall asleep. Eventually your baby should learn to go to sleep with you at the other side of the room, and then with you out of the room altogether.

Controlled crying involves soothing your baby in the cot with stroking and patting, but each time they cry leaving them to wait a little longer before you go in, the idea being that eventually the baby learns to self-soothe back to sleep. Many experts, though, feel controlled crying is not advisable on the grounds that it is stressful for babies and parents.

With all the different methods, consistency is essential.

Restful sleep Babies need a good night's sleep so the brain can consolidate the day's learning and the body can recharge for more action tomorrow.

IN BED TOGETHER

There's little doubt that a baby in their parents' bed is less likely to wake up crying or be difficult to settle at night. However, even if at this point you are all getting a good night's sleep, as your baby gets older your nights are likely to be less peaceful. As your baby gets bigger (and stronger), they will move more, kick, and make a noise at night. There are also risks associated with co-sleeping, and it is not advised in certain circumstances (see pp.30–31). If you or your baby are not co-sleeping as soundly as before, you may wish to think about moving them into their own bed sooner rather than later. Some babies make the transition easily, others need to get used to the idea – you may have to keep your baby's cot in your room for a while, for example. Even if your baby moves out, your bed can still be a great place for cuddles in the morning!

Toy time

Choosing appropriate toys for your baby can be mind-boggling.
Observe them at play to help you select toys that will interest them.

Your baby's thinking and problem solving are geared for fun and discovery. Books, balls, building blocks, and stacking cups are all great for honing their ability to understand cause and effect and shape and size, and to develop their problem-solving skills. Make sure items are of a size that your baby can hold and pass from one hand to the other easily.

Any toys that encourage movement, or support your baby

Fun with learning Toys designed for this stage of your baby's development will help them enjoy and be enthusiastic about learning.

as they pull to standing, are also good choices. Check the age-range on new toys before you buy to make sure that they are suitable for your baby's age and stage of development. A toy should suit your baby's individual level of mobility, dexterity, and understanding. You don't need to spend lots on shop-bought toys, though – make use of bits you might have lying around the house. For example, the inner tubes of wrapping paper rolls make wonderful trumpets, and a cardboard box is great for climbing into and out of, or to use as a "net" for a thrown ball.

Shapes and sizes

You can start to introduce new concepts such as large and small now, but don't expect your baby to identify these all by themselves yet.

Comment on familiar objects and describe their properties using words such as "bigger", "smaller", "soft", and "hard". Your baby will start to grasp these concepts in the months to come.

Introduce shape-sorters, toys of different sizes and textures, and posting games and they'll be acting out concepts such as in and out and large and small without realizing. Play story games with their soft toys or teddies, talking about little baby

ted and big mummy or daddy teddy. Then you can show them the toys and ask, "Show me the big one." Soon they'll be experimenting with these ideas intentionally. Make use of stories that contain themes about shapes and sizes, especially those with sensory panels. Talk to your baby about big, small; round, square; high, low, and so on, bringing shape and size into conversation and observation on a regular basis.

AS A MATTER OF FACT

Don't be surprised if your baby's eyes are still changing colour. Although base eye colour is usually established between six and nine months, subtle changes in tone may still be noticed as more dark pigment is produced in the iris (green eyes turning more hazel, for example, or hazel eyes becoming deeper brown). Eye colour can keep changing into toddlerhood and sometimes even in adulthood.

Time away from your baby

You're bound to have mixed feelings about a night away from your baby. Leaving them with carers whom you trust will make it easier.

Now that you are so accustomed to having responsibility for your baby's welfare, it can be quite difficult to "let go" and hand over to someone else, especially for a whole night. For this reason, it's important to be comfortable with whomever you choose to look after them while you are away. And it helps if they're very familiar to your baby and have an idea of their routine and preferences.

Preparing your baby

In the week leading up to your absence, spend lots of time with the person or people who'll be looking after your baby. Ideally, have them come to stay with you, so your baby has the security of their own home as they get to know each other. If you can invite the carers to stay for the few days before you leave, all the better. Ask them to do some feeding, nap time, bedtime, and waking routines so your baby is used to their care by the time you leave.

Preparing the carers

By familiarizing themselves with your routines before you leave, your baby's carers will be well prepared. Ensure they know which foods to offer (leave prepared meals if you can) and which snacks. While, you may prefer they kept to your schedule, let them know it's okay to make changes in order to do keep your baby happy.

If your baby is staying with their carer, ensure they have a cot, their comfort object, and plenty of food, nappies, and changes of clothes. Cater for a day longer than your planned absence to guarantee your baby will be short of nothing. Ask the carer to perform a quick babyproofing check with you before you leave. Always leave emergency contact details.

Preparing yourself

Agree on times to call to check in before you go. When the time comes to leave, be cheerful, brave, and purposeful. If you sneak off, they may worry that you won't be back. Give them a wave, and hit the road.

MONTHS 10–12

ASK A CHILD PSYCHOLOGIST

Will my baby get out of their routine if they're with another carer overnight? It can be unsettling for your baby to be in a different environment, and no matter how hard their carers try, they won't get their routine spot on. However, your baby is able to tolerate brief variations to their usual schedule so long as their routine at home is well established. Once they're home, quickly settle them back into the usual pattern and don't be tempted to keep them up late or change things because you want extra time or want to "treat" them because you've been away.

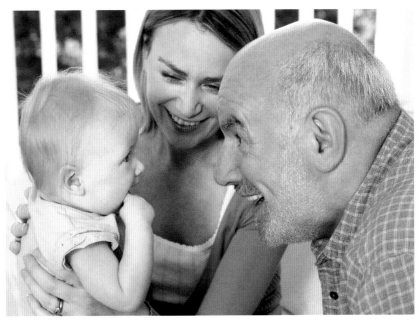

Preparation for your absence In the week before you go away, make sure your baby spends plenty of time with whomever will be taking care of them during your absence.

Building language skills

Around this time, you might want to use a bit less "parentese", start to lower your pitch, and make your intonation more adult in style.

At this stage, encourage all forms of communication between you and your baby. Whether your baby uses words you can understand or not, give them the space to say what they want to say, even if it appears to be gibberish. When your baby pauses in their babbling, respond with adult language. What they need to hear back from you is the correct way of saying things.

Ask quesitons to refine your understanding of what they are saying. For example, ask, "Are you asking me for a drink?", "Would you like to go out?" or, "Would you like the teddy?" Don't worry if you can't immediately tell what they mean; keep trying and you may get a smile to show you've got it right. Listen and respond, and show your delight so they'll know they're on the right track. Allowing them to speak, and then responding to them, encourages their language skills and builds their communication confidence.

My baby wakes during the night and wants a bottle of formula. How can I discourage this? Your baby shouldn't be hungry during the night now; they should have taken in all the calories they require during the day. Often, the only reason babies of this age demand a feed at night is for comfort. Make sure they have a good last feed before bedtime and offer them a bottle of cool boiled water if they wake in case they are thirsty.

Muscle development

Your baby's fine and gross motor skills have come a long way, but there's still plenty you can do to encourage their development.

The muscles of your baby's legs and arms continue to strengthen with every physical challenge. Encourage your baby to climb over and under soft pieces of furniture (with a soft landing), up stairs (with supervision), and in a soft-play environment. Playing games such as "Row, Row, Row the Boat" helps to develop upper-body strength. Also, try dancing with your baby by holding their body or their hands as they stand and bounce, which is great for developing their leg muscles.

Your baby is now more able to control their smaller muscles, such as those in their fingers. Get them used to paint and paper by making hand prints, or trying some finger painting. You can try giving them a fat crayon and guide their hand to make a mark. It might be a bit early for success with this yet, but you'll probably find that they have quite a strong grip – if you try to take the crayon away, they may not let go willingly!

Gripping a crayon Scribbling is fun and improves your baby's fine motor skills.

Encouraging healthy eating

Help your baby to develop a taste for healthy foods before they start to develop any particularly strong likes or dislikes.

Although your baby is too young to stir or chop, they can sit with you as you prepare their food and talk them through the process of what you're doing. If you can spark their interest in what they're eating and make them feel part of the preparation process, they're more likely to be open-minded about enjoying it.

Allow them to experience the textures of what you're feeding them before and after cooking and talk to them about the colours of the foods. For instance, say to them, "This is a carrot – look how orange it is! Shall I peel the carrot?"

Make it visually appealing

If you were presented with a plate of food in a restaurant that looked unappealing, it's unlikely you would want to eat it. Your baby's response to food is no different. Babies love bright colours, different shapes, and, once they can cope with small, soft lumps, a variety of textures. Use these facts to make the healthy foods you offer your baby look interesting and appetizing.

Arrange different types of foods in little piles on your baby's plate – for instance, put gently steamed vegetables that they can pick up with their fingers in one area, and their chicken casserole in another. Try serving their meals on plates that have separate compartments – these are often brightly coloured and decorated to appeal especially to babies and toddlers.

If you are feeling artistic, you can use finger foods to create fun faces, or make a train out of mini sandwiches. Use shaped biscuit cutters to make shaped sandwiches – your baby will love eating a star or flower!

Another good trick is to create swirls or other shapes of colourful fruit compote in a bowl of otherwise bland-looking breakfast porridge.

Sous chef Spark your baby's interest in their meals by talking to them about how they are made and getting them to "help" you.

FINGER-FOOD DUNKERS

Your baby loves to feed themself, so encourage this developing skill with finger-food dunkers. They'll enjoy this fun way of eating healthy foods. Below are ideas to get you started, but be warned – they are messy!

• **Homemade baby guacamole** Mix chopped tomatoes with mashed avocado and a teaspoon of lemon juice; serve with wholemeal toast.

• **Tomato sauce and pasta** Make a simple tomato pasta sauce and offer your baby a few very softly cooked pasta twists (chopped into smaller chunks, if necessary) to dunk in it.

• **Cheese fondue** Make a cheese fondue: gently heat in a pan 25g (1oz) butter, 25g (1oz) cream cheese, and 50g (2oz) grated mild Cheddar cheese until melting. Serve with chunks of bread or toast and lightly steamed vegetables for dipping (halved new potatoes are good).

• **Pancake dippers** Strips of pancake or banana can be dipped into plain yoghurt.

• **Meatball dippers** Dip meatballs into a fresh tomato sauce.

• **Yoghurt dippers** Dip chunks of steamed fish (check for bones) or chicken into a minty yoghurt dip made of creamy Greek yoghurt, chopped fresh mint, and a little lemon juice.

• **Homemade fish fingers** Dip in a homemade tomato sauce.

Work vs. home?

There are positives both to going back to work and to staying at home, so it's a good idea to remind yourself of these occasionally.

Going back to work is beneficial for more than just your finances:
• You will quickly re-learn all the important information and skills you need to do your job.
• It can be a confidence boost in your independence beyond your home.
• It can make a change to dress up in your work clothes.
• It allows you to socialize and see the colleagues whose company you enjoy but may have missed for a while.

Benefits to staying at home are:
• You're around to witness your baby's every milestone.
• You have time to reassess your career and look at new work opportunities.
• You have the opportunity to connect to your local community and network with parents.
• You have more time to get active, enjoying exercise on your own or together with your baby.

A NEW CAR SEAT

Your baby may outgrow their first infant Group 0 car seat between nine and 12 months, when they reach 9kg (20lb). If they have a Group 0+ seat, it may last longer – until they weigh at least 13kg (29lb). Only move to a bigger Group 1 car seat once your baby exceeds the maximum weight or their head is higher than the top of the seat. The next seat up should last until your baby is about four.

What's that noise?

Your baby is interested in all the sounds they hear around them, so help them to learn about the different noises in their world.

Say it out loud Sound out the noises of objects and animals in your baby's picture books.

You can have lots of fun teaching your baby about the many different noises they're likely to encounter. From cars to animals to the telephone or front door bell ringing, there's plenty of scope to hone your skills of imitation or engineer it so that your baby hears the real thing.

Play with toy animals with your baby and demonstrate the noises they make. If barking, moo-ing, and miaowing all gets a bit much, think about buying, or borrowing from the library, an animal sounds book so that you can help your baby push the animal buttons to hear "baas" or bird song. Or download an app designed to teach babies about animal noises.

You can teach your baby about everyday household noises too, so that they aren't startled when the front door bell rings, or you switch on the vacuum cleaner. Help them to push the doorbell so that they can hear the noise it makes. They'll soon start to remember who or what makes the noises they hear.

Extended breastfeeding

Extended or long-term breastfeeding means breastfeeding beyond your baby's first year – so is it for you?

The longer you breastfeed your baby, the longer they will benefit from the goodness in your breastmilk. Breastmilk becomes more concentrated in its nutritional benefits when your baby is feeding less often, and continues to provide them with vitamins A, C, B12, and large amounts of folate, calories, protein, and calcium. However, it is also true that by the time your baby reaches their first birthday, their primary source of nutrients will be the food that they eat.

The World Health Organization (WHO) has identified that toddlers between the ages of 16 and 30 months who breastfeed have been found to have fewer illnesses, as well as illnesses of shorter duration than non-breastfeeding toddlers.

Extended breastfeeding has benefits for the woman's health and wellbeing, too. There is a reduced risk of developing certain cancers, including breast, ovarian, uterine, and endometrial cancer. The WHO also suggests that it may reduce the risk of osteoporosis.

A decision for you

How long you choose to breastfeed should be entirely dependent on what feels right for you and your baby. Breastfeeding is a natural way to feed your baby, and as long as you are both enjoying and benefiting from the experience, there's no reason to stop. If you experience negative comments from those whose opinions matter to you, simply explain why you are continuing to breastfeed, giving particular emphasis to the benefits for your baby – cited as a greater sense of security and confidence.

Many mothers of older babies continue to partially breastfeed – offering breastmilk in the morning and evening as a comforting start and end to the day. This can be ideal as your baby shouldn't need regular nursing during the day if they are properly established on solids.

Still breastfeeding While it's more unusual in the West, breastfeeding older babies and toddlers is normal in many cultures.

AS A MATTER OF FACT

In Western culture, breastfeeding much beyond infancy is now relatively rare, despite the fact that the World Health Organization (WHO) recommends breastfeeding for at least the first two years of a child's life.

Until the 1960s, women in many cultures, including in Kenya, New Guinea, and Mongolia, routinely breastfed their babies until they reached 3–5 years old. However, extended breastfeeding is becoming less prevalent as women become more educated and go out to work in increasing numbers. Today, there are few societies where children are routinely breastfed until they are three or four years old, and these communities tend to be found in low-income countries, such as the Sincantea Indians in Mexico and the Sirionó people in Bolivia.

In the UK, initial breastfeeding rates have risen – 81 per cent of new mums breastfed according to the last NHS Infant Feeding Survey. However, it is estimated that only 25 per cent of women are still breastfeeding at six months.

Leading by example

By watching and copying you, your baby is starting to use you as a role model to follow. Keep setting them good examples.

FOCUS ON TWINS: TALKING

Do your twins give the impression that they understand each other's babbling? Most experts agree that twins don't share a "language" as such, but rather a "code", or series of shortcuts that they develop when conversing with each other. This usually starts in infancy, when twins copy one another's immature speech patterns, such as jumbled sounds and "made-up" words. Because both twins are developing at the same rate, they often reinforce each others' communicative attempts and increase their own language. Although "twin talk" may be cute, you should help your children learn to use correct language when speaking. You can do this by speaking to your twins individually rather than together, and reading to them so they hear plenty of words.

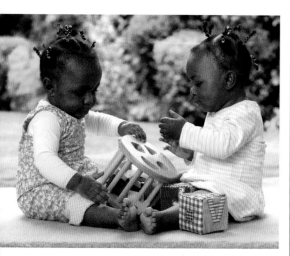

Say something then! Twins often like to copy each other's babble.

Your baby may not have uttered their first word yet, but may be shaking their head to say "no", pointing at items they want or want you to notice, and waving bye-bye. These are all actions we use as we communicate with our babies every day, and they have picked them up from you. If your baby isn't waving yet, don't worry – some babies don't do this until well into their second year. Capitalize on their copying behaviour by pointing things out to them, or expressing your meaning with actions as well as words. If you are telling them that something is big, open your arms wide. If you are telling them it's time for lunch, make an eating action.

Mimicking chores

Your baby will also want to play with the things they see you hold and use, from a harmless measuring cup to a dangerous kitchen knife. (Hazards should all be locked away by now, but it's always good to double-check you haven't become complacent and left anything lying about.)

Give your baby toy versions of grown-up tools. A toy iron allows them to be just like you, but without the danger of burns; a toy mobile phone makes your own far less appealing if it's left in reach.

You are the ultimate learning tool

Maximize on your baby's wonderfully suggestible nature. If they see you

Hello and goodbye Wave to your baby and they may wave back.

respond happily to a given situation, they are much more likely to respond happily in a similar situation, too. And if they see you using cutlery to eat your food, they'll want to use their spoon. Even if they don't mimic you immediately, they may well have processed what they've seen and do it another time – psychologists call this deferred imitation.

All this, does, of course, put parents in the spotlight, especially as learning from your behaviour takes precedence over any other kind of learning your baby will experience at this age. So whatever you do, be good!

Upside down

Your baby's increased coordination allows them to manoeuvre themself into different positions to gain new perspectives on their world.

At this age, your baby will probably pull up to standing, but getting down is more problematic as they still haven't worked out how to bend their knees, so if they see a toy on the floor that they want, they will either bend down from the waist with legs straight to grab it, or will simply sit down with a thud (although slightly less of a thud than previously!). When leaning down, they may peek between their legs and try to reach through them to grab toys and other objects. In fact, they have no real sense of their own abilities and limitations, and will try all sorts of manoeuvres to get what they want and may be surprised to end up in an unexpected position!

Help your baby to practise their balance and coordination by encouraging them to bend forwards and pick up toys on the floor from a standing position.

They may also push themself up on their legs when they're in a crawling position, and peek backwards. Every new position provides a new angle on the world, and they're developing spatial awareness. Encourage them to point to things that they see from their new vantage point, and watch them giggle with delight when they see their favourite items upside down.

Now that your baby is probably a very competent crawler, you can help them to master coming down the stairs (far harder than going up) – on their tummy, feet first, and sliding backwards. The same movement is used for sliding off the sofa.

OUTDOOR SAFETY

Once your baby is on the move, they will be keen to explore the great outdoors – starting with your garden! Plenty of outdoors play is hugely beneficial for your baby's health and wellbeing, but before you let them loose, take a good look around any outdoor space and ensure it's safe for your inquisitive, mobile baby. The following guidelines will help to keep your baby safe.

• **Check that there are no poisonous plants your baby could reach.** If you're unsure whether something is poisonous – perhaps flowers were planted by a previous owner – take a cutting or photo to your local garden centre to see if they can identify it.

• **Keep patio pot plants out of your baby's reach** so that they aren't tempted to eat the soil or pebbles, which are also a choking hazard.

• **Watch your baby all the time near water.** Fill in or fence off garden ponds and remove, or turn over, paddling pools that are not in use.

• **Make sure any play equipment is sturdily built.** If you are assembling it yourself, follow the instructions exactly. Keep play equipment away from fences and walls.

• **Cover sandpits** when not in use to prevent cats using them as a litter tray. Check the rest of the garden for cat and other animal faeces.

• **Most importantly, supervise your baby** at all times in the garden.

A different view The world looks different from various angles, and your baby now has the manoeuvrability to try out new positions as they straighten their legs and pivot down.

Getting their attention

Your busy baby may be so intent on exploring at times that they don't pay attention to your guidance or warnings.

Usually your baby will hang upon your every word, keen to interact, listen, and respond. Of course, they'll also spend time engrossed in play and it'll be more of a challenge to get them to listen, especially if you're asking them to stop or want to divert them onto something else. If you need to interrupt them, you'll get their attention most effectively if you get down to their level and make eye contact. Say their name first and then give a short, simple statement. For example, if they're annoying the cat and you can see a scratch coming, say, "Stop prodding the cat" and guide them away. Avoid long sentences or multiple requests and always guide them gently to move if they need to. There's no point listing dangers to them as they can't imagine the possible hazards that come so readily to your mind. Instead, if there's a problem, mime the consequences, for example if you need to show them your drink is hot, then mime touching the cup and say, "Ouch, hot, don't touch" while waving your fingers as if they're burnt. It will take many repetitions to teach this danger awareness so don't expect them to remember this for quite a while.

If they consistently doesn't respond when you talk to them out of their range of vision, it's worth asking your doctor to check their hearing.

No more bottles

Your baby is now able to master a beaker and take milk this way. Dropping the bottle early can help to protect their teeth.

The longer your baby drinks from a bottle, the harder it will be for them to move onto a cup and fall asleep without sucking. The sucking action causes milk to swirl around their mouth, bathing the teeth in the sugars contained in milk, causing tooth decay. If you wean them onto a cup early on, they won't be as likely to associate milk with comfort, so is less likely to comfort eat later in life.

Drinking from a cup Get your baby into the habit of taking their milk and other fluids in a cup to prevent tooth decay.

To make the transition, switch the teat on their bottle to a spout so they become used to drinking rather than sucking. Buy colourful beakers and let them choose which one they'd like to drink from. Habits can be established quickly in babies under a year, and if they feel they have a choice, the disappointment of not having a bottle will soon be forgotten.

If you're breastfeeding, work towards giving one or two smaller feeds a day and offering expressed breastmilk in a cup to make up the difference. Suckling breastmilk does not cause dental caries.

Your child's first teacher

You are your baby's first teacher. Your guidance and actions are their benchmark for understanding the world around them.

Your baby looks to you for guidance and information and will learn how to behave, interact, and negotiate their world by watching and listening to you. For this reason, it's important to do your best to model the type of behaviour you want your baby to learn, and present your family values to them through your actions.

While they are still too young to display any table manners (and digging in and making a mess is an important part of their learning to eat), you can exhibit good manners yourself. Sit and eat with them whenever you can. Studies show that the more frequently families eat together, the better their relationships. Your baby will learn that mealtimes are sociable, and will see how you and your partner listen when others are speaking and wait your turn to talk. This teaches them about relationships, respect, and acceptable behaviour.

Setting a good example

Babies who grow up hearing shouting or seeing adults lose their tempers will mimic this behaviour and consider it the norm. It certainly isn't always easy to cope with a single-minded baby, and you may find your nerves get frayed, but working out healthy ways to control your frustration when things go wrong or you're stressed is good for your baby.

However, while there's no doubt that setting a positive example is

Setting an example As well as being sociable occasions, family mealtimes offer the perfect opportunity to model good table manners.

beneficial (when your baby sees you socializing, reading, being organized and active, and enjoying fulfilling relationships, they will be likely to absorb these qualities, too), it's also healthy to recognize that there's no such thing as a "perfect" parent.

Don't be hard on yourself if you don't manage to get everything right, whether leaving the kitchen in a mess, ignoring a phone call, letting routines slip, or being niggly with your partner. Babies can cope with things not always being ideal. As long as you're in tune with your baby's needs, put these first, and give consistent care, then you're good enough. Providing a secure environment is the best thing you can do for your child.

ASK A CHILD PSYCHOLOGIST

My baby has temper tantrums already! Is this normal? While your baby is not yet emotionally capable of a proper "toddler"-style tantrum, babies can appear to lose their tempers. This is a sign that they are frustrated at being unable to express their needs. Try to remain calm and patient yourself. Many babies respond to being held and comforted when feeling out of sorts; sing a familiar song to calm them and try to distract them from the situation. Speak quietly so your baby is reassured that everything in their world is not out of control, and show them how to master whatever it was they were trying to do, or gently move them to another room where the trigger will no longer upset them.

Growing appetite

The more mobile your baby becomes, the more their appetite increases. They may need more food and regular snacks to sustain their energy.

By now your baby is eating two or three meals a day. They should be getting plenty of wholegrain carbohydrates, fresh vegetables and fruits, lean meats and fish, eggs, dairy products, and pulses. Continue to serve a variety of healthy foods, revisiting the foods that have been rejected every few days or so until they become familiar.

Don't offer unhealthy snacks between meals. Snacks should contribute to overall diet and make up for shortfalls. If they learn to satisfy their hunger with raisins, dried apricots, wholegrain toast with peanut butter, yoghurt, squares of cheese, strips of vegetables, fruit, a hard-boiled egg, or a few spoonfuls of tuna, they will develop healthy eating habits and associate good, fresh food with meals and snacks.

Encourage your baby to taste new appropriate foods from your plate.

Show them different foods when you are shopping or preparing meals, and let them touch, smell, and taste them. Let them eat until they feel full; they may eat lots at each sitting for a few days, then seem to want less for a while. Allow their hunger to decide how much they eat: while it is important that they get regular, healthy meals, these can be smaller or larger, as long as their weight remains stable (see p.278).

A different approach

Instead of racing to do chores when your baby is asleep, slow down and let them join in. You may be surprised to find you both have fun.

Little helper Unpacking the shopping doesn't have to be quick when it's this interesting.

When your baby begins a play session, you may have a few minutes to make a phone call, check emails, or make a list before they demand your attention. You may also be able to get a few things done while they nap. However, these small windows of opportunity are unlikely to provide all the time you need for chores.

Although it may take much longer, letting them participate in your practical activities will keep them occupied and teach them about the way in which a household runs. Pop them in a pile of washing while you sort the clothes and name the different colours; or make a game out of refilling your nappy changing stations and repacking your changing bag, letting them handle the items.

You might even want to include your baby in some of your other daily routines – for example, sharing a bath together. If you read your book or your emails out loud when they are happily playing on the floor, they'll simply enjoy the sound of your voice. You may get less done than you would like, but you'll have the satisfaction of working with your baby as a positive part of your day, leaving you more time for rest after their bedtime.

Outdoor play

It's important that your baby has plenty of outdoor playtime to ensure they get fresh air, sunlight, and lots of exercise.

Gross and fine motor skills, coordination, balance, and imagination are developed when children are given plenty of opportunities to climb and play, and to respond to the natural world with its multitude of textures, smells, activities, and possibilities.

Being outdoors is also helpful in giving your child experience of a different field of vision and new sensory stimulation. Seeing into the distance, feeling the wind on their skin, and noticing changes in the light all offer their senses new information.

Time spent outdoors in a natural environment is known to improve mood in adults, so taking your baby outside regularly will probably give you a boost and set them up in a habit that will be good for them as they grow. Time spent in sunlight also encourages the production of vitamin D in your baby's body (see p.221), which helps your baby to build healthy bones and teeth. Do, though, take steps to stop their skin burning.

Daily excursions

Make an effort to get outside at least once a day, and in fine weather, let your baby sit in the grass, crawl in the park, or amuse themself in the sandpit in your local playground. Push them on the baby swings, play ball, point out the squirrels, and take a bag of stale bread to feed the ducks. Give them a safe place to explore; hold their hands so that they can stand supported and splash in puddles; and let them crawl and get their hands dirty. Once they are on their feet, hold their hand and enjoy "mini" explorations of your local park or neighbourhood, letting them take their time and stop to examine nature along the way. Have their pushchair at the ready so they can rest when they get tired. Spending quality time outside will give your baby a fresh view of the world and will also do wonders for your own perspective.

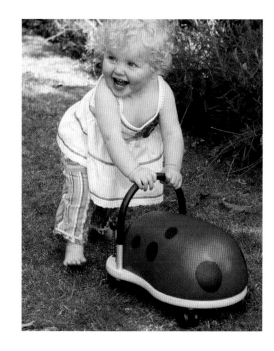

Outdoor fun Playing outdoors allows for exuberant fun and a change of scene.

DEVELOPMENT ACTIVITY: RAINY-DAY FUN

Your baby needs some time each day to move their body freely so that they can make those gross motor movements that teach them so much about what they can do with their body.

If you can't venture out due to rainy days or cold weather, think of ways in which you can keep them active at home. Encourage them to crawl up and down the stairs next to you, and have a crawling race across the living room floor. Hold their hands and dance to lively music; and set up an obstacle course with cushions, pillows, folded towels, and their favourite toys for them to climb up, over, and around.

You could make a drum kit with kitchen pots and pans and wooden spoons, or play a game of tag, chasing them as they crawl around the living room, and playing action rhymes when you catch them.

As long as they get a little out of breath and, ideally, are giggling too, they'll be using up energy and, of course, having plenty of fun.

12 months

AT FIRST, BABIES BELIEVE THAT THE IMPORTANCE OF A POINTING FINGER IS THE FINGER ITSELF.
Your baby's manual dexterity has come a long way and they are now adept at using their index finger to point to things of interest. They're also getting better at using a spoon to feed themself, but as their hand–eye coordination is not yet fully developed, mealtimes are bound to be messy!

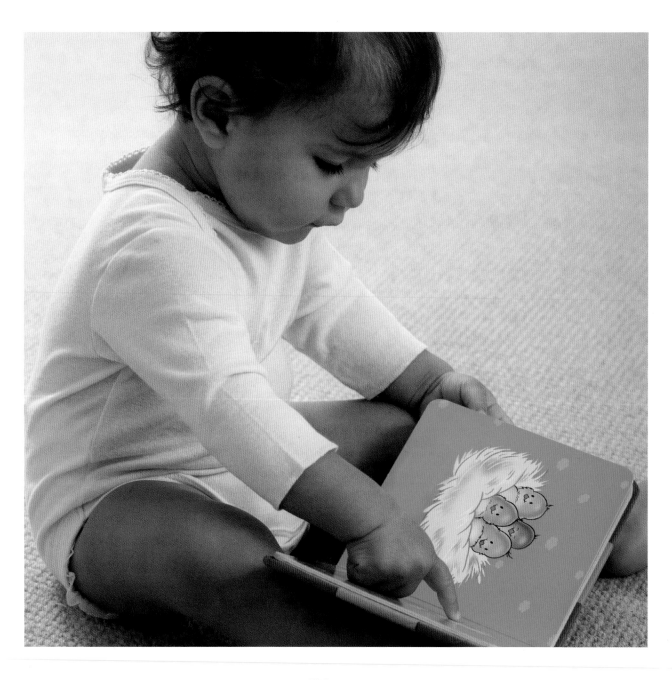

Practice makes perfect

It'll be a while before your baby can successfully feed themself with a spoon, but they'll enjoy trying to eat with one, just like the rest of you.

By now, your baby may be keen to feed themself, even though they don't yet have the motor skills and coordination to bring a spoon easily to their mouth. However, practice makes perfect. To make it easier, give them a short-handled plastic spoon rather than a long-handled weaning one. Give them a bowl, preferably one with a suction ring on the base which will hold the bowl in place as your baby dips their spoon into it. As they negotiate their own spoon and food, offer spoonfuls from a second bowl that you hold. They will eventually learn the art of picking up and holding a spoon, filling it with food, and placing it in their mouth.

Forget about etiquette

To begin with, your baby is likely to hold the spoon in one hand and use their other hand to scoop what's in front of them into their mouth. At this stage, let them do exactly as they please. Give them a bib (a wipe-clean one will save on washing), and put some newspaper or a splash mat on the floor under their high chair.

Even if most of the food ends up in their hair, don't discourage them. You can hold their fist as they grip the spoon and help them move it to their mouth, but remember that they don't yet have the coordination or the flexibility in their wrist to be able to do this themself. Don't underestimate the importance of providing your baby with guidance and a model to

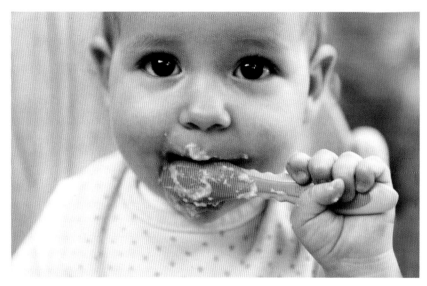

Self-feeding with a spoon Be prepared for a good proportion of the contents of your baby's bowl to end up in their lap, on the floor, and all over their face – even in their hair!

copy. Sit down to eat with them at mealtimes so they see how you operate your own cutlery.

The most important thing at the moment is that your baby is encouraged to get their food into their tummy in the easiest way possible and that they enjoy themself at mealtimes. Successful self-feeding is a big developmental leap for your baby. Now it's all about confidence – they will be unlikely to be able to feed themselves a full meal without any help until they are about three, so mealtimes need to be fun, positive, and full of praise in the meantime.

ASK A NUTRITIONIST

Why isn't my baby hungry at mealtimes?
At this age, they need no more than 500–600ml (17fl oz–1 pint) of milk a day, and some of this can be in the form of cheese, yoghurt, butter, and other dairy products. Offer them solid food before a milk feed so they start meals on an empty stomach. Work on cutting down daytime bottles or milk feeds. By now, they can manage on a feed in the morning and in the evening, with a little milk alongside meals. Ensure they don't have constant access to other drinks, especially juices or squash, which dull their appetite. Also avoid giving them too many snacks: a couple of healthy ones a day is enough.

Patting, poking, and pinching

Your baby's hand–eye coordination is improving constantly, and they are now capable of pointing and poking, and may even pinch, too!

Being gentle Teach your baby how to treat siblings with gentleness.

Your baby will begin to test their own strength and abilities and you may find them prodding, poking, pushing, and even pinching pets, toys, and people. In fact, any activity that offers a resounding reaction will attract their repeated interest.

Your baby's unwelcome behaviour is nothing more than an exercise undertaken to satisfy their curiosity and gauge the response they get. They're not being malicious, but are trying out their skills. When they do poke or hit, show them how to interact more gently. Show them how to pat or stroke your family pet. Provide words for these actions, such as "Nice cat, pat the cat", so they learn to understand the terminology for the actions you want to see. Soon enough you will be able to say the words, "Pat-pat" to get them to stroke rather than hit.

If they continue being too physical, distract. Find opportunities to put your baby's skilled little fingers to better use. Give them an activity board with buttons to push, dials to turn, and strings to pull.

When they won't go to bed

Your baby equates bedtime with being separated from their closest family – and all the fun – and they may resist attempts to settle at night.

Babies need less sleep as they get older. If your baby starts to put up a fight at bedtime, make sure that their evening routine continues to be relaxing and comforting so that they look forward to this time and associate it with enjoying close, quiet time with you.

Throughout the day, ensure your baby gets plenty of exercise and stimulation so that they are tired enough to go to sleep at bedtime. Consider moving their nap to an earlier slot, or their bedtime later, so that they are ready to settle.

Try not to become frustrated at a reluctant sleeper, especially if they start to learn that reluctance leads to attention. Simply settle them in their cot as usual and return when they call you. Stroke them and pat them, sing their familiar night-time song or say the usual "good night", then leave. Be upbeat so that they don't feel that bedtime is a punishment. Keep other noise to a minimum during this phase so that your baby isn't distracted by what's going on elsewhere.

If all else fails, at bedtime put your baby in their cot with a few toys and their usual comfort items, and allow them to occupy themself quietly until sleep descends, then remove the toys.

Limits and boundaries

As your baby nears their first birthday, you may be wondering what you can expect of their behaviour, and what parenting style to develop.

Most parents are concerned about what sort of parent they will be, and most aim for a middle ground focused on being warm and loving, and firm, but fair, when it comes to guiding their child's behaviour. The challenge is often to get the right balance between giving your child the freedom to explore the world, yet ensure that they grow up to be well-behaved individuals with a proper sense of right and wrong.

You are already setting boundaries, by moving your baby away or distracting them if they snatch toys from another child. You probably also hold their hands firmly and say, "No", if they do something they shouldn't. So by 10 months, your baby may have worked out that "no" means "stop", but they haven't grasped the ideas of right and wrong, and may not heed your instructions simply because curiosity has got the better of them.

Types of discipline

Discipline tends to fall into two main categories – that needed for safety and that needed for good behaviour.

When it comes to safety, it's important to remove your child physically from danger. If, for example, they go to touch the oven door, or grab a lamp from the table, move them away, hold their hands firmly, and, kneeling at their eye level, tell them, "No" and explain why – "The oven is hot, it will burn you. Ow!" or "The lamp is heavy, it will bump

you." Once won't be enough with explanations, but repetition and consistent responses will help your baby get the message.

When it comes to good behaviour, don't expect too much. Your baby still considers themselves to be the centre of the world and has only the shakiest idea that they could upset others. At this age, they learn by watching, and you are their key role model. When you show good manners and speak calmly, they'll absorb this and start to show this behaviour too as they

develop. They don't understand the concept of saying sorry yet, but it's not too early to demonstrate how it's done so that they get to know what's expected.

Whatever parenting style you develop, there are some key points to remember. Your child will be more responsive if you are consistent; spend more time and energy praising and encouraging rather than telling off; and, when the time comes to use discipline and consequences, you do so calmly and without anger.

DEVELOPMENT ACTIVITY: SOFT AND HARD

Help your baby to understand the different properties of the objects they encounter each day. Give them different textured toys and household items to hold and handle, and describe each one, talking about whether it is smooth, hard, soft, or furry, as well as what colour it is. Talking to them in this way helps to extend their vocabulary and understand that not only do things have names, but they also have different characteristics. This in turn helps them start to make connections and comparisons. They're not ready to name all these things themself, but you are helping them to understand.

Exploring through touch Fill a basket with different textured toys and objects, and encourage them to dive in and explore.

In your baby's own time

It can be tempting to want your baby to meet the same milestones as their peers, but remember that every baby is different.

Milestones are designed to give you a rough idea of when your baby will be physically, mentally, and/or emotionally ready to master those challenges or skills that are acquired across infancy and childhood. They are not tests to establish intelligence or define future prowess. In fact, achieving milestones such as walking or sleeping through the night early is no indication that they will do everything else early. It's important to realize, too, that, just as milestones act as a guide rather than a rule, the order in which they are reached can vary from baby to baby. Some babies leap ahead physically and are slower to talk. Others gain hand–eye coordination earlier, while walking happens further into the second year. So while your friend's baby of the same age may be busy climbing stairs, yours may be far more preoccupied with making different sounds.

Your baby is unique. They will meet their milestones when they are good and ready, and unless they are obviously lagging well behind their peers of the same age, there is no reason for you to be concerned. If you genuinely think there could be a problem, you should check with a health professional.

It's me!

Your baby is developing a sense of independence, and over the coming months, their self-awareness will grow.

Hello! Your baby will enjoy using a mirror to explore their senses, particularly their visual sense.

Your baby is beginning to understand that you are separate from them. The earliest signal of this was a few months ago, around the time they realized that you weren't always there and that you sometimes moved out of sight. This is when they grasped the concept of "person permanence": the idea that you exist even when they can't see or hear you.

As they discovered their own body, their self-awareness grew, alongside their increasing control over, and consciousness of, how their body moved. They are also developing a mental picture of themselves and others. At around 12 months, they'll be able to tell the difference between a photograph of themselves and that of another baby, and from 15 months comes the revelation that the image in the mirror is their reflection.

Your baby's involvement in some basic fantasy play is another sign that they're aware of self and others. When the two of you act out cuddling a teddy, or pretend to give it a drink, they're copying others' behaviour.

As they move through their second year, their awareness that they're a separate person from you will grow, so watch out for them asserting their personality. Soon, "no" will be their favourite word!

Working parent

Juggling work and parenting can be stressful, and you may feel that you cannot give 100 per cent to either. These feelings are normal.

Despite any concerns you may have as a working parent, be reassured that you can most certainly raise a healthy, happy baby and enjoy your work. The secret is to be organized and flexible, and to get your priorities right. If you put your job first when you are at work, and your baby and family first at home, you are bound to get things right. The other parts of your life that surround this, including household chores and socializing, may need to go on the back burner for a while – certainly until you establish a routine that works for everyone – and it is equally important that you lower the expectations you hold for yourself. If you are just about keeping all of the balls in the air, then well done!

Work–life balance

While it's undeniably tricky to keep work and family life ticking over, there are several things you can do to help your days go smoothly. First, get organized. Make sure you know what needs to happen when, and stick to the same routine each day so you can streamline events and your baby knows what's going on, which will help them to feel secure. Set out everything required for the morning the night before so that you can relax knowing that everything is ready, no matter what happens the following morning. Batch cooking and bulk-buying are other organizational godsends that save you a great deal of

DEVELOPMENT ACTIVITY: HOMEMADE FUN!

Your baby will be just as excited by a big, empty box that they can crawl into or tip over as they will be by the latest and most expensive new toys. Scrunch up paper into balls to fill the box, then encourage them to tip the contents out and reload the box. Pop in a few toys for them to discover while they play. Equally, a sturdy laundry basket makes a great toy car or train – your baby will enjoy playing the part of the driver or passenger when you push them around.

These games will help to stretch your baby's imagination and improve their gross and fine motor skills. What's more, they'll keep them occupied for stretches of time!

Improvised toys Even a piece of paper taped into a cone shape will be "useful".

time in the long run – and probably some money, too.

It's important to have back-up plans, too, in case your baby is sick or your carer is away. Try to organize a support network that you can turn to for when things don't go to plan.

If at times you feel overwhelmed, focus on the positives. Feeling guilty for not being there to see all of your baby's "firsts" or tend to their daily needs won't help you. Instead, celebrate the fact that your baby is healthy and happy and you're able to

go out and earn a living. Concentrate on the most important areas of your life and only agree to things that enhance your life. An exhausted, unhealthy, and emotional parent isn't going to be effective in any area of their life.

Lastly, don't feel guilty about relaxing work ambitions for the time being if you find a young family isn't conducive to a go-getting mentality. There will be plenty of time to chase those goals when your baby is more independent.

New skills

In addition to their milk feeds, your baby should now be eating three meals a day, and the occasional snack on days where they are particularly active.

Your little one's fine motor control is improving all the time and they are becoming adept at manipulating objects accurately. They are also more interested in trying to use tools, such as a spoon or fork, for their intended purpose.

Pre-load a spoon with food, then support your baby in bringing the spoon to their mouth. Let your baby do the rest of the work, putting the spoon into their mouth themselves. It may get messy! Use sticky or lumpy foods like mashed potato or porridge. Remember to praise your baby when they successfully feed themselves.

Self-feeding Be patient while your baby learns and explores. They may not get it right every time.

Working it out

Your baby now shows an increased ability to solve problems, and enjoys creative activities and toys that test their developing skills.

DEVELOPMENT ACTIVITY: ARTS AND CRAFTS

Encourage your baby's creativity as well as their hand–eye coordination and fine motor skills with regular arts-and-crafts sessions. Purchase some chunky non-toxic crayons, tape a large piece of paper to the kitchen floor, and show them how to make marks with their crayons. Create patterns and scribbles. Talk about the colours you are using and guide your baby's hand to make straight lines or circles, naming all the different shapes you make. Every couple of months, save one of their creations in a scrapbook or art portfolio so you can see how their skills progress over the coming years. In the summer, go outside and use chalk to create pictures and scribbles on the pavement or deck.

Free flow Your baby will enjoy being expressive with colours and shapes.

Toys such as shape-sorters, simple first jigsaw puzzles, musical instruments, and building blocks help your baby to improve their analytical thinking, which, in turn, will develop their ability to work out how things in their environment operate. They will encourage your baby to reason, deduce, analyze, and use logical thought and then to put their ideas to the test. They are also learning to problem solve when their ideas do not work immediately. For example, if they have chosen a slot in which to fit their wooden puzzle piece and it doesn't fit, they may persevere to create the right match. Although they can become frustrated, most babies enjoy a challenge and repeat things until they get them right.

To encourage your baby to develop and hone their problem-solving skills, give them puzzles and activities they can master before moving them on to more challenging toys. Early successes breed confidence for the harder tasks. If they struggle to master a new toy, bring back simpler toys to rebuild their confidence first.

Observation and imitation

Your baby will solve problems by observing and copying. This is one reason why it's worth spending lots of time playing with them and showing them how things work. Demonstrate new toys and then let them have a go, applauding their efforts.

Analyzing Your baby's ability to work out what fits, and their new fine motor skills, allow them to solve more complex puzzles.

Encourage your baby's socialization skills; give them the chance to play alongside other children on a regular basis. Seek out local playgroups, or a community crèche or nursery, so they get used to being with other babies. Or arrange a regular get-together with parents and babies you've met, rotating who hosts. All of these opportunities offer your baby the chance to observe other babies doing things in different ways, allowing your baby to observe and learn.

Planning your baby's birthday

You may wish to celebrate your baby's first birthday with a party. But don't be surprised if they don't show much interest in the proceedings!

Keep your baby's first birthday party simple – you can't celebrate their transition to toddlerhood if you are busy serving canapés or clearing up spills, and they will prefer to have you by their side, particularly if there are more people than usual in your home. On that note: choose a few people your baby knows well.

Forget about themes and party games – they will have no interest in them. Balloons may be fun, but tape them out of reach to avoid your baby popping them (the fright could ruin the day!). Or use helium balloons and cut the strings so the little ones can't reach them.

Keep the party short – an hour or 90 minutes is plenty. Aim to start it half an hour after they wake from their nap so that they're refreshed, but not grumpy, and ensure they have something to eat and drink as they'll be too excited to eat much once the guests arrive. Ensure food intended for adults is out of reach.

Don't be worried if your baby finds the colourful gift paper more exciting than the gifts themselves! If guests ask for gift ideas, a good choice is books to build up your baby's library. If there are lots of gifts, open them over several days to prolong the fun.

Sleeping less

Your baby may resist settling down at bedtime and need less sleep than before, but it's important they get enough to stay healthy.

Routine A consistent bedtime ritual helps your baby to prepare for impending sleep.

As they approach one year of age, your baby needs about 14 hours of sleep in a 24-hour period. They may have one long nap of around two hours, but may continue to need two daily naps totalling 2–3 hours, which is fine. Don't worry about meeting a specific sleep goal.

Your baby will benefit now from having a comfort object, which will help to soothe them if they wake in the night. You can also place a few cot-safe toys at the end of their cot: they may be happier to settle in their cot if they can see something fun to keep them occupied. They'll likely fall asleep mid-activity.

Work out the best nap system for your baby. A late-afternoon nap might make it hard for them to settle at night – a quiet, gentle playtime instead may relax them. A single longer nap at around lunchtime may keep them going all afternoon, as long as they're in bed early.

The time of your baby's bedtime is not so important, as long as it is consistent. Be aware, though, that if you settle them down before 6pm, they're going to rise before 6am the next morning. If you're a night owl rather than a lark, you may need to adjust their bedtime accordingly to fit in with yours.

Outdoor pursuits

Now that your baby is one year old, you can start to enjoy some new outdoor activities that you will both enjoy doing together.

Your baby is old enough to enjoy taking part in some of the outdoor activities you enjoyed before they were born, but may have avoided for practical reasons since.

If you like to walk or hike, buy a baby backpack carrier. Take your baby with you to buy it so that you're happy that you both find it comfortable. It needs to have adequate back support for you, with a sturdy, front-closing strap, and to be the right size for your baby, with sufficient head support if they fall asleep. Most are waterproof with sun and rain shields, and have a pouch to carry essentials such as a drink, snack, nappy-changing kit, and sun cream. Check that it has the safety kite mark to show it has been tested for babies, and inspect all the straps and fixtures regularly for wear and tear. Ideally, walk with at least one other adult so that someone can check on your baby and help get the carrier on and off, as well as share the carrying. A sturdy, thick-wheeled buggy is good for longer walks over uneven terrain.

Cycling as a family

If you're keen to get back on your bicycle, you can fit a bike trailer to your bike. The age at which a baby can sit in a trailer is determined by the strength of their head and neck development, and the weight of the helmet. Ideally, they should have been sitting well without support for at least two months. Some countries have laws that state babies must be at least one year old before riding as a passenger on a bike, and make it compulsory for babies to wear helmets, including when in a trailer. Avoid putting your baby in a bike seat until they are at least one year of age, as they won't have sufficient muscle strength before then to support their head while wearing a helmet.

To get your baby used to a trailer, and help you to adjust to carrying them behind you, start with short rides on smooth paths to avoid jolts, and steer clear of roads. Take your partner or a friend with you at first, and build up to longer trips.

Don't put your baby in a backpack or a trailer if it's very hot or cold as it will be difficult to regulate their temperature. On longer trips, have frequent breaks to check them, and take them out at intervals so they can move freely.

Easy rider Baby carriers are a great way to enjoy walking with your baby – and they get to see the world on your level.

ASK A NUTRITIONIST

Should I encourage my baby to eat everything in front of them? It's best to let your baby's appetite be the guide. Encouraging them to finish up their plate may lead to negative food associations and increase resistance. At this age, the appetite of some babies wanes slightly. In the first year, your baby tripled their birth weight, but they gain weight more slowly in their second year, so while more active, they may not need to eat and feed as often. Bear in mind, too, that they still gain a proportion of their calories from milk. Also, as they are more mobile, it may be harder to get them to stay still long enough to finish every last morsel. On the other hand, if your baby is less interested in their milk now, you may find that they wolf down their food. Either way, as long as you offer a variety of healthy foods (ideally concentrated around mealtimes), they will gain the necessary nutrients they need to thrive.

Mind those Ps and Qs

This is the ideal time to demonstrate good manners to your baby by showing them the polite responses you would like them to mimic.

Your baby will pick up on phrases you use regularly and start to understand their meaning, so being polite and considerate towards them and other people can only have a positive effect.

Say, "Thank you" when your baby hands you a toy, and "Please" when you ask for something from them so that they get used to the sounds of these words. It doesn't matter that they won't be saying, "Please" or "Thank you" themself for a while, just hearing them as part of conversation will help them begin to make sense. Say ,"Excuse me", "You're welcome", and even "I'm sorry" appropriately. They'll grow up understanding that these words are part of normal behaviour, and will adopt them more easily when they start to talk.

Be polite to people around you, too, including your partner. Be generous with praise and appreciation, and always show empathy for others. On those occasions when you can't be a paragon, just be aware that your baby may be listening – try to keep rude remarks to a minimum!

As your baby's vocabulary expands, prompt them to say "please" and "thank you" by asking, "What do you say?", and repeating either "please" or "thank you" so they get into the habit.

Dressing for the weather

While your baby's clothing needs are fairly modest, there are a few wardrobe basics that will equip them for all weather conditions.

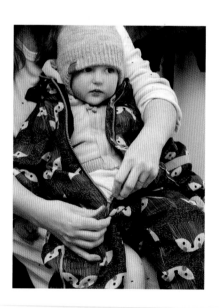

Comfortable clothing Opt for simple styles that are easy to add or remove to keep them the right temperature in all weathers.

Layer your baby's clothing so that you can adapt what they're wearing as conditions change, or they move between inside and outdoors.

In colder months, dress them in several layers, including a vest, top, and then warmer fleece or jumper. They'll need a warm outer jacket (waterproof if it's wet) for outdoors, as well as mittens and a hat. All-in-one snowsuits are perfect for nippy days. If they're sitting in a fleecy cover or blanket it will keep them cosy. If you go into a shop, remove their blanket and hat, and remove layers and hats indoors at home.

In the warmer months, a few light layers are sufficient, with a summer cardigan to put on and take off as needed. A sunhat is essential: opt for a floppy one or Legionnaire-style hat with a brim and back flap to cover their neck. Always protect their shoulders from the sun. Keep a long-sleeved T-shirt on them, and, on the beach, buy a baby lycra swimsuit that covers them and blocks most UVA rays. When they're indoors on a hot day, a nappy may be all they need.

Too sick for nursery?

It can be tempting for working parents to dose up an unwell baby with medicine and send them to nursery, but they should be kept at home.

A child's immune system gradually builds up antibodies to infection, so your baby will probably catch every bug going among their peers. For this reason, parents have an obligation to keep children who are ill away from a nursery environment until they are no longer contagious. Also, your sick baby's immune system is already hard at work fighting off an infection, so they'll be in danger of acquiring a secondary infection if they're in contact with another set of bugs.

Feeling unwell A sick baby should be cared for at home until they're back on form.

If your baby is ill, be honest – staff looking after them will soon know if they are off-colour! Have a back-up plan, with a list of family members or friends who can step in to care for your baby; or aim to work from home or temporarily swap hours.

Ensure your baby is comfortable at home and gets plenty of fluids to flush out infection. Expect some grizzling, tearfulness, and irritability, as well as a few broken nights, and be patient. When in doubt, call your doctor who can assess the situation, reassure you, and provide guidance about the right time for a return to nursery.

ASK A DOCTOR

When should I keep my baby at home from nursery?

• Most babies and children suffer from regular colds (you can expect anywhere between one and six a year in the early years). If nasal discharge is thick and sticky, your baby may be more susceptible to further infections, including ear infections. It's best to keep them at home until the cold has cleared completely.

• If your baby has a fever, they should stay at home for at least 24 hours after it has ended. They will need plenty of rest and fluids to recover.

• Most rashes can be treated at home after a consultation with a pharmacist. Rashes have many causes, including infectious diseases; if your baby has chickenpox, don't take them to the nursery

for around five days, or until the spots crust over. Your baby may continue to attend nursery if they have slapped cheek syndrome as they're no longer infectious; just make sure the nursery is informed.

• Flu and other respiratory illnesses can become serious in babies if they are not monitored, so it's worth taking your baby to the doctor if they have flu symptoms (see p.376). These illnesses can easily spread around a nursery, so a baby with the flu must be kept at home.

• A baby with diarrhoea or vomiting should always be kept at home. Your baby will be sent home if they experience these symptoms at the nursery. They'll need to stay at home for at least 48 hours after the last episode, no matter how well they seem to be feeling.

• Bacterial eye infections, such as conjunctivitis (see p.370), are highly contagious. Keep your baby at home until symptoms clear and they have been taking antibiotics for at least 36 hours.

• Keep your baby at home if they catch whooping cough, or another childhood illness such as measles, rubella, or mumps. Although in the early months whooping cough is routinely vaccinated against, it's still possible to catch, but is less severe. Keep them at home, too, with roseola, scarlet fever, and hand, foot and mouth disease.

• If your baby has impetigo or another contagious skin disease, keep them at home for at least 48 hours after starting antibiotics. Scabies needs to be treated before your baby can return.

Making savings

Having a baby is an expensive business, as you no doubt well know by now, but there are ways to save money as you go along.

New baby items such as your Moses basket and its blankets and sheets, your newborn baby bath, and a top-and-tail bowl are probably now redundant. If you're thinking about extending your family, they may come in useful the next time around; if not, you might want to think about raising a little cash for the next phase by selling them at a local nearly new sale (these are often run by mother-and-baby groups). Then, think about buying secondhand for the next phase – especially for clothing, which your baby will quickly outgrow and is likely to get mucky with all that play! If buying new, make the most of sales – and consider bargains that future proof your growing baby. Collect the coupons and money-off vouchers given away with baby products – they can add up to considerable savings.

Sibling support

Older siblings may feel a little sidelined by a baby who is demanding of your attention, so make sure they get special time with you, too.

Older siblings may adore their little brother or sister and be thrilled to be involved in looking after them, but as the baby gets older and more interested in their toys and games, they may find them a nuisance. At times, they may become cross or frustrated, even physically unkind. If this happens, intervene straight away and reinforce the notion that hitting, pushing, biting or hair-pulling, for example, is not the way to behave towards other people.

See how it's done Older siblings will enjoy helping their new brother or sister to play, but do supervise them when they're together.

As your baby demands more, their sibling's needs will also increase. The closer in age they are, the more difficult they might find it to have to share you. However, even much older siblings can feel left out.

Make time to be with your baby's bigger siblings on a one-to-one basis. When your baby has a sleep, avoid rushing around getting jobs done. Instead, spend time playing with their siblings. Regularly arrange a time when someone else can look after your baby, and plan a treat or activity with your older children in advance so they can look forward to their special time with you.

Toys for 11 months up

As your baby approaches their first birthday, they'll be ready for some exciting new toys that will stimulate their growing curiosity and confidence.

FOCUS ON TWINS: PLAYTIME

Entertaining two babies is definitely challenging, but not impossible. Make sure you put out enough toys for both of them. This doesn't mean dragging everything out (which would be overwhelming) or going overboard purchasing twice as many toys, but ensure there's a variety of toys to keep both occupied. Toys that can be easily split, such as soft blocks, are perfect, too. It's important to treat them as individuals. Be aware of each twin's likes and dislikes, and provide toys to suit their different needs. Lastly, do enjoy one-to-one time with each baby. Don't assume that because they have each other, they have less need of you. You are their number-one playmate and teacher, so it's vital that you and your partner spend quality time with each baby.

Side by side As with other babies this age, your twins will be happily preoccupied in their own pursuits.

Your baby may have outgrown many of their old toys by now. If you are having a party to celebrate their first birthday, you may be thinking of gift ideas and, no doubt, you'd like to get them one or two age-appropriate toys. There are many toys on the market that are suitable for one-year-olds, so you've plenty to choose from. Try to give a variety of toys to help your baby develop different skills.

Toys that encourage physical activity are a good idea, as your baby's motor skills are developing rapidly. Babies make the most of push-along baby walkers, which support them as they push them around, but make sure your baby doesn't become over-reliant on them for walking. Balls are also popular now; your baby may enjoy batting one and passing it back and forth to you.

This is also a good age for sorting toys, such as shape-sorters and stacking cups, which help your baby to hone their problem-solving skills and explore how smaller objects fit into bigger ones.

Very basic and sturdy wooden puzzles with knobs to lift the pieces in and out of position will appeal to your older baby, and they may spend a long time turning them to try to make them fit into the different holes. Choose simple shapes and show your baby how the puzzle pieces fit.

Toys with a string to pull will also delight your baby as they can grasp and pull quite easily now. Try a toy

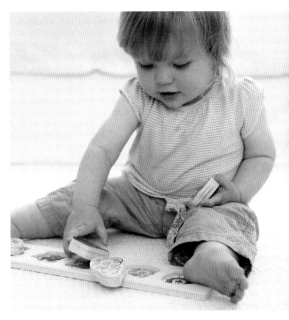

Puzzles Chunky puzzles with simple shapes will appeal to your one-year-old baby.

that climbs up its string, or makes a sound, or plays a song when its string is pulled.

If it's warm outside, water or sand tables or pits provide endless enjoyment as your baby fills buckets, empties them, and makes a real mess! Never leave your baby unsupervised near water.

Finding a balance

Happy, fulfilled parents are good for babies, so you both need to have time and space for all those aspects of your lives that are important.

By now, you and your partner may both be back at work, on a full or part-time basis, having arranged additional care for your baby. Or one of you may have decided to stay at home to look after your baby while the other one works. Or you may both be working part-time and juggling the sharing of childcare between you. Whatever you have decided to do will probably be the result of planning and discussion between you.

There's no doubt that life now is different to your life before your baby. If one of you is looking after your baby at home, you may be thrilled with your new role in raising them the way you want, sharing activities with them each day, and proudly watching them develop. However, you may also miss some aspects of your pre-baby life.

A different person

If you have given up work, you may feel that your image of yourself has changed and that you feel a different person. It's easy for your confidence to falter, even though you are doing what you chose to do and recognize the valuable role you are playing. It's important that you don't give yourself selflessly over to what you think your baby needs. You need to develop a new life for yourself in which you find a routine that works for you and to feel confident in your parenting.

Take some time for yourself each week, perhaps asking your partner or a family relative to have your baby for a morning or a few hours at the weekend so you can do something you enjoy. You may decide to book your baby into a regular session at the local nursery or childminder or employ a part-time nanny to give yourself a break. Never feel guilty about this. Being happy and fulfilled as a person will make you a better, more evenly balanced parent.

Most of all, nurture friendships with other parents with babies of a similar age. You will be an invaluable support to each other. If you feel isolated, use playgroups to meet other parents. Your health visitor or local library will have details of what's available in your area.

If you have gone back to work, you may miss your baby or feel guilty that you're not at home. Rest assured: your baby will be fine. Create special times together when you aren't at work. If your partner is the main carer, make sure you have time to talk each day. Your partner will need to tell you everything your baby is up to; this will boost your partner's sense of achievement and ensure you feel part of your baby's development.

You are growing in your role as parents – try not to be too rigid. You may find one or the other of you does not have the work or childcare options they expected, or changes their mind about their role. Discuss anything that doesn't feel right and be open to making changes.

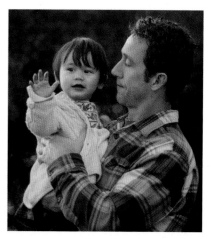

Bye It's important to find a routine that works for both you and your partner and one that offers a life with and away from your baby.

ASK A PARENT

I keep having to get up at night to replace my baby's dummy. Is now a good time to wean them off it? Yes, it is generally recommended that babies stop using dummies by the age of one, partly because habits are less ingrained before then and partly because of concerns that relying too much on dummies when babies start babbling could affect their speech development. Start by limiting its use: let your baby have it to fall asleep, then take it out of their mouth so they get used to it not being there when they wake. When you get rid of the dummy, offer another comfort object, such as a blanket or toy as a distraction. Your baby might object for a night or two, but most adapt quickly.

Changing tastes

Your baby's palate is becoming more sophisticated, so this is the ideal age to expand their diet and get them interested in new foods.

If your baby is curious about what the rest of the family is eating, let them try, as it is one of the best ways to encourage healthy eating habits. They'll learn to enjoy the flavours of the food they will grow up on, and will also enjoy feeling part of the social experience of eating as a family.

Although your baby is still learning to feed themselves, offer them a plate of their own with a selection of foods customized from your meal. (Separate your baby's portion before adding any salt when cooking.) Soups, casseroles, pasta, meatballs, and family roasts are perfect for older babies. If your baby is a picky eater, you can hide a selection of vegetables in sauces and soups.

Using wine in cooking is fine now – just ensure that you cook it off long enough for the alcohol to evaporate.

Leave salt and whole nuts off the menu still, but you can add new seasonings (herbs and spices) and cheeses to flavour your baby's food.

If your baby is still reluctant to eat very lumpy foods, offer finger foods as well as regular foods in a lumpier form. Give, say, finely chopped poached chicken and mashed vegetables with chunks and strips of each to encourage experimentation.

When your baby dreams

At this age, your baby begins to dream a little less than they used to, but their brain is still consolidating what it has learned during the day.

Sleep tight Through the night, your baby has periods of deep, restful sleep, and phases of lighter sleep, during which they dream.

As your baby approaches one year of age, they will have less "REM" or dream sleep (see p.109) than before. During this phase of sleep your baby's brain works hard to process and consolidate information acquired during that day. (Premature babies still have more dream sleep than babies born at full term, and continue to need more for several more months.) When your baby dreams, their central nervous system enters an "active" state and their temperature may rise a little, while brain-wave activity and heart rate both increase. During this lightest stage of sleep, they may wake up briefly, or seem restless in their sleep.

Try to avoid responding too quickly if they cry slightly or sound disturbed in their sleep, as they will usually settle themselves. Periods of dream sleep are followed by phases of deep sleep, and most babies have about five periods of each type of sleep, occurring in a cycle, throughout the night. In deep sleep, your baby's breathing will be regular, and they may sigh and make sucking motions.

A little reader

Your baby will have definite favourites on the bookshelf now, and will love having the same stories read over and over again.

Books keep babies occupied for long periods of time, with pages to peruse, and then turn to see what's next – but they offer much more than just a way of passing time. Books enhance vocabulary, language acquisition, and concentration. As the months pass, your baby will be more able to follow a story – a skill that will one day help them to read on their own.

Babies love to have familiar stories read to them. Research has found that every time you read the same story to a baby, they pick up new information from the narrative, and their memory is improved. You may find that your baby "follows" the story with you when you read a familiar book to them, as they anticipate what's coming next and begin to respond to what is about to happen. If you miss out a page or even a sentence or a word, they'll probably look perplexed!

Old and new

Old favourites encourage your baby's development, but it's important, too, to introduce a variety of books and, once they are able, to encourage your baby to choose their own stories.

Keep their books on a safe, low shelf in an accessible bookcase or basket, so that they can select themselves the ones they would like to look at. Pack a few books for long car journeys and shopping trips. Give your baby as many opportunities as you can to use books as a distraction and to keep themself occupied. When reading with your baby, engage them in the story. Ask them to point to different elements, and make noises or sounds for the characters. As well as stories, find books with a single word on a page to encourage word recognition. Offer interactive books with flaps, textures, or buttons.

Consider creating a special book for your baby full of photographs of their favourite people, places, toys, and activities. Use an online provider or simply laminate the pages and sew them together. As they get older, encourage them to tell stories about what they see in their special book.

Story time Reading daily to your baby will help develop their language and communication skills.

DEVELOPMENT ACTIVITY : SPLISH, SPLASH, SPLOSH!

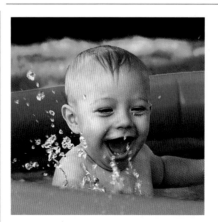

Summertime fun Older babies love to splash about in paddling pools in warm weather. Make sure, though, that you never leave them unattended in a paddling pool, even for a few seconds.

Once your baby is on their feet, it's time to invest in some Wellington boots. Babies love nothing better than a good splash in puddles on outdoor walks! Or get the paddling pool out in the summer and supervise them while they learn about how water moves in response to their actions, and how things float. Playing with water makes swimming fun for your baby and develops their senses and confidence. Best of all, it allows them to explore their environment while making a splendidly satisfying splash! However, never leave them unattended near any garden pond, paddling pool, or swimming pool.

Becoming more mobile

Mobility is a part of every toddler's development, and even the most reluctant crawlers or walkers will make a move in the coming months.

Early walkers may now move on to running, but most babies are still working towards their first steps.

Once your baby does start to walk, they will test their skills by trying to walk backwards, sideways, and up and down the stairs, before lurching forwards at speed – and usually taking plenty of tumbles on the way.

Try to spend some time outdoors on grass, which will cushion your baby's falls and help them to develop balance on a slightly uneven surface. They will have no sense of distance, nor will their depth perception be mature (so they may walk off the end of landings and porches), so keep a close eye on them.

Multiples mayhem

As with all babies, give your twins or other multiples a safe environment to practise walking – often in different directions! Remember that they may develop at different rates to each other. This simply reflects different developmental traits.

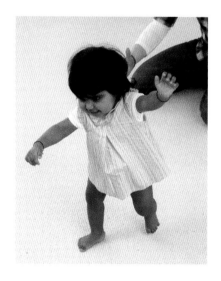

Full steam ahead! Your baby may find it difficult to stop once they get going, so ensure your home is fully toddler-proofed!

Changing the routine

Over the coming months, your baby will need slightly less sleep. Let their needs, not their routine, dictate how much sleep they get.

Over the coming year, your baby will need to sleep for between 10 and 13 hours in a 24-hour period. Whether this requirement is met entirely during the night, or is divided between daytime and night-time sleeps, will be determined by your baby's individual needs. However, very few babies manage a whole day without at least one restorative nap.

You may also find that your baby is more tired on some days than on others, and will need a morning nap just a few hours after they wake up. They may also develop a habit of sleeping across lunchtime, so you'll need to tweak your routine to ensure they get a good meal before they settle down so that they don't wake early through hunger.

Once your baby has settled down for an afternoon nap, wake them only if they sleep past 4pm – the point at which daytime sleep usually interferes with a good night's sleep.

If your baby copes better with a nap during the day, ensure they get some physical activity beforehand to help them settle well, and continue with your usual pre-nap routine. Beware that at this age, they're more likely to wake up and want to play after their nap, and may make an attempt to escape, too, so ensure that their cot is safe (see p.279), with the base on its lowest setting.

Cow's milk as a drink

Once your baby is one year old, they are old enough to have cow's milk. Choose full-fat milk until they're two, after which you can give semi-skimmed.

Up until now, breast- and formula milk have been the most suitable to meet your baby's nutritional needs. Once your baby is a year old, though, it is safe for them to drink cow's milk, which will provide them with healthy fats, protein, calcium, vitamin A, and essential fatty acids (EFAs), along with other key minerals.

If you are bringing up your baby as a vegetarian, or if they are a fussy eater, consider a "growing up" formula, which contains extra iron and vitamins. Aim to expand their food repertoire so that, eventually, their food alongside full-fat cow's milk meet their nutritional needs.

All dairy products are high in the nutrients in cow's milk, so don't panic if your baby doesn't take to it. Simply increase their intake of other dairy products and calcium-containing foods, such as almonds, leafy green vegetables, pulses, tofu, and soya.

Babies need far more fat in their diets than adults, so give your baby full-fat milk. This provides the energy and fat-soluble vitamins needed for growth. Under the age of two, fats should make up about half their calorie intake. After that, alongside a varied, nutritious diet, you can change to semi-skimmed milk.

Baby still wants to breastfeed

Whether or not you have other ideas, your baby may want to continue breastfeeding and show no signs of being ready to stop.

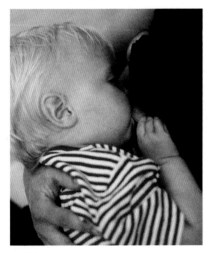

Still natural For a one-year-old, breastfeeding still feels natural and comforting.

There's no right time to stop breastfeeding. Many mums find that their babies often "wean" themselves around now as they get distracted by the world around them. Others seem happy to continue. This is fine, too – unless you would like to stop.

Take your time weaning your older baby off the breast as this is a well-established habit for them that provides much comfort. Give them lots of cuddles and reassurance. You'll need to replace breastfeeds with formula (until they are one year old; see above) as they still need 500–600ml (17–20fl oz) of milk a day, even once they're established on solids.

However, they'll probably get what they need in two feeds a day, plus a little milk on their breakfast and alongside meals if necessary. If you want to keep the morning or evening breastfeeds, this is good for you both on every level (see also p.331).

For an older baby, breastmilk can be a valuable source of nutrients. One study found that in a baby's second year, just 450ml (15fl oz) of breastmilk can provide 29 per cent of their energy needs; 43 per cent of their protein; 36 per cent of their calcium; 75 per cent of their vitamin A; 94 per cent of their vitamin B12; and 60 per cent of their vitamin C needs, a day.

First times

Your baby will face many new experiences in the coming months. A little preparation will help them negotiate them comfortably.

At some point over the coming year, your baby will have their first visit to the dentist or hairdresser, or perhaps their first sleepover with family outside your home. Some babies happily adjust to new experiences; others need a little warming up. Either way, if your baby knows what to expect from a new situation, they'll feel more secure about it.

If you need a relatively quick trip to the dentist, doctor, or hairdresser yourself – or are taking an older sibling – take your baby along, too, to get them used to the surroundings.

While the hairdresser is cutting your hair, hold your baby on your lap and explain what's being done in an upbeat tone of voice. Let them see the dentist examining your teeth, or the doctor taking your blood pressure, while you sit back calmly.

If you think your baby might be fazed by a new upcoming experience, borrow a library book that tells them all about it. If they're going to stay at Granny's or Grandpa's on their own, plan a trip or two in advance for the pair of you to enjoy together so that they get used to being there with you first (see also p.327).

On the day

When the time comes for your baby's first haircut or other new experience, make sure they're not hungry or tired, and give them their comfort object or a toy or book to distract them if they look a little worried. Explain very

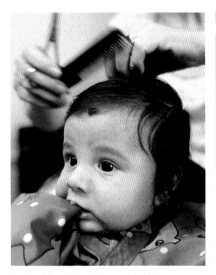

Hair raising A first haircut shouldn't worry your baby if they've visited the salon with you.

simply where you are going and what's going to happen. Remind them of the story you read (about the scenario they're going to encounter), or recall that just like Mummy or Daddy had their hair cut, now it's their turn to be fussed over and look smart. Let them know that afterwards you plan to round off the experience with something fun, such as a trip to the soft play centre or park. This will help to create positive associations with the event whatever it may be. Above all, stay calm and upbeat yourself – if you show a fear of the dentist, for example, your baby will quickly pick up on this and be worried for themselves.

ASK A DOCTOR

When does my baby need their first dental appointment? It's a good idea to have your baby's teeth checked at around six months, or whenever the first teeth emerge, so that they become accustomed to the experience of visiting the dentist, and to check that all is well. They won't need a full check-up until around their first birthday. Your dentist will give you plenty of advice about your baby's oral health, including brushing and using fluoride toothpastes, and will check that there are no signs of early decay.

Treat the first appointment like a social occasion, getting your baby used to the new environment and different smell. At first, and maybe for the first few appointments, your baby can sit in your lap while the dentist looks at their teeth. Your baby will probably love the attention. Try not to panic, though, if this isn't the case and they create a fuss; you can always reschedule an appointment for a later date.

My baby was distraught after having their injections. Does this mean they'll be terrified of future vaccinations? Your baby won't remember their first sets of injections, so rest assured that they won't have developed a fear of the doctor's surgery! However, it may be in their nature to react loudly: some babies do scream loudly, while others are quiet or more easily comforted.

Words with meaning

By now, many babies have a small repertoire of words that they can use with meaning, and a rapidly increasing vocabulary.

First words tend to be those that are most relevant for your baby, such as "mama", "dada", and "bottle" (which often comes out as "baba"). Your baby may not be able to say many of these words accurately, but you'll know what they mean. Don't be surprised if your baby changes their words for various people and items. They may call their bottle a "baba" one week, then "bobo", or "mik" (milk), the next.

Your baby learns language by listening and, at this point, they'll understand far more than they can say. Continue to chat to them and offer the correct words for items. However, being able to repeat words doesn't mean using them in the right way. Listen and watch when your baby speaks – their intonation and gestures may give you a clue to the intended meaning.

Some babies don't use their first words until well into their second year, but by the age of 20 months, you can expect your baby to have 30–40 words in their repertoire. These will be mixed in with a stream of babbling. After 20 months, they'll begin to pick up words at an amazing rate – even one or two a day – and you'll be in absolutely no doubt about what they're saying... and what they want!

Reflecting on your year

So have you loved the past year – or just about survived it? All parents are different and some are more "ga-ga" about babies than others...

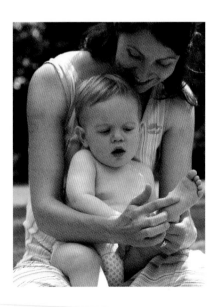

Now you have almost 12 months' experience under your belt, how would you describe yourself as a parent? Has it been an otherwordly, sublime experience in each and every way, or are you finding the mountain of nappies a constant battle? Or, more likely, a mixture of both?

If you haven't enjoyed the past year as much as you had hoped, try not to feel disheartened – loving your baby themselves doesn't mean you have to love the baby "stage". For some,

Apple of your eye Your baby is adorable, but they can be hard work at times, too!

parenthood becomes more rewarding as babies become better able to interact. As your child's personality develops, you'll probably find that the more mundane practicalities of parenting are outweighed by the joy of the little person who is emerging. It's a cliché, but babies really do grow up incredibly fast: one day you have a toddler, the next thing you know you're taking them to reception class at school – so try to appreciate every moment. There will always be weak spots and pinch points, but the bond you share with your child is precious and unique – wherever you happen to be on the parenting journey.

Your baby is one today

Congratulations – your baby is officially a toddler! You have many exciting changes to look forward to in the coming year.

Your baby's first birthday can be a time of mixed emotions for you – they are becoming more independent, and will depend less on you for feeding and even getting around. They may have clear ideas of what they can and want to do, and for the first time you may find yourself locking horns with a contrary little person. As they head towards the age of two, you can expect them to become much more reluctant to accept your intervention!

Paradoxically, separation anxiety continues well into your toddler's second, or even third, year, and they will seek out your presence and find security in their routines. Continue to reassure them with regular physical affection and enjoy plenty of activities together to reinforce your bond.

Their speech will develop hugely in the coming year, and you will soon have the knack of working out what they're saying. Reading, singing, and chatting will continue to support their language acquisition. Over the next year, they'll start to string together short sentences and, with a combination of gestures and words, make their needs easily known.

Your toddler's safety remains a top priority, and you will have to check their environment and activities continually to ensure they aren't putting themselves in danger as they explore their expanding world. Make sure they understand the basics of stair safety, and keep an eye on them always when you are out and about.

Happy birthday! Your baby's birthday marks the end of a miraculous year of development, and you may choose to celebrate this wonderful journey with your family and closest friends.

Support their developmental skills with games and pursuits that keep them entertained and stimulated. Your input remains crucial to their continued development.

Your baby will hold their own at the dinner table now, and the more often you can eat together, the better their food choices, table manners, and social skills will become. Try not to pass on your own dislikes – a varied diet will give them the best chance of good health and development.

Take time to stop and enjoy the small things – write down their amazing firsts, capture their activities on camera, save their first artistic creations, and record their attempts at speech. The coming years will pass with lightning speed. You've created a unique little person with a world of opportunity in front of them. Take pride in their achievements and rest assured that all of your hard work has produced the best possible results.

YOUR BABY'S
HEALTH

The health and wellbeing of your baby are prime concerns, and the more informed and confident you feel about recognizing and treating illness when it happens, the easier it is to cope. Most babies experience at least one bout of sickness in their first year, so this chapter clearly explains all the common illnesses and how best to treat your child. Of course, there's no substitute for a parent's instinct, so if you are worried about your baby's health, always call your doctor straight away.

Your unwell baby

THE BETTER INFORMED YOU ARE, THE MORE CONFIDENT YOU WILL FEEL CARING FOR YOUR SICK BABY.
Your baby's immune system is still developing, so they are susceptible to a number of illnesses during this first year. Most of these will be minor, but occasionally a more serious illness may develop. It's vital that you know what to look out for so that you can take the right action.

When your baby is ill

As a new parent, it can be hard to tell if your baby is unwell, but as you get to know them, you'll recognize when something is wrong.

Prolonged crying can be a sign that your baby feels unwell or has pain, especially if you can't pacify them. Listen out for a hoarse cry or one of a higher pitch than usual. Conversely, a very ill baby may cry much less than usual, so take note if your baby is unusually quiet and subdued, especially if they also have other symptoms (see p.369).

Your baby may lose interest in feeding when feeling poorly, or they may take less than usual. Vomiting is a common symptom, and it doesn't always mean a tummy upset.

Once your baby starts smiling, they're likely to smile a lot. If your baby looks grumpy or won't smile at you when you talk, there may be something wrong. In much the same way, older babies often lose interest in playing. Instead, your baby may become more clingy, hanging onto you when you are near and not wanting you to leave the room. If your baby's breathing is noisier or faster than usual, there's likely to be something wrong. A slightly ill baby may also sleep more than usual. However, you should be able to rouse them; if they're unresponsive, call an ambulance or take them to hospital yourself if you can get there quickly.

Dehydration

Many common illnesses cause serious fluid loss, and fever compounds the problem. Babies can quickly become dehydrated, which is a major concern, so it's vital to recognize the signs. At first, dry lips may be the only symptom visible. As dehydration worsens, your baby's nappies may be drier than usual. Their skin may feel dry and loose. Your baby may be a bit lethargic. You may also notice that their fontanelle (the soft spot on the top of the head) looks slightly sunken. Contact your doctor at once.

With severe dehydration, your baby may pass dark yellow urine, have fewer wet nappies, and their eyes may appear sunken. Your baby may have a fast heart rate or be breathing rapidly. They require urgent treatment: call 111 and book an emergency appointment with the GP.

To avoid dehydration, offer your baby plenty of breast- or formula milk. They will need extra fluids to replace those lost through illness, especially if they have diarrhoea or vomiting. If your baby is under six months and formula-fed, you can also offer them water, boiled, and cooled. If your baby is vomiting, ask your doctor about giving an oral rehydration solution, which is easier for them to keep down. This replaces fluids, and the sugars and salts lost due to an upset tummy.

TAKE YOUR BABY'S TEMPERATURE

Fever is the body's normal response to infection, so a raised temperature can help to tell you if your baby is ill. Normal body temperature is 37°C (98.6°F) and about 0.5°C (1°F) lower when taken in the armpit. The best way to take your baby's temperature is from the ear or armpit, although the latter can be problematic if you have a wriggly baby because you need to hold them still for at least a couple of minutes to get a reading. Oral thermometers cannot be used for babies in case they bite them.

Ear thermometer Hold your baby firmly and place the thermometer in your baby's ear, following the instructions to make sure you position it correctly (left). **Under-arm thermometer** Settle your baby on your lap and hold them still to get a more accurate reading.

Getting medical help

If your baby is ill, you may need to take them to the doctor or – if you are seriously concerned about their health – to hospital.

Seeing the doctor

Parents see their family doctor on average nine times during their baby's first year. Most practices fit in sick babies between appointments and offer emergency appointments. When you call to make an appointment, let the receptionist know your baby's age. If your baby

WHEN TO CALL THE DOCTOR

As you get to know your baby, you'll find it easier to recognize when they need medical help. The younger your baby, the more promptly you should consult a doctor. Very young babies can become critically ill quickly. Call a GP if your baby:

• Runs a fever of 39°C (102.2°F) or higher; or 38°C (100.4°F) for babies under 3 months.
• Has a fever that persists for longer than five days.
• Refuses to feed.
• Appears drowsy and off-colour.
• Vomits persistently, bringing up green or blood-streaked vomit.
• Shows signs of severe dehydration (see p.363).
• Has six or more episodes of diarrhoea in a period of 24 hours, or continues to have diarrhoea for longer than five days.
• Passes blood or mucus in their stools.
• Has bleeding that will not stop.
• Produces discharge from their ears, eyes, or genitals in the past 24 hours.
• Has difficulty breathing, or is panting or breathing rapidly.
• Has a rash.
• Has a seizure (fit or convulsion).
• Has a minor burn or scald.

has a rash, mention this – an infection may put others at risk, so the doctor may prioritize you. Take a spare nappy with you so that you can put a clean one on after the doctor examines your baby. If your baby has diarrhoea, take a dirty nappy with you in case your doctor needs a sample to send for tests. You can get 24-hour advice by phoning or using the online NHS 111 helpline; you'll be able to speak to someone who can advise whether your baby needs medical attention or should be admitted to the hospital.

Getting the most from your visit

Describe your baby's symptoms clearly, giving details of their temperature and any medicines or home remedies you have tried. Always tell your doctor what's on your mind, whether you're concerned about a cough or worried about the possibility of meningitis. This puts you both on the same wavelength.

Make sure you understand any instructions as to what to do, and how to give any medicines. Your doctor should also tell you what to look out for and what to do if your baby doesn't improve, and when to return for a follow-up. Don't worry about being a bit of a nuisance; occasional false alarms are inevitable when you're finding your way as a new

parent. Many doctors have children themselves and will be able to identify with your situation. They should understand your concerns about your precious little bundle, and will know that one or two unnecessary consultations are far better than leaving things too late.

If you feel you can't communicate with your doctor, perhaps this isn't the right doctor for your family. Every professional has different interests and skills, and after a few consultations you may decide you would be better with a different doctor, either within the same practice or another one altogether.

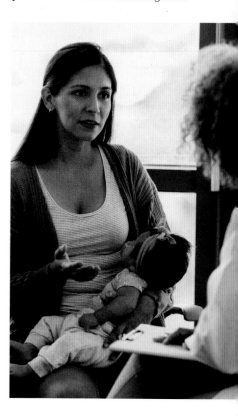

Making an appointment Talk to your doctor if your baby is showing signs of illness, or you are not sure of their condition.

If you just want advice

You can get 24-hour advice by phoning NHS 111; you'll speak to a nurse who can advise you whether your baby should see a doctor. Try your health visitor for issues such as breastfeeding and minor concerns like colic, or your pharmacist for advice on treating minor ailments such as nappy rash. Many areas have walk-in centres, where you can drop in any time and see a nurse, but before you go, check that they have facilities for babies. If you need to see a doctor when your surgery is closed, phone your GP's out-of-hours service.

Going to A&E

Most parents take their little one to A&E at some point. In the majority of cases, there's nothing seriously wrong. Occasionally, though, worries about a baby's health may mean they need to stay in hospital.

However worried you feel, try to stay calm. When you arrive at the A&E department, find your way to the A&E reception. You may be redirected to a children's A&E if there is one; otherwise there should be a dedicated children's nurse to assess your child. Be as clear as you can about what has happened and your baby's symptoms. The nurse will assess the severity of your child's illness, and you will either be seen by a doctor straight away or asked to wait.

If you aren't seen immediately by a doctor, it can be difficult to predict how long you will have to wait as A&E departments prioritize the most urgent cases. However, as a general rule, young babies are usually seen within a few hours at the most. Because you may be waiting some time, don't forget to take your baby's comfort object, a dummy, if needed, plus any milk, bottles, or nappies.

WHEN TO CALL 999

Call 999 for an ambulance, or take your baby to the hospital yourself (if you can get there quickly) if your baby:
• has stopped breathing or is having difficulty breathing, has blue skin, lips or tongue
• is unresponsive, floppy, drowsy or will not wake up
• has had a fit (convulsion) or febrile seizure
• has severe bleeding that will not stop
• has a purple-red spotty rash that doesn't fade when a glass is rolled over it
• has a severe allergic reaction (anaphylaxis)
• has severe scalds or burns
• appears to become unwell after swallowing something harmful, such as a household product or medication.

STAYING IN HOSPITAL

Children's hospital wards are now much brighter, friendlier, and less formal places than they used to be. Paediatricians don't wear white coats and are often very approachable. You'll find all staff have a genuine interest in their little patients.

Staying with your baby If your baby has to stay in hospital, you can almost always stay in too, though expect facilities for parents to be basic. From your baby's point of view, the most important thing is that you can be there to reassure them throughout most tests and procedures. If they have to have blood taken, local anaesthetic cream is usually applied first. If your baby needs an operation under local anaesthetic, your presence is usually welcome. You won't be allowed in for procedures under general anaesthetic, but you can be there holding your baby

until they are asleep. Bringing in your baby's favourite toys, comfort object, or blanket may help settle your baby.

Planned hospital admissions If an older baby needs to go into hospital, there'll be time to forewarn them. Tell them a little about it so that it doesn't come as a huge surprise. Babies are very aware of their parents' moods and emotions, so try to stay positive whatever's happening. If you have negative feelings about hospitals or needles, do your best to keep them to yourself. Use a soft voice to help calm your baby. You can also sing their favourite songs or nursery rhymes.

Being informed Understanding the treatment your child is being given will help to prevent unnecessary anxiety. If you're not sure what's happening, ask,

and never feel intimidated. There are usually doctors and nurses on hand who will be happy to answer your queries. It can be useful to write down any questions you have, as it's easy to forget when there is so much going on.

When it's time for your baby to go home, make sure you understand the discharge plan and have contact details if you need to seek help.

Looking after your sick baby

Your baby is likely to need all your attention when they're feeling ill. Knowing what to do can make all the difference to their recovery.

YOUR HOME MEDICINE CUPBOARD

Stocking a cupboard with essential medical supplies will enable you to deal with common ailments quickly and effectively. Keep medicines out of your baby's reach, ideally in a cool, dark place, and check expiry dates. Make sure medicines are right for your baby's age.
• Liquid paracetamol.
• Baby ibuprofen.

• Calamine lotion, for bites and rashes.
• Rehydrating solution/sachets.
• Antibacterial ointment for cuts and scrapes.
• Infant topical pain-relief gel, to relieve teething discomfort.
• Medicine syringe and/or spoon.
• Thermometer.
• Plasters and a bandage.

ADMINISTER DROPS

In all cases, wash your hands, ensure the medicine dropper does not come into direct contact with your baby, and sterilize it between uses.

Nose drops Lay your baby on their back on your lap, tilting their head back gently if they are an older baby. Be sure to support your baby's head and drip the nose drops into each nostril.

Eye drops Lay your baby down on your lap and hold their head steady with one arm. Gently pull down the lower eyelid and instil the drops into the space between the lid and the eyeball. Then wipe the excess drops off their cheek. If you have trouble managing, get another adult to help hold your baby.

Ear drops Warm the ear drops by holding in your palm for a few minutes, then lay your baby down on their side on your lap. They need to be comfortable as they will have to stay in this position for a little

while. Hold their head firmly, yet gently, and let the drops fall from the dropper into the ear. Keep them still for a few minutes as you don't want the drops to spill out right away. When your baby sits up again, a little excess may leak out, so have a tissue ready to catch it.

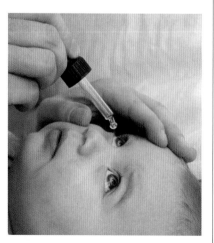

Putting in eye drops Holding your hand steady, squeeze the bulb of the dropper to instil the medication behind the lower lid.

You can expect sick babies to be demanding and to need your presence. Prioritize things so you can spend time cuddling your little one, or at least sitting with them. A good baby-minder or trusted relative can fit the bill, but your baby will prefer to have the reassurance of a parent.

A sick baby may still want to play simple games, or to hear you tell a favourite story. Often this is the same story over and over again. They may also enjoy listening to pre-recorded stories and rhymes, though it's your voice that has significance for them.

Keep an eye on your baby's temperature (see p.363) and check it regularly. There's no need to treat every fever, but try to lower it if they are uncomfortable, their temperature is very high, or your doctor has advised you to do so. Paracetamol or ibuprofen may be suitable (read the instructions). Use one of these medicines only, not both together.

Babies usually need extra fluids when they're ill, especially if they're feverish. Fever is a normal response to infection, but it contributes to dehydration. This in turn can make fever worse, so it's something of a vicious circle. If you're breastfeeding, continue with this. They may or may not need water too – check with your doctor or health visitor. Older babies may need encouragement to drink more. Make sure there's always a drink within reach.

If your baby is on solids, don't worry too much if they won't eat much while they're unwell. Right now fluids matter more than food.

There's no need for your baby to be in their cot when ill, though it may be convenient to keep them in night-time clothing as this is often simpler to change in and out of. At night, it's a good idea to keep your baby close by. If they already sleep in their own room, you might want to move their cot or crib into your room as a temporary measure. This makes it easier to attend to them if they need anything in the night, and you may sleep more easily knowing that they are near you.

While your baby is ill, you could skip bathtime in favour of topping and tailing, or a simple wash with a flannel. It all depends on how unwell they are and how much they enjoy a bath. Some older babies relax in the bath. You can then put them into fresh clothing, which could make them feel a lot better. Tepid sponging is no longer recommended as a treatment for fever.

It can be tiring looking after a poorly baby, so put your feet up and rest when your baby sleeps. Don't spend too much time rushing around doing chores. If you need help, don't be afraid to ask friends or relatives to take over for a little while so that you can get some rest. However tired you are, never fall asleep on the sofa with your sick baby in your arms.

Giving medication

If your baby has been prescribed medication, such as antibiotics, it's very important to give the correct dosages and to finish the full course as directed. This applies to topical treatments, such as steroid creams, too. You'll need to give any medications to your baby in liquid form and there are several different methods for doing this easily (see below).

GIVE YOUR BABY MEDICINE

There are several techniques for giving a baby medicine by mouth, whether it's a prescription from your doctor or an over-the-counter remedy. Wash your hands before you start, and make sure you know what the dose is meant to be. An overdose can be dangerous, especially for young babies. When giving medicine, hold your baby so that they are slightly upright. Don't lay them down flat because there's a risk that they may inhale the medicine into their lungs.

Using a syringe This is probably the best method for very young babies, who haven't learned to swallow from a spoon, and for medicines for which small, precise doses are needed. For a baby under six months, sterilize the syringe before use. Fill the syringe from the bottle, then pick up and hold your baby in the crook of your arm. Put the mouthpiece of the medicine syringe on your baby's lower lip and gently push the plunger so the medicine goes into their mouth.

Using a dropper Sterilize first, for a baby under six months, then take up the right amount of medicine in the dropper before picking up your baby. Lean your baby back slightly, and place the tip of the dropper into the corner of their mouth, or just inside the lower lip. Squeeze the medicine out, making sure the dropper empties completely into your baby's mouth and that they swallow the liquid.

Using a spoon This is the most common method for babies over 12 weeks or so of age, especially if the dose is at least 2.5ml. Measure the dose before picking up your baby. Holding your baby upright, touch the lower part of the spoon to their bottom lip, then gently tip the spoon up so that the medicine goes into their mouth.

Syringe For very young babies, you'll probably find it easiest to give medicines with a syringe .

Dropper When using a dropper, make sure all the medicine goes into your baby's mouth.

Spoon Babies over 12 weeks can usually manage a spoon.

Illnesses & injuries

AN ILL OR INJURED BABY NEEDS LOTS OF COMFORT COMBINED WITH THE RIGHT ACTION.
When your baby is poorly or has fallen and bumped themself, it's important that you know
when it's fine to treat them at home, which measures are appropriate, and when you need to
seek medical advice. If you're confident about what to do, you'll be calmer and more effective.

Common conditions

When your baby isn't feeling at their best, it could be any one of a number of conditions. Babies often can't signal what's wrong.

Fever

Fever is not an illness, but a symptom. It is the body's normal response to infection or inflammation, so always take notice of a fever, especially if your baby is under six months old.

Causes include flu, chest infection, gastroenteritis, urine infection, and infectious diseases such as roseola (see p.374). Fever can also occur after a routine immunization.

You may suspect your baby has a fever by touch, especially if the back of their neck feels hot or sweaty, but you can only know for sure by taking their temperature (see p.363).

Dealing with fever Fever can make your baby uncomfortable and can also have a dehydrating effect. That's why it's important to give plenty of fluids when a baby or child is feverish, and to look out for any possible signs of dehydration (see p.363).

Don't overdress your baby as this makes it harder for body temperature to drop back down to normal. When indoors, a nappy and a vest may be enough, but keep a close eye on your baby, as young babies are poor at controlling their body temperature and can also get cold quickly.

There's no point in sponging your baby down or giving them a bath as it is only likely to make them miserable. You can relieve fever in babies over three months with infant paracetamol or ibuprofen (check the dosage for the age of your baby). Do not give both at the same time. However, if one of them doesn't work, try the other.

When to see the doctor In young babies, fever is less common and therefore more significant. As a rule, the younger your baby, the more swiftly you need to get medical attention, but use your instincts, too. In older babies, their actual temperature or how long they have had it often does not indicate how unwell they are. Contact your doctor if:
• Your baby has a temperature of 39°C (102.2°F) or more (38°C /100.4°F or more if under three months old).
• Your baby seems unwell in themselves, even if the fever is mild.
• There are any worrying symptoms such as vomiting or trouble breathing.
• They are unresponsive.

Your doctor may ask for a urine sample because urine infection is relatively common in babies yet does not cause any of the typical symptoms adults get. Get medical attention urgently if:
• Your baby has a rash that doesn't fade on pressure.
• Your baby has a seizure.
• Their general condition worsens.

Reflux

Gastro-oesophageal reflux (GOR) is a condition in which the stomach contents flow up the oesophagus (gullet) and cause symptoms. It's estimated that around half of all babies under three months have it, but few have severe symptoms. Both breastfed and formula-fed babies may be affected. Reflux occurs because the valve at the lower end of the oesophagus is lax. However, this

---

FEBRILE SEIZURES

In babies over six months and young children, a high fever can lead to a fit (seizure or convulsion) known as a febrile seizure.

Fever can be stressful for a youngster's brain and can temporarily disrupt the signals between brain cells, in some cases triggering a seizure. This usually occurs at a time when body temperature rises rapidly. Your baby is more likely to be affected if there is a family history of febrile seizures or other types of seizure.

A seizure can be frightening to see even though it usually lasts less than two minutes. The baby loses consciousness, stops breathing momentarily, and tends to wet or soil themself. The limbs and face may twitch and the eyes often roll upwards. When it stops, the baby regains consciousness, but may be very sleepy.

During a fit, lie them on their side but don't try to restrain them, but do make sure they are safe and cannot fall. If possible, note the time of onset of the fit. Call an ambulance if your baby's fit carries on for over five minutes: any seizure lasting longer than this is likely to be more serious than a febrile convulsion.

If your baby has had a seizure, call your doctor. If this is their first seizure, they are likely to need hospital tests to rule out a serious cause. For any subsequent seizures, they should still have a check-up to find out the cause of their high fever.

corrects itself in time. The symptoms to look out for include:
• bringing up large amounts of feed
• vomiting
• coughing
• irritability
• feeding poorly
• rarely, blood in the stools or vomit (seek urgent medical help).

You may suspect reflux in your baby if they scream during feeds as if in pain, or they posset a lot. However, many babies posset without having reflux. Occasionally, reflux has more serious effects such as breathing problems or poor growth because a baby is unable to keep down feeds.

Giving smaller, more frequent feeds can help reflux. Burping and holding your baby upright for 20 minutes after each feed can also relieve symptoms.

Your doctor may prescribe a thickened feed or thickener that you add to feeds, and also an infant antacid, which helps the action of the valve in the gullet. If neither of these approaches helps or your baby has severe symptoms, you may need to see a paediatrician who may suggest tests or a different prescription.

Tongue-tie

There is normally a strip of tissue between the floor of the mouth and the underside of the tongue (this is called the frenulum). In tongue-tie, this strip is shorter and often thicker than usual, which can restrict tongue movements. Most cases of tongue-tie are mild, but in some babies it may prevent successful breastfeeding.

It's debatable whether tongue-tie can interfere with learning to speak. Most experts believe it does not, mainly because it has often improved by the time that speech starts. However, if you do think that your baby has tongue-tie, see your doctor. A few babies may need a minor procedure, performed under local anaesthetic, to release the tie.

Conjunctivitis

This is inflammation of the lining of the eyeball and/or eyelids. It can be bacterial, viral, or allergic. Bacterial conjunctivitis is the most common type in babies under six months. They often get conjunctivitis because their tear ducts are still immature, so germs can easily collect and set up infection.

You may notice that your baby's eyelids are crusty in the morning or after a nap, or there may be a blob of pus in the corner of the eye. Your baby's eyes can also become bloodshot and the eyelids may be swollen.

If symptoms are mild, and the white of the eye isn't red, wipe your baby's eyes with cotton wool dipped in cooled, boiled water or your own breastmilk. Wash your hands before you begin, and wipe from the nose towards the outer side of the eye, using a clean piece of cotton wool for each eye. Avoid touching their eyeball.

If pus accumulates again, consult your health visitor or doctor. Your baby may need eye drops or ointment containing antibiotic. It's usual to treat both eyes if you are given drops, even if only one eye is affected.

If your baby has frequent attacks of conjunctivitis, your health visitor may

Conjunctivitis Blobs of pus in the corner a baby's eyes, as seen here, are often a sign of conjunctivitis caused by bacterial infection.

show you how to massage the tear ducts to help the flow of tears.

Vomiting

All babies posset – bring up a little milk – but in vomiting the stomach contracts, and the amount brought up is much greater. Vomiting is most often related to a problem with feeding or something affecting the stomach or gut, as in:
• overfeeding
• gastroenteritis (see opposite)
• allergy to food (see p.372)
• reflux (see p.369)
• pyloric stenosis (see below)
• bowel obstruction (see right).

However, vomiting doesn't necessarily mean that the trouble is anywhere near the tummy. Babies can also vomit when they're unwell with an infection, especially a serious one like urine infection (see p.377), meningitis (see p.377), middle ear infection (see p.378), or chest infection (see p.377). Whooping cough also causes vomiting, most often at the end of a bout of coughing.

If your baby is well in themselves and only vomits once, you may not need the doctor. However, babies get dehydrated easily and can become unwell quickly, so as a rule consult your doctor if your baby vomits more than once or twice. Specific treatment depends on the cause.

Pyloric stenosis In this condition, there is overgrowth of the muscle of the pylorus, the valve at the stomach outlet. As a result, the outlet is too narrow for stomach contents to pass through and instead they are vomited out. Around one baby in 400 or so develops the condition. It's most common in boys between four and six weeks old.

Vomiting occurs right after a feed and can be so forceful that the regurgitated feed shoots across the room – so-called projectile vomiting.

INTUSSUSCEPTION

In this condition, part of the bowel telescopes into itself, as if being swallowed. This creates a blockage. Symptoms include:
• screaming from pain (often intermittent)
• fever
• vomiting
• dehydration or shock
• blood and mucus in the stools (often described as looking like redcurrant jelly).

It's a rare condition that affects babies 3–12 months old, sometimes just when they're recovering from gastroenteritis. However, it's worth knowing about as it can be very serious if untreated. It is often possible to treat without surgery, but some babies will need an operation.

The baby is usually hungry and may appear well, but dehydration sets in as the condition progresses. Doctors and health visitors sometimes check for a lump in the stomach area after a feed, but ultrasound scanning is a much more reliable test. Treatment involves a small operation to release the overgrown muscle, sometimes achieved using keyhole surgery.

Bowel obstruction This is not common, but it is very serious. Normally vomit looks like milk or food, but in bowel obstruction the vomit is bile-stained, so it looks green. If your baby's vomit is green, contact your doctor urgently or go to A&E.

Gastroenteritis

This means inflammation or infection in the stomach and gut, and can be caused by bacteria or viruses. It causes vomiting and often diarrhoea too, though some infections, such as norovirus ("winter vomiting disease"), cause vomiting without diarrhoea.

Rotavirus infection is the most common cause of gastroenteritis in babies. Bacterial causes include E.coli, salmonella, shigella, and campylobacter. On the whole, gastroenteritis is more common in bottle-fed babies. Symptoms include:
• vomiting and/or diarrhoea
• stomach ache, especially before a bowel movement
• fever.

Always talk to your doctor if you think your baby has gastroenteritis, as babies get dehydrated very quickly. Seek urgent help if your baby has had any blood in their stool. This can occur with some types of gastroenteritis, but it is also typical of intussusception (see left), a form of bowel blockage in babies under a year. In an attack of gastroenteritis, it isn't usually essential to know which bacteria or viruses started it off. However, occasionally your doctor will ask you to provide a sample for analysis in the lab.

The main aim of treatment is to replace lost fluids and, in many cases, your doctor will be happy for you to treat your baby at home. Your doctor will probably advise you to give your baby an oral rehydration solution, which contains the right balance of salts and sugar to prevent dehydration. Give small sips at a time, or your baby won't keep it down. If you're breastfeeding, you can continue. If your baby is bottle-fed, use rehydration solution instead of formula.

Keep plenty of paper towels to hand, and possibly a bowl for an older baby. Maintain good hygiene, and keep away from other people. Most causes of gastroenteritis are very contagious. Keep a close eye on your baby's progress. If they don't improve, they may need a visit to hospital.

Diarrhoea

Every baby passes loose motions sometimes. Breastfed babies often have loose stools, and this is normal. Diarrhoea means the frequent passing of stools that are looser than usual. In some cases, the motion will be very runny and may leak out of the nappy. Causes include:
• gastroenteritis (see left)
• allergy or milk intolerance (see p.372)
• cystic fibrosis.

The most common cause of diarrhoea is gastroenteritis, but in babies almost any feverish illness, even an ear infection, can trigger diarrhoea. Some antibiotics can cause diarrhoea too, as they can kill off some of the beneficial bacteria in the gut. As with vomiting, diarrhoea can make your baby dehydrated very quickly, so call your doctor if your baby has more than 4–6 runny motions in 24 hours, or has other symptoms that concern you. Look out for signs of dehydration (see p.363), bearing in mind that when a baby in nappies has diarrhoea, you can't tell if they're passing urine or not. You'll probably be advised to:
• Give rehydration solution. You can continue breastfeeding. If your baby is bottle-fed, you may also be able to continue, but this depends on how bad the diarrhoea is. Your health visitor or doctor will guide you.
• Take strict hygiene precautions and keep away from others.
• Avoid taking your baby into a swimming pool for 14 days after the last episode of diarrhoea.

Constipation

This means the passage of hard, infrequent motions. Breastfed babies can pass stools less often, but if the motion looks normal, then it's not constipation. The most common causes of constipation in babies are:
• starting on solid food

• lack of fibre in the diet
• ;ack of fluid (for example, during an illness)
• incorrectly made formula feeds.

In very young babies, constipation can be caused by a rare congenital condition called Hirschsprung's disease in which there is an abnormal segment of bowel.

When a baby is constipated, they may only pass a motion two or three times a week. The motions may be hard and pellet-like or much bulkier. They can be painful to pass, and may even tear the edge of the anal canal, causing bleeding. As a result, the baby avoids passing a motion, constipation worsens, and tummy pain can develop.

Consult your health visitor or GP if your baby is constipated. Avoid home remedies or laxatives for older children or adults; these are unsuitable for babies.

Hirschsprung's disease may be suspected if your baby did not pass meconium (black sticky stool) in their first day of life. Further tests and surgery may be needed. However, in most cases, the cause is more likely to be dehydration or a diet low in fruit and vegetables. Your doctor may prescribe a mild laxative to begin with, but the long-term answer is for your baby to have a well-balanced diet.

Jaundice

Jaundice means a yellow tinge to the skin and the whites of the eyes caused by a build-up of a chemical called bilirubin in the blood. Bilirubin comes from the breakdown of red blood cells – it's the reason why bruises go through a yellow phase.

Normally the liver clears bilirubin from the bloodstream, but the liver is immature in newborn babies and they also have more red blood cells. That's why over half of all babies develop slight jaundice during the first week after birth. In most cases, no

Neonatal jaundice This is a common and usually harmless condition. Look for a yellow discolouration of your baby's skin and eyes.

treatment is needed and the jaundice gets better on its own within a few weeks. Premature babies are more likely to become jaundiced as their livers cope less easily with bilirubin. This can occasionally cause problems, so if your baby is born prematurely, they may be placed under a blue light (phototherapy), which speeds up the removal of bilirubin. Breastfed babies are more likely to get jaundiced – factors in the milk seem to block enzymes in the liver, and it can run in families. It does not need treatment.

Jaundice can be serious:
• If it begins before 24 hours: Causes include bleeding due to a difficult delivery, infections, and blood group incompatibility. Urgent treatment in a neonatal unit will be needed.
• If it lasts longer than two weeks: See the doctor promptly to rule out a serious liver problem. Look out for pale motions and dark yellow urine as these are also significant symptoms.

Allergy

Allergies are becoming increasingly common, and if there are allergies in your family, your baby is more likely to develop them. However, there's more to it than genetics – even identical twins don't necessarily have the same allergies. The most common symptoms of an allergy include:
• swollen lips and throat
• runny or blocked nose
• coughing and wheezing
• itchy skin or rash
• reflux, nausea and vomiting
• diarrhoea and abdominal pain
• blood and mucus in stools.

Occasionally, an allergy can cause a severe reaction called anaphylaxis (see below).

Eczema (see p.375) is the most common allergic reaction in babies. It often starts around 3–12 months of age. In one in 10 children, eczema is linked with an underlying food allergy even though the food allergy may not be obvious yet.

ANAPHYLACTIC SHOCK

This is a severe, overwhelming allergic reaction. Luckily, it is rare in babies. Possible triggers include foods such as milk, nuts, and eggs, as well as insect venom and drugs. There could be vomiting or a rash at first, then:
• noisy breathing or wheezing
• swelling of the tongue
• a hoarse cry
• collapse
• widespread rash.

However, anaphylaxis is difficult to spot in the very young, and your baby may just go very floppy. Immediate hospital care is vital. If you have been prescribed an adrenaline (epinephrine) injection for your baby, give it right away.

The most common food allergy in babies is cow's milk allergy (specifically to cow's milk protein). About 2–7 per cent of babies under a year have it. A reaction can occur immediately after taking cow's milk, or it can take several days to develop, making diagnosis tricky.

See your doctor if you think your baby may have cow's milk allergy. Tests can help diagnose it, but they don't always. You may be advised to change your baby's formula, or, if you are breastfeeding, to avoid dairy products yourself. Babies usually outgrow this type of allergy by their third birthday. However, some do not and will need to continue to avoid milk products.

Milk intolerance is not a true allergy. It is an intolerance to lactose, a sugar present in milk, caused by an enzyme deficiency. Symptoms can include diarrhoea and vomiting. An intolerance can develop after gastroenteritis and is usually resolved by changing to lactose-free milk for a month, after which your baby should be able to resume normal milk.

Other true food allergies include reactions to eggs, peanuts, tree nuts, wheat, soya, and fish. If your baby is allergic to egg, they will need egg-free vaccines or to have certain vaccines given in a hospital environment in case they have an allergic reaction.

There is no known way of preventing allergies from occurring but current advice is to exclusively breastfeed for the first six months and to wean your baby no earlier than six months, slowly introducing new foods, such as milk, eggs, peanuts, fish, soya and gluten one at a time so you can spot any reaction.

Nappy rash

Even with modern, highly absorbable nappies nappy rash is still common. Affected skin will be inflamed and sore, and may look pimply. A wet or dirty nappy is the main cause of nappy rash, so the longer you can leave their nappy off, the better. You'll find that letting air get to the rash makes it less irritated. Try nappy-free playtime a couple of times a day for about 20 minutes, or as much as you can manage. Before putting on a clean nappy, apply a little barrier cream.

Get advice from your health visitor or doctor if the rash looks very angry, is weeping or blistered, or has small spots outside the main area of redness.

Chickenpox

Chickenpox is more usual in toddlers, but babies under a year can get it too. The varicella-zoster virus that causes chickenpox is a very contagious and highly transmissible disease. The incubation period (time to develop the illness) is 14–21 days, but one attack usually gives immunity for life.

Your baby may feel unwell for a day or so before the rash. Spots then appear as small red dots, mostly over the trunk. They quickly develop into blisters, which may appear over a few days. Then they crust over and fall off. However, your baby remains

Chickenpox A chickenpox rash starts as small red dots. These turn into fluid-filled blisters with red bases, which then crust over.

contagious until all the spots have gone. Chickenpox is extremely itchy and your baby may be irritable and feel unwell, especially if they have spots inside the mouth. These are ulcers rather than blisters, and they can make feeding very uncomfortable for them.

In most cases, you'll be able to treat your baby at home. The following measures may help your baby to feel more comfortable.
• Soothe skin with calamine lotion.
• Keep your baby's skin cool as this can help prevent further spots.
• You can try bathing your baby in lukewarm water with a tablespoon of sodium bicarbonate (baking soda).
• Keep your baby's nails short to reduce damage from scratching.
• If your baby has a sore mouth, give cooler feeds than usual, or else soft foods if they are on solids.
• Treat fever with paracetamol or ibuprofen (always read the leaflet, found inside the packaging, to ensure the medication is age appropriate. If in doubt ask the pharmacist).
• If your baby is exposed to chickenpox under four weeks of age, talk to your doctor as they may need specialist treatment to stop them developing severe symptoms.

Keep your baby away from anyone who hasn't had the disease. Chickenpox can be very serious for adults who have never had the infection.

Thrush

This is caused by a yeast called Candida albicans (also known as monilia), which is normally present in the lower bowel. Most of the time, it causes no symptoms, but if it's present in larger amounts than usual, then it can cause thrush.

In babies, the most common areas for thrush are the nappy area and the mouth because these areas are warm and moist, so they encourage the growth of candida. Recent antibiotic treatment is also a factor, as some antibiotics suppress the beneficial bacteria that keep candida in check. Candida can infect your nipples if you breastfeed, but this is no reason to stop nursing. In the nappy area, you may see:

• A red rash, often with a glazed appearance.
• A scattering of small spots (satellites) outside the main area of rash.

If your baby has thrush in the mouth, there may be:

• Soreness when feeding from the breast or bottle, and poor feeding or crying during feeds.
• Redness of the inside of the mouth
• White or creamy patches on the mouth or gums.

In most cases, thrush responds quickly to antifungal drops or gel prescribed by your doctor or health visitor. Sometimes your baby needs a swab first to make sure that candida is the right diagnosis.

Roseola

Caused by herpesvirus 6, this viral infection affects babies who are over six months old. Its other names are exanthema subitum, sixth disease, and three-day fever. Although it's common, not many parents know about it. It is highly contagious with an incubation period of 5–15 days.

• The first symptom is a high temperature, often over 40°C (104°F). There can be febrile seizures (see p.369), but despite this your baby may seem remarkably well.
• After three days of fever, a rash of

Roseola rash This common infection causes pinkish-red spots or patches, and are usually found on the tummy, chest, and back.

pale reddish spots appears over the trunk and then spreads to the arms and legs, and sometimes the face. The spots may have a lighter halo around them. Because the rash may last only for 12 hours, it can be easy to miss.

• Your baby may also be irritable and tired, and have mild diarrhoea and decreased appetite.

There's no specific treatment for roseola other than keeping your baby comfortable, giving fluids, and controlling fever. Most babies recover quickly.

Laryngomalacia

Laryngomalacia (floppy larynx) is a common condition experienced in infancy and normally presents with symptoms of noisy breathing during inspiration (stridor), difficulty feeding, or increased effort breathing. If babies continue to feed well and gain weight, then no treatment or operation is necessary as the condition will usually improve by itself or go away by 18 months. If it does not and you suspect your baby has a floppy larynx, consult your doctor who may refer you to see an Ear, Nose and Throat (ENT) specialist.

THE MMR VACCINATION

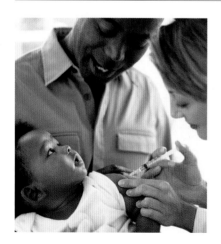

Getting jabbed Just before the jab is given, distract your baby by calling their name or by singing their favourite nursery rhyme.

To protect against measles, mumps, and rubella, your baby will be offered the MMR vaccination at around 13 months, and again at between three and five years of age. Contact your doctor for advice should you suspect your baby has any one of these three infections.

Measles is a highly contagious viral infection that can lead to serious complications, including pneumonia and brain damage. Before the vaccine, measles caused many deaths in children. Mumps is usually a mild viral infection if contracted during childhood (it's rare in babies under two years old), but it can have serious complications, including deafness. In adults, the illness is usually much more severe and can lead to inflammation of the testes in men or ovaries in women.

Rubella (German measles) is usually a mild illness. However, immunization is important to protect pregnant women, as if they contract the disease, their unborn baby can be seriously affected.

Hand-foot-and-mouth disease

This is an infection caused by a type of coxsackievirus. It has no link with foot-and-mouth disease in animals. The illness is very contagious, but not usually serious. The incubation period is about 10 days. Because there are several coxsackieviruses that can cause this illness, it can recur.

• The typical rash appears on the palms, soles, and buttocks as small red spots, which can be flat or raised. Sometimes, there's blistering.
• There may be ulcers in the mouth, which make feeding difficult. The spots can take two days to develop.
• Your baby may also feel unwell and run a fever.

The infection is easy to diagnose from the rash. There's no specific treatment other than keeping your baby comfortable, but it is wise to speak to your doctor, especially if your baby is very young.

Slapped cheek disease

Also called parvovirus, fifth disease, and erythema infectiosum, slapped cheek disease is usually mild. It's caused by parvovirus B19 and is very contagious. School-aged children are

Slapped cheek disease A bright red rash on the cheeks is characteristic of this viral infection and accounts for the name.

more likely to get it, but it can occur at any age. The incubation period seems to be 13–21 days, and it's no longer catching once the rash appears.

• The typical rash is a red facial rash with a sharply defined edge on one or both cheeks. There may also be a fine lacy rash on the arms and legs.
• Sometimes there's a mild fever.

On the whole, a youngster with slapped cheek disease will be well in themselves. However, someone with sickle-cell disease can get very ill with parvovirus. The infection can also be dangerous if caught during pregnancy, with a small chance of miscarriage in the early stages. In adults, parvovirus can also cause joint pains, but these are transient.

Eczema

This is a common skin condition in babies. It's also known as atopic eczema, atopic referring to the tendency for the immune system to over-react. Babies affected by eczema usually have a relative with eczema or another atopic condition, such as asthma or hay fever. Eczema can clear up completely in time, but sometimes it becomes chronic.

Common sites for eczema are the ankles, elbows, wrist, face, neck, and back of the knees, but it can appear almost anywhere. The skin can look dry and cracked, or raw and weepy.

Your baby is likely to find their skin itchy, and may scratch, especially at night. Keeping their nails short will help. Otherwise put scratch mittens on before bedtime. Simple emollients are almost always needed for eczema.

Emollients come in the form of sprays, creams, ointments, leave-on products, and soap substitutes. You can buy these from a pharmacy without a prescription. However, if the skin condition is severe and a stronger treatment is needed, speak to your GP, nurse, or health visitor.

Try changing to a different (non-biological) washing powder or liquid to see if this makes any difference. Your baby may also need a mild steroid cream prescribed by your doctor. Eczema can become infected because bacteria easily enters through small cracks. If your baby's eczema gets worse, see your doctor.

Heat rash

Also known as prickly heat, this is common in babies in warm weather. It's caused by excess sweat and is a sign that your baby is too hot. The typical small red pimples can appear almost anywhere, but most often on the neck, arms, face, trunk, or near the nappy area. Your baby can find them irritating or itchy.

Cool your baby down by taking their clothes off, or swapping them for lighter, cotton clothes. You can also apply calamine lotion if the rash seems to irritate your baby. The rash of prickly heat subsides within a day or two. Contact your doctor if it doesn't clear up quickly, or your baby seems unwell.

SUNBURN

Sunlight is good for babies and it helps the body to produce vitamin D, but sunburn is not. Prevention is better than cure. If your baby does get too much sun, immediately put them in the shade and give them fluids to drink. Soothe the skin with a lukewarm bath or tepid sponging. Make sure they don't go out in the sun again, even with sunscreen, until all the redness has gone. Call the doctor if your baby:

• has severe sunburn
• has swelling on their face
• has any signs of infection
• starts to blister early on
• is feverish
• vomits, appears listless, or seems ill to you.

375

Colds

Babies often have colds because they are born with little immunity to the 200 or so different cold viruses. Acquiring resistance to them is a matter of gradually becoming exposed to the range of these viruses. Colds have a short incubation period of around two days. Your baby is most likely to have a cold in winter, when more people spend time indoors with each other – and with their viruses.

Symptoms in babies are much the same as in older children. Your baby is likely to sneeze and have a runny or blocked nose, which makes feeding more difficult. Be patient during feeds and give your baby plenty of time. Your baby may also have a slight cough. This isn't usually serious, but it can develop into a chest infection (see opposite) or bronchiolitis (see right).

You can help your baby keep their nose clean by wiping it gently for them. Cotton wool may be softer than a tissue. Safely raising the head of their cot at night can help keep their nasal passages clear.

Antibiotics do not treat colds (which are viral), but some over-the-counter decongestant ointments are suitable for young babies. Saline drops can help unblock a baby's nose, but not all doctors think they're useful. A moist atmosphere makes it easier for your baby to breathe; place wet towels over a chair near a radiator, or you can buy a special baby humidifier. See your doctor if your baby:
• seems unwell in themselves
• refuses feeds
• coughs a lot
• has trouble breathing
• runs a high fever of 39°C (102.2 F) or above and that doesn't go down after giving age-appropriate paracetamol or ibuprofen and lasts more than five days.

These may be signs of a more serious infection or that your baby has flu rather than a cold.

Bronchiolitis

This is an infection of the tiny air passages (bronchioles) in the lungs. It almost always affects babies and can be serious, especially in the very young. The most common cause is respiratory syncytial virus (RSV), but other viruses (such as adenovirus and flu virus) can cause the same symptoms. It is very contagious and often spreads in day nurseries.
• Bronchiolitis usually begins like a cold, then quickly progresses to cough, wheeze, and rapid breathing.
• Your baby's breathing may sound crackly or bubbly.
• A mild fever is usual.

Many babies with bronchiolitis seem happy in themselves, but some become very unwell. One sign to watch out for is indrawing of the chest between the ribs (or below the ribcage) during breathing. This suggests that your baby is fighting for breath. In severe cases, a baby may turn blue from lack of oxygen.

Always consult your doctor if you think your baby has bronchiolitis. Get medical help urgently if your baby is going blue or fighting for breath.

In many cases, it is possible to care for your baby at home, with your doctor's advice, but sometimes a baby with bronchiolitis needs to go into hospital, especially if they:
• are very distressed
• are not taking fluids or becomes dehydrated
• are working hard to breathe
• have a very rapid respiratory rate
• turn blue.

Wheezing

Babies can wheeze and cough during or after viral infections. They may start with a cold but then develop a wheeze, cough, or noisy, rattly breathing that lasts a week or more. These symptoms occur as a result of inflammation and narrowing of the airways. Babies have narrow airways making them more likely to wheeze. It can be hard to tell

Treating wheezing Drugs to relieve symptoms by widening the airways are given to babies via a face mask and spacer attached to an inhaler.

These medicines are not recommended for babies or for children under six years. Research conducted by the Medicines and Healthcare products Regulatory Agency (MHRA) has shown that taking these medicines has no proven benefits for babies and children, and that in very rare cases there may actually be a risk of some form of allergic reaction.

The medicines concerned are over-the-counter cough and cold remedies (including oral preparations and nasal drops) containing the following ingredients: nasal decongestants (pseudoephedrine, ephedrine, phenylephrine, oxymetazoline, and xylometazoline), antihistamines (diphenhydramine, chlorphenamine bromopheniramine, promethazine, triprolidine, and doxylamine), antitussives (dextromethorphan and pholcodine), and expectorants (guaifenesin or ipecacuanha).

the difference between this and bronchiolitis (see left). Seek urgent medical help if your baby is fighting for breath or looks blue. Wheezing may be treated with drugs given through an inhaler to open the airways. It is too early to tell if wheezing might lead to asthma because asthma is a chronic, long-term condition that isn't diagnosed until babies are over one year of age.

Chest infection

This means any infection affecting the large air passages (bronchial tubes) leading to the lungs or the lung tissue itself. It includes pneumonia and bronchitis. Doctors often use the term "chest infection" when they can't be sure exactly where the problem lies. Both bacteria and viruses can cause chest infections. There are various symptoms that can accompany a

chest infection, including:
• feeling unwell in themself
• high fever
• rapid breathing and distress
• shortness of breath
• cough (though many youngsters with a chest infection do not have a cough)
• they may feed almost normally, or they may be off food and drink, at the risk of becoming dehydrated.

Always see your doctor if you think your baby might have a chest infection. This usually needs antibiotics. They may also need oxygen and fluids in hospital.

Croup

This is a form of laryngitis that affects babies over six months. It is very common in winter, and is usually caused by the para-influenza virus. Like bronchiolitis (see opposite), croup usually begins with cold symptoms and then progresses to wheezing and a typical barking cough. Your baby's voice may be hoarse. They may also have "stridor" – a noise on breathing in, suggesting the airways are partly blocked.

If you think your baby has croup, get advice from your doctor. A baby with mild croup can often be treated at home. Your doctor may prescribe an inhaler and steroids, and suggest you steam the room to help reduce swelling in your baby's airways. If your child's symptoms are severe and they are having difficulty breathing go to the hospital or call 999.

Urine infection

Urinary tract infections (UTI) are surprisingly common in young babies. Most infections are bacterial and get into the system via the urethra – the opening that leads from the bladder to the outside. But the symptoms in young babies are very different to UTIs in adults. A baby with a UTI may experience the following:

• fever
• irritability
• vomiting
• refusing feeds.

Very young babies can simply have prolonged jaundice, or they may fail to put on weight.

Always see your doctor if your baby has these symptoms. Only a urine sample can determine if it's a UTI.

It's vital to get a clean sample of urine for examination. You may be able to catch some urine in a sterile bottle when your baby wees. However, this can be difficult in small babies. Your doctor or health visitor will give you a uribag to stick onto your baby's bottom to collect a urine sample. Ensure you deliver the sample to the doctor without delay.

UTIs need prompt treatment with antibiotics to avoid kidney damage and other complications. In most cases, a specialist will suggest a scan to rule out any abnormalities of the urinary system that could have led to the infection. In some cases, you may need to give your baby a small daily dose of antibiotic to prevent further attacks.

Meningitis

This means inflammation or infection in the meninges, the layers of tissue that wrap the brain, due to viruses or bacteria. Bacterial meningitis is more serious than viral. Many of the germs that cause meningitis live harmlessly in the back of the throat in healthy people. It's not certain exactly why they cause disease in some babies and children, but factors include overcrowding and passive smoking.

Since Hib, pneumococcal, and meningitis C immunization, many of the worst forms of meningitis have become less common. All the same, meningitis is a very serious disease and it often goes hand in hand with septicaemia (blood poisoning). By the time a baby has reached this stage,

treatment is vital to save their life and you mustn't lose a minute. That's why every parent needs to know how to recognize it and what to do.
Symptoms in a baby can include:
• a high-pitched cry or moan
• refusing feeds
• irritability
• drowsiness
• limp or floppy limbs
• having a fever, but with cold hands or feet.
• a tense or bulging fontanelle (soft spot on the top of the head)
• pale, blotchy, or clammy skin
• a rash of small red or brownish

THE GLASS TEST

Rashes are common in babies, so it's hard to tell by looking at one if it's a rash linked with meningitis and septicaemia (see p.377). However, the rash of meningococcal septicaemia (sepsis or blood poisoning) does not fade when you press it, and a good way to check this is to carry out the glass (tumbler) test. Press the side of a glass firmly against your baby's skin where you see the rash. If you can still see the rash through the side of the glass, your baby may have meningitis/septicaemia and needs urgent hospital treatment. It is harder to see on dark skin so check against paler areas.

The glass test Press a glass firmly against your baby's skin where you see a rash. If the rash doesn't fade, call an ambulance.

pin-prick spots, which can turn into large bruises and purplish marks. If you see this rash, it could be septicaemia. Carry out the glass test (see below).

Call for an ambulance if your baby is unwell with any of the above symptoms. Never wait for all the symptoms to develop. The rash and other skin changes are signs that a baby is already critically ill. Treatment is much more successful when given in the early stages. Tell the ambulance and the hospital that you suspect your baby may have meningitis.

Ear canal infection

Infection of the ear canal, also known as otitis externa, can occur when milk or food gets into the ear, or sometimes when the ear isn't dried after bathtime. Babies that crawl may poke dirty fingers into their ears. Your baby may try scratching the ear, and you may see some redness or a little discharge. Generally, there's no fever and your baby remains well. See your doctor, who may prescribe ear drops. You can use paracetamol or ibuprofen for pain relief, although discomfort is usually mild.

Middle ear infection

Also known as otitis media, infection of the middle ear, behind the eardrum, can be due to viruses or bacteria. It often happens after a cold when the infection spreads up the Eustachian tubes that lead from the back of the nose to the ear. In babies and children, the Eustachian tubes are short and run horizontally, which means that they get more middle ear infections than adults. Sometimes only one ear is affected, but it's often both. Babies often have no symptoms that suggest the trouble is in the ear, but they may:
• feel very unwell
• be irritable or cry inconsolably
• have a high fever.

GLUE EAR

The medical term for glue ear is secretory otitis media. Normally, the middle ear space contains air. In glue ear, there's a build-up of sticky fluid instead. It occurs after repeated attacks of middle ear infection (see right), though there's no agreement on how many infections may cause glue ear. Some babies are more likely to develop it than others, and there can be a family history of the condition.

The most obvious symptom is hearing loss. Your baby may fail to hear you clearly, may not turn to look at you when you speak, or may look surprised when you suddenly appear over the side of the cot because they haven't heard you approach. Babies are learning all the time, and hearing is vital to most of their development. If untreated, glue ear can lead to problems with speech and behaviour. Always see your doctor if you think your baby may have glue ear or any other hearing problem.

Treatment may involve a minor operation to put in grommets. These are tiny tubes to let air in and equalize the pressure on each side of the eardrum. After a few months, the grommets usually fall out, by which time hearing is back to normal.

• Refuse feeds
• Vomit.
Some babies pull at the affected ear, but many babies also do this when they are tired.

If your baby has any of the symptoms above, see your doctor promptly so the infection can be treated at an early stage. If the infection is untreated, the eardrum can burst, causing a discharge. This relieves the pressure in the middle ear so the baby may feel better as soon as this happens. However, they still need treatment for the infection.

COMMON COMPLAINTS: QUICK REFERENCE

See a doctor if your baby's temperature is 39°C (102.2F) or 38°C (104.4F) if under three months or more and does not go down after giving age-appropriate paracetamol or ibuprofen or persists for more than five days.

SYMPTOM	POSSIBLE CAUSE	WHAT TO DO
Fever	Fever is not a very specific symptom as babies can become feverish for all sorts of reasons. It is most commonly a sign of a viral or bacterial infection (see also Fever, p.369).	Offer plenty of fluids (breastfeeds, if breastfeeding); keep room cool. See your doctor if your baby's temperature is 39°C (102.2°F) or more (38°C/100.4°F if under three months).
Runny nose	A runny nose, commonly producing clear mucus that thickens and turns yellow, green, or grey over about a week, is often caused by a cold (see p.376) and sometimes by flu. Other causes include allergy (see p.372), the early stages of bronchiolitis (see p.376), or croup (see p.377).	For a cold, make sure your baby has plenty of rest and fluids (breastfeeds, if breastfeeding). Ease their breathing by tilting the head end of the cot, if it's safe to do so. Ask your doctor about using saline drops.
Cough	A common symptom, it can be due to a cold (see p.376). Coughing can also be a symptom of a chest infection (see p.377); allergy (see p.372); bronchiolitis (see p.376) or wheezing (see p.376). A deep cough with a barking sound could be croup (see p.377), and bouts of coughing that end with a big breath in may indicate whooping cough.	Give plenty of fluids (breastfeeds, if breastfeeding). See a doctor if a cough persists for more than one week or is accompanied by a high fever or wheeze, if your baby is short of breath, makes a crackling breathing sound, refuses feeds, or is listless.
Rash	Once your baby is on solids, a rash around the mouth is often due to irritation from food. If their lips look swollen or they has other symptoms, suspect an allergy (see p.372). A rash can be a symptom of many common childhood viral infections, such as chickenpox (see p. 373). A rash can also occur with meningitis and septicaemia (see p.377). Around the nappy area, the most likely cause is nappy rash (see p.373). Little bumps, or tiny blisters, particularly in skin folds, may be heat rash (see p.375). Eczema (see p.375) causes patches of dry skin.	Treatment depends on the cause of the rash. Do the glass test (see opposite) if the rash appears quickly or your baby is unwell. The more ill your baby seems, the more serious their rash is likely to be, so contact the doctor if you are concerned.
Vomiting	Vomiting affects most babies at some stage and is not usually serious. It is most often due to a problem in the digestive tract, but can indicate a serious infection elsewhere in the body (see also Vomiting, p.371).	Offer plenty of fluids (breastfeeds, if breastfeeding). If vomiting lasts longer than 12–24 hours, take your baby to the doctor, who may prescribe an oral rehydration solution.
Diarrhoea	Diarrhoea is a common symptom most often due to infection of the digestive tract (see also Diarrhoea, p.370).	Treat as for vomiting (above). Use a barrier cream when changing their nappy – loose stools can cause their bottom to become irritated.
Loss of appetite	Babies are sometimes reluctant to feed when teething, but other causes might be gastroenteritis (see p.371), or almost any other acute infection, including middle ear infection (see opposite).	Keep offering fluids (breastfeeds, if breastfeeding) and food, and keep checking of the number of wet nappies to make sure they aren't becoming dehydrated. If they refuse several feeds in a row, contact the doctor.

Developmental concerns

Treating milestones just as helpful guidelines prevents unnecessary anxiety, but do seek reassurance if you have persistent concerns.

Babies are all different and even identical twins develop in their own unique way. Even so, there is a pattern of progression, and babies acquire new skills in the same order (see development charts, below). As a parent, you spend most time with your baby and are often the first person to notice if they aren't developing as expected. A slight delay in one area of development isn't always significant, but delay in two or more areas is important. If your baby was born prematurely, remember to allow for that. A baby born six weeks prematurely won't reach the stage of a six-week-old baby until 12 weeks after the birth.

As your baby grows up and does more, the different areas of development become increasingly interlinked. A baby may not wave bye-bye, for instance, unless they can also see, hear, and understand that someone is leaving.

It can be tempting to compare your baby with others. While other people's babies can give you an overall idea of what happens when, you can't expect your baby to do things at exactly the same time as others. If you have other children, don't expect this baby to have the same development timetable as your previous babies. Some traits do run in families. Bottom shuffling, for instance, can be familial, but most other achievements vary hugely from one child to the next. Your baby's development will be checked routinely at 6–8 weeks and again before their first birthday.

Signs to watch out for

Speak to your doctor or health visitor if your baby displays any of the

DEVELOPMENTAL MILESTONES

KEY
The four key areas of development are shown in different colours. Coloured bands (right) are development windows, which show when your baby is most likely to acquire each skill.

- Gross motor development
- Vision and fine motor development
- Hearing and language
- Social and intellectual development

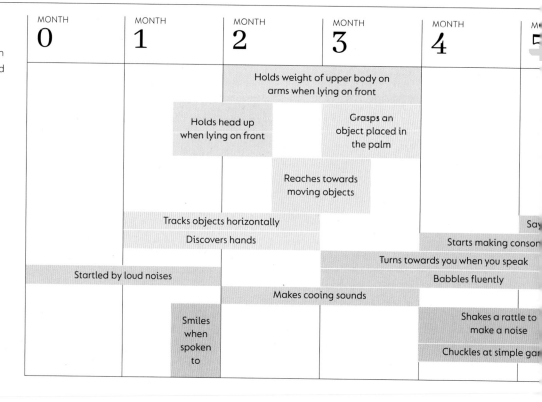

	MONTH 0	MONTH 1	MONTH 2	MONTH 3	MONTH 4	M 5
			Holds weight of upper body on arms when lying on front			
		Holds head up when lying on front		Grasps an object placed in the palm		
			Reaches towards moving objects			
		Tracks objects horizontally				Say
		Discovers hands			Starts making conson	
				Turns towards you when you speak		
	Startled by loud noises			Babbles fluently		
			Makes cooing sounds			
					Shakes a rattle to make a noise	
		Smiles when spoken to			Chuckles at simple gam	

following signs, or if they regress in any area. Your baby will be examined and you may be asked to bring them back. Babies can vary from day to day, depending on their mood or whether they are hungry or tired, so it is not always easy to give a definite answer on the first consultation. Alternatively, your baby may be referred to a paediatrician for assessment. There may be cause for concern if your baby:
• Has a persistent squint (cross-eyed) after six weeks
• Isn't smiling by 9–10 weeks
• Tilts their head persistently to one side
• Doesn't make cooing sounds at about three months
• Makes no eye contact by three months
• Doesn't turn their head towards sounds by three months

• Still has a floppy head by three months (when awake)
• Has any squint after three months
• Doesn't reach for objects by six months
• Won't turn around when you speak to them at six months
• Isn't babbling by 10 months or stops babbling after having previously done

so (this can be a sign of deafness)
• Won't sit up by 10 months
• Won't bear weight on legs at 10 months
• Doesn't grasp objects at 10 months
• Doesn't try feeding themself at 12 months
• Has asymmetry of the limbs, or any movement, at any stage.

YOUR BABY'S VISION

Parents are often concerned about whether their baby can see properly or will need glasses. While conditions such as glaucoma, astigmatism, and short-sightedness can run in families, you don't generally need to be concerned at this stage. However, if you are in doubt or need reassurance, talk to your doctor.

A newborn baby has a very close range of vision, but you should be able to tell whether they can focus on your face at a distance of around 20–25cm (8–10in). Also, their pupils should be dark (or red in a flash photograph). Always see the doctor if you notice a white mass in either pupil.

Take note, too, if you note any abnormal eye movements, such as a squint, or any wandering or jerking movement, talk to your doctor.

MONTH 6	MONTH 7	MONTH 8	MONTH 9	MONTH 10	MONTH 11	MONTH 12

Sits unsupported

Walks unaided

Crawls or bottom-shuffles

Pulls up to standing position

Rolls from front to back, and back to front

Cruises around furniture

Drops things on purpose

Bangs bricks together

Can transfer objects from one hand to the other

Can point using index finger

Da
ds

Can grasp object between finger and thumb

Puts toys in and takes them out of containers

Sounds begin to resemble real words

Waves bye-bye

Responds to own name

n as peek-a-boo

Becomes shy with strangers

Everyday first aid

It's important you know what to do if your baby is injured. Consider taking a practical first aid course to prepare you for an emergency.

Cuts and grazes

Babies can become very upset if they get a cut or graze, so reassure them while you have a look at the injury.

If it's a small graze or cut, gently clean the area with soap and water using a gauze pad (or, you can use any soft, non-fluffy material). If the wound looks dirty, rinse it under running water, pat dry with clean pieces of material, then cover with a clean dressing that is larger than the area of the wound. For a cut lip, apply an ice cube wrapped in a clean piece of muslin for about five minutes.

If there is a lot of bleeding, place a clean pad or piece of non-fluffy material over the cut and press down firmly on the wound. If possible, raise the injured part above the level of the heart to reduce blood flow. Keep pressing until the bleeding slows down or stops, then apply a dressing large enough to cover the wound.

Take your baby to A&E if·
• bleeding isn't under control in 10 minutes
• the wound is gaping
• there may be a foreign body in the wound.

Bites and stings

If your baby has been bitten or stung by an insect, they will be shocked and in pain, so comfort them. Bites and stings are not usually serious, but in rare cases, a bee or wasp sting can cause a serious reaction, known as anaphylactic shock (see p.372). A bite or sting in or on the mouth can be serious; if this happens, take your baby to hospital immediately.

If you can see a sting left in the skin, scrape it off with your fingernail. Don't use tweezers as you'll inject more venom into the skin. You can reduce swelling and relieve itching by applying a flannel or towel soaked in cold water, or an ice cube wrapped in a dry cloth. Hold it on for five minutes while you hug your baby. You can give your baby infant paracetamol if they're in pain.

Falls, bumps, and bruises

Babies often fall and hurt themselves. Most of the time, all you need to do is comfort your baby and apply a cold compress to the area to relieve swelling and pain (see Bites and stings, left).

Go to A&E if your baby·
• has a head injury
• cannot move one of their limbs
• is bleeding and you can't control it within 10 minutes with direct pressure, or has a gaping wound (see Cuts and grazes, left)
• is or was unconscious
• you're not sure if it's serious.

Burns

Fire, hot water, steam, sunlight, electricity, and chemicals can all cause burns. The damage depends on the site, size, thickness, and type of burn. The deepest burns are often fairly painless. Cool the burn under cold running water for at least 10 minutes. Remove (or cut off) clothing around the burn, unless it is stuck to the burn. After cooling, apply a clean dressing or kitchen film and take your baby to hospital for assessment. If the area of the burn is small, see your doctor, but do not delay.

Take your baby to A&E right away if·
• It's a large burn (larger than the palm of your baby's hand).
• It's on the face/in the mouth, on the hands, or the genitals.
• The burn is chemical or electrical (take the chemical container with you)
• Your baby seems unwell.
• You're unsure what to do.

Foreign objects

Dirt, dust, or other bits can easily get into babies' eyes, and babies may push small objects, such as beans or buttons, into their ears or nose.

Object in eye Anything in the eye usually causes discomfort and crying. If it's a small speck on the surface of the eye, it can generally be washed out.

Fill a jug with warm water. Hold your baby with their head tilted upwards and pour the water into their eye, aiming for the inner corner. The eyelids need to be separated so you'll need assistance.

Take your baby to A&E if·
• An object is embedded in or stuck to the eye. Do not attempt to remove it.
• You've tried to wash out an object on the surface of the eye, but have been unsuccessful.
• The eye remains irritated and sore after the object has been removed.

Object in ear or nose If your baby gets something stuck in their ear or nose, reassure them that there's nothing to worry about. Do not try to remove the object even if you can see it because you risk pushing it further in. Take your baby to A&E, where doctors will be able to remove the object, using tiny forceps or a suction machine. Sometimes, a baby may not realize there's something stuck in their ears or nose. They may not hear well or one side of their nose may run or have a smelly discharge. If you have any concerns that there could be something in your baby's ear or nose, see your doctor right away.

Choking

Small objects, such as beans or coins, are often responsible for choking as babies put everything into their mouths. Babies can also choke on food, or on mucus or milk. Coughing is nature's way of trying to dislodge an obstruction in the airway, so if your baby is choking but coughing effectively, let them be. If, after two or three minutes, your baby continues to cough, call 999.

If your baby cannot breathe, cough, or cry, the choking is severe. They may make strange noises and their face may turn blue. You need to act immediately (see box, below).

Poisoning

If your baby has ingested something toxic, call an ambulance or take them to A&E. Tell the medical team what your baby has swallowed, how much, and when, and keep a sample. Do not try to make your baby vomit as this can cause more harm. Wipe off any corrosive substances on or around their mouth. If they've eaten a toxic plant or berries, look in their mouth and remove any remaining pieces.

DEAL WITH CHOKING

If your baby is choking and unable to breathe, take emergency action to clear their airways.
• Lay the baby face down on your forearm, with their head lower than their body. Support their head with your hand. Using the heel of your other hand, give up to five sharp blows to their upper back.
• Check their mouth and, if you can clearly see a loose object, remove it carefully. Do not sweep the inside of their mouth with your fingers or feel blindly down their throat as you may push an object further in or damage their throat.
• If the obstruction is still there, turn your baby over onto their back and give up to five chest thrusts, by pushing down with two fingers in the middle of the chest.
• Check quickly after each chest thrust to see if the obstruction has been dislodged. If the obstruction does not clear after three cycles of five back blows and five chest thrusts, call for an ambulance.
• Continue giving back blows and chest thrusts until help arrives.

Even if you have successfully dealt with the emergency, any baby who has had chest thrusts must be seen by a doctor to check that no damage has been done to delicate bones.

Back blows Make sure the baby's head is lower than their body. Use the heel of your hand to give back blows, making sure the blows land between their shoulder blades.

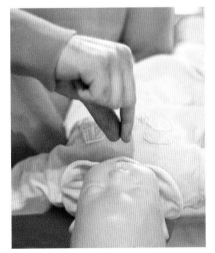

Check mouth Look inside your baby's mouth. If a dislodged object is clearly visible, fish it out gently with your fingertips, being careful not to push it further in.

Chest thrusts To avoid injury when giving chest thrusts, your fingers should be on the breastbone, not ribs. Push inwards and upwards, being firm but not jerky.

Resources

Feeding & nutrition

www.abm.me.uk
The Association of Breastfeeding Mothers is a charitable organization providing counselling and information.
Helpline: 08444 122949

www.babyfriendly.org.uk
The Baby Friendly Initiative, developed by the WHO and Unicef, has information on breastfeeding and babycare.

www.nct.org.uk
The National Childbirth Trust offers information on breastfeeding (as well as parenting and first aid for babies).
Breastfeeding helpline: 0300 330 0771

www.nhs.uk/Planners/birthtofive/Pages/bottle-feeding.aspx
NHS guide to bottle-feeding.

https://www.nhs.uk/conditions/baby/breastfeeding-and-bottle-feeding/breastfeeding/
NHS breastfeeding guide. National breastfeeding helpline: 0300 100 0212

www.nhs.uk/start4life
News and advice on nutrition and activity – to help parents build healthy habits for their babies.

www.nutrition.org.uk
British Nutrition Foundation website; includes advice on nutrition for babies.

Parenting

www.babycentre.co.uk
Pregnancy and parenting website.

www.bbc.co.uk/parenting
Advice and information on all aspects of parenting from the BBC.

www.direct.gov.uk/surestart
Information about Government-run children's centres in your area. Most offer parenting courses, childcare, health services, and opportunities to socialize with other parents.

www.familylives.org.uk
Support and advice for parents on all aspects of family life, from relationships to running a household.
Parentline: 0808 800 2222

www.fatherhoodinstitute.org
Campaigns on behalf of fathers and offers information and support.

www.gingerbread.org.uk
Practical advice and support for single parents.
Helpline: 0808 802 0925

www.mumsnet.com
Online community for parents offering advice, information, and reviews.

www.netmums.com
Online community for parents; advice, information, and local listings.

www.relate.org.uk
Advice and relationship counselling for couples, individuals, and families.

Childcare

www.daycaretrust.org.uk
National childcare charity providing factsheets on childcare issues and a newsletter for parents.

www.ncma.org.uk
The National Childminding Association provides information on choosing childminders and nannies.

www.ofsted.gov.uk
Government inspection body providing information on childcare and reports on childcare providers.

www.workingfamilies.org.uk
Charitable organization campaigning for a better work–life balance for parents. Advice on employment rights, flexible working, and rights and benefits.

Health & safety

www.actionforsickchildren.org
Action for Sick Children is a healthcare charity that offers guidance for parents on getting the best for their child when dealing with healthcare services.

www.capt.org.uk
The Child Accident Prevention Trust seeks to protect children from injury due to accidents. It has a comprehensive guide to keeping your baby safe, both inside and outside the home.

www.lullabytrust.org.uk
The website of the Lullaby Trust, (formerly the Foundation for the Study of Infant Death) provides up-to-date baby safety advice.

www.nhs.uk
Check symptoms online, find your nearest GP or A&E department, and get health information and advice.
Helpline: 0845 4647 (7 days, 24 hours).

www.nspcc.org.uk
The National Society for the Prevention of Cruelty to Children works to protect children from harm. Resources for parents range from how to keep babies safe to coping with parenthood.

www.redcross.org.uk
The British Red Cross website has advice on what to do in a range of baby first aid emergencies. You can also find out about courses and events in your area.

www.sja.org.uk
Find out about the practical first aid courses run by St John Ambulance and read first aid advice online.

www.postnatalexercise.co.uk
Guild of Pregnancy and Postnatal Exercise Teachers, providing details of instructors in your area.

Rights & benefits

www.citizensadvice.org.uk
Get advice online or find your local
Citizens Advice Bureau.

www.direct.gov.uk
This Government website enables you
to access information about all public
services, from employment rights and
benefits to healthcare.

www.hmrc.gov.uk
HM Revenue and Customs' website
providing information on child
benefit and tax credits.

www.hse.gov.uk
The Health and Safety Executive's
guide to health and safety law
at work.

www.maternityaction.org.uk
A charity working on behalf of
vulnerable parents, especially
migrants and asylum seekers.
Offers information on rights
and benefits.

www.moneyadviceservice.org.uk
Set up by the Government, this site
offers free, independent advice to
parents on managing their finances.

www.turn2us.org.uk
A charitable service helping people
to access money available to them
through welfare benefits, grants,
and other help.

www.worksmart.org.uk
TUC guide to employee rights at work,
with information on parental leave
and family-friendly working.

Support groups

www.allergyuk.org
Allergy UK is a medical charity
offering information and advice on
allergies, food intolerance, and
chemical sensitivity.
Helpline: 01322 619898

www.apni.org
The Association for Postnatal Illness
provides information and support.
Helpline: 020 7386 0868

www.asthma.org.uk
Charity dedicated to improving the
health and wellbeing of those whose
lives are affected by asthma.
Helpline: 0800 121 62 44

www.bda.org.uk
The British Deaf Association
campaigns on behalf of deaf people
and promotes British Sign Language.

www.bliss.org.uk
Special-care baby charity, providing
information and support to parents of
premature and sick babies.
Helpline: 0500 618140

www.cafamily.org.uk
Charity supporting parents of disabled
children and providing guidance on all
aspects of caring for a disabled child.
Helpline: 0808 808 3555

www.cry-sis.org.uk
National charity advising parents
of babies with excessive crying
and sleep problems.
Helpline: 08451 228 669

www.downs-syndrome.org.uk
The Down's Syndrome Association
supports people with Down's and
their families.
Helpline: 0208 614 5100

www.eczema.org
The National Eczema Society
provides advice on treating and
managing eczema.
Helpline: 0800 089 1122

www.home-start.org.uk
Support for families, for example
those who feel isolated or who are
struggling to cope with caring for
twins or triplets.

www.meningitis-trust.org
Information about meningitis,
including symptoms.
Helpline: 0800 028 18 28

www.mind.org.uk
Information and advice about mental
health, including anxiety, depression,
and postnatal depression.
Helpline: 0300 123 3393

www.pelvicpartnership.org.uk
The Pelvic Partnership is run by
women volunteers who have
experienced Symphysis Pubis
Dysfunction (SPD), now known as
Pelvic Girdle Pain (PGP).

www.scope.org.uk
Practical advice and support
for families of children with
cerebral palsy.
Helpline: 0800 800 3333

www.sense.org.uk
On-going support and advice for
families of deafblind children.

www.steps-charity.org.uk
Information and advice on talipes
(club foot) and other lower limb
conditions. Helpline: 01925 750271

www.tamba.org.uk
The Twins and Multiple Births
Association (Tamba) offers support
services for multiple birth families.
Helpline: 0800 138 0509

Index

A

A&E departments 365, 382–3
abdominal muscles
    pelvic tilts 65, 169
    tummy time 88, 116, 124, 139
accidents 170, 279
acne, neonatal 123
action rhymes 158
activity centres 209
adenovirus 376
ADHD 265
adrenaline 131
advice, conflicting 76
aerobic exercise 97
affection
    need for 313
    responding to 176
agencies
    babysitting 261
    nanny 114–15
air travel, young babies 125
airways
    bronchiolitis 376
    chest infections 377
    croup 377
    wheezing 376–7
alcohol
    in baby's food 200, 353
    and breastfeeding 62
    and mother's sleep 101
alleles, genetics 21
allergies 372–3
    anaphylactic shock 372, 382
    antibacterial cleaning products
        and 112
    asthma 233, 375, 377
    bee and wasp stings 382
    breastfeeding and 25
    cow's milk 100, 229
    eczema 267, 372, 375
    food allergies 225, 241
    soya milk 229
    stopping breastfeeding 254
    symptoms 372, 373
    and weaning 154–5, 179, 200,
        216
ALTE (Apparent Life-Threatening
    Event) 227
ambulance, when to call 365
anaemia 130, 156
anaesthetics 365
analytical thinking 345
anaphylactic shock 225, 241, 372,
    382
anger 295, 335
animals 312
    animal noises 165, 253, 288, 330

    see also pets
antacids 370
antibacterial cleaning products,
    and allergies 112
antibiotics 245, 367
    and breastfeeding 63
    and colds 376
    effects on teeth 306
    and thrush 374
antibodies
    breastfeeding 25, 103, 255
    breastfeeding during illness 63
    in colostrum 26, 27, 44
    and food allergies 241
    in frozen breastmilk 83
    immune system 103
    vaccinations 99
anti-depressants 110
antihistamine 241
antitussives 377
anxiety
    about strangers 298
    see also separation anxiety
Apgar test 41
appetite, loss of 143, 339, 379
"approach" cues 118
areola, breastfeeding 26, 27, 41, 46
arms, muscle development 328
artistic activities 345
    drawing 328, 345
    flour "painting" 323
    painting 262
asthma 233, 375, 377
atopic eczema 375
attachment theory 138, 313
au pairs 115
avocados, guacamole 329

B

babbling
    imitating pitch and intonation
        245
    importance of 253
    older babies 206, 226, 274
    twins 332
    young babies 86, 133
baby blues 49, 61, 110
baby classes 163
baby gyms 98, 116
baby-led weaning 178–9, 217
baby massage 119
baby monitors 34, 211
baby nests 30
babyproofing home 180, 205, 243,
    301
babysitting 261

grandparents 80, 144
    and "me-time" 80, 256, 316
    at night 327
"baby talk" (parentese) 84, 86, 328
baby walkers 197, 351
background noise 264, 322
backpack carriers 347
bacteria 103
    antibiotics 245
    breastfeeding and 25
    chest infections 377
    gastroenteritis 371
    meningitis 377–8
    middle ear infection 378
    urine infections 377
baking soda 373
balance
    cruising 269, 300
    standing 333
    vestibular system 151, 211
    walking 319
baldness 196
balloons 346
balls 235, 283, 351
banisters, safety 258
barrier cream 73, 373
batch cooking 272
bathing
    dislike of 135
    and dry skin 123
    equipment 35, 189
    newborn babies 57
    nursing sick babies 367
    topping and tailing 45
    using big baths 189
    water temperature 189, 290
    young babies 101
batteries 205
beakers see cups
bedding 31, 86
bedrooms
    equipment 34–5
    positioning cots 108
    safety 277
    sleeping alone 211
    temperature 31, 73, 106, 231, 290
beds, co-sleeping 30, 242, 325
bedtime routines
    early or late bedtimes 224
    falling asleep on own 156, 166
    one-year-olds 346
    problems 135, 262, 340
    and sleeping through the night
        324–5
    stopping breastfeeding 255
    young babies 89
bee stings 382

behaviour
    encouraging good behaviour
        256, 266
    helpfulness 315
    manners 348, 359
    poking and pinching 340
    role models 341
    testing your reactions 266
belly buttons 92
benefits 18–19
bibs 35, 154
bike trailers 347
"bikini nappies" 32, 51
bilateral coordination 199
bilingual babies 151
bilirubin 27, 51, 372
bird feeders 312
birth
    registering 18, 52
    talking about 64
birth certificates 18, 52
birth control 73, 92, 257
birthdays 346, 359
birthmarks 41, 61
bites, insect 382
biting 143, 322
black-and-white patterns 67
blankets 31
    comfort objects 282, 317
    kicking off 248
    in pushchairs 290, 348
bleeding
    after birth 42, 50, 92
    after sexual intercourse 113
    cuts and grazes 382
    gums 110
    serious wounds 382
blisters, chickenpox 373
blood
    in bowel movements 218, 232,
        371
    see also bleeding
blood poisoning 377
blood pressure, after birth 92
blood tests
    for food allergies 225, 241
    newborn bloodspot test 50
board books 117, 137, 354
body clock 81, 131
body language 171, 174
bonding 42–3, 45, 52
    bottle-feeding and 29
    breastfeeding and 25
    eye contact and 57
bones
    breastfeeding and 110
    number of 78

osteoporosis 25, 110, 331
rickets 158, 219
six-week checks 93
books 235, 354
  board and fabric books 117, 137, 354
  as gifts 346
  libraries 318
  and new experiences 357
  nursing sick babies 366
  reading to babies 145, 202, 223
  secondhand 350
  story time sessions 318
  textures 310
bootees 231, 290
boots 354
boredom
  and crying 69
  snacks and 247
bottle-feeding 29
  after birth 44
  anti-colic bottles 75
  demand feeding 75
  and diarrhoea 100
  dropping night feeds 325
  equipment 29, 34
  establishing a routine 100
  follow-on milk 207, 229
  formula for hungry babies 164, 207, 229
  and growth spurts 91, 127
  on holiday 289
  increasing feeds 152
  introducing cups 190, 334
  making up formula 48
  newborn babies 47, 49, 53
  and night waking 214, 328
  positions for 59
  reducing feeds 184
  sharing with partner 84
  skin-to-skin contact 45
  and stopping breastfeeding 254–5
  supplementing breastfeeding 85, 91, 207
  and teething 143
  and weaning 164, 269
  and weight gain 60, 124, 186
bottles, sterilizing 29, 34, 306
bottom shuffling 204, 209, 240, 300
bouncers 197
bouncing 303
bouncy chairs 34
boundaries, setting 16, 341
bowel movements
  after weaning 218
  blood in 371
  constipation 118, 171, 371–2
  grimacing during 232
  meconium 27, 41, 45, 47, 372

newborn babies 44–5
potty training 296
teething and 133
see also diarrhoea
bowels
  intussusception 371
  obstructions 371
Bowlby, John 313
bow-leggedness 204
boys
  changing nappies 44, 47
  circumcision 47
  developmental differences 23, 161
  erections 95
  playing with girls' toys 235
  undescended testes 93, 95
brain
  and babbling 253
  bilingual babies 151
  cells 182, 278
  development of 22–3, 182, 278
  febrile seizures 369
  and handedness 184
  memory 104, 192, 291
  meningitis 377–8
  "mirror neurons" 120
  music and 87
  during sleep 109, 353
  vestibular system 151, 211
  and vision 95, 212
bras
  nursing bras 26, 34, 107, 321
  stopping breastfeeding 255
breakfast 185, 236, 287, 299
breastfeeding 25–8
  after birth 41, 44
  antibodies 25, 27, 103
  benefits of 25, 27, 255
  biting 143
  and bone loss 110
  changes to breasts 321
  clothes 107
  cluster feeds 214
  colic and 75
  colostrum 26–7, 41, 44, 46, 49
  as comfort 184
  and contraception 73
  co-sleeping and 30
  cultural differences 331
  demand feeding 27–8, 49, 75, 152
  diet and 62, 105
  distracted babies 111, 299
  drinking water 105
  dropping night feeds 325
  emptying breasts 58
  equipment 34
  establishing a routine 100
  extended breastfeeding 331
  foremilk and hindmilk 27, 58

  and growth spurts 91, 127
  during illness 63
  and immune system 168
  and jaundice 372
  latching on 26, 27, 41, 46
  length of feeds 58
  milk production 26
  and mother's weight loss 25, 226
  newborn babies 46, 49, 50, 53
  and night waking 156
  one-year-olds 356
  and periods 25, 82, 257
  positions for 58
  postnatal checks 92
  problems 28, 59
  in public 72
  reducing feeds 184
  and returning to work 160, 185
  skin-to-skin contact 45
  sore nipples 46, 58, 59
  stopping 185, 207, 254–5
  supplementing with bottles 85, 91, 207
  and teething 143
  transitional milk 49
  twins 51, 59
  vitamins 331
  and weaning 25, 154–5, 229, 269
  weaning onto cups 334
  and weight gain 60, 124, 186
  see also expressing breastmilk
breast pads 34
breasts
  after breastfeeding 82, 255
  cancer 25, 27
  changes in pregnancy 26, 321
  engorged 27, 49, 207
  mastitis 255
  nursing bras 26, 34, 107, 321
  and return of periods 257
breast shells 34
breathing
  ALTE (Apparent Life Threatening Event) 227
  bronchiolitis 376
  croup 377
  instant energy fixes 183
  irregular 227
  laryngomalacia 374
  signs of illness 363
  during sleep 47
  sleep apnoea 54
  wheezing 376–7
  when to call doctor 308
bricks, stacking 315
bronchiolitis 167, 376
bronchitis 377
brothers see siblings
bruises 279, 382
bubbles, blowing 267
buggies see pushchairs and

buggies
buoyancy, arm bands 267
burns 382
burping babies 49
bye-bye, waving 274, 332

C

Caesarean section
  and air travel 125
  breastfeeding after 27, 49
  discharge from hospital 46
  exercise after 62
  pelvic floor exercises 65
  postnatal checks 93
  recovery from 42, 113
  sexual intercourse after 96
  stitches 50, 65
cafés, feeding babies in 251
caffeine
  and breastfeeding 62
  drinks 217, 229
  and mother's sleep 101
calamine lotion 373
calcium
  in breastmilk 25, 331, 356
  in cow's milk 356
  and diet for breastfeeding 110
  and post-pregnancy weight loss 259
  preventing tooth decay 285
calendula cream 73
calories
  for breastfeeding 105
  in shop-bought baby food 251
campylobacter 371
cancer, and breastfeeding 25, 27, 331
candida see thrush
canine teeth 198
carbohydrates
  introducing lumpier foods 237
  nutritional requirements 193
  for older babies 286
cardigans 348
carers see childcare
carrying newborn babies 46, 71
car travel
  car seats 35, 330
  dislike of 135
  overheating 73
  young babies 121, 125
casein, in formula milk 29, 164, 229
catching games 283
cat nets 122
cats see pets
caution 309
cells, brain 182, 278
cereals, "baby" 251
cervix

bleeding after intercourse 113
smear tests 92
chairs
bouncy chairs 34
climbing on 258
high chairs 154, 206, 238
changing bags 35, 61, 239
changing stations 32, 34
charity shops 350
cheese fondue 329
chest infections 308, 377
chest press 321
chest stretch 321
chewing 236, 245, 276, 299
chickenpox 203, 349, 373
chicken, weaning 216, 217
child benefit 18–19
childcare 114–15
babysitting 144
and baby's milestones 288
leaving baby at night 327
partner as main provider 215
relationship with carers 214, 273
separation anxiety 213, 263
at sports centres 142
childminders 114
babysitting 261
relationship with 273
children
meeting other children 316
see also siblings
children's centres 181
child tax credit 19
chlamydia 113
chloride, in cow's milk 356
chlorine, swimming pools 267
chlorphenamine
bromopheniramine 377
choking 276, 383
circumcision 47
clapping hands 146, 223
classes, baby 163
cleaners 239
cleaning products, and allergies 112
climbing 258, 269
muscle development 328
stairs 258, 279, 333
clingy babies 277
anxiety about strangers 298
separation anxiety 228, 233
clinics, weighing babies 124
clothes
and baby's temperature 73
for breastfeeding 26, 107
breastfeeding in public 72
cold weather 348
dressing babies 272
hot weather 348
older babies 231, 290
in the past 296

secondhand 104, 350
for special occasions 104
for twins 104
washing 123
young babies 91
club foot 204
cluster feeds 214
co-bedding twins 63
coeliac disease 155, 179
coffee tables, safety 301
cognitive development
object permanence 233, 263
problem solving 264
colds 308, 376
complications 308
snoring and snuffling 47, 227
staying home from nursery 349
treatment 308
young babies 103
cold weather 290, 348
colic 136
crying and 68, 96
dealing with 75
lactose intolerance 100
colostrum
antibodies in 26, 27, 41
starting breastfeeding 26–7, 44, 46
transitional milk 49
colour
of eyes 21, 147, 326
of food 329
colourings, in shop-bought baby food 251
colour vision 95, 98, 112, 147
combs 290
comfort
comfort eating 334
and crying 69
pick-ups 159
sucking as 184
thumb sucking 147, 194
comfort objects 86, 123, 138, 282
at bedtime 346
problems with 317
and separation anxiety 213, 263
communication
babbling 86, 133, 245, 253, 274
body language 171, 174
eye contact and 57
gestures 232
importance of repetition 159
newborn babies 70
parentese ("baby talk") 84, 86, 328
pointing 284, 332
reading baby's cues 118
responding to baby 266
saying "no" 191, 341, 342
smiling 94
sociability 119

waving bye-bye 274, 332
young babies 151
see also crying
competitive parenting 17, 173
complementary feeding see weaning
conditioner, washing hair 252, 290
confidence
building self-esteem 160
developing 22
parenting 320
conflict, effects on baby 234
conflicting advice 76
conjunctivitis 349, 370
constipation 118, 171, 371–2
contraception 73, 92, 257
contracts, nannies 115
controlled crying 325
convulsions 369
cooking 242, 329
cooperation 246
cortisol 230
co-sleeping 30, 242, 325
cot death see Sudden Infant Death Syndrome (SIDS)
cots 30–1, 34
bedding 31
climbing out of 258
co-bedding twins 63
on holiday 125, 289
mattresses 30, 108, 277
moving baby into 108
safety 86, 277
teething rails 108, 277
toys in 346
cotton wool 35
coughs 376
causes 379
cough medicines 377
croup 308, 377
at night 167
treatment 379
when to call doctor 308
counting 159
cow's milk 356
allergy to 100, 229, 254, 373
cooking with 207
coxsackievirus 375
cracked nipples 59
cradle cap 76
cradles 30, 34
crawling 22, 209
climbing stairs 333
getting ready for 157
outdoor play 337
crayons 328, 345
creativity
drawing 328, 345
flour "painting" 323
painting 262

crèches 142, 345
"creeping" 131
criticism, positive parenting and 17
croup 308, 377
cruising 209, 269, 300, 319
shoes 269, 300, 302
crying 96
clingy babies 277
empathy 270
and mother's accent 70
newborn babies 48, 57, 68–9
and night waking 156, 166, 325
reading baby's cues 118
reasons for 68–9
separation anxiety 213
signs of illness 363
sleep 'training' 325
cuddles, clingy babies 277
cupboards, safety 301
cups 154, 190, 232, 334
curiosity 224, 256, 279
curly hair 252, 290
cutlery 339, 344
cuts and grazes 382
cycling 347
cystic fibrosis, newborn bloodspot test 50

D

"Dada," saying 206
dairy products 356
allergies 179
calcium content 285
and colic 75
fat content 193, 200
and post-pregnancy weight loss 259
unpasteurized 217
weaning 237
dancing 122, 281, 303, 328
danger see safety
dark, fear of 309
death see Sudden Infant Death Syndrome (SIDS)
decongestants 63, 377
deferred imitation 332
defrosting purées 179
dehydration 213
colds and 308
diarrhoea and 167, 213, 363
fevers and 366–7, 369
signs of 97, 363
vomiting and 370
when to call doctor 308
demand feeding 27–8, 49, 75, 152
dens 278
dental care 110, 198, 357
depression
fathers and 163

postnatal 49, 61, 110
depth perception 112, 128, 212, 355
determination 322
development see milestones
developmental dysplasia of the
  hip (DDH) 204
dextromethorphan 377
diabetes
  breastfeeding and 25
  weaning and 155, 179
diaries
  and food allergies 241
  and weaning 179
diarrhoea 167
  breastfeeding and 25
  causes 250, 371, 379
  and dehydration 167, 213, 363
  gastroenteritis 371
  lactose intolerance 100
  staying home from nursery 349
  teething and 133, 198
  treatment 371, 379
dieting, and post-pregnancy
  weight loss 105, 259
dimmer switches 309
dinners 287
diphenhydramine 377
diphtheria vaccination 99, 152
dippers and dunkers 272, 329
discharges, from ear 103
discipline
  diversion tactics 182
  encouraging good behaviour
    256
  introducing 16–17
  and negative behaviour 266
  and safety 341
  saying "no" 191
  setting boundaries 16, 341
disease see illness
dishwashers
  bottle-feeding equipment in 29
  safety 301
dislikes 135, 171
disposable nappies 32, 44, 77
distractions, young babies and 111
distraction techniques 182,
  186, 234
  dealing with baby dislikes 135
  dressing babies 272
DNA 21
doctors
  changing 364
  postnatal checks 77, 92–3
  registering with 70
  visiting 357, 364
  when to call 308, 364, 369
dogs, fear of 279
  see also pets
dominant genes 21
doors, safety 301

downtime, for babies 88
doxylamine 377
drawing 328, 345
dreams 109, 227, 353
dressing babies 272
dried fruit 302
drinks 229
drooling 138, 306
dropping things 283, 295
drops, administering 366, 367
drowsiness, when to call
  doctor 308
drugs
  administering 366, 367
  and breastfeeding 28, 63
  cough medicines 376
  lowering fevers 366
  medicine cupboards 366
  for postnatal depression 110
  see also antibiotics
drums 281
dry skin 123
dummies 31, 69, 352
dunkers and dippers 272, 329
dust mites 112
duvets 31, 248

E

eardrum, perforated 103, 378
early waking 187
ears
  administering drops 366
  cleaning 310
  foreign objects 382–3
  glue ear 378
  infections 103, 349, 378
  rubbing 308
  thermometers 363
  see also hearing
echo "talk" 245
E. coli 25, 371
eczema 267, 372, 375
eggs
  allergy to 155, 179, 373
  introducing lumpier foods 237
  safety 217
electricity, safety 301
emergencies
  A&E departments 365, 382–3
  ALTE (Apparent Life
    Threatening Event) 227
  babysitting 261
  dehydration 213
  meningitis 377–8
  when to call 999 365
emollients 375
emotions 192
  after birth 49, 61
  coping with your own 335
  developing emotional

intelligence 159, 234
empathy 270, 348
  making faces 301
  new mothers 82
  outdoor play and 337
  postnatal checks 92–3
  postnatal depression 110
  sensitivity to 205
  strong emotions 250
empathy 270, 348
employment see work
enamel, teeth 285, 306
energy
  active play 337
  diet and 105
  instant fixes 183
  lack of 156
  and post-pregnancy weight
    loss 259
engorged breasts 27, 49, 207
environmental factors, nurture
  versus nature 23
ephedrine 377
episiotomy 50, 92, 271
equipment
  bathing 35
  bedrooms 34–5
  bottle-feeding 29, 34
  for breastfeeding 34
  high chairs 154, 206, 238
  nappies 32–3
  for outdoor activities 333, 347
  selling 350
  travel 35
  for weaning 154
erections 95
erythema infectiosum 375
essential fatty acids (EFAs)
  in breastmilk 25, 255
  in cow's milk 356
eucalyptus oil 308
Eustachian tubes, middle ear
  infection 378
exanthema subitum 374
exercise 142
  after birth 62, 97
  boosting energy levels 105
  instant energy fixes 183
  pectoral muscles 321
  pelvic floor exercises 65, 79, 169
  postnatal checks 92
  and post-pregnancy weight
    loss 226, 259
expectorants 377
expressing breastmilk 71, 83
  engorged breasts 207
  pumps 28, 34, 54, 83
  for special-care babies 54
  at work 185
extended family 15
extroverts 252

extrusion reflex 155, 178
eyes
  administering drops 366
  colour 21, 147, 326
  conjunctivitis 349, 370
  development of 22
  foreign objects 382
  jaundice 372
  newborn babies 41, 57
  signs of dehydration 363
  six-week checks 93
  squint 128, 147
  sticky eyes 64
  teary eyes 232
  see also vision

F

fabric books 117, 137
faces
  breastfeeding and development
    of 25
  looking at 95, 98, 197
  recognition memory 104
  on toys 137
facial expressions
  looking in mirrors 218
  making faces 301
  mimicry 70, 121, 171
  reading baby's cues 118, 171
faddy eaters 217, 336, 353
falls 258, 279, 355, 382
family life 14–15
  extended family 111
  mealtimes 297
  with newborn babies 66
fantasy play 342
farm animals 312
fathers see partners
fats
  in cow's milk 356
  low-fat products 200
  nutritional requirements 193
  for older babies 286, 287
  and post-pregnancy weight
    loss 259
  in shop-bought baby food 251
fears
  of dark 309
  of strangers 309
  of vaccinations 357
febrile seizures 369
feeding
  special-care babies 54–5
  bottle-feeding; breastfeeding
feet
  club foot 204
  cruising 269, 319
  flat feet 204
  intoeing 243
  manipulative movement 223

newborn baby checks 43
shoes 269, 300, 302
walking 238, 249, 319
walking in bare feet 302
fertility 257
fevers 369
causes 379
and dehydration 366–7, 369
febrile seizures 369
nursing sick babies 366
staying home from nursery 349
taking temperature 73, 363
and teething 143
treatment 369, 379
when to call doctor 308
fibre, in diet 200, 287
fifth disease 375
finances
child benefit 18–19
home-made versus shop-
bought baby food 251
loss of independence 113
maternity benefit 19
planning baby's future 140
tax credits 19
finger foods 299
baby-led weaning 217
digestion of 218
dippers and dunkers 272, 329
encouraging independence
307, 312
stage three weaning 286
stage two weaning 236, 237
fingernails, trimming 60
finger puppets 275
fingers see hands
first aid 279, 382–3
fish
allergies 155, 179, 373
introducing lumpier foods 237
safety 217
weaning 216, 217
fish fingers 329
fits 369
flannels 35
flat feet 204
fleeces 348
floors
safety 301
washing 306
flour, "painting" with 323
flu
bronchiolitis 376
staying home from nursery 349
swine flu 232
vaccination 99, 164
fluoride
in toothpaste 198, 285
in water 285
folate, in breastmilk 331
follow-on milk 207, 229

fondue, cheese 329
fontanelles 97
closure 238, 276
meningitis 378
newborn checks 43
signs of dehydration 363
food
birthday parties 346
boosting energy levels 105
comfort eating 334
cooking 272, 329
eating in restaurants 310
encouraging baby to clear
plate 347
encouraging independence 307
faddy eaters 336, 353
family meals 297
gagging on 248
on holiday 289
home-made versus shop-
bought 251
hygiene 238
increasing size of pieces 299
instant energy fixes 183
introducing new foods 272, 312
and lack of energy 156
lack of hunger and 339
making food appealing 329
mealtimes 287
mother's diet 62, 105
nursing sick babies 366
nutritional requirements 193
for one-year-olds 353
picking up 295
postnatal checks 92
and post-pregnancy weight
loss 259
self-feeding 312, 339
stage one weaning 216–17
stage three weaning 286–7
stage two weaning 236–7
storing leftovers 238
sweet foods 302
toddlers 359
vegetarian diet 193, 236, 356
vitamins 219
see also finger foods; snacks;
weaning
food allergies 225, 241, 373
food colourants 217
food diaries 179, 241
food intolerances 225
foreign objects 382–3
foremilk 27, 58
foreskin 47
formula milk
and allergies 254
choosing 29
and colic 75
follow-on milk 207, 229
fully hydrolyzed formula 254

"growing up" formula 356
on holiday 289
for hungry babies 164, 207, 229
making up feeds 48
types of 229
freezing
breastmilk 83
purées 179
friendships
new parents 147
support networks 88, 352
fruit
finger foods 237
high-fibre foods 200
on holiday 289
introducing lumpier foods 237
mashed 299
for older babies 286
purées 178, 179, 216
vitamins and minerals 193
fruit juice 179, 229, 232, 285, 302
frustration 180, 250, 256
and first words 288
temper tantrums 335
fungal infections see thrush
furniture
climbing on 258, 269
cruising 269
fussy eaters 217, 336, 353

G

gagging 248
games see play
gardens 201, 333, 337
gastroenteritis 25, 167, 371
gastro-oesophageal reflux (GOR)
369–70
gender differences 161, 235
genetics 21
nurture versus nature 23, 161
genitals, newborn babies 41, 47
gentleness 313, 340
German measles see rubella
germs 306, 308
gestures 232, 270
gifts, birthday parties 346
giggling 138, 168, 298, 318
girls
changing nappies 44, 47
developmental differences
23, 161
glass, safety 301
glass test, meningitis 378
gloves 290
glue ear 378
gluten 155, 179
goat's milk 229, 254
golden hour, after birth 42–3
GPs see doctors
grandparents

babysitting 80, 144
childcare by 115, 273
family life 15, 66
and loneliness 72
long-distance communication
144
as role models 175
sleepovers with 357
"spoiling" babies 246
grasp reflex 47, 94, 102
grazes 382
grazing 247
gripe water 75
grommets, glue ear 378
growth factors, in breastmilk 25
growth potential 350
growth spurts 90, 91, 96, 124, 127
guacamole 329
guaifenesin 377
guilt, work/life balance 305
gums
bleeding 110
teething 143, 306
gymnastics 158

H

haemangiomas 61
Haemophilus influenzae type b
(Hib) vaccination 99, 152
haemorrhoids 92
hair 238, 290
baby baldness and changes
89, 196
cutting 252, 357
genetics 21
hair analysis tests 225
hairdressers 357
lanugo 41
mother's hair after birth 110
washing 57, 189, 252, 290
handbags 205
hand-foot-and-mouth disease
349, 375
hands
clapping 146, 223
drawing 328
dropping things 283, 295
gaining control of 22, 94, 106
gestures 232
gloves 290
grasp reflex 47, 94, 102
handedness 184
hand-eye coordination 76, 116
manipulative movement 223
newborn baby checks 43
picking things up 162
pincer grip 188, 276, 286, 295,
311
playing with 76
poking and pinching 340

reaching and grasping 146, 158, 228

two-handed activities 199, 223, 228

waving bye-bye 274, 332

harnesses

high chairs 206

pushchairs 117

supermarket trolleys 300

hats 73, 129, 290, 348

hay fever 375

head

cradle cap 76

fontanelles 43, 97, 238, 276

head-banging 227

injuries 382

muscle control 22

neck muscles 124

newborn babies 41, 43

six-week checks 93

tummy time 116

health visitors 365

clinics 124

help with breastfeeding 28

home visits after birth 46, 50–1

hearing

development of 22, 87

filtering out background noise 264

glue ear and 378

hearing tests 87, 253

learning about noises 330

making sense of sounds 165

heart

newborn baby checks 43

six-week checks 93

heart disease, breastfeeding and 25

heat rash 123, 375

height, genetics 21

helium balloons 346

helmets, cycling 347

helpfulness 315

hepatitis vaccination 99, 152

herbal teas, and breastfeeding 62

heredity 21

hernia, umbilical 92

hide and seek 307

high chairs 154, 206, 238

hiking 347

hindmilk 27, 58

hips

developmental dysplasia of the hip (DDH) 204

newborn baby checks 43

reusable nappies and 77

Hirschsprung's disease 372

holding newborn babies 46, 71

holidays 260, 289, 316

home safety 180, 205, 243, 301

honey 217

hormones

after birth 110

and baby blues 49, 110

and bonding 52

breastfeeding 25, 26

and changes to breasts 321

return of periods 257

stress hormones 230

hospitals

A&E departments 365, 382–3

after birth 43

discharge from 46

special-care babies 54–5

staying in 365

hotels 125

hot weather 290, 348

housework

establishing roles 113

lowering standards 239

with newborn baby 71

as play sessions 315, 336

and returning to work 130

sharing 84, 170

time-saving strategies 242

hunger

and crying 68

demand feeding 75

formula milk for hungry babies 164, 207, 229

and growth spurts 91

lack of 339

reading baby's cues 118

and weaning 152, 154

young babies 152

hydration see dehydration

hygiene

and animals 122, 312

bottle-feeding 29

food preparation 238

on holiday 289

older babies 306

preventing illness 103

young babies 112

hypothyroidism, newborn bloodspot test 50

I

ibuprofen, lowering fevers 366, 369

identical twins, telling apart 79

identity, sense of 194

illness

A&E departments 365, 382–3

antibiotics 245

breastfeeding and 25, 27, 63

and breastfeeding toddlers 331

and crying 69

fevers 369

NHS 111 365

nursing sick babies 349, 366–7

signs of 168, 363

staying home from nursery 349

visiting doctors 364

and weight loss 304

when to call doctor 364, 369

young babies 168

see also vaccinations and specific illnesses

imitation see mimicry

immune system

and allergies 112, 225, 241

breastfeeding and 25, 27, 103

and colds 308

germs and 306

secondary infections 349

vaccinations 99

young babies 103, 168

immunisation see vaccinations

impetigo 349

incisors 198

incontinence, stress 65, 79

incubation periods see specific diseases

incubators 54–5

independence 359

encouraging 307

mobility and 209

parent's loss of 14

self awareness 194, 342

self-feeding 312

separation anxiety 229, 233

trial and error learning 202

infections see illness

inheritance 21

insect bites and stings 382

instincts 13

insurance, travel 289

Internet, social networking 181

intestines, breastfeeding and 27

introverts 252

intussusception 371

investment trusts 140

ipecacuanha 377

iron

in breast milk 255

deficiency 130, 154, 156

in formula milk 207, 356

in meat 217

sources of 219

isolation 15, 352

itching, eczema 375

IUD devices 257

J

jackets 348

jaundice 51, 66, 372

jealousy 122, 195

joints 93, 97

juice, fruit 179, 229, 232, 285, 302

jumpers 348

K

kangaroo care 43, 54

Kegel exercises 65, 79, 169

kicking 131

kidneys, and urine infections 377

kitchens 238, 301

L

lactation see breastfeeding

lactation counsellors 28

lactose 193

lactose intolerance 100, 373

language see speech development

lanugo 41

laryngitis 377

laryngomalacia 374

larynx 226, 374

latching on, breastfeeding 26, 27, 41, 46

laughter 138, 166, 298, 318

laundry, time-saving strategies 242

laxatives 372

learning

curiosity and 224

importance of repetition 159

mimicry and 191

trial and error 202

understanding shapes and sizes 326

using objects correctly 311

young babies 188

left-handedness 184

legs 131, 328

bow-leggedness 204

developmental dysplasia of the hip (DDH) 204

reusable nappies and 77

slender legs 204

strengthening 204

walking 319

let-down reflex 26, 59, 96

libraries 318

ligaments

after birth 97, 169

chest 321

lighting

bedrooms 34

dimmer switches 309

night lights 309

light, phototherapy 372

liners, nappy 33

liver, jaundice 51, 66, 372

lochia 42, 50

locks, cupboards 301

loneliness 69, 72, 82

long-term memory 291

love 22, 176, 313

lovemaking see sexual intercourse

lullabies 230
lunches 236, 287
lungs
  bronchiolitis 376
  chest infections 377
  newborn baby checks 43
  wheezing 376–7
lymphocytes 103

M

malaria 125
"Mama," saying 206
manners 335, 348, 359
massage 119
mastitis 59, 207, 255
Maternity Allowance (MA) 19
maternity benefit 19
maternity leave 130
maternity pads 42
mattresses 30, 108, 277
mattress protectors 31
MCADD 50
mealtimes 287, 297, 335, 359
measles 99, 349, 374
meat
  introducing lumpier foods
    237
  meatball dippers 329
  mincing 299
  nutrition 193
  weaning 216, 217
meconium 27, 41, 45, 47, 372
medicine see drugs
medicine cupboards 366
Medicines and Healthcare
  products Regulatory Agency
    (MHRA) 377
memory boxes 185
memory, development of 104, 192,
  284, 291
meningitis 377–8
  vaccination 99, 130, 152
menstruation see periods
mercury poisoning, fish 217
messy play 291
metanium ointment 73
"me-time" 195, 199, 256
microwave ovens 29, 179
middle ear infection 378
midwives 28, 46, 50–1
milestones 22–3, 380–1
  competitive parenting 17, 173
  differences in meeting 342
  pincer grip 311
  premature babies 173
  slow development 275
  twins 173
walking 319
  milk
    milk intolerance 167, 373

possetting 74
  see also bottle-feeding;
    breastfeeding; cow's milk;
    formula milk
milk sinuses 26
milk teeth see teeth
millet, weaning 178
mimicry
  babbling 253
  deferred imitation 332
  empathy 270
  facial expressions 70, 171
  and learning 191
  making faces 301
  "mirror neurons" 120
minerals
  in breast milk 255
  nutritional requirements 193
  in shop-bought baby food 251
mint tea 62
mirroring, helping baby accept
  strong emotions 250
"mirror neurons" 120
mirrors 121, 194, 218, 342
mites, dust 112
mittens 290, 348
MMR vaccination 99, 374
mobiles 76, 81, 98
mobility 209
  bottom shuffling 204, 209,
    240, 300
  cruising 269, 300, 302, 319
  dancing 122, 281, 303, 328
  older babies 333
  pulling up to standing 243
  rolling over 22, 128, 139,
    180, 209
  toys to encourage 326
  see also crawling; walking
moisturizers 123
molars 198, 306
monitors 34, 211
Montgomery's tubercles 26
moods see emotions
Moro reflex 47
Moses baskets 30, 34, 108
mother-and-baby groups see
  parent-and-baby groups
motions see bowel movements
mouth
  chickenpox in 373
  exploring world with 123, 276
  hand-foot-and-mouth disease
    375
  newborn baby checks 43
  thrush 373–4
  tongue-tie 370
mucus, in stools 218
multiple births see twins
mumps 99, 349, 374
muscles

development of 22, 155, 328
  gaining control of 94
  legs 131, 204, 328
  pectoral 321
  pelvic floor exercises 65, 79, 169
  six-week checks 93
  tummy time 88, 116, 124, 139
music 281
  baby classes 163
  background noise 264
  benefits of 230
  dancing 122, 281, 303
  musical ability 21
  musical instruments 281
  newborn babies and 80, 87
  young babies and 98
  see also songs
muslin squares 35, 61
mustard 297

N

nails, trimming 60
nakedness 296
names, recognition of 253, 260
nannies 114–15, 273
nappies 32–3
  and crying 68
  disposable nappies 32, 44, 77
  distracting babies while
    changing 111
  leaking 167
  liners 33
  nappy-free periods 296
  newborn babies 44–5
  reusable nappies 77
  swim nappies 267
nappy rash 373–4
  and crying 68
  dealing with 73, 296
  disposable nappies and 32
  preventing 45, 296
  thrush and 73
nappy sacks 32
naps
  body clock 81
  changing routines 260
  consistency 296
  dropping 176, 270, 340
  and early or late bedtimes 224
  and early waking 187
  instant energy fixes 183
  length of 296
  older babies 208, 284, 346
  one-year-olds 355
  routines 31, 89, 136, 355
  settling babies 74
  and sleeping through the
    night 325
  young babies 131
  see also sleep

National Association of Family
  Information Services 181
National Health Service (NHS)
  numbers 18, 70
nature 201
nature versus nurture 161
naughtiness 182, 256, 266
navel 92
neck muscles 124, 158
neonatal acne 123
neurons (brain cells) 182, 278
newborn babies 40–77
  appearance 41
  bathing 57
  bonding with 52
  bottle-feeding 47, 53
  breastfeeding 46, 49, 50, 53
  carrying and holding 46, 71
  checks 41, 42, 43
  crying 48, 57, 68–9
  eyes 57
  feeding 44, 46–7
  genitals 41, 47
  nappies 44–5
  outings 61
  playing with 67
  reflexes 47
  sleep 47, 53
  special-care babies 54–5
  topping and tailing 45
  weight gain 60
newborn bloodspot test 50
Nexplanon 257
NHS 111 365
NHS numbers 18, 70
night
  body clock 81
  comfort feeds 328
  fear of dark 309
  leaking nappies 167
  leaving baby with someone
    else 327
  nursing sick babies 367
  reluctance to go to bed 340
  sleeping through night 324–5
night lights 35, 309
night waking 101
  early waking 187
  feeding and 214
  separation anxiety 214
  young babies 156
nipple cream 34, 46
nipples
  breastfeeding 26, 27
  inverted 28
  sore 46, 58, 59
  thrush 59, 374
nipple shields 62
noises
  animal noises 165, 253, 288, 330
  background noise 264, 322

dropping things 283
learning about 330
startling babies 264, 309
norovirus 371
"no," saying 191, 230, 341, 342
nose
administering drops 366
colds 376
foreign objects in 382–3
runny nose 379
nudity 296
numbers, counting 159
nurseries 114, 115, 345, 349
nursery rhymes
action rhymes 164
animals in 312
and speech development
253, 281
tickling games 263
nurses, walk-in health
centres 365
nursing bras 26, 34, 107, 321
nursing sick babies 349, 366–7
nutrition 193, 219
nutritionists 241
nuts
peanut allergy 225, 373
safety 217, 353

O

oat drinks 229
obesity 186
breastfeeding and 25
demand feeding and 75
object permanence
and dropping things 283
hide and seek 233, 307
peek-a-boo games and 134
and separation anxiety 263
oesophagus, reflux 68, 369–70
oestrogen, and vaginal dryness 96
Ofsted 114
omega oils, in formula milk 29
oral contraceptives 257
oral rehydration solution 363, 371
orchidopexy 95
orgasm 113
osteoporosis 25, 110, 331
otitis externa 378
otitis media 378
outdoor activities 333, 337, 347
outings
changing routines 260
family outings 121
holidays 260, 289, 316
newborn babies 61
older babies 203
for parents 316
pushchairs 117
watching animals 312

see also travel
ovarian cancer 25, 27
ovens, safety 301
overhead press 321
overheating 73
over-stimulated babies 69, 177
overweight babies 186, 304
breastfeeding and 25
demand feeding and 75
snacks and 247
oxygen, ALTE (Apparent
Life-Threatening Event) 227
oxymetazoline 377
oxytocin 26, 52

P

paddling pools 354
pain
body language 171
breastfeeding 58
periods 257
sexual intercourse 271
painkillers, and breastfeeding 63
paint, cots 108
painting 262, 323
palmar grasp reflex 162
pancake dippers 329
parabens, in shampoo 252
paracetamol
for colds 308
lowering fevers 366, 369
para-influenza virus 377
parallel play 282
parasites, on pets 122
parent-and-baby groups 72, 181
benefits for babies 145
nearly new sales 350
story time sessions 318
support networks 88
parentese ("baby talk") 84, 86, 328
parenting
adjusting to parenthood 13, 358
approaches to parenthood
16–17
confidence 320
connecting with other parents
181
establishing own style 152
limits and boundaries 341
positive parenting 17
"pushy" parenting 17, 173
and sense of self 195, 358
ten good things about being a
parent 174
parks 337
parties, birthday 346
partners
adapting to change 113
baby showing preference for
214, 240

bonding with baby 45, 52
and breastfeeding 28
giving mother a break 74
and loneliness 72
main childcare provider 215
paternity leave 19
physical play with baby 141
quality time with baby 318
relationship with 14
and returning to work 130
sex 271
sharing babycare 84, 170
time out with 80, 316
part-time work 115
parvovirus 375
passive immunity 103
passports 18, 125
pasta 329
paternity leave 19, 130
patterns, black-and-white 67
peanut allergy 225, 373
pectoral muscles 321
peek-a-boo games 134, 233
pelvic floor exercises 65, 79, 169
pelvic tilts 65, 169
penis
changing nappies 44, 47
circumcision 47
erections 95
perfume, in shampoo 252
periodic breathing 47
periods 257
after birth 73
breastfeeding and 25, 82, 257
personality
development of 23, 129
nature versus nurture 161
older babies 252, 303
twins 305
person permanence 342
pertussis vaccination 99, 152
pets
and allergies 112
faeces 333
hygiene 306
safety 122, 301
pharmacists 365
phenylephrine 377
phenylketonuria (PKU) 50
pholcodine 377
photographs
memories 121
and self awareness 342
social networking sites 15
special book for baby 354
phototherapy 372
Piaget, Jean 134
pick-ups 159
picky eaters 353
piles 92
pillows

in cots 31, 248
feeding pillows 34
pincer grip 276, 286, 295, 311
pineal gland 81
pituitary gland, breastfeeding 26
plants, poisonous 333
plaque, on teeth 285
play
action rhymes 164
active play 337
activity centres 209
and analytical thinking 345
catching games 283
clapping games 146
clear-up time 239
dens 278
encouraging independence 307
fantasy play 342
hide and seek 307
with household items 153, 191
housework as 336
importance of 153
messy play 291
newborn babies 67
object permanence 233
with other babies 194, 282, 345
outdoor play 333, 337
parallel play 282
and parental attention 266, 313
peek-a-boo games 134, 233
physical play 141
reading baby's cues 118
sandpits 201, 351
soft-play centres 258
solo play 160, 177
with sounds 253
stacking toys 315
taking turns 246
tickling games 263
tipping and tilting 211
toddlers 359
in tunnels 317
twins 135, 351
understanding shapes and
sizes 326
washing-up 241
water play 169, 219, 351, 354
word recognition 260
young babies 136, 137, 175
playgroups 323, 345, 352
playpens 209
"please" 348
PMS 199, 257
pneumococcal infections,
vaccination 99
pneumonia 377
pointing 232, 284, 332
poisons
emergencies 383
poisonous plants 333
poking 340

polio vaccination 99, 152
polygenic traits 21
ponds, safety 333, 354
poos see bowel movements
positive parenting 17
possetting 74, 370
postnatal checks 77, 92–3
postnatal depression (PND) 49
    fathers and 163
    signs of 110
    sunlight and 61
    treatment of 110
postnatal psychosis 110
potassium, in cow's milk 356
potty training 296
poultry, introducing lumpier
    foods 237
praise 17, 230, 256, 266
prams 35
pregnancy
    changes in breasts 321
    parvovirus and 375
    planning second baby 257
    rubella and 374
premature babies
    appearance 41
    and cot death 31
    development 355
    dream sleep 353
    expressing breastmilk for 28
    jaundice 372
    lactose intolerance 100
    milestones 173, 275
    special-care babies 54–5
    vitamin supplements 158
    weaning 155
presents, birthday parties 346
preservatives, in shop-bought
    baby food 251
prickly heat 375
probiotics, in formula milk 29
problem solving
    learning by trial and error 202
    play and 264, 345
progesterone, contraception
    257
projectile vomiting 370
prolactin 26, 110
promethazine 377
protein
    in breastmilk 255, 331, 356
    in cow's milk 356
    in formula milk 29
    in goat's milk 254
    nutritional requirements 193
    for older babies 286
    and post-pregnancy weight
        loss 259
    in shop-bought baby food 251
pseudoephedrine 377
psychosis, postnatal 110

public transport 203
puddles 354
pulling up to standing 243
pulses, introducing lumpier
    foods 237
pumps, expressing breastmilk 28,
    34, 54, 83
puppets 275
purées
    first tastes 178, 210, 216
    freezing 179
    making 179
    reheating in microwave 179
pushchairs and buggies
    choosing 35, 117
    in cold weather 290, 348
    on public transport 203
    for uneven terrain 347
push ups 321
"pushy" parenting 17, 173
puzzles 351
pyloric stenosis 370–1

Q

quality time, working parents 318
"quiet" time 264

R

rainy-day fun 337
rashes
    causes 379
    chickenpox 203, 373
    hand-foot-and-mouth disease
        375
    heat rash 123, 375
    measles 374
    meningitis 377–8
    roseola 374
    rubella 374
    slapped cheek disease 375
    staying home from nursery 349
    thrush 373–4
    treatment 379
    when to call doctor 308
    see also nappy rash
raspberries, blowing 274
rattles 107, 137
reading to babies 223, 354
    benefits of 145, 202
    nursing sick babies 366
    repetition 354
    story time sessions 318
    twins 202
reasoning skills 188, 235
recessive genes 21
recognition 104, 284
red blood cells 372
reflexes
    breastfeeding 26, 27, 59

newborn babies 47
six-week checks 93
reflexive crying 270
reflux 68, 74, 369–70
registering birth 18, 52
rehydration solution 363, 371
relationships
    adapting to change 113, 305
    attachment theory 313
    with extended family 111
    family mealtimes 335
    friendships 147
    see also partners
relaxation
    for parents 195, 199
    prioritizing activities 242
relaxin 110
repetition
    and brain development 278
    cause and effect 283
    first words 358
    importance of 159
    and learning 188
    memory development 192
    reading books 354
    sounds 201
    trial and error learning 202
reptiles, as pets 122
respect, learning about 348
respiratory illnesses, staying
    home from nursery 349
respiratory syncytial virus
    (RSV) 376
restaurants 310
    breastfeeding in 72
    feeding babies in 251
    on holiday 289
reusable nappies 32–3, 77
rhymes see nursery rhymes
rice 178, 210
rickets 158, 219
right-handedness 184
rights, parental 19
rocking 227
role models
    good behaviour and 341
    managing strong emotions 250
    at mealtimes 339
    parents as 175, 335
role play
    encouraging gentleness 313
    using objects correctly 311
rolling over 128, 209
    back-to-front rolls 139
    encouraging 139
    milestones 22
    safety 128, 139, 180
    during sleep 231, 248
rooting reflex 27, 47, 59
root vegetables 299
roseola 349, 374

rotavirus
    infection 371
    vaccination 99
"Round and Round the Garden"
    263
routines
    changing 260
    establishing 136, 141
    feeding 100
    leaving baby at night 327
    naps 136, 141, 284, 296
    recognition of 284
    security and 260
    separation anxiety 213
    sleep 31, 136, 141
    work/life balance 343
    young babies 136, 141
    see also bedtime routines
"Row, Row, Row the Boat" 328
RSV (respiratory syncytial virus)
    376
rubella (German measles) 374–5
    staying home from nursery 349
    symptoms 374
    vaccination 99, 374
rugs, safety 301
runny nose 379

S

safety
    babyproofing home 180, 205,
        243, 301
    baby walkers 197
    bedrooms 277
    birthday parties 346
    button batteries 205
    choking risks 276
    cots 108, 277
    cruising 269
    and discipline 341
    diversion tactics 182
    getting his attention 334
    high chairs 206
    on holiday 289
    outdoors 333
    pets 122
    pushchairs 117
    rolling over 128, 139, 180
    stairs 258, 279, 333
    sun protection 129
    toddlers 359
    toys 137
    vitamin supplements 219
    walking 249
    water 354
    weaning 217
    young babies 86
saline drops 376
saliva
    drooling 138, 306

and tooth care 285
salmonella
  breastmilk and 25
  in eggs 217
  gastroenteritis 371
  and pet food 122
salt
  dangers of 200
  family meals 297, 353
  introducing solids 210, 217
  in shop-bought baby food 251
sandpits 201, 337
  hygiene 312
  for one-year-olds 351
  safety 333
savings accounts 140
savoury foods 302
scabies 349
scalding 301
scalp, cradle cap 76
scarlet fever 349
scars, Caesarean section 65, 93
scratch mittens 375
screen time 265
scrotum, undescended testes
  93, 95
second-hand shoes 302
secretory otitis media 378
security
  attachment theory 313
  comfort objects 317
  and development of confidence
    22
  effects of parental stress 234
  and night waking 156
  pick-ups 159
  and routines 260
  setting boundaries 16
seizures 369
self awareness 194, 342
self-confidence, parents 320
self-employment, maternity
  benefits 19
self-esteem 160
senses
  touch 169, 310
  see also hearing; vision
sensory development classes 163
separation anxiety 23, 263
  anxiety about strangers 298
  bedtime problems 262
  comfort objects and 282
  dealing with 233
  encouraging independence 307
  object permanence and 233
  returning to work 213
  showing caution 309
  and sleeping through the night
    214, 324
  toddlers 359
septicaemia 377–8

sexual intercourse 271
  after birth 92, 96
  bleeding after 113
  loss of libido 96, 271
  painful 271
shampoo 189, 290
  all-in-one bath products 35
  choosing 252
  rinse cups 189
shapes, understanding 326
sharenting 88
sheep's milk 229
sheets 31
shigella 371
shoes 231
  for cruising 269, 300, 302
  second-hand 302
shopping 248
  supermarket trips 300
  time-saving strategies 242
showers, instant energy fixes 183
shyness 194, 252
siblings
  adjusting to new baby 14–15, 66
  play with 194
  rivalry 14–15
  sharing your attention 350
  step-children 15
sick babies, nursing 349, 366–7
sickle-cell disease 375
  newborn bloodspot test 50
SIDS see Sudden Infant Death
  Syndrome (SIDS)
sight see vision
singing see songs
single parents
  adjusting to parenthood 15
  and extended family 111
  maternity benefits 19
  websites 181
sinuses, blocked 308
sisters see siblings
sitting
  milestones 22
  young babies 124, 134
sixth disease 374
six-week checks 77, 92–3
sizes, understanding 326
skin
  burns 382
  cuts and grazes 382
  diseases 349
  eczema 372, 375
  jaundice 372
  signs of dehydration 363
  strawberry marks 61
  stretch marks 82
  sunburn 375
  topping and tailing 45
  vernix 41, 45
  young babies 123

see also nappy rash; rashes
skin-prick tests 225, 241
skin-to-skin contact
  and bonding 43, 45
  kangaroo care 43, 54
skull, fontanelles 43, 97, 238, 276
slapped cheek disease 375
sleep
  air travel 125
  amount needed 346
  bedroom temperature 106
  bedtime routines 89
  body clock 81
  changing routines 131, 260
  changing sleep patterns 270
  co-bedding twins 63
  co-sleeping 30, 242, 325
  dreams 109, 227, 353
  dropping naps 176, 340
  early or late bedtimes 224
  early waking 187
  falling asleep on own 156, 166
  fear of dark 309
  in first year 23
  and growth spurts 127
  on holiday 289
  and immune system 168
  instant energy fixes 183
  kangaroo care 54
  and lack of energy 156
  new babies 30–1, 47, 53
  night waking 101, 156
  noises during 227
  one-year-olds 355
  reluctance to go to bed 340
  rolling over during 231, 248
  routines 31, 131, 136, 141, 355
  self settling 324
  settling baby 74, 109
  signs of illness 363
  at six months 214
  sleep cycles 109
  sleeping alone 211
  sleeping through the night 80,
    324–5
  sleep 'training' 109, 325
  types of 109
  waking for a feed 51
  see also naps
sleep apnoea 54, 227
sleeping bags 31, 98, 106, 248
sleepovers 357
slings 35, 48, 69, 71
smear tests 92
smiling 77, 90, 94, 119–20
smoking
  and asthma risk 233
  and breastfeeding 62
  and cot death 31
snacks
  boosting energy levels 105

encouraging independence 307
  healthy snacks 336
  on holiday 289
  for older babies 247, 286, 299
  and post-pregnancy weight loss
    259
  and tooth care 285
snoring 227
snowsuits 348
snuffling 227
sociability
  anxiety about strangers 298
  empathy 270
  laughter 298
  making faces 301
  mealtimes 297, 335
  meeting other children 316
  personality development 252
  playgroups 323
  play with other babies 194,
    282, 345
  young babies 119, 145
social media 88, 195
social networking 15, 181
sock puppets 275
socks 231, 269
sodium, in cow's milk 356
sofas, safety 258
soft-play centres 258
solids see weaning
songs 230
  action rhymes 164
  calming babies 165
  clapping games 146
  dancing to 122
  nursery rhymes 281
  and speech development 253
  word recognition 260
soothing babies 69
  comfort items 86
  sleep 'training' 325
  with touch 71
sorry, saying 341
sounds
  animal noises 165, 253, 288, 330
  learning about noises 165, 330
  mimicry 191
  newborn babies and 80
  rattles 107
  repetition 86, 87, 201
soya allergy 373
soya milk 229, 254
special-care babies 54–5
speech development
  animal noises 165, 253, 288, 330
  "baby talk" 84
  background noise and 322
  bilingual babies 151
  first words 288, 304, 322, 358
  and gestures 232
  hearing tests 253

"Mama" and "Dada" 206
milestones 22
mimicry and 191
music and 230
pitch and intonation 245, 274
"please" and "thank you" 348
repetition of sounds 201
saying "no" 191, 342
screen time 265
talking to herself 274
toddlers 359
tongue-tie and 370
twins 332
using adult language 328
word recognition 253, 260
young babies 151
see also babbling
spices 286–7, 297
spine, newborn baby checks 43
"spoiling" babies 22, 48, 246
spoons
administering drugs 367
self-feeding 286, 307, 339, 344
weaning babies 154, 178
sporting ability 21
spots 123
squint 128, 147
stacking toys 315, 351
stairs
climbing 258, 279, 333
safety 333
stair gates 258
standing 22
cruising 269, 300
pulling up to standing 243
strengthening legs 204
starchy foods, weaning 216
startle reflex 47, 53
startling 309
statutory maternity pay (SMP) 19
steaming vegetables 179
step-children, adjusting to new
baby 15
stepping reflex 47
sterilization
cups 190
feeding equipment 306
sterilizers 29, 34
toys 180
steroid creams 367, 375
"stickability" 322
sticky eyes 64
stimulation
and brain development 278
over-stimulated babies 69, 177
stings, insect 382
stitches
Caesarean section 50
tears and episiotomy 50, 92
stomach
gastroenteritis 371

gastro-oesophageal reflux
(GOR)
68, 369–70
pyloric stenosis 370–1
vomiting 370
storage
purées 179
toys 239
stories see books; reading to
babies
stork marks 41
strangers
anxiety about 298
fear of 309
strawberry marks 61
stress
controlling 335
effects on emotions 234
stress hormones 230
stress incontinence 65, 79
stretch marks 82
stridor 377
sucking, bottle-feeding 334
sucking reflex 47
sucking thumb 147, 194
Sudden Infant Death Syndrome
(SIDS, cot death) 31
breastfeeding and 25
co-sleeping and 30
overheating and 73 rolling
over and 231, 248
sugar 200, 302
family meals 297
in shop-bought baby food 251
and tooth care 285, 302
and weaning 210
sulphates, in shampoo 252
sunburn 375
sunhats 129, 290, 348
sunlight, and vitamin D
production 61, 129, 212, 219, 337
sunscreen 129, 212, 290
supermarkets 300
supplements, vitamin 219
support networks
finding 181
friendships 352
importance of 88
new parents 72
working parents 343
Sure Start children's centres 181
surgery 365
swaddling 53, 106, 248
sweating, dehydration 213
sweeteners 200, 217
sweet foods see sugar
sweets, and tooth care 285
swimming 267
swimming pools, safety 354
swimsuits 348
swine flu 232

syringes, administering drugs
367

T
table manners 335, 359
taking turns 246
talipes 204
talking see speech development
tampons 42
tangles, washing hair 252, 290
tantrums 335
tax
nannies 114
tax credits 19
tears
healing 92
pain after 271
teary eyes 232
teats, bottle-feeding 29, 34, 85
tea, weaning suggestions 236
teenagers, babysitting 261
teeth
biting 143, 322
care of baby's 198, 285, 311
care of mother's 110
dentists 110, 198, 357
first teeth 162
milk and 334
molars 306
mottling 306
preventing tooth decay 198, 285
sugar and 302
thumb sucking and 147
teething
and diarrhoea 133, 198
loss of appetite 143
molars 306
order of teeth 198
and sleep 133
teething rails for cots 108, 277
teething rings 123, 143, 276
telephones, toy 332
television 264, 265
temper
losing your 335
temper tantrums 335
temperament see personality
temperature
bath water 35, 101, 189, 290
bedrooms 31, 73, 106, 231, 290
and crying 68
mother's after birth 42
normal body temperature 290
older babies 290
regulation by baby 73
swimming pools 267
taking 73, 363
see also fevers
terry nappies 33
testes, descent into scrotum 93, 95

tetanus vaccination 99, 152
tetracycline, effects on teeth 306
texture
finger foods 312
food for older babies 299, 329
lumpier foods 236–7
messy play 291
sense of touch 310
soft and hard objects 341
"thank you" 348
thawing purées 179
thermometers
bath 35
taking baby's temperature 363
thirst
and breastfeeding 105
in hot weather 290
and weaning 229
"This Little Piggy" 263
three-day fever 374
throwing 283
thrush
and nappy rash 73, 373–4
on nipples 59
and painful sex 271
signs of 123, 373–4
treatment 374
thumb sucking 147, 194
thyroid problems 130, 156
tickling games 263
tidy-up time 239, 315
time out, for parents 195, 256
time-saving strategies 242
tipping and tilting 211
tiptoes, cruising on 269
tiredness
changing sleep patterns 270
and crying 69
mother's 96, 130, 156
overtiredness 131, 224
reading baby's cues 118
settling babies 74
toddlers 359
breastfeeding 331
toenails, trimming 60
toilet training 296
tomato sauce and pasta 329
tongue
extrusion reflex 155, 178
tongue-tie 370
tooth see teeth
toothbrushes 162, 198
toothpaste 162, 198, 285, 311
topping and tailing 45
touch
development of sense of 169
importance of 71
and learning 310
soft and hard objects 341
special-care babies 55
young babies 106

towels 35
toxocariasis 122
toys
　for 12 months up 351
　activity centres 209
　and analytical thinking 345
　baby gyms 98, 116
　chewing 123
　comfort objects 282
　in cots 346
　and crawling 157
　distraction techniques 234
　encouraging gentleness 313
　encouraging independence 307
　gender differences 235
　on holiday 289
　household items as 153, 191
　improvised 343
　and mimicry 191
　mouthing 276
　musical instruments 281
　for older babies 235, 326
　parallel play 282
　picking up 162
　and problem-solving skills 264
　puppets 275
　rattles 107
　in restaurants 310
　safety 137
　secondhand 350
　snatching 256
　solo play 177
　stacking toys 315
　sterilizing 112, 180
　storage 239
　taking turns 246
　tidying up 239, 315
　treasure boxes 235
　for twins 351
　two-handed activities 199,
　　223, 228
　washing 112, 306
　for young babies 137
tracking, vision 76, 79, 128
trailers, bike 347
trainer cups 190
travel
　equipment 35
　food 247
　holidays 289, 316
　insurance 289
　older babies 203
　passports 18, 125
　young babies 125
　see also outings
treasure boxes 235
trial and error learning 202
triprolidine 377
tryptophan 101
tumble dryers, safety 301
tummy time 116

and crawling 157
dislike of 88
and rolling over 139
strengthening neck 124
tunnels 317
twins 13
　allergies 372
　bonding with 52
　breastfeeding 51, 59
　clothes 104
　co-bedding 63
　early waking 187
　genetic studies 21
　growth spurts 127
　milestones 173
　personalities 303, 305
　play 135, 351
　reading to 202
　speech development 332
　taking turns 246
　telling apart 79
walking 355

U

umbilical cord 51, 92
umbilical hernia 92
under-arm thermometers 363
urine
　infections 377
　leaking nappies 167
　newborn babies 47
　potty training 296
　signs of dehydration 363
　stress incontinence 65, 79
　taking samples 377
urination after birth 42
uterus
　after birth 42, 50
　breastfeeding and 41

V

vaccinations
　egg allergy and 373
　fear of 357
　first immunisations 99
　flu jabs 99, 164
　MMR vaccination 374
　overseas travel 125
　second immunisations 99, 130
　swine flu 232
　third immunisations 99, 152
vagina, dryness 96
varicella-zoster 373
VEGA tests, food allergies 225
vegetables
　calcium content 285
　finger foods 237
　high-fibre foods 200
　on holiday 289

introducing lumpier foods 237
　mashed 299
　for older babies 286
　purées 178, 179, 210, 216
　vitamins and minerals 193
vegetarian diet 193, 236, 356
vernix 41, 45
vestibular system 151, 211
vinegar 297
viruses
　antibiotics and 245
　bronchiolitis 376
　chest infections 377
　chickenpox 373
　colds 308, 376
　croup 377
　definition 245
　gastroenteritis 371
　hand-foot-and-mouth disease
　　375
　measles 374
　meningitis 377–8
　middle ear infection 378
　roseola 374
　rubella 374–5
　slapped cheek disease 375
　wheezing 376–7
vision
　black-and-white patterns 67
　colour vision 95, 98, 112
　cross-eyes 79
　depth perception 112, 128,
　　212, 355
　development of 22
　hand-eye coordination 76, 116
　looking at faces 95, 98
　mobiles 81
　seeing small things 188
　shapes 98
　squint 128, 147
　tracking 76, 79, 128
　up and down 163
　young babies 95, 128, 147
　see also eyes
vitamin A
　in breastmilk 331, 356
　in cow's milk 356
　functions 219
　sources of 219
　supplements 158
vitamin B12 331, 356
vitamin C
　in breastmilk 331, 356
　functions 219
　sources of 219
vitamin D
　functions 219
　sources of 219
　sunlight and 61, 129, 212, 219,
　　337
　supplements 158, 212

vitamins 219
　in breastmilk 255, 331
　functions 219
　in "growing up" formula 356
　nutritional requirements 193
　in shop-bought baby food 251
　sources of 219
　supplements 219
vocabulary see words
voice
　mimicry 191
　recognizing 85
　recording baby's 144
vomiting 370–1
　bowel obstructions 371
　breastfeeding and 25
　causes 379
　and dehydration 213, 363
　gastroenteritis 371
　lactose intolerance 100
　pyloric stenosis 370–1
　signs of illness 363
　staying home from nursery 349
　treatment 379

W

walking 355
　backpack carriers 347
　bare feet 302
　cruising 209, 269, 300, 319
　first steps 249, 319
　instant energy fixes 183
　milestones 22
　and post-pregnancy weight
　　loss 259
　safety 249
　and shoes 269
　twins 355
washing
　clothes 123
　floors 306
　hair 57, 189, 252, 290
　time-saving strategies 242
　toys 112, 306
　see also bathing
washing machines, safety 301
washing-up 241
wasp stings 382
water
　fluoride in 285
　playing in 354
　playing with 169, 219, 351
　safety 333, 354
　swimming 267
　washing-up 241
water, drinking
　bottled water 229
　and breastfeeding 62, 105
　instant energy fixes 183
　introducing cups 190, 232

older babies 229

and post-pregnancy weight loss 259

at snack time 247

young babies 72

waterproof jackets 348

waving bye-bye 274, 332

wax, in ears 310

weaning 25, 154–5

and allergies 200, 216, 254

baby-led weaning 179, 217

bowel movements 218

equipment 154

first tastes 178–9, 216–17

food allergies 225

food diaries 179

introducing cups 190

introducing lumpier foods 236–7, 248

nutritional requirements 193

premature babies 155

purées 179, 210

reducing milk feeds 184

refusing spoon feeding 216–17, 229

stage one 216–17

stage three 286–7

stage two 236–7

stopping breastfeeding 254–5

unsuitable foods 200, 217

webcams 15

websites

for single parents 181

social networking 181

weight gain

breastfeeding and 26

newborn babies 50, 60

older babies 238, 276, 304

by six months 197

six-week checks 93

snacks and 247

young babies 124, 186

weight loss (baby) 47, 304

weight loss (mother) 259

breastfeeding and 25, 226

diet and 105, 259

realism about 226

welfare benefits 18–19

Wellington boots 354

wheat allergy 155, 179, 373

wheezing 376–7

whey, in formula milk 29, 229

white blood cells 103

whooping cough

staying home from nursery 349

vaccination 99, 152

wind

and colic 68, 75

possetting 74

winding babies 49

wine, in baby's food 353

winter vomiting disease 371

wipes 35

"withdrawal" cues 118

words

first words 288, 304, 322, 358

"Mama" and "Dada" 206

"please" and "thank you" 348

word recognition 253, 260

see also speech development

work

adjusting to parenthood 14

benefits of 331

"breadwinner" and main childcare provider 215

breastfeeding and 160, 185, 254

flexible hours 115

at home 115

part-time 115

paternity leave 19

planning childcare 114–15

and quality time with baby 318

returning to 19, 130, 213

and separation anxiety 263

work/life balance 305, 343, 352

working tax credits 19

World Health Organisation (WHO) 331

wounds

Caesarean section 65, 93

first aid 382

wraps, nappy 33

X

xylometazoline 376

Y

yawning 74

yeast infections see thrush

yellow fever vaccination 125

yoga 97

baby classes 163

yoghurt 251, 329

Z

zinc oxide cream 73

zoos 312

Contributors

INDEX

Acknowledgments

Thanks to the models: Sarah and Kaiden Asamoa; Nina and Jamie Bradburn; Unity Brennan, Amelie Grace, and Benjamin Wolski; Selina Chand and Faith Lucy O'Brien; Narae Cho and Alex Park; Nicola and Freya Church; Anna and Eliana Clarke; Archie Clements; Philippa and Noah Dovar; Joe and Dagan Drahota; Jenny and Harry Duggin; Laura and Zoe Forrest; Rachael and Samuel Grady; Kate Heavenor and Nicolas Diaz; Olga and Mia Gelev; Beatriz de Lemos and Isabel Walker; Jordan McRobie, Jenny Parr and Reuben McRobie; Eden Martin-Osakwe; Poppy Mitchell and Oaklee Wealands; Amelie Victoria Morris; Victoria and Arthur Morton; Oreke Mosheshe and Carter Mbamali; Gabriela and Alba Nardi; Miriam Nelken and Mala Shahi; Laura and Charlie Nickoll; Amie and Rosie Niland; Lauren Overs and Grayson Andrews; Yoan Petkov; Suzy Richards and Max Snead; Heidi Robinson and Elias Crosby; Jenny Sharp and Joshua Tyler; Matthew, Angela, and Jacob Smith; Eve Spaughton and Genevieve Long; Rose and Brooke Thunberg; Anggayasti Trikanti and Carissa Afila; Rachel Weaver and Jacob Marcus; Karen and Milly Westropp; Georgie and Harriet Willock.

Picture credits

The publisher would like to thank the following for their kind permission to reproduce their photographs:

(Key: a-above; b-below/bottom; c-centre; f-far; l-left; r-right; t-top)

2 Alamy Stock Photo: Cultura Creative RF / Sporrer / Rupp (cra). **Getty Images**: DigitalVision / Jon Feingersh Photography Inc (clb); DigitalVision / Jessie Casson (cb); The Image Bank / Glasshouse Images (bc); Moment / Oscar Wong (br). **Getty Images / iStock**: E+ / enigma_images (tr); E+ / Pekic (cla). **5 Getty Images**: Stone / Catherine Delahaye. **6 Getty Images**: Moment / Oscar Wong. **8-9 Getty Images / iStock**: E+ / AJ_Watt. **13 Getty Images**: Cavan Images (cr). **15 Getty Images / iStock**: E+ / JohnnyGreig. **18 Getty Images**: Westend61. **23 Shutterstock.com**: imageBROKER.com (bl). **28 Getty Images**: Moment / Emilija Manevska (bc). **34 Dreamstime.com**: Pojoslaw (bc). **35 Getty Images / iStock**: E+ / Stefan Tomic. **39 Getty Images / iStock**: E+ / Anchiy (c). **40 Getty Images**: Frank Herholdt (c). **41 Corbis**: Cameron (cra). **42 Getty Images**: Photodisc / Daniel Tardif. **44 Getty Images / iStock**: E+ / lostinbids (bl, bc, br). **47 Getty Images**: Anthony Bradshaw (c). **49 Getty Images**: Collection Mix: Subjects / Guerilla (cra). **Getty Images / iStock**: E+ / FatCamera (ca). **55 Alamy Images**: Peter Usbeck (br). **Getty Images**: Louie Psihoyos (tr). **57 Getty Images**: Moment / d3sign (fbl, bl, bc). **58 Getty Images / iStock**: E+ / CocoSan (bc); E+ / FatCamera (fbl). **59 Getty Images / iStock**: Vetta / SelectStock (bl). **Photolibrary**: Philippe Dannic (tc). **60 Getty Images**: Ian Hooton / Spl (br). **Photolibrary**: Gyssels (bc). **61 Dreamstime.com**: Polina Zubko (cr). **Science Photo Library**: Dr P. Marazzi (bc). **63 Mother & Baby Picture Library**: Ruth Jenkinson (br). **69 Dreamstime.com**: Pojoslaw (br). **75 Getty Images / iStock**: E+ / DonnaDiavolo (br). **81 Alamy Stock Photo**: Jennie Hart (cl). **82 Getty Images / iStock**: E+ / FatCamera. **83 Dorling Kindersley**: Antonia Deutsch (cr). **90 Getty Images / iStock**: E+ / enigma_images. **96 Dreamstime.com**: Thitaree Mahawong. **97 Getty Images / iStock**: E+ / Isbjorn. **100 Getty Images**: Moment / skaman306. **101 Getty Images**: DigitalVision / Kohei Hara. **102 Getty Images / iStock**: E+ / pixdeluxe. **103 Getty Images / iStock**: Westend61. **105 Getty Images / iStock**: E+ / damircudic. **106 Getty Images**: Moment / Karl Tapales. **107 Alamy Stock Photo**: Addictive Stock Creatives (cr). **110 Getty Images**: Westend61. **111 Corbis**: Sean Justice (cra). **114 Getty Images / iStock**: E+ / FatCamera. **117 Getty Images**: Image Source / Manuela Larissegger. **122 Getty Images**: Westend61. **129 Getty Images / iStock**: E+ / Anchiy (cra); Prostock-Studio (ca). **130 Getty Images**: Tetra images / Blend Images - JGI / Tom Grill. **135 Getty Images**: Corbis Documentary / Andria Patino. **136 Getty Images**: Tetra images / Inti St Clair. **138 Getty Images**: Maskot.

140 Getty Images / iStock: E+ / lechatnoir. **142 Corbis**: Fabrik Studios / Index Stock (cra). **146 Getty Images**: Moment / Kevin Liu (c). **152 Getty Images / iStock**: PeopleImages. **156 Getty Images / iStock**: E+ / hsyncoban. **160 Getty Images**: Moment Open / Kevin Liu. **161 Alamy Stock Photo**: Cultura Creative RF / Sporrer / Rupp. **164 Getty Images / iStock**: E+ / FG Trade. **166 Getty Images / iStock**: E+ / AJ_Watt. **167 Getty Images**: IndiaPix / IndiaPicture. **170 Getty Images**: Jozef Polc / 500px. **173 Getty Images / iStock**: E+ / SDI Productions (cl). **175 Getty Images / iStock**: E+ / urbazon. **178 Getty Images**: Stone / Catherine Delahaye. **181 Getty Images / iStock**: E+ / SolStock. **183 Getty Images**: Moment / Oscar Wong. **185 Getty Images / iStock**: MonthiraYodtiwong (cra). **187 Getty Images**: Westend61. **189 Alamy Stock Photo**: Irina Sapozhnikova. **195 Getty Images / iStock**: E+ / FreshSplash. **201 Corbis**: Lisa B. (bl). **202 Getty Images**: Moment / Images by Jazmyn Luo. **203 Getty Images / iStock**: E+ / mgstudyo. **207 Getty Images**: Moment / Davide Casarini. **210 Getty Images**: DigitalVision / Jon Feingersh Photography Inc. **213 Getty Images**: DigitalVision / MoMo Productions. **215 Getty Images / iStock**: petrunjela. **218 Getty Images**: Photodisc / Mitch Diamond. **225 Getty Images**: Moment / d3sign. **231 Getty Images**: The Image Bank / Cecile Lavabre. **232 Getty Images / iStock**: E+ / Miodrag Ignjatovic. **234 Getty Images**: Moment / Yasser Chalid. **240 Getty Images**: DigitalVision / Willie B. Thomas. **241 Getty Images / iStock**: E+ / SolStock. **242 Getty Images**: Moment / Oscar Wong. **246 Getty Images / iStock**: E+ / FatCamera. **248 Mother & Baby Picture Library**: Ian Hooton (bl). **254 Getty Images / iStock**: E+ / Onfokus. **256 Getty Images**: Moment / Catherine Falls Commercial. **259 Getty Images**: Westend61. **260 Getty Images**: DigitalVision / Oliver Rossi. **261 Getty Images / iStock**: E+ / PixelsEffect. **263 Getty Images**: Westend61. **265 Getty Images**: Stone / Catherine Delahaye. **266 Getty Images / iStock**: E+ / SolStock. **267 Getty Images / iStock**: E+ / SolStock. **269 Getty Images**: Moment / Oscar Wong (c, cr). **271 Getty Images / iStock**: E+ / Pekic. **273 Getty Images / iStock**: romrodinka. **277 Getty Images**: Moment / Oscar Wong. **279 Corbis**: Image Source (bl). **280 Getty Images**: Brand X Pictures / BFG Images. **289 Getty Images**: Moment / Laura Olivas. **295 Getty Images**: Moment / Oscar Wong (cra). **297 Getty Images**: Cavan Images. **298 Getty Images**: Moment / Tanja Ivanova. **301 Getty Images**: DigitalVision / Jessie Casson. **303 Getty Images / iStock**: Tatiana Dyuvbanova (cr). **307 Getty Images**: The Image Bank / Glasshouse Images. **308 Getty Images**: Fabrice LEROUGE (cla). **312 Getty Images**: Tetra images / Jamie Grill. **314 Getty Images / iStock**: E+ / SolStock. **316 Getty Images / iStock**: E+ / Drs Producoes. **317 Getty Images / iStock**: E+ / Tempura. **320 Corbis**: Jose Luis Pelaez, Inc. / Blend Images (cla). **327 Alamy Images**: moodboard (br). **330 Getty Images**: Tetra images / Jessica Peterson. **331 Corbis**: Brigitte Sporrer (cra). **335 Getty Images / iStock**: E+ / SolStock. **342 Getty Images**: Westend61. **347 Getty Images**: Stone / Bjarte Rettedal. **348 Getty Images / iStock**: Andrey Zhuravlev. **349 Getty Images**: Stone / Tony Anderson. **352 Getty Images**: Moment / Layland Masuda. **354 Getty Images**: DigitalVision / Solskin (cra). **Getty Images**: David M. Zuber (bc). **357 Alamy Images**: Ian nolan (ca). **359 Getty Images**: Moment / Oscar Wong. **362 Getty Images / iStock**: E+ / Pekic. **364 Getty Images / iStock**: E+ / SDI Productions. **367 Dorling Kindersley**: dave king (bc). **368 Mother & Baby Picture Library**: Ian Hooton (c). **370 Science Photo Library**: Dr P. Marazzi (bc). **372 Getty Images**: DigitalVision / Justin Paget. **373 Science Photo Library**: Chris Knapton (bc). **374 Getty Images**: Brand X Pictures / Science Photo Library - IAN HOOTON. (bl). **Science Photo Library**: (c). **375 Science Photo Library**: Dr H. C. Robinson (bl). **376 Getty Images**: Ruth Jenkinson / Spl (br). **378 Meningitis Trust** www.meningitis-trust.org: (bl).

Cover images: Front: **Getty Images**: DigitalVision / Jose Luis Pelaez Inc fbr, Stone / Jade Albert Studio, Inc. bl; **Getty Images / iStock**: Digital Vision / Photodisc br, Tom Merton / OJO Images fbl

All other images © Dorling Kindersley

DK UK
Senior Editor Sophie Blackman
Senior Acquisitions Editor Becky Alexander
Senior Designer Glenda Fisher
Picture Researchers Jo Chukualim, Amy Moss
Jacket Designer Glenda Fisher
Production Editor David Almond
Senior Production Controller Stephanie McConnell
Assistant Editor Jasmin Lennie
Editorial Manager Ruth O'Rourke
Art Director Maxine Pedliham
Publishing Director Katie Cowan

Consultants Aiwyne Foo, Helen Moore, Holly Markham
Editors Judy Barratt, Nicola Deschamps
Designer Hannah Moore

DK INDIA
Editor Ankita Gupta
DTP Designers Umesh Singh Rawat, Anurag Trivedi
DTP Coordinator Pushpak Tyagi
Senior Picture Researcher Aditya Katyal
Assistant Picture Research Administrator Manpreet Kaur
Pre-production Manager Balwant Singh
Creative Head Malavika Talukder

This edition published in 2023
Based on content first published in Great Britain in 2012 in
The Day-by-Day Baby Book by
Dorling Kindersley Limited
DK, One Embassy Gardens, 8 Viaduct Gardens,
London, SW11 7BW

The authorised representative in the EEA is
Dorling Kindersley Verlag GmbH. Arnulfstr. 124,
80636 Munich, Germany

Printed and bound in China.

www.dk.com

THE DAY-BY-DAY BABY BOOK

DK UK
Senior Editors Victoria Heyworth-Dunne, Amanda Lebentz
Senior Designers Nicola Rodway, Pamela Shiels
Editorial Assistant Kathryn Meeker
Senior Production Editor Clare McLean
Production Controller Seyhan Esen
Creative Technical Support Sonia Charbonnier
New Photography Vanessa Davies
Art Direction for Photography Emma Forge
Managing Editor Penny Smith
Managing Art Editor Marianne Markham
Publishing Manager Anna Davidson
Publisher Peggy Vance

DK INDIA
Senior Editor Alicia Ingty
Editors Janashree Singha, Himanshi Sharma
Art Editor Ira Sharma
Assistant Art Editor Ridhi Khanna
Managing Editor Glenda Fernandes
Managing Art Editor Navidita Thapa
DTP Manager Sunil Sharma
DTP Designers Anurag Trivedi, Satish Chandra Gaur

Publisher notes

The publisher would like to thank Naorem Anuja for editorial
support, Kathy Steer for the proofread, and Ruth Ellis for
the index.

Every effort has been made to ensure that the information
in this book is complete and accurate. However, neither
the publisher nor the authors are engaged in rendering
professional advice or services to the individual reader.
The contents of this book are not intended as a substitute
for consulting with your healthcare provider. All matters
regarding the health of you and your baby require medical
supervision. Neither the publisher nor the authors shall be
liable or responsible for any loss or damage allegedly arising
from any information or suggestions in this book.

Gender identities

DK recognises all gender identities, and acknowledges that
the sex someone was assigned at birth based on their sexual
organs may not align with their own gender identity. People
may self-identify as any gender or no gender (including, but
not limited to, that of a cis or trans woman, of a cis or trans
man, or of a non-binary person).

As gender language, and its use in our society evolves, the
scientific and medical communities continue to reassess their
own phrasing. Most of the studies referred to in this book use
"women" to describe people whose sex was assigned as
female at birth, and "men" to describe people whose sex
was assigned as male at birth.